Logic Programming

Logic Programming

Proceedings of the 1997 International Symposium

edited by Jan Małuszyński

The MIT Press
Cambridge, Massachusetts
London, England

ISBN 978-0-262-63180-8 (pb.   )

The MIT Press is pleased to keep this title available in print by manufacturing single copies, on demand, via digital printing technology.

Contents

Refereed Papers

Post-Conference Workshops

Program Committee

Conference Chairs

I. V. Ramakrishnan	State University of New York at Stony Brook, USA
Terrance Swift	State University of New York at Stony Brook, USA

Committee

Frédéric Benhamou	Université d'Orléans, France
Annalisa Bossi	Universitá di Venezia Cá Foscari, Italy
Maurice Bruynooghe	Katholiekie Universiteit Leuven, Belgium
Michael Codish	Ben Gurion University of the Negev, Israel
Frank de Boer	Universiteit Utrecht, The Netherlands
Saumya Debray	University of Arizona, USA
Pierre Deransart	INRIA-Rocquencourt, France
Burkhard Freitag	Universität Passau, Germany
María García de la Banda	Monash University, Australia
Gopal Gupta	New Mexico State University, USA
Michael Hanus	RWTH Aachen, Germany
Seif Haridi	SICS, Sweden
Michael Leuschel	Katholiekie Universiteit Leuven, Belgium
Jonathan Lever	IC-Parc, UK
Giorgio Levi	Universitá di Pisa, Italy
Jan Małuszyński, Chair	Linköping University, Sweden
Stephen Muggleton	Oxford University, UK
Ulf Nilsson	Linköping University, Sweden
Andreas Podelski	Max-Planck-Institut f. Informatik, Germany
Teodor Przymusinski	University of California at Riverside, USA
Germán Puebla	Universidad Politécnica de Madrid, Spain
I. V. Ramakrishnan	State University of New York at Stony Brook, USA
Uday Reddy	University of Illinois at Urbana-Champaign, USA
Olivier Ridoux	IRISA, France
Vijay Saraswat	AT&T Research, USA
Robert Stärk	University of Fribourg, Switzerland
Leon Sterling	University of Melbourne, Australia
Terrance Swift	State University of New York at Stony Brook, USA
Paul Tarau	Université de Moncton, Canada
Kazunori Ueda	Waseda University, Japan
Pascal Van Hentenryck	Brown University, USA
David S. Warren	State University of New York at Stony Brook, USA
Carlo Zaniolo	UCLA, USA

The Association for Logic Programming

The Association for Logic Programming (ALP) was founded in 1986. In addition to this conference (ICLP'97) the ALP has sponsored International Conferences and Symposia in Melbourne (1987), Seattle (1988), Lisbon (1989), Cleveland (1989), Jerusalem (1990), Austin (1990), Paris (1991), San Diego (1991), Washington, D.C. (1992), Budapest (1993), Vancouver (1993), Santa Margherita Ligure (1994), Ithaca (1994), Tokyo (1995), Portland (1995), Bad Honnef, Germany (1996), and Leuven, Belgium (1996). The proceedings of all these meetings are published by the MIT Press.

The Association sponsors workshops, contributes support to other meetings related to logic programming, and provides limited support for attendance at its sponsored conferences and workshops by participants in financial need. Members receive the Association's newsletter quarterly and can subscribe to the Journal of Logic Programming at a reduced rate.

The affairs of the Association are overseen by the Executive Council. Current members are Mats Carlsson, Veronica Dahl, Danny De Schreye, Maurizio Martelli, Lee Naish, Joxan Jaffar, and Peter Szeredi; Association President Krzysztof Apt; and Past President David Scott Warren. The current officers of the Association are: Robert Kowalski, Secretary; Francesca Toni, Treasurer and Conference Budget Auditor; and Andrew Davison, Newsletter Editor.

Further information about the Association may be obtained from:

Dania Kowalska
ALP Administrative Secretary
Department of Computing
Imperial College
180 Queen's Gate
London SW7 2BZ, UK

Tel: +44 (171) 594 8226/7
Fax: +44 (171) 589 1552
E-mail: alp@doc.ic.ac.uk

Series Foreword

The logic programming approach to computing investigates the use of logic as a programming language and explores computational models based on controlled deduction.

The field of logic programming has seen a tremendous growth in the last several years, both in depth and in scope. This growth is reflected in the number of articles, journals, theses, books, workshops, and conferences devoted to the subject. The MIT Press Series in Logic Programming was created to accommodate this development and to nurture it. It is dedicated to the publication of high-quality textbooks, monographs, collections, and proceedings in logic programming.

Ehud Shapiro
The Weizmann Institute of Science
Rehovot, Israel

Preface

This volume contains the papers presented at the 1997 International Logic Programming Symposium (ILPS'97), held Port Washington, Long Island, NY, October 13–16, 1997. The 1997 conference is the fourteenth in the series of symposia on logic programming initiated in the US in 1984 and was sponsored primarily by the Association for Logic Programming in cooperation with the State University of New York at Stony Brook. Industrial sponsors included CASP, Dayton T. Brown Inc., and Eshare Technologies. The aim of ILPS'97 was to discuss new accomplishments in logic programming, together with new research directions where the ideas originating from logic programming can play a fundamental role in other fields of computer science.

There were 63 submissions, and 22 papers were accepted by the Program Committee. The selection meeting was held at Linköping University. The joint number of submissions to this symposium and to 1997 International Logic Programming Conference (62) is almost identical as the number of submissions to the 1996 Joint International Conference and Symposium on Logic Programming (122).

I would like to thank the authors of the submitted papers for supporting this meeting. I am very grateful to the Program Committee and to the other reviewers (listed separately) for their hard work. My special thanks go to Ulf Nilsson, who, in addition to his reviewing work as a PC member, developed Prolog-based web tools supporting the work of the PC. The tools were invaluable help for me during the whole reviewing process and were extensively used by almost of PC members in the final stage of reviewing. Ulf Nilsson also designed and, in cooperation with Juliana Freire, supported the ILPS'97 web home page. I am very grateful to Juliana and to Ulf for this and for the substantial other work done by them as the publicity chairs.

Some of the submitted papers have been forwarded for consideration to the Poster Review Committee. They have been considered together with the independently submitted posters. The abstracts of the posters presented at the ILPS are contained in this volume. I am very grateful to C. R. Ramakrishnan, the Chairman of the Poster Review Committee, and to the members of the committee—Roland Bol, Steven Dawson, Phan Min Dung, Josh Hodas, Lee Naish, and Enrico Pontelli—for their work in preparation of the poster session.

I would like to thank the invited speakers Ed Clarke, Heikki Mannila, and Thomas Reps. I am also very grateful to the tutorial speakers Veronica Dahl, Rob Gerth, Michael Hanus, Manuel Hermenegildo, Michael Kifer, Andreas Podelski, Gert Smolka, and Paul Tarau.

During the last years the ILPS/ICLP post-conference workshops have been gaining increased attendance, and, in many cases, they developed into mini-conferences with their own reviewing procedures and proceedings. In preparation of ILPS'97, this trend has been supported by early planning of workshops. A call for workshop proposals was issued in the early stage of preparation. As a result six workshops were announced in February 1997. The coordinators of the workshops were invited to join the Program Committee (if they were not yet PC members). This volume contains information about the post-conference workshops and, in particular, the web addresses of the electronic proceedings of the workshops. I am very grateful to all people involved in the organization of the workshops, especially to Frédéric Benhamou, Annalisa Bossi, Burkhard Freitag, Michael Leuschel, Teodor Przymusinski, and Germán Puebla, who not only chaired the respective workshops but also worked hard as PC members. I would also like to thank Vítor Santos Costa for coordinating the more recently announced additional workshop.

I am very grateful to Conference Chairs I. V. Ramakrishnan and Terrance Swift for their perfect handling of all ILPS'97 matters and, in particular, for their involvement in the work of the Program Committee. I would also like to thank Bob Prior and Julie Grimaldi of the MIT Press for their help and advice in preparing this volume.

Jan Małuszyński

Referees

Mira Balaban
Chitta Baral
François Barthélémy
Rachel Ben-Eliyahu
Michel Bergére
Roland N. Bol
Alan Borning
Pierre Boullier
Gerhard Brewka
Antonio Brogi
Francisco Bueno
Daniel Cabeza
Manuel Carro
Serena Cerrito
Witold Charatonik
Nicoletta Cocco
Philippe Codognet
Simone Contiero
Agostino Cortesi
Veronica Dahl
Dennis Dams
Andrew Davison
Jean-Paul Delahaye
Bart Demoen
Marc Denecker
Danny De Schreye
José de Siqueira
Yves Deville
Alessandra Di Pierro
Guozhu Dong
Agostino Dovier
Wlodek Drabent
Denys Duchier
Andreas Eisele
Thomas Eiter
Sandro Etalle
François Fages
Moreno Falaschi
Amy Felty
Alfred Fent

Christian G. Fermüller
Maurizio Gabbrielli
Pedro López-García
Michael Gelfond
Sameer Genaim
Dale Gerdemann
Fosca Giannotti
Rix Groenboom
Frédéric Goualard
James Harland
Manuel Hermenegildo
Koen Hindriks
Yan-Nong Huang
Frank Huch
Petra Hofstedt
Jean-Louis Imbert
François Jacquenet
Jean Marie Jacquet
Sverker Janson
Gerda Janssens
David Kemp
Andy King
Naoki Kobayashi
Vitaly Lagoon
Arnaud Lallouet
Evelina Lamma
Baudouin Le Charlier
Yves Lespérance
Renwei Li
Seng Wai Loke
Andrew Macdonald
Bernard Malfon
Paolo Mancarella
Elena Marchiori
Massimo Marchiori
Kim Marriott
Luis Monteiro
Johan Montelius
Maria Chiara Meo
Laurent Michel

Dale Miller
Kuniaki Mukai
Hiroshi Nakashima
Mauricio Osorio
Dino Pedreschi
Enrico Pontelli
Alessandra Raffaetà
Desh Ranjan
Francesco Ranzato
Prasad Rao
Stephen Rochefort
Robert Rodosek
David A. Rosenblueth
Abhik Roychoudhury
Pasquale Rullo
Konstantinos Sagonas
Chiaki Sakama
Vítor Santos Costa
Taisuke Sato
Peter Schachte
Richard Scherl
Joachim Schimpf
Heribert Schütz
Dietmar Seipel
Solomon Eyal Shimony
Zoltan Somogyi
Liz Sonenberg
Harald Søndergaard
Karl Stroetmann
Peter Stuckey
Cochavit Taboch
Henk Vandecasteele
Wiebe van der Hoek
Peter Van Roy
Michael Winikoff
Cees Witteveen
Frank Zartmann
Jianyang Zhou
Neng-Fa Zhou
Ulrich Zukowski

Invited Talks

Temporal Logic Model Checking

Edmund M. Clarke

School of Computer Science

Carnegie Mellon University

Pittsburgh, PA 15213-3890

Abstract

Logical errors in finite state reactive systems are an important problem for designers. They can delay getting a new product on the market or cause the failure of some critical device that is already in use. My research group has developed a verification method called temporal logic model checking for this class of systems. In this approach specifications are expressed in a propositional temporal logic, and reactive systems are modeled as state-transition graphs. An efficient search procedure is used to determine automatically if the specifications are satisfied by the state-transition graph. The technique has been used in the past to find subtle errors in a number of non-trivial circuit and protocol designs.

During the last few years, the size of the reactive systems that can be verified by model checking techniques has increased dramatically. By representing sets of states and transition relations implicitly using Binary Decision Diagrams (BDDs), we are now able to check examples that are many orders of magnitude larger than was previously the case. In this lecture we describe how the BDD-based model checking techniques work and illustrate their power by verifying the Space Shuttle Contingency Guidance Protocol. This protocol specifies what happens when the shuttle has to abort its flight during take-off.

Program Analysis via Graph Reachability

Thomas Reps
Computer Sciences Department
University of Wisconsin
1210 West Dayton Street
Madison, WI 53706, USA
reps@cs.wisc.edu
http://www.cs.wisc.edu/~reps/

Abstract

This paper describes how a number of program-analysis problems can be solved by transforming them to graph-reachability problems. Some of the program-analysis problems that are amenable to this treatment include program slicing, certain dataflow-analysis problems, and the problem of approximating the possible "shapes" that heap-allocated structures in a program can take on. Relationships between graph reachability and other approaches to program analysis are described. Some techniques that go beyond pure graph reachability are also discussed.

1. Introduction

The purpose of program analysis is to ascertain information about a program without actually running the program. For example, in classical dataflow analysis of imperative programs, the goal is to associate an appropriate set of "dataflow facts" with each program point (*i.e.*, with each assignment statement, call statement, I/O statement, predicate of a loop or conditional statement, *etc.*). Typically, the dataflow facts associated with a program point p describe some aspect of the execution state that holds when control reaches p, such as available expressions, live variables, reaching definitions, *etc.* Information obtained from program analysis is used in program optimizers, as well as in tools for software engineering and re-engineering.

Program-analysis frameworks abstract on the common characteristics of some class of program-analysis problems. Examples of analysis frameworks range from the gen/kill dataflow-analysis problems described in many compiler textbooks to much more elaborate frameworks [6]. Typically, there is an "analysis engine" that can find solutions to all problems that can be specified within the framework. Analyzers for different program-analysis problems are created by "plugging in" certain details that specify the program-analysis problem of interest (*e.g.*, the dataflow functions associated with the edges of a program's control-flow graph, *etc.*).

For many program-analysis frameworks, an instantiation of the framework for a particular program-analysis problem yields a set of equations. The analysis engine underlying the framework is a mechanism for solving a particular family of equation sets (*e.g.*, using chaotic iteration to find a least or greatest solution). For example, each gen/kill dataflow-analysis problem instance yields a set of equations that are solved over a domain of finite sets, where the variables in the equations correspond to program points and each equation is of the form $val_p = ((\bigcup_{q \in pred(p)} val_q) - kill_p) \cup gen_p$. The values $kill_p$ and gen_p are constants associated with program point p: gen_p represents dataflow facts "created" at p, and $kill_p$ represents dataflow facts "removed" by p.

This paper presents a program-analysis framework based on a somewhat different principle: Analysis problems are posed as graph-reachability problems. As will be discussed below, we express (or convert) program-analysis problems to *context-free-language reachability problems* ("CFL-reachability problems"), which are a generalization of ordinary graph-reachability problems. CFL-reachability is defined in Section 2. Some of the program-analysis problems that are amenable to this treatment include:

- Interprocedural program slicing.
- Interprocedural versions of a large class of dataflow-analysis problems.
- A method for approximating the possible "shapes" that heap-allocated structures can take on.

There are a number of benefits to be gained from expressing a program-analysis problem as a graph-reachability problem:

- We obtain an efficient algorithm for solving the program-analysis problem. In a case where the program-analysis problem is expressed as a single-source ordinary graph-reachability problem, the problem can be solved in time linear in the number of nodes and edges in the graph; in a case where the program-analysis problem is expressed as a CFL-reachability problem, the problem can be solved in time cubic in the number of nodes in the graph.
- The difference in asymptotic running time needed to solve ordinary reachability problems and CFL-reachability problems provides insight into possible trade-offs between accuracy and running time for certain program-analysis problems: Because a CFL-reachability problem can be solved in an approximate fashion by treating it as an ordinary reachability problem, this provides an automatic way to obtain an approximate (but safe) solution, via a method that is asymptotically faster than the method for obtaining the more accurate solution.

- In program optimization, most of the gains are obtained from making improvements at a program's "hot spots", such as the innermost loops, which means that dataflow information is really only needed for selected locations in the program. Similarly, software-engineering tools that use dataflow analysis often require information only at a certain set of program points (in response to user queries, for example). This suggests that applications that use dataflow analysis could be made more efficient by using a *demand* dataflow-analysis algorithm, which determines whether a given dataflow fact holds at a given point [1,39,27,7,31,14]. For program-analysis problems that can be expressed as CFL-reachability problems, demand algorithms are typically obtained by solving single-target CFL-reachability problems [14].

- The graph-reachability approach provides insight into the prospects for creating parallel program-analysis algorithms. The connection between program analysis and CFL-reachability has been used to establish a number of results that very likely imply that there are limitations on the ability to create efficient parallel algorithms for interprocedural slicing and interprocedural dataflow analysis [29]. Specifically, it was shown that

  – Interprocedural slicing is log-space complete for $\mathcal{P}$.
  – Interprocedural dataflow analysis is $\mathcal{P}$-hard.
  – Interprocedural dataflow-analysis problems that involve finite sets of dataflow facts (such as the classical "gen/kill" problems) are log-space complete for $\mathcal{P}$.

  The consequence of these results is that, unless $\mathcal{P} = \mathcal{NC}$, there do not exist algorithms for interprocedural slicing and interprocedural dataflow analysis in which (i) the number of processors is bounded by a polynomial in the input size, and (ii) the running time is bounded by a polynomial in the log of the input size.

- The graph-reachability approach offers insight into ways that more powerful machinery can be brought to bear on program-analysis problems [27,31].

The remainder of the paper is organized into five sections, as follows: Section 2 defines CFL-reachability. Section 3 discusses how the graph-reachability approach can be used to tackle interprocedural dataflow analysis, interprocedural program slicing, and shape analysis. Section 4 discusses algorithms for solving CFL-reachability problems. Section 5 concerns demand versions of program-analysis problems. Section 6 describes some techniques that go beyond pure graph reachability.

2. Context-Free-Language Reachability Problems

The theme of this paper is that a number of program-analysis problems can be viewed as instances of a more general problem: *CFL-reachability*. A CFL-reachability problem is not an ordinary reachability problem (*e.g.*, transitive closure), but one in which a path is considered to connect two nodes only if the concatenation of the labels on the edges of the path is a word in a particular context-free language:

Definition 2.1. Let L be a context-free language over alphabet Σ, and let G be a graph whose edges are labeled with members of Σ. Each path in G defines a word over Σ, namely, the word obtained by concatenating, in order, the labels of the edges on the path. A path in G is an *L-path* if its word is a member of L. We define four varieties of CFL-reachability problems as follows:

(i)   The *all-pairs L-path problem* is to determine all pairs of nodes n_1 and n_2 such that there exists an L-path in G from n_1 to n_2.

(ii) The *single-source L-path problem* is to determine all nodes n_2 such that there exists an L-path in G from a given source node n_1 to n_2.

(iii) The *single-target L-path problem* is to determine all nodes n_1 such that there exists an L-path in G from n_1 to a given target node n_2.

(iv) The *single-source/single-target L-path problem* is to determine whether there exists an L-path in G from a given source node n_1 to a given target node n_2. □

Other variants of CFL-reachability include the multi-source L-path problem, the multi-target L-path problem, and the multi-source/multi-target L-path problem.

Example. Consider the graph shown below, and let L be the language that consists of strings of matched parentheses and square brackets, with zero or more e's interspersed:

$$L: \; matched \;\rightarrow\; matched\; matched$$
$$\mid\; (\; matched\;)$$
$$\mid\; [\; matched\;]$$
$$\mid\; e$$
$$\mid\; \varepsilon$$

In this graph, there is exactly one L-path from s to t: The path goes exactly once around the cycle, and generates the word "$[(e[])eee[e]]$". □

It is instructive to consider how CFL-reachability relates to two more familiar problems:

- An ordinary graph-reachability problem can be treated as a CFL-reachability problem by labeling each edge with the symbol e and letting L be the regular language e^*. For instance, transitive closure is the all-pairs e^*-problem. (Thus, ordinary graph reachability is an example of *regular-*

language reachability—the special case of CFL-reachability in which the language L referred to in Definition 2.1 is a regular language.)

- The *context-free-language recognition problem* (CFL-recognition) answers questions of the form "Given a string ω and a context-free language L, is $\omega \in L$?" The CFL-recognition problem for ω and L can be formulated as the following special kind of single-source/single-target CFL-reachability problem: Create a linear graph $s \rightarrow \cdots \rightarrow t$ that has $|\omega|$ edges, and label the ith edge with the ith letter of ω. There is an L-path from s to t iff $\omega \in L$ [37].

There is a general result that all CFL-reachability problems can be solved in time cubic in the number of nodes in the graph (see Section 4). This method provides the "analysis engine" for our program-analysis framework. Again, it is instructive to consider how the general case relates to the special cases of ordinary reachability and CFL-recognition:

- A single-source ordinary reachability problem can be solved in time linear in the size of the graph (nodes plus edges) using depth-first search.
- Valiant showed that CFL-recognition can be performed in less than cubic time [34]. Unfortunately, the algorithm does not seem to generalize to arbitrary CFL-reachability problems.

From the standpoint of program analysis, the CFL-reachability constraint is a tool that can be employed to filter out paths that are irrelevant to the solution of an analysis problem. In many program-analysis problems, a graph is used as an intermediate representation of a program, but not all paths in the graph represent potential execution paths. Consequently, it is desirable that the analysis results not be polluted (or polluted as little as possible) by the presence of such paths. Although the question of whether a given path in a program representation corresponds to a possible execution path is, in general, undecidable, in many cases certain paths can be identified as being infeasible because they correspond to "execution paths" with mismatched calls and returns.

In the case of interprocedural dataflow analysis, we can characterize a superset of the feasible paths by introducing a context-free language ($L(realizable)$, defined below) that mimics the call-return structure of a program's execution: The only paths that can possibly be feasible are those in which "returns" are matched with corresponding "calls". These paths are called *realizable paths*.

Realizable paths are defined in terms of a program's *supergraph* G^*, an example of which is shown in Fig. 1. A supergraph consists of a collection of control-flow graphs, one for each procedure in the program. Each procedure call in the program is represented in G^* by two nodes, a *call* node and a *return-site* node. In addition to the ordinary intraprocedural edges that connect the nodes of the individual control-flow graphs, for each procedure call—represented, say, by call node c and return-site node r—G^* contains three edges: an intraprocedural *call-to-return-site* edge from c to r; an interprocedural *call-to-start* edge from c to the start node of the called procedure; an interprocedural *exit-to-return-site* edge from the exit node of the called procedure to r.

Let each call node in G^* be given a unique index from 1 to *CallSites*, where *CallSites* is the total number of call sites in the program. For each call site c_i, label the call-to-start edge and the exit-to-return-site edge with the symbols "$($i$" and "$)i", respectively. Label all other edges with the symbol e. A path in G^* is a *matched path* iff the path's word is in the language $L(matched)$ of balanced-parenthesis strings (interspersed with strings of zero or more e's) generated from nonterminal *realizable* according to the following context-free grammar:

$$
\begin{aligned}
matched \rightarrow\ & matched\ matched \\
| \ & (_i\ matched\ )_i \qquad\qquad \text{for } 1 \le i \le CallSites \\
| \ & e \\
| \ & \varepsilon
\end{aligned}
$$

A path is a *realizable path* iff the path's word is in the language $L(realizable)$:

$$
\begin{aligned}
realizable \rightarrow\ & matched\ realizable \\
| \ & (_i\ realizable \qquad\qquad \text{for } 1 \le i \le CallSites \\
| \ & \varepsilon
\end{aligned}
$$

The language $L(realizable)$ is a language of *partially* balanced parentheses: Every right parenthesis "$)$i$" is balanced by a preceding left parenthesis "$($i$", but the converse need not hold.

To understand these concepts, it helps to examine a few of the paths that occur in Fig. 1.

- The path "$start_{main} \rightarrow n1 \rightarrow n2 \rightarrow start_P \rightarrow n4 \rightarrow exit_P \rightarrow n3$", which has word "$ee(_1ee)_1$", is a matched path (and hence a realizable path, as well). In general, a matched path from m to n, where m and n are in the same procedure, represents a sequence of execution steps during which the call stack may temporarily grow deeper—because of calls—but never shallower than its original depth, before eventually returning to its original depth.
- The path "$start_{main} \rightarrow n1 \rightarrow n2 \rightarrow start_P \rightarrow n4$", which has word "$ee(_1e$", is a realizable path but not a matched path: The call-to-start edge $n2 \rightarrow start_P$ has no matching exit-to-return-site edge. A realizable path from the program's start-node s_{main} to a node n represents a sequence of execution steps that ends, in general, with some number of activation records on the call stack. These correspond to unmatched $(_i$'s in the path's word.
- The path "$start_{main} \rightarrow n1 \rightarrow n2 \rightarrow start_P \rightarrow n4 \rightarrow exit_P \rightarrow n8$", which has word "$ee(_1ee)_2$", is neither a matched path nor a realizable path: The exit-to-return-site edge $exit_P \rightarrow n8$ does not correspond to the preceding call-to-start edge $n2 \rightarrow start_P$. This path represents an infeasible execution path.

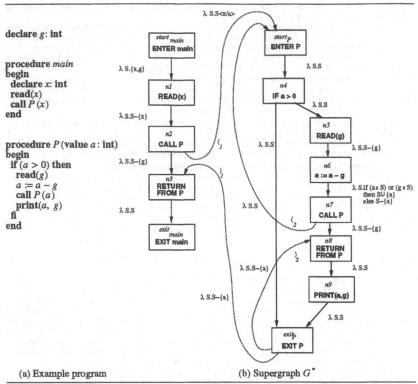

declare *g*: int

procedure *main*
begin
  declare *x*: int
  read(*x*)
  call *P* (*x*)
end

procedure *P* (value *a* : int)
begin
  if (*a* > 0) then
    read(*g*)
    a := *a* − *g*
    call *P* (*a*)
    print(*a*, *g*)
  fi
end

(a) Example program   (b) Supergraph G^*

Fig. 1. An example program and its supergraph G^*. The supergraph is annotated with the dataflow functions for the "possibly-uninitialized variables" problem. The notation S<x/a> denotes the set S with x renamed to a.

3. Three Examples

In this section, we show how three program-analysis problems can be transformed into partially balanced parenthesis problems (using languages similar to the language $L(realizable)$ defined in Section 2). Although these examples illustrate the use of only a limited class of context-free languages, the full power of the CFL-reachability framework is also useful in some situations. That is, there are other program-analysis problems that can be solved by expressing them as L-path problems, where L is a context-free language that is something other than a language of partially balanced parentheses [22].

3.1. Interprocedural Dataflow Analysis

Dataflow analysis is concerned with determining an appropriate dataflow value to associate with each point p in a program to summarize (safely) some aspect of the execution state that holds when control reaches p. To define an instance of a dataflow problem, one needs

- The control-flow graph for the program.
- A domain V of dataflow values. Each point in the program is to be associated with some member of V.
- A meet operator $\sqcap$, used for combining information obtained along different paths.
- An assignment of dataflow functions (of type $V \rightarrow V$) to the edges of the control-flow graph.

   Example. In Fig. 1, the supergraph G^* is annotated with the dataflow functions for the "possibly-uninitialized variables" problem. The possibly-uninitialized variables problem is to determine, for each node n in G^*, a set of program variables that may be uninitialized just before execution reaches n. Thus, V is the power set of the set of program variables. A variable x is possibly uninitialized at n either if there is an x-definition-free path from the start of the program to n, or if there is a path from the start of the program to n on which the last definition of x uses some variable y that itself is possibly uninitialized. For example, the dataflow function associated with edge $n6 \rightarrow n7$ shown in Fig. 1 adds a to the set of possibly-uninitialized variables after node $n6$ if either

a or g is in the set of possibly-uninitialized variables before node $n6$. $\square$

Below we show how a large class of interprocedural dataflow-analysis problems can be handled by transforming them into realizable-path reachability problems. This is a non-standard treatment of dataflow analysis. Ordinarily, a dataflow-analysis problem is formulated as a *path-function problem*: The path function pf_q for path q is the composition of the functions that label the edges of q; the goal is to determine, for each node n, the "meet-over-*all*-paths" solution: $MOP_n = \underset{q \,\in\, \text{Paths}(\textit{start},\, n)}{\sqcap} pf_q(\bot)$, where Paths$(\textit{start}, n)$ denotes the set of paths in the control-flow graph from the start node to n [16].[1] MOP_n represents a summary of the possible execution states that can arise at n; $\bot \in V$ is a special value that represents the execution state at the beginning of the program; $pf_q(\bot)$ represents the contribution of path q to the summarized state at n.

In *inter*procedural dataflow analysis, the goal shifts from the meet-over-*all*-paths solution to the more precise "meet-over-*all-realizable-paths*" solution: $MRP_n = \underset{q \,\in\, \text{RPaths}(\textit{start}_{\textit{main}},\, n)}{\sqcap} pf_q(\bot)$, where RPaths$(\textit{start}_{\textit{main}}, n)$ denotes the set of realizable paths from the main procedure's start node to n (and "realizable path" means a path whose word is in the language $L(\textit{realizable})$ defined in Section 2) [32,5,19,17,28,7]. Although some realizable paths may also be impossible execution paths, none of the non-realizable paths are possible execution paths. By restricting attention to just the realizable paths from $\textit{start}_{\textit{main}}$, we exclude some of the impossible execution paths. In general, therefore, MRP_n characterizes the execution state at n more precisely than MOP_n.

The *interprocedural, finite, distributive, subset problems* (*IFDS problems*) are those interprocedural dataflow-analysis problems that involve a finite set of dataflow facts, and dataflow functions that distribute over the confluence operator (either set union or set intersection, depending on the problem). Thus, an instance of an IFDS problem consists of the following:

- A supergraph G^*.
- A finite set D (the universe of dataflow facts). Each point in the program is to be associated with some member of the domain 2^D.
- An assignment of distributive dataflow functions (of type $2^D \to 2^D$) to the edges of G^*.

We assume that the meet operator is union; problems in which the meet operator is intersection can always be converted into an equivalent problem in which the meet operator is union.

The IFDS framework can be used for languages with a variety of features (including procedure calls, parameters, global and local variables, and pointers). The call-to-return-site edges are included in G^* so that the IFDS framework can handle programs with local variables and parameters. The dataflow functions on call-to-return-site and exit-to-return-site edges permit the information about local variables and value parameters that holds at the call site to be combined with the information about global variables and reference parameters that holds at the end of the called procedure. The IFDS problems include, but are not limited to, the classical "gen/kill" problems (also known as the "bit-vector" or "separable" problems), *e.g.*, reaching definitions, available expressions, and live variables. In addition, the IFDS problems include many non-gen/kill problems, including possibly-uninitialized variables, truly-live variables [10], and copy-constant propagation [9, pp. 660].

Expressing a problem so that it falls within the IFDS framework may, in some cases, involve a loss of precision. For example, there may be a loss of precision involved in formulating an IFDS version of a problem that must account for aliasing. However, once a problem has been cast as an IFDS problem, it is possible to find the MRP solution with no further loss of precision.

One way to solve an IFDS problem is to convert it to a realizable-path reachability problem [28,14]. For each problem instance, we build an *exploded supergraph* $G^\#$, in which each node $\langle n, d \rangle$ represents dataflow fact $d \in D$ at supergraph node n, and each edge represents a dependence between individual dataflow facts at different supergraph nodes.

The key insight behind this "explosion" is that a distributive function f in $2^D \to 2^D$ can be represented using a graph with $2D + 2$ nodes; this graph is called f's *representation relation*. Half of the nodes in this graph represent f's input; the other half represent its output. D of these nodes represent the "individual" dataflow facts that form set D, and the remaining node (which we call Λ) essentially represents the empty set. An edge $\Lambda \to d$ means that d is in $f(S)$ regardless of the value of S (in particular, d is in $f(\varnothing)$). An edge $d_1 \to d_2$ means that d_2 is not in $f(\varnothing)$, and is in $f(S)$ whenever d_1 is in S. Every graph includes the edge $\Lambda \to \Lambda$; this is so that function composition corresponds to compositions of representation relations (this is explained below).

Example. The main procedure shown in Fig. 1 has two variables, x and g. Therefore, the representation relations for the dataflow functions associated with this procedure will each have six nodes. The function associated with the edge from $\textit{start}_{\textit{main}}$ to $n1$ is $\lambda S.\{x, g\}$; that is, variables x and g are added to the set of possibly-uninitialized variables regardless of the value of S. The representation relation for this function is shown in Fig. 2(a).

---

[1] For some dataflow-analysis problems, such as constant propagation, the meet-over-all-paths solution is uncomputable. A sufficient condition for the solution to be computable is for each edge function f to distribute over the meet operator; that is, for all $a, b \in V$, $f(a \sqcap b) = f(a) \sqcap f(b)$. The problems amenable to the graph-reachability approach are distributive.

10

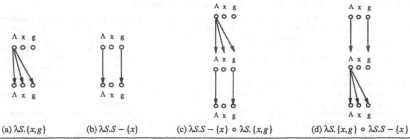

(a) $\lambda S.\{x,g\}$ (b) $\lambda S.S - \{x\}$ (c) $\lambda S.S - \{x\} \circ \lambda S.\{x,g\}$ (d) $\lambda S.\{x,g\} \circ \lambda S.S - \{x\}$

Fig. 2. Representation relations for two functions and the two ways of composing the functions.

The representation relation for the function $\lambda S.S - \{x\}$ (which is associated with the edge from $n1$ to $n2$) is shown in Fig. 2(b). Note that x is never in the output set, and g is there iff it is in S. □

A function's representation relation captures the function's semantics in the sense that the representation relation can be used to evaluate the function. In particular, the result of applying function f to input S is the union of the values represented by the "output" nodes in f's representation relation that are the targets of edges from the "input" nodes that represent either Λ or a node in S. For example, consider applying the dataflow function $\lambda S.S - \{x\}$ to the set $\{x\}$ using the representation relation shown in Fig. 2(b). There is no edge out of the initial x node, and the only edge out of the initial Λ node is to the final Λ node, so the result of this application is $\emptyset$. The result of applying the same function to the set $\{x,g\}$ is $\{g\}$, because there is an edge from the initial g node to the final g node.

The composition of two functions is represented by "pasting together" the graphs that represent the individual functions. For example, the composition of the two functions discussed above, $\lambda S.S - \{x\} \circ \lambda S.\{x,g\}$, is represented by the graph shown in Fig. 2(c). Paths in a "pasted-together" graph represent the result of applying the composed function. For example, in Fig. 2(c) there is a path from the initial Λ node to the final g node. This means that g is in the final set regardless of the value of S to which the composed function is applied. There is *no* path from an initial node to the final x node; this means that x is not in the final set, regardless of the value of S.

To understand the need for the $\Lambda \rightarrow \Lambda$ edges in representation relations, consider the composition of the two example functions in the opposite order, $\lambda S.\{x,g\} \circ \lambda S.S - \{x\}$, which is represented by the graph shown in Fig. 2(d). Note that both x and g are in the final set regardless of the value of S to which the composed functions are applied. In Fig. 2(d), this is reflected by the paths from the initial Λ node to the final x and g nodes. However, if there were no edge from the initial Λ node to the intermediate Λ node, there would be no such paths, and the graph would not correctly represent the composition of the two functions.

Returning to the definition of the exploded supergraph $G^\#$: Each node n in supergraph G^* is "exploded" into $D + 1$ nodes in $G^\#$, and each edge $m \rightarrow n$ in G^* is "exploded" into the representation relation of the function associated with $m \rightarrow n$. In particular:

(i)   For every node n in G^*, there is a node $\langle n, \Lambda \rangle$ in $G^\#$.
(ii) For every node n in G^*, and every dataflow fact $d \in D$, there is a node $\langle n, d \rangle$ in $G^\#$.

Given function f associated with edge $m \rightarrow n$ of G^*:

(iii) There is an edge in $G^\#$ from node $\langle m, \Lambda \rangle$ to node $\langle n, d \rangle$ for every $d \in f(\emptyset)$.
(iv) There is an edge in $G^\#$ from node $\langle m, d_1 \rangle$ to node $\langle n, d_2 \rangle$ for every d_1, d_2 such that $d_2 \in f(\{ d_1 \})$ and $d_2 \notin f(\emptyset)$.
(v)   There is an edge in $G^\#$ from node $\langle m, \Lambda \rangle$ to node $\langle n, \Lambda \rangle$.

Because "pasted together" representation relations correspond to function composition, a path in the exploded supergraph from node $\langle m, d_1 \rangle$ to node $\langle n, d_2 \rangle$ means that if dataflow fact d_1 holds at supergraph node m, then dataflow fact d_2 holds at node n. By looking at paths that start from node $\langle start_{main}, \Lambda \rangle$ (which represents the fact that no dataflow facts hold at the start of procedure *main*) we can determine which dataflow facts hold at each node. However, we are not interested in *all* paths in $G^\#$, only those that correspond to *realizable* paths in G^*; these are exactly the realizable paths in $G^\#$. (For a proof that a dataflow fact d is in MRP_n iff there is a realizable path in $G^\#$ from node $\langle start_{main}, \Lambda \rangle$ to node $\langle n, d \rangle$, see [25].)

Example. The exploded supergraph that corresponds to the instance of the "possibly-uninitialized variables" problem shown in Fig. 1 is shown in Fig. 3. The dataflow functions are replaced by their representation relations. In Fig. 3, closed circles represent nodes that are reachable along realizable paths from $\langle start_{main}, \Lambda \rangle$. Open circles represent nodes not reachable along realizable paths. (For example, note that nodes $\langle n8, g \rangle$ and $\langle n9, g \rangle$ are reachable only along non-realizable paths from $\langle start_{main}, \Lambda \rangle$.) This information indicates the nodes' values in the meet-over-all-realizable-paths solution to the dataflow-analysis problem. For instance, the meet-over-all-realizable-paths solution at node $exit_P$ is the set $\{g\}$. (That is, variable g is the only possibly-

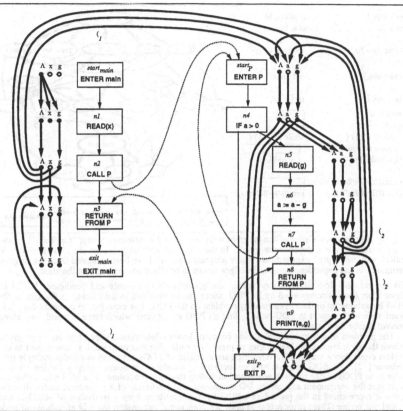

Fig. 3. The exploded supergraph that corresponds to the instance of the possibly-uninitialized variables problem shown in Fig. 1. Closed circles represent nodes of $G^{\#}$ that are reachable along realizable paths from $\langle start_{main}, \Lambda \rangle$. Open circles represent nodes not reachable along such paths.

uninitialized variable just before execution reaches the exit node of procedure P.) In Fig. 3, this information can be obtained by determining that there is a realizable path from $\langle start_{main}, \Lambda \rangle$ to $\langle exit_P, g \rangle$, but not from $\langle start_{main}, \Lambda \rangle$ to $\langle exit_P, a \rangle$. □

3.2. Interprocedural Program Slicing

Slicing is an operation that identifies semantically meaningful decompositions of programs, where the decompositions consist of elements that are not necessarily textually contiguous [36,24,8,12,26,33]. Slicing, and subsequent manipulation of slices, has applications in many software-engineering tools, including tools for program understanding, maintenance, debugging, testing, differencing, specialization, reuse, and merging. (See [33] for references to the literature.)

There are two kinds of slices: a *backward slice* of a program with respect to a set of program elements S is the set of all program elements that might affect (either directly or transitively) the values of the variables used at members of S; a *forward slice* with respect to S is the set of all program elements that might be affected by the computations performed at members of S. A program and one of its backward slices is shown in Fig. 4.

The value of a variable x defined at p is directly affected by the values of the variables used at p and by the predicates that control how many times p is executed; the value of a variable y used at p is directly affected by assignments to y that reach p and by the predicates that control how many times p is executed. Consequently, a slice can be obtained by following chains of dependences in the directly-affects relation. This observation is due to Ottenstein and Ottenstein [24], who noted that *program dependence graphs* (PDGs), which were originally devised for use in parallelizing and vectorizing compilers, are a convenient data structure for slicing. The PDG for a program is a directed graph whose nodes are connected by several kinds of edges. The nodes in the PDG represent the individual statements and predicates of the program. The edges of a PDG represent

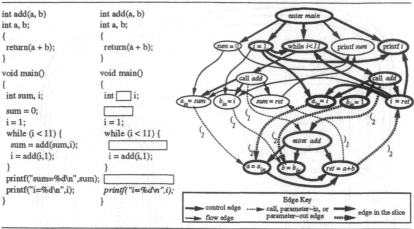

```
int add(a, b)          int add(a, b)
int a, b;              int a, b;
{                      {
  return(a + b);         return(a + b);
}                      }

void main()            void main()
{                      {
  int sum, i;            int [    ] i;

  sum = 0;              [        ]
  i = 1;               i = 1;
  while (i < 11) {     while (i < 11) {
    sum = add(sum,i);    [              ]
    i = add(i,1);         i = add(i,1);
  }                      }
  printf("sum=%d\n",sum);  [                    ]
  printf("i=%d\n",i);    printf("i=%d\n",i);
}                      }
```

Edge Key

→ control edge ----▶ call, parameter-in, or ➡ edge in the slice
→ flow edge   parameter-out edge

Fig. 4. A program, the slice of the program with respect to the statement *printf("i = %d\n", i)*, and the program's system dependence graph. In the slice, the starting point for the slice is shown in italics, and the empty boxes indicate where program elements have been removed from the original program. In the dependence graph, the edges shown in boldface are the edges in the slice.

the control and flow dependences among the procedure's statements and predicates [18,24,8]. Once a program is represented by its PDG, slices can be obtained in time linear in the size of the PDG by solving an ordinary reachability problem on the PDG. For example, to compute the backward slice with respect to PDG node v, find all PDG nodes from which there is a path to v along control and/or flow edges.

The problem of *inter*procedural slicing concerns how to determine a slice of an entire program, where the slice crosses the boundaries of procedure calls. For this purpose, it is convenient to use *system dependence graphs* (SDGs), which are a variant of PDGs extended to handle multiple procedures [12]. An SDG consists of a collection of procedure dependence graphs (which we will refer to as PDGs)—one for each procedure, including the main procedure. In addition to nodes that represent the assignment statements, I/O statements, and predicates of a procedure, each call statement is represented in the procedure's PDG by a call node and by a collection of actual-in and actual-out nodes: There is an actual-in node for each actual parameter; there is an actual-out node for the return value (if any) and for each value-result parameter that might be modified during the call. Similarly, procedure entry is represented by an entry node and a collection of formal-in and formal-out nodes. (Global variables are treated as "extra" value-result parameters, and thus give rise to additional actual-in, actual-out, formal-in, and formal-out nodes.) The edges of a PDG represent the control and flow dependences in the usual way. The PDGs are connected together to form the SDG by *call* edges (which represent procedure calls, and run from a call node to an entry node) and by *parameter-in* and *parameter-out* edges (which represent parameter passing, and which run from an actual-in node to the corresponding formal-in node, and from a formal-out node to all corresponding actual-out nodes, respectively). In Fig. 4, the graph shown on the right is the SDG for the program that appears on the left.

One algorithm for interprocedural slicing was presented in Weiser's original paper on slicing [36]. This algorithm is equivalent to solving an ordinary reachability problem on the SDG. However, Weiser's algorithm is imprecise in the sense that it may report effects that are transmitted through paths that have mismatched calls and returns (and hence do not represent feasible execution paths). The slices obtained in this way may include unwanted components. For example, there is a path in the SDG shown in Fig. 4 from the node of procedure *main* labeled "*sum*=0" to the node of *main* labeled "printf *i*." However, this path corresponds to an "execution" in which procedure *add* is called from the first call site in *main*, but returns to the second call site in *main*. This could never happen, and so the node labeled "*sum*=0" should not be included in the slice with respect to the node labeled "printf *i*".

Although it is undecidable whether a path in the SDG actually corresponds to a possible execution path, we can again use a language of partially balanced parentheses to exclude from consideration paths in which calls and returns are mismatched. The parentheses are defined as follows: Let each call node in SDG G be given a unique index from 1 to *CallSites*, where *CallSites* is the total number of call sites in the program. For each call site c_i, label the outgoing parameter-in edges and the incoming parameter-out edges with the symbols "$(_i$" and "$)_i$", respectively; label the outgoing call edge with "$(_i$". Label all other edges in G with the symbol e. (See Fig. 4.)

Slicing is slightly different from the CFL-reachability problems defined in Definition 2.1. For instance, a backward slice with respect to a given target node t consists of the set of nodes that *lie on* a realizable path from the entry node of *main* to *t* (*cf.* Definition 2.1). However, as long as *t* is located within a procedure that is transitively callable from *main*, we can change this problem into a single-target CFL-reachability problem (in the sense of Definition 2.1(iii)). We say that a path in an SDG is a *slice path* iff the path's word is in the language *L*(*slice*):

$$
\begin{aligned}
\textit{unbalanced-right} \ &\rightarrow \ \textit{unbalanced-right matched} \\
&| \ \ \textit{unbalanced-right} \ )_i \qquad \text{for } 1 \le i \le \textit{CallSites} \\
&| \ \ \varepsilon \\
\textit{slice} \ &\rightarrow \ \textit{unbalanced-right realizable}
\end{aligned}
$$

The nodes in the backward slice with respect to *t* are all nodes *n* such that there exists an *L*(*slice*)-path between *n* and *t*. That is, the nodes in the backward slice are the solution to the single-target *L*(*slice*)-path problem for target node *t*.

To see this, suppose that $r\|s$ is an *L*(*slice*)-path that connects *n* and *t*, where *r* is an *L*(*unbalanced-right*)-path and *s* is an *L*(*realizable*)-path. As long as *t* is located within a procedure that is transitively callable from *main*, there exists a path $p\|q$ (of control and call edges) that connects the entry node of *main* to *n*, where *p* is an *L*(*realizable*)-path and *q* "balances" *r*; that is, the path $q\|r$ is an *L*(*matched*)-path. It can be shown that the path $p\|q\|r\|s$ is an *L*(*realizable*)-path.

3.3. Shape Analysis

Shape analysis is concerned with finding approximations to the possible "shapes" that heap-allocated structures in a program can take on [30,15,23]. This section addresses shape analysis for imperative languages that support non-destructive manipulation of heap-allocated objects. Similar techniques apply to shape analysis for pure functional languages.

We assume we are working with an imperative language that has assignment statements, conditional statements, loops, I/O statements, goto statements, and procedure calls; the parameter-passing mechanism is either by value or value-result; recursion (direct and indirect) is permitted; the language provides atomic data (*e.g.*, integer, real, boolean, identifiers, *etc.*) and Lisp-like constructor and selector operations (nil, cons, car, and cdr), together with appropriate predicates (equal, atom, and null), but not rplaca and rplacd operations. Because of the latter restriction, circular structures cannot be created; however, dag structures (as well as trees) can be created. We assume that a read statement reads just an atom and not an entire tree or dag. For convenience, we also assume that only one constructor or selector is performed per statement (*e.g.*, "y := cons(car(x), y)" must be broken into two statements: "*temp* := car(x); y := cons(*temp*, y)"). (The latter assumption is not essential, but simplifies the presentation.)

Example. An example program is shown in Fig. 5. The program first reads atoms and forms a list *x*; it then traverses *x* to assign *y* the reversal of *x*. This example will be used throughout the remainder of this section to illustrate our techniques. □

```
x := nil
read(z)
while z ≠ 0 do
    x := cons(z, x)
    read(z)
od
y := nil
while x ≠ nil do
    temp := car(x)
    y := cons(temp, y)
    x := cdr(x)
od
```

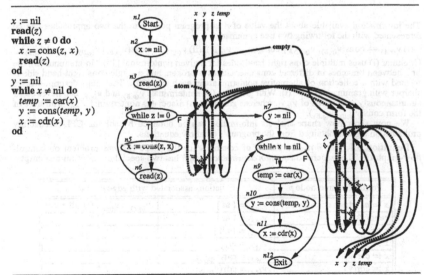

Fig. 5. A program, its control-flow graph, and its equation dependence graph. All edges of the equation dependence graph shown without labels have the label *id*. The path shown by the dotted lines is a *hd_path* from **atom** to node ⟨*n12,y*⟩.

A collection of dataflow equations can be used to capture an approximation to the shapes of a superset of the terms that can arise at the various points in the program [30,15]. The domain Shape of shape descriptors is the set of selector sequences terminated by **at** or **nil**: Shape = $2^{L((\mathbf{hd}+\mathbf{tl})^*(\mathbf{at}+\mathbf{nil}))}$. Each sequence in $L((\mathbf{hd}+\mathbf{tl})^*(\mathbf{at}+\mathbf{nil}))$ represents a possible root-to-leaf path. Note that a single shape descriptor in Shape may contain both the selector sequences **hd.tl.at** and **hd.tl.hd.at**, even though the two paths cannot occur together in a single term.

Dataflow variables correspond to ⟨*program-point,program-variable*⟩ pairs. For example, if x is a program variable and p is a point in the program, then $v_{\langle p,x \rangle}$ is a dataflow variable. The dataflow equations are associated with the control-flow graph's edges; there are *several* dataflow equations associated with each edge, one per program variable. The equations on an edge $p \rightarrow q$ reflect the execution actions performed at node p. Thus, the value of a dataflow variable $v_{\langle q,x \rangle}$ approximates the shape of x just *before* q executes. The dataflow-equation schemas are shown in Fig. 6.

Procedure calls with value parameters are handled by introducing equations between dataflow variables associated with actual parameters and dataflow variables associated with formal parameters to reflect the binding changes that occur when a procedure is called. (By introducing equations between dataflow variables associated with formal out-parameters and dataflow variables associated with the corresponding actuals at the return site, call-by-value-result can also be handled.)

When solved over a suitable domain, the equations define an abstract interpretation of the program. The question, however, is: "Over what domain are they to be solved?" One approach is to let the value of each dataflow variable be a *set* of shapes (*i.e.*, a set of sets of root-to-leaf paths) and the join operation be union [30,15]. Functions **cons**, **car**, and **cdr** are appropriate functions from shape sets to shape sets. For example, **cons** is defined as:

$$\mathbf{cons} =_{df} \lambda S_1.\lambda S_2.\{\,\{\,\mathbf{hd}.p_1 \mid p_1 \in s_1\,\} \cup \{\,\mathbf{tl}.p_2 \mid p_2 \in s_2\,\} \mid s_1 \in S_1, s_2 \in S_2\,\}.$$

In our work, however, we use an alternative approach: The value of each dataflow variable is a *single* Shape (*i.e.*, a single set of root-to-leaf paths), and the join operation is union [23]. Functions **cons**, **car**, and **cdr** are functions from Shape to Shape. For example, **cons** is defined as:

$$\mathbf{cons} =_{df} \lambda S_1.\lambda S_2.\{\,\mathbf{hd}.p_1 \mid p_1 \in S_1\,\} \cup \{\,\mathbf{tl}.p_2 \mid p_2 \in S_2\,\}.$$

With both approaches, solutions to shape-analysis equations are, in general, infinite. Thus, in practice, there must be a way to report the "shape information" that characterizes the possible values of a program variable at a given program point *indirectly*—*i.e.*, in terms of the values of other program variables at other program points. This indirect information can be viewed as a *simplified set of equations* [30], or, equivalently, as a *regular-tree grammar* [15,23].

The use of domain Shape in place of 2^{Shape} does involve some loss of precision. A feeling for the kind of information that is lost can be obtained by considering the following program fragment:

> **if** $\cdots$ **then** p: $A := \text{cons}(B, C)$
> **else** q: $A := \text{cons}(D, E)$
> **fi**
> r: $\cdots$

The information available about the value of A at program point r in the two approaches can be represented with the following two tree grammars:

(i) $v_{\langle r,A \rangle} \rightarrow \mathbf{cons}(v_{\langle p,B \rangle}, v_{\langle p,C \rangle}) \mid \mathbf{cons}(v_{\langle q,D \rangle}, v_{\langle q,E \rangle})$ (ii) $v_{\langle r,A \rangle} \rightarrow \mathbf{cons}(v_{\langle p,B \rangle} \mid v_{\langle q,D \rangle}, v_{\langle p,C \rangle} \mid v_{\langle q,E \rangle})$

Grammar (i) uses multiple **cons** right-hand sides for a given nonterminal [15]. In grammar (ii), the link between branches in different **cons** alternatives is broken, and a single **cons** right-hand side is formed with a collection of alternative nonterminals in each arm [23]. The shape descriptions are sharper with grammars of type (i): With grammar (i), nonterminals $v_{\langle p,B \rangle}$ and $v_{\langle q,E \rangle}$ can never occur simultaneously as children of $v_{\langle r,A \rangle}$, whereas grammar (ii) associates nonterminal $v_{\langle r,A \rangle}$ with trees of the form $\mathbf{cons}(v_{\langle p,B \rangle}, v_{\langle q,E \rangle})$.

We now show how shape-analysis information can be obtained by solving CFL-reachability problems on a graph obtained from the program's dataflow equations.

Definition 3.1. Let Eqn$_G$ be the set of equations for the shape-analysis problem on control-flow-graph G. The associated *equation dependence graph* has two special nodes **atom** and **empty**,

Form of source-node p	Equations associated with edge $p \rightarrow q$	
$x := a$, where a is an atom	$v_{\langle q,x \rangle} = \{\,\mathbf{at}\,\}$	$v_{\langle q,z \rangle} = v_{\langle p,z \rangle}$, for all $z \neq x$
$\mathbf{read}(x)$	$v_{\langle q,x \rangle} = \{\,\mathbf{at}\,\}$	"
$x := \mathbf{nil}$	$v_{\langle q,x \rangle} = \{\,\mathbf{nil}\,\}$	"
$x := y$	$v_{\langle q,x \rangle} = v_{\langle p,y \rangle}$	"
$x := \text{car}(y)$	$v_{\langle q,x \rangle} = \mathbf{car}(v_{\langle p,y \rangle})$	"
$x := \text{cdr}(y)$	$v_{\langle q,x \rangle} = \mathbf{cdr}(v_{\langle p,y \rangle})$	"
$x := \text{cons}(y, z)$	$v_{\langle q,x \rangle} = \mathbf{cons}(v_{\langle p,y \rangle}, v_{\langle p,z \rangle})$	"

Fig. 6. Dataflow-equation schemas for shape analysis.

together with a node $\langle p,z \rangle$ for each variable $v_{\langle p,z \rangle}$ in Eqn_G. The edges of the graph, each of which is labeled with one of $\{\ id,\ hd,\ tl,\ hd^{-1},\ tl^{-1}\ \}$, are defined as shown in the following table:

Form of equation	Edge(s) in the equation dependence graph	Label
$v_{\langle q,x \rangle} = \{\ \mathbf{at}\ \}$	$\mathbf{atom} \rightarrow \langle q,x \rangle$	id
$v_{\langle q,x \rangle} = \{\ \mathbf{nil}\ \}$	$\mathbf{empty} \rightarrow \langle q,x \rangle$	id
$v_{\langle q,x \rangle} = v_{\langle p,y \rangle}$	$\langle p,y \rangle \rightarrow \langle q,x \rangle$	id
$v_{\langle q,x \rangle} = \mathbf{cons}(v_{\langle p,y \rangle},\ v_{\langle p,z \rangle})$	$\langle p,y \rangle \rightarrow \langle q,x \rangle$ $\langle p,z \rangle \rightarrow \langle q,x \rangle$	hd tl
$v_{\langle q,x \rangle} = \mathbf{car}(v_{\langle p,y \rangle})$	$\langle p,y \rangle \rightarrow \langle q,x \rangle$	hd^{-1}
$v_{\langle q,x \rangle} = \mathbf{cdr}(v_{\langle p,y \rangle})$	$\langle p,y \rangle \rightarrow \langle q,x \rangle$	tl^{-1}

□

The equation dependence graph for this section's example is shown in Fig. 5.

Shape-analysis information can be obtained by solving *three* CFL-reachability problems on the equation dependence graph, using the following context-free grammars:

$$L_1: \quad id\_path \rightarrow id\_path\ id\_path$$
$$| \quad hd\ id\_path\ hd^{-1}$$
$$| \quad tl\ id\_path\ tl^{-1}$$
$$| \quad id$$
$$| \quad \varepsilon$$
$$L_2: \quad hd\_path \rightarrow id\_path\ hd\ id\_path$$
$$L_3: \quad tl\_path \rightarrow id\_path\ tl\ id\_path$$

The language L_1 represents paths in which each hd (tl) is balanced by a matching hd^{-1} (tl^{-1}); these paths correspond to values transmitted along execution paths in which each cons operation (which gives rise to a hd or tl label on an edge in the path) is eventually "taken apart" by a matching car (hd^{-1}) or cdr (tl^{-1}) operation. Thus, the second and third rules of the L_1 grammar are the grammar-theoretic analogs of McCarthy's rules: "car(cons(x, y)) = x" and "cdr(cons(x, y)) = y" [21].

The language L_2 represents paths that are slightly unbalanced—those with one unmatched hd; these paths correspond to the possible values that could be accessed by performing one additional **car** operation (which would extend the path with an additional hd^{-1}). The language L_3 also represents paths that are slightly unbalanced—in this case, those with one unmatched tl; these paths correspond to the possible values that could be accessed by performing one additional **cdr** operation (extending the path with tl^{-1}).

Example. Suppose we are interested in characterizing the shape of program variable y just before the **exit** statement of the program shown in Fig. 5. We can determine information about the possible origin of the root constituent of y at $n12$ by solving the single-target L_1-path problem for $\langle n12,y \rangle$. This yields the set $\{\ \langle n12,y \rangle,\ \langle n8,y \rangle,\ \langle n11,y \rangle,\ \mathbf{empty}\ \}$. This indicates that y is either nil or was allocated at $n10$ during an execution of the second while loop. Similarly, the solution to the single-target L_2-path problem for $\langle n12,y \rangle$ is the set $\{\ \langle n10,temp \rangle,\ \langle n5,z \rangle,\ \langle n4,z \rangle,\ \mathbf{atom}\ \}$. This indicates that the atom in car(y) is one originally read in as the value of z. (See Fig. 5, which shows an L_2-path from **atom** to $\langle n12,y \rangle$.) Finally, the solution to the single-target L_3-path problem for $\langle n12,y \rangle$ is the set $\{\ \langle n10,y \rangle,\ \langle n9,y \rangle,\ \langle n8,y \rangle,\ \langle n11,y \rangle,\ \mathbf{empty}\ \}$. This indicates that the tail of y is either nil or was allocated at $n10$ during an execution of the second while loop.

This information can be interpreted as the following regular-tree grammar:

$$\langle n12,y \rangle \rightarrow \langle n12,y \rangle\ |\ \langle n8,y \rangle\ |\ \langle n11,y \rangle\ |\ \mathbf{empty}$$
$$|\ \mathbf{cons}(\langle n10,temp \rangle\ |\ \langle n5,z \rangle\ |\ \langle n4,z \rangle\ |\ \mathbf{atom},\ \langle n10,y \rangle\ |\ \langle n9,y \rangle\ |\ \langle n8,y \rangle\ |\ \langle n11,y \rangle\ |\ \mathbf{empty}) \quad □$$

4. Algorithms for Solving CFL-Reachability Problems

CFL-reachability problems can be solved via a simple dynamic-programming algorithm. The grammar is first normalized by introducing new nonterminals wherever necessary so that the right-hand side of each production has at most two symbols (either terminals or nonterminals). Then, additional edges are added to the graph according to the patterns shown in Fig. 7 until no more edges can be added. The solution is obtained from the edges labeled with the grammar's root symbol. When an appropriate worklist algorithm is used, the running time of this algorithm is cubic in the number of nodes in the graph [22]. (This algorithm can be thought of as a generalization of the

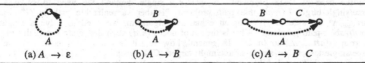

(a) $A \rightarrow \varepsilon$ (b) $A \rightarrow B$ (c) $A \rightarrow B\ C$

Fig. 7. Patterns for adding edges to solve a CFL-reachability problem. In each case, the dotted edge is added to the graph.

CYK algorithm for CFL-recognition [38].)

Although all CFL-reachability problems can be solved in time cubic in the number of graph nodes, one can sometimes do asymptotically better than this by taking advantage of the structure of the graph that arises in a program-analysis problem. For instance, with IFDS problems, the number of nodes in the exploded supergraph is ND, where N is the number of nodes in the supergraph and D is the size of the universe of dataflow facts. However, by taking advantage of the structure of the exploded supergraph, IFDS problems can be solved in time $O(ED^3)$, which is asymptotically better than the general-case time bound of $O(N^3D^3)$ [28,14]. A similar improvement over the general-case time bound can be obtained for interprocedural slicing, as well [26].

5. Solving Demand Versions of Program-Analysis Problems

An exhaustive dataflow-analysis algorithm associates with each point in a program a set of "dataflow facts" that are guaranteed to hold whenever that point is reached during program execution. By contrast, a *demand* dataflow-analysis algorithm determines whether a single given dataflow fact holds at a single given point [1,27,7,14]. Demand analysis can sometimes be preferable to exhaustive analysis for the following reasons:

- *Narrowing the focus to specific points of interest.* Software-engineering tools that use dataflow analysis often require information only at a certain set of program points. Similarly, in program optimization, most of the gains are obtained from making improvements at a program's "hot spots"—in particular, its innermost loops. The use of a demand algorithm has, in some cases, the potential to reduce greatly the amount of extraneous information computed.
- *Narrowing the focus to specific dataflow facts of interest.* Even when dataflow information is desired for every program point p, the full set of dataflow facts at p may not be required. For example, for the uninitialized-variables problem we are ordinarily interested in determining only whether the variables *used* at p might be uninitialized, rather than determining that information at p for *all* variables.
- *Reducing work in preliminary phases.* In problems that can be decomposed into separate phases, not all of the information from one phase may be required by subsequent phases. For example, the MayMod problem determines, for each call site, which variables may be modified during the call. This problem can be decomposed into two phases: computing side effects disregarding aliases (the so-called DMod problem), and computing alias information [3]. Given a demand (*e.g.*, "What is the MayMod set for a given call site c?"), a demand algorithm has the potential to reduce drastically the amount of work spent in earlier phases by propagating only relevant demands (*e.g.*, "What are the alias pairs (x, y) such that x is in DMod(c)"?).
- *Sidestepping incremental-updating problems.* A transformation performed at one point in the program can affect previously computed dataflow information at other points in the program. In many cases, the old information at such points is no longer safe; the dataflow information needs to be updated before it is possible to perform further transformations at such points. Incremental dataflow analysis could be used to maintain complete information at all program points; however, updating all invalidated information can be expensive. An alternative is to demand only the dataflow information needed to validate a proposed transformation; each demand would be solved using the current program, so the answer would be up-to-date.
- *Demand analysis as a user-level operation.* It is desirable to have program-development tools in which the user can ask questions interactively about various aspects of a program [20]. Such tools are particularly useful when debugging, when trying to understand complicated code, or when trying to transform a program to execute efficiently on a parallel machine. Because it is unlikely that a programmer will ask questions about all program points, solving just the user's sequence of demands is likely to be significantly less costly than performing an exhaustive analysis.

Of course, determining whether a given fact holds at a given point may require determining whether other, related facts hold at other points (and those other facts may not be "facts of interest" in the sense of the second bullet-point above). It is desirable, therefore, for a demand-driven program-analysis algorithm to minimize the amount of such auxiliary information computed.

For program-analysis problems that have been transformed into graph-reachability problems, demand algorithms are obtained for free, by solving a single-target or multi-target graph-reachability problem. For instance, the problem transformation described in Section 3.1 has been used to devise demand algorithms for interprocedural dataflow analysis [25,14,13]. Because an algorithm for solving single-target (or multi-target) reachability problems focuses on the nodes that reach the specific target(s), it minimizes the amount of extraneous information computed.

In the case of IFDS problems, to answer a single demand we need to solve a single-source/single-target $L(realizable)$-path problem: "Is there a realizable path in $G^\#$ from node $\langle start_{main}, \Lambda \rangle$ to node $\langle n, d \rangle$?" For an exhaustive algorithm, we need to solve a single-source $L(realizable)$-path problem: "What is the set of nodes $\langle n, d \rangle$ such that there is a realizable path in $G^\#$ from $\langle start_{main}, \Lambda \rangle$ to $\langle n, d \rangle$?" In general, however, it is not known how to solve single-source/single-target (or single-source/multi-target) CFL-reachability problems any faster than single-source CFL-reachability problems. Experimental results showed that in situations when only a small number of demands are made, or when most demands are answered *yes*, a demand algorithm for IDFS problems (*i.e.*, for the single-source/single-target or single-source/multi-target $L(realizable)$-path problems) runs faster than an exhaustive algorithm (*i.e.*, for the single-source

L (*realizable*)-path problem) [14,13].

In the case of partially balanced parenthesis problems, it is possible to use a hybrid scheme; that is, one in between a pure exhaustive and a pure demand-driven approach. The hybrid approach takes advantage of the fact that there is a natural way to divide partially balanced parenthesis problems into two stages. The first stage is carried out in an exhaustive fashion, after which individual queries are answered on a demand-driven basis. In the description that follows, we explain the hybrid technique for backward interprocedural slicing [12,26]. A similar technique also applies in the case of IFDS problems.

The preprocessing step adds *summary edges* to the SDG. Each summary edge represents a matched path between an actual-in and an actual-out node (where the two nodes are associated with the same a call site). Let P be the number of procedures in the program; let E be the maximum number of control and flow edges in any procedure's PDG; and let *Params* be the the maximum number of actual-in vertices in any procedure's PDG. There are no more than *CallSites Params^2* summary edges, and the task of identifying all summary edges can be performed in time $O((P \times E \times Params) + (CallSites \times Params^3))$ [26]. By the *augmented SDG*, we mean the SDG after all appropriate summary edges have been added to it.

The second, demand-driven, stage involves only *regular-reachability* problems on the augmented SDG. In the second stage, we use the following two linear grammars:

unbalanced-right' → *unbalanced-right' summary*	*realizable'* → *summary realizable'*
| *unbalanced-right' e*	| *e realizable'*
| *unbalanced-right'*)$_i$ 1≤*i*≤*CallSites*	| ($_i$ *realizable'* 1≤*i*≤*CallSites*
| ε	| ε

Suppose we wish to find the backward slice with respect to SDG node n. First, we solve the single-target L (*realizable'*)-path problem for node n, which yields a set of nodes S. Let S' be the subset of actual-out nodes in S. The set of nodes in the slice is S together with the solution to the multi-target L (*unbalanced-right'*)-path problem with respect to S'.

An advantage of this approach is that each regular-reachability problem—and hence each slice—can be solved in time linear in the number of nodes and edges in the augmented SDG; *i.e.*, in time $O((P \times E) + (CallSites \times Params^2))$.

This approach is used in the Wisconsin Program-Slicing Tool, a slicing system that supports essentially the full C language. (The system is available under license from the University of Wisconsin. It has been successfully applied to slice programs as large as 51,000 lines.)

6. Program Analysis Using More Than Graph Reachability

The graph-reachability approach offers insight into ways that machinery more powerful than the graph-reachability techniques described above can be brought to bear on program-analysis problems [27,31].

One way to generalize the CFL-reachability approach stems from the observation that CFL-reachability problems correspond to a restricted class of Datalog programs, so-called "chain programs": Each edge $m \to n$ labeled e is represented by a fact "$e(m,n)$."; each production $A \to B\ C$ is encoded as a chain rule "$a(X,Z) :- b(X,Y), c(Y,Z)$." A CFL-reachability problem can be solved using bottom-up semi-naive evaluation of the chain program [37]. This observation provides a way for program-analysis tools to take advantage of the methods developed in the logic-programming and deductive-database communities for the efficient evaluation of recursive queries in deductive databases, such as tabulation [35] and the Magic-sets transformation [2,4]. For instance, algorithms for demand versions of program-analysis problems can be obtained from their exhaustive counterparts essentially for free by specifying the problem with Horn clauses and then applying the "Magic-sets" transformation [27]. The fact that CFL-reachability problems are related to chain programs, together with the fact that chain programs are just a special case of the logic programs to which tabulation and transformation techniques apply, suggests that more powerful program-analysis algorithms can be obtained by going outside the class of pure chain programs [27].

A different way to generalize the CFL-reachability approach so as to bring more powerful techniques to bear on interprocedural dataflow analysis was presented in [31]. This method applies to problems in which the dataflow information at a program point is represented by a finite environment (*i.e.*, a mapping from a finite set of *symbols* to a finite-height domain of *values*), and the effect of a program operation is captured by a distributive "environment-transformer" function. Two of the dataflow-analysis problems that this framework handles are (decidable) variants of the constant-propagation problem: *copy-constant propagation* and *linear-constant propagation*. The former interprets assignment statements of the form $x = 7$ and $y = x$. The latter also interprets statements of the form $y = -2*x + 5$.

By means of an "explosion transformation" similar to the one utilized in Section 3.1, an interprocedural distributive-environment-transformer problem can be transformed from a meet-over-all-realizable-paths problem on a program's supergraph to a meet-over-all-realizable-paths problem on a graph that is *larger*, but in which every edge is labeled with a much *simpler* edge function (a so-called "micro-function") [31]. Each micro-function on an edge $d_1 \to d_2$ captures the effect that the value of symbol d_1 in the argument environment has on the value of symbol d_2 in the result environment. Fig. 8 shows the exploded representations of four environment-transformer functions used in constant propagation. Fig. 8(a) shows how the identity function $\lambda env.env$ is represented. Figs. 8(b)–(d) show the representations of the functions $\lambda env.env[x \mapsto 7]$, $\lambda env.env[y \mapsto env(x)]$, and $\lambda env.env[y \mapsto -2*env(x)+5]$, which are the functions for the statements $x = 7$, $y = x$, and $y = -2*x+5$, respectively. (Λ is used to represent the effects of a function that are independent of the argument environment. Each graph includes an edge of the form $\Lambda \rightarrow \Lambda$, labeled with $\lambda v.v$; as in Section 3.1, these edges are needed to capture function composition properly.)

Dynamic programming on the exploded supergraph can be used to find the meet-over-all-realizable-paths solution to the original problem: An exhaustive algorithm can be used to find the values for all symbols at all program points; a demand algorithm can be used to find the value for an individual symbol at a particular program point [31]. An experiment was carried out in which the exhaustive and demand algorithms were used to perform constant propagation on 38 C programs, which ranged in size from 300 lines to 6,000 lines. The experiment found that

- In contrast to previous results for numeric Fortran programs [11], linear-constant propagation found more constants than copy-constant propagation in 6 of the 38 programs.
- The demand algorithm, when used to demand values for all uses of scalar integer variables, was faster than the exhaustive algorithm by a factor ranging from 1.14 to about 6.

Acknowledgements

This paper is based in part on joint work with S. Horwitz, M. Sagiv, G. Rosay, and D. Melski. The work was supported in part by a David and Lucile Packard Fellowship for Science and Engineering, by NSF under grants DCR-8552602, CCR-9100424, and CCR-9625667, by DARPA (monitored by ONR under contracts N00014-88-K-0590 and N00014-92-J-1937), and by the Univ. of Wisconsin through a Vilas Associate Award.

References

1. Babich, W.A. and Jazayeri, M., "The method of attributes for data flow analysis: Part II. Demand analysis," *Acta Inf.* **10**(3) pp. 265-272 (Oct. 1978).

2. Bancilhon, F., Maier, D., Sagiv, Y., and Ullman, J., "Magic sets and other strange ways to implement logic programs," pp. 1-15 in *Proc. of the Fifth ACM Symp. on Princ. of Database Syst.*, (Cambridge, MA, Mar. 1986), (1986).

3. Banning, J.P., "An efficient way to find the side effects of procedure calls and the aliases of variables," pp. 29-41 in *Conf. Rec. of the Sixth ACM Symp. on Princ. of Prog. Lang.*, (San Antonio, TX, Jan. 29-31, 1979), ACM, New York, NY (1979).

4. Beeri, C. and Ramakrishnan, R., "On the power of magic," pp. 269-293 in *Proc. of the Sixth ACM Symp. on Princ. of Database Syst.*, (San Diego, CA, Mar. 1987), (1987).

5. Callahan, D., "The program summary graph and flow-sensitive interprocedural data flow analysis," *Proc. of the ACM SIGPLAN 88 Conf. on Prog. Lang. Design and Implementation*, (Atlanta, GA, June 22-24, 1988), *SIGPLAN Not.* **23**(7) pp. 47-56 (July 1988).

6. Cousot, P. and Cousot, R., "Abstract interpretation: A unified lattice model for static analysis of programs by construction or approximation of fixpoints," pp. 238-252 in *Conf. Rec. of the Fourth ACM Symp. on Princ. of Prog. Lang.*, (Los Angeles, CA, Jan. 17-19, 1977), ACM, New York, NY (1977).

7. Duesterwald, E., Gupta, R., and Soffa, M.L., "Demand-driven computation of interprocedural data flow," pp. 37-48 in *Conf. Rec. of the Twenty-Second ACM Symp. on Princ. of Prog. Lang.*, (San Francisco, CA, Jan. 23-25, 1995), ACM, New York, NY (1995).

8. Ferrante, J., Ottenstein, K., and Warren, J., "The program dependence graph and its use in optimization," *ACM Trans. Program. Lang. Syst.* **9**(3) pp. 319-349 (July 1987).

9. Fischer, C.N. and LeBlanc, R.J., *Crafting a Compiler*, Benjamin/Cummings Publishing Company, Inc., Menlo Park, CA (1988).

10. Giegerich, R., Möncke, U., and Wilhelm, R., "Invariance of approximative semantics with respect to program transformation," pp. 1-10 in *GI 81: 11th GI Conf., Inf.-Fach. 50*, Springer-Verlag, New York, NY (1981).

11. Grove, D. and Torczon, L., "Interprocedural constant propagation: A study of jump function implementation," pp. 90-99 in *Proc. of the ACM SIGPLAN 93 Conf. on Prog. Lang. Design and Implementation*, (Albuquerque, NM, June 23-25, 1993), ACM, New York, NY (June 1993).

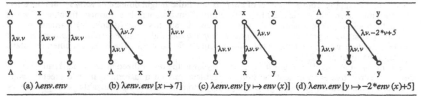

Fig. 8. The exploded representations of four environment-transformer functions used in constant propagation.

12. Horwitz, S., Reps, T., and Binkley, D., "Interprocedural slicing using dependence graphs," *ACM Trans. Program. Lang. Syst.* **12**(1) pp. 26-60 (Jan. 1990).

13. Horwitz, S., Reps, T., and Sagiv, M., "Demand interprocedural dataflow analysis," TR-1283, Comp. Sci. Dept., Univ. of Wisconsin, Madison, WI (Aug. 1995).

14. Horwitz, S., Reps, T., and Sagiv, M., "Demand interprocedural dataflow analysis," *SIGSOFT 95: Proc. of the Third ACM SIGSOFT Symp. on the Found. of Softw. Eng.*, (Wash., DC, Oct. 10-13, 1995), *ACM SIGSOFT Softw. Eng. Notes* **20**(4) pp. 104-115 (1995).

15. Jones, N.D. and Muchnick, S.S., "Flow analysis and optimization of Lisp-like structures," pp. 102-131 in *Program Flow Analysis: Theory and Applications*, ed. S.S. Muchnick and N.D. Jones,Prentice-Hall, Englewood Cliffs, NJ (1981).

16. Kildall, G., "A unified approach to global program optimization," pp. 194-206 in *Conf. Rec. of the First ACM Symp. on Princ. of Prog. Lang.*, ACM, New York, NY (1973).

17. Knoop, J. and Steffen, B., "The interprocedural coincidence theorem," pp. 125-140 in *Proc. of the Fourth Int. Conf. on Comp. Construct.*, (Paderborn, FRG, Oct. 5-7, 1992), *Lec. Notes in Comp. Sci.*, Vol. 641, ed. U. Kastens and P. Pfahler,Springer-Verlag, New York, NY (1992).

18. Kuck, D.J., Kuhn, R.H., Leasure, B., Padua, D.A., and Wolfe, M., "Dependence graphs and compiler optimizations," pp. 207-218 in *Conf. Rec. of the Eighth ACM Symp. on Princ. of Prog. Lang.*, (Williamsburg, VA, Jan. 26-28, 1981), ACM, New York, NY (1981).

19. Landi, W. and Ryder, B.G., "Pointer-induced aliasing: A problem classification," pp. 93-103 in *Conf. Rec. of the Eighteenth ACM Symp. on Princ. of Prog. Lang.*, (Orlando, FL, Jan. 1991), ACM, New York, NY (1991).

20. Masinter, L.M., "Global program analysis in an interactive environment," Tech. Rep. SSL-80-1, Xerox Palo Alto Res. Cent., Palo Alto, CA (Jan. 1980).

21. McCarthy, J., "A basis for a mathematical theory of computation," pp. 33-70 in *Computer Programming and Formal Systems*, ed. Braffort and Hershberg,North-Holland, Amsterdam (1963).

22. Melski, D. and Reps, T., "Interconvertibility of set constraints and context-free language reachability," pp. 74-89 in *Proc. of the ACM SIGPLAN Symp. on Part. Eval. and Sem.-Based Prog. Manip. (PEPM 97)*, (Amsterdam, The Netherlands, June 12-13, 1997), ACM, New York, NY (1997).

23. Mogensen, T., "Separating binding times in language specifications," pp. 12-25 in *Fourth Int. Conf. on Func. Prog. and Comp. Arch.*, (London, UK, Sept. 11-13, 1989), ACM, New York, NY (1989).

24. Ottenstein, K.J. and Ottenstein, L.M., "The program dependence graph in a software development environment," *Proc. of the ACM SIGSOFT/SIGPLAN Softw. Eng. Symp. on Practical Softw. Develop. Env.*, (Pittsburgh, PA, Apr. 23-25, 1984), *SIGPLAN Not.* **19**(5) pp. 177-184 (May 1984).

25. Reps, T., Sagiv, M., and Horwitz, S., "Interprocedural dataflow analysis via graph reachability," TR 94-14, Datalogisk Institut, Univ. of Copenhagen, Copenhagen, Denmark (Apr. 1994).

26. Reps, T., Horwitz, S., Sagiv, M., and Rosay, G., "Speeding up slicing," *SIGSOFT 94: Proc. of the Second ACM SIGSOFT Symp. on the Found. of Softw. Eng.*, (New Orleans, LA, Dec. 7-9, 1994), *ACM SIGSOFT Softw. Eng. Notes* **19**(5) pp. 11-20 (Dec. 1994).

27. Reps, T., "Demand interprocedural program analysis using logic databases," pp. 163-196 in *Applications of Logic Databases*, ed. R. Ramakrishnan,Kluwer Academic Publishers, Boston, MA (1994).

28. Reps, T., Horwitz, S., and Sagiv, M., "Precise interprocedural dataflow analysis via graph reachability," pp. 49-61 in *Conf. Rec. of the Twenty-Second ACM Symp. on Princ. of Prog. Lang.*, (San Francisco, CA, Jan. 23-25, 1995), ACM, New York, NY (1995).

29. Reps, T., "On the sequential nature of interprocedural program-analysis problems," *Acta Inf.* **33** pp. 739-757 (1996).

30. Reynolds, J.C., "Automatic computation of data set definitions," pp. 456-461 in *Information Processing 68: Proc. of the IFIP Congress 68*, North-Holland, New York, NY (1968).

31. Sagiv, M., Reps, T., and Horwitz, S., "Precise interprocedural dataflow analysis with applications to constant propagation," *Theor. Comp. Sci.* **167** pp. 131-170 (1996).

32. Sharir, M. and Pnueli, A., "Two approaches to interprocedural data flow analysis," pp. 189-233 in *Program Flow Analysis: Theory and Applications*, ed. S.S. Muchnick and N.D. Jones,Prentice-Hall, Englewood Cliffs, NJ (1981).

33. Tip, F., "A survey of program slicing techniques," *J. Program. Lang.* **3** pp. 121-181 (1995).

34. Valiant, L.G., "General context-free recognition in less than cubic time," *J. Comp. Syst. Sci.* **10**(2) pp. 308-315 (Apr. 1975).

35. Warren, D.S., "Memoing for logic programs," *Commun. ACM* **35**(3) pp. 93-111 (Mar. 1992).

36. Weiser, M., "Program slicing," *IEEE Trans. on Softw. Eng.* SE-**10**(4) pp. 352-357 (July 1984).

37. Yannakakis, M., "Graph-theoretic methods in database theory," pp. 230-242 in *Proc. of the Ninth ACM Symp. on Princ. of Database Syst.*, (1990).

38. Younger, D.H., "Recognition and parsing of context-free languages in time $n^{**}3$," *Inf. and Cont.* **10** pp. 189-208 (1967).

39. Zadeck, F.K., "Incremental data flow analysis in a structured program editor," *Proc. of the SIGPLAN 84 Symp. on Comp. Construct.*, (Montreal, Can., June 20-22, 1984), *SIGPLAN Not.* **19**(6) pp. 132-143 (June 1984).

Inductive Databases and Condensed Representations for Data Mining

Extended abstract

Heikki Mannila

University of Helsinki, Department of Computer Science
P.O. Box 26 (Teollisuuskatu 23), FIN-00014 Helsinki, Finland
Heikki.Mannila@cs.helsinki.fi
http://www.cs.helsinki.fi/~mannila

Abstract

Knowledge discovery in databases and *data mining* aim at semiautomatic tools
for the analysis of large data sets. It can be argued that several data mining
tasks consist of locating interesting sentences from a given logic that are true
in the database. Then the task of the user/analyst is to is to query this set,
the theory of the database. This view gives rise to the concept of of *inductive
databases*, i.e., databases that in addition to the data contain also inductive
generalizations about the data. We describe a rough framework for inductive
databases, and consider also *condensed representations*, data structures that
make it possible to answer queries about the inductive database approximately
correctly and reasonably efficiently.

1 Introduction

Knowledge discovery in databases (KDD), often called data mining, aims
at the discovery of useful information from large collections of data. The
discovered knowledge can be rules describing properties of the data, frequently
occurring patterns, clusterings of the objects in the database, etc. Current
technology makes it fairly easy to collect data, but data analysis tends to
be slow and expensive. There is a suspicion that there might be nuggets of
useful information hiding in the masses of unanalyzed or underanalyzed data,
and therefore semiautomatic methods for locating interesting information from
data would be useful. Data mining has in the 1990's emerged as visible
research and development area; see [6] for a recent overview of the area.

The motivation for data mining comes from applications, and it is not
clear whether the area has any identity of its own; it has been argued that
"data mining is just machine learning on large datasets" or that "data mining
is just statistics on large datasets".

However, certain emerging trends in data mining point to the possibility
of a general theory that would be applicable to a reasonable selection of data
mining tasks. In this paper we argue that several data mining tasks can be
formulated as locating interesting sentences from a given logic that are true

in the database. Using this viewpoint, the task of the user/analyst is to is to query this set, the theory of the database.

This view gives rise to the concept of of *inductive databases*, i.e., databases that contain inductive generalizations about the data, in addition to the usual data. In this paper we describe a draft framework for inductive databases, and consider also *condensed representations*, data structures that make it possible to answer queries about the inductive database approximately correctly and reasonably efficiently.

The rest of this paper is organized as follows. In Section 2 we review an example of a data mining task, the discovery of association rules. Section 3 discusses the view of data mining as querying the knowledgebase induced by the database. In Section 4 we give tentative definitions of inductive databases, and discuss possible query languages for such databases. Section 5 considers condensed representations. Section 6 is a short conclusion.

2 An example: association rules

This section describes association rules, a simple concept class that has received much attention in the data mining literature. We also discuss briefly how the same idea can be extended to finding patterns from sequences of events. This section can be considered as a brief introduction to a typical data mining task.

Given a schema $R = \{A_1, \ldots, A_p\}$ of attributes with domain $\{0, 1\}$, and a relation r over R, an *association rule* [1] about r is an expression of the form $X \Rightarrow B$, where $X \subseteq R$ and $B \in R \setminus X$. The intuitive meaning of the rule is that if a row of the matrix r has a 1 in each column of X, then the row tends to have a 1 also in column B.

Examples of data where association rules might be applicable include the following.

- A student database at a university: rows correspond to students, columns to courses, and a 1 in entry (s, c) indicates that the student s has taken course c.

- Data collected from bar-code readers in supermarkets: columns correspond to products, and each row corresponds to the set of items purchased at one time.

- A database of publications: the rows and columns both correspond to publications, and $(p, p') = 1$ means that publication p refers to publication p'.

- A set of measurements about the behavior a system, say exchanges in a telephone network. The columns correspond to the presence or absence of certain conditions, and each row correspond to a measurement: if entry (m, c) is 1, then at measurement m condition c was present.

Given $W \subseteq R$, we denote by $s(W, r)$ the *frequency* of W in r: the fraction of rows of r that have a 1 in each column of W. The *frequency* of the rule $X \Rightarrow B$ in r is defined to be $s(X \cup \{B\}, r)$, and the *confidence* of the rule is $s(X \cup \{B\}, r)/s(X, r)$.

In the discovery of association rules, the task is to find all rules $X \Rightarrow B$ such that the frequency of the rule is at least a given threshold σ and the confidence of the rule is at least another threshold θ. In large retailing applications the number of rows might be 10^6 or even 10^8, and the number of columns around 5000. The frequency threshold σ typically is around 10^{-2} — 10^{-4}. The confidence threshold θ can be anything from 0 to 1. From such a database one might obtain thousands or hundreds of thousands of association rules. (Of course, one has to be careful in assigning any statistical significance to findings obtained from such methods.)

Note that there is no predefined limit on the number of attributes of the left-hand side X of an association rule $X \Rightarrow B$, and B is not fixed, either; this is important so that unexpected associations are not ruled out before the processing starts. It also means that the search space of the rules has exponential size in the number of attributes of the input relation. Handling this requires some care for the algorithms, but there is a simple way of pruning the search space.

We call a subset $X \subseteq R$ *frequent* in r, if $s(X, r) \geq \sigma$. Once all frequent sets of r are known, finding the association rules is easy. Namely, for each frequent set X and each $B \in X$ verify whether the rule $X \setminus \{B\} \Rightarrow B$ has sufficiently high confidence.

How can one find all frequent sets X? This can be done in a multitude of ways; see, e.g., [1, 2, 8, 20, 21]. A typical approach [2] is to use the fact that all subsets of a frequent set are also frequent: first find all frequent sets of size 1 by reading the data once and recording the number of times each attribute A occurs. Then form *candidate* sets of size 2 by taking all pairs $\{B, C\}$ of attributes such that $\{B\}$ and $\{C\}$ both are frequent. The frequency of the candidate sets is again evaluated against the database. Once frequent sets of size 2 are known, candidate sets of size 3 can be formed; these are sets $\{B, C, D\}$ such that $\{B, C\}$, $\{B, D\}$, and $\{C, D\}$ are all frequent. This process is continued until no more candidate sets can be formed.

The algorithm has to read the database at most $K + 1$ times, where K is the size of the largest frequent set. In the applications K is small, typically at most 10, so the number of passes through the data is reasonable.

The algorithms work quite nicely on large input relations. Their running time is approximately $O(NF)$, where $N = np$ is the size of the input and F is the sum of the sizes of the sets in the candidate collection $\mathcal{C}$ during the operation of the algorithm [15]. This is nearly linear, and the algorithms seem to scale nicely to tens of millions of examples. Typically the only case when they fail is when the output is too large, i.e., there are too many frequent sets.

Association rules are a simple formalism and they produce nice results for binary data. The information about the frequent sets can actually be used to approximate fairly accurately the confidences and supports of a far wider set of rules, including negation and disjunction [14]. The basic restriction for the use of association rules is that the relation should be sparse in the sense that there are no frequent sets that contain more than about 15 attributes. Namely, the framework of finding all association rules generates typically at least as many rules as there are frequent sets, and if there is a frequent set of size K, there will be at least 2^K frequent sets.

The basic ideas of the frequent set finding algorithm are fairly widely applicable. For example, they can be used to find repeated *episodes* in sequences of events [16, 13].

3   Data mining as querying the theory of the database

The goal of knowledge discovery is to obtain useful knowledge from large collections of data. Such a task is inherently interactive and iterative: one cannot expect to obtain useful knowledge simply by pushing a lot of data to a black box. The user of a KDD system has to have a solid understanding of the domain in order to select the right subsets of data, suitable classes of patterns, and good criteria for interestingness of the patterns. Thus KDD systems should be seen as interactive tools, not as automatic analysis systems.

Discovering knowledge from data should therefore be seen as a process containing several steps: understanding the domain, preparing the data set, discovering patterns (data mining), postprocessing of discovered patterns, and putting the results into use. See [5] for a slightly different process model and an excellent discussion. The KDD process is necessarily iterative: the results of a data mining step can show that some changes should be made to the data set formation step, postprocessing of patterns can cause the user to look for some slightly modified types of patterns, etc. Efficient support for such iteration is one important development topic in KDD.

Within this process model, our special interest is in the combined pattern discovery and postprocessing steps. Instead of thinking about discovery as something qualitatively different from normal processing, one can also view the discovery task simply as querying. Provocatively, one might say that there is no such thing as discovery: it is all a question of the expressive power of the query language.

Consider as an example the search for association rules. Is there a magical "discovery" step somewhere? Definitely not: the task of finding all association rules with sufficient frequency and confidence can be described quite simply: go through all possible rules, evaluate there frequencies and confidences, and output the rules that satisfy the selection conditions. Looked this way, there is no conceptual difference between this process and the evaluation of ordinary queries in databases.

More formally, what is happening in rule querying is that we have a language $\mathcal{L}$ of sentences and view data mining as the problem of finding the sentences in $\mathcal{L}$ that are "sufficiently true" in the data and furthermore fulfill the user's other criteria for interestingness. That is, the task of data mining is to find the theory of the database with respect to the language:

$$Th(\mathbf{r}, \mathcal{L}, q) = \{\theta \in \mathcal{L} \mid q(\mathbf{r}, \theta)\}$$

where $\mathbf{r}$ is the database and q is a satisfaction predicate indicating whether the sentence of the language describes an interesting property of the data. This point of view has either implicitly or explicitly been used in discovering integrity constraints from databases, in inductive logic programming, and in machine learning [3, 4, 10, 11, 12]; some theoretical results can be found in [15]. A suggested logical formalism for this approach is given in [9], where we argue that the logic $\mathcal{L}$ should be a slice of a probabilistic first-order logic.

In such querying of rules, the user often wants to cross the boundary between data and rules several times. For example, the user might want to view some rules, select one of them, look at the exceptions to this rule, form a set of rules describing these exceptions, etc. To make such moves between data and rules possible we have to combine them together to a whole, such that the queries satisfy a closure property: the result of a KDD query should be an object of a similar type than the arguments. (Recall that relational databases satisfy this: answers to queries are relations.) This requirement partially motivates the following definition of inductive databases.

4 Inductive databases

In this section we describe a way of formalizing our view of data mining. Our framework is called *inductive databases*, as the idea is that the database consists of the raw data and some more or less inductively obtained rules etc. The term "inductive databases" should be compared with the term "deductive databases": deductive databases use some simple forms of deduction to augment fact databases to contain a potentially infinite set of derived/deduced facts. The goal for inductive databases is that in addition to the facts, the database will contain a potentially infinite set of induced rules (or some other form of more general information). It is not clear yet how useful this framework is, but it seems to offer some benefits.

We start with simple definitions of the schema and the instance of an inductive database. The *schema of an inductive database* is a pair $\mathcal{R} = (\mathbf{R}, \mathcal{Q})$, where $\mathbf{R}$ is a (relational, object, or nested) database schema, and $\mathcal{Q}$ is a collection $(Q_i \mid i \in I)$ of queries over $\mathbf{R}$; for simplicity we assume that each query has the same answer schema of S. An inductive database $\hat{\mathbf{r}} = (\mathbf{r}, s)$ over the schema $\mathcal{R}$ consists of a database $\mathbf{r}$ over $\mathbf{R}$ plus a nested relation s over the schema (J, S), where $dom(J) = I$. The relation s contains the rows $(i, Q_i(\mathbf{r}))$ for $i \in I$.

As an example, consider the discovery of association rules. We first define the schema $\mathcal{R}_a = (R, (J, S))$ of the inductive database. We start with a relational database schema consisting of one relation schema $R = \{A_1, \ldots, A_p\}$ of attributes with domain $\{0, 1\}$. The collection of queries J is defined by

$$J = \{(X, B) \mid X \subseteq R \wedge B \in R\}.$$

For each $(X, B) \in J$ there is a query $Q_{(X,B)}$ in the inductive database. Applied to a relation r over R, the query $Q_{(X,B)}$ returns the frequency and confidence of the rule $X \Rightarrow B$. Thus the result schema of the query is $S = (F, C)$, where both F and C are real-valued attributes.

Consider an instance (r, s) of the inductive database schema $\mathcal{R}_a$. Then s is a nested relation, and each entry is of the form $((X, B), (c, f))$. With this database at hand, we can do association rule discovery simply by querying it. For example, finding all rules of the form $X \Rightarrow C$ such that X contains D but not E, the frequency of the rule is at least 0.1 and the confidence at least 0.9 is easy to transform to any query language for nested relations. In this simple example even SQL would do, since each of the queries of the schema of the inductive database returns actually only a single row, and hence no true nesting is needed.

Queries on an inductive database can now be defined in a similar way as for a relational database. For example, given an inductive database $\hat{r} = (\mathbf{r}, s)$ and a selection query Q on the schema $\mathbf{R}$ of the usual database $\mathbf{r}$, the result of applying Q to $\hat{r}$ is the inductive database $(Q(\mathbf{r}), Q(s))$, where $Q(s)$ is the nested relation where for index i the corresponding relation is $Q_i(Q(\mathbf{r}))$. Likewise, selection conditions on the set of queries are easy to formulate. These query operations make it possible to do the rule/data querying typical of the KDD process.

The drawback of the above formulation is that the set of queries in the original inductive database was given explicitly, which can cause problems. A simple way of getting around this would be to view the set of queries as another nested relation, which is generated by a set of Datalog-like rules, i.e., by using deductive database techniques to specify the inductive database. We omit the details.

5 Condensed representations

Given a schema for an inductive database and the original data inside the relational database, how should one implement the query operations for the inductive database? An explicit evaluation of all the queries of the schema against the database (and all databases resulting from it by queries) is not feasible for large data sets. We need some methods that make it possible to answer the queries faster than by evaluating each of the queries individually.

There are two issues here: how to evaluate a class of similar queries faster than by looking at each of them individually, and how to evaluate queries without looking at the whole data set.

Looking at the search for association rules, the frequency of a collection of attribute sets can be evaluated very efficiently in one pass through the data. Similar, but less ad hoc, methods should be possible for more complex situations; see [22] for some interesting ideas.

The second problem is to evaluate queries from a query class without looking at the whole data. Given a class of structures $\mathcal{D}$, a data collection $d \in \mathcal{D}$, and a class of patterns $\mathcal{P}$, a *condensed representation* for d and $\mathcal{P}$ is a data structure that makes it possible to answer queries of the form "How many times does $p \in \mathcal{P}$ occur in d" approximately correctly and more efficiently than by looking at d itself.

A simple example of a condensed representation is obtained by taking a sample from the data: by counting the occurrences of the pattern in the sample, one gets an approximation of the number of occurrences in the original data.

Another, less obvious example is given by the collection of frequent sets of a 0-1 valued relation [14]: the collection of frequent sets can be used to give approximate answers to arbitrary boolean queries about the data, even though the frequent sets represent only conjunctive concepts. The approximation can be fairly accurate.

The data cube [7] can also be viewed as a condensed representation for a class of queries. One can also consider a "frequent" variation of the data cube, i.e., a cube where the computation is halted for any cell whose frequency falls below a given threshold. Similarly, in computational geometry the notion of an ε-approximation [19] is closely related.

Developing condensed representations for various classes of patterns seems a promising way of implementing inductive databases and more generally improving the effectiveness of data mining algorithms. Whether this approach is generally useful is still open. Condensed representations have connections to maximum entropy approaches, as well as to some recent ideas in machine learning [17, 18].

6   Conclusions

We have presented a draft framework for inductive databases, based on the ideas that parts of data mining can be viewed as querying the theory of a database, and that the querying of rules and data have to be mixed in the data mining process. For efficient implementation of inductive databases it seems that concepts like condensed representations are useful.

Obviously, the framework is currently very rough. However, it seems that there are some advantages in it.

Acknowledgments

Comments from Hannu Toivonen on the manuscript are gratefully acknowledged.

References

[1] R. Agrawal, T. Imielinski, and A. Swami. Mining association rules between sets of items in large databases. In P. Buneman and S. Jajodia, editors, *Proceedings of ACM SIGMOD Conference on Management of Data (SIGMOD'93)*, pages 207 – 216, Washington, D.C., May 1993. ACM.

[2] R. Agrawal, H. Mannila, R. Srikant, H. Toivonen, and A. I. Verkamo. Fast discovery of association rules. In U. M. Fayyad, G. Piatetsky-Shapiro, P. Smyth, and R. Uthurusamy, editors, *Advances in Knowledge Discovery and Data Mining*, pages 307 – 328. AAAI Press, Menlo Park, CA, 1996.

[3] L. De Raedt and M. Bruynooghe. A theory of clausal discovery. In *Proceedings of the Thirteenth International Joint Conference on Artificial Intelligence (IJCAI–93)*, pages 1058 – 1053, Chambéry, France, 1993. Morgan Kaufmann.

[4] L. De Raedt and S. Džeroski. First-order jk-clausal theories are PAC-learnable. *Artificial Intelligence*, 70:375 – 392, 1994.

[5] U. M. Fayyad, G. Piatetsky-Shapiro, and P. Smyth. From data mining to knowledge discovery: An overview. In U. M. Fayyad, G. Piatetsky-Shapiro, P. Smyth, and R. Uthurusamy, editors, *Advances in Knowledge Discovery and Data Mining*, pages 1 –34. AAAI Press, Menlo Park, CA, 1996.

[6] U. M. Fayyad, G. Piatetsky-Shapiro, P. Smyth, and R. Uthurusamy, editors. *Advances in Knowledge Discovery and Data Mining*. AAAI Press, Menlo Park, CA, 1996.

[7] J. Gray, S. Chaudhuri, A. Bosworth, A. Layman, D. Reichart, M. Venkatrao, F. Pellow, and H. Pirahesh. Data Cube: A relational aggregation operator generalizing group-by, cross-tab, and sub-totals. *Data Mining and Knowledge Discovery*, 1(1):29 – 53, 1997.

[8] J. Han and Y. Fu. Discovery of multiple-level association rules from large databases. In *Proceedings of the 21st International Conference on Very Large Data Bases (VLDB'95)*, pages 420 – 431, Zurich, Swizerland, 1995.

[9] M. Jaeger, H. Mannila, and E. Weydert. Data mining as selective theory extraction in probabilistic logic. In R. Ng, editor, *SIGMOD'96 Data Mining Workshop, The University of British Columbia, Department of Computer Science, TR 96-08*, pages 41–46, 1996.

[10] J.-U. Kietz and S. Wrobel. Controlling the complexity of learning in logic through syntactic and task-oriented models. In S. Muggleton, editor, *Inductive Logic Programming*, pages 335 – 359. Academic Press, London, 1992.

[11] W. Kloesgen. Efficient discovery of interesting statements in databases. *Journal of Intelligent Information Systems*, 4(1):53 – 69, 1995.

[12] H. Mannila and K.-J. Räihä. Design by example: An application of Armstrong relations. *Journal of Computer and System Sciences*, 33(2):126 – 141, 1986.

[13] H. Mannila and H. Toivonen. Discovering generalized episodes using minimal occurrences. In *Proceedings of the Second International Conference on Knowledge Discovery and Data Mining (KDD'96)*, pages 146 – 151, Portland, Oregon, Aug. 1996. AAAI Press.

[14] H. Mannila and H. Toivonen. Multiple uses of frequent sets and condensed representations. In *Proceedings of the Second International Conference on Knowledge Discovery and Data Mining (KDD'96)*, pages 189 – 194, Portland, Oregon, Aug. 1996. AAAI Press.

[15] H. Mannila and H. Toivonen. Levelwise search and borders of theories in knowledge discovery. *Data Mining and Knowledge Discovery*, 1(3), 1997.

[16] H. Mannila, H. Toivonen, and A. I. Verkamo. Discovery of frequent episodes in event sequences. *Data Mining and Knowledge Discovery*, 1(3), 1997.

[17] A. Moore and M. Lee. Cached sufficient statistics for efficient machine learning with large datasets. Technical Report CMU-RI-TR-97-27, Robotics Institute, Carnegie-Mellon University, 1997.

[18] A. W. Moore, J. Schneider, and K. Deng. Efficient locally weighted polynomial regression predictions. In *Proceedings of the 1997 International Machine Learning Conference*, 1997.

[19] K. Mulmuley. *Computational Geometry: An Introduction Through Randomized Algorithms*. Prentice Hall, New York, 1993.

[20] A. Savasere, E. Omiecinski, and S. Navathe. An efficient algorithm for mining association rules in large databases. In *Proceedings of the 21st International Conference on Very Large Data Bases (VLDB'95)*, pages 432 – 444, Zurich, Swizerland, 1995.

[21] H. Toivonen. Sampling large databases for association rules. In *Proceedings of the 22nd International Conference on Very Large Data Bases (VLDB'96)*, pages 134 – 145, Mumbay, India, Sept. 1996. Morgan Kaufmann.

[22] J. D. Ullman. A system for managing query flocks. Available from http://www-db.stanford.edu/~ullman/pub/flocks.html, 1997.

Advanced Tutorials

Logic Programming Tools for Advanced Internet Programming

Paul Tarau
Université de Moncton
Département d'Informatique
Moncton, N.B. Canada E1A 3E9,
tarau@info.umoncton.ca

Abstract

The tutorial is intended to introduce logic programmers to advanced Internet programming. Our tools, encapsulated in a small set of very high-level primitives, will enable the participants to program basic client-server applications in a few lines of code, interact with http servers and Java applets, and put on the Web their favorite programs.

The tutorial also gives a glimpse on mobile code and multi-agent programming with special emphasis on using essential Prolog features like meta-programming to implement complex remote execution mechanisms, while language extensions like hypothetical assumptions and Linda coordination primitives are used to elegantly deal with the complexities of network and agent programming, at a very high level. Mobile threads are implemented by capturing first order continuations in a compact data structure sent over the network. Code is fetched lazily from its original base turned into a server as the continuation executes at the remote site. Combined with a dynamic recompilation scheme ensuring that heavily used code moves up smoothly in a speed hierarchy, our techniques are shown to be an effective means for implementing mobile agents in a natural programming style.

We will also describe our experience with building a comprehensive Internet programming infrastructure [3] on top of **BinProlog** [2] and its Java peer - a multithreaded unification based Linda client and server, using Prolog terms and unification for associative search.

Among the applications, we review LogiMOO[5, 4], a shared multi-user virtual world prototype with a controlled natural language interface, executing under Java and VRML enabled browsers like Netscape Communicator.

The tutorial is organized around a set of "how to do it" examples, among which the following:

- simple CGI-scripts, client-server applications on the WWW

- a multi-user chat program

- an applet: from Prolog to Java and back

- distributed programming with BinProlog engines and threads

- mobile code: "take the continuation and run"
- LogiMOO: crafting shared virtual objects on the Web
- Talking to VRML: BinProlog-driven 3D-avatar animation

We conclude with an analysis of the practical application development and promising future directions of work. With the paradigm shift to highly interconnected computers and programming tools, logic programming languages have a unique opportunity to contribute to practical Internet application development. Simplicity, robustness, automatic memory management, code and object mobility [1] are among the features some LP languages [6, 3] share with emerging tools like Java. Superior meta-programming and high-level networking, built-in grammars and dynamic databases, declarative semantics are among their competitive advantages. In this context, we discuss some strategies about how to integrate this technology in the (real!) world of software development.

References

[1] K. A. Bharat and L. Cardelli. Migratory applications. In *Proceedings of the 8th Annual ACM Symposium on User Interface Software and Technology*, Nov. 1995. http://gatekeeper.dec.com/pub/DEC/SRC/research-reports/abstracts/src-rr-138.html.

[2] P. Tarau. BinProlog 5.75 User Guide. Technical Report 97-1, Département d'Informatique, Université de Moncton, Apr. 1997. Available from *http://clement.info.umoncton.ca/BinProlog*.

[3] P. Tarau, V. Dahl, and K. De Bosschere. A Logic Programming Infrastructure for Remote Execution, Mobile Code and Agents. In *Proceedings of IEEE WETICE'97*, Boston, MA, June 1997.

[4] P. Tarau, V. Dahl, S. Rochefort, and K. De Bosschere. LogiMOO: a Multi-User Virtual World with Agents and Natural Language Programming. In S. Pemberton, editor, *Proceedings of CHI'97*, pages 323–324, Mar. 1997. ACM ISBN 0-8979-926-2.

[5] P. Tarau and K. De Bosschere. Virtual World Brokerage with BinProlog and Netscape. In P. Tarau, A. Davison, K. De Bosschere, and M. Hermenegildo, editors, *Proceedings of the 1st Workshop on Logic Programming Tools for INTERNET Applications*, JICSLP'96, Bonn, Sept. 1996. http://clement.info.umoncton.ca/ lpnet.

[6] P. Van Roy, S. Haridi, P. Brand, G. Smolka, M. Mehl, and R. Scheidhouer. Mobile Objects in Distributed Oz. *ACM TOPLAS*, 1997. to appear.

Set-based analysis of logic programs and reactive logic programs

Andreas Podelski

Max-Planck-Institut für Informatik,
Im Stadtwald, D-66123 Saarbrücken, Germany
www.mpi-sb.mpg.de/~podelski
podelski@mpi-sb.mpg.de

Question: what is a logic program?
Answer: a set constraint.

We will give an introduction to set constraints and to the set-based analysis of logic programs (i.e., with the least-model semantics) [2] and of reactive logic programs (i.e., with the greatest-model semantics) [1], which uses *definite* and *co-definite* set constraints, respectively.

A set constraint φ_P is inferred from the program P (by a syntactical transformation of P). Then, φ_P is solved, which means: the least [greatest] solution α of φ_P is computed. This again means the construction of effective presentations of the sets $\alpha(p)$ of (tuples of) trees. Since the sets $\alpha(p)$ are possibly recursively defined (but, as one can show, always regular), one uses tree automata or some equivalent formalism for their representation.

The relationship between logic programs and their inferred set constraints is best understood if one enlargens the standard, syntactic notion of set constraints to a semantic notion. *A set constraint is a formula that expresses a relation between sets of trees.* We will next present the view of logic programs as set constraints.

A logic program P defines predicates $p \in \mathsf{Pred}$ through clauses of the form $p(t_i){:}{-} \bigwedge_j p_{ij}(t_{ij})$ where i and j range over suitable index sets. The logical semantics of P is given by the formula below.

$$P \equiv \bigwedge_{p \in \mathsf{Pred}} \forall x \ p(x) \leftrightarrow \bigvee_i \exists_{-x} \ x = t_i \wedge \bigwedge_j p_{ij}(t_{ij})$$

For better readability, we assume that all predicates are unary (for the general case we can, for example, extend the signature of function symbols with symbols forming tuples). For the logical interpretation of P, we view predicate symbols $p, q, \ldots \in \mathsf{Pred}$ as (second-order) variables ranging over sets of trees. The (first-order) variables $x, y, \ldots \in \mathsf{Var}$ range over trees; note that they are all bound in P. We use $\exists_{-x}$ to denote the existential quantification of all tree variables but x.

A model (sometimes called interpretation) is a subset ρ of the Herbrand base $\mathcal{B}_P = \{p(t) \mid p \in \mathsf{Pred}, t \in T_\Sigma\}$. We can identify a model ρ with a valuation $\rho : \mathsf{Pred} \to 2^{T_\Sigma}$ from predicate symbols to sets of trees (where $\rho(p) = \{t \in T_\Sigma \mid p(t) \in \rho\}$). A *model of the program* P is a solution of P, i.e., a valuation such that the formula P is valid in the usual logical sense. Hence, a program is a formula (with free variables $p \in \mathsf{Pred}$) expressing a relation between predicate variables $p, q, \ldots$. Hence, P is a set constraint.

The least solution $lm(P)$ and greatest solution $gm(P)$ of the set constraint P (i.e., the least model and the greatest model of P) are generally not effectively representable. They are, however, approximated by the least solution α_{ψ_P} of the definite set constraint ψ_P inferred from P, and by the greatest solution α_{φ_P} of the co-definite set constraint φ_P inferred from P, respectively, and the values $\alpha_{\psi_P}(p)$ and $\alpha_{\varphi_P}(p)$ of these two solutions are regular sets of trees. Formally,

$$(lm(P))(p) \subseteq \alpha_{\psi_P}(p)$$

$$(gm(P))(p) \subseteq \alpha_{\varphi_P}(p)$$

for all $p \in \mathsf{Pred}$. Note that the constraints ψ_P and φ_P are generally not logically weaker than the formula P (i.e, the implications $P \to \psi_P$ and $P \to \varphi_P$ are generally not valid). The soundness of the abstraction given by the inclusions above is shown via the characterizations of the models by the respective fixpoints of the T_P operator. Roughly, the constraints ψ_P and φ_P are reformulations of the fixpoint equations (which may be written as inequalities according to the two cases of least and greatest fixpoints).

The set-based analysis of logic programs wrt. least and greatest models is interesting because temporal logic (CTL) properties of reactive infinite-state systems can be characterized by logic programs with oracles and, hence, be approximated via the solutions of the inferred set constraints [1].

For an extensive list of references, see our home page.

References

[1] W. Charatonik, A. Podelski, and M. Müller. Set-based analysis of reactive infinite-state systems. Submitted for publication, 1997.

[2] N. Heintze and J. Jaffar. A finite presentation theorem for approximating logic programs. In *Seventeenth Annual ACM Symposium on Principles of Programming Languages*, pages 197–209, January 1990.

Constraint Programming in Oz

Gert Smolka
DFKI and Universität des Saarlandes
Saarbrücken, Germany
http://www.ps.uni-sb.de/~smolka/

This tutorial will introduce the constraint programming facilities of Oz 2. The audience is expected to have a passing acquaintance with finite domain constraint logic programming.

Oz 2 is a lexically scoped language with first-class procedures, cells, threads, logic variables, and a constraint store. It supports finite domain constraints and feature constraints. Oz is not based on backtracking but has a space primitive from which a variety of encapsulated search engines can be programmed. Spaces can express sequential and concurrent engines for one, incremental all, and best solution search. They can also express specialized engines for chart parsing of constraint grammars and polymorphic type inference.

The beta version of DFKI Oz 2 is available under a GNU-style licence. On a Pentium, DFKI Oz 2 finds and proves an optimal solution of the MT 10 job shop scheduling problem in less than 3 minutes. DFKI Oz 2 has a C++ interface for adding new propagators and comes with innovative tools facilitating the development of constraint programs.

The outline of the tutorial is as follows:

1. Review of finite domain constraint programming

2. Finite domain constraint programming in Oz

3. Programming search engines with spaces

4. Case study: parsers for constraint grammars.

The tutorial will include system demos.

The following papers are related to the tutorial:

1. Gert Smolka, The Oz Programming Model. In: Jan van Leeuwen (ed.), Computer Science Today, LNCS, Volume 1000, pages 324-343, 1995.

2. Gert Smolka, Finite Domain Constraint Programming in Oz. Draft of a chapter of the Oz Primer, available at http://www.ps.uni-sb.de/~smolka/drafts/fd.ps.

3. Christian Schulte, Programming Constraint Inference Engines. In: Gert Smolka, editor, Proceedings of the Third International

Conference on Principles and Practice of Constraint Programming, Lecture Notes in Computer Science, October 1997, Springer-Verlag.

4. Christian Schulte, Oz Explorer: A Visual Constraint Programming Tool. In: Lee Naish, editor, Proceedings of the Fourteenth International Conference on Logic Programming, Leuven, Belgium, pages 286-300. The MIT Press, July 1997.

5. Jörg Würtz, Constraint-Based Scheduling in Oz. Operations Research Proceedings 1996. Springer-Verlag, 1997.

6. Tobias Müller and Jörg Würtz, Extending a Concurrent Constraint Language by Propagators. In: Jan Maluszynski, editor, Proceedings of the International Logic Programming Symposium 1997, The MIT Press.

The DFKI Oz system is available at http://www.ps.uni-sb.de/oz2/.

Model Checking

Rob Gerth

Eindhoven University of Technology

NL-5600 MB Eindhoven

The Netherlands

Abstract

Model checking is increasingly being perceived as the prime industrially relevant approach to (formal) system verification. This is due partly to the high level of automation it allows and partly to the ease with which it can be inserted in existing design-flows. Its natural application domain is systems that are primarily control (as opposed to data) driven and that have a high level of interaction with an only partly controllable environment. Indeed, model checking has seen most use in telecommunication and in hardware design. Moreover, companies such as Siemens and Intel have incorporated these methods into their system design-flows.

Conceptually, model checking explores the space of all possible system behaviors in search for an illegal one that refutes some system requirement. Indeed, in some implementations this exploration resembles an SLD refutation with a depth-first search rule. Accordingly, a major issue is the efficiency of such searches, which entails questions of compact representation of behaviors, early pruning of the search space (e.g., automatic insertion of safe cuts) and the use of abstract interpretation. A second example is in the application of model checking to systems that have a continously varying component. Behaviors of such systems cannot be enumerated anymore and one uses a constraint system instead to describe the behavior space and searches for a refuting behavior in the solution set.

This tutorial aims to give an introduction and overview of model checking; its methods, its applications, its limits. Secondly, it aims to indicate those spots where model checking and logic programming touch and where awareness of results and research directions can be mutually beneficial.

Logic Programming for Processing Natural Language

Veronica Dahl
Logic and Functional Programming Group
Department of Computing Sciences
Simon Fraser University
Burnaby, B.C. Canada V5A 1S6
veronica@cs.sfu.ca

Abstract

We uncover a natural alliance between natural language and logic programming, which was apparent in the beginnings of the latter and is becoming again apparent in a more mature state-of-the-art way.

We first present a short historic overview, from the origins of Prolog as a "man-machine" system for communicating in natural language, to the present promise, implicit in recent developments, that natural language for controlling various AI applications may not be too far away after all.

We then briefly describe three important families of linguistically principled approaches to natural language processing: unification-based (also known as constraint-based), logico-mathematical, and principles-and-parameters. We stress common points between the areas of natural language processing through logic programming and linguistic theory, such as the ideas of inferencing, unification and constraints. We also note cross-fertilizations among these fields, such as memoization, which was born from David D. H. Warren's observation that the Earley algorithm ideas about parsing should be transfered into logic programming proper; as well as with other fields (e.g. connections with parametric L-systems, which were developed for visual models of plant development and constitute an interesting parallel grammar paradigm; Datalog grammars, inspired by database theory, and with interesting termination properties).

Among the latest developments, we describe in some more detail Assumption Grammars, which we believe to be the best compromise to date between expressive and linguistic power. These are basically Definite Clause Grammars, augmented with linear and intuitionistic implication, and which handle multiple streams (as in Peter Van Roig's Extended Definite Clause Grammars, but without the need of a preprocessing technique).

We then show how Assumption Grammars are useful for typical hard problems in natural language processing: anaphora, coordination, co-specification free word order. We also show two recent results which were surprising to us, namely: a) Assumption grammars allow a direct and efficient implementation of *link grammars* -a context-free like formalism developed independently from logic grammars; and b) they offer the flexibility of switching between data-driven or goal-driven reasoning, at no overhead in terms of either syntax or implementation.

Next, we discuss several interesting applications, most of them briefly but the last one in some detail: concept-based retrieval through natural language, driving robots through Natural Language, error diagnosis and repair, machine translation, language front ends to knowledge based systems, and controlling virtual worlds through natural language. We argue that we can exploit the characteristics of virtual worlds and of Assumption Grammars to develop untraditional but extremely expressive natural language analysers (with complete non-determinism, partial formula evaluation through consulting world knowledge gleaned from the net, easy extensibility both in terms of language coverage and of transfer into other natural languages), and that these new techniques might soon lead to the direct use of some form of controlled language input, together with speech recognition, as a language front end to many AI applications, with Prolog as an invisible mediator.

References

[1] A. Colmerauer. Metamorphosis grammars. *Lecture Notes in Computer Science*, Springer-Verlag, N. Y., 1978.

[2] J. Y. Girard. Linear Logic. *Theoretical Computer Science*, 50:1–102, 1987.

[3] E. Stabler Representing Knowledge with Theories About Theories. *Journal of Logic Programming*, vol. 9, No. 11, 1990.

[4] O. Zaiane, A. Fall, S. Rochefort, V. Dahl and P. Tarau Concept-Based Retrieval using Controlled Natural Language. *Proc. NLDB'97*, Vancouver, 1997.

[5] V. Dahl, P. Tarau and R. Li Assumption Grammars for Natural Language Processing. *Proc. 1997 International Conference on Logic Programming*, 256:270, Belgium, July 1997.

[6] S. Rochefort, V. Dahl and P. Tarau. Controlling Virtual Worlds through Extensible Natural Language. *Proc. AAAI Symposium on NLP for the WWW*, Stanford, CA, 1997.

[7] V. Dahl, A. Fall and M. C. Thomas. Driving Robots through Natural Language. *Proc. 1995 IEE International Conference on Systems, Man and Cybernetics*, Vancouver, 1995.

Multi-Paradigm Declarative Programming

Michael Hanus

RWTH Aachen, Informatik II, D-52056 Aachen, Germany

hanus@informatik.rwth-aachen.de

Abstract

This tutorial provides a survey on the integration of functional and logic programming and sketches the main features of the multi-paradigm declarative language Curry, a new programming language aiming to integrate functional, logic, and concurrent programming paradigms. This could also lead to a new perspective for logic programming, since most of the impure features of Prolog could be replaced by declarative elements in a multi-paradigm language.

1 Functional Logic Programming

Since more than ten years, the integration of the functional and logic programming paradigms have been studied (see [10] for a survey). Functional logic languages offer features from functional programming (reduction of nested expressions, higher-order functions, lazy evaluation, polymorphic type systems) and logic programming (logical variables, partial data structures, goal solving, built-in search). Compared to purely functional languages, functional logic languages are more expressive due to the use of logical variables and built-in search mechanisms. Compared to purely logic languages, they have more efficient evaluation mechanisms due to the deterministic reduction of functional expressions. However, there are quite different ways to combine the non-deterministic search principle of logic programming with reduction mechanisms from functional programming. Therefore, the research on integrated declarative languages lead to the development of various programming languages (e.g., ALF [9], Babel [14], Escher [13], K-Leaf [8], Le Fun [2], Life [1], LPG [4], Mercury [18], NUE-Prolog [15], Oz [17], SLOG [7]).

A simple method to integrate functional and logic programming styles is the translation of function definitions and functional expressions into logic programs by flattening nested function calls [6, 15]. Since the flattened programs are evaluated as purely logic programs, the flattening approach provides a functional syntax but has no real advantage w.r.t. logic programming. A more sophisticated method is the integration of functions and predicates in one language but separating reduction and search such that function calls are deterministically reduced and all search and non-determinism is covered by predicates. This operational principle, called *residuation*, is used, for instance, in Escher [13], Le Fun [2], Life [1]), NUE-Prolog [15], and Oz [17]. Roughly speaking, residuation suspends function calls during unification if they are not sufficiently instantiated for a deterministic reduction step. The residuation principle keeps the deterministic nature of functions, supports a concurrent programming style and provides an elegant amalgamation with external functions [5]. On the other hand, it is incomplete (computations may flounder) and it is not clear whether this strategy is better than Prolog's resolution strategy since there are examples where residuation has an infinite search space in contrast to equivalent (flattened) Prolog programs.

Functional logic languages with a complete operational semantics, e.g., ALF [9], Babel [14], K-Leaf [8], LPG [4], SLOG [7], are mainly based on *narrowing*, a combination of the reduction principle of functional languages with unification for parameter passing. Narrowing provides completeness in the sense of functional programming (normal forms are computed if they exist) as well as logic programming (solutions are computed if they exist). However, in order to compete with Prolog's resolution strategy, sophisticated narrowing strategies are required. Recently, a lazy narrowing strategy, called *needed narrowing* [3], has been developed which is optimal w.r.t. the length of derivations and the number of computed solutions. This also shows an advantage of integrating functions into logic programs: by transferring and extending results from functional programming to logic programming, we obtain better and, for particular classes of programs, optimal evaluation strategies without loosing the search facilities.

2 The Multi-Paradigm Language Curry

Due to the diversity of integrated functional logic languages and the recent improvements in this area, a number of people felt that the time is ripe to develop a multi-paradigm language which can serve as a common basis for further developments. This language, called Curry [11, 12], combines features from functional programming (nested expressions, higher-order functions, lazy evaluation, types) and logic programming (logical variables, partial data structures, constraints, built-in search), and concurrent programming (concurrent evaluation of expressions with synchronization on logical variables).

Curry's operational semantics is based on a single computation model, described in [11], which combines lazy reduction of expressions with a possibly non-deterministic binding of free variables occurring in expressions. Thus, purely functional programming, purely logic programming, and concurrent (logic) programming are obtained as particular restrictions of this model. It also amalgamates the residuation and narrowing principles of existing functional logic languages in a seamless way. Due to the use of an integrated functional logic language, one can choose the best of the two worlds in application programs. For instance, input/output (implemented in logic languages by side effects) can be handled with the monadic I/O concept [16] in a declarative way. Basic arithmetic and other primitive functions can be cleanly implemented by the residuation principle [5]. Furthermore, most applications of the "cut" operator of Prolog are subsumed by the use of functions.

References

[1] H. Aït-Kaci. An Overview of LIFE. In *Proc. Workshop on Next Generation Information System Technology*, pp. 42–58. Springer LNCS 504, 1990.

[2] H. Aït-Kaci, P. Lincoln, and R. Nasr. Le Fun: Logic, equations, and Functions. In *Proc. 4th IEEE Int. Symp. on Logic Programming*, pp. 17–23, 1987.

[3] S. Antoy, R. Echahed, and M. Hanus. A Needed Narrowing Strategy. In *Proc. 21st ACM Symp. on Principles of Programming Languages*, pp. 268–279, 1994.

[4] D. Bert and R. Echahed. Design and Implementation of a Generic, Logic and Functional Programming Language. In *Proc. European Symposium on Programming*, pp. 119–132. Springer LNCS 213, 1986.

[5] S. Bonnier and J. Maluszynski. Towards a Clean Amalgamation of Logic Programs with External Procedures. In *Proc. 5th Conference and Symposium on Logic Programming*, pp. 311–326. MIT Press, 1988.

[6] P.H. Cheong and L. Fribourg. Implementation of Narrowing: The Prolog-Based Approach. In *Logic programming languages: constraints, functions, and objects*, pp. 1–20. MIT Press, 1993.

[7] L. Fribourg. SLOG: A Logic Programming Language Interpreter Based on Clausal Superposition and Rewriting. In *Proc. IEEE Internat. Symposium on Logic Programming*, pp. 172–184, Boston, 1985.

[8] E. Giovannetti, G. Levi, C. Moiso, and C. Palamidessi. Kernel LEAF: A Logic plus Functional Language. *Journal of Computer and System Sciences*, Vol. 42, No. 2, pp. 139–185, 1991.

[9] M. Hanus. Compiling Logic Programs with Equality. In *Proc. of the 2nd Int. Workshop on Programming Language Implementation and Logic Programming*, pp. 387–401. Springer LNCS 456, 1990.

[10] M. Hanus. The Integration of Functions into Logic Programming: From Theory to Practice. *Journal of Logic Programming*, Vol. 19&20, pp. 583–628, 1994.

[11] M. Hanus. A Unified Computation Model for Functional and Logic Programming. In *Proc. of the 24th ACM Symp. on Principles of Programming Languages*, pp. 80–93, 1997.

[12] M. Hanus (ed.). Curry: An Integrated Functional Logic Language. Available at http://www-i2.informatik.rwth-aachen.de/~hanus/curry, 1997.

[13] J.W. Lloyd. Combining Functional and Logic Programming Languages. In *Proc. of the International Logic Programming Symposium*, pp. 43–57, 1994.

[14] J.J. Moreno-Navarro and M. Rodríguez-Artalejo. Logic Programming with Functions and Predicates: The Language BABEL. *Journal of Logic Programming*, Vol. 12, pp. 191–223, 1992.

[15] L. Naish. Adding equations to NU-Prolog. In *Proc. of the 3rd Int. Symposium on Programming Language Implementation and Logic Programming*, pp. 15–26. Springer LNCS 528, 1991.

[16] S.L. Peyton Jones and P. Wadler. Imperative Functional Programming. In *Proc. 20th Symp. on Principles of Programming Languages*, pp. 71–84, 1993.

[17] G. Smolka. The Oz Programming Model. In J. van Leeuwen, editor, *Computer Science Today: Recent Trends and Developments*, pp. 324–343. Springer LNCS 1000, 1995.

[18] Z. Somogyi, F. Henderson, and T. Conway. The execution algorithm of Mercury, an efficient purely declarative logic programming language. *Journal of Logic Programming*, Vol. 29, No. 1-3, pp. 17–64, 1996.

Transaction Logic: An Introduction

Michael Kifer
Department of Computer Science
University at Stony Brook
Stony Brook, NY 11794-4400, USA
kifer@cs.sunysb.edu

Abstract

The status of update operators in logic programming, such as assert and retract, has been a sore spot from the very inception of Prolog. Unlike much of the language, the update operators persistently defied the logical semantics, and their non-backtrackable nature was in stark contradiction with Prolog's operational semantics.

The result of this unsatisfactory state of affairs is that Prolog programs that rely on backtracking through assert and retract are notoriously hard to debug and maintain. This theoretical weakness becomes even more apparent when declarative programming tries to take a bite out of the object-oriented pie, where state-changing methods are commonplace.

Although it is not hard to hack up backtrackable updates in Prolog and the technique for doing so has been known for a long time, the logic behind this such updates remained unclear. Unclear, that is, until Transaction Logic came along.

Transaction Logic [7, 4, 5, 6, 2, 1, 3] is a conservative extension of classical predicate calculus. It has a natural model theory, a sound and complete proof theory and, unlike many other logics, it allows users to program state-changing actions by combining simple actions into complex ones. The semantics of Transaction Logic leads naturally to features whose amalgamation in a single logic has proved elusive in the past. Apart from composable, "backtrackable updates," these features include non-deterministic actions, dynamic constraints on execution, tentative (non-committed) execution, concurrent and communicating processes, and more. Transaction Logic holds promise as a logical model of hitherto non-logical phenomena, including so-called procedural knowledge in AI, active databases, and the behavior of object-oriented databases, especially methods with side effects.

This tutorial is intended as an introduction to Transaction Logic, which will provide a glimpse into the model theory, the proof theory, and some of the applications of the logic.

Acknowledgements

Transaction Logic was developed jointly with Anthony B. Bonner.

References

[1] A.J. Bonner and M. Kifer. Transaction logic programming. In *Intl. Conference on Logic Programming (ICLP)*, pages 257–282, Budapest, Hungary, June 1993. MIT Press.

[2] A.J. Bonner and M. Kifer. Applications of transaction logic to knowledge representation. In *Proceedings of the International Conference on Temporal Logic (ICTL)*, number 827 in Lecture Notes in Artificial Inteligence, pages 67–81, Bonn, Germany, July 1994. Springer-Verlag.

[3] A.J. Bonner and M. Kifer. An overview of transaction logic. *Theoretical Computer Science*, 133:205–265, October 1994.

[4] A.J. Bonner and M. Kifer. Transaction logic programming (or a logic of declarative and procedural knowledge). Technical Report CSRI-323, University of Toronto, November 1995. Available at http://www.db.toronto.edu:8020/transaction-logic.html.

[5] A.J. Bonner and M. Kifer. Concurrency and communication in transaction logic. In *Joint Intl. Conference and Symposium on Logic Programming (JICSLP)*, pages 142–156, Bonn, Germany, September 1996. MIT Press.

[6] A.J. Bonner, M. Kifer, and M. Consens. Database programming in transaction logic. In A. Ohori C. Beeri and D.E. Shasha, editors, *Proceedings of the International Workshop on Database Programming Languages (DBPL)*, Workshops in Computing, pages 309–337. Springer-Verlag, February 1994. Workshop held on Aug 30–Sept 1, 1993, New York City, NY.

[7] M. Kifer. Deductive and object-oriented data languages: A quest for integration. In *Intl. Conference on Deductive and Object-Oriented Databases (DOOD)*, Lecture Notes in Computer Science, pages 187–212, Singapore, December 1995. Springer-Verlag. Keynote address at the 3d Intl. Conference on Deductive and Object-Oriented databases.

Programming with Global Analysis

Manuel Hermenegildo
The CLIP Group
School of Computer Science
Technical University of Madrid
herme@fi.upm.es

Abstract

Global data-flow analysis of (constraint) logic programs, which is generally based on abstract interpretation [7], is reaching a comparatively high level of maturity. A natural question is whether it is time for its routine incorporation in standard compilers, something which, beyond a few experimental systems, has not happened to date. Such incorporation arguably makes good sense only if:

- the range of applications of global analysis is large enough to justify the additional complication in the compiler, and

- global analysis technology can deal with all the features of "practical" languages (e.g., the ISO-Prolog built-ins) and "scales up" for large programs.

We present a tutorial overview of a number of concepts and techniques directly related to the issues above, with special emphasis on the first one. In particular, we concentrate on novel uses of global analysis during program development and debugging, rather than on the more traditional application area of program optimization.

The idea of using abstract interpretation for validation and diagnosis has been studied in the context of imperative programming [2] and also of logic programming. The latter work includes issues such as using approximations to reduce the burden posed on programmers by declarative debuggers [6, 3] and automatically generating and checking assertions [4, 5] (which includes the more traditional type checking of strongly typed languages, such as Gödel or Mercury [1, 8, 9])

We also review some solutions for scalability including modular analysis, incremental analysis, and widening. Finally, we discuss solutions for dealing with meta-predicates, side-effects, delay declarations, constraints, dynamic predicates, and other such features which may appear in practical languages.

In the discussion we will draw both from the literature and from our experience and that of others in the development and use of the CIAO system analyzer. In order to emphasize the practical aspects of the solutions discussed, the presentation of several concepts will be illustrated by examples run on the CIAO system, which makes extensive use of global analysis and assertions.

Acknowledgments

This tutorial was prepared in close collaboration with F. Bueno and G. Puebla. The work presented was supported in part by ESPRIT project DiSCiPl and has benefited greatly from discussions with P. Deransart, W. Drabent, J. Małuszyński, and other DiSCiPl project members, as well as other members of the CLIP group at UPM.

References

[1] K. R. Apt and E. Marchiori. Reasoning about Prolog programs: from modes through types to assertions. *Formal Aspects of Computing*, 6(6):743–765, 1994.

[2] F. Bourdoncle. Abstract debugging of higher-order imperative languages. In *Programming Languages Design and Implementation'93*, pages 46–55, 1993.

[3] J. Boye, W. Drabent, and J. Małuszyński. Declarative diagnosis of constraint programs: an assertion-based approach. In *Proc. of the 3rd. Int'l Workshop on Automated Debugging–AADEBUG'97*, pages 123–141, Linkoping, Sweden, May 1997. U. of Linkoping Press.

[4] F. Bueno, D. Cabeza, M. Hermenegildo, and G. Puebla. Global Analysis of Standard Prolog Programs. In *European Symposium on Programming*, number 1058 in LNCS, pages 108–124, Sweden, April 1996. Springer-Verlag.

[5] F. Bueno, P. Deransart, W. Drabent, G. Ferrand, M. Hermenegildo, J. Maluszynski, and G. Puebla. On the Role of Semantic Approximations in Validation and Diagnosis of Constraint Logic Programs. In *Proc. of the 3rd. Int'l Workshop on Automated Debugging–AADEBUG'97*, pages 155–170, Linkoping, Sweden, May 1997. U. of Linkoping Press.

[6] M. Comini, G. Levi, M. C. Meo, and G. Vitiello. Proving properties of logic programs by abstract diagnosis. In M. Dams, editor, *Analysis and Verification of Multiple-Agent Languages, 5th LOMAPS Workshop*, number 1192 in Lecture Notes in Computer Science, pages 22–50. Springer-Verlag, 1996.

[7] P. Cousot and R. Cousot. Abstract Interpretation: a Unified Lattice Model for Static Analysis of Programs by Construction or Approximation of Fixpoints. In *Fourth ACM Symposium on Principles of Programming Languages*, pages 238–252, 1977.

[8] P. Hill and J. Lloyd. *The Goedel Programming Language*. MIT Press, Cambridge MA, 1994.

[9] Z. Somogyi, F. Henderson, and T. Conway. The execution algorithm of Mercury: an efficient purely declarative logic programming language. *JLP*, 29(1–3), October 1996.

Refereed Papers

A Lazy Narrowing Calculus for Functional Logic Programming with Algebraic Polymorphic Types

P. Arenas-Sánchez, M. Rodríguez-Artalejo
Dpto. Sistemas Informáticos y Programación
Universidad Complutense de Madrid
Av. Complutense s/n, Madrid (SPAIN), E-28040
{puri,mario}@eucmos.sim.ucm.es

Abstract

In a recent work, we have proposed a semantic framework for lazy functional logic programming with algebraic polymorphic types, i.e., polymorphic types whose data constructors must obey a finite set C of equational axioms. That framework included C-based rewriting calculi and a notion of model, proving soundness and completeness of C-based rewriting w.r.t. models, existence of free models for all programs and type preservation results, but no goal solving mechanism was presented. The present paper extends the previous one by developing a sound and complete procedure for goal solving, which is based on the combination of lazy narrowing with unification modulo C. The resulting language is quite expressive for many kinds of problems, as e.g. action and change problems.
KEYWORDS: functional logic programming, polymorphic types, algebraic data constructors, lazy narrowing.

1 Introduction

The combination of different declarative programming paradigms (specially functional and logic) has been widely treated in the literature (see [11] for a survey). In particular, some *lazy functional logic languages* such as K-LEAF [7] and BABEL [18] were designed to combine lazy evaluation with unification by presenting programs as rewriting systems and using *lazy narrowing* (a notion introduced in [20]) as a goal solving mechanism.

Classical equational logic does not supply an adequate semantics for the behaviour of lazy functions. An alternative semantic framework for lazy functional logic languages has been proposed in [8], and it was extended in [3] with the incorporation of *algebraic polymorphic types*, i.e. polymorphic datatypes whose data constructors must obey a given set C of equational axioms[1]. In [3], C-based rewriting calculi and a notion of model are presented, getting soundness and completeness for C-based rewriting calculi w.r.t. models, existence of free models for all programs and type preservation results.

The aim of the present paper is to extend the approach in [3] by providing a lazy narrowing calculus (named LNCEC) for goal solving. In comparison to narrowing calculi for languages based on free constructors, as e.g. [8], LNCEC must

---

[1]Note that user-defined datatypes are also called "algebraic" in Haskell [19]. In spite of this terminology, Haskell's data constructors are free.

work modulo the equational axioms C which govern the data constructors. In fact, we have borrowed ideas from several previous works, such as [8, 10, 15, 21]. As the main novelty w.r.t. [8] and [10] our lazy narrowing calculus includes *mutation* rules (in the line of [15]) for applying equational axioms in C. With respect to works like [14, 6, 12, 9, 17] which use non-free data constructors (specially sets and multisets) for extended logic programming and multiparadigm declarative programming languages, we introduce lazy functions and parametric polymorphism. We view a program as a set of C-based conditional rewrite rules to define the behaviour of lazy functions on top of a given finite set C of equational axioms for data constructors. Both constructors and defined functions have polymorphic principal types. As in [8], defined functions can be partial and possibly *non-deterministic* in the spirit of [13]. For instance, a simple program consisting of a non-deterministic partial function which selects an arbitrary element from a non-empty set can be defined by a single rewrite rule:

datatypes	constructors		equations
$Set(\alpha)$	$\{\,\}:\to Set(\alpha)$		$\{x\lvert\{y\lvert zs\}\} \approx \{y\lvert\{x\lvert zs\}\}$
	$\{\cdot\lvert\cdot\}:(\alpha, Set(\alpha)) \to Set(\alpha)$		$\{x\lvert\{x\lvert zs\}\} \approx \{x\lvert zs\}$

functions
    $select : Set(\alpha) \to \alpha$
    $select(\{x\lvert xs\}) \to x$

where the set constructors $\{\,\}$ (to build an empty set) and $\{\cdot\lvert\cdot\}$ (to add an element to a set) are governed by the two given equations. Note that by omitting the second one, we can obtain a datatype for polymorphic multisets.

Our goal solving calculus LNCEC is presented as a system of goal transformations. Thanks to the combination of lazy narrowing and C-based mutations, it can cope with infinite data structures and algebraic constructors simultaneously. For instance, assume that we extend the little program above by adding the datatype *Nat*, the constructors $Zero :\to Nat$ and $Suc : Nat \to Nat$, and the defining rule: $gen\_set\_nat(n) \to \{n\lvert gen\_set\_nat(Suc(n))\}$. Then, LNCEC is able to solve the goal $Suc(Suc(Suc(Zero))) \bowtie select(gen\_set\_nat(Zero))$. In fact, we can prove soundness and completeness of LNCEC w.r.t. the proof-theoretic and model-theoretic semantics from [3]. Since these two semantics were proved equivalent in [3], we will refer only to the first one in this paper. Our completeness proof splits the goal solving process in two phases, like in [10]. The first phase allows to transform a goal into a quasi-solved goal only containing variables, whereas the second phase transforms quasi-solved goals into solved goals representing a computed answer for the initial goal. Unfortunately, the resulting goal solving procedure is not satisfactory as a basis for an efficient implementation, due to the high degree of nondeterminism and the possibility of computing redundant answers. However, for particular cases such as sets and multisets, and using techniques similar to those in [1], it should be possible (although difficult) to develop many optimizations, without loss of soundness and completeness. This and other topics are left for future work.

The rest of the paper is organized as follows: Sect. 2 sets the basic formalism, defining polymorphic signatures, (well-typed) expressions and equational axioms C for data constructors. In Sect. 3 we recall C-based rewrite rules and a goal-oriented rewriting calculus for defining lazy functions on top of a given set C of equational axioms, as defined in [3]. This section also includes some simple but illustrative programming examples and type preservation results. Sect. 4 presents our goal solving calculus, showing that it preserves well-typing of goals, as well as soundness and completeness w.r.t. the goal-oriented rewriting calculus. Some topics for future research are pointed in the concluding Sect. 5.

Proofs have been omitted due to lack of space. They can be found in [2].

2 Signatures, Expressions, Types and Equations

Let $TC = \bigcup_{n \geq 0} TC^n$ be a ranked alphabet of type constructors and $\alpha, \beta, \ldots \in TVar$ a denumerable set of type variables. The set of *polymorphic types* $\tau, \tau', \ldots \in Type_{TC}(TVar)$ is defined by $\tau ::= \alpha \mid C(\tau_1, \ldots, \tau_n)$, where $\tau_i \in Type_{TC}(TVar)$, $1 \leq i \leq n$, $C \in TC^n$. Given $\tau \in Type_{TC}(TVar)$, $tvar(\tau)$ is the set of type variables occurring in τ.

A *polymorphic signature* Σ over TC is a triple $\langle TC, DC, FS \rangle$, where DC is a set of type declarations for *data constructors*, of the form $c : (\tau_1, \ldots, \tau_n) \rightarrow \tau_0$ with $\bigcup_{i=1}^{n} tvar(\tau_i) \subseteq tvar(\tau_0)$ (so-called *transparency* property), and FS is a set of type declarations for *defined function symbols*, of the form $f : (\tau_1, \ldots, \tau_n) \rightarrow \tau_0$. We require that Σ does not include multiple type declarations for the same symbol. The types given by declarations in $DC \cup FS$ are called *principal types*. We will write $h \in DC^n \cup FS^n$ to indicate the arity of a symbol according to its type declaration.

In the following, $DC_\perp$ will denote DC extended by a new constant constructor declaration $\perp :\rightarrow \alpha$. The bottom constant $\perp$ is intended to represent an undefined value. Analogously, $\Sigma_\perp$ will denote the result of replacing DC by $DC_\perp$ in Σ.

Given a denumerable set $x, y, \ldots \in DVar$ of data variables, the set of *partial expressions* $e, r, l, \ldots \in Expr_{\Sigma_\perp}(DVar)$ is defined by $e ::= x \mid h(e_1, \ldots, e_n)$, where $h \in FS^n \cup DC_\perp^n$ and $e_i \in Expr_{\Sigma_\perp}(DVar)$. The set $Term_{\Sigma_\perp}(DVar)$ of *partial data terms* is defined as $Expr_{\Sigma_\perp}(DVar)$, but now $h \in DC_\perp^n$ and $e_i \in Term_{\Sigma_\perp}(DVar)$. Using DC instead of $DC_\perp$, the sets $Expr_\Sigma(DVar)$ of *total expressions* and $Term_\Sigma(DVar)$ of *total data terms* can be defined analogously. In the sequel, we reserve t, s to denote possibly partial data terms, and we write $dvar(e)$ for the set of all data variables occurring in an expression e. The notation $h(\bar{e}_n)$ will stand for $h(e_1, \ldots, e_n)$, where $h \in DC^n \cup FS^n$ and $e_i \in Expr_{\Sigma_\perp}(DVar)$, $1 \leq i \leq n$.

Type substitutions $\theta \in TSub$ are mappings from $TVar$ to $Type_{TC}(TVar)$. *Partial data substitutions* $\delta \in DSub_\perp$ are mappings from $DVar$ to $Term_{\Sigma_\perp}(DVar)$. *Total data substitutions* $\delta \in DSub$ are mappings from $DVar$ to $Term_\Sigma(DVar)$. We say that $\delta \in DSub_\perp$ is *idempotent* iff $\delta(\delta(x)) = \delta(x)$, for all $x \in DVar$.

The notions of *instance*, *renaming* and *variant* have the usual definitions (see e.g. [4]) and can be trivially extended to declarations in $DC_\perp \cup FS$. In the sequel, we will use postfix notation for applying substitutions.

For any $\delta, \delta' \in DSub_\perp$, the notation $\delta = \delta'[S]$ and $\delta = \delta'[\backslash S]$ (where $S \subseteq DVar$) will indicate respectively that $x\delta = x\delta'$ for all $x \in S$ and $x\delta = x\delta'$ for all $x \in DVar \backslash S$. The *subsumption ordering* over $DSub_\perp$ is defined as: $\delta \leq \delta'$ (read δ is more general than δ') iff $\delta' = \delta\delta''$, for some $\delta'' \in DSub_\perp$. Furthermore, the notation $\delta \leq \delta'[S]$ will mean that δ is more general than δ' over the variables in S.

An *environment* is defined as any set V of type-annotated data variables $x : \tau$, such that V does not include two different annotations for the same variable. The set $Expr_{\Sigma_\perp}^\tau(V)$ of all partial expressions that admit type τ w.r.t. the environment V

is defined in the usual way; see [3]. A partial expression e is called *well-typed* w.r.t. V iff $e \in Expr^\tau_{\Sigma_\perp}(V)$ for some type τ.

We will specify the behaviour of data constructors by means of a set $\mathcal{C}$ of *equational axioms* $s \approx t$, where s and t are total data terms. Such an axiom is called *strongly regular* iff $dvar(s) = dvar(t)$ and $s, t \notin DVar$. In the rest of the paper we focus on strongly regular axioms, because strong regularity is needed to prove some type preservation results, as shown in [3].

We say that a strongly regular axiom $c(t_1, \ldots, t_n) \approx d(s_1, \ldots, s_m)$ is *well-typed* iff the declared principal types for c and d have variants $c : (\tau_1, \ldots, \tau_n) \to \tau$ and $d : (\tau'_1, \ldots, \tau'_m) \to \tau$ such that $c(t_1, \ldots, t_n), d(s_1, \ldots, s_m) \in Term^\tau_\Sigma(V)$, for some environment V. For instance, it is easy to check that equational axioms $\{x | \{y | zs\}\} \approx \{y | \{x | zs\}\}$ and $\{x | \{x | zs\}\} \approx \{x | zs\}$ for the set constructor, are well-typed. In the following, we will say that two data constructors c, d have *compatible types* iff their declared principal types admit variants $c : (\tau_1, \ldots, \tau_n) \to \tau$ and $d : (\tau'_1, \ldots, \tau'_m) \to \tau$, respectively.

Given a set $\mathcal{C}$ of equational axioms for data constructors, $c \in DC^n$ is called *algebraic* (or *equational*) iff $\mathcal{C}$ contains some axiom $s \approx t$ such that s or t is of the form $c(t_1, \ldots, t_n)$. Otherwise, c is called *free*.

3 Defining Rules, Programs and a Rewriting Calculus

On top of a given set $\mathcal{C}$ of equational axioms for data constructors, we introduce constructor-based rewrite rules for defined functions. More precisely, assuming a principal type declaration $f : (\tau_1, \ldots, \tau_n) \to \tau \in FS$, a *defining rule* for f must have the form $f(t_1, \ldots, t_n) \to r \Leftarrow a_1 \bowtie b_1, \ldots, a_m \bowtie b_m$, where the left-hand side is *linear* (i.e. without multiple occurrences of variables), $t_i \in Term_\Sigma(DVar)$, $1 \leq i \leq n$, and $a_j, b_j, r \in Expr_\Sigma(DVar)$, $1 \leq j \leq m$. *Joinability conditions* $a_j \bowtie b_j$ are intended to hold iff a_j, b_j can be reduced to some common total $t \in Term_\Sigma(DVar)$, as in [8]. A more formal definition will be given below. A defining rule is called *regular* iff r includes no extra variables, i.e. $dvar(r) \subseteq dvar(t_1) \cup \ldots \cup dvar(t_n)$. Extra variables in the condition are allowed, as well as the unconditional case $m = 0$.

Programs are intended to solve *goals* composed of joinability conditions; i.e. goals will have the same form as conditions for defining rules. Formally a *program* is defined as a triple $\mathcal{P} = \langle \Sigma, \mathcal{C}, \mathcal{R} \rangle$, where Σ is a polymorphic signature, $\mathcal{C}$ is a finite set of equational axioms for data constructors in Σ, and $\mathcal{R}$ is a finite set of defining rules for defined functions symbols in Σ. We will say that a program $\mathcal{P}$ is *strongly regular* iff all axioms in $\mathcal{C}$ are strongly regular and all rules in $\mathcal{R}$ are regular.

The expressive power of algebraic constructors in our programs can be used to model *action and change* problems declaratively, avoiding the so-called *frame problem* [16]. In [9, 12], it has been already shown that *planning problems* can be modeled by means of *equational logic programs*, using a binary *ACI* operation $\circ$, to represent situations as multisets of facts $fact_1 \circ \ldots \circ fact_n$, and a ternary predicate $execPlan(initialSit, plan, finalSit)$ to model the transformation of an initial situation into a final situation by the execution of a plan. Action and change problems can be also tackled by means of non-classical logics such as Girard's linear logic and Meseguer's rewriting logic; see [16]. In our framework we can follow the same idea quite naturally, using multisets of facts to represent situations, and a non-deterministic function execPlan : $(List(Action), Mset(Fact)) \rightarrow Mset(Fact)$ to represent the effect of plan execution. The next little program adapted from [12], shows how to solve a very simple planning problem in our setting. More complicated action and change problems could be treated analogously.

Example 3.1 *The following typical blocksworld problem consists in finding a plan for transforming situation (A) into situation (B) (see figure below) by means of a robot's hand. The possible facts are:*

- $O(b_1, b_2)$: *block b_1 is over block b_2;*
- $C(b)$: *block b is clear; i.e. there is no block over it;*
- $T(b)$: *block b is over the table;*
- $H(b)$: *the robot's hand holds block b;*
- E: *the robot's hand is empty.*

   The available actions are $Stack(b_1, b_2)$, $Pickup(b)$, $Unstack(b_1, b_2)$ and Put-down(b). Their behaviour can be easily deduced from the definition of the function execAction *below.*

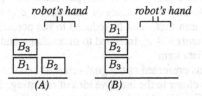

(A)   (B)

   The problem of finding a plan for transforming situation (A) into (B) can be described in our framework by means of the following simple program:

datatypes $Block/0, Fact/0, Action/0, Mset/1, List/1$

constructors

$B_1, B_2, B_3 :\rightarrow Block$
$C, T, H : Block \rightarrow Fact$ $\{\ \} :\rightarrow Mset(\alpha)$
$O : (Block, Block) \rightarrow Fact$ $\{\cdot|\cdot\} : (\alpha, Mset(\alpha)) \rightarrow Mset(\alpha)$
$E :\rightarrow Fact$ $[\ ] :\rightarrow List(\alpha)$
$Pickup, Putdown : Block \rightarrow Action$ $[\cdot|\cdot] : (\alpha, List(\alpha)) \rightarrow List(\alpha)$
$Stack, Unstack : (Block, Block) \rightarrow Action$

equations

$$\{x, y|xs\} = \{y, x|xs\}$$

functions

execPlan : $(List(Action), Mset(Fact)) \rightarrow Mset(Fact)$
$execPlan([\ ], sit) \rightarrow sit$
$execPlan([act|ract], sit) \rightarrow execPlan(ract, execAction(act, sit))$

execAction : $(Action, Mset(Fact)) \rightarrow Mset(Fact)$
$execAction(Pickup(v), \{C(v_1), T(v_2), E|facts\}) \rightarrow \{H(v)|facts\}$
$\qquad \Leftarrow v \bowtie v_1, v \bowtie v_2$
$execAction(Unstack(v, w), \{C(v_1), O(v_2, w_1), E|facts\}) \rightarrow \{H(v), C(w)|facts\}$
$\qquad \Leftarrow v \bowtie v_1, v \bowtie v_2, w_1 \bowtie w$
$execAction(Putdown(v), \{H(v_1)|facts\}) \rightarrow \{T(v), C(v), E|facts\} \Leftarrow v \bowtie v_1$
$execAction(Stack(v, w), \{H(v_1), C(w_1)|facts\}) \rightarrow \{O(v, w), C(v), E|facts\}$
$\qquad \Leftarrow v \bowtie v_1, w \bowtie w_1$

Note that we have used $\{\!\{x, y | xs\}\!\}$ as abbreviation for $\{\!\{x | \{\!\{y | xs\}\!\}\}\!\}$. In the sequel we will continue using such notation. The appropriate goal for getting a plan which solves the planning problem at hand is $execPlan(plan, \{\!\{C(B_2), C(B_3), O(B_3, B_1),$
$T(B_2), T(B_1), E\}\!\}) \bowtie \{\!\{C(B_1), O(B_1, B_2), O(B_2, B_3), T(B_3), E\}\!\}$.

Using the lazy narrowing calculus presented in Sect. 4, the answer plan $=[Uns\text{-}$
$tack(B_3, B_1), Putdown(B_3), Pickup(B_2), Stack(B_2, B_3), Pickup(B_1), Stack(B_1, B_2)]$
can be computed. Of course, other possible plans for solving the same planning problem can be also computed. ∎

Some of our subsequent results will refer to well-typed programs. A strongly regular program $\mathcal{P} = \langle \Sigma, \mathcal{C}, \mathcal{R} \rangle$ is *well-typed* iff $\mathcal{C}$ is well-typed and every defining rule $f(t_1, \ldots, t_n) \to r \Leftarrow C$ is well-typed in the following sense: there exists an environment V such that $t_i \in Term_\Sigma^{\tau_i}(V), 1 \leq i \leq n$ and $r \in Expr_\Sigma^\tau(V)$, where $f : (\tau_1, \ldots, \tau_n) \to \tau$ is the principal type declaration for f in Σ. Moreover, for each $a \bowtie b \in C$ there must be some type τ' such that $a, b \in Expr_\Sigma^{\tau'}(V)$. For instance, it is easy to check that the program given in example 3.1 is well-typed.

In the rest of the section we present a Goal-Oriented Rewriting Calculus $GORC$ which plays the role of a proof-theoretical specification of programs' semantics. $GORC$ is designed to derive two kinds of statements: *approximation statements* $e \to t$, intended to mean that e can be reduced to the possibly partial data term t and *joinability statements* $e \bowtie e'$, intended to mean that e and e' can be reduced to some common total data term.

In [3], $GORC$ was presented as the goal-oriented version of an equivalent calculus BRC, which is closer to the intuitive idea of rewriting. In this paper we use a new presentation of $GORC$ which is equivalent to that given in [3], but more convenient for our present purposes. As a technical device, we need the "linearization" $\mathcal{C}_\to$ of $\mathcal{C}$, which is obtained by transforming each equation $s \approx t \in \mathcal{C}$ into two rewrite rules $s' \to t \Leftarrow C_s$ and $t' \to s \Leftarrow C_t$, built as follows: s' is the result of replacing repeated occurrences of variables x in s by different new variables x_i, and C_s includes conditions $x \bowtie x_i$. The construction of t' and C_t is similar. For instance, $c(x, x, x, y) \approx d(y, y, y, x)$ gives rise to the rewrite rules:

- $c(x, x_1, x_2, y) \to d(y, y, y, x) \Leftarrow x \bowtie x_1, x \bowtie x_2$ and
- $d(y, y_1, y_2, x) \to c(x, x, x, y) \Leftarrow y \bowtie y_1, y \bowtie y_2$.

For a given program $\mathcal{P} = \langle \Sigma, \mathcal{C}, \mathcal{R} \rangle$, the rewriting calculus $GORC$ is defined as shown in figure 1, where $e, e', c(e_1, \ldots, e_n), f(e_1, \ldots, e_n) \in Expr_{\Sigma_\bot}(DVar)$, $t, c(t_1, \ldots, t_n) \in Term_{\Sigma_\bot}(DVar), x \in DVar$ and

$$
\begin{aligned}
[\mathcal{R}]_\to &= \{(l \to r \Leftarrow C)\delta \mid l \to r \Leftarrow C \in \mathcal{R}, \delta \in DSub_\bot\} \\
[\mathcal{C}]_\to &= \{(s \to t \Leftarrow C)\delta \mid s \to t \Leftarrow C \in \mathcal{C}_\to, \delta \in DSub_\bot\}
\end{aligned}
$$

$GORC$ does not specify rewriting in the usual sense. Rule Bottom shows that $e \to t$ is intended to mean "t approximates e", and the construction of $[\mathcal{R}]_\to, [\mathcal{C}]_\to$ reflects a "call-time choice" treatment of non-determinism, as explained in [13]. As the main novelty w.r.t. [8], we find the rule Outer $\mathcal{C}$-mutation to deal with equations between constructors.

The next theorem ensures that $GORC$ preserves types. The strong regularity of $\mathcal{C}$ is needed for this result. See [3] for an example.

$$\begin{array}{ll} \text{Bottom}: \ \dfrac{}{e \to \perp} & \text{Restricted reflexivity}: \ \dfrac{}{x \to x} \end{array}$$

$$\text{Decomposition}: \ \dfrac{\ldots, e_i \to t_i, \ldots}{c(e_1, \ldots, e_n) \to c(t_1, \ldots, t_n)}$$

$$\text{Outer } \mathcal{C}\text{-mutation}: \ \dfrac{\ldots, e_i \to t_i, \ldots, C, s \to t}{c(e_1, \ldots, e_n) \to t} \ \text{if } t \neq \perp, c(\bar{t}_n) \to s \Leftarrow C \in [\mathcal{C}]_\to$$

$$\text{Outer } \mathcal{R}\text{-reduction}: \ \dfrac{\ldots, e_i \to t_i, \ldots, C, r \to t}{f(e_1, \ldots, e_n) \to t} \ \text{if } t \neq \perp, f(\bar{t}_n) \to r \Leftarrow C \in [\mathcal{R}]_\to$$

$$\text{Join}: \ \dfrac{e \to t', e' \to t'}{e \bowtie e'} \ \text{if } t' \in Term_\Sigma(DVar) \text{ is a } total \text{ data term}$$

Figure 1: The Goal-Oriented Rewriting Calculus $GORC$

Theorem 3.2 (Type preservation) *Let* $\mathcal{P} = \langle \Sigma, \mathcal{C}, \mathcal{R} \rangle$ *be a well-typed strongly regular program. Let* V *be an environment. If* $e \to t$ *is GORC-derivable and* $e \in Expr^\tau_{\Sigma_\perp}(V)$ *then* $t \in Term^\tau_{\Sigma_\perp}(V)$. $\qquad\square$

The model-theoretic semantics of our framework was presented in [3]. Here, we only recall that the intended meaning of any program is given by its *free term model*, which includes exactly the information provided by $GORC$-derivability.

4 A Lazy Narrowing Calculus for Goal Solving

This section presents a *Lazy Narrowing Calculus based on Equational Constructors* (LNCEC for short). This calculus is the main contribution of the paper. It provides a goal solving procedure that combines lazy narrowing (in the spirit of of [8] and [10]) with unification modulo a set of equational axioms $\mathcal{C}$ (in the line of [15] and [21]). Differently to [8] and [10] (where data constructors are free) we require the introduction of mutation rules (as in [15]) for applying equational axioms to data constructors. With respect to [15] and [21] we need the incorporation of *narrowing* for applying program rules.

As in [8], goals are finite conjunctions of approximation and joinability statements whereas solutions will be partial data substitutions such that the goal affected by such a substitution is provable in $GORC$. Due to technical reasons that will become apparent later, we divide LNCEC in two main phases, as in [10]. The first one transforms an initial goal G into a quasi-solved goal G' (only containing variables) by applying goal transformation rules in figures 2 and 3. The second one takes the resulting G' and using transformation rules in figure 5, transforms it into a solved goal which represents a solution in the sense of definition 4.3 below. Each transformation step using a rule of figures 2 and 3 is noted as $G \hookrightarrow_\mathcal{P} G'$ whereas $G \hookrightarrow_{DVar} G'$ represents a transformation step using variable elimination rules from figure 5. A *derivation* for a goal is a finite sequence of $\hookrightarrow_\mathcal{P}$-steps (named $\hookrightarrow_\mathcal{P}$-derivation) followed by a finite sequence of $\hookrightarrow_{DVar}$-steps (named a $\hookrightarrow_{DVar}$-derivation). *FAIL* represents an irreducible inconsistent goal used to write *failure rules* (see figure 4). Of course, since we work with static types, LNCEC preserves types in the case of a well-typed admissible goal and program (see theorem 4.11). As notation, $dvar(L)$ stands for the set of variables occurring in L, where L is either a goal, a multiset of joinability/approximation statements, a program rule or an equational axiom.

Next definition introduces formally the notion of (well-typed) *admissible goal*. Admissible goals fulfill a number of technical requirements needed to achieve the effect of lazy unification with *sharing*. As explained in [13, 8], *sharing* is needed for correctness in our semantics.

Definition 4.1 (Well-typed admissible goals) *Let* $\mathcal{P} = \langle \Sigma, \mathcal{C}, \mathcal{R} \rangle$ *be a program. An admissible goal* G *for* $\mathcal{P}$ *has the structure* $G \equiv \exists \bar{u} S \square P \square E$, *where:*

- $\mathsf{evar}(G) \equiv \bar{u}$ *is the set of existential variables;*
- S *is a system of equations in solved form; i.e.* $S \equiv x_1 = t_1, \ldots, x_n = t_n$, *where* $t_i \in Term_\Sigma(DVar)$, $1 \leq i \leq n$ *and* x_i *occurs exactly once in the whole goal,* $1 \leq i \leq n$;
- $P \equiv e_1 \to t_1, \ldots, e_k \to t_k$ *is a multiset of approximation statements.* $\mathsf{pvar}(P)$ $=_{Def} \bigcup_{i=1}^k dvar(t_i)$ *is called the set of produced variables;*
- $E \equiv e_1 \bowtie e'_1, \ldots, e_m \bowtie e'_m$ *is a multiset of joinability statements, and must fulfill the following conditions:*
  - $(t_1, \ldots, t_k)$ *is linear;*
  - $\mathsf{pvar}(P) \subseteq \mathsf{evar}(G)$, *i.e. all produced variables are existentially quantified;*
  - *the transitive closure of the relation* $\gg$ *defined as:* $x \gg y$ *iff there exists* $1 \leq i \leq k$ *such that* $x \in dvar(e_i)$ *and* $y \in dvar(t_i)$, *must be irreflexive (i.e. a strict partial order);*
  - $dvar(S) \cap \mathsf{pvar}(P) = \emptyset$, *i.e. the solved part does not contain produced variables.*

G *is well-typed iff there exists an environment* V *such that for all* $e \diamond e' \in S \cup P \cup E$, $\diamond \in \{\to, \bowtie, =\}$, *there exists some type* τ *such that* $e, e' \in Expr_\Sigma^\tau(V)$. $\qquad \square$

In the following, *initial goals* will be admissible goals of the form $\exists \bar{u} \square \square E$ whereas *quasi-solved goals* will be admissible goals such that for all $e \to t \in P$ and $e' \bowtie e'' \in E$ it holds that $e, t, e', e'' \in DVar$. Finally, *goals in solved form* will be also admissible goals with the following structure: $\exists \bar{u} S \square \square$. It is easy to check that solved goals with $S \equiv x_1 = t_1, \ldots, x_n = t_n$, determine an associated *answer data substitution* δ_S defined as $\delta_S(x_i) = t_i$, for all $1 \leq i \leq n$ and $\delta_S(x) = x$ for all $x \neq x_i$, which is idempotent.

Some brief comments are needed in order to clarify the above definition. Intuitively, each equation $x = t$ in the solved part S denotes a computed answer for x. As we will show later, if an admissible goal G has a solution δ, our lazy narrowing calculus is able to transform G into a solved goal $G' \equiv \exists \bar{u} S' \square \square$ in such a way that the solved system S', viewed as a data substitution $\delta'_{S'}$, denotes a solution for G more general than δ. Approximation statements $e \to t$ in goals indicate that e must be narrowed to match t. In particular, statements of the form $e \to x$ can be thought as delayed bindings x/e. The transformation rules in figure 3 deal with these statements in such a way that e is narrowed lazily, and the data term obtained as result is shared via x with the rest of the goal. Irreflexivity of $\gg$ allows to avoid occur-check in some of our transformations.

Definition 4.2 (Demanded variables) *Let* $G \equiv \exists \bar{u} S \square P \square E$ *be an admissible goal. A variable* $x \in dvar(G)$ *is demanded iff* $x \bowtie e \in E$ *or* $e \bowtie x \in E$. *In the following* $\mathsf{demandvar}(G)$ *will denote the set of demanded variables in* G. $\qquad \square$

Decomposition : $\exists \bar{u} S \Box P \Box c(\bar{e}_n) \bowtie c(\bar{e'}_n), E \hookrightarrow_P \exists \bar{u} S \Box P \Box \ldots, e_i \bowtie e'_i, \ldots, E$

Mutation : $\exists \bar{u} S \Box P \Box c(\bar{e}_n) \bowtie e', E \hookrightarrow_P \exists \bar{x} \ \bar{u} S \Box \ldots, e_i \to t_i, \ldots, P \Box C, s \bowtie e', E$

    where $Eq : c(\bar{t}_n) \to s \Leftarrow C$ is a variant of a rule in $\mathcal{C}_{\to}$

    with $\bar{x} = dvar(Eq)$ fresh variables.

Imitation+Decomposition : $\exists \bar{u} S \Box P \Box x \bowtie c(\bar{e}_n), E \hookrightarrow_P$

        $\exists \bar{x}_n \bar{u}[x = c(\bar{x}_n)], (S \Box P \Box \ldots, x_i \bowtie e_i, \ldots, E) \delta$

    where $\delta = \{x / c(\bar{x}_n)\}$, $\bar{x}_n$ fresh variables.

Imitation+Mutation : $\exists \bar{u} S \Box P \Box x \bowtie c(\bar{e}_n), E \hookrightarrow_P$

        $\exists \bar{z} \ \bar{x}_m \bar{u}[x = d(\bar{x}_m)], (S \Box \ldots, x_i \to t_i, \ldots, P \Box C, s \bowtie c(\bar{e}_n), E) \delta$

    if c is algebraic, principal types of c and d are compatible,

    $Eq : d(\bar{t}_m) \to s \Leftarrow C$ is a variant of a rule in $\mathcal{C}_{\to}$

    with $\bar{z} = dvar(Eq)$ and $\bar{x}_m$ fresh variables, where $\delta = \{x / d(\bar{x}_m)\}$.

Narrowing : $\exists \bar{u} S \Box P \Box f(\bar{e}_n) \bowtie e', E \hookrightarrow_P \exists \bar{x} \ \bar{u} S \Box \ldots, e_i \to t_i, \ldots, P \Box C, r \bowtie e', E$

    where $Rul : f(\bar{t}_n) \to r \Leftarrow C$ is a variant of a rule in $\mathcal{R}$

    with $\bar{x} = dvar(Rul)$ fresh variables.

Figure 2: $\hookrightarrow_P$-rules for $\bowtie$

As we will see in definition 4.3, any solution (partial data substitution δ) for G must guarantee the existence of $GORC$-proofs for all joinability and approximations statements in G affected by δ. Due to the semantics of joinability and approximation statements, solutions must bind demanded variables to total data terms. Thus, in statements of the form $f(\bar{e}_n) \to x$, $f \in FS^n$ or $c(\bar{e}_n) \to x$, $c \in DC^n$ with $x \in \text{demandvar}(G)$, the evaluation of $f(\bar{e}_n)$ or $c(\bar{e}_n)$, respectively, is needed (see transformation rules Mutation, Imitation and Narrowing in figure 3). Otherwise (x is not demanded) such evaluation is delayed until the application of another transformation rule transforms x into a demanded variable or the approximation statement can be eliminated by using rule Elimination. As a consequence *laziness* is achieved.

4.1 LNCEC transformation rules. Correctness and Completeness

As commented before at the beginning of this section, LNCEC is divided in two different processes. The first one handles transformation rules only applicable to those approximation/joinability statements one of whose sides is not a variable (see figures 2, 3 and 4). These rules transform any admissible goal either into a quasi-solved goal G' (only containing variables) or *FAIL* (indicating that G has no solutions). The second process applies variable elimination rules in figure 5 to G', getting a solved goal representing a computed answer for G. Remark that no particular strategy is used to select an element of $G \equiv \exists \bar{u} S \Box P \Box E$ to be reduced. On the other hand we see conditions $e \bowtie e' \in E$ as symmetric for the purpose of applying goal transformations. All bracketed equations $[x = t]$ occurring in S mean that $x = t$ only occurs in S if $x \notin \text{pvar}(P)$.

Differently to [8], $\hookrightarrow_P$ needs *don't know choice* in the application of transformation rules[2]. The reason is the incorporation of equational axioms for algebraic constructors. Thus, when a statement $c(\bar{e}_n) \bowtie c(\bar{e'}_n)$ (respect. $c(\bar{e}_n) \to c(\bar{e'}_n)$), where c is algebraic, has to be reduced it is unknown which transformation rule (Decomposition or Mutation) will succeed. For instance, considering $c(a) \approx c(b) \in \mathcal{C}$,

---

[2]Of course this kind of non-determinism also appears in the election of $\mathcal{C}$-equations and program rules to be applied.

where a and b are free constant symbols, we get that $c(a) \bowtie c(b)$ must be reduced using Mutation but $c(a) \bowtie c(a)$ should be reduced using Decomposition. However in both cases, both rules are applicable. Some other times, frequently in presence of variables, both rules are able to capture a solution, even the same. For instance, consider the goal $\Box\Box c(a) \bowtie c(x)$ which clearly has as possible solutions $\{x = a\}$ and $\{x = b\}$. Using Decomposition and Imitation+Decomposition we get the solution $\{x = a\}$. Now, applying Mutation to $c(a)$ with $c(a) \to c(b) \in \mathcal{C}_\to$, Decomposition and Imitation+Decomposition we get another solution $\{x = b\}$. Furthermore, applying Mutation to $c(x)$ with $c(a) \to c(b) \in \mathcal{C}_\to$ we can again capture the solution $\{x = a\}$ computed previously. This shows that LNCEC can compute repeated solutions, something undesirable from a practical point of view. For particular cases, such as the equational axioms for sets and multisets, and using similar techniques to those presented in [1], it should be possible (although complicated) to get a goal solving procedure able to enumerate all the independent solutions without repetitions. However this topic is out of the scope of this paper and left for future work.

The *failure rules* in figure 4 must be applied before the rest of $\hookrightarrow_\mathcal{P}$-rules in order to detect failures as soon as possible. The set $\mathsf{svar}(e)$ in rule Cycle denotes the set of *safe variables* occurring in e, i.e. the set of variables x such that x occurs in e at some position whose ancestor positions are all occupied by free constructors. In [8], a different notion of safe variable is used: "x is safe in e iff x occurs in e at some position whose ancestor positions are all occupied by constructors". This notion wouldn't lead to a correct Cycle rule in a language with algebraic constructors. For instance, in our framework, if $c(a) \approx a \in \mathcal{C}$ then $x \bowtie c(x)$ has a solution $x = a$.

Let us now introduce the notion of solution for admissible goals.

Definition 4.3 (Solution) *Let* $\mathcal{P} = \langle \Sigma, \mathcal{C}, \mathcal{R} \rangle$ *be a program. Let* $G \equiv \exists \bar{u} S \Box P \Box E$ *be an admissible goal for* $\mathcal{P}$ *and* $\delta \in DSub_\perp$. *We say that* δ *is a solution of* G *iff*

(TOT) $x\delta \in Term_\Sigma(DVar)$ *for all* $x \in DVar - \mathsf{pvar}(P)$;

(EQ) $x\delta \equiv s\delta$ *for all* $x = s \in S$;

(GORC) *For all* $e \bowtie e' \in E$ *and* $e'' \to t \in P$ *there exists a GORC-proof of* $e\delta \bowtie e'\delta$ *and* $e''\delta \to t\delta$ *respectively. The multiset composed of all such GORC-proofs will be called a* witness $\mathcal{M}$ *for* G *and* δ.

In the following $\mathsf{Sol}(G)$ *will denote the set of all solutions for* G. $\qquad\qquad\square$

Solutions for goals are *partial data substitutions*. This is because of the presence of produced variables. Such variables, which are not present in initial goals, can appear (existentially quantified) in intermediate goals of a computation. Since they occur in right-hand sides of approximation statements, they serve to express approximation and thus may need to be given only partial values. For instance, consider the functions $duo : Set(\alpha) \to Bool$ and $om :\to \alpha$ defined respectively by the rewriting rules $duo(\{x, y\}) \to True$ and $om \to om$. Consider now the admissible goal $G \equiv \Box\Box duo(\{om\}) \bowtie True$ which has the empty substitution as solution. By applying Narrowing using the program rule variant $duo(\{x_1, y_1\}) \to True$, we get $G' \equiv \exists x_1, y_1 \Box \{om\} \to \{x_1, y_1\} \Box True \bowtie True$. Clearly, any solution δ' for G' must map x_1 and y_1 (produced variables) into $\perp$. Otherwise there is no witness for $\{om\} \to \{x_1, y_1\}\delta'$. Notice that for initial goals (where only E is present), solutions are *total data substitutions*. The same can be said for goals in solved form due to **(TOT)** and **(EQ)**.

Decomposition : $\exists \bar{u} S \square c(\bar{e}_n) \to c(\bar{t}_n), P \square E \hookrightarrow_{\mathcal{P}} \exists \bar{u} S \square \ldots, e_i \to t_i, \ldots, P \square E$

Mutation : $\exists \bar{u} S \square c(\bar{e}_n) \to t, P \square E \hookrightarrow_{\mathcal{P}} \exists \bar{x} \ \bar{u} S \square \ldots, e_i \to t_i, \ldots, s \to t, P \square C, E$
   if $t \notin DVar$ or $t \in$ demandvar(G), where $Eq : c(\bar{t}_n) \to s \Leftarrow C$ is a variant
   of a rule in $\mathcal{C}_\to$ with $\bar{x} = dvar(Eq)$ fresh variables.

Imitation+Decomposition : $\exists \bar{u} S \square x \to c(\bar{t}_n), P \square E \hookrightarrow_{\mathcal{P}}$
$$\exists \bar{x}_n \bar{u}[x = c(\bar{x}_n)], (S \square \ldots, x_i \to t_i, \ldots, P \square E)\delta$$
   where $\delta = \{x/c(\bar{x}_n)\}$, $\bar{x}_n$ fresh variables.

Imitation+Mutation : $\exists \bar{u} S \square x \to c(\bar{t}_n), P \square E \hookrightarrow_{\mathcal{P}}$
$$\exists \bar{z} \ \bar{x}_m \bar{u}[x = d(\bar{x}_m)], (S \square \ldots, x_i \to s_i, \ldots, s \to c(\bar{t}_n), P \square C, E)\delta$$
   if c is algebraic, principal types of c and d are compatible,
   $Eq : d(\bar{s}_m) \to s \Leftarrow C$ is a variant of a rule in $\mathcal{C}_\to$
   with $\bar{z} = dvar(Eq)$ and $\bar{x}_m$ fresh variables, where $\delta = \{x/d(\bar{x}_m)\}$.

Imitation : $\exists x \bar{u} S \square c(\bar{e}_n) \to x, P \square E \hookrightarrow_{\mathcal{P}} \exists \bar{x}_n \bar{u} S \square (\ldots, e_i \to x_i, \ldots, P \square E)\delta$
   if $x \in$ demandvar(G), where $\delta = \{x/c(\bar{x}_n)\}$, $\bar{x}_n$ fresh variables.

Elimination : $\exists x \bar{u} S \square e \to x, P \square E \hookrightarrow_{\mathcal{P}} \exists \bar{u} S \square P \square E$
   if $x \notin dvar(P \square E)$.

Narrowing : $\exists \bar{u} S \square f(\bar{e}_n) \to t, P \square E \hookrightarrow_{\mathcal{P}} \exists \bar{x} \ \bar{u} S \square \ldots, e_i \to t_i, \ldots, r \to t, P \square C, E$
   if $t \notin DVar$ or $t \in$ demandvar(G), where $Rul : f(\bar{t}_n) \to r \Leftarrow C$ is a variant
   of a rule in $\mathcal{R}$ with $\bar{x} = dvar(Rul)$ fresh variables.

Figure 3: $\hookrightarrow_{\mathcal{P}}$-rules for $\to$

Finally, notice that (**EQ**) can appear surprising in presence of equational axioms $\mathcal{C}$ for data constructors. The reason is that LNCEC enumerates non-deterministically all the possible solutions to any admissible goal, even those being equivalent modulo $\mathcal{C}$. This justifies rules Imitation, Imitation+Decomposition and Imitation+Mutation. In particular, we can always propagate bindings x/t in such a way that the resulting goal G' has always a solution δ' such that $x\delta'$ is syntactically identical to $t\delta'$. The following example will clarify this situation.

Example 4.4 *Consider an admissible goal of the form* $G \equiv \exists \bar{u} S \square x \to c(\bar{t}_n), P \square E$ *having a solution* δ. *Let us analyze the witness* $\mathcal{M}$ *associated to* G *and* δ. *If the GORC-proof in* $\mathcal{M}$ *for* $x\delta \to c(\bar{t})\delta$ *uses:*

(1) Decomposition *as last inference step, then* $x\delta = c(\bar{s}_n)$. *By applying the propagation rule* Imitation+Decomposition, *the resulting goal has a solution* δ' *defined as:* $\delta'(x_i) = s_i$ *and* $\delta' = \delta[\backslash\{x_1, \ldots, x_n\}]$ *and verifying that* $x\delta'$ *is syntactically equal to* $c(\bar{x}_n)\delta'$;

(2) Outer $\mathcal{C}$-mutation *as last inference step, then* $x\delta = d(\bar{s}_m)$ *and there exists* $Eq :$ $d(s_1', \ldots, s_m') \to s'' \Leftarrow C \in [\mathcal{C}]_\to$ *such that the GORC-proof for* $x\delta \to c(\bar{t}_n)\delta$ *in* $\mathcal{M}$ *contains subproofs for* $s_i \to s_i'$, C *and* $s'' \to c(\bar{t}_n)\delta$ *respectively. Trivially there exists a fresh variant* $Eq' : d(s_1^*, \ldots, s_m^*) \to s^* \Leftarrow C^*$ *in* $\mathcal{C}_\to$ *such that* $Eq = Eq'\delta_0$ *for some* $\delta_0 \in DSub_\perp$. *By applying the propagation rule* Imitation+Mutation *with* Eq', *the resulting goal has as solution* δ' *defined as* $\delta'(x_i) = s_i$, $\delta'(z) = \delta_0(z)$, *for all* $z \in dvar(Eq')$ *and* $\delta'(z) = \delta(z)$ *otherwise, where* δ' *verifies that* $x\delta'$ *is syntactically equal to* $d(\bar{x}_m)\delta'$. ∎

Similar considerations motivate the design of all the transformation rules in our goal solving mechanism LNCEC. They are chosen to enable a completeness proof that relies on a multiset ordering for witnesses. The definition of this ordering is borrowed from [8].

Conflict : $\exists \bar{u} S \square P \square c(\bar{e}_n) \bowtie d(\bar{e'}_m), E \hookrightarrow_{\mathcal{P}} FAIL$
> if $c \not\equiv d$ and c, d are free constructors, or c is free and d algebraic,
> or c is algebraic and d is free.

Cycle : $\exists \bar{u} S \square P \square x \bowtie e, E \hookrightarrow_{\mathcal{P}} FAIL$
> if $e \notin DVar$ and $x \in \text{svar}(e)$.

Conflict : $\exists \bar{u} S \square c(\bar{e}_n) \to d(\bar{t}_m), P \square E \hookrightarrow_{\mathcal{P}} FAIL$
> if $c \not\equiv d$ and c, d are free constructors, or c is free and d algebraic,
> or c is algebraic and d is free.

Figure 4: Failure rules

Definition 4.5 (Multiset ordering for proofs) *Let* $\mathcal{P} = \langle \Sigma, \mathcal{C}, \mathcal{R} \rangle$ *be a program and* $\mathcal{M} \equiv \{\!\{ \Pi_1, \ldots, \Pi_n \}\!\}$, $\mathcal{M}' \equiv \{\!\{ \Pi'_1, \ldots, \Pi'_m \}\!\}$ *multisets of GORC-proofs of approximation and joinability statements. We define* $\mathcal{M} \triangleleft \mathcal{M}' \Leftrightarrow \{\!\{ |\Pi_1|, \ldots, |\Pi_n| \}\!\} \prec \{\!\{ |\Pi'_1|, \ldots, |\Pi'_m| \}\!\}$, *where* $|\Pi|$ *is the size (i.e. the number of inference steps) of* Π, *and* $\prec$ *is the multiset extension [5] of the usual ordering over the natural numbers.* □

Then, in order to prove that LNCEC is complete, we can argue as follows: Given any non-quasi-solved admissible goal $G \equiv \exists \bar{u} S \square P \square E$ and $\delta \in \text{Sol}(G)$ with witness $\mathcal{M}$, there exists a $\hookrightarrow_{\mathcal{P}}$-transformation rule T such that $G \hookrightarrow_{\mathcal{P}} G'$ by applying T and G' has a solution δ' with witness $\mathcal{M}' \triangleleft \mathcal{M}$. Note that this is clear for example 4.4, since in (1) $\mathcal{M}'$ loses one application of the $GORC$-rule Decomposition whereas in (2) $\mathcal{M}'$ loses one application of the $GORC$-rule Outer $\mathcal{C}$-mutation. Analyzing all the possible forms of an admissible goal and reasoning as suggested by example 4.4, we can prove the following progress lemma:

Lemma 4.6 (Progress lemma for $\hookrightarrow_{\mathcal{P}}$) *Let* $\mathcal{P} = \langle \Sigma, \mathcal{C}, \mathcal{R} \rangle$ *be a program where* $\mathcal{C}$ *is strongly regular. Let* G *be a non quasi-solved admissible goal (different from FAIL),* $\delta \in \text{Sol}(G)$ *and* $\mathcal{M}$ *a witness for* G *and* δ. *Then, there exists a* $\hookrightarrow_{\mathcal{P}}$-*transformation rule* T *such that* $G \hookrightarrow_{\mathcal{P}} G'$ *using* T *and:*

- G' *is admissible;*
- *there exists* $\delta' \in \text{Sol}(G')$ *such that* $x\delta = x\delta'$, *for all* $x \in DVar - (\text{evar}(G) \cup \text{evar}(G'))$;
- *there exists* $\mathcal{M}'$ *a witness for* G' *and* δ' *such that* $\mathcal{M}' \triangleleft \mathcal{M}$;
- *if* G *and* $\mathcal{P}$ *are well-typed then* G' *is well-typed.* □

Note that the last item of the above lemma holds trivially due to the form of $\hookrightarrow_{\mathcal{P}}$-rules and the fact that all equational axioms and program rules in $\mathcal{P}$ are well-typed. Using this lemma, we can prove now the following completeness result for $\hookrightarrow_{\mathcal{P}}$:

Theorem 4.7 (Completeness of $\hookrightarrow_{\mathcal{P}}$) *Let* $\mathcal{P} = \langle \Sigma, \mathcal{C}, \mathcal{R} \rangle$ *be a program with* $\mathcal{C}$ *strongly regular,* G *an initial goal and* $\delta \in \text{Sol}(G)$. *Then there exist a quasi-solved goal* G' *and* $\delta' \in \text{Sol}(G')$ *such that* $G \hookrightarrow_{\mathcal{P}}^* G'$ *and* $\delta = \delta'[dvar(G)]$. *Furthermore, if* G *and* $\mathcal{P}$ *are well-typed then* G' *is well-typed.* □

Remark that $\hookrightarrow_{\mathcal{P}}$-rules involving algebraic constructors and propagating bindings have two versions. The first one is a standard imitation whereas the second one combines imitation of the outermost constructor in some $\mathcal{C}$-equation with mutation via that $\mathcal{C}$-equation. With these rules the termination of $\hookrightarrow_{\mathcal{P}}$ is ensured since

---

Produced variable elimination : $\exists y \bar{u} S \Box x \to y, P \Box E \hookrightarrow_{DVar} \exists \bar{u} S \Box (P \Box E) \delta$
  where $\delta = \{y/x\}$.
Identity : $\exists \bar{u} S \Box P \Box x \bowtie x, E \hookrightarrow_{DVar} \exists \bar{u} S \Box P \Box E$
  if $x \notin \mathsf{pvar}(P)$.
Non-produced variable elimination : $\exists \bar{u} S \Box P \Box x \bowtie y, E \hookrightarrow_{DVar} \exists \bar{u} x = y, (S \Box P \Box E) \delta$
  if $x, y \notin \mathsf{pvar}(P)$, where $\delta = \{x/y\}$.

Figure 5: Variable elimination rules

the election of the transformation rule for getting G' from G depends very directly on the witness associated to the given solution (as illustrated by example 4.4). The calculus obtained by adding mutation rules in the spirit of [15] to the constructor-based lazy narrowing calculus presented in [8] could solve goals in our framework more efficiently. This calculus is presented in [2], and it is correct in the sense of theorem 4.13 below. However its termination is not clear when bindings are propagated, since such propagation could afterwards impose a big number of mutations as shown in [2]. We conjecture that such a goal solving calculus is also complete, but we were unable to find a termination ordering for the completeness proof. To prove completeness of this calculus is an interesting open problem, since its behaviour is less wildly indeterministic. Therefore, it is much better suited as a basis for implementations.

Let us now present several results related to $\hookrightarrow_{DVar}$-rules (figure 5). For that, we define the following well-founded ordering, useful for proving that any $\hookrightarrow_{DVar}$-derivation always terminates (see lemma 4.9).

Definition 4.8 (Order for quasi-solved goals) *Let $G = \exists \bar{u} S \Box P \Box E$ and $G' = \exists \bar{u}' S' \Box P' \Box E'$ be quasi-solved goals. We say that $G' \sqsubset G$ iff $n < m$, where n and m are the number of approximation and joinability statements occurring in $P' \Box E'$ and $P \Box E$ respectively.* $\square$

Finally we state the lemma which ensures the termination of $\hookrightarrow_{DVar}$ along with the preservation of types, quasi-solved goals and solutions. The proof is easy to obtain by inspection of the $\hookrightarrow_{DVar}$-rules.

Lemma 4.9 (Progress lemma for $\hookrightarrow_{DVar}$) *Let $\mathcal{P} = \langle \Sigma, \mathcal{C}, \mathcal{R} \rangle$ be a program with $\mathcal{C}$ strongly regular. Let G be a quasi-solved goal (different from FAIL). Then there exists a $\hookrightarrow_{DVar}$-transformation rule T such that $G \hookrightarrow_{DVar} G'$ using T and:*

- *G' is quasi-solved;*
- *there exists $\delta' \in \mathsf{Sol}(G')$ such that $\delta = \delta'[\backslash \mathsf{evar}(G)]$;*
- *$G' \sqsubset G$;*
- *if $\mathcal{P}$ and G are well-typed then G' is well-typed.* $\square$

Using this lemma we get:

Theorem 4.10 (Completeness of $\hookrightarrow_{DVar}$) *Let $\mathcal{P} = \langle \Sigma, \mathcal{C}, \mathcal{R} \rangle$ be a program with $\mathcal{C}$ strongly regular. Let G be a quasi-solved goal and $\delta \in \mathsf{Sol}(G)$. There exists a solved goal $\exists \bar{u} S \Box \Box$ such that $G \hookrightarrow^{*}_{DVar} \exists \bar{u} S \Box \Box$ and $\delta_S \leq \delta[\backslash \mathsf{evar}(G)]$.* $\square$

From theorems 4.7 and 4.10 we get LNCEC completeness.

Theorem 4.11 (Completeness of LNCEC) *Let* $\mathcal{P} = \langle \Sigma, \mathcal{C}, \mathcal{R} \rangle$ *be a program with* $\mathcal{C}$ *strongly regular. Let* G *be an initial goal and* $\delta \in \mathsf{Sol}(G)$. *There exist a quasi-solved goal* G' *and a solved goal* $G'' = \exists \bar{u} S \square \square$ *such that* $G \hookrightarrow_{\mathcal{P}}^* G' \hookrightarrow_{DVar}^* G''$ *and* $\delta_S \leq \delta[dvar(G)]$. *Furthermore, if* G *and* $\mathcal{P}$ *are well-typed then* $G\delta_S$ *is well-typed.* □

To conclude we state the soundness of LNCEC. Previously, we present a correctness lemma which ensures that $\hookrightarrow_{\mathcal{P}}$-steps fail only in case of unsatisfiable goals and $\hookrightarrow_{\mathcal{P}}$ and $\hookrightarrow_{DVar}$ steps do not introduce new solutions. The proof proceeds by inspecting all $\hookrightarrow_{\mathcal{P}}$ and $\hookrightarrow_{DVar}$ transformation rules.

Lemma 4.12 (Correctness lemma) *Let* $\mathcal{P} = \langle \Sigma, \mathcal{C}, \mathcal{R} \rangle$ *be a program where* $\mathcal{C}$ *is strongly regular. Let* G *be an admissible goal. Then:*

(a) if $G \hookrightarrow_{\mathcal{P}} FAIL$ *then* $\mathsf{Sol}(G) = \emptyset$;

(b) If $G \hookrightarrow_{\mathcal{P}} G'$ *or* $G \hookrightarrow_{DVar} G'$ *and* $\delta' \in \mathsf{Sol}(G')$ *then there exists* $\delta \in \mathsf{Sol}(G)$ *with* $\delta = \delta'[\backslash\mathsf{evar}(G)]$. □

By applying repeatedly (b) of lemma 4.12, considering that $\delta_S \in \mathsf{Sol}(\exists \bar{u} S \square \square)$ and that G has no existential variables, we can prove the following correctness theorem.

Theorem 4.13 (Correctness of LNCEC) *Let* $\mathcal{P} = \langle \Sigma, \mathcal{C}, \mathcal{R} \rangle$ *be a program with* $\mathcal{C}$ *strongly regular. Let* G *be an initial goal and* G' *a quasi-solved goal such that* $G \hookrightarrow_{\mathcal{P}}^* G' \hookrightarrow_{DVar}^* \exists \bar{u} S \square \square$. *Then* $\delta_S \in \mathsf{Sol}(G)$. □

5 Conclusions

We have developed a sound and complete goal solving procedure which provides a formal basis for the implementation of functional logic languages with algebraic polymorphic types, according to the framework presented in [3], which supports lazy evaluation, non-deterministic functions and algebraic constructors. The combination of all these features is not found in other related works we are aware of [6, 9, 12, 14, 17], and it is useful for many kinds of problems, e.g. *action and change* problems, as shown in Sect. 3. Our goal solving procedure combines lazy narrowing and unification modulo equations for data constructors in a highly non-deterministic fashion. The completeness of the alternative, less non-deterministic goal solving procedure shown in [2] is an unproved conjecture.

In the near future, we plan to implement the instance of our framework given by the equational axioms for multisets, which is expected to allow for many optimizations w.r.t. the general case. We are also looking forward enriching our framework with constraints, coming from a constraint system given as a suitable extension of the equational axioms for the data constructors. For instance, in the case of sets and multisets, disequality and membership constraints should be introduced, in analogy to [6].

Acknowledgments: This research has been partially supported by the Spanish National Project TIC95-0433-C03-01 *CPD* and the Esprit BRA Working Group EP-22457 *CCL II*. The authors are also indebted to their colleagues A. Gil-Luezas and F.J. López-Fraguas for their contributions to the development of this work.

References

[1] Arenas-Sánchez P., Dovier A.: *Minimal Set Unification*. In Proc. PLILP'95. Springer LNCS 982, pp. 397–414, 1995.

[2] Arenas-Sánchez P., Rodríguez-Artalejo M.: *A Lazy Narrowing Calculus for Functional Logic Programming with Algebraic Polymorphic Types*. TR DIA97/56, http://mozart.mat.ucm.es/ papers/1997/TR97-56.ps.gz

[3] Arenas-Sánchez P., Rodríguez-Artalejo M.: *A Semantic Framework for Functional Logic Programming with Algebraic Polymorphic Types*. In Proc. TAPSOFT'97 (CAAP'97), Springer LNCS 1214, pp. 453–464, 1997. Full version available as TR DIA96/39, http://mozart.mat.ucm.es/ papers/1996/TR96-39.ps.gz

[4] Dershowitz N., Jouannaud J.P.: *Rewrite Systems*. In J. van Leeuwen (Ed.), *Handbook of Theoretical Computer Science*, Vol. B, Chapter 6. Elsevier North-Holland, 1990.

[5] Dershowitz N., Manna Z.,: *Proving Termination with Multiset Ordering*. Comm. of the ACM 22(8), 1979, pp. 465–476.

[6] Dovier A., Rossi G.: *Embedding Extensional Finite Sets in CLP*. In Proc. ILPS'93, the MIT Press, pp. 540–556, 1993.

[7] Giovannetti G., Levi G., Moiso C., Palamidessi C.: *Kernel K-LEAF: A Logic plus Functional Language*. JCSS 42 (2), pp. 139–185, 1991.

[8] González-Moreno J.C., Hortalá-González T., López-Fraguas F.J, Rodríguez-Artalejo M.: *A Rewriting Logic for Declarative Programming*. In Proc. ESOP'96, Springer LNCS 1058, pp. 156–172, 1996. Full version available as TR DIA95/10, http://mozart.mat.ucm.es/papers/1996/full-esop96.ps.gz

[9] Große G., Hölldobler J., Schneeberger J., Sigmund U., Thielscher M.: *Equational Logic Programming, Actions, and Change*. In Proc. ICLP'92, the MIT Press, pp. 177–191, 1992.

[10] Hanus, M.: *Lazy Unification with Inductive Simplification*. TR MPI-93-215, April 1993.

[11] Hanus M.: *The Integration of Functions into Logic Programming*. A Survey. JLP (19:20). Special issue *Ten Years of Logic Programming*, pp. 583–628, 1994.

[12] Hölldobler S., Schneeberger J.: *A New Deductive Approach to Planning*. New Generation Computing, 8, pp. 225–244, 1990.

[13] Hussmann H.: *Non-determinism Algebraic Specifications and Nonconfluent Term Rewriting*. JLP 12, pp. 237–255, 1992.

[14] Jayaraman B., Plaisted D.A.: *Programming with Equations, Subsets, and Relations*. In Proc. ICLP'89, Vol. 2, the MIT Press, pp. 1051–1068, 1989.

[15] Jouannaud J.P., Kirchner C.: *Solving Equations in Abstract Algebras: A Rule-Based Survey of Unification*. Computational Logic Essays in Honor of Alan Robinson. The MIT Press, pp. 257–321, 1991.

[16] Martí-Oliet N., Meseguer J.: *Action and Change in Rewriting Logic*. In R. Pareschi & B. Fronhöfer (eds.). Theoretical Appoaches to Dynamic Worlds in Computer Science and Artificial Intelligence. Cambridge M.P., 1995.

[17] Meseguer J.: *A Logical Theory of Concurrent Objects and Its Realization in the Maude Language*. In Agha A., Wegner P. and Yonezawa A. (Eds), Research Directions in Concurrent Object-Oriented Programming, the MIT Press, 1993.

[18] Moreno-Navarro J.J., Rodríguez-Artalejo M.: *Logic Programming with Functions and Predicates: The Language BABEL*. JLP 12, pp. 191–223, 1992.

[19] Peterson J., Hammond K. (eds.): *Report on the Programming Language Haskell. A Non-strict, Purely Functional Language*. Version 1.3., May 1, 1996.

[20] Reddy U.: *Narrowing as the Operational Semantics of Functional Languages*. In Proc. IEEE Symposium on Logic Programming, pp. 138–151, 1985.

[21] Socher-Ambrosius R.: *A Refined Version of General E-Unification*. In Proc. CADE-12, Springer LNAI, pp. 665–677, 1994.

References

[1] Alonso-Sanabria H. De-..., A..., Maxwell...? ..., ..., ..., C.H.M., J.S. Spronk.
ICES 93. Pp. 101-135, 1995.

[2] Amanda Jecloa... The Negative Argument Wo... Interval-based Computing for Fuzzy
Ratio-Logic Types... A. ... at ... a supplier's ... ... Ryote, ...

[3] Amanda Jecloa J. C..., Sohagen..., ... n... A.Sher, ... Thes to ... ... Crithon...
Logic Programs... P..., R.A.A. Robot, Prog... Symposium, Lie... ..., ... 1790-1792.
(LA/RS/..., Series 1285/SAA, pp. ... Jorge-Reel, 1992. Tod... Systems ... ... P.
D.L/9643 Entry... information and news. FW1/WRP ... Bloe... ...

[4] Duggan A..., ... R. and J.T. ... representation, in A. ... al al..., ... J. Biederbek
of Plural... and ... ... Supper, Vol. b: Cham... Electronic ... Chemical, 1974.
Dordrecht, in ... Mee... ... An ... ...-... on ... M... Medicine, Conter, e
relations... Wk... 1, 1994, pp. 465-470.

[5] ... ... Mode... C... ... and ... J... ..., bl... ... J. W...-R... in Re... M... ...
L... ... ... 105, pp. ... ...

[6] T. ... Jorge-S... ...-... Arith-O-10...-J, Me... J. ... c... 127-M... pyr... T...
... 13 nm... ... Re-... In ... ..., Geni-... c...

[7] ... ... Ashton... I... dem...e fasther ... ...-... Sure, ..., Pa... Reis... or
Program... II... ..., ... Hap-... ..., ...-R-... e ... In... ... in Plural. RSOP' in
Speci... Vol/... ... Sea-... T..., ... in Cha... and ... world, in HLR ...-DIA-754,
... J... ... ... in ... ... Pro... ... ...

[8] ... ... Y... B. Time J. ... ... or Gr.or... ... A... ...-... ... ... Sup-... ... ...
W... vol... Frisco... ... ... and ... ... the CMG...M... Wes... pp. ...

[10] ... ... pe-... ... ...

[11] ... ... H. Wu tragem-... ... ... um... ... ... Jorge-... A. Luce... J.E.
Ro-... and ... Vi... ... We...t, Co... ... U... ... h... Pp. Pl... Plal...
[12] ... and ... ... Sul... ...je... Pl... vo... ... ... Pp. ... Lu... ... Op... in ... Clo-... Coo-
... ... put... K...r... ... ... 561-570.

[13] ... ... w... ... R... ... ... n... ... Vi... ... Impa... t So-...
... ... 12, pp. ... P. 3... ...

[14] ... ... a ... D... ... ... Hu... ... ... w... ... ... or ...
... ... C. P p., M... W... ... ... H..., ..., ...
[15] ... ... H. R... ... ..., ...
... ... w... ... of ... ... m... ... ... for
... ... 15-73... ...

[16] ... ... D... ... ... P... ...
... ... Pl... ... ... A... ... ... work... ... ... Compute... Scien...
... ... in ... ... 1... ...

[17] ... ... Op... pl... ... ... and ... ... Comput...
... ... P... ... 2... ... ... U.S.A., ... pert...hbor
... ... Chome-V... igr... an... ... ...

[18] ... ... W... ... the ... I... wment,
... ...

[19] ... ...
... ...

[20] ... ... N.
... ...

[21] ... ... CAM
... ...

Answer Sets for Prioritized Logic Programs

Yan Zhang
Department of Computing
University of Western Sydney, Nepean
Kingswood, NSW 2747, Australia
E-mail: yan@st.nepean.uws.edu.au

Norman Y. Foo
School of Computer Science and Engineering
University of New South Wales
Sydney, NSW 2052, Australia
E-mail: norman@cse.unsw.edu.au

Abstract

Conflict resolution is an important issue in knowledge representation and reasoning. A common idea of solving conflicts in reasoning is to add preferences in the underlying reasoning mechanism. This paper describes extensions of Gelfond and Lifschitz's extended logic programs [5] by adding preference information. We first propose prioritized logic programs (PLPs) in which the preference is expressed *statically*. An extended answer set semantics is provided for PLPs. We then extend PLPs to dynamic PLPs (DPLPs) in which the preference can be expressed *dynamically*. The semantics of DPLPs is defined in terms of answer sets of the corresponding PLPs. By illustrating typical examples, we show how conflicts between rules are resolved in PLPs and DPLPs. We also investigate basic properties of PLPs and DPLPs in detail.

1 Introduction

Conflict resolution is an important issue in knowledge representation and reasoning. A common idea of solving conflicts in reasoning is to add preferences in the underlying reasoning mechanism. The goal of this paper is to investigate this problem in the framework of logic programs. In particular, we extend Gelfond and Lifschitz's extended logic programs by adding preference information. We first consider logic programs with *static* preferences which we call *prioritized logic programs* or PLPs, and then describe logic programs with *dynamic* preferences (dynamic PLPs or DPLPs). Formal semantics for PLPs and DPLPs is provided based on extensions of Gelfond and Lifschitz's answer set semantics for extended logic programs [5].

The paper is organized as follows. Next section introduces the syntax of

PLPs. Section 3 provides an answer set semantics of PLPs. By illustrating several typical examples, this section also shows how conflicts are resolved in PLPs. Section 4 defines syntax and semantics for dynamic PLPs (DPLPs), and presents simple applications of DPLPs, while section 5 investigates basic properties of PLPs and DPLPs. Finally, section 6 discusses some related work and concludes the paper.

2 Syntax of Prioritized Logic Programs (PLPs)

In this section we provide a formal description of prioritized logic programs (PLPs).

Our language $\mathcal{L}$ includes the following vocabulary:

- *Variables*: $x, y, z, \cdots$.

- *Constants*: $C, C_1, C_2, \cdots$, including logical constants *True* and *False*.

- *Predicates*: $P, Q, R, \cdots$.

- *Names*: $N, N_1, N_2, \cdots$.

- A strict partial ordering (i.e. antireflexive, antisymmetric and transitive) $<$ on names.

- A naming function $\mathcal{N}$, which maps a *rule* (see below) to a name.

- A symbol $\leftarrow$, which is used to represent a rule.

- Connectives $\neg$ and *not*, where $\neg$ represents the classical negation (strong negation), and *not* represents *negation as failure* (weak negation).

We also require that the sets of variables, constants, predicates and names be disjoint.

A *term* is either a constant or a variable. An *atom* is $P(t_1, \cdots, t_k)$, where P is a predicate of arity k and $t_1, \cdots, t_k$ are terms. A *literal* is either an atom P or a negation of an atom $\neg P$. A *rule* is a statement of the form

$$L_0 \leftarrow L_1, \cdots, L_m, not\ L_{m+1}, \cdots, not\ L_n,$$

where L_i $(0 \leq i \leq n)$ is a literal. L_0 is the *head* of the rule, while $L_1, \cdots, L_m, not\ L_{m+1}, \cdots, not\ L_n$ is the *body* of the rule. Obviously, the body of a rule could be empty.

A term, an atom, a literal, or a rule is *ground* if no variable occurs in it.

For the naming function $\mathcal{N}$, we require that for any rules r and r' in a PLP (see the following definition), $\mathcal{N}(r) = \mathcal{N}(r')$ iff r and r' indicate the same rule.

An *extended logic program* Π is a collection of rules [5]. A *prioritized logic program* (PLP) $\mathcal{P}$ is a triplet $(\Pi, \mathcal{N}, <)$, where Π is an extended logic program, $\mathcal{N}$ is a naming function mapping each rule in Π to a name, and $<$ is a relation representing all strict partial orderings on names.

The following is an example of prioritized extended logic program.

$\mathcal{P}_1 = (\{P \leftarrow not\ Q,\ not\ R,\ Q \leftarrow not\ P,\ R \leftarrow not\ P\},\ \{\mathcal{N}(P \leftarrow not\ Q,\ not\ R) = N_1,\ \mathcal{N}(Q \leftarrow not\ P) = N_2,\ \mathcal{N}(R \leftarrow not\ P) = N_3\},\ \{N_1 < N_2, N_2 < N_3\})$.

To simplify our presentation, we usually represent $\mathcal{P}_1$ as the following form:

$\mathcal{P}_1$:
$N_1 : P \leftarrow not\ Q,\ not\ R,$
$N_2 : Q \leftarrow not\ P,$
$N_3 : R \leftarrow not\ P,$
$N_1 < N_2, N_2 < N_3.$

We also use notations $\mathcal{P}_1(\Pi)$, $\mathcal{P}_1(\mathcal{N})$, and $\mathcal{P}_1(<)$ to denote the sets of rules, naming function's values and $<$-relation of $\mathcal{P}_1$ respectively.

Consider the following program:

$\mathcal{P}_2$:
$N_1 : P \leftarrow not\ Q,\ not\ R,$
$N_2 : Q \leftarrow not\ P,$
$N_3 : R \leftarrow not\ P,$
$N_1 < N_2, N_2 < N_3, N_1 < N_3.$

Obviously, the only difference between $\mathcal{P}_1$ and $\mathcal{P}_2$ is that there is one more relation $N_1 < N_3$ in $\mathcal{P}_2$. As we mentioned earlier, since $<$ is a strict partial ordering (i.e., antireflexive, antisymmetric and transitive), we would expect that $\mathcal{P}_1$ and $\mathcal{P}_2$ are identical in some sense. Furthermore, if we rename rules in $\mathcal{P}_2$ as follows,

$\mathcal{P}'_2$:
$N'_1 : P \leftarrow not\ Q,\ not\ R,$
$N'_2 : Q \leftarrow not\ P,$
$N'_3 : R \leftarrow not\ P,$
$N'_1 < N'_2, N'_2 < N'_3, N'_1 < N'_3,$

$\mathcal{P}'_2$ would be also identical to $\mathcal{P}_2$ and hence to $\mathcal{P}_1$ too from our intuition. To make this precise, we first introduce $<$-closure as follows.

Definition 1 *Given a program* $\mathcal{P} = (\Pi, \mathcal{N}, <)$. $\mathcal{P}(<^+)$ *is the* $<$-closure *of* $\mathcal{P}$ *iff* $\mathcal{P}(<^+)$ *is the smallest set containing* $\mathcal{P}(<)$ *and closed under transitivity.*

We also need to define a renaming function as follows. A *renaming function Rn* maps a PLP $\mathcal{P} = (\Pi, \mathcal{N}, <)$ to another PLP $\mathcal{P}'$, i.e. $Rn(\mathcal{P}) = \mathcal{P}' = (\Pi', \mathcal{N}', <')$, such that (i) $\mathcal{P}(\Pi) = \mathcal{P}'(\Pi')$; (ii) for each rule $r \in \mathcal{P}(\Pi)$[1], $\mathcal{N}(r) = N \in \mathcal{P}(\mathcal{N})$ iff $\mathcal{N}'(r) = N' \in \mathcal{P}'(\mathcal{N}')$ (N and N' are not necessarily

---

[1]Of course, r is also in $\mathcal{P}'(\Pi')$.

different); (iii) for any rules r_1 and r_2 in $\mathcal{P}(\Pi)$, $\mathcal{N}(r_1) = N_1$, $\mathcal{N}(r_2) = N_2 \in$ $\mathcal{P}(\mathcal{N})$, and $N_1 < N_2 \in \mathcal{P}(<)$ iff $\mathcal{N}'(r_1) = N_1'$, $\mathcal{N}'(r_2) = N_2' \in \mathcal{P}'(\mathcal{N}')$, and $N_1' < N_2' \in \mathcal{P}'(<')$. It is easy to see that applying a renaming function to a PLP will only change the names of rules in the PLP.

Two prioritized extended logic programs $\mathcal{P}_1$ and $\mathcal{P}_2$ are *identical* iff there exists a renaming function Rn, mapping $\mathcal{P}_2$ to $\mathcal{P}'_2$ such that $\mathcal{P}_1(\Pi) = \mathcal{P}'_2(\Pi')$, $\mathcal{P}_1(\mathcal{N}) = \mathcal{P}'_2(\mathcal{N}')$, and $\mathcal{P}_1(<^+) = \mathcal{P}'_2(<'^+)$.

We have defined that a prioritized extended logic program is a Gelfond and Lifschitz's extended logic program [5] by associating with a partial ordering $<$ to it. Intuitively such ordering represents a preference of applying rules during the evaluation of the program. In particular, if in a program $\mathcal{P}$, relation $\mathcal{N}(r) < \mathcal{N}(r')$ holds, rule r would be preferred to apply over rule r' during the evaluation of $\mathcal{P}$ (i.e. rule r is more preferred than rule r'). Consider the following classical example represented in our formalism:

$\mathcal{P}_3$:
$N_1 : Fly(x) \leftarrow Bird(x), not \neg Fly(x),$
$N_2 : \neg Fly(x) \leftarrow Penguin(x), not\ Fly(x),$
$N_3 : Bird(Tweety) \leftarrow,$
$N_4 : Penguin(Tweety) \leftarrow,$
$N_2 < N_1.$

Obviously, rules N_1 and N_2 conflict with each other as their heads are complementary literals[2], and applying N_1 will defeat N_2[3] and *vice versa*. However, as $N_2 < N_1$, we would expect that rule N_2 is preferred to apply first and then defeat rule N_1 after applying N_2 so that the desired solution $\neg Fly(Tweety)$ could be derived.

3 Semantics of PLPs

In this section, we develop the semantics of PLPs. Our method is based on an extension of answer set semantics for extended logic programs [5]. Before we present our idea in detail, we need to introduce this answer set semantics first.

3.1 Answer Sets for Extended Logic Programs: A Review

Let Π be an extended logic program. For simplicity, we treat a rule r in Π with variables as the set of all ground instances of r formed from the set of ground literals of the language of Π. We will also adopt this assumption in our prioritized extended logic programs. In the rest of paper, we will

---

[2]Precisely, N_2 is the name of rule $\neg Fly(x) \leftarrow Penguin(x), not\ Fly(x)$. Whenever there is no confusion in the context, we just simply refer a rule by its name.

[3]Informally, when we say that a rule is defeated in a program, it simply means that this rule is unapplicable in the evaluation of the program. A precise definition of defeatness is given in the following section.

not explicitly declare this assumption whenever there is no ambiguity in our discussion.

Let Π be an extended logic program not containing *not* and *Lit* the set of all ground literals in the language of Π. The *answer set* of Π, denoted as $Ans(\Pi)$, is the smallest subset S of *Lit* such that

(i) for any rule $L_0 \leftarrow L_1, \cdots, L_m$ from Π, if $L_1, \cdots, L_m \in S$, then $L_0 \in S$;

(ii) if S contains a pair of complementary literals, then $S = Lit$.

Now consider Π be an extended logic program. For any subset S of *Lit*, let Π^S be the logic program obtained from Π by deleting

(i) each rule that has a formula *not* L in its body with $L \in S$, and

(ii) all formulas of the form *not* L in the bodies of the remaining rules.

We define that S is an *answer set* of Π, denoted $Ans(\Pi)$, iff S is an answer set of Π^S, i.e. $S = Ans(\Pi^S)$.

Consider $\mathcal{P}_3$ presented in last section. It is not difficult to see that extended logic program $\mathcal{P}_3(\Pi)$ has two answer sets: $\{Bird(Tweety),$ $Penguin(Tweety), \neg Fly(Tweety)\}$ and $\{Bird(Tweety), Penguin(Tweety),$ $Fly(Tweety)\}$.

3.2   Answer Sets for PLPs

In program $\mathcal{P}_3$, we have seen that rules N_1 and N_2 conflict with each other. Since $N_2 < N_1$, we try to solve the conflict by applying N_2 first and defeating N_1. However, in some programs, even if one rule is more preferred than the other, these two rules may not affect each other at all during the evaluation of the program. In this case, the preference relation between these two rules does not play any role in the evaluation and should be simply ignored. This is illustrated by the following program:

$\mathcal{P}_4$:
$\quad N_1 : P \leftarrow not\ Q_1,$
$\quad N_2 : \neg P \leftarrow not\ Q_2,$
$\quad N_1 < N_2.$

Although heads of N_1 and N_2 are complementary literals, applying N_1 will not affect the applicability of N_2 and *vice versa*. Hence $N_1 < N_2$ should not be taken into account during the evaluation of $\mathcal{P}_4$. The following definition provides a formal description for this intuition.

Definition 2 *Let Π be an extended logic program and r a rule with the form $L_0 \leftarrow L_1, \cdots, L_m, not\ L_{m+1}, \cdots, not\ L_n$ (r does not necessarily belong to Π). Rule r is defeated by Π iff for any answer set $Ans(\Pi)$ of Π, there exists some $L_i \in Ans(\Pi)$, where $m + 1 \le i \le n$.*

Now our idea of evaluating a PLP is as follows. Let $\mathcal{P} = (\Pi, \mathcal{N}, <)$. If there are two rules r and r' in $\mathcal{P}(\Pi)$ and $\mathcal{N}(r) < \mathcal{N}(r')$, r' will be ignored in the evaluation of $\mathcal{P}$, *only if* keeping r in $\mathcal{P}(\Pi)$ and deleting r' from $\mathcal{P}(\Pi)$ will result in a defeat of r', i.e. r' is defeated by $\mathcal{P}(\Pi) - \{r'\}$. By eliminating all such potential rules from $\mathcal{P}(\Pi)$, $\mathcal{P}$ is eventually reduced to an extended logic program in which the partial ordering $<$ has been removed. Our evaluation for $\mathcal{P}$ is then based on this extended logic program.

Let us consider program $\mathcal{P}_3$ once again. Since $N_2 < N_1$ and N_1 is defeated by $\mathcal{P}_3 - \{N_1\}$ (i.e. the unique answer set of $\mathcal{P}_3 - \{N_1\}$ is $\{Bird(Tweety)$, $Penguin(Tweety)$, $\neg Fly(Tweety)\}$), rule N_1 should be ignored during the evaluation of $\mathcal{P}_3$. For program $\mathcal{P}_4$, on the other hand, although $N_1 < N_2$, relation $N_1 < N_2$ will not affect the solution of evaluating $\mathcal{P}_4$ as $\mathcal{P}_4(\Pi) - \{N_2\}$ does not defeat N_2 (i.e. the unique answer set of $\mathcal{P}_4(\Pi) - \{N_2\}$ is $\{P\}$).

Definition 3 *Let $\mathcal{P} = (\Pi, \mathcal{N}, <)$ be a prioritized extended logic program. $\mathcal{P}^<$ is a reduct of $\mathcal{P}$ with respect to $<$ if and only if there exists a sequence of sets Π_i ($i = 0, 1, \cdots$) such that:*

(i) $\Pi_0 = \Pi$;

(ii) $\Pi_i = \Pi_{i-1} - \{r_1, \cdots, r_k \mid$ (a) there exists $r \in \Pi_{i-1}$ such that for every j ($j = 1, \cdots, k$), $\mathcal{N}(r) < \mathcal{N}(r_j) \in \mathcal{P}(<^+)$ and $r_1, \cdots, r_k$ are defeated by $\Pi_{i-1} - \{r_1, \cdots, r_k\}$, and (b) there does not exist a rule $r' \in \Pi_{i-1}$ such that $N(r_i) < N(r')$ for some j ($j = 1, \cdots, k$) and r' is defeated by $\Pi_{i-1} - \{r'\}\}$;

(iii) $\mathcal{P}^< = \bigcap_{i=0}^{\infty} \Pi_i$.

In Definition 3, clearly $\mathcal{P}^<$ is an extended logic program obtained from Π by eliminating some rules from Π. In particular, if $\mathcal{N}(r) < \mathcal{N}(r')$ and $\Pi - \{r'\}$ defeats r', then rule r' will be eliminated from Π if there is no *less preferred rule* can be eliminated (i.e. conditions (a) and (b)). This procedure is continued until a fixed point is reached. Note that due to the transitivity of $<$, we need to consider each $\mathcal{N}(r) < \mathcal{N}(r')$ in the $<$-closure of $\mathcal{P}$.

Example 1 Using Definition 1 and 3, it is not difficult to conclude that $\mathcal{P}_1$, $\mathcal{P}_3$ and $\mathcal{P}_4$ have unique reducts as follows respectively:

$$\mathcal{P}_1^< = \{P \leftarrow not\ Q,\ not\ R\},$$
$$\mathcal{P}_3^< = \{\neg Fly(x) \leftarrow Penguin(x),\ not\ Fly(x),$$
$$Bird(Tweety) \leftarrow, Penguin(Tweety) \leftarrow\},$$
$$\mathcal{P}_4^< = \mathcal{P}_4(\Pi).$$

■

It is quite obvious to note that the reduct of a PLP may not be unique as the following example shows.

Example 2 Consider a PLP $\mathcal{P}_5$:

> $\mathcal{P}_5$:
> $N_1 : P \leftarrow,$
> $N_2 : Q \leftarrow not\ R,$
> $N_3 : T \leftarrow,$
> $N_4 : R \leftarrow not\ Q,$
> $N_1 < N_2, N_3 < N_4.$

According to Definition 3, it is easy to see that $\mathcal{P}_5$ has two reducts: $\{P \leftarrow,$ $T \leftarrow,\ R \leftarrow not\ Q\}$ and $\{P \leftarrow,\ Q \leftarrow not\ R,\ T \leftarrow\}$. ∎

We should also mention that the condition (b) in the construction of Π_i in Definition 3 is necessary. Without ths condition, some unintuitive results may be derived. For instance, if we have additional preference information $N_3 < N_2$ in program $\mathcal{P}_3$, then using a modified version of Definition 3 without condition (b) in the construction of Π_i, we will conclude that $\{Fly(x) \leftarrow$ $Bird(x),\ not\ \neg Fly(x),\ Bird(Tweety) \leftarrow, Penguin(Tweety) \leftarrow\}$ is also a reduct of $\mathcal{P}_3$, which, as will be followed by Definition 4 next, leads to an unintuitive result saying that Tweety can fly.

Now it is quite straightforward to define the answer set(s) for a prioritized extended logic program.

Definition 4 *Let $\mathcal{P} = (\Pi, \mathcal{N}, <)$ be a PLP and Lit the set of all ground literals in the language of $\mathcal{P}$. For any subset S of Lit, S is an answer set of $\mathcal{P}$, denoted as $Ans^P(\mathcal{P})$, iff $S = Ans(\mathcal{P}^<)$ for some reduct $\mathcal{P}^<$ of $\mathcal{P}$.*

Example 3 Immediately from Definition 4 and Examples 1 and 2, we have the following solutions:

> $Ans^P(\mathcal{P}_1) = \{P\},$
> $Ans^P(\mathcal{P}_3) = \{Bird(Tweety),$
> $\qquad\qquad\qquad Penguin(Tweety), \neg Fly(Tweety)\},$
> $Ans^P(\mathcal{P}_4) = Lit,$
> and two answer sets for $\mathcal{P}_5$:
> $Ans^P(\mathcal{P}_5) = \{P, R, T\},$
> $Ans^P(\mathcal{P}_5) = \{P, Q, T\},$

which, respectively, are also consistent with our intuitions. ∎

3.3 More Examples

Now let us examine more examples to illustrate some features of PLPs.

Example 4 Let $\mathcal{P}_6$ be:

> $\mathcal{P}_6$:
> $N_1 : P \leftarrow not\ Q,$
> $N_2 : \neg P \leftarrow not\ P,$
> $N_2 < N_1.$

This program was originally presented in [2]. The reduct of $\mathcal{P}_6$ is $\mathcal{P}_6(\Pi)$. So the unique answer set of $\mathcal{P}_6$ is $\{P\}$. Note that even if the heads of N_1 and N_2 are complementary literals and $N_2 < N_1$, rule N_1 can not be deleted from $\mathcal{P}_6(\Pi)$ as $\mathcal{P}_6(\Pi) - \{N_1\}$ does not defeat N_1. ∎

Example 5 Let $\mathcal{P}_7$ be:

$\mathcal{P}_7$:
$\quad N_1 : P \leftarrow not\ Q,$
$\quad N_2 : Q \leftarrow not\ P,$
$\quad N_3 : R \leftarrow not\ Q,\ not\ S,$
$\quad N_4 : S \leftarrow not\ R,$
$\quad N_1 < N_2, N_3 < N_4.$

$\mathcal{P}_7(\Pi)$ has three answer sets: $\{P, R\}$, $\{Q, S\}$, and $\{P, S\}$. The unique reduct of $\mathcal{P}_7$ is $\{P \leftarrow not\ Q,\ R \leftarrow not\ Q,\ not\ S\}$. Therefore, the unique answer set of $\mathcal{P}_7$ is $Ans^P(\mathcal{P}_7) = \{P, R\}$. Note that this solution is consistent with our intuition since $N_1 < N_2$ and $N_3 < N_4$, and applying N_1 and N_3 causes N_2 and N_4 inapplicable respectively. ∎

Example 6 Let $\mathcal{P}_8$ be:

$\mathcal{P}_8$:
$\quad N_1 : P \leftarrow not\ Q,\ not\ R,$
$\quad N_2 : Q \leftarrow not\ P,$
$\quad N_3 : R \leftarrow not\ P,$
$\quad N_1 < N_2.$

$\mathcal{P}_8(\Pi)$ has two answer sets $\{P\}$ and $\{Q, R\}$. Obviously, N_2 is not defeated by $\mathcal{P}_8(\Pi) - \{N_2\}$ as P only belongs to one of two answer sets $\{P\}$ and $\{R\}$ of $\mathcal{P}_8(\Pi) - \{N_2\}$. Therefore, the unique reduct $\mathcal{P}_8^<$ of $\mathcal{P}_8$ is the same as $\mathcal{P}_8(\Pi)$. So $\mathcal{P}_8$ has two answer sets $\{P\}$ and $\{Q, R\}$.

It is worth observing that if we add $N_1 < N_3$ to $\mathcal{P}_8$, $\mathcal{P}_8$ will then has a unique answer set $\{P\}$. On the other hand, if we add $N_3 < N_1$ instead of $N_1 < N_3$, the unique answer set of $\mathcal{P}_8$ will then have $\{Q, R\}$. ∎

4 Logic Programs with Dynamic Preferences

So far, preferences specified in our prioritized logic programs are *static* in the sense that the partial ordering $<$ among rules is pre-defined from *outside*. Using PLPs to represent knowledge of a domain, the user must explicitly specify his/her preference information about the domain. However, as observed by Brewka recently [2], in many situations, preferences are context-dependent, and there may not exist a feasible way to specify such preferences explicitly. Consider the following extended logic program:

$\mathcal{P}_9$:

$N_1 : \neg Employed(x) \leftarrow Student(x),$
$\qquad\qquad\qquad not\ Employed(x),$
$N_2 : Employed(x) \leftarrow Age(x, > 25),$
$\qquad\qquad\qquad not\ \neg Employed(x),$
$N_3 : Student(x) \leftarrow FT\text{-}Student(x),$
$N_4 : Student(x) \leftarrow PT\text{-}Student(x),$
$N_5 : Student(Peter) \leftarrow,$
$N_6 : Age(Peter, > 25) \leftarrow.$

Obviously, $\mathcal{P}_9$ has two answer sets, from one we conclude $\neg Employed(Peter)$ and from the other we conclude $Employed(Peter)$. By specifying $N_1 < N_2$ or $N_2 < N_1$, we can retain one answer set and exclude the other, and hence resolve the conflict as it may occur. However, the reason for specifying $N_1 < N_2$ (or $N_2 < N_1$) rather than $N_2 < N_1$ (or $N_1 < N_2$) is completely motivated by the user. There is no way in our PLPs to express the preference about preference. For instance, with a more natural way, we may hope to express that "if x is a full-time student, then N_1 is more preferred than N_2, while if x is a part-time student, then N_2 is more preferred than N_1". Therefore, if we obtain further information knowing that Peter is a full-time student, we would expect to conclude that Peter is unemployed, otherwise Peter's employment status will remain indefinite.

Hence, to make our system more flexible, we need to reason about preferences. In other words, we hope to specify the preference information *dynamically* in our prioritized logic programs. In this section, we will discuss the dynamic PLPs (or DPLPs for short). We provide an answer set semantics for DPLPs based on the answer set semantics of PLPs.

4.1 Syntax of DPLPs

A language $\mathcal{L}^D$ of DPLPs is a language $\mathcal{L}$ of PLPs except the following modifications:

- *Variables* consist of variables $x, y, z, \cdots$ of $\mathcal{L}$ and name variables $n, n_1,$ $n_2, \cdots$, where $\{x, y, z, \cdots\}$ and $\{n, n_1, n_2, \cdots\}$ are disjoint.

- *Constants* consist of constants $C, C_1, C_2, \cdots$ of $\mathcal{L}$ and name constants $N, N_1, N_2, \cdots$, where $\{C, C_1, C_2, \cdots\}$ and $\{N, N_1, N_2, \cdots\}$ are disjoint.

- *Names* consist of name variables and name constants. The naming function $\mathcal{N}$ maps each rule to a name constant.

- A special predicate $<$ takes two names as arguments, where $<$ is used to represent a strict partial ordering among rules.

Terms, atoms, literals and rules are defined as the same in PLPs but under the language $\mathcal{L}^D$. Since $<$ is a special predicate in $\mathcal{L}^D$, $<$ can occur in any rules of $\mathcal{L}^D$. For instance, $N_1 < N_2 \leftarrow not\ N_2 < N_1$ and $n_1 < n_2 \leftarrow P(n_1), Q(n_2),\ not\ n_2 < n_1$ could be valid rules of $\mathcal{L}^D$.

A *dynamic* PLP (DPLP) is a pair $\mathcal{P} = (\Pi, \mathcal{N})$, where Π is a collection of rules of $\mathcal{L}^D$ and $\mathcal{N}$ is a naming function that maps each rule of Π to a name constant. Given a DPLP $\mathcal{P}$, Lit^D denotes the set of all ground literals of the language $\mathcal{L}^D$ of $\mathcal{P}$.

To keep the partial ordering $<$ consistent, we assume that any DPLP includes the following two rules[4]:

$$n_1 < n_3 \leftarrow n_1 < n_2, n_2 < n_3, \tag{1}$$

$$\neg n_2 < n_1 \leftarrow n_1 < n_2{}^5. \tag{2}$$

Example 7 Consider a DPLP as follows.

> $\mathcal{P}_{10}$:
> $N_1 : \neg Employed(x) \leftarrow Student(x),$
> $\qquad\qquad\qquad\qquad not\ Employed(x),$
> $N_2 : Employed(x) \leftarrow Age(x, > 25),$
> $\qquad\qquad\qquad\qquad not\ \neg Employed(x),$
> $N_3 : Student(x) \leftarrow FT\text{-}Student(x),$
> $N_4 : Student(x) \leftarrow PT\text{-}Student(x),$
> $N_5 : FT\text{-}Student(Peter) \leftarrow,$
> $N_6 : Age(Peter, > 25) \leftarrow,$
> $N_7 : N_1 < N_2 \leftarrow FT\text{-}Student(x), not\ N_2 < N_1,$
> $N_8 : N_2 < N_1 \leftarrow PT\text{-}Student(x), not\ N_1 < N_2.$

$\mathcal{P}_{10}$ is similar to $\mathcal{P}_9$ except that there are two rules N_7 and N_8 in $\mathcal{P}_{10}$ which express conditional preferences and we know Peter is a full-time student (i.e. rule N_5)[6]. Intuitively, rule N_7 is interpreted as "if x is a full-time student and there is no explicit knowledge to conclude that N_2 is more preferred than N_1, then rule N_1 is more preferred than rule N_2". A similar interpretation can be stated for N_8. It should be also noted that in a DPLP, preference relations on rules are not explicitly represented like PLPs. They have been encoded into the rules of the DPLP. ∎

4.2 Answer Set Semantics for DPLPs

Now we try to provide a formal semantics for DPLPs. Our method of evaluating a DPLP is based on a transformation of each DPLP into a PLP in language $\mathcal{L}^D$ under a sequence of reductions with respect to the partial ordering $<$[7].

---

[4]To simplify our presentation, we will not explicitly represent these two rules in our DPLPs.

[6]Note that implicitly other two rules (1) and (2) should be also included in $\mathcal{P}_{10}$.

[7]In the rest of the paper, whenever there is no confusion, we will simply refer $<$ as a partial ordering rather than a special predicate in $\mathcal{L}^D$ used to present a partial ordering.

Before to present our method formally, we first introduce some useful notations. Firstly, a DPLP $\mathcal{P} = (\Pi, \mathcal{N})$ can be treated as a special PLP *in* language $\mathcal{L}^D$ with the form $(\Pi, \mathcal{N}, <_0)$, where $<_0 = \emptyset$. Generally, we say that a logic program $\mathcal{P}$ is a PLP in language $\mathcal{L}^D$ if the program is specified as the form $(\Pi, \mathcal{N}, <)$, where Π is a set of rules of $\mathcal{L}^D$, $\mathcal{N}$ is a naming function mapping each rule in Π to a name constant and $<$ is a set of ground atoms of the form $N < N'$. In this case, we can compute each of $\mathcal{P}$'s *PLP answer sets*, denoted as $Ans^{P,D}(\mathcal{P})$, by using the approach proposed in section 3. Consider the following program.

$\mathcal{P}_{11}$:
$\quad N_1 : P \leftarrow not\ Q,$
$\quad N_2 : Q \leftarrow not\ P,$
$\quad N_3 : N_1 < N_2 \leftarrow not\ N_2 < N_1,$
$\quad N_4 : N_2 < N_1 \leftarrow not\ N_1 < N_2,$
$\quad N_3 < N_4.$

Note that $\mathcal{P}_{11}$ is not a DPLP but a PLP in language $\mathcal{L}^D$ as $N_3 < N_4$ is specified from *outside* of the rules of $\mathcal{P}_{11}$. Clearly, under the answer set semantics of PLPs, $\mathcal{P}_{11}$ has two answer sets: $\{P, N_1 < N_2\}$ and $\{Q, N_1 < N_2\}$.

Now we give the formal descriptions of the semantics of DPLPs.

Definition 5 *Let $\mathcal{P} = (\Pi, \mathcal{N})$ be a DPLP. A PLP $\mathcal{P}^*$ in $\mathcal{L}^D$ is a transformation of $\mathcal{P}$ to PLP if and only if there exists a sequence of sets Ψ_i $(i = 0, 1, \cdots)$ such that*

(i) $\Psi_0 = (\Pi_0, \mathcal{N}, <_0)$, where $\Pi_0 = \Pi$ and $<_0 = \emptyset$;

(ii) $\Psi_i = (\Pi_i, \mathcal{N}, <_i)$, where $\Pi_i = \Psi_{i-1}^{<_{i-1}}$ is a
reduct[8] of Ψ_{i-1} with respect to $<_{i-1}$, and
$<_i = \{N < N' \mid N < N'$ belongs to all
PLP answer sets of $\Psi_{i-1}\}$;

(iii) $\mathcal{P}^* = (\Pi_\infty, \mathcal{N}, <_\infty)$.

Definition 6 *Let $\mathcal{P} = (\Pi, \mathcal{N})$ be a DPLP. For any subset S of Lit^D, S is an answer set of $\mathcal{P}$, denoted as $Ans^D(\mathcal{P})$, iff $S = Ans^{P,D}(\mathcal{P}^*)$ for some transformation $\mathcal{P}^*$ of $\mathcal{P}$ to PLP as defined in Definition 5.*

Let us examine the above definitions more closely. The basic idea of evaluating a DPLP $\mathcal{P}$ is to transform $\mathcal{P}$ to a corresponding PLP $\mathcal{P}^*$ in $\mathcal{L}^D$, and then use the PLP answer set semantics to evaluate $\mathcal{P}^*$ (eg. Definition 6). From Definition 5, we can see that during this transformation, $\mathcal{P}$ is first treated as a special PLP in $\mathcal{L}^D$, i.e. Ψ_0. Then for each i $(i = 1, 2, \cdots)$, $\Psi_i = (\Pi_i, \mathcal{N}, <_i)$ is a PLP in $\mathcal{L}^D$ and generated from $\Psi_{i-1} = (\Pi_{i-1}, \mathcal{N}, <_{i-1}$

---

[8]See Definition 3.

). Intuitively, $<_i$ presents all ground instances of the partial ordering $<$ derived from Ψ_{i-1} under the semantics of PLP, and Π_i is a reduct of Ψ_{i-1} by eliminating defeated rules from Π_{i-1} with respect to $<_{i-1}$ (eg. $\Pi_i = \Psi_{i-1}^{<_{i-1}}$). This transformation procedure is continued until a fixed point is reached. To show how the answer set(s) of a DPLP can be computed, let us consider the following examples.

Example 8 Consider a DPLP $\mathcal{P}_{12}$ as follows.

$\mathcal{P}_{12}$:
$N_1 : P \leftarrow not\ Q,$
$N_2 : Q \leftarrow not\ P,$
$N_3 : N_1 < N_2 \leftarrow not\ N_2 < N_1,$
$N_4 : N_2 < N_1 \leftarrow not\ N_1 < N_2,$
$N_5 : N_3 < N_4 \leftarrow.$

According to Definition 5, we get the following sequence of Ψ_i $(i = 1, 2, 3)$[9]:

Ψ_1:
$N_1 : P \leftarrow not\ Q,$
$N_2 : Q \leftarrow not\ P,$
$N_3 : N_1 < N_2 \leftarrow not\ N_2 < N_1,$
$N_4 : N_2 < N_1 \leftarrow not\ N_1 < N_2,$
$N_5 : N_3 < N_4 \leftarrow,$
$N_3 < N_4.$

Ψ_2:
$N_1 : P \leftarrow not\ Q,$
$N_2 : Q \leftarrow not\ P,$
$N_3 : N_1 < N_2 \leftarrow not\ N_2 < N_1,$
$N_5 : N_3 < N_4 \leftarrow,$
$N_1 < N_2, N_3 < N_4.$

Ψ_3:
$N_1 : P \leftarrow not\ Q,$
$N_3 : N_1 < N_2 \leftarrow not\ N_2 < N_1,$
$N_5 : N_3 < N_4 \leftarrow,$
$N_1 < N_2, N_3 < N_4.$

Then it is easy to verify that $\Psi_4 = \Psi_3$. So the transformation of $\mathcal{P}_{12}$ to PLP is $\mathcal{P}_{12}^* = \Psi_3$[10]. Therefore, from Definition 6, $\mathcal{P}_{12}$ has a unique answer set $Ans^D(\mathcal{P}_{12}) = \{P, N_1 < N_2, N_3 < N_4, \neg N_2 < N_1, \neg N_4 < N_3\}$[11]. ∎

Example 9 Example 7 continued. Ignoring the detail, it is not difficult to see that $\mathcal{P}_{10}$ has a unique answer set $Ans^D(\mathcal{P}_{10}) = \{Age(Peter, > 25),$ $FT\text{-}Student(Peter),\ Student(Peter),\ \neg Employed(Peter),\ N_1 < N_2, \neg N_2 < N_1\}$, which presents the desired result for $\mathcal{P}_{10}$. ∎

---

[9] Ψ_0 is trivial.

[10] In this example, the transformation is unique.

[11] Recall that any DPLP must include rules (1) and (2).

Example 10 Consider a DPLP $\mathcal{P}_{13}$ as follows.

$\mathcal{P}_{13}$:
$\quad N_1 : n_1 < n_2 \leftarrow P(n_1), Q(n_2),\ not\ n_2 < n_1,$
$\quad N_2 : R(C) \leftarrow not\ R(C'),$
$\quad N_3 : R(C') \leftarrow not\ R(C),$
$\quad N_4 : P(N_2) \leftarrow,$
$\quad N_5 : Q(N_3) \leftarrow.$

This program is a bit different from those DPLPs discussed above. Intuitively, N_1 can be viewed as a general rule about the preference of the domain - "for any two rules n_1 and n_2, if n_1 and n_2 satisfy properties P and Q respectively, and there is no explicit knowledge to conclude that n_2 is more preferred than n_1, then n_1 is more preferred than n_2", while N_2 - N_5 present explicit knowledge of the domain[12]. Clearly, using the approach described above, $\mathcal{P}_{13}$ has a unique answer set $\{R(C), P(N_2), Q(N_3), N_2 < N_3, \neg N_3 < N_2\}$. ∎

5 Properties of Prioritized Logic Programs

In this section we discuss some properties of PLPs and DPLPs in detail. We first discuss the property of PLPs. To simplify our presentation, let us introduce some useful notations.

Let Π be an extended logic program. We use $ANS(\Pi)$ to denote the class of answer sets of Π. Suppose $\mathcal{P} = (\Pi, \mathcal{N}, <)$ is a PLP. From Definition 3, we can see that a reduct $\mathcal{P}^<$ of $\mathcal{P}$ is generated from a sequence of extended logic programs: $\Pi = \Pi_0, \Pi_1, \Pi_2, \cdots$. We use notation $\{\Pi_i\}$ $(i = 0, 1, 2, \cdots)$ to denote this sequence and call it a *reduct chain* of $\mathcal{P}$. Then we can prove the following useful result[13].

Theorem 1 *Let* $\mathcal{P} = (\Pi, \mathcal{N}, <)$ *be a PLP, and* $\{\Pi_i\}$ $(i = 0, 1, 2, \cdots)$ *a reduct chain of* $\mathcal{P}$. *Suppose each* Π_i *has answer set(s). Then for any i and j where $i < j$, $ANS(\Pi_j) \subseteq ANS(\Pi_i)$.*

Theorem 1 shows an important property of the reduct chain of $\mathcal{P}$: each Π_i is consistent with Π_{i-1} but becomes more *specific* than Π_{i-1} in the sense that all answer sets of Π_i are answer sets of Π_{i-1} but some answer sets of Π_{i-1} are filtered out if they conflict with the preference partial ordering $<$. The following theorem shows the answer set relation between a PLP and its corresponding extended logic programs.

Theorem 2 *Let* $\mathcal{P} = (\Pi, \mathcal{N}, <)$ *be a PLP. Then a subset S of Lit is an answer set of $\mathcal{P}$ iff S is an answer set of each Π_i for some reduct chain $\{\Pi_i\}$ $(i = 0, 1, 2, \cdots)$ of $\mathcal{P}$, where each Π_i has answer set(s).*

---

[12] An application of this kind of program in legal reasoning was addressed in [2].

[13] All proofs of theorems presented in this paper were given in our full paper [9].

Now we investigate properties of DPLPs. Let $\mathcal{P}$ and $\mathcal{P}'$ be a DPLP and a PLP in $\mathcal{L}^D$ respectively. We use $ANS^{P,D}(\mathcal{P}')$ to denote the class of PLP answer sets of $\mathcal{P}'$. From Definition 5, we can see that a transformation $\mathcal{P}^*$ of $\mathcal{P}$ is generated from a sequence of PLPs in $\mathcal{L}^D$: Ψ_0, Ψ_1, Ψ_2, $\cdots$. We use notation $\{\Psi_i\}$ $(i = 0, 1, 2, \cdots)$ to denote this sequence and call it a *PLP-reduct chain* of $\mathcal{P}$. Then, similarly to the case of PLPs described earlier, we have the following results for DPLPs.

Theorem 3 *Let $\mathcal{P} = (\Pi, \mathcal{N})$ be a DPLP, and $\{\Psi_i\}$ $(i = 0, 1, 2, \cdots)$ a PLP-reduct chain of $\mathcal{P}$. Suppose each Ψ_i has PLP answer set(s). Then for any i and j where $i < j$, $ANS^{P,D}(\Psi_j) \subseteq ANS^{P,D}(\Psi_i)$.*

Theorem 4 *Let $\mathcal{P} = (\Pi, \mathcal{N})$ be a DPLP. Then a subset S of Lit^D is an answer set of $\mathcal{P}$ iff S is a PLP answer set of each Ψ_i for some PLP-reduct chain $\{\Psi_i\}$ $(i = 0, 1, 2, \cdots)$ of $\mathcal{P}$, where each Ψ_i has PLP answer set(s).*

6 Related Work and Conclusions

The issue of logic programs with preferences has been explored recently also by other researchers [4, 6, 7]. However, most of these proposals are not completely satisfactory. One of the major limitations of their work, as pointed by Brewka [2], is that the priority can only be expressed statically. Another restriction of some previous proposals is that only one type of negation was considered in their logic programs (eg. [4, 7]).

Our work described in this paper is most related to Brewka's recent work on prioritized logic programs [2], while Brewka proposed a well-founded semantics for logic programs with dynamic preferences.

Due to the space limitation, we will not compare these two semantics in detail. A thorough investigation of the relationship between these two approaches was presented in our technical report. In brief, our method inherits some advantages and drawbacks from answer set semantics, while Brewka's approach inherits some advantages and drawbacks from well-founded semantics as well. For instance, our answer set semantics can derive reasonable conclusions in most cases, but some reasonable solutions can not be obtained from Brewka's well-founded semantics (see page 35 in [2]). On the other hand, reasoning under our semantics is intractable in the general case while it can be done in polynomial time under Brewka's semantics. However, based on recent results of computations of stable models, eg. [3], it is possible to locate a reasonably broad tractable subclass of our prioritized logic programs so that the applicable range of our method can be identified. Detailed work concerning the computational analysis about our PLPs and DPLPs was presented in [9].

The prioritized logic programs proposed in this paper can be used to solve some important problems in reasoning about change. In [8] and [9], we also investigated the applications of PLPs to deal with generalized rule-based updates and actions in domains including defeasible and causal constraints. These results have enhanced our expectation of using prioritized logic programs as a general tool to formalize and implement dynamic knowledge systems in the real world.

Acknowledgements

We thank Chitta Baral for valuable comments on an earlier draft of this paper. Thanks are also due to anonymous referees for their criticisms and useful comments, especially the one of suggestion in revising Definition 3 to avoid some unintuitive results. This research is supported in part by a research grant from University of Western Sydney, Nepean and a grant from the Australian Research Council.

References

[1] C. Baral and M. Gelfond, Logic programming and knowledge representation. *Journal of Logic Programming*, **19,20** (1994) 73–148.

[2] G. Brewka, Well-founded semantics for extended logic programs with dynamic preferences. *Journal of Artificial Intelligence Research*, **4** (1996) 19–36.

[3] R. Ben-Eliyahu, A hierarchy of tractable subsets for computing stable models. *Journal of Artificial Intelligence Research*, **6** 1996 27–52.

[4] F. Buccafurri, N. Leone, and P. Rullo, Stable models and their computation for logic programming with inheritance and true negation. *Journal of Logic Programming*, **27** 1996 5–43.

[5] M. Gelfond and V. Lifschitz, Classical negation in logic programs and disjunctive databases. *New Generation Computing*, **9** (1991) 365–386.

[6] R. Kowalski and F. Sadri, Logic programs with exceptions. *New Generation Computing*, **9** (1991) 387–400.

[7] X. Wang, J.H. You, and L.Y. Yuan, Circumscription by inference rules with priority. In *Proceedings of ECAI'96*, pp 111–114, 1996.

[8] Y. Zhang and N.Y. Foo, Towards generalized rule-based updates. In *Proceedings of the 15th International Joint Conference on Artificial Intelligence (IJCAI'97)*. Morgan Kaufmann Publishers Inc., 1997.

[9] Y. Zhang and N.Y. Foo, Prioritized logic programs and their applications. *Manuscript*. July 1997.

Generated Models and Extensions of Nonmonotonic Systems

Joeri Engelfriet
Faculty of Mathematics and Computer Science
Vrije Universiteit Amsterdam
De Boelelaan 1081a
1081 HV Amsterdam, The Netherlands
joeri@cs.vu.nl

Heinrich Herre
Institut für Informatik
University of Leipzig
Augustusplatz 10-11
04109 Leipzig, Germany
herre@informatik.uni-leipzig.de

Abstract

Stable generated models provide a general semantics for logic programming. Although equal for normal programs, they differ from the answer set semantics on disjunctive programs. We show that stable generated semantics coincide with the semantics obtained by translating programs into a minimal partial temporal logic into which a subsystem of default logic can be embedded. This leads us to a new version of disjunctive default logic, based on generated extensions. These results establish a close relation between three different approaches to non-monotonic reasoning: stable generated models of logic programs, default logic, and minimal partial temporal logic.

1 Introduction

The stable model semantics of [4] is one of the prominent semantics for normal logic programs. There is a straightforward translation of normal logic programs into default theories ([10]), and under this translation, stable models of a program correspond to extensions of the translation of the program. Stable generated models were introduced in [7] as a semantics for the most general kind of logic programs. On normal (non-disjunctive) programs, this semantics coincides with the stable models of [4]. In [2] it was shown that default theories can be translated into temporal theories. With a suitable (nonmonotonic) temporal semantics, temporal models of the translation correspond to extensions of the original default theory. So far we have a homogeneous picture of various coinciding semantics.

When considering disjunctive rules, however, the approaches diverge. In [5], (see also [8]) answer sets were introduced as a generalization of stable models to disjunctive logic programs, in which the head of a rule may be a disjunction. The intention of the disjunctive conclusion is that a commitment should be made to one of the disjuncts, i.e., not only should the disjunction be a conclusion, but (at least) one of the disjuncts should also be a conclusion. In [6] a variant of default logic was introduced with disjunctive conclusions of rules, and it was shown that an embedding of disjunctive logic programs into disjunctive default logic existed under which answer sets correspond to extensions.

Stable generated models are defined for a very general class of logic programs, and we can easily restrict ourselves to the class of (normal) disjunctive logic programs. It was shown in [7] that answer sets of normal disjunctive logic programs are stable generated models. It turned out, however, that there may be stable generated models which are not answer sets. The translation of default logic into the temporal logic of [2] can also easily be extended to the disjunctive case, and again it turns out that the translation may have (temporal) models which have no corresponding extensions. We will show that for super logic programs ([9]), the temporal approach coincides with stable generated models. We also introduce a variant of disjunctive default logic by extending the semi-constructive definition in [10] (shown to be equivalent to the fixed-point definition in the non-disjunctive case), and show that this variant is related to the stable generated models and the temporal approach.

This difference shows that there are at least two ways of extending the stable (default) semantics to the disjunctive case: one based on fixed-points, and one based on (semi-) generated models.

The paper has the following structure. After introducing some basic notation in section 2, we recall the notion of a stable generated model in section 3. Section 4 describes the temporal logic and its link with stable generated models. In section 5, we introduce the notion of a generated extension of a disjunctive default theory and give an appropriate translation of super logic programs into disjunctive default logic.

2 Preliminaries

A *signature* $\sigma = \langle Rel, Const, Fun \rangle$ consists of a set of relation symbols, a set of constant symbols, and a set of function symbols. U_σ denotes the set of all ground terms of σ. For a tuple $t_1, \ldots, t_n$ we will also write $\vec{t}$ when its length is of no relevance. The logical functors are $\neg, \wedge, \vee, \rightarrow, \forall, \exists$; where $\rightarrow$ is called *material implication*. $L(\sigma)$ is the smallest set containing the atomic formulas of σ, and being closed with respect to the following conditions: if $F, G \in L(\sigma)$, then $\{\neg F, F \wedge G, F \vee G, F \rightarrow G, \exists x F, \forall x F\} \subseteq L(\sigma)$.

$L^0(\sigma)$ denotes the corresponding set of sentences (closed formulas). For sublanguages of $L(\sigma)$ formed by means of a subset $\mathcal{F}$ of the logical functors, we write $L(\sigma; \mathcal{F})$. With respect to a signature σ we define the following sublanguages: $At(\sigma) = L(\sigma; \emptyset)$, the set of all atomic formulas (also called *atoms*); Lit$(\sigma) = L(\sigma; \neg)$, the set of all *literals*. We introduce the following conventions. When $L \subseteq L(\sigma)$ is some sublanguage, L^0 denotes the corresponding set of sentences. We will sometimes omit the signature and write, e.g., L instead of $L(\sigma)$. $Cn(X)$ denotes the deductive closure of the set X of sentences within classical logic.

If $(Y, <)$ is a partially ordered set, then Min$(Y, <)$ denotes the set of all minimal elements of $(Y, <)$, i.e. Min$(Y, <) = \{x \in Y \mid \neg \exists x' \in Y : x' < x\}$. If the ordering is clear from the context, we will omit it.

A *Herbrand interpretation* of the language $L(\sigma)$ is one for which the universe equals U_σ, and the function symbols are interpreted canonically. We identify Herbrand interpretations over σ with subsets of At$^0(\sigma)$. The class of all Herbrand σ-interpretations is denoted by $I_H(\sigma) = 2^{\text{At}^0(\sigma)}$. The standard ordering on interpretations is set inclusion. In the sequel we shall also simply say 'interpretation' instead of 'Herbrand interpretation'. A *valuation* over an interpretation I is a function ν from the set of all variables *Var* into the Herbrand universe U_σ, which can be naturally extended to arbitrary terms by $\nu(f(t_1, \ldots, t_n)) = f(\nu(t_1), \ldots, \nu(t_n))$. Analogously, a valuation ν can be canonically extended to arbitrary formulas F, where we write $F\nu$ instead of $\nu(F)$. Note that for a constant c, being a 0-ary function, we have $\nu(c) = c$. The model relation $\models \subseteq I_H(\sigma) \times L^0(\sigma)$ between an interpretation and a sentence is defined inductively as follows.

Definition 2.1 (Model Relation)   *1. $I \models r(\vec{t})$ iff $r(\vec{t}) \in I$.*

2. $I \models F \wedge G$ iff $I \models F$ and $I \models G$.

3. $I \models F \vee G$ iff $I \models F$ or $I \models G$.

4. $I \models \exists x F(x)$ iff $I \models F(t)$ for some $t \in U_\sigma$.

5. $I \models \forall x F(x)$ iff $I \models F(t)$ for all $t \in U_\sigma$.

6. $I \models \neg F$ iff $I \not\models F$.

7. $I \models F \to G$ iff $I \models \neg F \vee G$.

The model relation between an interpretation $I \in I_H(\sigma)$ and a formula $F \in L(\sigma)$ is defined by $I \models F$ iff $I \models F\nu$ for every valuation $\nu : Var \to U_\sigma$. I is a model of a set X of formulas iff $I \models F$ for all $F \in X$. Mod$_H(X) = \{I \in I_H : I \models X\}$ denotes the Herbrand model operator, and $\models_H$ denotes the corresponding consequence relation, i.e. $X \models_H F$ iff Mod$_H(X) \subseteq$ Mod$_H(F)$. Let $I \in I_H(\sigma)$, and $F \in L(\sigma)$. Then Sat$_I(F) = \{\nu : I \models F\nu\}$.

Definition 2.2 (Minimal Models)   *For $F \in L(\sigma) \supseteq X$, we define* Mod$_m(X)$ Min$((\text{Mod}_H(X), \subseteq))$, *and* $X \models_m F$ *iff* Mod$_m(X) \subseteq$ Mod$_H(F)$.

Definition 2.3 (Sequent)   *A sequent s is an expression of the form*

$$F_1, \ldots, F_m \Rightarrow G_1, \ldots, G_n$$

where $F_i, G_j \in L(\sigma)$ for $i = 1, \ldots, m$ and $j = 1, \ldots, n$. The body of s, denoted by Bs, is given by $\{F_1, \ldots, F_m\}$, and the head of s, denoted by Hs, is given by $\{G_1, \ldots, G_n\}$. $\mathrm{Seq}(\sigma)$ denotes the class of all sequents s such that $Hs, Bs \subseteq L(\sigma)$, and for a given set $S \subseteq \mathrm{Seq}(\sigma)$, $[S]$ denotes the set of all ground instances of sequents from S.

Definition 2.4 (Model of a Sequent)   *A Herbrand interpretation $I \in \boldsymbol{I}_H$ is a model of the sequent s, denoted $I \models F_1, \ldots, F_m \Rightarrow G_1, \ldots, G_n$ iff $\bigcap_{i \le m} Sat_I(F_i) \subseteq \bigcup_{j \le n} Sat_I(G_j)$.*

We define the following classes of sequents corresponding to normal, normal disjunctive, super and generalized logic programs, respectively.

1. $\mathrm{NLP}(\sigma) = \{s \in \mathrm{Seq}(\sigma) : Hs \subseteq \mathrm{At}(\sigma),\ \#Hs = 1,\ Bs \subseteq \mathrm{Lit}(\sigma)\}$.

2. $\mathrm{NDLP}(\sigma) = \{s \in \mathrm{Seq}(\sigma) : Hs \subseteq \mathrm{At}(\sigma),\ Bs \subseteq \mathrm{Lit}(\sigma), Hs \ne \emptyset\}$.

3. $\mathrm{SLP}(\sigma) = \{s \in \mathrm{Seq}(\sigma) : Hs \subseteq At(\sigma), Hs \ne \emptyset, Bs \subseteq At(\sigma) \cup \{\neg K : K \in L(\sigma; \wedge)\}\}$.

4. $\mathrm{GLP}(\sigma) = \{s \in \mathrm{Seq}(\sigma) : Hs, Bs \subseteq L(\sigma; \neg, \wedge, \vee, \rightarrow)\}$.

Super logic programs were introduced in [9]. Let $S \subseteq \mathrm{GLP}$ be a generalized logic program. Then, obviously, $\mathrm{Mod}_H(S) = \mathrm{Mod}_H([S])$ where $[S]$ is the Herbrand instantiation of S. With respect to a class of interpretations $\boldsymbol{K}$, we write $\boldsymbol{K} \models F$ iff $I \models F$ for all $I \in \boldsymbol{K}$. We denote the set of all sequents from a sequent set S which are applicable in $\boldsymbol{K}$ by

$$S_{\boldsymbol{K}} = \{s \in [S] : \boldsymbol{K} \models Bs\}$$

If $\boldsymbol{K}$ is a singleton, we omit brackets.

3   Stable Generated Models

In this section we recall the definition of stable generated model introduced in [7]. Let $I_1, I_2 \in \boldsymbol{I}_H$. Then, $[I_1, I_2] = \{I \in \boldsymbol{I}_H : I_1 \subseteq I \subseteq I_2\}$.

Definition 3.1 *[7]   Let $S \subseteq \mathrm{GLP}(\sigma)$. A model M of S is called* stable generated *(s.g. for short), symbolically $M \in \mathrm{Mod}_{sg}(S)$, if there is a chain of Herbrand interpretations $I_0 \subseteq \ldots \subseteq I_\kappa$ such that $M = I_\kappa$, and*

1. $I_0 = \emptyset$.

2. *For successor ordinals α with $0 < \alpha \leq \kappa$, I_α is a minimal extension of $I_{\alpha-1}$ satisfying all sequents which are applicable in $[I_{\alpha-1}, M]$, i.e. $I_\alpha \in \text{Min}\{I \in \boldsymbol{I}_H(\sigma) : I \supseteq I_{\alpha-1}, \text{ and } I \models \bigvee Hs, \text{ for all } s \in S_{[I_{\alpha-1},M]}\}$.*

3. *For limit ordinals $\lambda \leq \kappa$, $I_\lambda = \sup_{\alpha < \lambda} I_\alpha$.*

We also say that M is generated by the S-stable chain $I_0 \subseteq \ldots \subseteq I_\kappa$.

The set of stable generated models of S is denoted by $\text{Mod}_{sg}(S)$, and the stable entailment relations is defined as follows:

$$S \models_{sg} F \quad \text{iff} \quad \text{Mod}_{sg}(S) \subseteq \text{Mod}(F)$$

Stable generated models do not exist in all cases. For instance, $S = \{\neg p \Rightarrow p\}$ has exactly one minimal model, $\text{Mod}_m(S) = \{\{p\}\}$, which is not stable, however. A satisfiable sequent set, resp. logic program, without s.g. models will be called *unstable*.

Example 1 $S = \{(p \rightarrow q) \Rightarrow r; \ r \Rightarrow p\}$ *is unstable.*

Proposition 3.1 *[7] If M is an s.g. model of $S \subseteq$ GLP, then there is either a finite S-stable chain, or an S-stable chain of length ω, generating M.*

For $B \subseteq Lit$, let B^- denote the set of atoms which occur negated in B, i.e. $B^- = \{a \in At : \neg a \in B\}$, and let $B^+ = \{a \in At : a \in B\}$.

Definition 3.2 *[4] Let $I \subseteq$ At, and $S \subseteq$ NLP. Then the Gelfond-Lifschitz transformation of S with respect to I is defined as*

$$S^I = \{B^+ \Rightarrow a : (B \Rightarrow a) \in [S], \text{ and } B^- \cap I = \emptyset\}$$

and the Gelfond-Lifschitz operator Γ_S is defined as follows: $\Gamma_S(I)$ is the unique minimal model of S^I, denoted M_{S^I}, i.e. $\Gamma_S(I) = M_{S^I}$. We also define the fixpoint set $\text{Fix}(\Gamma_S) = \{I : I = \Gamma_S(I)\}$.

Claim 3.2 *[7] Stable generated semantics coincides with Gelfond-Lifschitz semantics on normal logic programs, i.e. for every $S \subseteq$ NLP, we have that $\text{Fix}(\Gamma_S) = \text{Mod}_{sg}(S)$*

Definition 3.3 *Let $I \subseteq$ At, and $S \subseteq$ NDLP. Then the Gelfond-Lifschitz transformation of S with respect to I is defined as*

$$S^I = \{B^+ \Rightarrow H : (B \Rightarrow H) \in [S], \text{ and } B^- \cap I = \emptyset\}$$

and the generalized Gelfond-Lifschitz operator Γ_S is defined as follows: $\Gamma_S(I)$ collects all minimal models of S^I, i.e. $\Gamma_S(I) = \text{Mod}_m(S^I)$. We also define the fixpoint set $\text{Fix}(\Gamma_S) = \{I : I \in \Gamma_S(I)\}$.

The relationship between the fixpoints of Γ_S, i.e. the answer sets of a normal disjunctive logic program S as defined in [5], and the stable generated models of S is clarified by the following claim.

Claim 3.3 *[7] Let $S \subseteq \text{NDLP}$. Every fixpoint of Γ_S is a stable generated model of S, i.e. $\text{Fix}(\Gamma_S) \subseteq \text{Mod}_{sg}(S)$.*

The converse of this claim is not true, i.e. not every stable generated (even minimal) model of a NDLP S is a fixpoint of Γ_S.

Example 2 *Let $S = \{\Rightarrow a, b;\ a \Rightarrow b;\ \neg a \Rightarrow a\}$. We show that $\{a, b\}$ is a stable generated and minimal model of S. Obviously, $\{a, b\}$ is a minimal model of S. $\{a, b\}$ is also stable generated: $I_0 = \emptyset$, $S_{[\emptyset, \{a,b\}]} = \{\Rightarrow a, b\}$. A minimal extension of $\emptyset$ is either $\{a\}$ or $\{b\}$. Take $I_1 = \{a\}$. Then $S_{[\{a\}, \{a,b\}]} = \{a \Rightarrow b;\ \Rightarrow a, b\}$, and a minimal extension of $\{a\}$ satisfying b gives finally $I_2 = \{a, b\}$. On the other hand, $\{a, b\}$ is not a minimal model of $S^{\{a,b\}} = \{\Rightarrow a, b;\ a \Rightarrow b\}$, since $\{b\}$ is a model of $S^{\{a,b\}}$. In fact, Γ_S does not have any fixpoint.*

4 Minimal partial temporal logic

In this section we will describe a partial temporal semantics for logic programs. The semantics is obtained by translating a logic program into a nonmonotonic partial temporal logic. This logic was first used to give a temporal semantics to default logic ([2]). The idea behind the temporal framework is that a temporal theory describes the reasoning process of a (nonmonotonic) agent. A number of different forms of reasoning were treated in this fashion in [3]. Although the full temporal logic is more general (it uses S5 models instead of partial models, and temporal operators may be stacked), we will describe a simpler variant here that is sufficient to give semantics to logic programming. First we will formally introduce minimal partial temporal logic.

Definition 4.1 (Partial model)

1. *A partial model M for the signature σ is an assignment of a truth value from $\{0, 1, u\}$ to each of the atoms of $At^0(\sigma)$. Using the strong Kleene semantics, this assignment can be extended to arbitrary sentences.*

2. *The ordering of truth values is defined by $u \leq 0$, $u \leq 1$, $u \leq u$, $1 \leq 1$, $0 \leq 0$. This is extended to partial models by: $M \leq N$ if for all atoms $a \in At^0(\sigma)$ we have $M(a) \leq N(a)$.*

A partial model describes which formulae the agent knows (or, has derived) at any point in time. To give an account of the total reasoning process of an agent, we have to describe what the agent knows (has derived) at all points in time. We assume that the reasoning of the agent starts at some point, and continues in a discrete manner: based on what the agent knows, it may apply some (nonmonotonic) inference steps to arrive at a new state of knowledge (described by a partial model), from which it may again apply inference steps. We will take the natural numbers (ω) as our flow of time.

Definition 4.2 (Partial temporal model)   *A partial temporal model $\mathcal{M}$ is a sequence $\{\mathcal{M}_t\}_{t \in \omega}$ of partial models. We will assume all partial temporal models are* conservative, *which means that for all t, we have $\mathcal{M}_t \leq \mathcal{M}_{t+1}$. The ordering $\leq$ is extended to partial temporal models by*

$$\mathcal{M} \leq \mathcal{N} \Leftrightarrow \mathcal{M}_t \leq \mathcal{N}_t \; \forall t \in \omega$$

In conservative models, the knowledge of the agent may only increase over time: the agent does not forget and does not revise its knowledge. Whenever we have $\mathcal{M} \leq \mathcal{N}$, then this means that $\mathcal{M}$ contains less (or equal) knowledge than $\mathcal{N}$, *at each time point.* The temporal language in which the reasoning of an agent can be described, is a restricted version of the language introduced in [2]. For each closed formula $\alpha \in L^0(\sigma)$, there are three basic expressions in the language that describe the truth of α in time: $C\alpha$, which states that the agent *currently* knows α, $F\alpha$, which states that the agent will know α *sometimes in the future*, and $G\alpha$, stating that the agent knows α *always in the future*; these basic expressions are called temporal atoms. The set of temporal formulas, denoted by $TF(\sigma)$, is the smallest set of expressions containing the temporal atoms and closed with respect to the propositional connectives $\{\wedge, \neg, \vee, \rightarrow\}$.

Definition 4.3 (Semantics)   *Let $\mathcal{M}$ be a partial temporal model, and let $t \in \omega$.*

1. *For a sentence $\alpha \in L^0(\sigma)$:*

   - $(\mathcal{M}, t) \models C\alpha \Leftrightarrow \mathcal{M}_t(\alpha) = 1$
   - $(\mathcal{M}, t) \models F\alpha \Leftrightarrow \mathcal{M}_s(\alpha) = 1$ *for some $s > t$*
   - $(\mathcal{M}, t) \models G\alpha \Leftrightarrow \mathcal{M}_s(\alpha) = 1$ *for all $s > t$*

2. *For two temporal formulae ϕ, ψ:*

   - $(\mathcal{M}, t) \models \phi \wedge \psi \Leftrightarrow (\mathcal{M}, t) \models \phi$ *and* $(\mathcal{M}, t) \models \psi$
   - $(\mathcal{M}, t) \models \neg\phi \Leftrightarrow (\mathcal{M}, t) \not\models \phi$

3. *Implication ($\rightarrow$) and disjunction ($\vee$) are defined as usual from conjunction and negation.*

4. *A formulae ϕ is true in $\mathcal{M}$, denoted $\mathcal{M} \models \phi$, if $(\mathcal{M}, t) \models \phi$ for all $t \in \omega$. A set of formulae Th is true in a model $\mathcal{M}$, denoted $\mathcal{M} \models Th$, if $\mathcal{M} \models \phi$ for all $\phi \in Th$.*

Even though we want to describe the reasoning process of an agent, we are of course still interested in the *final outcomes* of this reasoning process. This is expressed by the *limit* of a partial temporal model.

Definition 4.4 (Limit model)   *Let $\mathcal{M}$ be a (conservative) partial temporal model. Then the limit of $\mathcal{M}$, denoted $lim\,\mathcal{M}$, is the partial model defined by:*

$$lim\,\mathcal{M}(a) = \begin{cases} 1 \text{ if there exists } t \in \omega \text{ such that } \mathcal{M}_t(a) = 1 \\ 0 \text{ if there exists } t \in \omega \text{ such that } \mathcal{M}_t(a) = 0 \\ u \text{ otherwise} \end{cases}$$

for all $a \in At^0(\sigma)$.

Using the temporal language, we can describe the reasoning behavior of the agent. The temporal formulae prescribe when the agent should make an inference. But we also want the agent to know (or derive) nothing more than that (we do not want to describe explicitly what it should *not* derive. So we want to make sure that the knowledge of the agent over time satisfies the temporal formulae, but otherwise is *minimal*. The following definition formalizes this.

Definition 4.5 (Minimal model)   *Let Th be a temporal theory and let $\mathcal{M}$ be a partial temporal model. Then $\mathcal{M}$ is a* minimal model *of Th if*

- *$\mathcal{M} \models Th$, and*

- *for any partial temporal model $\mathcal{N}$, if $\mathcal{N} \models Th$ and $\mathcal{N} \leq \mathcal{M}$, then $\mathcal{N} = \mathcal{M}$.*

The minimal temporal models of a theory describe the intended possible behavior of the agent over time. We are now ready to give the translation of a logic program to a temporal theory. We have to consider what the agent should do with a rule (of $SLP(\sigma)$) $a_1 \wedge \ldots \wedge a_n \wedge \neg K_1 \wedge \ldots \neg K_m \Rightarrow c_1 \vee \ldots \vee c_k$, where the K_i are conjunctions (we will consider only clauses from the Herbrand instantiation of a program). If the agent has already derived a_1 through a_n (it *currently* knows them), and the K_1 through K_m are *not* derived, then it should derive one of the c_i (and hence know it from the next point in time on). The subtlety lies in the reading of the $\neg K_i$. The K_i should not only not have been derived *now*, but also never in the future (otherwise the applicability of this rule at this moment is undermined later on). Since the models are conservative, this is equivalent to requiring that the K_i are never known in the future. The temporal translation of this rule becomes:

$$Ca_1 \wedge \ldots \wedge Ca_n \wedge \neg FK_1 \wedge \ldots \wedge \neg FK_m \to Gc_1 \vee \ldots \vee Gc_k$$

This leads us to the temporal translation of a program.

Definition 4.6 (Temporal translation)   *Let $P \subseteq SLP(\sigma)$. Define the translation Temp by*

- $Temp(a_1 \wedge \ldots \wedge a_n \wedge \neg K_1 \wedge \ldots \neg K_m \Rightarrow c_1 \vee \ldots \vee c_k) = Ca_1 \wedge \ldots \wedge Ca_n \wedge \neg FK_1 \wedge \ldots \wedge \neg FK_m \rightarrow Gc_1 \vee \ldots \vee Gc_k$

- $Temp(P) = \{Temp(s) \mid s \in [P]\}$

It has been shown in [2] that a similar translation can capture default logic (meaning that the limit models of minimal models of the translation correspond to extensions). Since one can similarly embed the stable semantics of normal logic programs into such default theories, it is easy to see that this temporal translation gives the stable model semantics for normal programs (limit models of minimal models of the translation *Temp* correspond to stable models of the original program). In the disjunctive case, however, the limit models do not correspond in a one-to-one fashion with the answer sets, but they correspond to stable generated models. In the sequel, we will consider only P-stable chains of length ω. This may always be done; remember that a stable generated model always has either a P-stable chain of length ω, or a finite one. These finite ones can always be made of length ω by repeating the last interpretation in the chain. Herbrand interpretations are not the same as partial models, but there is a clear connection.

Definition 4.7 *Let a Herbrand interpretation I and a partial model M be given. We say that I and M correspond to each other, if*
$$M(a) = \begin{cases} 1 \text{ if } a \in I \\ u \text{ otherwise} \end{cases}$$

Before we proceed with the main result of this section, we will first give a useful lemma.

Lemma 4.1 *Let $\mathcal{M}$ be a partial temporal model, $t \in \omega$, and $a_1, \ldots, a_n \in At^0(\sigma)$, then*

$$(\mathcal{M}, t) \models \neg F(a_1 \wedge \ldots \wedge a_n) \Leftrightarrow \exists i \in \{1, \ldots, n\} : \forall s > t \, (\mathcal{M}_s(a_i) \neq 1)$$

Proof: The right to left direction is easy. For the other direction, suppose that for every a_i there is a timepoint t_i such that $\mathcal{M}_{t_i}(a_i) = 1$, then let $t = max\{t_1, \ldots, t_n\}$. By conservativity we have $\mathcal{M}_u(a_i) = 1$ for every a_i and $u \geq t$, which implies that $(\mathcal{M}, s) \models F(a_1 \wedge \ldots \wedge a_n)$. $\square$

We will use this lemma in the proof of the following proposition without mentioning.

Proposition 4.2 (Equivalence)   *Let $P \subseteq SLP(\sigma)$. If I is a consistent stable generated model of P, then there is a minimal partial temporal model of $Temp(P)$ such that its limit corresponds to I. If M is the limit of a* *minimal partial temporal model of $Temp(P)$, then there is a stable generated model I that corresponds to it. Moreover, if $I_0 \subseteq I_1 \subseteq \ldots \subseteq I$ is a P-stable chain generating I, then there is a minimal partial temporal model $\mathcal{M}$ with limit M that corresponds to the chain in a pointwise fashion. Also, for every minimal partial temporal model $\mathcal{M}$ with limit M, there is a P-stable chain generating I that corresponds to it pointwise.*

Proof: "$\Rightarrow$": Suppose I is a stable generated model of P, with chain $\{I_i\}_{i\in\omega}$. This means that $I = \bigcup_{i=0}^{\infty} I_i$ and

- $I_0 = \emptyset$

- $I_{n+1} \in \mathrm{Min}\{J \in I_H(\sigma) : J \supseteq I_n, \text{ and } J \models \bigvee Hs, \forall s \in P_{[I_n,I]}\}$

Now define the partial temporal model $\mathcal{M}$ by

$$\mathcal{M}_i = \begin{cases} 1 \text{ if } a \in I_i \\ u \text{ otherwise} \end{cases}$$

We will show that $\mathcal{M}$ is a minimal model of $Temp(P)$. First we will show that it is a model of $Temp(P)$. In the sequel we will assume that $K_j = b_1^j \wedge \ldots \wedge b_{p_j}^j$.

Take any rule $Ca_1 \wedge \ldots \wedge Ca_n \wedge \neg FK_1 \wedge \ldots \wedge \neg FK_m \to Gc_1 \vee \ldots \vee Gc_k$ in $Temp(P)$, and take $t \in \omega$. Suppose $(\mathcal{M},t) \models Ca_1 \wedge \ldots \wedge Ca_n \wedge \neg FK_1 \wedge \ldots \wedge \neg FK_m$. Then $a_1,\ldots,a_n \in I_t$ and for every K_j there is a $h_j \in K_j$ such that $h_j \notin I_s \, \forall s > t$, in particular $h_1,\ldots,h_m \notin I$ so $I_{t+1} \models c_1 \vee \ldots \vee c_k$, so $c_{k_0} \in I_{t+1}$ for some $1 \leq k_0 \leq k$, but then $c_{k_0} \in I_s \, \forall s > t$. This implies that $(\mathcal{M},t) \models Gc_{k_o}$ so $(\mathcal{M},t) \models Gc_1 \vee \ldots \vee Gc_k$. Now suppose that $\mathcal{M}$ is not minimal, then there is a model $\mathcal{N}$ with $\mathcal{N} < \mathcal{M}$ and $\mathcal{N} \models Temp(P)$. Take the smallest $i_0 \in \omega$ such that $\mathcal{N}_{i_0} < \mathcal{M}_{i_0}$. First remark that $i_0 > 0$, since $\mathcal{M}_0$ assigns u to each atom ($I_0 = \emptyset$). Now define $J = \{a \in At^0(\sigma) \mid N_{i_0} = 1\}$. Then we claim that $I_{i_0-1} \subseteq J$. For suppose $a \in I_{i_0-1}$, then $\mathcal{M}_{i_0-1}(a) = 1$, so $\mathcal{N}_{i_0-1}(a) = 1$ (since i_0 was the smallest index for which $\mathcal{M}$ and $\mathcal{N}$ differ). As $\mathcal{N}$ is a conservative model, we have $N_{i_0}(a) = 1$, so $a \in J$. Now take a sequent $a_1 \wedge \ldots \wedge a_n \wedge \neg K_1 \wedge \ldots \neg K_m \Rightarrow c_1 \vee \ldots \vee c_k$ whose body holds in $[I_{i_0-1},I]$, then $(\mathcal{N}, i_0 - 1) \models Ca_1 \wedge \ldots \wedge Ca_n$, and for every K_j there is $h_j \in K_j$ such that $h_j \notin I$ so $(\mathcal{M}, i_0 - 1) \models \neg FK_1 \wedge \ldots \wedge \neg FK_m$ but then $(\mathcal{N} < \mathcal{M} \,!)$ $(\mathcal{N}, i_0 - 1) \models \neg FK_1 \wedge \ldots \wedge \neg FK_m$. As $\mathcal{N} \models Temp(P)$, we have $(\mathcal{N}, i_0 - 1) \models Gc_1 \vee \ldots \vee Gc_k$ so there is $k_0 \in \omega$ such that $N_{i_0}(c_{k_0}) = 1$. Therefore $J \models c_1 \vee \ldots \vee c_k$. This would mean that I_{i_0} is not a minimal extension of I_{i_0-1} satisfying the heads of rules whose bodies is satisfied. This leads to a contradiction, so we conclude that $\mathcal{M}$ is a minimal model of $Temp(P)$. It is easy to see that $\lim \mathcal{M}$ corresponds to I.

"$\Leftarrow$": Suppose $\mathcal{M}$ is a minimal model of $Temp(P)$. First of all, remark that $\mathcal{M}$ never assigns a 0 to any literal. If this were the case, then we could make a smaller model by changing this 0 to u. It can easily be seen that this smaller model would not invalidate any of the rules of $Temp(P)$. Define $I_i = \{a \in At^0(\sigma) \mid \mathcal{M}_i(a) = 1\}$ and $I = \{a \in At^0(\sigma) \mid \lim \mathcal{M}(a) = 1\}$. From the first remark it now follows that I_i corresponds to $\mathcal{M}_i$ and I corresponds to $\lim \mathcal{M}$. Then since $\mathcal{M}$ is conservative, we have $I_0 \subseteq I_1 \subseteq \ldots \subseteq I$ and $I = sup\{I_i\}$. We will show that the sequence $\{I_i\}$ is a P-stable chain generating I. First of all, $I_0 = \emptyset$. For if not, then define $\mathcal{N}$ by $\mathcal{N}_0(a) = u \; \forall a \in At^0(\sigma)$, and $\mathcal{N}_i = \mathcal{M}_i \; \forall i > 0$. Then $\mathcal{N} < \mathcal{M}$, and it is easy to check that $\mathcal{N} \models Temp(P)$. Now we will prove that the sequence satisfies the other requirement of Definition 3.1. Firstly, we have already established that I_{i+1} is an extension of I_i. Now take any rule $a_1 \wedge \ldots \wedge a_n \wedge \neg K_1 \wedge \ldots \neg K_m \Rightarrow c_1 \vee \ldots \vee c_k$ in $[P]$, and suppose the body holds in $[I_i, I]$. This means that $a_1, \ldots, a_n \in I_i$, and for every K_j there is a $h_j \in K_j$ such that $h_j \notin I$. Then $(\mathcal{M}, i) \models Ca_1 \wedge \ldots \wedge Ca_n \wedge \neg FK_1 \wedge \ldots \wedge \neg FK_m$ but as $\mathcal{M} \models Temp(P)$, $(\mathcal{M}, i) \models Gc_1 \vee \ldots \vee Gc_k$. Then in particular, for some $1 \leq k_0 \leq k$, $\mathcal{M}_{i+1}(c_{k_0}) = 1$, so $c_{k_0} \in I_{i+1}$. This means that I_{i+1} is an extension of I_i satisfying all heads of clauses whose bodies are satisfied. Now let us show that for all i_0, I_{i_0} is a minimal such extension. Suppose it is not, suppose J is a smaller such extension. Define the partial temporal model N by $\mathcal{N}_i = \mathcal{M}_i \; \forall i \neq i_0$, and $\mathcal{N}_{i_0}(a) = \begin{cases} 1 \text{ if } a \in J \\ u \text{ otherwise} \end{cases}$

Then obviously $\mathcal{N}$ is a conservative partial temporal model and $\mathcal{N} < \mathcal{M}$. But also $\mathcal{N} \models Temp(P)$. Take any rule $Ca_1 \wedge \ldots \wedge Ca_n \wedge \neg FK_1 \wedge \ldots \wedge \neg FK_m \rightarrow Gc_1 \vee \ldots \vee Gc_k$, and let $j \in \omega$. First consider the case when $j \geq i_0$; if $(\mathcal{N}, j) \models Ca_1 \wedge \ldots \wedge Ca_n \wedge \neg FK_1 \wedge \ldots \wedge \neg FK_m$, then $(\mathcal{M}, j) \models Ca_1 \wedge \ldots \wedge Ca_n \wedge \neg FK_1 \wedge \ldots \wedge \neg FK_m$, so $(\mathcal{M}, j) \models Gc_1 \vee \ldots \vee Gc_k$, so $(\mathcal{N}, j) \models Gc_1 \vee \ldots \vee Gc_k$, since $\mathcal{N}_i = \mathcal{M}_i$ for $i > i_0$. Second, if $j < i_0 - 1$, then $(\mathcal{N}, j) \models Ca_1 \wedge \ldots \wedge Ca_n \wedge \neg FK_1 \wedge \ldots \wedge \neg FK_m$ if and only if $(\mathcal{M}, j) \models Ca_1 \wedge \ldots \wedge Ca_n \wedge \neg FK_1 \wedge \ldots \wedge \neg FK_m$, but also $(\mathcal{N}, j) \models Gl$ if and only if $(\mathcal{M}, j) \models Gl$: if $(\mathcal{M}, j) \models Gl$, then $\mathcal{M}_{j+1}(l) = 1$, but $\mathcal{M}_{j+1} = \mathcal{N}_{j+1}$ $(j + 1 < i_0)$, and since $\mathcal{N}$ is conservative, $(\mathcal{N}, j) \models Gl$. The other direction is trivial, since $\mathcal{N} \leq \mathcal{M}$.

Now suppose $j = i_0 - 1$. Suppose $(\mathcal{N}, j) \models Ca_1 \wedge \ldots \wedge Ca_n \wedge \neg FK_1 \wedge \ldots \wedge \neg FK_m$. Then $a_1, \ldots, a_n \in I_{i_0-1}$. Also, $(\mathcal{M}, i_0 - 1) \models \neg FK_1 \wedge \ldots \wedge \neg FK_m$, so for each K_j there is $h_j \in K_j$ such that so $h_j \notin I$. But this means that the body of the rule is satisfied in $[I_{i_0-1}, I]$, so $J \models c_1 \vee \ldots \vee c_k$, so for some k_0 we have that $J \models c_{k_0}$, but then $(\mathcal{N}, i_0) \models Cc_{k_0}$, and as $\mathcal{N}$ is conservative, $(\mathcal{N}, i_0 - 1) \models Gc_{k_0}$. We conclude that $(\mathcal{N}, i_0 - 1) \models Gc_1 \vee \ldots \vee Gc_k$. From these cases we have that $\mathcal{N} \models Temp(P)$, and we already had that $\mathcal{N} < \mathcal{M}$, which contradicts the assumption that $\mathcal{M}$ was a minimal model of $Temp(P)$. Therefore, I_{i_0} is a minimal extension of I_{i_0-1} satisfying the heads of rules whose body is satisfied in $[I_{i_0-1}, I]$. This means that $I_0 \subseteq I_1 \subseteq \ldots \subseteq I$ is a P-stable chain generating I. It is easy to see that I corresponds to $\lim \mathcal{M}$. $\square$

Remark that the minimal models never assign 0 to any literal. We could have made them two-valued, but we have not done this in order to retain compatibility with the original definition in [2], but also in order to be able to capture explicit negation easily. This will not be done in the present paper.

Let us have a look at the example from the previous section.

Example 3 (Continued Example) *The temporal translation of the example is:*

$$\{Ga \vee Gb, Ca \to Gb, \neg Fa \to Ga\}$$

This theory has only one minimal model:

		time				
		0	1	2	3	...
atoms	a	u	1	1	1	...
	b	u	u	1	1	...

It is easy to see that this model corresponds to the stable generated model of the original program and to the stable chain generating it.

5 Disjunctive Defaults and Generated Extensions

Disjunctive default logic is an extension of Reiter's default logic ([10]), meant to deal more aptly with disjunctive information. When disjunctive information is added, a commitment has to be made to one of the disjuncts. We will restrict ourselves to the propositional case.

Definition 5.1 *A disjunctive default is an expression of the form (α : $\beta_1, \ldots, \beta_n$ / $\gamma_1 | \ldots | \gamma_n$), where α, β_i and γ_j are propositional formulae.*

Disjunctive defaults were first treated in [6], from which we repeat the following definition.

Definition 5.2 *[6] Let D be a set of disjunctive defaults and E a set of sentences. $Min_E(D)$ is the set of all minimal deductively closed sets M satisfying the following condition for every $(\alpha : \beta_1, \ldots, \beta_m/\gamma_1 | \ldots | \gamma_n) \in D$: if $\alpha \in M$, and $\neg \beta_1, \ldots, \neg \beta_m \notin E$, then $\{\gamma_1, \ldots, \gamma_n\} \cap M \neq \emptyset$. E is an extension of D if $E \in Min_E(D)$.*

This definition is clearly a generalization of the original fix-point definition of an extension. However, there is also a semi-constructive definition, which is equivalent in the non-disjunctive case. It turns out that if we generalize this semi-constructive definition (which is more in the spirit of s.g. models, the minimal temporal models, and Reiter's original semi-constructive characterization of extensions), we get a somewhat different notion.

Definition 5.3 *Let D be a set of disjunctive defaults. A set E of sentences is a generated extension of D if there is a sequence $E_0 \subseteq E_1 \subseteq \ldots \subseteq E_n \subseteq \ldots$ of deductively closed sets of sentences such that*

1. $E_0 = Cn(\emptyset)$;

2. E_{n+1} *is a minimal extension of E_n satisfying the following condition: if $(\alpha : \beta_1, \ldots, \beta_k \,/\, \gamma_1 | \ldots | \gamma_l) \in D$, $\alpha \in E_n$, and $\neg\beta_1, \ldots, \neg\beta_k \notin E$ then $\{\gamma_1, \ldots, \gamma_l\} \cap E_{n+1} \neq \emptyset$.*

and $E = \bigcup_{i=0}^{\infty} E_i$.

Proposition 5.1 *Let D be a set of disjunctive defaults. Every extension of D is a generated extension of D.*

Proof: Let E be an extension of D. Then $E \in Min_E(D)$. We can construct a sequence $E_0 \subseteq E_1 \subseteq \ldots \subseteq E_n \subseteq \ldots$ such that:
(1) $E_0 = Cn(\emptyset)$;
(2) E_{n+1} is a minimal extension of E_n closed w.r.t.:
if $(\alpha : \beta_1, \ldots, \beta_m \,/\, \gamma_1 | \ldots | \gamma_n) \in D$, $\alpha \in E_n$, and $\neg\beta_1, \ldots, \neg\beta_m \notin E$ then $\{\gamma_1, \ldots \gamma_n\} \cap E_{n+1} \neq \emptyset$.
The sets E_n are chosen such that $E_n \subseteq E$. By induction one can show that this is possible. Now it is sufficient to show that
(3) $\bigcup_{n=0}^{\infty} E_n = E$. Let $E_\omega = \bigcup_{n=0}^{\infty} E_n$. Obviously, the set E_ω is closed w.r.t. the default rules; since E is minimal, and $E_\omega \subseteq E$, it follows that $E_\omega = E$.
□.

Remark: The converse of the preceding proposition is not true: there are disjunctive default theories D having generated extensions but without any extension in the sense of [6].

Example 4 *This is the translation of the earlier example, $D = \{(: \,/\, a|b) \, (a : \,/\, b) \, (: \neg a \,/\, a)\}$. Then $E = Cn(\{a, b\})$ is a generated extension of D: $E_0 = Cn(\emptyset)$, $E_1 = Cn(\{a\})$, $E_2 = Cn(\{a, b\})$. But E is not an extension. It does satisfy the closure condition with respect to itself, but $Cn(\{b\})$ also satisfies it, so $Min_E(D) = \{Cn(\{b\})\}$.*

We now relate super logic programs to disjunctive defaults theories. Let $r := a_1, \ldots, a_l, \neg K_1, \ldots, \neg K_m \Rightarrow c_1, \ldots, c_n$ be a super rule; where $K_j = b_1^j \wedge \ldots \wedge b_{p_j}^j$, $j \leq m$. We translate such a rule in the following disjunctive default rule: $tr(r) := (a_1 \wedge \ldots \wedge a_l : \neg K_1, \ldots, \neg K_m \,/\, c_1 | \ldots | c_n)$. Let $At(E) = \{a : a$ is a ground atom with $E \models a\}$.

Proposition 5.2 *Let P be a super logic program, $tr(P)$ the default theory given by the above translation of P.*
If a set I of ground atoms is a stable generated model of P then there is a generated extension E of $tr(P)$ such that $I = At(E)$. If E is a generated extension of $tr(P)$, then $At(E)$ is a stable generated model of P.

Proof: 1) Assume I is a stable generated model of P. Then there is a stable chain $I_0 \subseteq I_1 \subseteq \ldots \subseteq I_n \subseteq \ldots$, $I = \bigcup_{n<\omega} I_n$. Let $E = Cn(I)$, $E_n = Cn(I_n)$. We show that E is a generated extension of $tr(P)$ via the sequence $\{E_n\}_{n<\omega}$. It is sufficient to show that E_{n+1} is a minimal extension of E_n closed w.r.t. the rules in $tr(P)$. Let $(a_1 \wedge \ldots \wedge a_m : \neg K_1, \ldots, \neg K_n) / c_1 | \ldots | c_s) \in tr(P)$, and $\{a_1, \ldots, a_m\} \subseteq E_n$, and $\neg\neg K_j \notin E$, $j \leq n$, i.e. $b_1^1 \wedge \ldots \wedge b_{p_1}^1, b_1^2 \wedge \ldots \wedge b_{p_2}^2, \ldots, b_1^n \wedge \ldots \wedge b_{p_n}^n \notin E$, hence for every $j \leq n$ there is an element $h_j \in K_j$ such that $h_j \notin E$, and from this follows $h_j \notin I$ and $I \models \neg h_j$; this implies $[I_n, I] \models \neg K_1, \ldots, \neg K_n$, and by definition of I_{n+1}, we get $I_{n+1} \models c_1 \vee \ldots \vee c_s$. Then, there is a $k \leq s$ such that $c_k \in I_{n+1}$, and this implies $\{c_1, \ldots, c_s\} \cap E_{n+1} \neq \emptyset$. We now show that E_{n+1} is a minimal extension of E_n satisfying these properties. Let F be a deductively closed set such that $E_n \subseteq F \subseteq E_{n+1}$, and F closed w.r.t. to rule application. Then, $I_{n+1} \subseteq F$, and hence $F = E_{n+1}$.

2) Let E be an generated extension of $tr(P)$. We have to show that $I = At(E)$ is a stable generated model of P. Let $E_0 \subseteq E_1 \subseteq \ldots$ be a generated sequence generating E. Define $I_n = At(E_n)$, we show that $(I_n)_{n<\omega}$ is stable chain for I and I is a model of P. Obviously, $I_0 = \emptyset$, since $E_0 = Cn(\emptyset)$. We show that I_{n+1} is a minimal extension of I_n being a model of the set $\{\bigvee Hr : r \in [P], [I_n, I] \models \bigwedge Br\}$. Let $r := a_1, \ldots, a_l, \neg K_1, \ldots, \neg K_m \Rightarrow c_1, \ldots, c_n$ a super rule; where $K_j = b_1^j \wedge \ldots \wedge b_{p_j}^j$. Define $tr(r) \in \Delta(n)$ iff $\{a_1, \ldots, a_l\} \subseteq E_n$ and $\neg\neg K_1, \ldots, \neg\neg K_m \notin E$, i.e. there are $h_j \in K_j$ such that $h_j \notin E$, $j \leq m$. Define $\Omega(n) = \{r : r \in [P]$ and $[I_n, I] \models \bigwedge Br\}$. Then $\Delta(n) = \{tr(r) : r \in \Omega(n)\}$. We show that $I_{n+1} \models Heads(\Omega(n))$ (where $Heads(S)$ is the set of the disjunctions of the heads of the rules in S), and if $I_n \subseteq J \subseteq I_{n+1}$, $J \models Heads(\Omega(n))$, then $J = I_{n+1}$. Let $r \in \Omega(n)$, then $tr(r) \in \Delta(n)$, hence $\{c_1, \ldots, c_n\} \cap E_{n+1} \neq \emptyset$, and thus $I_{n+1} \models \bigvee Hr$. Let $I_n \subseteq J \subseteq I_{n+1}$, and $J \models Heads(\Omega(n))$. Then $Cn(J)$ satisfies the second closure condition of Definition 5.3, and since E_{n+1} is minimal it follows $Cn(J) = E_{n+1}$, and hence $J = At(E_{n+1})$. $\square$

This version of disjunctive default logic can be captured by the full version of minimal temporal logic as described in [1].

6 Conclusion and Future Research

By introducing the notion of a generated extension for disjunctive default theories, we have established a close relation between three different approaches to non-monotonic reasoning: default logic, stable generated models of logic programs and minimal temporal partial models. This connection adds further evidence to the naturalness of stable generated models as the intended semantics for generalized logic programs. The main topic for future research is to extend this result to the broader class of extended generalized logic programs with two kinds of negations.

References

[1] J. Engelfriet Minimal Temporal Epistemic Logic. *Notre Dame Journal of Formal Logic*, 37(2):233–259, 1996.

[2] J. Engelfriet and J. Treur. A Temporal Model Theory for Default Logic. In M. Clarke, R. Kruse, S. Moral, editors, *Proceedings ECSQARU'93*, Lecture Notes in Computer Science 747, Springer-Verlag, 1993, pp. 91–96. Revised and extended version to appear as "An Interpretation of Default Logic in Minimal Temporal Epistemic Logic" in the *Journal of Logic, Language and Information*.

[3] J. Engelfriet and J. Treur. Temporal Theories of Reasoning. In C. Mac-Nish, D. Pearce, L.M. Pereira, editors, *Proceedings JELIA'94*, Lecture Notes in Artificial Intelligence **838**, Springer-Verlag, 1994, pp. 279–299; Also in: *Journal of Applied Non-Classical Logics*, 5(2):239–261, 1995.

[4] M. Gelfond and V. Lifschitz. The Stable Model Semantics for Logic Programming. In R.A. Kowalski and K.A. Bowen, editors, *Proc. of ICLP*, MIT Press, 1988, pp. 1070–1080.

[5] M. Gelfond and V. Lifschitz. Classical Negation in Logic Programs and Disjunctive Databases. *New Generation Computing*, 9:365–385, 1991.

[6] M. Gelfond, V. Lifschitz , H. Przymusinska , M. Truszczynski. Disjunctive Defaults. In *Proceedings 2nd KR*, 1991 , pp. 230–237.

[7] H. Herre and G. Wagner. Stable Models are Generated by a Stable Chain. *Journal of Logic Programming*, 30(2):165–177, 1997.

[8] T.C. Przymusinski. Stable Semantics for Disjunctive Programs. *New Generation Computing*, 9:401–424, 1991.

[9] T.C. Przymusinski. Super Logic Programs and Negation as Belief. In R. Dyckhoff, H. Herre, P. Schroeder-Heister, editors, *Proc. of the 5th Int. Workshop on Extensions of Logic Programming*, Lecture Notes in Artificial Intelligence 1050, Springer-Verlag, pp. 229–236.

[10] R. Reiter. A Logic for Default Reasoning. *Artificial Intelligence*, 13:81–132, 1980.

Comparative Metric Semantics for Commit in Or-Parallel Logic Programming

Eneia Todoran
Department of Computer Science, Technical University of Cluj-Napoca
26 Baritiu Street, 3400 Cluj-Napoca, Romania
e-mail: Eneia.Todoran@cs.utcluj.ro

Jerry den Hartog and Erik de Vink
Faculty of Mathematics and Computer Science, Vrije Universiteit
De Boelelaan 1081a, NL-1081 HV Amsterdam, the Netherlands
e-mail: {jerry,vink}@cs.vu.nl

Abstract

For the control flow kernel of or-parallel Prolog with commit an operational
and a denotational model are constructed and related using techniques from
metric semantics. By maintaining explicit scope information a compositional
handling of the commit for the denotational model is established. By application of an abstraction function, which deletes this extra information, the
operational semantics is recovered.

1 Introduction

In recent years substantial progress has been reported on or-parallel logic
programming systems, on successful experiments with extensive test sets
performed on it, as well as on and-parallel extensions of these systems. See,
e.g., [11, 13, 5, 10]. However, [7] discusses the lack of semantical consensus,
at least for the Gödel language, about what should be considered as acceptable implementations of pruning operators. In general, semantical methods,
in particular compositional ones, seem somewhat lacking behind in the understanding of concurrency in logic programming together with extra-logical
control flow operators. Only a few references are known to us, e.g. [2, 8]
to mention two of them. Paraphrasing the mantra of logic programming
one can argue that concerning the semantical analysis of concurrent logic
programming one has to deal with logic*control instead of with their sum.

   In this paper we report on a comparative semantics for the control flow
kernel of or-parallel logic programming with a commit operator. The comparison is made for a step-oriented operational semantics and a continuation-
style denotational one. The restriction to the control flow follows the 'logic

programming without logic' approach as advocated in [2]. It turns out that already in this relatively simple case intricate modeling tricks have to be applied, both for a succinct description (encoding of scope information) and for the justification of the denotational semantics (the technical aspect of using finitely non-empty and closed sets instead of non-empty compact ones). Taking all together one can not characterize this as 'a trivial exercise in semantics'. The present paper though is only a modest contribution to the enterprise of a complete compositional modeling of the class of concurrent logic programming languages with all meta-logical pruning operators that one would like to have to combine parallel systems and declarative program construction.

Starting point of our investigations are the metric techniques for comparative semantics as developed by De Bakker and co-workers (cf. [3, 4]). Main technical advantage of the usage of complete metric spaces over exploitation of complete partial orders is the existence of *unique* fixed points of contractions (Banach's Fixed Point Theorem) rather than *least* fixed points of continuous functions (Knaster-Tarski). Although the class of order-theoretical domains strictly subsumes that of metric ones, the latter provides sufficient structure for the modeling of concurrent logic programming.

Acknowledgments The work reported here was in part carried out while the first author visited Vrije Universiteit Amsterdam. We are indebted to Jaco de Bakker and his research group for their contribution to this. We are grateful to all four ILPS'97 referees for their honest opinion and their valuable comments on the earlier version of this paper.

2 Mathematical preliminaries

In this paper complete metric spaces are used as underlying mathematical structure for the semantical models. We assume known the definitions and basic facts of the following notions: complete metric space, compactness, non-expansive function and contractive function, standard metric on function spaces and products. The reader may inspect any standard textbook on metric topology or the monograph [4] for further details.

Main tool in metric semantics in general and, in particular, for the development of the operational and denotational semantics for or-parallel Prolog below, is the following classical result.

Theorem 2.1 *(Banach's Fixed Point Theorem) Let M be a complete metric space and $f: M \to M$ a contraction. Then f has a unique fixed point $\text{fix}(f)$.*

Below we will work with strings and certain sets of strings. For any alphabet $\mathcal{A}$ we let $\mathcal{A}_\delta^\infty = \mathcal{A}^* \cup \mathcal{A}^* \cdot \delta \cup \mathcal{A}^\omega$ be the collection of finite strings over $\mathcal{A}$, finite strings over $\mathcal{A}$ followed by δ and infinite strings over $\mathcal{A}$. The notation ϵ is employed to denote the empty string. We use $a \cdot x$ to denote the prefixing of a to the string x and, likewise, $a \cdot X$ for the set $\{\, a \cdot x \mid x \in X \,\}$.

Collections of strings come equipped with the Baire-distance. The Baire-distance between two strings x and y is governed by the length of their common prefix, i.e.,

$$d(x,y) = 2^{-\sup\{n \mid x[n]=y[n]\}}$$

where $x[n]$, $y[n]$ denote the prefix of x, y of length n. As key property of the Baire-distance we have $d(a \cdot x, a \cdot y) = \frac{1}{2}d(x,y)$ for all strings x, y. We have that $\mathcal{A}_\delta^\infty$ is a complete metric space. In fact, the metric on this collections is an *ultra-metric*, i.e. it satisfies the strong triangle inequality $d(x,z) \leq \max\{ d(x,y), d(y,z) \}$. This property, typical for the structures modeling computational behaviors, will be needed later.

The notation $\mathcal{P}_{nco}(M)$ denotes the hyperspace of all non-empty compact subsets of a metric space M. The distance on M induces a metric on $\mathcal{P}_{nco}(M)$, the so-called Hausdorff-distance as follows:

$$d(X,Y) \leq \varepsilon \iff$$
$$\forall x \in X \exists y \in Y : d(x,y) \leq \varepsilon \wedge \forall y \in Y \exists x \in X : d(y,x) \leq \varepsilon,$$

for $\varepsilon \geq 0$ and $X, Y \in \mathcal{P}_{nco}(M)$. It holds that completeness of M implies completeness of $\mathcal{P}_{nco}(M)$. If $f : M_1 \to M_2$ is a non-expansive function, then the 'lifting' $F : \mathcal{P}_{nco}(M_1) \to \mathcal{P}_{nco}(M_2)$ of the function f is defined as $F(X) = \{ f(x) \mid x \in X \}$. It holds that F is well-defined, i.e. delivers non-empty and compact sets, and that F is also non-expansive. This result is called the Lifting Lemma.

Below we will employ the space $\mathcal{P}_{nco}(Act_\delta^\infty)$. For *nonempty* $X, Y \subseteq Act_\delta^\infty$ we have $d(a \cdot X, a \cdot Y) = \frac{1}{2}d(X,Y)$.

3 The language $\mathcal{L}$

In this section the abstract programming language $\mathcal{L}$ is introduced and its computational intuition is discussed. The language $\mathcal{L}$ captures the control flow of or-parallel Prolog: it provides sequential composition, both a sequential and a parallel don't know nondeterministic choice and a commit operator.

Definition 3.1 *Fix a set Act of actions and a set PVar of procedure variables, having typical elements a and x, respectively. Distinguish a special symbol* fail. *The class Stat of statements, ranged over by s, is given by the BNF*

$$s ::= a \mid \text{fail} \mid x \mid s \cdot s \mid s + s \mid s \oplus s \mid s{:}s.$$

The class Decl of declarations, with meta-variable D, is given by Decl $=$ PVar $\to$ Stat and, finally, the language $\mathcal{L}$ is defined by $\mathcal{L} = $ Decl $\times$ Stat.

Actions are schematic versions of unifications. Together with procedure calls the two notions represent the usual concept of a goal. Failure is modeled in the abstract setting by the token fail. The operator '$\cdot$' is sequential conjunction, '$+$' sequential disjunction, '$\oplus$' parallel disjunction and '$:$' the pruning operator of commitment.

A program (D, s) of $\mathcal{L}$ consists of a declaration part D and a program body s. The declaration, conceptually a function, associates to each procedure variable a procedure body. For technical reasons we assume to have guarded recursion. However, in the setting of logic programming this is always fulfilled.

Next we discuss two problems that are encountered in the modeling of $\mathcal{L}$. The first one is caused by the presence of the don't know nondeterminism, which means that, in general, a goal $x = s_1 + s_2$ or $x = s_1 \oplus s_2$ can not be evaluated locally if it is followed by another goal x'. Rather, in executing $x \cdot x'$ first we must expand x according to its declaration and then replicate x' for each alternative of x as suggested by the following sequence of rewriting steps:

$$x \cdot x' \rightsquigarrow (s_1 + s_2) \cdot x' \rightsquigarrow (s_1 \cdot x' + s_2 \cdot x').$$

The second problem we face is how to formalize the meaning of *commit*. Intuitively, this primitive should make the current procedure deterministic, by removing the nondeterminism collected since the beginning of its execution. In this section we only explain our solution to this problem informally.

In order to define the precise scope of each commit we use a tag set *Tag*. A tag θ, σ, ρ is a non-empty sequence consisting of the natural numbers 1 and 2. Defining '$\preccurlyeq$' by $\theta \preccurlyeq \sigma$ if θ is a prefix of σ gives a partial order on tags.

The partial order $\preccurlyeq$ on *Tag* can be represented as a tree as is done in the following picture. Each node in the tree is larger then its predecessors, smaller than its successors and incomparable to nodes in other branches of the tree.

In the example above $\theta \leq \theta 1 \leq \theta 12$ and $\theta 1$ is not comparable with $\theta 2$ (i.e. neither $\theta 1 \leq \theta 2$ nor $\theta 2 \leq \theta 1$).

We will use the tags to identify the dynamic context of each recursive procedure call. Consider, for example, the following $\mathcal{L}$-programs $(D, x), (D, y)$ where x and y are the initial goals and the declaration D is given by

$$\begin{array}{llll}
D(x) & = & (a_1 \cdot x_1) : a_2 + a_3 & \qquad D(y) & = & (a_1 \cdot y_1) \cdot y_2 + a_2 \\
D(x_1) & = & b_1 + b_2 & \qquad D(y_1) & = & b_1 + b_2 \\
& & & \qquad D(y_2) & = & c_1 : c_2
\end{array}$$

In the example above we have implicitly used that $\cdot$ and $:$ bind stronger than $+$, i.e. $s_1 \cdot s_2 + s_3 = (s_1 \cdot s_2) + s_3$. Given tags ρ for x and σ for y we label $D(x), D(y)$ as follows:

$$\begin{array}{lll}
D(x^\rho) & = & (a_1 \cdot x_1^{\rho 112}) :_\rho a_2 +_\rho a_3 \\
D(y^\sigma) & = & (a_1 \cdot y_1^{\sigma 112}) \cdot y_2^{\sigma 12} +_\sigma a_2
\end{array}$$

The commit and choice operators get the same tag as the procedure in which they occur. For each recursive call in the procedure a new labels ($\rho 1$, $\rho 2$, $\rho 11$, etc.) is created such that each recursive call is receives a label larger than the label of the current procedure and incomparable with the labels of other recursive calls. This is achieved by adding a 1 or a 2 to the label depending on whether the recursive call is on the left or the right of the operator. For example the label of x_1 above is constructed as follows: First a 1 is added to ρ since x_1 is on the right of the '$+_\rho$'. Next a 1 is added since x_1 is on the right of '$:_\rho$'. Finally a 2 is added since x_1 is on the left of '$\cdot$'.

The operator '$:_\rho$' removes all the other alternatives of the choice operators '$+$' and '$\oplus$' with a tag having ρ as a prefix. This means that the commit '$:_\rho$' will exactly remove all non-deterministic alternatives created in this procedure (arguments of an operators labeled with ρ) or sub-procedures (arguments of operators labeled with a label greater then ρ). The alternatives created by other procedures will not be affected since they will have a label that is incomparable with ρ.

Below we present (possible) execution traces of the above programs. The notations are as yet informal. $s \xrightarrow{a} s'$ means that in 'state' s we can make an a-step and then continue execution in state s'. The notation $s \rightsquigarrow s'$ indicates that s is prepared for further execution by rewriting it to s'.

$$\begin{array}{ll}
x^\rho \rightsquigarrow (a_1 \cdot x_1^{\rho 112}) :_\rho a_2 +_\rho a_3 & \qquad y^\sigma \rightsquigarrow (a_1 \cdot y_1^{\sigma 112}) \cdot y_2^{\sigma 12} +_\sigma a_2 \\[4pt]
\xrightarrow{a_1} x_1^{\rho 112} :_\rho a_2 +_\rho a_3 & \qquad \xrightarrow{a_1} y_1^{\sigma 112} \cdot y_2^{\sigma 12} +_\sigma a_2 \\[4pt]
\rightsquigarrow (b_1 +_{\rho 112} b_2) :_\rho a_2 +_\rho a_3 & \qquad \rightsquigarrow (b_1 +_{\sigma 112} b_2) \cdot y_2^{\sigma 12} +_\sigma a_2 \\[4pt]
\rightsquigarrow (b_1 :_\rho a_2 +_{\rho 112} b_2 :_\rho a_2) +_\rho a_3 & \qquad \rightsquigarrow (b_1 \cdot y_2^{\sigma 12} +_{\sigma 112} b_2 \cdot y_2^{\sigma 12}) +_\sigma a_2 \\[4pt]
\xrightarrow{b_1[\rho]} a_2 & \qquad \xrightarrow{b_1} (y_2^{\sigma 12} +_{\sigma 112} b_2 \cdot y_2^{\sigma 12}) +_\sigma a_2 \\[4pt]
& \qquad \rightsquigarrow (c_1 :_{\sigma 12} c_2 +_{\sigma 112} b_2 \cdot y_2^{\sigma 12}) +_\sigma a_2 \\[4pt]
& \qquad \xrightarrow{c_1[\sigma 12]} (c_2 +_{\sigma 112} b_2 \cdot y_2^{\sigma 12}) +_\sigma a_2
\end{array}$$

The first four steps are similar in both cases. The first step is expanding a procedure according to its definition. The second step is taking an action. The third step is again expanding a procedure and the fourth step is replication for each alternative as explained above.

The next step for x is the action b_1 after which we must commit to the current alternative. This is denoted by $b_1[\rho]$. As described before the alternatives that have to be removed are those with labels which have prefix ρ. This means that both other alternatives are removed since the labels of the operators are $\rho 112$ and ρ.

For y the next steps are b_1 and then again expanding a procedure. The final step given is $c_1[\sigma 12]$. In this case no alternative is removed since the neither $\sigma 112$ nor σ has $\sigma 12$ as a prefix.

4 Operational semantics

In this section the computational intuition behind the examples discussed above is formally described using a labeled transition system. From the transition system an operational semantics is derived in the standard way. Main technicality concerns the encoding of the scope of the commit operator.

We define the set set $\mathit{Tag'} = \mathit{Tag} \cup \{\infty\}$. The special symbol ∞ will be used to label actions that do not commit. Note that (since $\infty \notin \mathit{Tag}$) we have $\neg(\infty \preccurlyeq \rho)$ for any $\rho \in \mathit{Tag}$. ϱ will range over $\mathit{Tag'}$.

Definition 4.1 *The collection Res of (syntactic) resumptions with typical element r, and the collection Conf of configurations, ranged over by t, are given as follows:*

$$r ::= \mathrm{E} \mid \langle s, \theta, \sigma \rangle :_\varrho r \quad and \quad t ::= r \mid t_1 +_\rho t_2 \mid t_1 \oplus_\rho t_2 \,.$$

The collection of tagged actions, with meta-variable α, is simply $\mathit{Act} \times \mathit{Tag'}$. We write $a[\varrho]$ for a pair (a, ϱ) in $\mathit{Act} \times \mathit{Tag'}$ and put $\mathrm{tag}(a[\varrho]) = \varrho$.

The special symbol E denotes proper termination. Generally, resumptions are sequences of triples of the form $\langle s, \theta, \sigma \rangle$. The basic idea is that $\langle s, \theta, \sigma \rangle :_\varrho r$ starts its computation with executing $\langle s, \theta, \sigma \rangle$. After having finished this it continues the computation with that of r. A triple $\langle s, \theta, \sigma \rangle$ consists of a statement $s \in \mathit{Stat}$ and two tags $\theta, \sigma \in \mathit{Tag}$. In the definition of the transition system below we will use θ to identify the context of the current procedure, and σ to generate fresh tags for each recursive procedure call.

The token '$:_\rho$' is used to model a commit with scope ρ. If an action is executed it complies to the scope information and results, in case ρ is the current context, in a tagged action $a[\rho]$. The tag on the action can then be employed to kill possible other alternatives, thus having a net effect of a commitment. The token '$:_\infty$' is used to model the and ('$\cdot$') operator. Actions labeled with ∞ take the place of the unlabeled actions used in the previous section. Configurations are either simple resumptions or composite structures defined by means of the binary operator symbols '$+_\rho$' and '$\oplus_\rho$' that also incorporate some appropriate scoping information.

The computation steps for $\mathcal{L}$ are given by a transition system, i.e. a relation defined by axioms and rules, on $\mathit{Conf} \times \mathit{Act} \times \mathit{Tag'} \times \mathit{Conf}$. For clarity of presentation we will suppress the global declaration part of a program by assuming some fixed declaration D (instead of working with pairs of declarations and configurations).

Definition 4.2 *The transition system for $\mathcal{L}$ is given by the following axiom and rules:*

- $$\langle a, \theta, \sigma \rangle :_\varrho r \xrightarrow{a[\varrho]} r \qquad\qquad\qquad (Act)$$

- $$\frac{\langle D(x), \sigma, \sigma \rangle :_\varrho r \xrightarrow{\alpha} t}{\langle x, \theta, \sigma \rangle :_\varrho r \xrightarrow{\alpha} t} \qquad\qquad\qquad (Rec)$$

- $$\frac{\langle s_1, \theta, \sigma 1 \rangle :_\infty (\langle s_2, \theta, \sigma 2 \rangle :_\varrho r) \xrightarrow{\alpha} t}{\langle s_1 \cdot s_2, \theta, \sigma \rangle :_\varrho r \xrightarrow{\alpha} t} \qquad\qquad (And)$$

- $$\frac{(\langle s_1, \theta, \sigma 1 \rangle :_\varrho r) \, \mathsf{op}_\theta \, (\langle s_2, \theta, \sigma 2 \rangle :_\varrho r) \xrightarrow{\alpha} t}{\langle s_1 \, \mathsf{op} \, s_2, \theta, \sigma \rangle :_\varrho r \xrightarrow{\alpha} t} \quad \mathsf{op} \in \{+, \oplus\} \qquad (Op)$$

- $$\frac{\langle s_1, \theta, \sigma 1 \rangle :_\theta (\langle s_2, \theta, \sigma 2 \rangle :_\varrho r) \xrightarrow{\alpha} t}{\langle s_1 : s_2, \theta, \sigma \rangle :_\varrho r \xrightarrow{\alpha} t} \qquad\qquad (Commit)$$

- $$\frac{t_1 \xrightarrow{\alpha} t_1'}{t_1 +_\rho t_2 \xrightarrow{\alpha} t_1'} \quad \text{if } tag(\alpha) \preccurlyeq \rho \qquad\qquad (SeqOr\ 1)$$

- $$\frac{t_1 \xrightarrow{\alpha} t_1'}{t_1 +_\rho t_2 \xrightarrow{\alpha} t_1' +_\rho t_2} \quad \text{if } \neg(tag(\alpha) \preccurlyeq \rho) \qquad (SeqOr\ 2)$$

- $$\frac{t_1 \not\rightarrow \quad t_2 \xrightarrow{\alpha} t_2'}{t_1 +_\rho t_2 \xrightarrow{\alpha} t_2'} \qquad\qquad\qquad (SeqOr\ 3)$$

- $$\frac{t_1 \xrightarrow{\alpha} t_1'}{t_1 \oplus_\rho t_2 \xrightarrow{\alpha} t_1'} \quad \text{if } tag(\alpha) \preccurlyeq \rho \qquad\qquad (ParOr\ 1)$$

- $$\frac{t_1 \xrightarrow{\alpha} t_1'}{t_1 \oplus_\rho t_2 \xrightarrow{\alpha} t_1' \oplus_\rho t_2} \quad \text{if } \neg(tag(\alpha) \preccurlyeq \rho) \qquad (ParOr\ 2)$$

- $$\frac{t_1 \xrightarrow{\alpha} t_1' \quad t_2 \not\rightarrow}{t_1 \oplus_\rho t_2 \xrightarrow{\alpha} t_1'} \qquad\qquad\qquad (ParOr\ 3)$$

three symmetric rules $\qquad\qquad\qquad\qquad$ *(ParOr 4,5,6)*

In the axiom (Act), the action a is augmented with the scope information of the commit, in this case with ϱ. This way the action turns into a committing action. Note that there is no axiom or rule available for fail. The rule (Rec) is basically the usual copy rule which embodies handling of recursion by body replacement. In addition, the context information is updated, the tag σ replaces the tag θ. In the rules (And), (Op) and (Commit) new tags $\sigma1$ and $\sigma2$ are generated, so that the recursive calls in s_1 and s_2 will be executed in different contexts. Each commit is adorned with a tag that identifies the context of the current goal. In the (Op)-rule the resumption r is replicated for each alternative of the leftmost goal.

The notation $t_1 \not\rightarrow$ in the sets of rules (SeqOr) and (ParOr) means that t_1 has no transitions, i.e. there is no (tagged) action α and no configuration t_1' such that $t_1 \xrightarrow{\alpha} t_1'$. In case t_1 or t_2 has no transitions it is dropped from the configuration providing other options are available. The rules (SeqOr 1) and (ParOr 1,4) capture, in fact, the behavior of the commit. If one of the alternatives successfully performs a tagged action $a[\theta]$ then the computation commits to this choice. Therefore other possibilities will be discarded. These are exactly generated by the subconfigurations in the scope of '$+_\rho$' and '$\oplus_\rho$' for which $\theta \preccurlyeq \rho$. In case ρ is independent from θ, i.e. $\neg(\theta \preccurlyeq \rho)$, the execution of the action induces no commitment for the or-parallelism at level ρ and the alternative remains available. Since ∞ is incomparable with any tag ρ an action with label ∞ will not commit. Note that, as is to be expected, the (SeqOr)-rules are asymmetric in t_1 and t_2. Transitions possible for t_2 only get propagated to $t_1 +_\rho t_2$ provided t_1 itself fails, i.e. has no transitions.

As an aside, it could in principle be the case that the transition system as given above would not be well-defined, due to the presence of so-called negative premises, viz. the conditions of the format $t \not\rightarrow$. However, by stratification techniques borrowed from the model-theoretic semantics for logic programming with negation, one can assure that the underlying set operator —corresponding to the T-operator— is monotone and that therefore a smallest subset satisfying the axiom and rules, i.e. a least fixed point, exists. See, e.g., [6].

One can define a so-called complexity measure for configurations such that the premises of the rules are less complex than their conclusions. (See, e.g., [2] or [4] for more details.) This implies strong normalization of the transition system as a deductive theory. More importantly though, it provides us with an induction principle that we refer to as induction on complexity measure. A straightforward application of this principle amounts to the next result. (In the comparison of the operational and denotational semantics the principle will be used again.)

Lemma 4.3 *The transition relation '$\longrightarrow$', as given in Definition 4.1, is finitely branching, i.e. it holds that $\{(\alpha, t') \mid t \xrightarrow{\alpha} t'\}$ is a finite set, for all configurations $t \in Conf$.*

The operational semantics $\mathcal{O}[\![\cdot]\!]$ for $\mathcal{L}$ simply collects all the finite and infinite completed computations for a configuration. For convenience we employ an auxiliary mapping $\mathcal{O}$. The model $\mathcal{O}[\![\cdot]\!]$ is obtained from this $\mathcal{O}$ by initializing the proper tags and lifting a statement to a resumption.

Definition 4.4 *The semantical mapping $\mathcal{O}\colon Conf \to \mathcal{P}(Act_\delta^\infty)$ is given by $\mathcal{O}(\mathrm{E}) = \{\epsilon\}$ and for $t \neq \mathrm{E}$*

$$\mathcal{O}(t) = \begin{cases} \{\delta\} & \text{if } t \not\to \\ \bigcup\{ a \cdot \mathcal{O}(t') \mid \exists \varrho \colon t \xrightarrow{a[\varrho]} t' \} & \text{otherwise.} \end{cases}$$

The operational semantics $\mathcal{O}[\![\cdot]\!]\colon \mathcal{L} \to \mathcal{P}(Act_\delta^\infty)$ is defined as

$$\mathcal{O}[\![s]\!] = \mathcal{O}(\langle s, 1, 1\rangle :_\infty \mathrm{E}).$$

Note that the above definition is reflexive. A standard way in metric semantics to overcome this is by characterization of the object to be defined as the fixed point of a suitable contraction on a complete metric space using Banach's theorem. For $\mathcal{O}$ above we have the following fixed point description.

Theorem 4.5 *Let $Sem = Conf \to \mathcal{P}_{nco}(Act_\delta^\infty)$. Define the transformation $\Phi\colon Sem \to Sem$ by $\Phi(S)(\mathrm{E}) = \{\epsilon\}$ and for $t \neq \mathrm{E}$*

$$\Phi(S)(t) = \begin{cases} \{\delta\} & \text{if } t \not\to \\ \bigcup\{ a \cdot S(t') \mid \exists \varrho \colon t \xrightarrow{a[\varrho]} t' \} & \text{otherwise,} \end{cases}$$

for all $S \in Sem$. Then it holds that Φ is a contraction and $\mathcal{O} = \mathrm{fix}(\Phi)$.

5 Denotational semantics

The next step is the development of the denotational semantics for $\mathcal{L}$. For a correct handling of the commit the semantical operator corresponding to sequential and parallel disjunction are parameterized with scope information. Justification of the various definitions can be obtained using appropriate fixed point characterizations.

Definition 5.1 *Let the complete metric spaces $\mathbb{P}$ and $\mathbb{Q}$ be given by $\mathbb{P} = \mathcal{P}_{nco}(\mathbb{Q})$ and $\mathbb{Q} = (Act \times Tag')_\delta^\infty$. We use p and q to range over $\mathbb{P}$ and $\mathbb{Q}$, respectively. Define, for $\rho \in Tag$, the semantical operator $+_\rho \colon \mathbb{P} \times \mathbb{P} \to \mathbb{P}$ by*

$$p +_\rho p' = \{ q +_\rho' q' \mid q \in p, q' \in p' \}$$

where '$+_\rho'$' is given as $\epsilon +_\rho' q' = q'$, $\delta +_\rho' q' = q'$, $(\alpha \cdot q) +_\rho' q' = \alpha \cdot q$ if $tag(\alpha) \preccurlyeq \rho$, and $(\alpha \cdot q) +_\rho' q' = \alpha \cdot (q +_\rho' q')$ otherwise. The semantical operator $\oplus_\rho \colon \mathbb{P} \times \mathbb{P} \to \mathbb{P}$, for $\rho \in Tag$, is given by

$$p \oplus_\rho p' = (p +_\rho p') \cup (p' +_\rho p).$$

The above definitions can be justified using so-called higher-order operations and by application of the Lifting Lemma. One can additionally show that the resulting fixed point, i.e. the operators $+_\rho$ and $\oplus_\rho$ on $\mathbb{P}$, are non-expansive. A property that we will need for the justification of the definition of the denotational semantics. Note that we do not define semantical counterparts of sequential conjunction and the commit itself. These constructions will be modeled using the tag-information explicitly.

The compositional model that we propose for $\mathcal{L}$ is a continuation semantics. Continuations $\gamma \in Cont$, which in fact coincide with the processes $p \in \mathbb{P}$, represent the further behavior of a process after completion of the part pertaining to the execution of the particular statement. Scope information θ, σ, ρ concerning the commit, can be easily propagated as they are arguments of the semantical mapping.

Definition 5.2 *Let Cont, ranged over by γ, be the collection of continuations given by $Cont = \mathbb{P}$. Let Tags be short for $Tag \times Tag \times Tag'$. The semantical mapping $\mathcal{D} \colon Stat \to Cont \to Tags \to \mathbb{P}$ is given by*

$$\mathcal{D}(a)(\gamma) = \lambda(\theta, \sigma, \varrho). \, a[\varrho] \cdot \gamma$$
$$\mathcal{D}(\mathsf{fail})(\gamma) = \lambda(\theta, \sigma, \varrho). \, \{\delta\}$$
$$\mathcal{D}(x)(\gamma) = \lambda(\theta, \sigma, \varrho). \, \mathcal{D}(D(x))(\gamma)(\sigma)(\sigma)(\varrho)$$
$$\mathcal{D}(s_1 \cdot s_2)(\gamma) = \lambda(\theta, \sigma, \varrho). \, \mathcal{D}(s_1)(\mathcal{D}(s_2)(\gamma)(\theta, \sigma 2, \varrho))(\theta, \sigma 1, \infty)$$
$$\mathcal{D}(s_1 + s_2)(\gamma) = \lambda(\theta, \sigma, \varrho). \, (\mathcal{D}(s_1)(\gamma)(\theta, \sigma 1, \varrho)) +_\theta (\mathcal{D}(s_1)(\gamma)(\theta, \sigma 2, \varrho))$$
$$\mathcal{D}(s_1 \oplus s_2)(\gamma) = \lambda(\theta, \sigma, \varrho). \, (\mathcal{D}(s_1)(\gamma)(\theta, \sigma 1, \varrho)) \oplus_\theta (\mathcal{D}(s_1)(\gamma)(\theta, \sigma 2, \varrho))$$
$$\mathcal{D}(s_1 : s_2)(\gamma) = \lambda(\theta, \sigma, \varrho). \, \mathcal{D}(s_1)(\mathcal{D}(s_2)(\gamma)(\theta, \sigma 2, \varrho))(\theta, \sigma 1, \theta).$$

The denotational semantics $\mathcal{D}[\![\cdot]\!] \colon \mathcal{L} \to \mathbb{P}$ is given by

$$\mathcal{D}[\![s]\!] \;=\; \mathcal{D}(s)(\{\epsilon\})(1, 1, \infty).$$

The meaning of an action a is the action itself together with the scoping information of a possible commitment with respect to this action. Since the model is compositional we have to take the possibility of evaluation of a in a context of a sequential or parallel disjunction into account. After $a[\varrho]$ the process continues with the behavior encoded in the continuation γ. Syntactic failure results in semantic failure independent of the continuation. Recursion is here also modeled by body replacement. Note that the right-hand side is syntactically not simpler than the left-hand side. An additional argument based on a suitable complexity measure can handle this.

The sequential conjunction amounts in the update of the continuation, since the computation for the second component has to be performed after the one for the first component has finished. The clause for the commit is similar. The two definitions differ in the way the scoping information is dealt with. For the sequential case the ρ set to ∞, since a commitment made for s_1 will have no effect on the search space for s_2, whereas it does for the case of a commit. The sequential and parallel disjunction are treated by the semantical operators given in definition 5.1 above.

Well-definedness of the function $\mathcal{D}$ can be obtained by characterizing $\mathcal{D}$ as a fixed point of a higher-order transformation on a suitable subspace of $Stat \rightarrow Cont \rightarrow Tags \rightarrow \mathbb{P}$. In order to show contractivity of the transformation one uses non-expansiveness of the semantical operators, contractivity of the transformation in the continuation and ultra-metricity of the distance of $\mathbb{P}$. (See for a similar argument, e.g., [1, 4].)

6 Relating $\mathcal{O}$ and $\mathcal{D}$

Having defined both an operational and a denotational semantics the question about there relationship will be addressed in this section. A compositional treatment forced us to deal with explicit scope information concerning the commit for the denotational semantics. In the step-oriented operational model there seems no point in delivering this tags to the meaning of a program. We will argue that the operational and denotational semantics coincide once the superfluous scope information has been removed from the latter. The proof of this takes advantage of the metric machinery, in particular the uniqueness of fixed point, underlying the semantical modeling of the paper.

First of all we will introduce an operational semantical mapping $\mathcal{O}^*$ that, in contrast to $\mathcal{O}$, yields outcomes in $\mathcal{P}_{nco}((Act \times Tag')^\infty_\delta)$, as is the case for the denotational semantics. The function $\mathcal{O}^*$ acts on configurations and is given as the fixed point of a transformation Φ^*. Also an abstraction function abs is given which deletes the tags from strings over $Act \times Tag$ resulting in strings over Act only.

On the one hand, it is shown that $\mathcal{O} = abs \circ \mathcal{O}^*$ employing the fixed point characterization of $\mathcal{O}$ of Section 4. On the other hand, the denotational semantics can be massaged to a mapping $\mathcal{D}^*$ on configurations (as is the case for $\mathcal{O}^*$). It is claimed that $\mathcal{D}^*$ is a fixed point of Φ^*, which, by definition, equals $\mathcal{O}^*$. So $\mathcal{O}^* = \mathcal{D}^*$. Combining the two result yields $\mathcal{O}[\![\cdot]\!] = abs \circ \mathcal{D}[\![\cdot]\!]$ for programs of $\mathcal{L}$. This is exactly the contents of Theorem 6.4.

Definition 6.1 *Put* $Sem = Conf \rightarrow \mathcal{P}_{nco}((Act \times Tag')^\infty_\delta)$. *Define* $\Phi^*: Sem \rightarrow Sem$ *by* $\Phi^*(S)(\mathrm{E}) = \{\epsilon\}$ *and*

$$\Phi^*(S)(t) = \left\{ \begin{array}{ll} \{\delta\} & \text{if } t \not\rightarrow \\ \bigcup \{ \alpha \cdot S(t') \mid t \xrightarrow{\alpha} t' \} & \text{otherwise,} \end{array} \right.$$

for all $S \in Sem$. *Let* $\mathcal{O}^* = fix(\Phi^*)$.

The abstraction function $abs: \mathcal{P}_{nco}((Act \times Tag')^\infty_\delta) \rightarrow \mathcal{P}_{nco}(Act^\infty_\delta)$ *is given by* $abs(p) = \{ abs'(q) \mid q \in p \}$ *where* $abs'(q)$ *is given by* $abs'(\epsilon) = \epsilon$, $abs'(\delta) = \delta$, *and* $abs'(a[\varrho] \cdot q) = a \cdot abs'(q)$.

The semantical mapping $\mathcal{D}^*: Conf \rightarrow \mathcal{P}_{nco}((Act \times Tag')^\infty_\delta)$ *is defined as*

$$\begin{aligned} \mathcal{D}^*(\mathrm{E}) &= \{\epsilon\} \\ \mathcal{D}^*(\langle s, \theta, \sigma \rangle :_\varrho r) &= \mathcal{D}(s)(\mathcal{D}^*(r))(\theta, \sigma, \varrho) \\ \mathcal{D}^*(t_1 \, op_\theta \, t_2) &= \mathcal{D}^*(t_1) \, op_\theta \, \mathcal{D}^*(t_2) \quad op \in \{+, \oplus\}. \end{aligned}$$

A technical complication arises with the justification of the above definition for the case of the abstraction function. To the other cases the standard techniques discussed earlier apply straightforwardly. The point concerning abs is that there is, in general, no guarantee that a compact sets of strings over $Act \times Tag$ remains compact when removing the tags, since the extra pieces of information separate tagged actions that are identified in Act. However, the methods available for finitary non-empty and closed sets can be used here instead (cf. [12, 4]).

The first building block for the comparison of $\mathcal{O}$ and $\mathcal{D}$ is the following.

Lemma 6.2 $\mathcal{O} = abs \circ \mathcal{O}^*$.

The lemma follows from the observation that the function $abs \circ \mathcal{O}^*$ is a fixed point of the transformation Φ of Theorem 4.5. Loosely speaking, the definition of Φ and Φ^* are the same modulo abstraction and the function abs behaves properly concerning set union. As a consequence of Theorem 4.5 we then have that $abs \circ \mathcal{O}^*$ coincides with $\mathcal{O}$ since the latter is the *unique* fixed point of the transformation Φ.

The second ingredient for establishing a relationship between $\mathcal{O}$ and $\mathcal{D}$ focuses on the equality of $\mathcal{O}^*$ and $\mathcal{D}^*$. We will sketch only one typical case in the proof of $\Phi^*(\mathcal{D}^*) = \mathcal{D}^*$ which, in general, goes by induction on a suitable complexity measure on configurations (as discussed also in Section 4). From the lemma it follows that $\mathcal{O}^* = \mathcal{D}^*$, again by uniqueness of fixed points.

Lemma 6.3 $\Phi^*(\mathcal{D}^*) = \mathcal{D}^*$.

Proof One shows, by induction on the complexity of a configuration, $\Phi^*(\mathcal{D}^*)(t) = \mathcal{D}^*(t)$. We only provide the case for $t \equiv t_1 +_\rho t_2$ where t_1 has one or more transitions:

$$\Phi^*(\mathcal{D}^*)(t_1 +_\rho t_2)$$

$= [\text{inspection transition system}]$

$$\bigcup\{\,\mathcal{D}^*(t_1') \mid t_1 \xrightarrow{\alpha} t_1' \wedge tag(\alpha) \preccurlyeq \rho\,\} \cup$$
$$\bigcup\{\,\mathcal{D}^*(t_1' +_\rho t_2) \mid t_1 \xrightarrow{\alpha} t_1' \wedge \neg(tag(\alpha) \preccurlyeq \rho)\,\}$$

$= [\text{property } \mathcal{D}^*]$

$$\bigcup\{\,\mathcal{D}^*(t_1') \mid t_1 \xrightarrow{\alpha} t_1' \wedge tag(\alpha) \preccurlyeq \rho\,\} \cup$$
$$(\bigcup\{\,\mathcal{D}^*(t_1') \mid t_1 \xrightarrow{\alpha} t_1' \wedge \neg(tag(\alpha) \preccurlyeq \rho)\,\} +_\rho \mathcal{D}^*(t_2))$$

$= [\text{definition } \Phi^*, \text{ not } t_1 \not\rightarrow]\ \Phi^*(\mathcal{D}^*)(t_1) +_\rho \mathcal{D}^*(t_2)$

$= [\text{induction hypothesis}]\ \mathcal{D}^*(t_1) +_\rho \mathcal{D}^*(t_2)$

$= [\text{definition } \mathcal{D}^*]\ \mathcal{D}^*(t_1 +_\rho t_2).$ $\qquad\qquad\square$

We are now in a position to prove the main result of this section.

Theorem 6.4 $\mathcal{O}[\![(D, s)]\!] = abs(\mathcal{D}[\![(D, s)]\!])$ *for all programs* $(D, s) \in \mathcal{L}$.

Proof Suppressing again the declaration part D we have

$$
\begin{aligned}
\mathcal{O}[\![s]\!] &= \text{[definition } \mathcal{O}[\![\cdot]\!]] \quad \mathcal{O}(\langle s, 1, 1, \rangle :_\infty \mathrm{E}) \\
&= \text{[by Lemma 6.2 and 6.3]} \quad abs(\mathcal{D}^*(\langle s, 1, 1 \rangle :_\infty \mathrm{E})) \\
&= \text{[definition of } \mathcal{D}^* \text{ and } \mathcal{D}] \quad abs(\mathcal{D}(s)(\{\epsilon\})(1, 1, \infty)) \\
&= \text{[definition } \mathcal{D}[\![\cdot]\!]] \quad abs(\mathcal{D}[\![s]\!]). \qquad \square
\end{aligned}
$$

Since we have hard-wired the scoping information into the denotational semantics —in particular concerning the semantical conjunction operators— we do not have a full-abstractness result for the compositional model. In fact, an easy example shows that two programs may behave the same in any context but are still being distinguished by the denotational semantics. It would be interesting to see how equality modulo scope encoding can be defined, and, subsequently, what relative full-abstractness result holds for the proposed models.

7 Concluding remarks

By using a suitable encoding of the scope information concerning the commit operator, an operational and a denotational semantics for or-parallel logic programming with commit can be constructed. The operational model is based on a transition system which captures the computational intuition; the denotational model takes compositionality as a starting point and resorts to fixed point arguments for its definition. In order to achieve compositionality for the denotational model scope information has to be maintained explicitly. By systematic use of Banach's fixed point theorem, as is available in the metric set-up of the paper, one proves a correctness result for the compositional model $\mathcal{D}$ relative to the transitional model $\mathcal{O}$ modulo a suitable abstraction function. The paper thus shows that the control flow of or-parallel Prolog with the meta-logical operation of commitment can be modeled using comparative metric semantics.

A question spawned of from the research reported here was triggered by the wish to incorporate independent and-parallelism into the models. The technical issue to be addressed concerns the combination, for the denotational semantics, of continuations and explicit parallelism. In current work of the third author with Franck van Breugel, in a setting of imperative-style distributed programming, a solution for this matter is studied. The result obtained there will help in paving the way for a compositional treatment of the control flow of and/or logic programming and associated pruning operators.

Logic programming carries its own promises and, consequently, its own focus in research interests. However, various proposals made in the context of logic programming go beyond the arbitrarily risen boarders of the field. E.g., Gregory's notion of 'wait_idle' given in [9] for speculative parallelism in Parlog may very well be interpreted for general concurrent programming. The distinguishing mixture of declarative and implementation oriented reasoning makes the concept 'in between' the programming and operating system level, as it abstracts away from the underlying machine architecture. At present analysis of such a notion seems out of reach of present-day compositional methods. The 'location' process algebras as advocated, e.g., by [14] go in part into this direction. It would be interesting to see if denotational methods, in particular the metric one, can be developed to capture this kind of constructs.

References

[1] P.H.M. America and J.W. de Bakker. Designing equivalent semantic models for process creation. *Theoretical Computer Science*, 60:109–176, 1988.

[2] J.W. de Bakker. Comparative semantics for flow of control in logic programming without logic. *Information and Computation*, 94:123–179, 1991.

[3] J.W. de Bakker and J.J.M.M. Rutten, editors. *Ten Years of Concurrency Semantics, selected papers of the Amsterdam Concurrency Group*. World Scientific, 1992.

[4] J.W. de Bakker and E.P. de Vink. *Control Flow Semantics*. Foundations of Computing Series. The MIT Press, 1996.

[5] A. Beaumont and D.H.D. Warren. Scheduling speculative work in or-parallel Prolog systems. In *Proc. ICLP'93*, pages 135–149. The MIT Press, 1993.

[6] R.N. Bol and J.F. Groote. The meaning of negative premises in transition system specifications. In *Proc. ICALP'91*, pages 481–494. LNCS 510, 1991.

[7] A. Brogi and C. Guarino. Pruning the search space of logic programs. In *Proc. ELP'96*, pages 35–49. LNAI 1050, 1996.

[8] A. Eliëns. *DLP: A Language for Distributed Logic Programming: Design, Semantics and Implementation*. Wiley, 1992.

[9] S. Gregory. Experiments with speculative parallelism in Parlog. In *Proc. ILPS'93*, pages 370–387. The MIT Press, 1993.

[10] G. Gupta and V. Santos Costa. Cuts and side-effects in and-or parallel Prolog. *Journal of Logic Programming*, 27:45–71, 1996.

[11] B. Hausman. *Pruning and Speculative Work in Or-Parallel Prolog*. PhD thesis, Royal Institute of Technology, Stockholm, 1990.

[12] E. Horita. A fully abstract model for a nonuniform concurrent language with parametrization and locality. In *Semantics: Foundations and Applications*, pages 288–317. LNCS 666, 1993.

[13] R. Karlsson. *A Higher Performance Or-Parallel Prolog System*. PhD thesis, Royal Institute of Technology, Stockholm, 1992.

[14] J. Riely and M. Hennessy. Distributed processes and location failures. In *Proc. ICALP'97*, pages 471–482 LNCS 1256, 1997.

The SBA: Exploiting Orthogonality in AND−OR Parallel Systems

Manuel E. Correia, Fernando Silva, Vítor Santos Costa
DCC-FC & LIACC, Universidade do Porto,
R. do Campo Alegre 823, 4150 Porto, Portugal
{mcc,fds,vsc}@ncc.up.pt

Abstract

One of the advantages of logic programming is the fact that it offers many sources of *implicit* parallelism, such as and-parallelism and or-parallelism. Recently, research has been concentrated on integrating the different forms of parallelism into a single combined system. In this work we concentrate on the problem of integrating or-parallelism and independent and-parallelism for parallel Prolog systems. We contend that previous data structures require *pure recomputation* and therefore do not allow for orthogonality between and-parallelism and or-parallelism. In contrast, we submit that a simpler solution, *the sparse binding array*, does guarantee this goal, and explain in detail how independent and-parallelism and or-parallelism can thus be efficiently combined.

1 Introduction

One of the advantages of logic programming is the fact that it offers many sources of *implicit* parallelism. The two major forms of implicit parallelism are and-parallelism and or-parallelism. *Or-parallelism* has been exploited successfully in systems such as Aurora [3] and Muse [1]. *And-parallelism* can be classified as *independent*, as exploited in &-Prolog [10], &-ACE [8], or *dependent*, as exploited in the committed-choice languages, in Andorra-I [14] or the DDAS [15]. More recently, research has been concentrated on integrating the different forms of parallelism into a single combined system. In this work we concentrate on the problem of integrating or- and independent and-parallelism.

Or-parallelism is arguably one of the most successful forms of parallelism available. It can obtain very good speedups for a large range of applications, such as applications that require search. It is therefore one of the main components to include in combined systems. Designers of or-parallel systems must address two main problems, scheduling and variable binding representation. As we shall see later, the scheduling problem can be addressed rather orthogonally to the other forms of parallelism. In contrast, binding representation affects all forms of parallelism.

The binding representation problem arises because the same variable may have several different bindings in different or-branches. A number of approaches have been presented to tackle the problem. Two successful ones are environment copying, as used in Muse [1], and binding arrays, as used in Aurora [3]. In the copying approach, each worker maintains its own copy of the path in the search tree it is exploring. Whenever work needs to be shared, the worker that is moving down the tree copies the stacks from the worker that is giving the work. In this approach, data sharing between workers only happens through an auxiliary data structure associated with choice-points.

In contrast, in the binding array approach work stacks are shared. To obtain efficient access, each worker maintains a private data structure, the binding array, where it stores its conditional bindings. To allow for quick access to the binding of a variable the binding array is implemented as an array, indexed by the number of variables that have been created in the current branch. This number is stored in the variable itself, thus giving constant-time access to private variable bindings.

Independent and-parallel systems use the same binding representation scheme as sequential Prolog, but require extensive changes to memory allocation, so that several workers can operate in and-parallel. They further require support for maintaining a pool of available work, for detecting successful completion of an and-parallel conjunction, and for propagating failure.

To fully exploit and-or parallelism, alternatives created by workers working in and-parallel must be made available to or-parallel execution. This introduces problems to the environment representation schemes developed for pure or-parallelism. In the case of environment copying approach, the main problem is now what to copy. Whereas in systems that exploit pure or-parallelism, execution for each branch proceeds in a contiguous stack, support for and-parallelism requires distributing execution of goals through different data areas. The ACE system [8] proposed the first copying-based solution for this problem, based on the C-tree model [7]. ACE must tackle a few difficult problems. The major one is that at copy-time ACE must find out which data areas to copy, making copying more complex than, say, for Muse. It is also likely that more copying than for pure or-parallel systems will be necessary. Moreover, and as we shall see later, ACE requires pure recomputation, that is, it prevents any reuse of independent and-parallel goals between or-parallel branches.

The binding array cannot be directly used for combined systems. The problem is that the same binding array has to be shared between computations that execute in and-parallel, creating a complex memory allocation problem. The first solution to this problem was the paged binding array PBA [9]. The PBA uses operating system technology to provide an elegant solution to the problem, at the cost of extra complexity in dereferencing bindings and in managing the BA. As we shall see later, the PBA also requires pure recomputation.

In this paper we describe how these schemes fare against simultaneous exploitation of OR-IAP Parallelism. The keystone of our work is the principle of *orthogonality*: or-parallel execution should be unaware of independent and-parallel execution, and independent and-parallel execution should be able to ignore the very existence of or-parallelism in the system. Orthogonality is required for simpler solutions, with the potential for easier implementation and lower overheads. We contend that *pure recomputation* does not allow for orthogonality. In contrast, we believe that a simpler solution, the sparse binding array, does guarantee this goal, and explain how independent and-parallelism and or-parallelism can thus be efficiently combined.

The paper is organized as follows. We first describe in more detail the binding array based schemes. Next, we concentrate on the orthogonality problem and the need for memory independence between or-parallel branches. We then describe how the data structures and algorithms for independent and-parallelism must be changed to support or-parallelism, and vice-versa. We last present the conclusions and future work.

2   From Or-Parallelism to And-Or Parallelism

We first define some terminology. Computations are executed by processing agents, that we will call *workers*, usually implemented as processes or threads running on separate processors.

Two major approaches have been proposed for combining independent and-parallelism with or-parallelism. In *reuse-based* models, the computation is seen as an and-or tree. Solutions for each goal in a conjunction are stored and then combined with the solutions from the other goals through a special operation, the cross-product calculation. This solution is very attractive because it can reduce the search space of logic programs, and was the basis for original proposals such as Conery's AND/OR Process model [4] and Kalé's Reduce Or Process model [11].

An alternative to this approach is the *recomputation* based models where and-goals may be recomputed in quite the same way as Prolog would. One major example of such models is the C-tree model. In this model, groups of workers, or *teams*, work together in and-parallel to explore branches from the search tree. Workers within the team execute and-parallel tasks in advance, as they would in pure and-parallel systems, such as &-Prolog. Note that as a result, different teams may be computing the same and-parallel goal in advance, and all generate the same solutions to this goal. Thus the model recomputes goals in much the same way as Prolog or &-Prolog would. Recomputation-based models have important advantages. First, their semantics are similar to Prolog's, thus enabling the support of side-effects in the presence of parallelism. Second, they avoid the overheads associated with implementing cross-product nodes and keeping the corresponding solutions. Often, the original programmers have written their programs in such a way as to avoid recomputing solutions, resulting in little gains for reuse [15]. Also, recomputation allows producer-consumer dependent and-parallelism [15].

The last major advantage of recomputation based approaches is that they *simplify* the task of extending or-parallel systems to incorporate and-parallelism. The two main proposals for doing so are copying, used in ACE, and binding arrays, that we describe in detail next.

2.1 Binding arrays for or-parallelism

The SRI model [17] was the first model to propose using binding arrays for or-parallelism. In this model, the stacks are shared by all the or-agents and form a search tree whose branch components are dynamically distributed between the stacks of all the workers participating in the computation. In this way, cactus stacks are formed for each of the heap, environment stack, choice-point stack and trail stack.

Each worker keeps a private set of bindings for shared variables. In the SRI model these bindings are stored in an array, the *binding array*. We say that a worker's binding array *shadows* the shared variables. The key idea in the binding array concept is that for each variable there is a single, uniquely identified, binding array slot that is the same for any or-worker.

The SRI model implements the BA by "binding" each variable, say X, to the number of variables N between X and the root of the computation tree. To find out the private binding of the variable X it is sufficient to search for the following value:

```
PRIVATE_VALUE = BA_BASE[*(SHARED_PTR)]
```

where `PRIVATE_VALUE` represents the value we are looking for, `BA_BASE` represents the origin of the corresponding binding array, and `SHARED_PTR` represents the position of the shared variable, with `*(SHARED_PTR)` giving the value `X`. This is a constant time operation, giving fast access. As an added benefit, `*(SHARED_PTR)` can be seen as the variable's age.

2.2 Binding Arrays for And-Or Parallelism

The key idea of recomputation-based systems is that a set of workers, a *team*, works in *and-parallel* to exploit a branch of the search tree. The team thus becomes the or-agent that computes a given branch of the search tree. Workers in a team will share the same bindings for the variables of the branch, and must thus share the same binding array. Or-parallelism is exploited by having these teams running in or-parallel, as in Andorra-I [14], or as in the C-tree model.

The question now arises of how to manage a binding array in the presence of several workers. The paged binding arrays data structure (PBA) [9] relies on the insight that this problem is similar to the problem that arises in operating systems when physical memory has to be shared between different processes. Their solution is to paginate the memory and have a memory page table for each process that translates the virtual address the process tries to access to a real memory address where the page containing the data to be accessed is located. A similar idea can be applied to the binding array of a team.

In PBA each shared variable is divided into two fields, `PG_NUMBER` and `OFFSET`. The position in the BA is determined by obtaining the page offset from the page table, PT, and adding the variable offset within the page.

PBA structures thus uses indirection to tackle the binding array management problem. The BA is paginated, with page size being implementation defined. A page table manages pages with synchronized access among the elements of the team. Each time an and-worker creates a variable and if there is no more space in its current page, or is just starting execution, a new page of size K is allocated from the binding array, a new page entry J is reserved from the page table, and a trail entry is pushed indicating the allocation of this page slot. The first two operations must be atomic within the team. The value of the variable now becomes the pair <PG_NUMBER,OFFSET>. Private values are obtained as follows:

```
PRIVATE_VALUE = BA_BASE[PAGE_TABLE[PG_NUMBER]+OFFSET]
```

3 Designing for And-Or Parallelism

A major goal in the design of recomputation based systems is to take the best advantage of research in and-parallel and or-parallel systems. To do so, one should try to obtain *orthogonality* between each component of the system. In an orthogonal design, or-parallel execution should be unaware of independent and-parallel execution, and vice-versa. Orthogonality implies that all the communication, synchronization, and data structures required to combine the two forms of parallelism can be designed independently. Moreover, orthogonality means that And-Scheduling and Or-Scheduling can be unaware of each other. This simplifies initial implementation and allows access to the substantial body of work available in scheduler design, while in no way it compromises the ability to eventually design more sophisticated scheduling strategies.

In the case of independent-and plus or-parallelism, orthogonality means that workers should only be aware of or-parallelism when they backtrack to shared public choice points. The converse is that even if a worker backtracks to a public part of the search tree, *the other workers in the team should be able to continue independent computations.* The same principle applies to extensions of independent and-parallelism that support dependent and-parallelism.

One important consequence of this principle is that workers working in and-parallel should be unaware of the fact that other workers have backtracked to choice-points, *even if they are shared.* This seems to be a form of reuse, as and-parallel computations that are produced while in a branch of the search-tree will actually be used when the team moves to another branch. We claim that this form of reuse is in fact *needed* for efficient execution, because otherwise searching for or-work will result in killing legitimate and-work, and will very much increase the overheads of moving any nontrivial and-parallel task in the search tree.

To be able to reuse work, we must be able to guarantee that all data structures used to store local values, allocated by another team doing work that we may want to share, *must never conflict with any of our own data-structures.* We call this property *memory independence.*

The requirement of orthogonality, and thus of memory independence, was not a major consideration in the original C-tree based models, such as the PBA and ACE. The question thus arises of whether we can guarantee this property with these models.

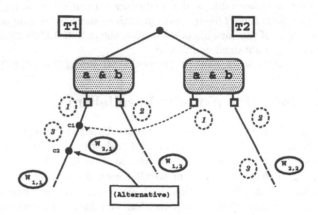

Figure 1: Structural problem in PBA.

Memory Independence in the PBA We first study an example for using the PBA. Consider the situation shown in figure 1. Team 1 (T_1) consists of two workers, $W_{1,1}$ and $W_{1,2}$. T_1 was the first team to exploit work from the parallel conjunction a & b. $W_{1,1}$ took the goal a and created the choice-points C_1 and C_2, whereas $W_{1,2}$ took the goal b. Note that initially $W_{1,1}$ allocated page 1 (as shown by the dotted circle) and that $W_{1,2}$ allocated page 2. Between creating choice-points C_1 and C_2 $W_{1,1}$ asked for a new binding-array page, receiving page 3.

Execution for team T_2 proceeds differently. The team also has two workers. $W_{2,1}$ first shares choice-point C_1 from T_1, whereas $W_{2,2}$ restarts execution of b. In this case, $W_{2,2}$ requires more variables more quickly than $W_{2,1}$ and asks for a new page receiving page 3.

At this point $W_{2,1}$ backtracks (an inside backtrack) to node C_1 and the Or-Scheduler decides that the worker will take from the closest node, in this case C_2. Notice that from node C_2 to C_1, T_1 used page table entry 3 that is now used by $W_{2,2}$ in its computation of goal b.

To move to node C_2, team T_2 must therefore rewind its computation of b in order to be able to install page 3 without conflicts. Notice that in general the problem may affect not just active computations, but in fact all independent and-parallel computations that were performed in advance.

Memory Independence in ACE The copying scheme used in ACE follows the same basic memory allocation principles of PBA.

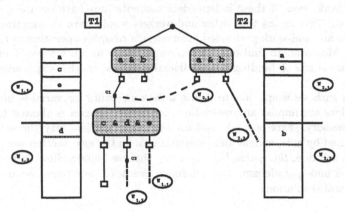

Figure 2: Structural problem in ACE.

Consider the situation shown in figure 2. As in the the previous case T_1 was the first team to exploit work from the parallel conjunction (a & b). In this case, $W_{1,1}$ took the goal a and created the choice point C_1. After a while, node C_1 is made public and team T_2 comes and takes work from this node relaunching goal b. $W_{2,1}$ takes goal a and $W_{2,2}$ takes goal b for execution. Meanwhile, worker $W_{1,1}$ starts parallel execution of (c & d & e) and takes for execution goal c. Worker $W_{1,2}$ moves to help and takes goal d for execution, eventually creating choice point C_2 in the process. Computation for goal c succeeds quickly and as a result node C_2 is made public. After succeeding goal c, $W_{1,1}$ takes goal e for execution. At this point arises the situation depicted in figure 2. Worker $W_{2,1}$ has failed and performs *inside backtracking* to node C_1. Since this is a public node the Or-Scheduler is called and it decides to install work from the now public node C_2.

The problem in ACE appears when T_2 tries to install work from C_2. In figure 2 this is easily seen by observing that in the stacks for team T_1 the space used for goal d can conflict with the space being used by worker $W_{2,2}$ when executing goal b. As a result $W_{2,2}$ has to rewind and deallocate the computation of b before the installation of or-work from node C_2 can proceed. Note however that these two situations are extreme cases. They only arise when a team picks up work from another team on failure, and they could be remedied to a large extent through careful scheduling. For example, by using a bottom most dispatching strategy the need to restart everything on public backtracking will be much reduced.

We have shown simple examples where teams conflict in their memory allocation. Much more complicated situations can and do arise. In the worst case, correct execution using the previous data representations requires a team to kill and fully rewind at least some of the independent-and private computations that are under the sharing choice point before installing public or-work, even if these independent computations have or are going to succeed. This means that other and-workers would have to backtrack and discard any and-work performed in advance, a complex operation in iap systems. Moreover, to find out which computations to kill we would need to compare stacks or binding arrays allocation tables, another expensive operation.

As such we would like to devise a data structure for variable bindings that does not impose any restrictions in the way a team is allowed to allocate memory, share or-work, and combine in an efficient way the solutions generated by independent and-computations. In the next section we present such a solution, *the sparse binding array*, that we believe allows support for or- and and- parallelism, at a minimum overhead over pure or-parallel or and-parallel solutions.

4   The Sparse Binding Array

The *sparse binding array* (hereafter SBA), is derived from the original binding array used in SRI based models. The key idea is that we can guarantee the memory independence principle if the index associated with a variable is unique in the whole search tree. This way, if several and-workers within a team create variables at the same time, they are guaranteed never to use the same binding array slot. Unique indexes also guarantee orthogonality, as variable slots allocated within the different teams, that is or-agents, can never interfere with each other when public or-work is being installed by a team.

To understand our proposed solution observe that in shared-stack parallel logic systems, memory objects are built with blocks taken from a pool of common shared memory. This initial shared address space is then used to build each worker's stacks. Variables, among other objects, are located in these stacks. The simplest way to implement the SBA is then to simply allocate for each team a private virtual address space with the same size as the whole system common memory pool. This address space is mapped at a fixed location for each team in the system. Bindings private to a team will be allocated there, whereas unconditional bindings can be placed in the shared data stacks. We can say that each SBA *shadows* the system shared address space. This is illustrated in figure 3.

To obtain private values, SBA based systems can use a direct mapping from the shared memory pool to the team's SBA. The mapping is from addresses in the shared address space to addresses in the corresponding team's SBA as follows:

$$\text{SHARED\_PTR} \Rightarrow \text{SHARED\_PTR} + (\text{SBA\_BASE} - \text{STACK\_BASE})$$

where STACK_BASE is the base address of the initially allocated System shared memory pool, and SBA_BASE is the base address of the corresponding SBA.

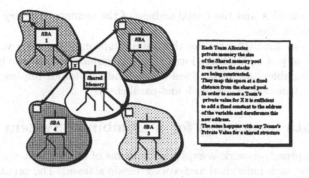

Figure 3: The Sparse binding array.

Most operating systems allow mapping memory at user-defined addresses. In these cases we can guarantee the difference SBA_BASE−STACK_BASE to be the same for all the teams in the system, and known as a constant at compile-time.

In these systems, the private value of a variable is thus obtained as follows:

PRIVATE_VALUE = SHARED_PTR[FIXED_DISTANCE]

where FIXED_DISTANCE is a constant value known at compile-time. Variable access is in this case a constant-time operation, giving fast access. In fact, variable access becomes faster than for the traditional binding array, as we just need to add a constant.

Notice that the value of the variable cell is no longer needed to find its binding array slot, although it can still be used for variable age maintenance. One option is to use the same scheme as for Aurora. In our implementation of the SBA [13] we introduced an alternative scheme based on the notion of *level*, where a level corresponds to the number of choice points and parallel conjunctions above a stack object in the search tree.

In the SBA, each cell in the local and global stacks will have at least as many "virtual" copies as there are teams. We use the word *virtual* because we are referring to virtual memory, managed by the operating system. Most of this memory will never be used during execution and will just be kept as reserved backing store. In fact, modern operating systems only allocate memory when really needed. The question thus becomes of how much more memory will our scheme *use* over traditional binding arrays, and whether this is an acceptable overhead for supporting and-parallelism and a simpler implementation.

Shadowing the whole stack and not just variable cells has another very important advantage. Any object whose memory has been allocated from the initial common shared memory pool can have a private value location in the SBA in exactly the same way a variable's private value has one. Just use the address of the object, add to this address a constant offset (the distance between the SBA and the initial address of the common memory pool) and access that address.

This way the SBA provides the system implementor with a very flexible and easy way of maintaining local values for objects in the search tree that are not variables. As we shall see this is fundamental for implementing the data structures associated with and-parallelism.

5 Data Structures for a Combined System

In our approach or-work is explored by teams of and-workers and iap-work is done by each individual and-worker inside a team. The organization of computing agents into teams has the following advantages:

- When workers fetch and-work they do not need to load their binding arrays, hash tables, or copy their new environment from other workers. For example, if the system is executing (a & b),c , any member of the team can take c. In systems where there is no concept of team, the worker that is going to execute c has to load the environments created during execution of a and b first.

- The team concept complies with the principle of orthogonality described previously. As such it allows the implementor to reuse code and ideas from previous implementations of other and- and or-systems.

One can see a team as an address space shared by several workers and composed of two parts, (i) the shared system memory pool, which is in fact shared by every team in the system, and (ii) the SBA, which is private to a team. One can also see the team as formed by and-workers (in the spirit of &-Prolog or &ACE), or *threads*, that together form a team, or *process*. This organization gives a natural mapping to operating systems processes and threads.

5.1 The Life of a Worker

The life of a worker is shown in figure 4. The white-background nodes correspond to purely and-work, and the shadowed area corresponds to occasions where the worker must be aware of or-parallelism. The worker interacts with the rest of the team by sending kill signals or publishing and-work. Note that when a worker is moving in an area shared with other teams the rest of the team will be working in and-parallel unaware of the fact that the worker is backtracking to and fetching work from the shared part of the search tree.

The distinction between shared and non-shared parts of the search tree corresponds to the distinction between public and private work. Workers must interface with the or-parallel system when they move through public work. Following the Aurora engine-scheduler interface [16], three basic interface operations are used.

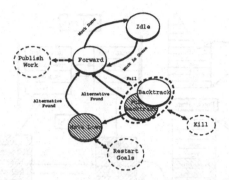

Figure 4: Worker Lifecycle.

The *MakeNodePublic* routine is called each time a choice point node is made public. As an engine routine it can have first-hand knowledge of the new data structures without interfering with the or-scheduler. *MakeNodePublic* must perform the same tasks as in the Aurora system, such as updating choice-point fields used by the or-scheduler to inform the work is shared. To do so the routine has to navigate through a choice-point stack that will also include markers and parcall-frames.

The *MoveUP* engine routine must be made aware of the new choice point stack objects and of the way memory is physically and logically connected so that it can be reused on backtracking. The basic scheme uses a reference counter for each object in the choice point stack. Each time a team moves down over an object its reference counter is atomically incremented. When a team moves up over an object its reference counter is atomically decremented. When that reference counter reaches zero then the object is no longer referenced by any team in the system and can be logically deallocated (same principle used in the Aurora system).

The *MoveDown* routine has to cope with the copying of computation slots from the shared heap to the SBA and update the slot pointers from the corresponding trail entries. The key idea here is that the routine actually moves from the bottom to the top of the shared tree. Thus, the first time it finds a parallel conjunction it has to initialize the SBA parallel conjunction values, copy to the SBA the state of the computations of the goals to its left [1], and restart all and-parallel goals to the right of the current goal, allocating new computations state data structures in the HEAP in the process.

5.2 The Execution Stacks

We have given an overview of how independent and-parallelism and or-parallelism interact in our proposal. We next explain how to adapt the data structures and execution models used in the implementation of SRI

---

[1] Only complete work can be shared, as such the correct values for this computations have already been copied to the shared stacks by the team that published work

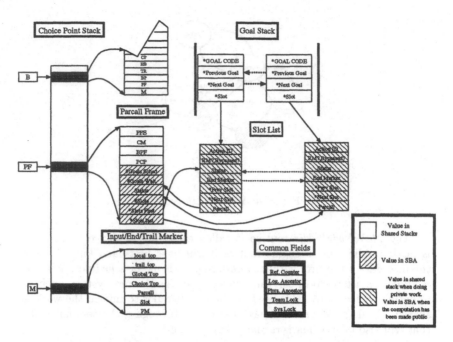

Figure 5: Data structures for or- and iap-and Parallelism.

derived Or-parallel systems (Aurora) and IAP-parallel RAP-WAM [10] derived systems (&-Prolog and &ACE) to obtain an SBA recomputation based
or-iap parallel execution model for full Prolog.

In figure 5 we can see the major data structures introduced by our or-iap
SBA based execution model. We extend the or-parallel WAM, as used in the
Aurora system, and combine it with the iap-parallel mechanisms developed
for &-Prolog and/or &ACE, using the SBA for environment representation.
We concentrate on the issues relevant for the combined system, please con-
sult [3, 10] for the issues in or-parallel and and-parallel systems.

The abstract machine registers closely follow the WAM registers. We introduce two new registers for independent and-parallelism. The *PF* register
always points to the current parcall frame should a failure occur. The *M*
register points to the Input Marker of the current iap-computation.

The two registers must be saved in choice-points only for shared work, as
they are fixed for private work. Hence we may always save them in the `try`
operations, or delay until a worker in a team makes the choice-point public.
In the latter case it will be up to that worker that is publishing the work to
give these fields the correct values.

The Parcall Frames Parcall frames are created whenever the conditions
in a CGE [10] succeed and and-parallelism is started. The corresponding

structure contains several fields. The Parcall-Frame Environment, *PFE*, is a pointer to the local environment when the parallel goals were activated, and is necessary to continue execution. The Continuation Input Marker, *CM*, is used to save the value of the M register at the time the frame was created. The previous parcall frame pointer, *BPF*, is used to propagate failure. The continuation of the Parcall Frame, *PCP*, is a pointer to the code to execute when the parcall-frame completes.

Several other fields control current execution status: *#Goals_Sched* gives the number of goals still to be scheduled, *#Goals_Wait* gives the number of goals that are executed but not yet reported success, *Parcall_Status*, is used to detect whether we are in inside or outside backtracking, *#Slots* is the number of goals in the parcall frame, *SlotFirst* and *SlotLast* point to the first and last computation slot.

As we explained before, parcall frames are shared. We therefore must keep private copies for the values that will be different for different teams. As shown in figure 5 the fields that change during execution are: *#Goals_Sched*, *#Goals_Wait*, and *Parcall_Status*.

The Slots Each and-parallel goal is represented by a *Computation Slot*. This is a data structure allocated in the heap that has the following fields. The *Id* of the agent working within the goal or that finished the computation is stored in *ActionID*. The *RM?Bypassed?* flag indicates whether the computation is rightmost and whether it has been bypassed [6] by the computation to its left. The *Status* field gives the computation status. The *End Marker* slot points to the end marker of the current computation, if it exists. The *PrevSlot* and *NextSlot* maintain a doubly linked list of slots, and the *Parcall* field gives fast access to the parcall-frame owning the slot. The *PrevSlot*, *NextSlot* and *Parcall* fields are public.

The *End Marker* field requires special processing. When exploring or-parallelism, the end-marker for a slot depends on which alternatives for the slot's goal are active in the current or-branch. To recover the correct end-marker when moving to fetch or-work an entry for this field is stored in the trail when the goal completes. Later on when or-work from this branch is taken by another team the proper value for the end-marker can be stored in the team's SBA location for the computation slot.

The Goal List The goal list provides a way for workers to share work. In &-Prolog each and-worker has a goal list, which is visible to other workers in the team. Each element of the list consists of four fields. The *Goal Code* field is a pointer to the code to execute, the *Slot* field is a pointer to the corresponding slot, and the *Next Goal* and *Prev Goal* fields maintain a doubly linked list.

Goal lists are structures for and-parallelism. They are only affected by or-parallelism when a team moves down the search tree to fetch new work and relaunches new computations for goals to the right in each parcall frame that it finds in a branch from where it is installing work. These goals are introduced in the goal list of the and-worker that is moving down the tree.

Choicepoint Stack Objects To support and-or parallelism all choice point stack objects contain extra entries labeled "Common Fields". These fields are shown in figure 5 and are required to support synchronization and scheduling under the and- and or-execution mechanisms. These fields include a *reference counter* that indicates if the objective is active, a *logical ancestor* for going up the tree, a *physical ancestor* for memory management, and *locks* that can be used only within the team or by any team. Each object pointer has an associated tag indicating its type.

6   Conclusions and Future Work

One of the major challenges in current logic programming research is how to exploit maximum parallelism in logic programs efficiently. We presented in this paper a model and data structures that allow the efficient combination of two major forms of parallelism, or-parallelism and independent and-parallelism. We show that to obtain orthogonality between or- and and-parallelism some reuse of goals between search branches is required. We thus propose a new data structure, the Sparse Binding Array, that guarantees this orthogonality by simplifying binding array management, and demonstrate that by using this approach the main data-structures for both or-parallelism and and-parallelism can be naturally adapted to support a combined system.

Work has already started in developing systems based on the sparse binding array. We have adapted the Aurora system to use this principle, and first results show that for or-parallelism only, this approach gives better single-processor performance and similar speedups as traditional binding arrays [13]. In the continuation, and in collaboration with the group at New Mexico State University, we are integrating the &ACE system with our or-parallel prototype. We expect that the combined system will not just exploit or- and independent and-parallelism, but it will also be able to support recent optimisations to and-parallelism such as LPCO [6] and dependent and-parallelism as in the extensions to &ACE [12].

Acknowledgments

The authors would like to acknowledge and thank for the contribution and support that Gopal Gupta, Enrico Pontelli, K. Shen, and Manuel V. Hermenegildo gave to this work. This work has been supported by the PRAXIS PROLOPPE project, the JNICT MELODIA project, and by the NATO MAPLE project.

References

[1] K. A. M. Ali and R. Karlsson. The Muse Or-parallel Prolog Model and its Performance. In *NACLP'90*, The MIT Press, 757–776, Oct. 1990.

[2] U. Baron and et. al. The Parallel ECRC Prolog System PEPSys: an Overview and Evaluation Results. In *ICFGCS'88*, ICOT, Japan, 841-850, Nov. 1988.

[3] M. Carlsson. *Design and Implementation of an OR-Parallel Prolog Engine*. PhD Thesis, SICS, The Royal Institute of Technology, 1990.

[4] J. S. Conery. *Parallel Execution of Logic Programs*. Kluwer Academic Publishers, 1987.

[5] M. E. Correia, F. Silva, and V. Santos Costa. SBA: Exploiting orthogonality in AND-OR Parallel Systems. DCC-97-3, DCC-FC & LIACC, University of Oporto, April 1997.

[6] G. G. D. Tang, E. Pontelli and M. Carro. Last Parallel Call Optimization and Fast Backtracking in and-parallel systems. In *Workshop on Parallel and Data-Parallel Execution of Logic Programs*, 93–109, 1994.

[7] G. Gupta, M. Hermenegildo, and V. Santos Costa. And-Or Parallel Prolog: A Recomputation based Approach. *New Generation Computing*, 11(3,4):770–782, 1993.

[8] G. Gupta, M. Hermenegildo, E. Pontelli, and V. S. Costa. ACE: And/Or-parallel Copying-based Execution of Logic Programs. In *ICLP'94*, The MIT Press, 93–109, 1994.

[9] G. Gupta and V. Santos Costa. And-Or Parallelism in Full Prolog with Paged Binding Arrays. In *PARLE'92*, LNCS 605, Springer-Verlag, 617–632, June 1992.

[10] M. V. Hermenegildo. An Abstract Machine for Restricted And-Parallel Execution of Logic Programs. In *ICLP'86*, Springer-Verlag, 25–39, July 1986.

[11] L. V. Kalé. The REDUCE OR process model for parallel evaluation of logic programming. In *ICLP'87*, The MIT Press, 616–632, May 1987.

[12] E. Pontelli and G. Gupta. Non dependent and-parallelism revisited. TR 1, Lab. for Logic, Databases and Advanced Programming, NMSU, Las Cruces, USA, Feb. 1996.

[13] V. Santos Costa, M. E. Correia, and F. Silva. Performance of Sparse Binding Arrays for Or-Parallelism. In *Proceedings of the VIII SBAC-PAD*, 1996.

[14] V. Santos Costa, D. H. D. Warren, and R. Yang. Andorra-I: A Parallel Prolog System that Transparently Exploits both And- and Or-Parallelism. In *PPOPP'91*, SIGPLAN Notices 26(7), July 1991.

[15] K. Shen. *Studies of AND/OR Parallelism in Prolog*. PhD thesis, University of Cambridge, 1992.

[16] P. Szeredi and M. Carlsson. The Engine–Scheduler Interface in the Aurora Or–Parallel Prolog System. TR-90-09, University of Bristol, Computer Science Department, April 1990.

[17] D. H. D. Warren. The SRI Model for Or-Parallel Execution of Prolog—abstract design and implementation issues. In *ILPS'87*, 92–102, 1987.

Using SimICS to Evaluate the Penny System

Johan Montelius, Peter Magnusson
Swedish Institute of Computer Science
Box 1263, SE-164 29 Kista, SWEDEN
{jm,psm}@sics.se
http://www.sics.se/

Abstract

We demonstrate the benefits of instruction-set simulation in the evaluation of a parallel programming system, Penny. The simulator is a reliable tool in exploring design alternatives for improving performance and can greatly help in understanding program behavior. The results obtained improved the performance of Penny and highlighted the importance of the caches.

1 Introduction

Instruction-set simulation is a useful tool both for performance debugging and for explaining the behavior of a system. In this paper we show how the instruction set simulator SimICS is used to improve and explain the performance of Penny, an implicit parallel programming system.

A tool such as SimICS can provide a wide range of statistics on hardware events triggered by software activity, including data cache hits and misses, instructions executed, and virtual memory performance. It can relate these events to particular lines of code, greatly simplifying the task of understanding the performance of software systems and, hopefully, improving it.

The simulator shows that the Penny system would scale almost perfectly if only the number of executed instructions are taken into account, i.e. for an idealized multiprocessor. The total number of executed instructions when sixteen processors are used increase only by 10% compared to the one processor execution. This would indicate a speedup of 15, in contrast to the actual speedup of 7.7. The study shows how important good cache performance is to a system such as Penny, and demonstrates how an instruction set simulator can relate cache events to program code.

1.1 The Penny system

The Penny system [12] is a implementation of AKL [7] on a shared memory architecture. It will automatically extract parallelism in an AKL program. No user annotations are required, thus relieving the programmer from adding explicit information to control parallelism. The system can utilize both *and*- and *or*-parallelism in the program. There is no compiler support to extract parallelism. All detection and scheduling of parallel tasks is done automatically at runtime. Penny is complete with a parallel garbage collector and, for an experimental system, is quite stable.

The heart of the system is a threaded code emulator implemented in C using the GNU C compiler (version 2.x) where labels can be handled as data. The machine only defines sixty-three abstract machine instructions so the emulator itself is rather small. The instruction set is very similar to the instruction set used in the WAM [14].

When a program is executed, a fixed set of *workers* are created. The number of workers will determine the level of parallelism, so there is no advantage to create more workers than available number of processors. Each worker will dynamically be assigned work during an execution. If a worker runs out of work it will steal tasks from another worker.

During an execution the workers build and modify a shared *execution state*. The execution state consists of a tree structure of *goals* and *continuations*, and a set of AKL *terms*. Each goal in the execution state is either ready to be executed or suspended on some AKL variable. When a variable is assigned a value the goals suspended on the variable will be scheduled for execution. It is the worker that assigned the value that is responsible for executing the goals.

Continuations represents sequences of un-executed goals and are in the same way owned by a particular worker. The right to execute a goal or to select a goal from a continuation can be stolen by another worker. The whole execution state is therefore accessible to all workers.

The data structures that are used to represent goals and continuations can be explicitly reclaimed by the workers. This improves cache performance since the same cache-lines can be reused immediately. AKL terms are not explicitly reclaimed although work on compile time analysis shows that this is quite possible [4]. The terms are therefore allocated on a *heap* that is subjected to garbage collection. A parallel stop-and-copy garbage collector is used. It is important that the garbage collector is parallel since the garbage collection time would otherwise increase in proportion to the execution time.

The Penny compiler compiles AKL programs to abstract machine instructions. The Penny compiler is itself written in AKL and consists of about three thousand lines of AKL code, that can in turn be executed on Penny itself with good parallel performance.

1.2   The SIMICS Simulator

There are a large number of techniques and tools available to analyzing the behavior of a software system. Regardless of how it is done, we need to solve three problems. First, we need to execute the actual instructions specified by the executable binary. Second, we need to perform the system services required by the program, if any. The first two problems thus involve recreating the execution environment. Third, we need to generate information about the execution over and above the actual program result.

There are essentially three starting-point strategies:

Instruction set simulation, also called instruction-level or program-driven simulation, is the naive brute-force approach, whereby each instruction in the program is simulated one at a time. This provides an accessible and in some sense correct target machine model for instrumentation, and places minimum restrictions on the architectural relationship between the host and target. Program-driven simulation is probably the oldest strategy [5].

Execution-driven simulation, also called program augmentation, involves running a modified program binary. The modifications can be induced at any stage during generation of the binary, either by modifying intermediate program formats (source code, assembly code, object file, or executable binary) or any of the compiler tools (preprocessor, compiler, assembler, or linker). Traditional profilers generally fall into this category.

Host-supported simulation, historically called emulation, requires hardware monitors or other special host hardware features which provide tools to gather statistics or otherwise control the execution of a program.

Naturally, as with any artificial taxonomy, the above classification is by no means strict—mixing methods is common.

It is beyond the scope of this paper to go into any detailed discussion of trade-offs between the various strategies. Simply put, instruction set simulation is the slowest and most flexible, host-supported simulation is the converse (fast but inflexible), and execution-driven simulation holds the middle ground.

SimICS [9, 10, 11] is an instruction set simulator that has borrowed many design principles from g88 [3]. SimICS takes the brute force approach, modelling the target architecture on an instruction-by-instruction level. This results in a lower performance compared to execution-driven or host-supported systems—namely a slow-down of approximately $25 - 100$ per simulated processor compared to the real execution.[1] We also need to deal with a significantly more complex software engineering problem in building the simulator. This effect is, of course, difficult to quantify, but it is significant.

On the plus side, SimICS provides full profiles—both of execution (instructions), data cache events, and virtual memory events—and does so within a traditional debugger environment. This allows a detailed, interactive analysis of parallel programs.

1.3 Our Target Machine

Our workhorses for Penny timings (and SimICS runs) have been two SPARC-center 2000 (SC2000) multiprocessors with 8 and 20 processors, respectively.

---

[1]Thus if an execution takes two seconds using one processor and one second using two processors the simulation will in both cases take between 50 and 200 seconds, i.e. a slowdown of $30 - 100$ per processor.

The SC2000 is a bus-based shared-memory multiprocessor from Sun Microsystems. Figure 1 is a sketch of a generic shared-memory multiprocessor—though the SC2000 is considerably more complex, the figure serves to highlight some principal features.

Each processor has two on-chip caches, one for instructions and one for data. These are generally small, because on-chip area is a scarce resource. On the SC2000's processors, 50MHz SuperSPARCs, the data cache is 16Kbytes, four-way associative with 32 byte long cache lines. The instruction cache is 20Kbytes, 5-way associative with 64 byte cache lines. Despite their small size, the first level caches consume half of the SuperSPARC's 3 million transistors.

The processors connect to an off-chip cache, the second level cache, which on the SC2000 is 2Mbytes, direct-mapped with 64-byte cache lines. These caches are connected to a bus, whereby they can communicate with the main memory and/or other caches. This communication is controlled by Super-Cache controllers and "Bus Watcher" chips. There are actually 2 buses on the SC2000, dual 40MHz XDBuses, with an effective read/write throughput of 500Mbytes per second.

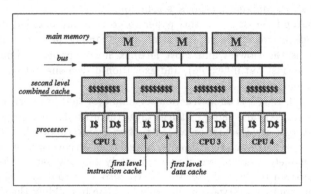

Figure 1: Generic shared-memory multiprocessor

A throughput of 500Mbytes per second may sound high, but each SuperSPARC processor is capable of executing three instructions per cycle, including supplying 64 bits per cycle from memory, so a 20-processor SC2000 could conceivably request 8 *billion* bytes per second from the memory system. Hence two layers of caches. The first level, being on-chip, can react with new data in one cycle. The second level takes 5-10 cycles, whereas accessing the main memory takes 20-60 cycles. A high cache hit rate is therefore crucial to good performance.

SimICS emulates the cache hierarchy in figure 1, which is close enough to real life to give a good prediction of performance of an application. In fact, during our profiling we initially had significant discrepancies between predicted performance and measured values, until we discovered that both the

SC2000 machines we used for timing measurements had faulty SuperSPARC processors with only 4Kbyte caches, not 16Kbyte. The faulty processors had gone unnoticed for several years, despite the machine being used extensively for benchmarking of parallel programs. To remain comparable to available hardware at the time of this study (autumn 1995), all simulated values in this paper assume a 4Kbyte first-level data cache with 32-byte cache lines, and a 2Mbyte second-level integrated cache with 64-byte cache lines, both direct-mapped. Instruction cache behavior is irrelevant in this study as the core interpreter in Penny is small.[2]

2 Using SIMICS

In this section, we show how we used SIMICS to study Penny from various perspectives. As input to Penny we used an implementation of the Smith-Waterman algorithm. The algorithm is used to compare DNA sequences and the benchmark has good parallel performance.

```
(gdb-simics) prof-weight 32 20
Weighted profiling results:
  Physical    Virtual     ( source )
  0x000ac860  0x00029860 (pid 1002)     285085.00
  0x000aca60  0x00029a60 (pid 1002)     282070.00
  0x000a61a0  0x000231a0 (pid 1002)     232325.00
  0x000a8540  0x00025540 (pid 1002)      95540.00
  0x000a8480  0x00025480 (pid 1002)      90155.00
  ...

Total profiled:   1644459.00 (56%)
Not shown:        1269168.00 (44%)
```

Figure 2: `prof-weight` listing

2.1 Performance debugging

The main concern when improving the performance of a system is to locate the code that consumes the most resources. SIMICS allows different costs to be assigned to events and can then generate statistics and display the most expensive parts of the program. Figure 2 shows the output from one such command.

---

[2]Interpreters in general have the effect of converting instruction cache pressure to data cache pressure.

For our benchmark set and on our target machine the second-level data cache and TLB misses turn out to be the most important events.[3] These misses easily stall the CPU if the result is needed soon, which is often the case. The output in figure 2 is from running the benchmark with 6 workers. The cost of a TLB miss and a read miss was set to 5 and a write miss to 1. The figure lists the 5 most expensive blocks of instructions where each block is 32 bytes long (8 SPARC instructions).

```
0x29868 :    0 54628 2388    63500   1 ld   [ %i2 + 4 ], %o0
0x2986c :    0     0    0    60500   1 cmp  %o0, 1
0x29870 :    0     0    0    65000   1 be,a    0x2992c
0x29874 :    0     0    1        0   1 ld   [ %i2 ], %i2
0x29878 :    0     0    0    68500   1 cmp  %o0, 1
0x2987c :    0     0    0    64000   1 bcs,a   0x2992c
0x29880 :    0  3481   33    57500   1 ld   [ %i2 ], %i2
0x29884 :    0     0    0     1000   1 cmp  %o0, 2
0x29888 :    0     0    0      500   1 bne,a   0x2992c
0x2988c :    0     0    1        0   1 ld   [ %i2 ], %i2
0x29890 :    0    36    0      500   1 ld   [ %i2 + 8 ], %l0
```

Figure 3: Assembler listing of the most expensive block

```
477 0   245   92    1000   4 for(tc = ta->trd; tc != NULL; tc = tc->nxt) {
478
479 0 58109 2423 380500  10   switch(tc->type) {
480                              case DEAD_CELL:
481                                  break;
482
483                              case FREE_CELL:
484                                  break;
485
486                              case CHB_CELL: {
487 0    36    0     500   1       templc = tc->box.chb;
```

Figure 4: Source code listing of the most expensive block

The listing shows that almost 10% of the cost is found in the block starting at virtual address 0x29868. The assembler listing of the block in figure 3 gives us: the number of write misses, the number of read misses, the

---

[3]The Translation Lookaside Buffer (TLB), also known as the Address Translation Cache (ATC), caches virtual-to-physical translations to improve the performance of virtual memory.

number of TLB misses, and the approximate number of times the instruction was executed and whether (1/0) the instruction was decoded.[4]

As the listing makes evident, the `ld` instruction on address `0x29868` causes a read miss almost every time it is executed. The instruction corresponds to the source code shown on line 479 in figure 4 where the profiling data has been accumulated for each source line.

The source code in figure 4 is from the garbage collector, and implements part of the algorithm for distributing tasks among workers. The read misses severely decreased overall performance, since the code is a part of a sequential phase of the garbage-collector.

Many profilers would have identified the procedure as a potential performance problem, but would not have explained why—namely that one line of assembler traversing a list misses the second-level cache over 80% of the time, and misses the TLB almost 4% of the time. This in turn was caused by the creation of the list having been spread across multiple processors, and would not have been a performance problem in a sequential version of Penny.

An implementation technique that avoids building the list had been sketched out a year earlier, but the previous benchmarking techniques had not seen the traversal as a potential problem. Making this correction to Penny improved performance significantly, as seen in figure 5.

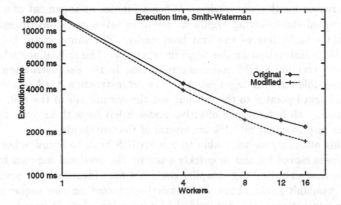

Figure 5: Improvements of the Smith-Waterman benchmark, following removal of sequential bottleneck in garbage collection (note: log-log scale)

2.2 Deciding on prefetching

By generating annotated source code the emulator could be studied in detail. We noticed an exceptionally high read miss rate in the decoding of the *unify*

---

[4]This corresponds closely with having been prefetched.

instructions.

The *unify* instructions are used to access the components of an AKL term. Terms are represented by tagged pointers and are accessed by first executing a *get* instruction. The *get* instruction will first look at the tag of the term and only after having verified the tag will it follow the pointer to verify the functor. A unique tag is used for list terms, so in this case only the tag needs to be verified. The following *unify* instructions will then access the arguments of the term.

The reason for the high miss rate in the *unify* instructions was that when the instructions were used they were often reading AKL terms that had been constructed by another worker. The terms had thus been constructed in one cache but were often read by another processor, forcing communication over the bus.

The remedy to this problem was to add a prefetch instruction (coded in C) in all *get* and *unify* instructions. The prefetch would read the next argument position so that the following *unify* instruction would find the value in the cache. The time to read the argument would hopefully overlap with useful work.

The fix did not work as expected. The read misses in the *unify* instructions did decrease but we had added a large number of read instructions, most of which contributed nothing since the data was already in the first-level cache. The net effect was slower execution.

The reason for this was obvious. When a functor or argument of a term was inspected the following argument would in seven cases out of eight be in the same cache line of the first level cache. The same would hold for any prefetch instruction in the *unify* instructions. The only place where a prefetch instruction would make any sense was in the *get* instruction that was responsible for verifying a list cell. The *get* instruction itself would only read the tagged pointer to the cell but not the *car* nor *cdr* of the cell.

Removing all but the one effective prefetch left us with an overall performance improvement of 3-4% for several of the workloads.

In this example, we were able to use SIMICS both to follow where the cache misses moved to, and to quickly quantify the overhead induced by the fix. Note that an optimizing compiler could not have identified this prefetch, since it wouldn't know about the restrictions placed on the sequences of abstract instructions—this required the intervention of the Penny designer, using SIMICS to explore trade-offs.

2.3   The danger of locking

The Penny system uses locks in two different situations. The first is in the internals when workers move between different parts of the execution state or steal tasks from each other. The second situation is when AKL variables are locked in order to add a new binding or suspension.

Both of these situations could cause a hot-spot in the implementation.

Since all locks are spin locks, a worker stalls if a lock is held by another worker, so it is interesting to know how often the locks are actually missed and how long it takes for a worker to acquire a missed lock.

To get an idea how often locks are missed, SIMICS *counters* were placed around the lock primitives. A SIMICS counter is a special SPARC instruction inserted in the source code that the hardware (the "real" processor) will treat as a no-op, but which SIMICS uses to start or stop event accumulators. The technique is thus similar to execution-driven simulation, but with much lower perturbation.

```
Counter 5:

    Number of times counter activated: 79949
    Total tick count spent in counter: 1729885

    Detailed counts:

        read operations            254074
        write operations           192874
        xmem (swap) operations     41178
        read cache misses          83
        write cache misses         6296
        xmem (swap) cache misses   4444
        cache replacements         184
        cache net invalidates      2424
        number of TLB misses       467

Counter 6:

    Number of times counter activated: 1
    Total tick count spent in counter: 6

    Detailed counts:

        read operations            2
        cache net invalidates      1
```

Figure 6: Example of a statistics vector (reported by counters)

We ran the Smith-Waterman benchmark with sixteen workers. The AKL variable lock counter statistics for one CPU are listed in figure 6. Counter 5 was entered when a worker examined a potential variable and counter 6 was entered if there was a collision. As we can see almost eighty-thousand variables were examined resulting in more than forty-thousand lock (swap) operations. In only one (!) case does a collision occur. The results were similar for all kinds of locks in the system.

These figures indicate that the locks in the Penny machinery are not a performance bottleneck. In fact, it might be worthwhile redesigning some of these locks to be more aggressive in assuming low contention.

The use of SIMICS counters in this analysis greatly simplified instrumentation of the locks. We added half a dozen different types of counters, to a few dozen different procedures and macros. Though it required modification in the source code and re-compilation, the binary can run on the real machine unchanged with an insignificant effect on performance. In fact, in the real execution this instrumentation adds less than 4 no-op instructions for every 10000 "real" instructions. Thus there is no real need to maintain separate versions.

3 The limiting factor

Though we managed to improve both the initial performance and speedup (parallelism) of the Penny system, there remains a significant sequential element that could not be easily explained. As seen earlier in figure 5 the speedup is not linear, but decreases. The limiting factor could of course be in the Smith-Waterman algorithm itself but there are no sequential components in the benchmark that could explain the limited speedup. The answer lies in the cache performance of the Penny system.

3.1 Perfect parallelism

Table 1 shows statistics gathered from executing the benchmark on the improved Penny system. The reported numbers are the sum of events generated by all the processors. The cache statistics are for a 2Mbyte cache, i.e. our target machines' second level cache.

	Number of workers				
	1	2	4	8	16
runtime (ms)	13822	7238	3996	2487	1789
read operations $(\times 10^6)$	124	124	125	127	129
read cache misses $(\times 10^3)$	8.63	257	287	384	467
write operations $(\times 10^6)$	47.5	47.5	47.6	48.1	48.1
write cache misses $(\times 10^3)$	137	271	294	412	418
executed instr. $(\times 10^6)$	630	631	634	656	669

Table 1: Profiling and timing for all processors

As the table shows, the increased number of processors does not induce a large overhead in the number of executed instructions. The instruction count only increases by 10% when sixteen workers are used and the number of read and write instructions increase even less.

In Table 2 we show the actual reduction in execution time with each doubling of workers, contrasted with the reduction in various operation types per processor. For example, in going from 4 to 8 workers, execution time is

	number of workers			
	1-2	2-4	4-8	8-16
runtime	0.52	0.55	0.62	0.72
read operations	0.50	0.50	0.51	0.51
write operation	0.50	0.50	0.51	0.50
executed instr.	0.50	0.50	0.52	0.51

Table 2: Actual execution time, contrasted with instruction counts.

cut by 38%, whereas the number of read and write instructions are reduced by 49% each and the instruction count is reduced by 48%, all on a per-CPU basis. In other words, the complexity and nature of the computation on a coarse level does not change much, but becomes evenly spread over an increasing number of workers. To account for the non-linear scaling of performance, we need to look for other effects.

3.2 Cache misses

The explanation is partly found in the number of read and write misses. Table 3 shows estimated reduced execution time based on the cache misses only. When going from one to two workers the number of read misses increases dramatically, which represents a small number of capacity misses changing to a large number of coherency misses caused by inter-processor communication. The write miss count also increases but not as dramatically. The increased number of read and write misses explains why the initial speedup is only 1.9 and not closer to 2.0 as indicated by the operation count.

	number of workers			
	1-2	2-4	4-8	8-16
runtime	0.52	0.55	0.62	0.72
read misses	15	0.56	0.67	0.61
write misses	0.99	0.54	0.70	0.51

Table 3: improvements of cache performance

Once the initial penalty of running in parallel has been taken the miss rate increases less dramatically. When going from two to four or from four to eight workers the increased miss rate appears sufficient to explain the actual limited speedup. But, when going from eight to sixteen workers the increased miss rate alone cannot explain the poor performance.

3.3 Explaining overall performance

We ran various combinations of Penny—using eight versions of Penny itself (with different improvements and modifications), several benchmark inputs in addition to Smith-Waterman, and three levels of parallelism (4, 8, and 16

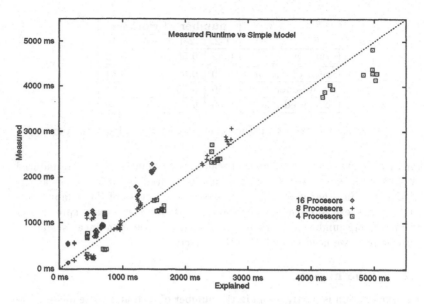

Figure 7: Results of explaining performance using a simple best-fit

workers). We measured the median time out of 31 runs, giving us 96 timing points. For each point, we used SIMICS to generate 12 aggregate values, covering the different cache and TLB miss types in the target system, for one of the processors.

We next selected three variables that we presumed to be important for explaining performance. A multiple regression of these variables against the database, and fudging, results in the following relation between the explained time T in milliseconds, read operations R, first-level read misses L_1, second-level read misses L_2:

$$T = 0.1 \times R + 0.33 \times L_1 + 10 \times L_2$$

In figure 7 we have plotted the explained time T against the measured time. The correlation is 0.96, not exceptional but clearly a good indicator. Observing the figure, we note that the performance of large configurations (16 processors) is overestimated and, conversely, the small configuration (4 processors) is underestimated. We suspect the reason for this is that we are lacking a fourth coefficient to measure bus contention, an issue that becomes significant as the number of communicating processors increase.

Misses to the second level cache cause the bus load to increase. The bus is a globally shared resource, so when it approaches saturation it stalls new accesses. As we increase parallelism, the miss rate of reads and writes both increase, which is natural since we are spreading work and communicating more. At the same time, execution time is decreasing, compounding pressure on the bus. This could explain the abnormally high coefficient for read misses to the second level cache (10), which of course is the one of the three closest correlated with bus contention and thus has to carry the bus contention load in the regression.

The conclusion is that the bus capacity starts affecting overall performance at 16 workers (something we could confirm over a year later by running the same benchmark on the next generation SPARC multiprocessor with a faster bus).

In this analysis, SIMICS reports sufficient detail to help us reconstruct what is causing speedup to begin trickling off. We now know that for larger configurations, we should focus on second-level cache misses. Many of the data structures in Penny have been optimized to be cache-line aligned, etc. The SIMICS' source-line profiling of second-level cache misses could be used to evaluate different design changes aimed at reducing the amount of data communicated.

4   Concluding remarks

The brief examples in this paper have been anecdotal, and were intended to underline SIMICS' ability to zoom in on and study performance problems, or to explore design alternatives. The criteria we used for deciding what was "good" were a small number of characteristics, essentially the type of data listed in the *counters* example in figure 6. That these relatively simple statistics are good guidelines can be shown by correlating them against a large number of performance measurements from the real target machine. The cache performance is so important for the overall performance of the system that it is very hard to tune a system without having access to cache miss statistics.

A parallel system can have a perfectly scalable behavior with respect to the number of instructions executed and still not show linear speedup. Only when the cache misses are taken into account can the performance of the system be understood. We have shown a strong correlation between the actual execution time and read operations. It indicates that a second level read miss is two order of magnitudes more expensive than a first level hit. This in turn suggests that a read miss rate of the second level cache of over one percent will dominate the execution time.

Analysis of cache performance of logic programming systems is not new [6] but our approach is quite different. We have analyzed the performance of a parallel system on an existing parallel architecture. The analysis is done not through a generated trace file of selected read and write operations but from all operations actually performed by the system.[5] The number of read and write operations performed by the larger benchmarks is over 100 mil-

---

[5]We have restricted ourselves to a user-level study, i.e. excluding the effects of an operating system.

lion. The total number of instructions executed is for some benchmarks over 600 million. SimICS also allows us to do interactive performance debugging since hot-spots are easily located. We know not only the overall cache performance but can pinpoint the instructions that generate misses.

In general, we note the importance of profiling tools keeping abreast of what hardware events are actually triggered by the software, why, and roughly what cost they correspond to. For the architecture modelled in this study, the performance of the memory hierarchy (data caches), the virtual memory system (TLB), and instruction count was adequate. Subsequent generations of parallel architectures will undoubtably introduce new events. For example, we would expect future large parallel machines to exhibit more complex memory hierarchy behavior, in which case we would need to extend SimICS to maintain separate profiles for a larger family of memory hierarchy events.

Acknowledgments

The parallel implementation of AKL has been developed using the AGENTS 1.0 [8] system as a starting point. Haruyasu Ueda did much of the implementation and analysis of the scheduler [13]. Gallal Atlam and Kahyri Ali, designed and implemented the garbage collector [1, 2].

Bengt Werner co-designed much of the SimICS front-end semantics. Anders Landin has been an enthusiastic supporter of SimICS and has contributed much to the discussion of what a user needs to know about program/architecture interaction. David Samuelsson wrote much of the SPARC V8 interpreter. Henrik Forsberg wrote much of the Unix emulation.

Thanks to Peter Fritzson at Linköping University for access to a 20-processor SC2000 for the Penny timings.

Various parts of this work have been sponsored by Ellemtel in the Enterprise and Hubble projects, Sun Microsystems in the SOS project, the European Commission in the GPMIMD project, ACCLAIM Esprit project, EP 7195 and SICS.

References

[1] K. A. M. Ali. A parallel copying garbage collection scheme for shared-memory multiprocessors. *New Generation Computing*, 13(4), December 1995.

[2] G. A. M. A. Atlam. *Parallel garbage collection in a multiprocessor implementation of a concurrent constraint programming system*. Phd thesis, Menoufia University, Egypt, January 1997.

[3] R. C. Bedichek. Some efficient architecture simulation techniques. In *Proceedings of Winter '90 USENIX Conference*, pages 53–63, January 1990.

[4] P. Brand, D. Sahlin, and T. Sjöland. Assessment of a storage optimization tool for AKL. Esprit, PARFORCE deliverable, D.WP2.3.5.M3.

[5] S. Gill. The diagnosis of mistakes in programmes on the EDSAC. In *Proceedings of the Royal Society Series A, Mathematical and Physical Sciences*, volume 206/1087, pages 538–554. Cambridge University Press, May 1951.

[6] M. Hermenegildo and E. Tick. Memory referencing characteristics and caching performance of and-parallel prolog on a shared-memory multiprocessor. *New Generation Computing*, 7(11):37–58, 1989.

[7] S. Janson. AKL a multiparadigm programming language. Uppsala Thesis in Computing Science 19, SICS Dissertation Series 14, Uppsala University, SICS, 1994.

[8] S. Janson and J. Montelius. The design of the AKL/PS 0.0 prototype implementation of the Andorra Kernel Language. ESPRIT deliverable, EP 2471 (PEPMA), SICS, 1992.

[9] P. S. Magnusson. A design for efficient simulation of a multiprocessor. In *Proceedings of MASCOTS*, pages 69–78, January 1993.

[10] P. S. Magnusson. Efficient instruction cache simulation and execution profiling with a threaded-code interpreter. In *Proceedings of the '97 Winter Simulation Conference*, 1997. (to appear).

[11] P. S. Magnusson and B. Werner. Efficient memory simulation in SimICS. In *Proceedings of the 28th Annual Simulation Symposium*, pages 62–73, 1995.

[12] J. Montelius. Exploiting fine-grain parallelism in concurrent constraint languages. Uppsala Thesis in Computing Science 28, SICS Dissertation Series 25, Uppsala University, SICS, 1997.

[13] H. Ueda and J. Montelius. Dynamic scheduling in an implicit parallel system. In *Ninth International Conference on Parallel and Distributed Computing Systems*, September 1996.

[14] D. H. D. Warren. An abstract prolog instruction set. Technical Report 309, SRI International, 1983.

Extending a Concurrent Constraint Language by Propagators

Tobias Müller and Jörg Würtz
Programming Systems Lab
Universität des Saarlandes and DFKI Saarbrücken
Postfach 15 11 50, D-66041 Saarbrücken, Germany
Email: {tmueller,wuertz}@ps.uni-sb.de

Abstract

To solve large and hard discrete combinatorial problems it is often necessary to design new constraints. Current systems either focus on the high-level modeling aspect or on very efficient implementation technology. While each approach lacks the advantages of the other one, this paper describes the combination of both approaches in the concurrent constraint language Oz. Through an interface to program new finite domain constraints efficiently in C++, the benefits of a high-level language to model a problem and of an efficient implementation technology for user-defined constraints are inherited.

Constraints and the Oz runtime system are linked together only by the interface abstractions. The interface supplies adequate abstractions to implement advanced algorithmic techniques. It provides, for example, also means to reflect the validity of a constraint and to control and inspect the state of the actual implementation of a constraint. This allows to solve demanding combinatorial problems, as for instance hard scheduling problems.

The described interface is not limited to concurrent constraint languages or a particular constraint system.

1 Introduction

Over the last years several approaches and systems were suggested to solve discrete combinatorial problems with finite domain constraints [4, 19, 3, 2, 5, 8]. To solve large and hard combinatorial problems it is often necessary to program new customized constraints and search strategies. Several approaches were suggested in literature.

A constraint logic programming (CLP) language like ECL^iPS^e [5] is well-suited to model constraint problems on a high-level. It provides certain primitives like attributed variables to design new constraints. But many techniques to solve hard problems require destructive low-level operations, which are difficult to program efficiently in this setting.

The indexical approach [19, 3] allows the user to program some new constraints. But it has no support to apply more sophisticated algorithmic techniques to implement new constraints (see also Section 8 and [13]).

On the other hand, combinatorial problems can be tackled in a language like C++ together with a dedicated library for constraint solving (see *e.g.* ILOG [8]). Although, many programming abstractions are provided through C++ classes, it is hard for a C++ library to prcvide an adequate level of abstraction to program the constraint model intended to solve the actual problem.

Each approach lacks the advantages of the others. In this paper we describe the combination of the advantages of these approaches by interfacing the high-level language Oz [17] with an interface to program new constraints efficiently in C++. Oz is a concurrent constraint programming (CCP) language [14] which comes with a rich predefined constraint library. By the concepts of a constraint store and entailment, new constraints can be programmed in the language itself. Furthermore, Oz provides means to program new search strategies [16].

Typically, the first step to solve a demanding problem consists in a prototypical implementation. In case of using Oz, rapid prototyping is supported by the features of a high-level language. After identifying the performance-critical parts of the program which are not covered by predefined library constraints, these parts should be re-casted in a very efficient implementation. To this aim an interface is provided which supports adequate abstractions to implement new constraints in C++. Thus, the application programmer can benefit from both a high-level language and an efficient C++ implementation.

The actual implementation of a constraint through the interface is called a propagator. The interface itself is called the Constraint Propagator Interface (CPI) of Oz. Propagators and the Oz runtime system are linked together only by the interface abstractions. The programmer is freed from tedious tasks like suspending or resuming propagators. Furthermore, the CPI provides abstractions to hide *resp.* handle specific features of Oz like computation spaces and equality constraints. That helps the programmer to concentrate on propagation techniques rather than on (in this context) irrelevant issues.

The implementation of advanced propagators is supported as follows. The validity of arbitrary constraints can be reflected into a 0/1-valued variable (also called reification) efficiently by a general and easy-to-use mechanism. The state of a propagator can be controlled and inspected by the programmer. For example, it is possible to extend the set of variables an already running propagator is constraining. Running propagators can spawn further propagators to strengthen constraint propagation. Furthermore, it is possible to keep a history of computation steps in the propagator's state. This can be used to avoid redundant computation.

The interface design can also be used for Prolog-based implementations providing for coroutining. Moreover, it can be extended by further constraint systems, as already done at the DFKI for set interval constraints.

We emphasise that to prove the practicability of our approach Oz's whole finite domain constraint library is implemented using the CPI. The resulting constraint solver shows competitive performance to state-of-the-art finite domain systems. It shows also competitive expressiveness and employs non-trivial algorithms for scheduling applications [20].

Plan of the paper. The following section introduces the computation model of Oz followed by the introduction of the CPI abstractions. Section 4 explains the implementation of a propagator. The advanced expressiveness of the CPI in conjunction with a case-study is discussed in Section 5 and 6. The specific features of Oz are considered in the following Section 7. The paper closes with related work, a performance evaluation, and a conclusion.

2 Computation with Constraints in Oz

As a particular instance of a CCP language we consider Oz [17, 16, 11]. Further, the paper focuses on *finite domain constraints* over non-negative integers (for short finite domain constraints, see [16] for details).

In Oz a distinction is made between those constraints which are basic and those which are not. For the purpose of this paper, a *basic constraint* takes the form $x = n$, $x = y$, or $x \in D$, where x and y are variables, n is an integer and D is a finite domain. A constraint $x \in D$ is called a *domain constraint*. We say a variable x is *determined* if the store entails a constraint $x = n$. The basic constraints reside in the *constraint store* C. Efficient algorithms to decide satisfiability and entailment are provided for basic constraints.

For more expressive constraints, like $x + y = z$, deciding their satisfiability is not computationally tractable. Such non-basic constraints are not held in the constraint store but are realized as *propagators*. A propagator is a computational agent which tries to narrow down the domains of variables by adding appropriate basic constraints to the store. The term *constraint propagation* refers to advancing the constraint store in this way. A propagator imposing the constraint P advances the store C to the store $C \wedge B$, if $C \wedge P$ entails B and B adds new and consistent information to C. The variables a propagator is narrowing are called its *parameters*.

The implementation of a propagator defines the amount of constraint propagation, *i.e.*, its operational semantics. Often a complete propagator which imposes the strongest basic constraint entailed by $C \wedge P$ is computationally too expensive. Thus, weaker propagation is usually employed. For some application areas domain-specific techniques can be exploited which lead to very good results (see also Section 9). A propagator may also cease to exist. If it ceases to exist, either P is entailed by C, or $C \wedge P$ is unsatisfiable.

As an example for constraint propagation, assume a store containing $x, y, z \in \{1, \ldots, 10\}$. The propagator for $x + y < z$ narrows the domains to $x, y \in \{1, \ldots, 8\}$ and $z \in \{3, \ldots, 10\}$ (since the other values cannot satisfy the constraint). Adding the constraint $z = 5$ causes the propagator to strengthen the store to $x, y \in \{1, \ldots, 3\}$ and $z = 5$. Imposing $x = 3$ lets the propagator narrow the domain of y to 1.

A *computation space* hosts a constraint store and a set of propagators. We first treat the case where only one computation space is given. The particularities of a hierarchy of computation spaces is described in Section 7.

3 Extending Oz with Propagators

The computational model sketched in Section 2 is realized by the Oz runtime system, which is implemented by an abstract machine [9], called the *emulator*. In the current section we explain the interface between the emulator and propagators. We introduce the provided CPI abstractions as consequence of the interaction between the emulator and propagators. Note that in the following we also speak of propagators if we mean the actual implementation of the computational agents.

Overview. A propagator exists in different execution states which are controlled by the emulator. Further, the emulator provides a propagator with resources like computation time and heap memory. To separate the emulator and the implementation of propagators, from the emulator's point of view a propagator is an opaque entity that requires resources *resp.* services.

In turn, a propagator synchronises on the constraint store and may amplify it with basic constraints. The emulator *resumes* a propagator, when the store has been amplified in a way the propagator is waiting for. For example, many propagators will only be resumed when the domain bounds of its parameters are narrowed. On resumption a propagator *reads* for its parameters the basic constraints which are contained in the store. In the course of constraint propagation it *writes* basic constraints to the store.

The CPI is a C++ interface and consequently, provides abstractions as C++ classes. A propagator is implemented by an instance of a C++ class which stores in its state references to the propagator's parameters. Operationally, resuming a propagator means running its propagation method. Note that in the following C++ identifiers which start with "OZ_" refer to CPI abstractions.

Handling a propagator. As mentioned above, the emulator regards a propagator as an opaque entity. Hence, the emulator needs a uniform way to refer to all instances of propagators. Further, the CPI must ensure that a programmer provides the minimal propagator functionality required by the emulator. The compiler should reject code which is incomplete in that sense. Technically, both requirements are realized in the interface by defining the class `OZ_Propagator` as *abstract base class*, which is the ancestor class of all propagator classes. An abstract base class provides only the declaration (*i.e.*, only the type signature) but not the definition for its virtual methods which are indicated by "=0" after the argument list. Virtual methods allow for dynamic binding of methods. This enables the emulator to control any concrete instance of a propagator only by having a pointer of type (`OZ_Propagator*`) to it and thus, separates completely propagators from the emulator.

```
enum OZ_Return {ENTAILED, FAILED, SLEEP};

class OZ_Propagator {
public:
    virtual OZ_Return propagate(void) = 0;
    virtual void updateHeapRefs(OZ_Boolean) = 0;
    ...
};
```

Imposing a propagator. Attaching a propagator instance to its parameters and introducing a reference to this instance to the emulator is called *propagator imposition*. This is done by a so-called *header function*. Such a function is connected via the Oz standard C interface [10] to an Oz procedure. A header function has to provide the following services.

1. A propagator is imposed as soon as its parameters are *sufficiently constrained*. For example, if a parameter which is expected to be an integer is not yet determined, the propagator should not be imposed yet. On the other hand, type errors should be detected by the header (*e.g.*, a parameter is an atom instead of an integer).

2. It is determined on imposition what events cause a propagator to be resumed. A propagator can be resumed if a parameter is determined, the bounds of the parameter's domain are narrowed, the size of the domain is shrunk, or a parameter is involved in a unification.

3. A reference to the newly created propagator instance has to be passed to the emulator.

The class OZ_Expect is provided for that purpose. It supplies a set of methods to test parameters to be sufficiently constrained. Further, they store the event (this is passed as extra argument to the test method) on which the propagator has to be resumed. Insufficiently constrained parameters cause the header function to be suspended such that it is resumed as soon as the parameters concerned are further constrained.

After creating a new instance of the propagator by invoking its constructor, a reference of type (OZ_Propagator*) is passed to the method impose() of OZ_Expect to introduce the propagator to the emulator. As a side-effect, impose() attaches *suspensions* to the appropriate *suspension lists* of the variable parameters. These parameters were previously stored in the state of the propagator by the test methods. The propagator is now *suspending* on its parameters and can be resumed if the parameters are further constrained. In fact, a variable can have several suspension lists such that the contained propagators are resumed on different events.

Scheduling a propagator by the emulator. In order to schedule propagators, the emulator maintains for each propagator an execution state which can take one of the following values: running, runnable, sleeping, entailed, and failed. The emulator's scheduler switches a propagator between the execution states as shown in Figure 1.

When a propagator is imposed, its execution state is immediately set running and the scheduler allocates a time slice for its first execution. After every execution, when the constraint propagation was performed by the appropriate propagation method, the emulator evaluates the propagator's return value.

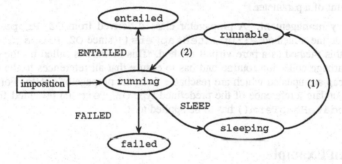

Figure 1: Execution states of a propagator

The value FAILED is returned if the propagator (according to its operational semantics) detects its inconsistency with the store. The emulator sets the propagator's execution state to failed and the computation is aborted. The propagator will be ignored by the emulator until it is eventually disposed by the next garbage collection. An immediate disposal is not desirable since there may be multiple references to a propagator.

The return value ENTAILED indicates that the propagator detects that the constraint it implements is entailed by the constraint store, *i.e.*, the propagator cannot further amplify the constraint store. The emulator sets the propagator's execution state to `entailed`. It happens the same as for a failed propagator: it will be ignored until it is disposed by garbage collection.

If the propagator can neither detect inconsistency nor entailment, it returns `SLEEP`. Its execution state is set to `sleeping`.

A propagator is resumed if at least one of its variable parameters was involved in unification or its domain was further narrowed. The emulator scans the suspension lists of the concerned variables and either deletes entries where the propagator's execution state is `failed` *resp.* `entailed` or switches the execution state of the suspending propagator to `runnable`. This is indicated by transition (1) in Figure 1. Now, the scheduler takes care of the propagator and will schedule it later on (the transition (2) from `runnable` to `running` is subject to the scheduler's policy and will be not discussed here). In fact, when the scheduler switches a propagator to `runnable` the propagator's method `propagate()` is executed.

Reading and writing constraints by a propagator. A propagator stores in its state references to its parameters. Constraint propagation in the implementation consists basically of the following stages: reading basic constraints of its parameters, writing further basic constraints to the store and resuming propagators suspending on these parameters. An instance of the class `OZ_FDIntVar` provides access to a parameter's representation in the constraint store. On construction it obtains access to a parameter's suspension lists and the parameter's finite domain representation of class `OZ_FiniteDomain`. Further, it stores a profile of the finite domain representation. A profile consists of the current domain size and the difference between the current largest and smallest element of the domain. Such a profile is used by the method `OZ_FDIntVar::leave()` to decide whether propagators suspending on this parameter have to be resumed or not. Instances of the class `OZ_FiniteDomain` provide methods to access the representation of the domain constraint of a parameter.

Memory management. A propagator class `P` derived from `OZ_Propagator` has to define a method `P::updateHeapRefs()` since `OZ_Propagator` declares this method as a pure virtual method. This method is called by the emulator's garbage collection routine and has to ensure that all references to the emulator's heap are updated which are reachable from the propagator's state. For example, to update a reference of the predefined type `OZ_Term` the provided function `OZ_updateHeapTerm()` has to be applied to it.

4   An Example

This section explains the constraint propagator interface of Oz by implementing the propagator for the constraint $x \leq y$.

The implementation of the $x \leq y$ propagator requires the definition of a new class inheriting from `OZ_Propagator`.

```
class LessEq : public OZ_Propagator {
private:
  OZ_Term x_ref, y_ref;
public:
  LessEq(OZ_Term x, OZ_Term y) : x_ref(x), y_ref(y) {}
  virtual OZ_Return propagate(void);
};
```

The propagator stores in its state references to its parameters (here x_ref and y_ref). A value of the predefined type OZ_Term refers to a parameter in the constraint store. The constructor of the class LessEq initialises the state and is used in the definition of the header function imposing the propagator (see at the end of this section).

The propagation method. When the emulator switches a propagator's state to running the method propagate() of the propagator is executed (see Figure 2). This method implements the propagation algorithm of the propagator.

```
 1  OZ_Return LessEq::propagate(void) {
 2    OZ_FDIntVar x(x_ref), y(y_ref);
 3    OZ_FiniteDomain * x_dom=x.getDom(), * y_dom=y.getDom();
 4    if (!x_dom->lowerUB(y_dom->getMaxElem())) goto failure;
 5    if (!y_dom->raiseLB(x_dom->getMinElem())) goto failure;
 6    if (x_dom->getMaxElem() <= y_dom->getMinElem()) {
 7      x.leave(); y.leave(); return ENTAILED;
 8    }
 9    x.leave(); y.leave(); return SLEEP;
10  failure:
11    x.fail(); y.fail(); return FAILED;
12  }
```

Figure 2: Method propagate() for the constraint $x \leq y$

To obtain access to the propagator's parameters the instances x and y of class OZ_FDIntVar are created. The function OZ_FDIntVar::getDom() returns a pointer to the representation of the domain constraint of the parameter (through its representation as an instance of OZ_FDIntVar). Therefore, x_dom and y_dom refer to the finite domain constraint representations of the respective parameters (3).[1]

The propagation algorithm for $x \leq y$ is straightforward. The upper bound of x's domain is constrained to be less than or equal to the upper bound of y's domain (4) and the lower bound of y's domain is constrained to be greater than or equal to the lower bound of x's domain (5). The method lowerUB(i) makes the upper bound of the domain less than or equal to i (4) and the method execution raiseLB(i) makes the lower bound of the domain greater than or equal to i (5). Both functions return the size of the resulting domain. The method getMinElem() *resp.* getMaxElem() returns the smallest *resp.* largest value of the domain (4,5). In case an empty domain is produced the execution branches to label failure.

The propagator cannot further amplify the store if the upper bound of x's domain is less than or equal to the lower bound of y's domain (6-8), *i.e.*, $x \leq y$ is entailed by the store. The returned value ENTAILED signals the emulator that the propagator can be discarded. Otherwise, returning SLEEP keeps the propagator suspending on its parameters. The method OZ_FDIntVar::leave() indicates for the emulator which suspending propagators should be resumed because of the occurred propagation.

The method OZ_FDIntVar::fail() has to be called to do some cleanups if the propagator is left because of a detected empty domain. The returned value FAILED signals the emulator that the current computation space is inconsistent.

Imposing the propagator. The header function to impose the $x \leq y$ propagator

---

[1]Note that in the sequel numbers in parentheses refer to program lines in Figure 2.

defines an instance of the class `OZ_Expect`. The following macro applications apply the test method `OZ_Expect::expectIntVarBounds()` to the 1st and 2nd parameter which causes the propagator to be imposed not before the parameters are constrained to finite domains. Additionally, it is determined that narrowing the bounds of domains will resume the propagator. A new instance of the propagator is created by calling the constructor with the 1st and 2nd parameter. The application of method `impose()` makes the propagator suspending on its parameters and introduces the propagator to the emulator.

```
OZ_C_proc_begin(lesseq, 2) {
  OZ_Expect pe;
  OZ_EXPECT(pe, 0, expectIntVarBounds);
  OZ_EXPECT(pe, 1, expectIntVarBounds);
  return pe.impose(new LessEq(OZ_args[0], OZ_args[1]));
} OZ_C_proc_end
```

5 Additional Expressiveness of the CPI

This section explains the extended expressiveness of the CPI which is desired to implement advanced propagators for demanding applications. All the discussed extensions are supported by adequate CPI-abstractions which fit smoothly in the setting presented before (see [12] for details).

Taking variable equality into account. Oz provides equality between variables, *i.e.* $x = y$, as basic constraint. The CPI deals with equality in two ways:

1. The CPI provides abstractions to check which parameters of a propagator are equal (see Section 6 for details). This can be applied to detect an inconsistency before variables are determined, as for the *alldiff*-constraint, which imposes the constraint that n variables must be pairwise different.

2. Different instances of `OZ_FDIntVar` associated with parameters which are equal refer to the same basic constraint. Therefore, updates to such a basic constraint are already visible via all other parameters while propagating and before leaving the propagator and telling the constraints to the store.

To avoid superficial equality treatment a propagator can check if an equality constraint was imposed on its parameters since the propagator's last run.

Exploiting statefulness. Because search in Oz is based on a copying-scheme, not only changes to variables are saved, but also complete computation spaces including propagators. That allows the modification of a propagator's state destructively since if an inconsistency occurs, the propagator can be fully recovered. This feature can be used to detect what parameter has been changed since the most recent execution of the propagation method by storing a profile (see Section 3) of the parameters before the propagation method is left. This allows the implementation of consistency algorithms like AC-5 [18]. Further, it can be used to store intermediate propagation results in the state which are expensive to recompute on each execution of the propagation method.

Replacing *resp.* imposing propagators while propagating. In the course of propagation a propagator may detect that it can replace itself by a more efficient one. For example, suppose $x = y$ is added to a store of a computation space where the constraint $x + y = z$ belongs to. It is more efficient to replace $x + y = z$ by $2x = z$ rather than to take care of equality every time propagation is done for $x + y = z$.

In scheduling applications a propagator for a specialized scheduling constraint may deduce in the course of propagation orderings betweens tasks. To maintain these task orderings propagators for constraints like $Start_{T_1} + Duration_{T_1} < Start_{T_2}$ can be imposed by the scheduling propagator with the side-effect that the scheduling propagator need not to care for these orderings anymore.

Encapsulated propagation. Typically, propagators tell the result of constraint propagation to the store. An instance of the class `OZ_FDIntVar` allows therefore to update the basic finite domain constraint of its associated parameter, such that the changes will become visible to the store. But, for example, propagators for reified (*resp.* meta) constraints [6] reflect only the validity of a constraint via a 0/1-variable to the store. The result of propagation is encapsulated in the propagator (*i.e.* not visible to the store) and only used to decide the validity of the constraint (for instance by comparing the basic constraints in the store with the result of propagation). The CPI supports encapsulated propagation by the method `OZ_FDIntVar::readEncap()`, so that reified constraints can be straightforwardly implemented in conjunction with propagator replacement.

Attaching a propagator with a stream. The CPI abstraction `OZ_Stream` allows to attach a propagator with a stream such that the propagator is able to read and write the stream. That enables communication between a propagator and other program parts independent from finite domain constraint propagation. This feature allows branching strategies to be guided by propagators. The propagator may suggest to an Oz procedure an ordering for tasks to be scheduled by using the shared stream. The Oz procedure may take the branching suggestion into account and may communicate back via the stream the actual branching decision to the propagator. The propagator in turn can use this information for the next ordering suggestion. Furthermore, it is possible to add extra parameters after a propagator is imposed to allow for propagators with dynamically increasing arity.

The discussed features have been applied to solve hard scheduling problems competive to the state-of-the-art [20]. The CPI enables the implementation of so-called global constraints. It is further possible to suspend the imposition of a propagator until the store contains certain required basic constraint, which is desired to implement, *e.g.*, an autonomous solver encapsulated in a propagator. The CPI allows the implementor of a propagator to determine the degree of propagation, *e.g.* domain consistency for a certain constraint.

6 A Case-study

This section outlines the implementation of a more advanced propagator using some of the previously discussed extensions. The example used is the constraint

$$\sum_{i=1}^{n} a_i x_i + c \leq 0 \tag{1}$$

Along this example, it is shown how the state of a propagator is used to avoid redundant computation, how constraints of arbitrary arity can be handled, and how equality between variables can be used.

Propagation rules. We assume for the presented formulas that for a given real number n, $\lfloor n \rfloor$ ($\lceil n \rceil$) denotes the largest (smallest) integer which is equal or smaller (larger) than n. Further, the current lower *resp.* upper bound of the domain of a variable x is denoted by $\underline{x}$ *resp.* $\overline{x}$. Resolving the inequation (1) for $a_k x_k$ yields.

$$a_k x_k \leq - \sum_{i=1, i \neq k}^{n} a_i x_i - c$$

The upper bound of the right hand side of this in-equation is

$$up_k = - \sum_{i=1, i \neq k, a_i > 0}^{n} a_i \underline{x}_i - \sum_{i=1, i \neq k, a_i < 0}^{n} a_i \overline{x}_i - c$$

For every k, the variable x_k is narrowed as follows until a fixed point is reached.

$$x_k \leq \left\lfloor \frac{up_k}{a_k} \right\rfloor, \text{ if } a_k > 0 \quad \text{and} \quad x_k \geq \left\lceil \frac{up_k}{a_k} \right\rceil, \text{ if } a_k < 0$$

This propagator ceases to exist if the following in-equation holds:

$$\sum_{i=1, a_i > 0}^{n} a_i \overline{x}_i + \sum_{i=1, a_i < 0}^{n} a_i \underline{x}_i + c \leq 0$$

Handling vectors. The CPI provides adequate abstractions to convert data structures of Oz (like lists) into C++ data structures. In Oz, a list, a tuple, or a record is denoted as a *vector*. To enable propagators with arbitrary arity, vectors are allowed as parameters too. The propagator for inequality (1) has three parameters, *i.e.*, the first parameter contains the coefficients, the second one the variables and the third one the constant.

The vectors of coefficients and finite domain variables are converted to C++ arrays of integers and elements of type OZ_Term, respectively. The class for the propagator implementing inequality constraints stores arrays for the coefficients a_i and the variables x_i, the constant c and the current size of the arrays.

```
class GenLessEqProp : public OZ_Propagator {
  int arr_sz, c, * a;
  OZ_Term * x;
public: ...
};
```

The header will check whether the arrays have the same size and whether the parameters have the correct type. For this aim, the class OZ_Expect can be customized to handle more complex data structures (like arrays or matrices).

Exploiting variable equality. The CPI provides the function

```
int * OZ_findEqualVars(int size, OZ_Term * v)
```

to detect equal variables, in an OZ_Term array. It expects v to be an array of size size. Assume the application

```
int * pa = OZ_findEqualVars(arr_sz, x);
```

where pa is called the position array. The array x is scanned with ascending index starting from 0 to determine the values of pa. If x[i] denotes a variable and this variable occurs the first time, the value of pa[i] is i. In case the variable occurs not the first time, pa[i] contains the index of the first occurrence. If x[i] denotes an integer, pa[i] contains -1.

As an example consider the constraint $2a + 3b - 4c - 5d + 4e + 8 \leq 0$ where at runtime the constraint $c = e \wedge d = 2$ is imposed. The result of checking for equal variables is as follows.

i:	0	1	2	3	4
x[i]:	a	b	c	d	e
pa[i]:	0	1	2	-1	2

The state of the propagator can now be updated to represent the equivalent constraint $2a + 3b - 2 \leq 0$. Thus, this simplification avoids tedious handling of equal variables in the propagation algorithm and it improves memory consumption and runtime behaviour.

7 Dealing with a Hierarchy of Computation Spaces

The main difference between constraint logic programming (CLP) and concurrent constraint programming (CCP) is the replacement of satisfiability detection by entailment checking. In Oz, computation spaces are used to implement entailment checking (recall that for this paper a computation space consists of a constraint store and a set of propagators attached to it). Furthermore, computation spaces are employed to implement different search strategies in Oz (see [16] for details). Thus a hierarchy of computation spaces may arise. Because constraint stores contain only basic constraints, entailment between stores can be decided efficiently. On the other hand, propagators should be taken into account, too. To this aim a propagator should cease to exist as soon as it can detect that the constraint it is imposing is entailed (but at last if all its parameters are determined). That all propagators in a computation space have ceased to exist is a necessary condition that a space, *i.e.*, its store and the constraints the propagators are imposing, is entailed.

While the implementors of the CPI have to take care of the handling of computation spaces, their existence and the resulting extra effort are *completely transparent* for the user of the CPI. This is due to the supplied functionality by appropriate methods which hide these issues from the programmer.

The fact that Oz computation may lead to a hierarchy of computation spaces has to be taken into consideration. In case a *global variable* (*i.e.*, a variable which is declared in a super-ordinated space) is further constrained in a subordinated space, the changes must be memorized. This is because the local information must not be visible in super-ordinated spaces and must be undone when the subordinated space is left. Second, the emulator can resume only those propagators which suspend in the current or in subordinated spaces. This is because constraints of a super-ordinated space are visible in all its subordinated spaces but not the other way around (note that this does not hold for propagators).

If a *local variable* (*i.e.*, a variable which is declared in the current space) is further constrained, the old domain need not be memorized. If a *global variable* is further constrained, it is bound to a fresh local variable. The old domain of the global variable is memorized (trailed) and the new domain is attached to the local variable. Furthermore, the suspension entries of a global variable which contain suspensions in the current or subordinated spaces are taken over. Propagators provide this functionality by the method `leave()` automatically, freeing the user from this task. Note that this technique avoids the usual time stamping where one ensures that a variable is trailed only once (see *e.g.* [2]).

8 Related Work

This section compares different constraint programming systems qualitatively rather than quantitatively with Oz (see Section 9 for benchmarks).

Comparison with ILOG SOLVER. ILOG SOLVER [8] is a commercial C++ library that allows to solve combinatorial problems in a constraint programming style in C++. ILOG SOLVER permits the user to add new constraints. Therefore, methods for the following tasks have to be implemented: posting the constraint, performing the constraint's propagation and detecting an inconsistency. In contrast to CPI propagators, an inconsistency is signalled to the solver by a separate method rather than by a return value. There is no way to inform the solver that a constraint is entailed which disallows early discard of the constraint. The implementation of reified (*resp.* meta) constraints requires to determine an "opposite" constraint which is automatically imposed if the 0/1-variable is constrained to 0. The CPI provides for that purpose its propagator replacement features (see Section 5). Further, constraints in ILOG SOLVER can employ so-called demons to propagate selectively, *i.e.*, every variable is assigned a separate propagation method. This trades speeding up execution against increasing memory consumption. The CPI supports this technique too by modelling a demon by a separate propagator. Both systems support the implementation of global constraints effectively.

Comparison with *ECL^iPS^e* and CHIP. *ECL^iPS^e* is a Prolog-based language with a variety of extensions, particularly it features a finite domain constraint solver. *ECL^iPS^e* features attributed variables and coroutining and is extended by primitives to manipulate finite domain variables which allows to implement constraints, even global ones, in *ECL^iPS^e* itself. The programmer has to take care of the suspension handling and propagator resumption himself. In contrast, the CPI abstraction `OZ_FDIntVar` fulfills this task in a self-acting way.

CHIP [4] is the forerunner of *ECL^iPS^e* and provides a set of powerful built-in constraints. Nevertheless, the constraints are hard-wired and the user has to define new constraints in CHIP itself.

Comparison with indexicals. The so-called indexical approach [19] allows the user to define new constraints by constructing them with indexicals. Indexicals are terms "x in r" where r defines how x is constrained and on what event an indexical is resumed. The indexicals which realize a single constraint exist independently of each other, *i.e.*, the constraint is not available first-class (see also [13]). Thus, algorithmic techniques employing global reasoning on all arguments of the constraint cannot be incorporated in this setting.

AKL(FD) [2] implements indexicals in a concurrent constraint setting where local computation spaces are employed in so-called deep guards. Hence, there are similarities in the handling of variables and suspensions of different computation spaces. The integration of constraints is not as tight as in Oz. In AKL(FD) a single constraint cannot be used simultaneously to amplify the store and be used for entailment checking as is possible for propagators.

9 Performance Evaluation

To evaluate the performance of the CPI we ran two sets of benchmarks with Oz 2.0.3 and set the results in relation to ILOG SOLVER 3.2 *resp.* ILOG SCHEDULER 2.2 [7]. We have chosen ILOG to compare with because they use also C++ as implementation language. Note that also the scheduling propagators for benchmarking the job-shop problems are implemented using the CPI.

The performance of Oz for small-size applications, like n-queens, is rather average due to the constant extra cost imposed by the very expressive first-class search facilities of Oz [15].

Propagation performance. The first set of benchmarks measures the performance of the CPI without search. Inconsistent constraints are imposed such that it requires a lot of propagation to detect the inconsistency. The time is taken until the inconsistency is detected. To keep the impact of propagation algorithms minimal we used the straightforward constraints $x < y$, $2x = y$, and $x + y = z$, which do not require sophisticated propagation techniques and reason only on the bounds of domains.

Inconsistent constraint	ILOG SOLVER 3.2 (sec)	Oz 2.0.3 (sec)	ILOG / Oz
$x, y \in \{0, \ldots, 1\,000\,000\} \wedge$ $u, v \in \{0, \ldots, 2\,000\,000\} \wedge$ $2x = u \wedge 2y = v \wedge u = v + 1$	26.71	24.35	1.09
$x, y \in \{0, \ldots, 10\,000\,000\} \wedge$ $x < y \wedge y < x$	28.09	29.65	0.95

Benchmarks ran on a Ultra Sparc 1, 170MHz, SunOs 5.5.

Table 1: Propagation performance

The results in Table 9 show that the propagation mechanism of the CPI is competitive with that of ILOG SOLVER. Comparing the quality of the propagation algorithms used for the supplied library constraints of ILOG SOLVER *resp.* Oz is beyond the scope of this paper.

Benchmarking job-shop problems. The following benchmarks compare Oz 2.0.3 with ILOG SCHEDULER 2.2 for classical 10x10 job-shop scheduling benchmarks for the proof of optimality [1]. In both systems we used the best strategy available in the corresponding libraries.[2]

In Table 2, the entry *Fails* denotes the number of failure nodes in the search tree needed for proving optimality. The entry *CPU* denotes the run time needed for proving optimality. The last two columns compare the run times between ILOG SCHEDULER and Oz.

To be able to solve job-shop problems we implemented special global constraints, *e.g.* edge-finding, and obtained results similar to ILOG SCHEDULER. The deviation between the results is due to the different propagation algorithms and

---

[2]In Oz, the capacity constraint was modeled by `FD.schedule.serialized` and the branching strategy by `FD.schedule.taskIntervalsDistP`. In ILOG, we used for the capacity constraint the provided edge-finding (with parameter 2 for the strongest pruning) and for the branching strategy `IlcSelResMinLocalSlack` to select the resource and `IlcSelFirstRCMinStartMax` to select the task to schedule first.

branching strategies.[3]

Problem	Oz		ILOG		ILOG/Oz	
	Fails	CPU	Fails	CPU	Fails	CPU
MT10	1 795	29.08	5 853	69.7	3.26	2.40
ABZ5	1 431	24.62	2 548	23.4	1.78	0.95
ABZ6	148	2.15	207	2.3	1.40	1.07
La19	1 066	18.43	3 786	35.1	3.56	1.90
La20	881	14.40	10 384	72.2	11.79	5.01
ORB1	7 533	124.93	3 925	42.9	0.52	0.34
ORB2	425	7.42	16 922	183.0	39.82	24.66
ORB3	22 590	345.28	16 845	211.3	0.75	0.61
ORB4	1 034	16.00	17 677	207.6	17.10	12.98
ORB5	871	14.84	3 031	27.2	3.48	1.83

Benchmarks ran on a Ultra Sparc 1, 170MHz, SunOs 5.5.

Table 2: Classical 10x10 job-shop problems

10 Conclusion

We have presented the interface CPI which extends the CCP language Oz by the possibility to implement efficient constraint propagators in C++. The interface abstractions are high-level enough to hide away low-level issues, like propagator resumption, from the programmer. The expressiveness of the CPI and the provided extensions (as discussed in Section 5) allow to easily implement, for example, complex global and reified constraints which make the interface suitable to tackle large and hard combinatorial problems. Further, the yielded interface performance is competitive with state-of-the-art constraint programming systems. The interface design can also be applied to Prolog-based implementations providing for coroutining. The CPI is also general enough to be extended by further constraint systems, as already proved for set interval constraints.

Acknowledgements. The authors would like to thank Martin Müller, Peter Van Roy, Christian Schulte, and the anonymous referees for their invaluable comments on earlier versions of this paper.

The research reported in this paper has been supported by the BMBF (FKZ-ITW-9105 and FTZ-ITW-9106), and the Esprit Working Group CCL-II (EP 22457).

References

[1] D. Applegate and W. Cook. A computational study of the job-shop scheduling problem. *Operations Research Society of America, Journal on Computing*, 3(2):149–156, 1991.

[2] B. Carlson, M. Carlsson, and S. Janson. The implementation of AKL(FD). In *Proceedings of the International Symposium on Logic Programming*, pages 227–241, 1995.

---

[3]A more thorough comparison (also with the Claire system) can be found through http://www.ps.uni-sb.de/~wuertz/Benchmarks/schedulingBenchs.html

[3] P. Codognet and D. Diaz. Compiling constraints in clp(FD). *Journal of Logic Programming*, 27(3):185–226, 1996.

[4] M. Dincbas, P. Van Hentenryck, H. Simonis, A. Aggoun, T. Graf, and F. Berthier. The constraint logic programming language CHIP. In *Proceedings of the International Conference on Fifth Generation Computer Systems FGCS-88*, pages 693–702, Tokyo, Japan, December 1988.

[5] ECRC. *ECL^{i}PS^e, User Manual Version 3.5.2*, December 1996.

[6] M. Henz and J. Würtz. Using Oz for college timetabling. In E.K. Burke and P. Ross, editors, *Practice and Theory of Automated Timetabling, First International Conference, Selected Papers, Edinburgh 1995*, volume 1153 of *Lecture Notes in Computer Science*, pages 162–178. Springer-Verlag, 1996.

[7] ILOG, URL: http://www.ilog.com. ILOG SCHEDULER 2.2, *User Manual, 1996*, 1996.

[8] ILOG, URL: http://www.ilog.com. ILOG SOLVER 3.2, *User Manual, 1996*, 1996.

[9] M. Mehl, R. Scheidhauer, and C. Schulte. An abstract machine for Oz. In *Programming Languages, Implementations, Logics and Programs, Seventh International Symposium, PLILP'95*, Lecture Notes in Computer Science, pages 151–168, Utrecht, The Netherlands, 20–22 September 1995. Springer Verlag.

[10] Michael Mehl, Tobias Müller, Konstantin Popov, Ralf Scheidhauer, and Christian Schulte. DFKI Oz user's manual. DFKI Oz documentation series, Deutsches Forschungszentrum für Künstliche Intelligenz GmbH, Stuhlsatzenhausweg 3, 66123 Saarbrücken, Germany, 1997.

[11] T. Müller and J. Würtz. A survey on finite domain programming in Oz. In *Notes on the DFKI-Workshop: Constraint-Based Problem Solving, To appear as Technical report D-96-02*, Kaiserslautern, Germany, 1996.

[12] T. Müller and J. Würtz. The constraint propagator interface. DFKI Oz documentation series, Deutsches Forschungszentrum für Künstliche Intelligenz GmbH, Stuhlsatzenhausweg 3, 66123 Saarbrücken, Germany, 1997.

[13] J.-F. Puget and M. Leconte. Beyond the glass box: constraints as objects. In *Proceedings of the International Symposium on Logic Programming*, pages 513–527, 1995.

[14] V. A. Saraswat. *Concurrent Constraint Programming Languages*. PhD thesis, School of Comp. Sc., Carnegie-Mellon University, Pittsburgh, CA, 1989.

[15] C. Schulte. Oz Explorer: A visual constraint programming tool. In Lee Naish, editor, *Proceedings of the Fourteenth International Conference on Logic Programming*, Leuven, Belgium, 8-11 July 1997. The MIT Press.

[16] C. Schulte, G. Smolka, and J. Würtz. Encapsulated search and constraint programming in Oz. In A.H. Borning, editor, *Principles and Practice of Constraint Programming*, volume 874 of *Lecture Notes in Computer Science*, pages 134–150, Orcas Island, Washington, USA, 1994. Springer-Verlag.

[17] G. Smolka. The Oz programming model. In Jan van Leeuwen, editor, *Computer Science Today*, Lecture Notes in Computer Science, vol. 1000, pages 324–343. Springer-Verlag, Berlin, 1995.

[18] P. Van Hentenryck, Y. Deville, and C.M. Teng. A generic arc-consistency algorithm and its specializations. *Artificial Intelligence*, 57:291–321, 1992.

[19] P. Van Hentenryck, V. Saraswat, and Y. Deville. Constraint processing in cc(FD). Technical report, Brown University, 1991. Unpublished.

[20] J. Würtz. Oz Scheduler: A workbench for scheduling problems. In M.G. Radle, editor, *Eighth International Conference on Tools with Artificial Intelligence*, pages 149–156, Toulouse, France, 1996. IEEE, IEEE Computer Society Press.

Remark. A copy of the DFKI Oz 2.0 implementation featuring the CPI can be obtained from http://www.ps.uni-sb.de/oz2/.

A Rational and Efficient Algorithm for View Deletion in Databases

Chandrabose Aravindan* and Peter Baumgartner†
Fachbereich Informatik, Universität Koblenz-Landau,
Rheinau 1, D-56075 Koblenz, Germany
<{arvind,peter}@informatik.uni-koblenz.de>

Abstract

In this paper, we show how techniques from disjunctive logic programming and classical first-order theorem proving can be used for efficient (deductive) database updates. The key idea is to tranform the given database
together with the update request into a disjunctive logic program and apply
disjunctive techniques (such as minimal model reasoning) to solve the original update problem. We present two variants of our algorithm both of which
are of polynomial space complexity. One variant, which is based on offline
preprocessing, is of polynomial time complexity. We also show that both
variants are rational in the sense that they satisfy certain rationality postulates
stemming from philosophical works on belief dynamics.

1 Introduction

View update in databases is an important problem that has recently attracted attention of researchers from both deductive and relational fields [6, 10, 13, 17, 24, 9,
18, 19, for example] ([1] provides a survey of works in this regard). One crucial
aspect of an algorithm for view update is the satisfaction of *rationality postulates*
stemming from philosophical works on rationality of change [11, 12, for example].
This aspect was studied in detail in [6, 4], where an algorithm for database deletion
that satisfies all rationality postulates was presented. However, a serious drawback
of this and other known rational algorithms (such as the one from Tomasic [24]) is
that they are of exponential space and time complexity.

In this paper, we present a radically different approach to rational view updates
in (definite datalog) databases, resulting in an algorithm of polynomial space complexity. We also show that, in a special case polynomial time complexity can be
achieved. For the simplicity of presenting the main ideas, in this paper we restrict
our attention to definite datalog programs (note that relational databases can be represented by definite programs) and view deletion only. The approach we present
here is very closely related to our diagnosis setup presented in [7], where hyper
tableaux calculus [8] was used for efficiently solving *model based diagnosis* tasks.

---

* Funded by the DFG ("Deutsche Forschungsgemeinschaft") under grant Fu 263/3-1
† Funded by the DFG within the research programme "Deduction" under grant Fu 263/2-2

This close relationship enables us to use our *existing*, efficient implementation for diagnosis applications for view updates as well.

The basic idea in [7] is to employ the *model generation* property of hyper tableaux to generate models and read off diagnosis from them. One specific feature of this diagnosis algorithm is the use of semantics (by transforming the system description and the observation using an "initial model" of the correctly working system) in guiding the search for a diagnosis. This semantical guidance by program transformation turns out to be useful for database updates as well. More specifically, we use a (least) Herbrand Model of the given database to transform it along with the update request into a disjunctive logic program in such a way that the models of this transformed program stand for possible updates. Thus known disjunctive logic programming and first-order theorem proving techniques are exploited for efficient and rational view updates.

We discuss two ways of transforming the given database together with the view deletion request into a disjunctive logic program, resulting in two variants of view deletion algorithm. In the first variant, a simple and straightforward transformation is employed. But unfortunately all models of the transformed program do not stand for rational deletions. In order to be rational, we show that a rationality axiom itself (strong relevance policy) could be used as a test to filter out models representing non-rational deletions. Interestingly, this test based on a rationality axiom turns out be equivalent to the *groundedness test* used by Ilkka Niemelä for generating minimal models of disjunctive logic programs [22]. These two concepts (strong relevance policy and groundedness test) come from two different fields (belief dynamics and minimal model reasoning resp.) and this equivalence provides more insights into the issue (minimization) common to both the fields. Further, this equivalence implies that all minimal models (minimal wrt the EDB atoms) of the transformed program stand for rational deletions. Not surprisingly, all deletions obtained through this algorithm result in minimal change.

The second variant of the algorithm uses the Least Herbrand Model of the given database for the transformation. In fact, what we referred to as offline preprocessing before is exactly this computation of the Least Herbrand Model. This variant is very meaningful in applications where views are materialized for efficient query answering. The advantage of using the Least Herbrand Model for the transformation is that all computed models of the transformed disjunctive logic program (not just the minimal ones) stand for rational deletions. No minimality test is required, and thus the runtime complexity is improved.

The rest of the paper is organized as follows: We first briefly recall the rationality of change and the hyper tableaux calculus in Section 2. We then present two variants of our rational and efficient algorithm for view deletion in Secion 3. The paper is concluded with some comments on our approach and indications for further work. Due to space limitation some technical details and proofs have been omitted. Interested readers are referred to the full version of this paper [5] for complete details.

2 Background

2.1 Rationality of change

Rationality of change has been studied at an abstract philosophical level by various researchers, resulting in well known *AGM Postulates* for revison [2, 11, 12, for example]. However, it is not clear how these rationality postulates can be applied in real world problems such as database updates and this issue has been studied in detail by works such as [6, 4]. In the sequel, we briefly recall the postulates and an algorithm for contraction based on abduction from [6, 4].

Formally, a knowledge base KB is defined as a finite set of sentences from language L, and divided into two parts: an immutable theory KB_I, which is the fixed part of the knowledge; and an updatable theory KB_U. Because of the duality of revision and contraction, it is enough to consider one, and rationality postulates for contracting a sentence α from KB, written as KB—α is produced below.

DEFINITION 2.1 Let KB be a knowledge base with an immutable part KB_I. Let α and β be any two sentences. Then, α and β are said to be *KB-equivalent* iff the following condition is satisfied: For all set of sentences E: $KB_I \cup E \vdash \alpha$ iff $KB_I \cup E \vdash \beta$ ∎

DEFINITION 2.2 (RATIONALITY POSTULATES)

(KB—1) (Inclusion)	KB—$\alpha \subseteq KB$	
(KB—2) (Immutable-inclusion)	$KB_I \subseteq KB$—α	
(KB—3) (Vacuity)	If $\alpha \notin Cn(KB)$, then KB—$\alpha = KB$	
(KB—4) (Immutable-success)	If $KB_I \nvdash \alpha$, then $\alpha \notin Cn(KB$—$\alpha)$	
(KB—5) (Preservation)	If α and β are KB-equivalent, then KB—$\alpha = KB$—β	
(KB—6.1) (Strong relevance)	If $\beta \in KB \backslash KB$—$\alpha$, then $(KB$—$\alpha) \cup \{\beta\} \vdash \alpha$	
(KB—6.2) (Relevance)	If $\beta \in KB \backslash KB$—$\alpha$, then $\exists KB'$ with KB—$\alpha \subseteq KB' \subseteq KB$ s.t. $\alpha \notin Cn(KB')$ and $\alpha \in Cn(KB' \cup \{\beta\})$	
(KB—6.3) (Weak relevance)	If $\beta \in KB \backslash KB$—$\alpha$, then $\exists KB'$ with $KB' \subseteq KB$ s.t. $\alpha \notin Cn(KB')$ and $\alpha \in Cn(KB' \cup \{\beta\})$	

∎

Note that we have three variants of the relevant postulate of varying strength. The weaker forms are motivated by various works of Hansson [16, 15].

Now we recall an algorithm for contraction based on abduction presented in [6, 4]. Some basic definitions required for the algorithm are presented first.

DEFINITION 2.3 Let KB be a knowledge base and α a sentence. An *abductive explanation* Δ for α wrt KB_I is a set of abducibles s.t. $\Delta \cup KB_I \models \alpha$ and $\Delta \cup KB_I$ is consistent. An explanation is *minimal* iff no proper subset of it is an explanation. It is said to be *locally minimal*, iff there exists a subset KB'_I of KB_I s.t. Δ is a minimal abductive explanation of α wrt KB'_I. Further, Δ is said to be *KB-Closed* iff $\Delta \subseteq KB_U$. ∎

The general contraction algorithm of [6, 4] is reproduced here as Algorithm 1. The basic idea behind this algorithm is to generate all (locally minimal) explanations for the sentence to be contracted and determine a hitting set for these explanations. Since all (locally minimal) explanations are generated this algorithm is of exponential space and time complexity.

DEFINITION 2.4 (HITTING SET) Let S be a set of sets. Then a set *HS* is a *hitting set* of S iff $HS \subseteq \bigcup S$ and for every non-empty element R of S, $R \cap HS$ is not empty. ∎

Algorithm 1 General contraction algorithm

Input: A knowledge base $KB = KB_I \cup KB_U$ and a sentence α to be contracted.

Output: A new knowledge base $KB' = KB_I \cup KB'_U$

1. Construct a set S = {X | X is a KB-closed locally minimal abductive explanation for α wrt KB_I}.

2. Determine a hitting set $\sigma(S)$.

3. Produce KB' = $KB_I \cup (KB_U \setminus \sigma(S))$ as a result.

THEOREM 1 *Let KB be a knowledge base and α a sentence.*

1. *If Algorithm 1 produces KB' as a result of contracting α from KB, then KB' satisfies all the rationality postulates (KB—1), (KB—2), (KB—3), (KB—4), (KB—5), (KB—6.3).*

2. *Suppose KB" statisfies all these rationality postulates for contracting α from KB, then KB" can be produced by Algorithm 1.*

2.2 Hyper Tableaux Calculus

In [8] a variant of clausal normal form tableaux called "hyper tableaux" is introduced. Since the hyper tableaux calculus constitutes the basis for our view update algorithm, we will briefly recall it. It is sufficient to restrict to the ground version here.

We assume that the reader is familiar with the basic concepts of propositional logic. *Clauses*, i.e. multisets of literals, are usually written as the disjunction $A_1 \vee \cdots \vee A_m \vee \neg B_1 \vee \cdots \vee \neg B_n$ or as an implication $A_1 \vee \cdots \vee A_m \leftarrow B_1 \wedge \cdots \wedge B_n$ ($m \geq 0$, $n \geq 0$). With $\overline{L}$ we denote the complement of a literal L. Two literals L and K are *complementary* if $\overline{L} = K$.

From now on D always denotes a finite ground clause set, also called *database*, and Σ denotes its signature, i.e. the set of all predicate symbols occurring in it. We consider finite ordered trees T where the nodes, except the root node, are labeled with literals. In the following we will represent a branch b in T by the sequence $b = L_1, \ldots, L_n$ ($n \geq 0$) of its literal labels, where L_1 labels an immediate successor of the root node, and L_n labels the leaf of b. The branch b is called *regular* iff $L_i \neq L_j$ for $1 \leq i, j \leq n$ and $i \neq j$, otherwise it is called *irregular*. The tree T is *regular* iff each of its branches is regular, otherwise it is *irregular*. The set of *branch literals* of b is $lit(b) = \{L_1, \ldots, L_n\}$. For brevity, we will write expressions like $A \in b$ instead of $A \in lit(b)$. A literal set is called *inconsistent* iff it contains a pair of complementary literals, otherwise it is called *consistent*. In order to memorize the fact that a branch contains a contradiction, we allow to label a branch as either *open* or *closed*. A tableau is *closed* if each of its branches is closed, otherwise it is *open*.

DEFINITION 2.5 (HYPER TABLEAU) *Hyper tableaux* for D are inductively defined as follows:

Initialization step: The empty tree, consisting of the root node only, is a hyper tableau for D. Its single branch is marked as "open".

Hyper extension step: If (1) T is an open hyper tableau for D with open branch b, and (2) $C = A_1 \vee \cdots \vee A_m \leftarrow B_1 \wedge \cdots \wedge B_n$ is a clause from D ($m \geq 0$, $n \geq 0$), called *extending clause* in this context, and (3) $\{B_1, \ldots, B_n\} \subseteq b$ (equivalently, we say that C is *applicable to b*) then the tree T' is a hyper tableau for D, where T' is obtained from T by *extension of b by C*: replace b in T by the *new* branches $(b, A_1) \ldots, (b, A_m), (b, \neg B_1) \ldots, (b, \neg B_n)$ and then mark every inconsistent new branch as "closed", and the other new branches as "open".

We say that a branch b is *finished* iff it is either closed, or else whenever C is applicable to b, then extension of b by C yields some irregular new branch. ∎

The applicability condition of an extension expresses that *all* body literals have to be satisfied by the branch to be extended (like in hyper *resolution*) From now on we consider only regular hyper tableaux. This restriction guarantees that for finite clause sets no branch can be extended infinitely often. But for one variant of our algorithm we need a weaker notion of regularity referred to as *strictness*. A tableau is said to be strict if for each branch every rule is applied at most once.

170

EXAMPLE 2.6 (HYPER TABLEAUX)

Consider the following database D:

$$D: \quad p \vee q \leftarrow t \wedge r \qquad t \leftarrow$$
$$q \leftarrow p \wedge t \qquad r \leftarrow$$

The figure on the right contains a hyper tableau for D. For economy of notation, closed branches are not displayed. This tableau is obtained as follows: starting with the empty tree, we can extend with $t \leftarrow$ and then with $r \leftarrow$. Then, since t and r are now on the branch, we can extend with $p \vee q \leftarrow t \wedge r$. The left branch is now finished, because $q \leftarrow p \wedge t$ is not applicable. Extension with $q \leftarrow p \wedge t$ at the right branch finishes this branch as well. ∎

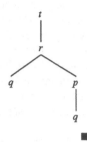

DEFINITION 2.7 (BRANCH SEMANTICS) As usual, we represent an interpretation I for given domain Σ as the set $\{A \in \Sigma \mid I(A) = true, A \text{ atom}\}$. *Minimality* of interpretations is defined via set-inclusion.

Given a tableau with consistent branch b. The branch b is mapped to the interpretation $[\![b]\!]_\Sigma := lit(b)^+$, where $lit(b)^+ = \{A \in lit(b) \mid A \text{ is a positive literal }\}$. Usually, we write $[\![b]\!]$ instead of $[\![b]\!]_\Sigma$ and let Σ be given by the context. ∎

For instance, the semantics of the left (right) branch b_1 (b_2) in the tableau in Example 2.6 is $[\![b_1]\!] = \{t,r,q\}$ ($[\![b_2]\!] = \{t,r,p,q\}$).

A refutational completeness result for hyper tableaux was given in [8]. For our purposes of computing database updates, however, we need a (stronger) model completeness result:

THEOREM 2 (MODEL COMPLETENESS OF HYPER TABLEAUX [7]) *Let T be a hyper tableau for D such that every open branch is finished. Then, for every minimal model I of D there is an open branch b in T such that $I = [\![b]\!]$.*

For example, since in the tableau in Example 2.6 every branch is finished, one of its branches contains a minimal model (the literals $\{t,r,q\}$ in the left branch constitute a minimal model).

The just presented calculus of hyper tableau has been adopted in [7] for model based diagnosis applications (cf. [23]). This diagnosis approach can be successfully used for database updates also, and in the sequel we discuss this in detail. For more details on the relationship between our approaches to diagnosis and database updates, see the full version of this paper [5].

3 An Algorithm for View Deletion

A *definite deductive database DDB* consists of two parts: an *intensional database IDB*, a set of definite program clauses; and an *extensional database EDB*, a set of ground facts. The intuitive meaning of *DDB* is provided by the *Least Herbrand model semantics*. The reader is referred to [20, and the references therein], for more information on definite programs, the least Herbrand model semantics, and SLD-derivations. All the predicates that are defined in *IDB* are referred to as *view predicates* and those defined in *EDB* are referred to as *base predicates*. Extending this notion, an atom with a view predicate is said to be a *view atom*, and similarly an atom with base predicate is a *base atom*. Further we assume that *IDB* does not contain any unit clauses and no predicate defined in a given *DDB* is both view and base. For the sake of simplicity we also assume that there are no integrity constraints associated with the given database.

Two kinds of view updates can be carried out on a *DDB*: An atom, that does not currently follow from *DDB*, can be *inserted*; or an atom, that currently follows from *DDB*, can be *deleted*. In this paper, we consider only deletion of an atom from a *DDB*. When an atom A is to be deleted, the view update problem is to delete only some relevant *EDB* facts, so that the modified *EDB* together with *IDB* will satisfy the deletion of A from *DDB*. View update problem, in the context of deductive and relational databases, has been studied by various authors and different algorithms have been proposed [6, 4, 10, 13, 17, 24, 9, 18, 19, for example].

Note that a *DDB* can be considered as a knowledge base to be revised. The *IDB* is the immutable part of the knowledge base, while the *EDB* forms the updatable part. In general, it is assumed that the language underlying a *DDB* is fixed and the semantics of *DDB* is the least Herbrand model over this fixed language. We assume that there are no function symbols impyling that the Herbrand Base is finite. Therefore, the *IDB* is practically a shorthand of its ground instantiation[1], written as IDB_G. In the sequel, technically we mean IDB_G when we refer simply to *IDB*. Thus, a *DDB* represents a knowledge base where the immutable part is given by IDB_G and updatable part is the *EDB*. Hence, the rationality postulates (KB—1), (KB—2), (KB—3), (KB—4), (KB—5), and (KB—6.3) provide an axiomatic characterization for deleting a view atom A from a definite database *DDB*.

An algorithm for view deletion, based on the general contraction algorithm (cf. Algorithm 1) was presented in [6, 4]. There, given a view atom to be deleted, set of all explanations for that atom has to be generated through a *complete* SLD-tree and a hitting set of these explanations is then deleted from the *EDB*. It was shown that this algorithm is rational. A serious drawback of this algorithm is that all explanations for the view atom to be deleted have to be generated and kept in memory. This means that this algorithm is of exponential space complexity. The same analysis holds for other known rational algorithms such as that of Tomasic [24].

In this paper, we present a radically different approach that runs on polynomial space. In contrast to our previous algorithm, this one directly computes a hitting set without explicitly generating all the explanations. Moreover the generation of hitting set is carried out through a hyper tableaux calculus that is focussed on the

---

[1] a ground instantiation of a definite program P is the set of clauses obtained by substituting terms in the Herbrand Universe for variables in P in all possible ways

goal.

3.1 An approach based on minimality test

The key idea of the algorithm presented in this paper is to transform the given database along with the view deletion request into a disjunctive logic program and apply known disjunctive techniques to solve the original view deletion problem. The intuition behind transformation is to obtain a disjunctive logic program in such a way that each (minimal) model of this transformed program represent a way of deleting the given view atom. We present two variants of our algorithm. The one that is discussed in this section employs a trivial transformation procedure but has to look for minimal models. The other variant (discussed in the next section) perfoms a costly transformation, but dispenses with the requirement of computing the minimal models.

We start presenting our algorithm by first defining precisely how the given database is tranformed into a disjunctive logic program for view deletion purposes.

DEFINITION 3.1 Given an *IDB* and a set of ground atoms S, the transformation of *IDB* wrt S is obtained by translating each clause $C \in IDB$ as follows: Every atom A in the body (resp. head) of C that is also in S is moved to the head (resp. body) as $\neg A$. ∎

DEFINITION 3.2 (*IDB** TRANSFORMATION) Let $IDB \cup EDB$ be a given database. Let $S_0 = EDB \cup \{A \mid A \text{ is a ground } IDB \text{ atom}\}$. Then, *IDB** is defined as the transformation of *IDB* wrt S_0. ∎

REMARKS 3.3 Note that *IDB** is in general a disjunctive logic program. The negative literals ($\neg A$) appearing in the clauses are intuitively interpreted as deletion of the corresponding atom (A) from the database. Technically, a literal $\neg A$ is to be read as a *positive* atom, by taking the $\neg$-sign as part of the predicate symbol. Note that there are no facts in *IDB**. So when we add a delete request such as $\neg A$ to this, the added request is the only fact and any bottom-up reasoning strategy is fully focused on the goal (here the delete request). ∎

Now, when we have a deletion request for a ground view atom A, represented as $\neg A$, the idea is to generate models of $IDB^* \cup \{\neg A\}$ and read the base atoms to be deleted from them. We propose to use the hyper tableaux calculus for this, and we state precisely how this is done. As mentioned in the above remark, $\neg A$ is the only fact and so the bottom-up hyper tableaux calculus for model generation is fully goal-oriented.

DEFINITION 3.4 (UPDATE TABLEAUX, HITTING SET) An *update tableau* for a database $IDB \cup EDB$ and delete request $\neg A$ is a hyper tableau T for $IDB^* \cup \{\neg A \leftarrow\}$ such that every open branch is finished. For every open finished branch b in T we define the *hitting set (of b in T)* as $HS(b) = \{A \in EDB \mid \neg A \in b\}$. ∎

REMARKS 3.5 The name "hitting set" is a misnomer here, but we use it in order to compare this approach with previous approaches that generate explanations and a hitting set of them. This new approach directly generates a "hitting set" without enumerating all the explanations. Also, what we call *hitting set* here, has been called — modulus some notation — *diagnosis* in [7]. ∎

EXAMPLE 3.6 Consider the following database:

IDB :	$p \leftarrow t$	EDB :	$t \leftarrow$	IDB^* :	$\neg t \leftarrow \neg p$
	$p \leftarrow q \wedge u$		$r \leftarrow$		$\neg q \vee \neg u \leftarrow \neg p$
	$q \leftarrow s$				$\leftarrow s \wedge \neg q$
	$u \leftarrow r$				$\neg r \leftarrow \neg u$

The set S_0 is determined by all the IDB atoms and the current EDB atoms and in our case it is $\{p,q,u,t,r\}$. IDB^* is the transformation of IDB wrt S_0 which is given at the right side of the bar. ∎

Suppose a ground view atom A is to be deleted. Then, an update tableau for IDB^* with delete request $\neg A$ is built. The open finished branches give us models for the renamed database. The intuition is that the set of EDB atoms appearing in a model (open branch) constitute a hitting set, and removing this set from EDB should achieve the required view deletion. Unfortunately, this does not result in a rational deletion, as relevance policy may be violated.

EXAMPLE 3.7
Let us continue with example 3.6. Suppose the view atom
p is to be deleted. Then according to the above proposal,
an update tableau for IDB^* and $\neg p$ is to be built. This is
illustrated in the accompanying figure at the right.
As shown, two open branches constitute two hitting sets
$\{t\}$ and $\{t,r\}$. It is not difficult to see that $\{t,r\}$ does
not satisfy any of the relevance policies (KB—6.1) or
(KB—6.2) or (KB—6.3). Hence simple model computation using hyper tableau calculus does not result in rational
hitting sets.

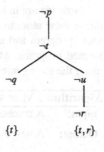

∎

To filter out only the rational hitting sets, the postulate (KB—6.1) can be used as a test! That is, after constructing each branch, the minimality condition of (KB—6.1) is checked (which is a theorem proving task). The branch is closed if the corresponding hitting set does not satisfy this strong relevance postulate.

DEFINITION 3.8 (MINIMALITY TEST) Let T be an update tableau for $IDB \cup EDB$ and delete request $\neg A$. We say that open finished branch b in T satisfies the strong minimality test iff $\forall s \in HS(b) : IDB \cup EDB \backslash HS(b) \cup \{s\} \vdash A$. ∎

DEFINITION 3.9 (UPDATE TABLEAU SATISFYING STRONG MINIMALITY) An update tableau for given $IDB \cup EDB$ and delete request $\neg A$ is transformed into an update tableau *satisfying strong minimality* by marking every open finished branch as closed which does not satisfy strong minimality. ∎

EXAMPLE 3.10 Continuing with the same example, after constructing the branch corresponding to the hitting set $\{t, r\}$, the strong minimality test is carried out as follows: It is checked if the resulting database with each member of hitting set implies the deleted atom p or not. For example, $IDB \cup EDB \backslash \{t, r\} \cup \{t\} \vdash p$. But the same does not hold for r, i.e. $IDB \cup EDB \backslash \{t, r\} \cup \{r\} \nvdash p$, and hence this branch fails the strong minimality test. ∎

Interestingly, this minimality test is equivalent to the *groundedness test* used by Ilkka Niemelä for generating minimal models of disjunctive logic programs [21, 22]. The key idea of the groundedness test is to check if the members in the model are implied by the program together with the negation of the atoms not present in the model. Interested readers are referred to [21, 22] for more information on this technique of generating minimal models. In our context, the groundedness test for generating minimal models can be stated as follows: Let T be an update tableau for $IDB \cup EDB$ and delete request $\neg A$. We say that open finished branch b in T *satisfies the groundedness test* iff $\forall s \in HS(b) : IDB^* \cup EDB \backslash HS(b) \cup \{\neg A\} \vdash \neg s$. It is not difficult to see that this is equivalent to the minimality test. This means that every minimal model (minimal wrt the base atoms) of $IDB^* \cup \{\neg A\}$ provides a minimal hitting set for deleting the ground view atom A.

Now we are in a position to formally present our algorithm. Given a database and a view atom to be deleted, we first transform the database into a disjunctive logic program and use hyper tableaux calculus to generate models of this transformed program. Models that do not represent rational deletions are filtered out using the strong minimality test. This is formalized in Algorithm 2.

Algorithm 2 View deletion algorithm based on minimality test

Input: A database $IDB \cup EDB$ and a ground view atom A to be deleted.

Output: A new database $IDB \cup EDB'$

1. Construct a branch b of an update tableau satisfying strong minimality (cf. Definition 3.9) for $IDB \cup EDB$ and delete request $\neg A$.

2. Produce $IDB \cup EDB \backslash HS(b)$ as a result. ($HS(b)$ of a branch b of an update tableau is defined in Definition 3.4)

To show the rationality of this approach, we study how this is related to the previous approach presented in the last section, i.e. generating explanations and computing hitting sets of these explanations. To better understand the relationship it is imperative to study where the explanations are in the hyper tableau approach. We first define the notion of cut in this direction.

DEFINITION 3.11 (CUT) Let T be a an update tableau. A set S is said to be a *cut* of T, if S has exactly one element from each open branch of T. ∎

A careful reader would have already realized that a cut across the tableau, that consists only of base atoms, constitutes an explanation for the view atom being deleted. This is formalized below.

LEMMA 3 *Let T be an update tableau for $IDB \cup EDB$ and delete request $\neg A$. Let S be the set of all EDB-closed minimal abductive explanations for A wrt IDB. Let S' be the set of all cuts of T that consist only of base atoms. Then the following hold:*

- $S \subseteq S'$

- $\forall \Delta' \in S' : \exists \Delta \in S s.t. \Delta \subseteq \Delta'$

The above lemma precisely characterizes what explanations are generated by an update tableau. It is obvious then that a branch cuts through all the explanations and constitutes a hitting set for all the generated explanations. This is formalized below.

LEMMA 4 ([6, 4]) *Let S and S' be sets of sets s.t. $S \subseteq S'$ and every member of $S' \backslash S$ contains an element of S. Then, a set H is a minimal hitting set for S iff it is a minimal hitting set for S'.*

LEMMA 5 *Let T be an update tableau for $IDB \cup EDB$ and delete request $\neg A$ that satisfies the strong minimality test. Then $HS(b)$ is a minimal hitting set for A, for every open finished branch b in T.*

So, Algorithm 2 generates a minimal hitting set (in polynomial space) of all *EDB*-closed locally minimal abductive explanations of the view atom to be deleted. From the belief dynamics results recalled in section 2, it immediately follows that Algorithm 2 is rational.

THEOREM 6 (MAIN THEOREM) *Algorithm 2 is rational, in the sense that it satisfies all the rationality postulates (KB—1), (KB—2), (KB—3), (KB—4), (KB—5), and (KB—6.1).*

3.2 A special case based on materialized view

In many situations, the view is materialized, i.e. the least Herbrand Model is computed and kept, for efficient query answering. When the given database is acyclic [3] and its view has been materialized, it is possible to compute the rational hitting sets without performing any minimality test. The idea is to transform the given *IDB* wrt the materialized view. In the sequel, whenever we refer to a database, we assume that it is acyclic.

DEFINITION 3.12 (IDB^+ TRANSFORMATION) Let $IDB \cup EDB$ be a given database. Let S_1 be the Least Herbrand Model of this database. Then, IDB^+ is defined as the transformation of IDB wrt S_1. ∎

Now every computed model of $IDB^+ \cup \{\neg A \leftarrow\}$ constitutes a rational hitting set for the deletion of ground view atom A.

DEFINITION 3.13 (UPDATE TABLEAU BASED ON MATERIALIZED VIEW) An update tableau based on materialized view for a database $IDB \cup EDB$ and delete request $\neg A$ is a strict hyper tableau T for $IDB^+ \cup \{\neg A \leftarrow\}$ such that every open branch is finished. ∎

So, the algorithm works as follows: Given a database and a view deletion request, we first transform the database wrt its Least Herbrand Model (computation of the Least Herbrand Model can be done as a offline preprocessing step. Note that it serves as materialized view for efficient query answering). Then the hyper tableaux calculus is used to compute models of this transformed program. Each model represent a rational way of accomplishing the given view deletion request. This is formalized in Algorithm 3.

Algorithm 3 View deletion algorithm based on materialized view

---

Input: An acyclic database $IDB \cup EDB$ and a ground view atom A to be deleted.

Output: A new database $IDB \cup EDB'$

1. Construct a branch b of an update tableau based on materialized view (cf. Definition 3.13) for $IDB \cup EDB$ and delete request $\neg A$.

2. Produce $IDB \cup EDB \backslash HS(b)$ as a result. ($HS(b)$ of a branch b of an update tableau is defined in Definition 3.4)

Like the approach with minimality test, this algorithm runs on polynomial space. Unlike the previous one, this does not require a minimality test and hence of polynomial time complexity too[2]. But, this requires some offline pre-processing of computing the Least Herbrand Model. Note that, unlike the other approach based on minimality test, this method may generate a non-minimal (but rational) hitting set.

EXAMPLE 3.14 Consider the following database:

$$IDB: \quad p \;\leftarrow\; q \wedge r \qquad\qquad EDB: \quad q \;\leftarrow$$
$$p \;\leftarrow\; r \qquad\qquad\qquad\qquad\quad r \;\leftarrow$$
$$p \;\leftarrow\; t$$
$$t \;\leftarrow\; s$$

The Least Herbrand Model of this database is $\{p, q, r\}$. The transformed database IDB^+ based on this model, together with an update tableaux for delete request $\neg p$

---

[2]This only holds because of our assumption that there are no integrity constraints to close a branch. So, the first (usually the leftmost) branch remains open and its length is limited by the number of clauses due to regularity. With integrity constraints, computing the first model is in NP

based on materialised view is as follows:

$$IDB^+: \quad \neg r \vee \neg q \;\leftarrow\; \neg p$$
$$\neg r \;\leftarrow\; \neg p$$
$$\leftarrow\; \neg p, t$$
$$t \;\leftarrow\; s$$

Observe that the last two clauses are never used and the necessarily failing attempt of deleting t to delete p is never made, thus greatly reducing the search space. Also note that the two cuts with only EDB atoms $\{q, r\}$ and $\{r\}$ are exactly the two locally minimal explanations for p. The two open branches provide the two models of $IDB^+ \cup \{\neg p\}$ which stand for the hitting sets $\{q, r\}$ and $\{r\}$. Clearly, $\{q, r\}$ is not minimal. ∎

So, this approach for view deletion may not satisfy (KB—6.1) in general. But, as shown in the sequel, conformation to (KB—6.3) is guaranteed and thus this approach results in rational deletion.

LEMMA 7 *Let T be an update tableau for an acyclic database $IDB \cup EDB$ and delete request $\neg A$ based on materialized view. Let S be the set of all EDB-closed locally minimal abductive explanations for A wrt IDB. Let S' be the set of all cuts of T that consist only of EDB atoms. Then the following hold:*

- $S \subseteq S'$

- $\forall \Delta' \in S' : \exists \Delta \in S \text{ s.t. } \Delta \subseteq \Delta'$

- $\forall \Delta' \in S' : \Delta' \subseteq \bigcup S$

LEMMA 8 ([6, 4]) *Let S and S' be sets of sets s.t. $S \subseteq S'$ and for every member X of $S' \backslash S$: X contains a member of S and X is contained in $\bigcup S$. Then, a set H is a hitting set for S iff it is a hitting set for S'.*

LEMMA 9 *Let T as in the lemma 7. Then $HS(b)$ is a rational hitting set for A, for every open finished branch b in T.*

THEOREM 10 (MAIN THEOREM) *The above algorithm is rational, in the sense that it satisfies all the rationality postulates (KB—1), (KB—2), (KB—3), (KB—4), (KB—5), and (KB—6.3).*

4 Concluding Remarks

We have presented two variants of an algorithm for deleting a view atom from a definite database. The key idea of this approach is to transform the given database into a disjunctive logic program in such a way that updates can be read off from the models of this transformed program. In contrast to the previous approaches, this algorithm is of polynomial space complexity. One variant based on materialized views is of polynomial time complexity. Moreover, we have also shown that this algorithm is rational in the sense that it satisfies the rationality postulates that are justified from philosophical angle.

As mentioned before, this algorithm is based on a diagnosis algorithm presented in [7]. An implementation exists for this diagnosis algorithm and has been tested extensively on real world examples. This implementation can be easily adopted for view updates as well and we are working on that now.

In the second variant, where materialized view is used for the transformation, after generating a hitting set and removing corresponding *EDB* atoms, how do we easily move to the new materialized view? An obvious way is to recompute the view from scratch using the new *EDB* (i.e. compute the Least Herbrand Model of the new updated database from scratch), but it is certainly interesting to look for more efficient methods. A reasonable answer for this question will greatly increase the significance of this approach. This is indeed the view maintenance problem studied by various researchers [14, for example].

Our approach works on the assumption that the *EDB* is available and the complete *EDB* is indeed used for the transformation. It is interesting to study whether this approach can be effectively used in situations where *EDB* is very huge or not completely known. It should not be difficult to work with only that part of the *EDB* upon which the current view update request depends on, but a formal study in this regard is necessary. We are also exploring how this approach can be extended for disjunctive databases, where there is generally no unique minimal model.

Acknowledgements The authors would like to thank all the members of the Artificial Intelligence Reseach Group at the University of Koblenz, Germany, for stimulating discussions on this topic. Thanks are also due to the anonymous referees for their helpful comments and suggestions.

References

1. S. Abiteboul. Updates: A new frontier. In M. Gyssens, J. Paredaens, and D. Van Gucht, editors, *Proceedings of the second international conference on database theory*, volume Lecture Notes in Computer Science 326, pages 1–18. Springer-Verlag, 1988.
2. C. E. Alchourrón, P. Gärdenfors, and D. Makinson. On the logic of theory change: Partial meet contraction and revision functions. *The Journal of Symbolic Logic*, 50(2):510–530, 1985.
3. K. R. Apt and M. Bezem. Acyclic programs (extended abstract). In D. H. D. Warren and P. Szeredi, editors, *Proceedings of International Conference on Logic Programming*, pages 617–633. The MIT Press, 1990.
4. Chandrabose Aravindan. *Dynamics of Belief: Epistemology, Abduction, and Database Updates*. PhD thesis, Computer Science Program, Asian Institute of Technology, Bangkok, Thailand, 1995.
5. Chandrabose Aravindan and Peter Baumgartner. A rational and efficient algorithm for view deletion in databases. Technical Report RR–10–97, Fachbereich Informatik, Universität Koblenz-Landau, Koblenz, Germany, 1997.

6. Chandrabose Aravindan and Phan Minh Dung. Knowledge base dynamics, abduction, and database updates. *Journal of Applied Non-Classical Logics*, 5(1):51–76, 1995.

7. Peter Baumgartner, Peter Fröhlich, Ulrich Furbach, and Wolfgang Nejdl. Semantically Guided Theorem Proving for Diagnosis Applications. In *15th International Joint Conference on Artificial Intelligence (IJCAI 97)*, Nagoya, 1997. International Joint Conference on Artificial Intelligence. To appear.

8. Peter Baumgartner, Ulrich Furbach, and Ilkka Niemelä. Hyper Tableaux. In *Proc. JELIA 96*, number 1126 in Lecture Notes in Aritificial Intelligence. European Workshop on Logic in AI, Springer, 1996.

9. U. Dayal and P. A. Bernstein. On the correct translation of update operations on relational views. *ACM Transactions on Database Systems*, 8(3):381–416, 1982.

10. Hendrik Decker. Drawing updates from derivations. In *Proceedings of the Third International Conference on Database Technology*. Springer-Verlag, 1990.

11. P. Gärdenfors. Belief Revision: An Introduction. In P. Gärdenfors, editor, *Belief Revision*, pages 1–28. Cambridge University Press, 1992.

12. P. Gärdenfors and H. Rott. Belief Revision. In D. M. Gabbay, C. J. Hogger, and J. A. Robinson, editors, *Handbook of Logic in AI and Logic Programming*, volume IV: Epistemic and Temporal Reasoning, pages 35–132. Oxford University Press, 1995.

13. A. Guessoum and J. W. Lloyd. Updating knowledge bases. *New Generation Computing*, 8, 1990.

14. Ashish Gupta and Inderpal Singh Mumick. Maintenance of materialized views: Problems, techniques, and applications. *IEEE DE Bulletin*, 18(2):3–19, 1995.

15. S. O. Hansson. *Belief base dynamics*. PhD thesis, Uppsala University, Sweden, 1991.

16. S. O. Hansson. Belief contraction without recovery. *Studia Logica*, 50(2):251–260, 1991.

17. A. C. Kakas and P. Mancarella. Database updates through abduction. Technical report, Department of Computing, Imperial College, London, U.K., 1990.

18. A. M. Keller. Algorithms for translating view updates to database updates for views involving selections, projections, and joins. In *Proceedings of the Fourth ACM Symposium on Prinsciples of Database Systems*, pages 154–163. ACM, 1985.

19. R. Langerak. View updates in relational databases with an independent scheme. *ACM Transactions on Database Systems*, 15(1):40–66, 1990.

20. J. W. Lloyd. *Foundations of Logic Programming*. Springer–Verlag, second extended edition, 1987.

21. Ilkka Niemelä. Implementing circumscription using a tableau method. In W. Wahlster, editor, *Proceedings of the 12th European Conference on Artificial Intelligence*, pages 80–84. John Wiley & Sons Ltd, 1996.

22. Ilkka Niemelä. A tableau calculus for minimal model reasoning. In P. Miglioli, U. Moscato, D. Mundici, and M. Ornaghi, editors, *Proceedings of the fifth workshop on theorem proving with analytic tableaux and related methods*, number 1071 in Lecture Notes in Artificial Intelligence, pages 278–294. Springer-Verlag, 1996.

23. Raymond Reiter. A Theory of Diagnosis from First Principles. *Artificial Intelligence*, 32(1):57–95, April 1987.

24. A. Tomasic. View update translation via deduction and annotation. In M. Gyssens, J. Paredaens, and D. van Gucht, editors, *Proceedings of the International Conference on Database Technology*, volume Lecture Notes in Computer Science 326, pages 338–352. Springer-Verlag, 1988.

NP Optimization Problems in Datalog

Sergio Greco
Domenico Saccà
DEIS Department
University of Calabria
87030 Rende, Italy
{greco,sacca}@si.deis.unical.it

Abstract

$\mathcal{NP}$ optimization problems can be formulated as `DATALOG`¬ queries under total stable model semantics using a max (or min) construct to select the model which maximizes (resp., minimizes) the number of tuples in the answer relation. We prove that the same expressive power is achieved by a 'disciplined' version of `DATALOG`¬, called `DATALOG`¬,ₛ,⊆,!, which uses stratified negation plus two additional types of 'controlled' negation, that are hard-wired into ad-hoc rules: (i) *subset* rule for performing a non-deterministic selection of a subset and (ii) *should_be rule* for enforcing constraints. The desired level of expressiveness for a query can be incrementally achieved by a suitable usage of the above extensions — e.g., if only subset rules are added to stratified negation then polynomial time execution as well as the capability of expressing every polynomial-time query are guaranteed. Thus our language ensures a polynomial behavior with polynomial problems but it does also provide the possibility of expressing harder problems. To enrich the modular structure and further tune in the expressive power and complexity of `DATALOG`¬,ₛ,⊆,!, we present simple syntactic restrictions in the usage of *subset* and *should_be* rules for capturing interesting subclasses of $\mathcal{NP}$ optimization queries, some of them consisting of approximable problems.

1 Introduction

$\mathcal{NP}$ optimization problems [23, 19] have recently received a renewed attention [17, 24, 22, 15, 16, 5], mainly with the aim of characterizing classes of problems that are constant or log approximable (i.e., there is a polynomial time algorithm that approximates the optimum value of the problem within a factor that is respectively constant or logarithmic in the size of the input).

In this paper we show that $\mathcal{NP}$ optimization problems can be formulated as `DATALOG`¬ queries [3] under a non-deterministic version [25] of total stable model semantics [9] using a max (or min) construct to select the model which maximizes (resp., minimizes) the number of tuples in the answer relation. Moreover, we show that the same expressive power is achieved by a language, denoted by `DATALOG`¬,ₛ,⊆,! which extends the simple, intuitive structure of `DATALOG`¬,ₛ (i.e., `DATALOG` with stratified negation [4]) by adding other two types of 'controlled' negation. The control is made by embedding the non-stratified negation into two specific rules: (i) *subset* rule for a non-deterministic selection of a subset and (ii) *should_be rule* for expressing constraints.

As an example of the language, take the *Min Vertex Cover* problem: *given a graph $G = (V, E)$, find the minimal cardinality of its vertex covers* — a subset V' of V is a *vertex cover* of G if for each pair edge (x, y) in E either x or y is in V'. The problem can be formulated by the query $\langle P_{vc}, min|v'(X)|\rangle$ where P_{vc} is the following DATALOG$^{\neg s, \subseteq, !}$program:

> $\mathtt{v'(X) \subseteq v(X)}.$
> $\mathtt{no\_cover \leftarrow e(X, Y), \neg v'(X), \neg v'(Y)}.$
> $\mathtt{should\_be(\neg no\_cover)}.$

The predicates $\mathtt{v}$ and $\mathtt{e}$ define the vertices and the edges of the graph by means a suitable number of facts. The first rule is a subset rule which non-deterministically selects a subset of the vertices. The second rule is a regular rule which verifies whether the selected subset is a vertex cover or not. If it is not then the selection is rejected by the third rule.

As confirmed by the above example, the advantage of expressing an $\mathcal{NP}$ optimization problem in our language rather than in plain DATALOG$^{\neg}$ (or, in the opposite direction, directly in logics) is that DATALOG$^{\neg s, \subseteq, !}$ is a 'modular' extension of stratified DATALOG$^{\neg}$ preserving its simple and intuitive structure as well as its mature technology for query optimization and execution. The language is 'modular' in the sense that the desired level of expressivity is achieved by enabling the constructs for non-stratified negation only when needed; in particular, if no such constructs are used at all then polynomial time computation is guaranteed. A similar approach was taken by [12] in designing another 'modular' extension of DATALOG$^{\neg s}$ for expressing decision problems ranging from the (whole) class $\mathcal{P}$ to the classes $\mathcal{D}^{\mathcal{P}}$ passing through $\mathcal{NP}$ and co$\mathcal{NP}$.

To further stress the modular characteristics of the language, we introduce simple syntactic restrictions to DATALOG$^{\neg s, \subseteq, !}$ to capture interesting hierarchies of minimization and maximization problems [15, 16, 6], including the ones which are approximable [24, 15, 16]. For instance, such restrictions confirm that the *Min Vertex Cover* problem is constant approximable.

The paper is organized as follows. In Section 2 we define $\mathcal{NP}$ optimization queries and we show that they correspond to $\mathcal{NP}$ optimization problems. In Section 3 we prove that $\mathcal{NP}$ optimization queries coincides with DATALOG$^{\neg}$ queries under non-deterministic total stable model semantics. We then present the language DATALOG$^{\neg s, \subseteq, !}$ in Section 4 and we show its capability of expressing all $\mathcal{NP}$ optimization problems. In Section 5 we introduce suitable restrictions to DATALOG$^{\neg s, \subseteq, !}$ in order to capture $\mathcal{NP}$ optimization subclasses and present meaningful examples. We draw the conclusion and discuss further work in Section 6.

2 NP Optimization queries

We assume that the reader is familiar with the basic terminology and notation of relational databases and of database queries [3, 28] as well as of complexity theory [8, 14, 21].

A *relational database scheme* $\mathcal{DB}$ over a fixed countable domain U is a set of relation symbols $\{r_1, ..., r_k\}$ where each r_i has a given arity, denoted by $a(r_i)$. A *database* D on $\mathcal{DB}$ is a finite structure $(A, R_1, ..., R_k)$ where $A \subseteq U$ is the *active domain* and $R_i \subseteq A^{a(r_i)}$ are the (finite) *relations* of the database, one for each relation scheme r_i — we denote A by $U(D)$ and R_i by $D(r_i)$. We assume that a database is suitably encoded by a string and the recognition of whether a string represents a database on $\mathcal{DB}$ is done in polynomial time.

Definition 1. Given a database scheme $\mathcal{DB}$ and an additional relation symbol f (the *goal*), a (*database*) *non-deterministic query* $NQ = \langle \mathcal{DB}, f \rangle$ is a (possibly partial) recursive function which maps every database D on $\mathcal{DB}$ to a finite (possibly empty) set of finite (possibly empty) relations $F \subseteq U(D)^{a(f)}$ and is invariant under an isomorphism on $U - W$, where W is any finite subset of U. Thus $NQ(D)$ yields a set of relations on the goal, that are the *answers* of the query; this set is empty iff the function is not defined on D.

The class of all queries is denoted **NQ**. The class $\mathbf{NQ}_{\mathcal{NPMV}}$ consists of all queries in **NQ** which can be computed in polynomial time by a non-deterministic transducer.[1] □

Observe that the class $\mathbf{NQ}_{\mathcal{NPMV}}$, first introduced in [18], corresponds to the class $\mathcal{NPMV}$ of multivalued functions [27] and is different from the class $\mathcal{NQPTIME}$ of [1, 2] — in fact, the latter class consists of all queries in $\mathbf{NQ}_{\mathcal{NPMV}}$ for which every computation path of the transducer ends into an accepting state.

Proposition 1. *Let* $NQ = \langle \mathcal{DB}, f \rangle$ *be a non-deterministic query. Then the following statements are equivalent:*

1. *NQ is in $\mathbf{NQ}_{\mathcal{NPMV}}$;*

2. *for each database D on $\mathcal{DB}$ and a relation $F \subseteq U(D)^{a(f)}$, deciding whether $F \in NQ(D)$ is in $\mathcal{NP}$;*

3. *there is a sequence $\mathcal{S}$ of relation symbols $s_1, \ldots, s_k$, distinct from those in $\mathcal{DB} \cup \{f\}$, and a closed first-order formula $\phi(\mathcal{DB}, f, \mathcal{S})$ such that for each database D on $\mathcal{DB}$, $NQ(D) = \{ F : F \subseteq U(D)^{a(f)}, S_i \subseteq U(D)^{a(s_i)} (1 \le i \le k), \text{ and } \phi(D, F, S) \text{ is true} \}.$*

---

[1]A transducer is a (deterministic or not) Turing machine T which, in addition to possibly accept a string x, writes a string y_i on an output tape before entering an accepting state. In our case, x corresponds to a suitable encoding of a database D and each output string y_i encodes an answer of the query.

PROOF (sketch).The equivalence of statements (1) and (2) has been proven in [18]. The equivalence of statements (2) and (3) can be easily derived from the well-known Fagin's result [7] that a class of finite structures is $\mathcal{NP}$-recognizable iff it is definable by a second order existential formula. $\square$

We shall use the equivalence with statement (3) to define a query in $\mathbf{NQ}_{\mathcal{NPMV}}$ as $NQ = \{\, f : (\mathcal{DB}, f, \mathcal{S}) \models \phi(\mathcal{DB}, f, \mathcal{S}) \,\}$.

Example 1. *CUT.* Let a database scheme $\mathcal{DB}_G = \{v, e\}$ represent a graph $G = (V, E)$ such that v has arity 1 and defines the vertices while e has arity 2 and defines the edges. The *CUT* problem consists to find a subset E' of the edges which induces a partition of V into two disjoint sets, say V_1 and V_2, such that each edge in E' has one endpoint in V_1 and one endpoint in V_2. The problem can be defined as the query NQ_{cut} below:

$$\{\, e' : (\mathcal{DB}_G, e', s) \models (\forall x, y)[e'(x, y) \leftrightarrow (\ (e(x, y) \wedge s(x) \wedge \neg s(y)) \vee$$
$$(e(x, y) \wedge \neg s(x) \wedge s(y))\ )\,]\,\}.$$

The query is total, the recognition of any answer can be done in polynomial time and an answer can be computed in polynomial time as well. The query is therefore in $\mathbf{NQ}_{\mathcal{NPMV}}$. $\square$

Example 2. *KERNEL.* The problem consists to find a kernel of the directed graph $G = (V, E)$, i.e., a subset V' of V such that (i) no two nodes in V' are joined by an edge and (ii) for each node x not in V', there is a node y in V' for which $(y, x) \in E$. The problem is defined by the query NQ_{kernel}:

$$\{\, v' : (\mathcal{DB}_G, v') \models (\forall x)[\ (v'(x) \wedge \forall y(\neg v'(y) \vee \neg e(x, y))) \vee$$
$$(\neg v'(x) \wedge \exists y(v'(y) \wedge e(y, x)))\,]\,\}$$

The query is not total, the recognition of any answer can be done in polynomial time but an answer cannot be computed in polynomial time unless $\mathcal{P} = \mathcal{NP}$ since deciding whether a graph has a kernel is $\mathcal{NP}$-complete [8]. Also this query is in $\mathbf{NQ}_{\mathcal{NPMV}}$.

The query $NQ_{\subseteq kernel}$ that returns any subset of a kernel is an example of a query in $\mathbf{NQ}_{\mathcal{NPMV}}$ for which the recognition of an answer is $\mathcal{NP}$-complete. $\square$

Definition 2. Given a query $NQ = \langle \mathcal{DB}, f \rangle$, a (*database*) *optimization query* $OQ = opt|NQ| = \langle \mathcal{DB}, opt|f| \rangle$, where opt is either max or min, is the total recursive function which maps every database D on $\mathcal{DB}$ to the integer $k = opt\{|F| : F \in NQ(D)\}$ defined as:

1. if $opt = max$ then k is equal to the maximal cardinality of the relations F if $NQ(D) \neq \emptyset$ or to 0 otherwise;

2. if $opt = min$ then k is equal to the minimal cardinality of the relations F if $NQ(D) \neq \emptyset$ or otherwise to $|U(D)^{a(f)}|$ (i.e., the size of the maximal relation on f).

The query NQ is called the *search query associated to OQ* and the relations in $NQ(D)$ are the *feasible solutions* of OQ.

The class of all optimization queries is denoted by $OPT\,\mathbf{NQ}$. The queries for which the associated search queries are in $\mathbf{NQ}_{\mathcal{NPMV}}$ are called $\mathcal{NP}$ optimization queries; their class is denoted by $OPT\,\mathbf{NQ}_{\mathcal{NPMV}}$. □

Proposition 2. *Let $OQ = \langle \mathcal{DB}, opt|f| \rangle$ be an optimization query. Then the following statements are equivalent:*

1. *OQ is an $\mathcal{NP}$ optimization query;*

2. *there is a closed first-order formula $\phi(\mathcal{DB}, f, \mathcal{S})$ over relations symbols $\mathcal{DB} \cup \{f\} \cup \mathcal{S}$ such that $OQ = opt_{f,\mathcal{S}}\{|f| : (\mathcal{DB}, f, \mathcal{S}) \models \phi(\mathcal{DB}, f, \mathcal{S})\}$;*

3. *there is a first-order formula $\phi(\mathbf{w}, \mathcal{DB}, \mathcal{S})$, where $\mathbf{w}$ is a $a(f)$-tuple of distinct variables, such that the relations symbols are those in $\mathcal{DB} \cup \mathcal{S}$, the free variables are exactly those in $\mathbf{w}$, and $OQ = opt_{\mathcal{S}}|\{\mathbf{w} : (\mathcal{DB}, \mathcal{S}) \models \phi(\mathbf{w}, \mathcal{DB}, \mathcal{S})\}|$.*

PROOF (sketch).The equivalence of statements (1) and (2) follows from Proposition 1 and Definition 2. The equivalence of (2) and (3) is shown in [16]. □

The above results pinpoint that the class $OPT\,\mathbf{NQ}_{\mathcal{NPMV}}$ corresponds to the class $OPT\,\mathcal{PB}$ of all optimization problems that can be logically defined [15, 16]. For simplicity but without substantial loss of generality, we use as objective function the cardinality rather than a generic polynomial-time computable function.

Example 3. *MAX-CUT*. The problem consists to find the cardinality of the largest cut in the graph $G = (V, E)$. The query coincides with $max|NQ_{cut}|$ (see Example 1) and can be also defined as:

$$max_s\,|\{\,(x,y) : (\mathcal{DB}_G, s) \models [(e(x,y) \wedge s(x) \wedge \neg s(y)) \vee (e(x,y) \wedge \neg s(x) \wedge s(y))]\}|.$$

The query is an $\mathcal{NP}$ maximization query. □

Example 4. *MIN-KERNEL*. In this case we want find the minimum cardinality of the kernels of a graph $G = (V, E)$. The query is $min|NQ_{kernel}|$ (see Example 2) and can be also defined as:

$$min_{v'}\,|\{\,w : (\mathcal{DB}_G, v') \models \quad v'(w) \vee (\forall x)[(v'(x) \wedge \forall y(\neg v'(y) \vee \neg e(x,y))) \\ \vee (\neg v'(x) \wedge \exists y(v'(y) \wedge e(y,x)))]\}|$$

This query is a $\mathcal{NP}$ minimization query. Observe that, for a graph without kernels, the query returns 0 and this answer implies no solutions for the associated search problem. However, it is not true that for every optimization query we can derive from its answer whether the associated search query is without solutions. For instance, for the query $max|NQ_{kernel}|$, an answer equal to the number of nodes has two meanings: (i) the set of all nodes is a kernel (i.e., the set of edges is empty) or (ii) there exists no kernel.

Finally, note that the query $max|NQ_{kernel}|$ equals the query $max|NQ_{\subseteq kernel}|$ although their search queries are distinct. □

3 Stable Models and NP Optimization DATALOG⁻ Queries

We assume that the reader is familiar with basic notions of logic programming and DATALOG⁻[3, 20, 28].

A *program P* is a finite set of rules r of the form $H(r) \leftarrow B(r)$, where $H(r)$ is an atom (*head* of the rule) and $B(r)$ is a conjunction of literals (*body* of the rule). A rule with empty body is called a *fact*. The *ground instantiation* of P is denoted by $ground(P)$; the *Herbrand universe* and the *Herbrand base* of P are denoted by U_P and B_P, respectively.

An interpretation $I \subseteq B_P$ is a *T-stable* (total stable) *model* [9] if $I = \mathbf{T}^{\infty}_{pos(P,I)}(\emptyset)$, where $\mathbf{T}$ is the classical *immediate consequence transformation* and $pos(P,I)$ denotes the positive logic program that is obtained from $ground(P)$ by (i) removing all rules r such that there exists a negative literal $\neg A$ in $B(r)$ and A is in I, and (ii) by removing all negative literals from the remaining rules. It is well-known that a program may have n T-stable models with $n \geq 0$.

A DATALOG⁻ program is a logic program with negation in the rule bodies but without functions symbols. Predicate symbols can be either extensional (i.e., defined by the facts of a database — *EDB predicate symbols*) or intentional (i.e., defined by the rules of the program — *IDB predicate symbols*).

A DATALOG⁻ program P has associated a relational database scheme $\mathcal{DB}_P$, which consists of all EDB predicate symbols of P. We assume that possible constants in P are taken from the same domain U of $\mathcal{DB}_P$.

Given a database D on $\mathcal{DB}_P$, the tuples of D are seen as facts added to P; so P on D yields the following logic program $P_D = P \cup \{q(t) : q \in \mathcal{DB}_P \wedge t \in D(q)\}$. Given a T-stable model M of P_D and a relation symbol r in P_D, $M(r)$ denotes the relation $\{t : r(t) \in M\}$.

Definition 3. A DATALOG⁻ *search query* $\langle P, f \rangle$, where P is a DATALOG⁻ program and f is an IDB predicate symbol of P, defines the query $NQ = \langle \mathcal{DB}_P, f \rangle$ such that for each D on DB_P, $NQ(D) = \{M(r) : M$ is a T-stable model of $P_D\}$. The set of all DATALOG⁻ search queries is denoted by $search(\text{DATALOG}^\neg)$.

The DATALOG⁻ *optimization query* $\langle P, opt|f| \rangle$ defines the optimization query $opt|NQ|$. The set of all DATALOG⁻ optimization queries is denoted by $opt(\text{DATALOG}^\neg)$. □

Observe that if the program P_D has no stable models then the query NQ is not defined on D whereas $opt|NQ|(D)$ yields 0 if $opt = max$ or $|U(D)^{a(r)}|$ if $opt = min$.

With a little abuse of notation and whenever no confusion arises, we blur the difference between a DATALOG⁻ query and the database query which is defined by it.

Proposition 3.

1. $search(\texttt{DATALOG}^{\neg}) = \mathbf{NQ}_{\mathcal{NPMV}}$;

2. $opt(\texttt{DATALOG}^{\neg}) = OPT\,\mathbf{NQ}_{\mathcal{NPMV}}$.

PROOF (sketch).In [25] it has been shown that a database query NQ is defined by a query in $search(\texttt{DATALOG}^{\neg})$ if and only if, for each input database, the answers of NQ are $\mathcal{NP}$-recognizable. Hence, by Proposition 1, $search(\texttt{DATALOG}^{\neg}) = \mathbf{NQ}_{\mathcal{NPMV}}$. Then $opt(\texttt{DATALOG}^{\neg}) = OPT\,\mathbf{NQ}_{\mathcal{NPMV}}$ follows from Proposition 2. □

Example 5. Take the queries NQ_{cut} and $max|NQ_{cut}|$ of Examples 1 and 3, respectively. Consider the following $\texttt{DATALOG}^{\neg}$ program P_{cut}

$$\begin{aligned}
\texttt{v}'(\texttt{X}) &\leftarrow \texttt{v}(\texttt{X}),\ \neg\hat{\texttt{v}}'(\texttt{X}). & \texttt{e}'(\texttt{X},\texttt{Y}) &\leftarrow \texttt{e}(\texttt{X},\texttt{Y}),\ \texttt{v}'(\texttt{X}),\ \neg\texttt{v}'(\texttt{Y}).\\
\hat{\texttt{v}}'(\texttt{X}) &\leftarrow \texttt{v}(\texttt{X}),\ \neg\texttt{v}'(\texttt{X}). & \texttt{e}'(\texttt{X},\texttt{Y}) &\leftarrow \texttt{e}(\texttt{X},\texttt{Y}),\ \neg\texttt{v}'(\texttt{X}),\ \texttt{v}'(\texttt{Y}).
\end{aligned}$$

We have that $NQ_{cut} = \langle P_{cut}, e' \rangle$ and $max|NQ_{cut}| = \langle P_{cut}, max|e'| \rangle$. □

Example 6. Take the queries NQ_{kernel} and $min|NQ_{kernel}|$ of Examples 2 and 4. Consider the following $\texttt{DATALOG}^{\neg}$ program P_{kernel}

$$\begin{aligned}
\texttt{v}'(\texttt{X}) &\leftarrow \texttt{v}(\texttt{X}),\ \neg\hat{\texttt{v}}'(\texttt{X}).\\
\hat{\texttt{v}}'(\texttt{X}) &\leftarrow \texttt{v}(\texttt{X}),\ \neg\texttt{v}'(\texttt{X}).\\
\texttt{joined\_to\_v}'(\texttt{X}) &\leftarrow \texttt{v}'(\texttt{Y}),\ \texttt{e}(\texttt{Y},\texttt{X}).\\
\texttt{no\_kernel} &\leftarrow \texttt{v}'(\texttt{X}),\ \texttt{joined\_to\_v}'(\texttt{X}).\\
\texttt{no\_kernel} &\leftarrow \hat{\texttt{v}}'(\texttt{X}),\ \neg\texttt{joined\_to\_v}'(\texttt{X}).\\
\texttt{constraint} &\leftarrow \neg\texttt{no\_kernel},\ \neg\texttt{constraint}.
\end{aligned}$$

We have that $NQ_{kernel} = \langle P_{kernel}, v' \rangle$ and $min|NQ_{kernel}| = \langle P_{kernel}, min|v'| \rangle$. Observe that P_{kernel} has no T-stable model iff NQ_{kernel} is nod defined on D (i.e., there is no kernel). □

4 A Language for NP Optimization Queries

In this section we show that $\mathcal{NP}$ optimization problems can be captured by a subset of $\texttt{DATALOG}^{\neg}$ that is stratified $\texttt{DATALOG}^{\neg}$ (i.e., , there is no recursion through negation [4]) plus two particular types of non-stratified negation captured by two ad-hoc rules: *subset* and *should_be*. After the proposal of [12, 13], the resulting language is $\texttt{DATALOG}^{\neg}$ with disciplined negation.

A *subset* rule is of the form

$$\mathbf{s}(\mathbf{X}) \subseteq \mathbf{A_1}, \ldots, \mathbf{A_n}.$$

where $\mathbf{s}$ is an IDB predicate symbol not defined elsewhere in the program (*subset predicate symbol*) and all literals $\mathbf{A_1}, \ldots, \mathbf{A_n}$ in the body are EDB. The rule enforces to select any subset of the relation that is derived from the body. The formal semantics of the rule is given by rewriting it into the following set of normal $\texttt{DATALOG}^{\neg}$ rules

$$s(\mathbf{X}) \leftarrow \quad \mathbf{A}_1, \dots, \mathbf{A}_n, \ \neg \hat{s}(\mathbf{X}).$$
$$\hat{s}(\mathbf{X}) \leftarrow \quad \mathbf{A}_1, \dots, \mathbf{A}_n, \ \neg s(\mathbf{X}).$$

where $\hat{s}$ is a new IDB predicate symbol with the same arity as s. Subset rules could be also rewritten using the choice construct of LDL [10, 26]; actually they can be thought off as a 'syntactic' specialization of the choice to subset selection.

A *should_be* rule [13] is of the form

$$should\_be(\mathbf{A}).$$

where $\mathbf{A}$ is a ground literal. The role of the rule is to take as intended models only those T-stable models for which A is true — thus, following the approach of mixed queries of [25], the rule works as a filter for the T-stable models of a program. This filtering can be enforced into the program by rewriting the rule as:

$$A\_constraint \leftarrow \neg\mathbf{A}, \ \neg A\_constraint.$$

where $A\_constraint$ is a new IDB 0-arity predicate symbol. It is easy to see that if A is false then $A\_constraint$ remains undefined and, therefore, there exist no T-stable models.

In the following we shall denote with $\mathtt{DATALOG}^{\neg s, \subseteq, !}$ the language $\mathtt{DATALOG}^{\neg}$ with stratified negation plus the rules *subset* and *should_be*. Moreover, $\mathtt{DATALOG}^{\neg s, \subseteq}$ denotes the restriction of the language to the programs without *should_be* predicates.

Theorem 1.

1. $search(\mathtt{DATALOG}^{\neg s, \subseteq, !}) = \mathbf{NQ}_{\mathcal{NPMV}}$;

2. $search(\mathtt{DATALOG}^{\neg s, \subseteq}) = \mathcal{NQPTIME} \subseteq \mathbf{NQ}_{\mathcal{NPMV}}$;

3. $opt(\mathtt{DATALOG}^{\neg s, \subseteq, !}) = opt(\mathtt{DATALOG}^{\neg s, \subseteq}) = OPT\,\mathbf{NQ}_{\mathcal{NPMV}}$.

PROOF (sketch). We have that $search(\mathtt{DATALOG}^{\neg s, \subseteq, !}) \subseteq \mathbf{NQ}_{\mathcal{NPMV}}$ since $\mathtt{DATALOG}^{\neg s, \subseteq, !} \subset \mathtt{DATALOG}^{\neg}$ by the mentioned rewriting rules for subset and *should_be* rules and $search(\mathtt{DATALOG}^{\neg}) = \mathbf{NQ}_{\mathcal{NPMV}}$ by Proposition 3. On the other hand, $search(\mathtt{DATALOG}^{\neg s, \subseteq, !}) \supseteq \mathbf{NQ}_{\mathcal{NPMV}}$ derives from the fact that the program used in [25] to prove that $\mathtt{DATALOG}^{\neg}$ with non-deterministic T-stable model semantics captures $\mathbf{NQ}_{\mathcal{NPMV}}$ is indeed in $\mathtt{DATALOG}^{\neg s, \subseteq, !}$. The proof that $search(\mathtt{DATALOG}^{\neg s, \subseteq, !}) = \mathcal{NQPTIME}$ is similar to the proof that $\mathtt{DATALOG}^{\neg s}$ plus choice captures $\mathcal{NQPTIME}$ [11]. The relationships of part (3) are straightforward. □

Example 7. The program P_{cut} of Example 5 can be replaced by the following program $P_{cut'}$:

$$\mathbf{v}'(\mathbf{X}) \subseteq \mathbf{v}(\mathbf{X}).$$
$$\mathbf{e}'(\mathbf{X}, \mathbf{Y}) \leftarrow \quad \mathbf{e}(\mathbf{X}, \mathbf{Y}), \ \mathbf{v}'(\mathbf{X}), \ \neg\mathbf{v}'(\mathbf{Y}).$$
$$\mathbf{e}'(\mathbf{X}, \mathbf{Y}) \leftarrow \quad \mathbf{e}(\mathbf{X}, \mathbf{Y}), \ \neg\mathbf{v}'(\mathbf{X}), \ \mathbf{v}'(\mathbf{Y}).$$

The query $\langle P_{cut'}, e' \rangle$ is in $search(\text{DATALOG}^{\neg s, \subseteq})$ and, therefore, the query $\langle P_{cut}, max|e'| \rangle$ is in $max(\text{DATALOG}^{\neg s, \subseteq})$. $\qquad\Box$

Example 8. The program P_{kernel} of Example 6 can be replaced by the following program $P_{kernel'}$:

```
v'(X) ⊆ v(X).
joined_to_v'(X) ← v'(Y),  e(Y,X).
no_kernel ← v'(X),  joined_to_v'(X).
no_kernel ← ¬v'(X),  ¬joined_to_v'(X).
should_be(¬no_kernel).
```

The query $\langle P_{kernel'}, v' \rangle$ is in $search(\text{DATALOG}^{\neg s, \subseteq, !})$ and, therefore, the query $\langle P_{kernel'}, min|v'| \rangle$ is in $min(\text{DATALOG}^{\neg s, \subseteq, !})$. $\qquad\Box$

5 Capturing Desirable Subclasses of NP Optimization Problems

We have shown in Proposition 2 that an NP optimization query $opt|NQ| = \langle \mathcal{DB}, opt|f| \rangle$ corresponds to a problem in the class $OPT \, \mathcal{PB}$ that is defined as $opt|NQ| = opt_S|\{\mathbf{w} : (\mathcal{DB}, \mathcal{S}) \models \phi(\mathbf{w}, \mathcal{DB}, \mathcal{S})\}|$. In addition to the free variables $\mathbf{w}$, the first order formula ϕ may also contain quantified variables so that the general formats of it are of two types:

$$(\exists \mathbf{x}_1)(\forall \mathbf{x}_2)\ldots(Q_k \mathbf{x}_k)\psi(\mathbf{w}, \mathcal{DB}, \mathcal{S}, \mathbf{x}_1, \ldots, \mathbf{x}_k), \text{ or}$$

$$(\forall \mathbf{x}_1)(\exists \mathbf{x}_2)\ldots(Q_k \mathbf{x}_k)\psi(\mathbf{w}, \mathcal{DB}, \mathcal{S}, \mathbf{x}_1, \ldots, \mathbf{x}_k),$$

where $k \geq 0$, Q_k is either $\exists$ or $\forall$, and ψ is a non-quantified formula. In the first case ϕ is a Σ_k formula while it is a Π_k formula in the latter case. (If ϕ has no quantifiers then it is both a Σ_0 and a Π_0 formula.) Accordingly, the class of all NP optimization problems for which the formula ϕ is a Σ_k (resp., Π_k) formula is called $OPT \, \Sigma_k$ (resp., $OPT \, \Pi_k$).

Kolaitis and Thakur [16] have introduced two hierarchies for the polynomially bounded NP minimization problems and for the polynomially bounded NP maximization problems:

$$MAX \, \Sigma_0 \subset MAX \, \Sigma_1 \subset MAX \, \Pi_1 = MAX \, \Sigma_2 \subset MAX \, \Pi_2 = MAX \, \mathcal{PB}$$
$$MIN \, \Sigma_0 = MIN \, \Sigma_1 \subset MIN \, \Pi_1 = MIN \, \Sigma_2 = MIN \, \mathcal{PB}$$

Observe that the classes $MAX \, \Sigma_0$ and $MAX \, \Sigma_1$ have been first introduced in [24] with the names $MAX \, \text{SNP}$ and $MAX \, \text{NP}$, respectively, whereas the class $MAX \, \Pi_1$ has been first introduced in [22].

A number of maximization problems have a desirable property: approximation. In particular, Papadimitriou and Yannakakis have showed that every problem in the class $MAX \, \Sigma_1$ is constant-approximable [24]. This is not the case for the complementary class $MIN\,\Sigma_1$ or other minimization subclasses: indeed the class $MIN\,\Sigma_0$ contains problems which are not log-approximable (unless $P = NP$) [16].

To single out desirable subclasses for minimization problems, Kolaitis and Thakur introduced a refinement of the hierarchies of NP optimization problems by means of the notion of *feasible NP optimization problem*, based on the fact that, as pointed out in Proposition 2, an NP optimization query $opt|NQ| = \langle \mathcal{DB}, opt|f| \rangle$ can be also defined as $opt_{f,\mathcal{S}}\{|f| : (\mathcal{DB}, f, \mathcal{S}) \models \phi(\mathbf{w}, \mathcal{DB}, f, \mathcal{S})\}$. Therefore, the class of all NP optimization problems for which the above formula ϕ is a Σ_k (resp., Π_k) formula is called $OPT\,F\Sigma_k$ (resp., $OPT\,F\Pi_k$). The following containment relations hold:

$$\left. \begin{array}{l} MAX\,\Sigma_0 \\ MAX\,F\Sigma_1 \end{array} \right\} \subset MAX\,\Sigma_1 \subset MAX\,F\Pi_1 = MAX\,F\Sigma_2 = MAX\,\Pi_1 =$$
$$MAX\,\Sigma_2 \subset MAX\,F\Pi_2 = MAX\,\Pi_2 = MAX\,\mathcal{PB}$$

$$\left. \begin{array}{l} MIN\,\Sigma_0 = MIN\,\Sigma_1 = MIN\,F\Pi_1 \\ MIN\,F\Sigma_1 \end{array} \right\} \subset MIN\,F\Sigma_2 \subset MIN\,\Pi_1 = MIN\,\Sigma_2 =$$
$$MIN\,F\Pi_2 = MIN\,\Pi_2 = MIN\,\mathcal{PB}$$

Observe that all problems in $MAX\,F\Sigma_1$ are const approximable since $MAX\,F\Sigma_1 \subset MAX\,\Sigma_1$.

A further refinement of feasible NP optimization classes can be obtained as follows. A first order formula $\phi(S)$ is *positive* w.r.t. the relation symbol S if all occurrences of S are within an even number of negation. The class of feasible NP minimization problems whose first order part is a positive Π_k formula ($1 \leq k \leq 2$) is denoted by $MIN\,F^+\Pi_k$. Particularly relevant is $MIN\,F^+\Pi_1$ as all optimization problems contained in this class are constant approximable [16].

We next show that it is possible to further discipline $\texttt{DATALOG}^{\neg s, \subseteq, !}$ in order to capture most of the above mentioned optimization subclasses.

Observe that feasible NP optimization problems can be captured in $\texttt{DATALOG}^{\neg s, \subseteq, !}$ by restricting the predicate appearing in the goal to be a subset predicate. For instance, the problem expressed by the query of Example 8 is feasible whereas the problem expressed by the query of Example 7 is not feasible.

5.1 $OPT\,\Sigma_0$ Problems

Definition 4. Let P be a $\texttt{DATALOG}^{\neg s, \subseteq, !}$ program, $p(\mathbf{y})$ be an atom and $\mathbf{X}$ a set of variables. We say that $p(\mathbf{y})$ is *free w.r.t.* $\mathbf{X}$ (in P) if

1. $var(p(\mathbf{y})) \subseteq \mathbf{X}$, where $var(p(\mathbf{y}))$ is the set of variables occurring in $\mathbf{y}$, and

2. $\forall r \in P$ such that the head $H(r)$ and $p(\mathbf{y})$ unify, then $var(B(r)) \subseteq var(H(r))$ (i.e., the variables in the body also appear in the head) and for each atom $q(\mathbf{w})$ in $B(r)$, either q is an EDB predicate or $q(\mathbf{w})$ is free w.r.t. $var(q(\mathbf{w}))$. $\quad\square$

We denote with $opt(\texttt{DATALOG}^{\neg_s,\subseteq})_{\exists}$ the class of all queries $\langle P, opt|f|\rangle$ in $opt(\texttt{DATALOG}^{\neg_s,\subseteq})$ such that $f(\mathbf{X})$ is free w.r.t. $\mathbf{X}$, where $\mathbf{X}$ is a list of distinct variables.

Theorem 2. $opt(\texttt{DATALOG}^{\neg_s,\subseteq})_{\exists} = OPT\,\Sigma_0$.

PROOF (sketch). Let $\langle P, opt|f|\rangle$ be a query in $opt(\texttt{DATALOG}^{\neg_s,\subseteq})_{\exists}$. Consider the rules that define directly or undirectly the goal f and let $\mathbf{X}$ be a list of $a(f)$ distinct variables. Since $f(\mathbf{X})$ is free w.r.t. $\mathbf{X}$ by hypothesis, it is possible to rewrite the variables in the above rules so that they are a subset of $\mathbf{X}$. It is now easy to show that the query can be written as a quantifier-free first-order formula with the free variables $\mathbf{X}$, i.e., the query is in $OPT\,\Sigma_0$. The proof that every query in $OPT\,\Sigma_0$ can be formulated as a query in $opt(\texttt{DATALOG}^{\neg_s,\subseteq})_{\exists}$ is straightforward. □

It turns out that all queries in $max(\texttt{DATALOG}^{\neg_s,\subseteq})_{\exists}$ are const approximable.

Example 9. *MAX CUT.* Consider the program $P_{cut'}$ of Example 7. The query $\langle P_{cut'}, max|e'|\rangle$ is in $MAX\,\Sigma_0$ since $e'(X,Y)$ is free w.r.t. $\langle X,Y\rangle$. □

5.2 $OPT\,\Sigma_1$ Problems

Definition 5. Let P be a $\texttt{DATALOG}^{\neg_s,\subseteq,!}$ program and $p(\mathbf{y})$ be an atom. We say that P is *semipositive* w.r.t. $p(\mathbf{y})$ if

1. p is an EDB or a subset predicate symbol, or

2. $\forall r \in P$ defining p, P is semipositive w.r.t. every positive literal in the body $B(r)$ while each negative literal is EDB or subset. □

We now denote with $opt(\texttt{DATALOG}^{\neg_s,\subseteq})_+$ the class of all queries $\langle P, opt|f|\rangle$ in $opt(\texttt{DATALOG}^{\neg_s,\subseteq})$ such that P is semipositive w.r.t. $f(\mathbf{X})$; moreover, $opt(\texttt{DATALOG}^{\neg_s,\subseteq})_{F,+}$ denotes the class of the queries in $opt(\texttt{DATALOG}^{\neg_s,\subseteq})_+$ for which f is a subset predicate symbol.

Theorem 3.

1. $opt(\texttt{DATALOG}^{\neg_s,\subseteq})_+ = OPT\,\Sigma_1$;

2. $opt(\texttt{DATALOG}^{\neg_s,\subseteq})_{F,+} = OPT\,F\Sigma_1$.

PROOF (sketch). Let $\langle P, opt|f|\rangle$ be a query in $opt(\texttt{DATALOG}^{\neg_s,\subseteq})_+$ and $\mathbf{X}$ be a list of $a(f)$ distinct variables. Consider the rules that define directly or undirectly the goal f. Since P is semipositive w.r.t. $f(\mathbf{X})$ by hypothesis, it is possible to rewrite the variables in the above rules so that each of them is either is $\mathbf{X}$ or existentially quantified. It is now easy to show that the query can be formulated into the $OPT\,\Sigma_1$ format. The proofs of the remaining relationships are straightforward. □

Then all queries in both $max(\texttt{DATALOG}^{\neg_s,\subseteq})_+$ and $max(\texttt{DATALOG}^{\neg_s,\subseteq})_{F,+}$ are const approximable.

Example 10. *MAX SATISFIABILITY.* We are given two unary relation c and a such that a fact $c(x)$ denotes that x is a clause and a fact $a(v)$ asserts that v is a variable occurring in some clause. We also have two binary relations p and n such that the facts $p(x,v)$ and $n(x,v)$ say that a variable v occurs in the clause x positively or negatively, respectively. A boolean formula in conjunctive normal form can be represented by means of the relations c, a, p, and n.

The maximum number of clauses simultaneously satisfiable under some truth assignment can expressed by the query $\langle P_{sat}, max|f| \rangle$ where P_{sat} is the following program:

$$s(X) \subseteq a(X) \qquad\qquad \begin{array}{l} f(X) \leftarrow c(X), \ p(X,V), \ s(V). \\ f(X) \leftarrow c(X), \ n(X,V), \ \neg s(V). \end{array}$$

Observe that $f(X)$ is not free w.r.t. $\{X\}$ (indeed the query is not in *MAX* Σ_0 but P_{sat} is semipositive w.r.t. $f(X)$ so that the query is in *MAX* Σ_1. Observe now that the query goal f is not a subset predicate: indeed the query is not in *MAX* $F\Sigma_1$. □

5.3 *OPT* Π_1 **Problems**

Definition 6. Let $r : should\_be(A)$ be a rule in a DATALOG$^{\neg s, \subseteq, !}$ program P. Then an atom C has

1. a *mark* 0 w.r.t. r if $C = A$ and A is positive;

2. a *mark* 1 w.r.t. r if $C = \neg A$ and A is negative;

3. a *mark* k w.r.t. r if there exists a rule r' in P and a substitution σ for the variables in C such that either (i) $H(r')$ has mark $(k-1)$ w.r.t. r and $C\sigma$ occurs negated in $B(r')$, or (ii) $H(r')$ has mark k w.r.t. r and $C\sigma$ is a positive literal in $B(r')$ □

Let us now define the class $opt(\text{DATALOG}^{\neg s, \subseteq, !})_{\exists}$ of all queries $\langle P, opt|f| \rangle$ in $opt(\text{DATALOG}^{\neg s, \subseteq, !})$ such that (i) $f(\mathbf{X})$ is free w.r.t. $\mathbf{X}$ and (ii) for each *should_be* rule r in P and for each atom C that has an even mark w.r.t. r, every rule r' in P whose head unifies with C, the variables occurring in the body $B(r')$ also occur in the head $H(r')$. Furthermore, $opt(\text{DATALOG}^{\neg s, \subseteq, !})_{\exists, F}$ denotes the subclass of feasible queries in $opt(\text{DATALOG}^{\neg s, \subseteq, !})_{\exists}$, i.e., the queries for which the query goal is a subset predicate symbol.

We are finally able to define a subclass which captures *OPT* $F^+\Pi_1$ that is approximable when *OPT* = *MIN*. To this end, we define the class $opt(\text{DATALOG}^{\neg s, \subseteq, !})_{\exists, F^+}$ as the subclass of $opt(\text{DATALOG}^{\neg s, \subseteq, !})_{\exists, F}$ consisting of those queries $\langle P, opt|f| \rangle$ such that for each *should_be* rule r in P, there exists no subset atom $s(\mathbf{x})$ which has an odd mark w.r.t. r.

Theorem 4.

1. $opt(\text{DATALOG}^{\neg s, \subseteq, !})_{\exists} = OPT$ Π_1;

2. $opt(\text{DATALOG}^{\neg s, \subseteq, !})_{\exists, F} = OPT\, F\Pi_1$;

3. $opt(\text{DATALOG}^{\neg s, \subseteq, !})_{\exists, F^+} = OPT\, F^+\Pi_1$.

PROOF (sketch). Let $\langle P, opt|f| \rangle$ be a query in $opt(\text{DATALOG}^{\neg s, \subseteq, !})_{\exists}$. Consider the rules that define directly or undirectly the goal f and let $\mathbf{X}$ be a list of $a(f)$ distinct variables. Since $f(\mathbf{X})$ is free w.r.t. $\mathbf{X}$ by hypothesis, it is possible to rewrite the variables in the above rules so that they are a subset of $\mathbf{X}$. Consider now the rules that define directly or undirectly the goal in a should-be rule. We can now rewrite the variables in the above rules so that they are universally quantified. It is now easy to show that the query can be written as a existential-free first-order formula with the free variables $\mathbf{X}$ and possibly additional variables universally quantified, i.e., the query is in $OPT\,\Pi_1$. The proofs of the other relationships are simple. □

Example 11. *MAX CLIQUE.* In this example we want find the cardinality of a maximum clique, i.e., a set of nodes V' such that for each pair of nodes (x, y) in V' there is an edge joining x to y. The maximum clique problem can be expressed by the query $\langle P_{clique}, max|v'| \rangle$ where the program P_{clique} is as follows:

> $\mathbf{v'(X) \subseteq v(X)}$.
> $\mathbf{no\_clique \leftarrow v'(X),\ v'(Y),\ X \neq Y,\ \neg e(X, Y)}$.
> $\mathbf{should\_be(\neg no\_clique)}$.

The query is in the class $max(\text{DATALOG}^{\neg s, \subseteq, !})_{\exists, F}$ and, therefore, the optimization query is in $MAX\, F\Pi_1\ (=\ MAX\,\Pi_1)$. On the other hand both atoms $\mathbf{v'(X)}$ and $\mathbf{v'(Y)}$ in the body of the rule defining the predicate $\mathbf{no\_clique}$ have mark 1 (i.e., , odd) w.r.t. the *should_be* rule. Therefore, the query $\langle P_{clique}, max|v'| \rangle$ is not in the class $max(\text{DATALOG}^{\neg s, \subseteq, !})_{\exists, F^+}$, thus it is not in $MAX\, F^+\Pi_1$. □

Example 12. *MIN VERTEX COVER.* As discussed in the introduction, the problem can be formulated by the query $\langle P_{vc}, min|v'(X)| \rangle$ where P_{vc} is the following program:

> $\mathbf{v'(X) \subseteq v(X)}$.
> $\mathbf{no\_cover \leftarrow e(X, Y),\ \neg v'(X),\ \neg v'(Y)}$.
> $\mathbf{should\_be(\neg no\_cover)}$.

Observe that both atoms $\mathbf{v'(X)}$ and $\mathbf{v'(Y)}$ in the rule defining $\mathbf{no\_cover}$ have a mark 2 (i.e., even) w.r.t. the *should_be* rule. Therefore, the query is in $min(\text{DATALOG}^{\neg s, \subseteq, !})_{\exists, F^+}$ and, then, in $MIN\, F^+\Pi_1$; so the problem is const approximable. □

5.4 Beyond *OPT* Π_1

Additional interesting subclasses can be captured in our framework but they are not investigated here for space reason. We just give an example of a query which is in the class *MIN* $F^+\Pi_2(1)$ — this class is a subset of *MIN* Π_2 where every subset predicate symbol occurs both positively and at most once in every disjunction of the formula ψ. Problems in this class are log-approximable [16].

Example 13. *MIN DOMINATING SET.* Let $G = (V, E)$ be a graph. A subset V' of V is a dominating set if every node either is in V' or has a neighbor in V'. The query $\langle P_{ds}, min|v'(X)| \rangle$ where P_{ds} is the following program, computes the cardinality of a minimum dominating set:

> v'(X) ⊆ v(X).
> q(X) ← v'(X).
> q(X) ← e(X, Y), v'(Y).
> no_ds ← v(X), ¬q(X).
> should_be(¬no_ds).

This problem belongs to *MIN* $F^+\Pi_2(1)$.   □

Observe that the problem *min kernel* as defined in Example 8 is in the class *MIN* $F\Pi_2$ but not in *MIN* $F^+\Pi_2$. as it contains occurrences of the subset predicate v' which have an odd mark w.r.t. the *should_be* rule.

6 Conclusions and future work

In this paper we have shown that $\mathcal{NP}$ optimization problems can be formulated as DATALOG¬ queries under a non-deterministic version of total stable model semantics. We have also presented an extension of DATALOG with stratified negation (called DATALOG¬ˢ,⊆,!) that is able to express all $\mathcal{NP}$ optimization queries. Our on-going research is concerning the efficient implementation schemes for the language, particularly to perform effective set selections by pushing down constraints and possibly adopting 'intelligent' search strategies and further extensions of the DATALOG¬ˢ,⊆,! language.

References

[1] S. Abiteboul, E. Simon and V. Vianu. Non-deterministic languages to express deterministic transformations. In *Proc. ACM PODS Symp.*, 1990, 218–229.

[2] S. Abiteboul and V. Vianu. Non-determinism in logic-based languages. *Annals of Mathematics and Artificial Intelligence 3*, 1991, 151–186.

[3] S. Abiteboul, R. Hull, V. Vianu. *Foundations of Databases*. Addison-Wesley, 1995.

[4] K. Apt, H. Blair and A. Walker. Towards a theory of declarative knowledge. In *Foundations of Deductive Databases and Logic Programming*, J. Minker (ed.), Morgan Kauffman, Los Altos, USA, 1988, 89–142.

[5] G. Ausiello, P. Crescenzi and M. Protasi. Approximate solution of NP optimization problems. In *Theoretical Computer Science*, No. 150, 1995, 1–55.

[6] T. Eiter, G. Gottlob, and Y. Gurevich. Normal forms for second-order logic over finite structures, and classification of NP optimization problems. *Annals of Pure and Applied Logic*, No. 78, 1996, 111–125.

[7] Fagin R., "Generalized First-Order Spectra and Polynomial-Time Recognizable Sets", in *Complexity of Computation (R. Karp, Ed.)*, SIAM-AMS Proc., Vol. 7, 1974, 43–73.

[8] M. Garey and D.S. Johnson. *Computers and Intractability — A Guide to the Theory of NP-Completeness*. W.H. Freeman, New York, USA, 1979.

[9] M. Gelfond and V. Lifschitz. The Stable Model Semantics for Logic Programming. In *Proc. Int. Conf. and Symp. on Logic Programming*, 1988, 1070–1080.

[10] F. Giannotti, D. Pedreschi, D. Saccà. and C. Zaniolo. Non-Determinism in Deductive Databases. In *Proc. DOOD Conf.*, 1991.

[11] F. Giannotti, S. Greco, D. Saccà. and C. Zaniolo. Programming with Nondeterminism in Deductive Databases. In *Annals of Mathem. and Art. Intell.*, No. 17, 1997, 97–125.

[12] S. Greco, D. Saccà and C. Zaniolo. Datalog with Stratified Negation and Choice: from P to D^P. In *Proc. ICDT Conf.*, 1995, 574–589.

[13] S. Greco and D. Saccà. "Possible is certain" is desirable and can be expressive. In *Annals of Mathem. and Art. Intell.*, 17, 1997, 147–168.

[14] D.S. Johnson. A Catalog of Complexity Classes. In *Handbook of Theoretical Computer Science*, Vol. 1, J. van Leewen (ed.), North-Holland, 1990.

[15] P. G. Kolaitis and M. N. Thakur. Logical Definability of NP Optimization Problems *Information and Computation*, No. 115, 1994, 321–353.

[16] P. G. Kolaitis and M. N. Thakur. Approximation Properties of NP Minimization Classes. *JCSS*, No. 50, 1995, 391–411.

[17] M. W. Krentel. The complexity of optimization problems. *JCSS*, No. 36, 1988, 490–509.

[18] N. Leone, L. Palopoli and D. Saccà. Much Ado about ... Non-Deterministic Queries. unpublished manuscript, 1996.

[19] E. Leggett and J. Moore. Optimization problems and the polynomial hierarchy. *Theoretical Computer Science*, No. 15, 1981, 279–289.

[20] Lloyd. *Foundations of Logic Programming*. Springer-Verlag, 1987.

[21] C. Papadimitriou. *Computational Complexity*. Addison-Wesley, 1994.

[22] A. Panconesi and D Ranjan. Quantifiers and Approximation. *Theoretical Computer Science*, No. 1107, 1992, 145–163.

[23] C. H. Papadimitriou and K. Steiglitz. *Combinatorial Optimization— Algorithms and Complexity*. Prentice-Hall, 1982.

[24] C. H. Papadimitriou and M. Yannakakis. Optimization, Approximation, and Complexity Classes. *JCSS*, No. 43, 1991, 425–440.

[25] D. Saccà. The Expressive Powers of Stable Models for Bound and Unbound Queries. *Journal of Computer and System Sciences*, to appear.

[26] D. Saccà and C. Zaniolo. Stable Models and Non-Determinism in Logic Programs with Negation. In *Proc. ACM PODS Symp.*, 1990, 205–218.

[27] A. Selman. A taxonomy of complexity classes of functions. *Journal of Computer and System Science*, No. 48, 1994, 357–381.

[28] J. Ullman. *Principles of Data and Knowledge-Base Systems*, volume 1 and 2. Computer Science Press, New York, 1988.

Prioritized Conflict Handling for Logic Programs

Benjamin N. Grosof

IBM T.J. Watson Research Center

P.O. Box 704, Yorktown Heights, NY 10598

http://www.research.ibm.com

(914) 784-7100

grosof@watson.ibm.com (or grosof@cs.stanford.edu)

http://www.research.ibm.com/people/g/grosof/

Abstract

We define courteous logic programs, an expressive superclass of general logic programs, for the acyclic case. Courteous LP's feature not only classical negation as in extended LP's (Gelfond & Lifschitz), but also prioritized conflict handling. We show courteous LP's always have a consistent and unique answer set, which can be computed in $O(m^2)$ time, where m is the size of the ground-instantiated program, as compared to $O(m)$ time for general LP's. Courteous LP's provide a method to resolve conflicts that arise in authoring (specifying), updating, and merging. This is especially useful for creation of rule-based intelligent agents by non-technical authors, e.g., for commercial applications such as personalized information filtering and workflow. Current work includes: implementing courteous LP's for such applications, in IBM's RAISE system; generalizing expressively, e.g., to permit recursion; and developing methods for interactive acquisition of rules, e.g., conflict analysis and inter-agent communication.

An extended version of this paper (with proofs) is available as IBM Research Report RC 20836, at http://www.research.ibm.com , as are additional other related papers and pages (see author's Web address above).

1 Introduction and Overview

Our aim in developing courteous logic programs is to improve the expressive convenience of logic programs, especially for applications in intelligent information agents. We call the formalism "courteous" for two reasons. First, it respects precedence, i.e., priority relationships between rules. Second, even in the presence of conflict between rules, it is "well-behaved" in the sense of there being a consistent, tractably computable, and unique set of conclusions.

An interesting application area for logic programming that motivates our work is "information-flow" applications enhanced by rule-based intelligent agents. In these applications, agents control the flow of information items. Their tasks include not only finding and filtering, but also categorizing, prioritizing for attention, storing and managing, monitoring and notifying, and selectively forwarding, disseminating and sharing.

IBM has released Agent Building Environment (ABE) as a toolkit product alpha, for building such applications. It is currently available free on the World Wide Web (see http://www.raleigh.ibm.com/iag/iaghome.html). ABE is based on our group's research system RAISE (Reusable Agent Intelligence Software Environment) [17] [18] [16] (also see author's Web address for more). ABE/RAISE's approach revolves around a logic program. In the currently released version of ABE, this logic program is acyclic (non-recursive), Datalog, and positive (without negation-as-failure). Inferencing is in the forward direction, and is exhaustive; i.e., all conclusions are generated. An innovative feature in ABE/RAISE is its patent-pending approach to "situating" the logic program's reasoning by augmenting it with clean and dynamic procedural attachments for perception and action. IBM has already built several practical intelligent agents applications based on ABE/RAISE: in e-commerce shopping, customer service, e-mail, and netnews. Several others are underway, mostly in cooperation with IBM's customers and business partners.

In this application area, it is valuable to facilitate authoring (i.e., specifying) of logic programs by relatively non-technical users, e.g., as part of personalizing rule-based intelligent agents. Rule sets are not "shrink-wrapped" with the application. Rather, a user is the "domain expert" for her own "workflow", e.g., for specifying her mail handling or shopping interests. These users specify their rule sets via forms and templates that are often application-specific. "Under the covers", the rules are then re-formatted as a more standard logic program.

We are attracted by the expressive power of classical negation as in extended logic programs [9]. There, classical negation is permitted in rule heads and bodies (in addition to negation-as-failure in the bodies). This offers the convenient capability to reason in a first-class way about both sides of a proposition p (say, "Highly Important" for e-mail): i.e., about $\neg p$ as well as about p, in particular to infer $\neg p$ from rules (as well as p from rules). However, a rule $p \leftarrow Body1$ may *conflict* with a rule $\neg p \leftarrow Body2$. I.e., informally, both *Body*1 and *Body*2 may succeed (fire), creating a conflict about whether p or $\neg p$ should succeed. In extended logic programs, such conflict results in global inconsistency ("blow-up"); every literal is a conclusion. This is similar to the situation in classical logic, in which an inconsistent theory implies any sentence as a conclusion.

A difficulty with employing extended logic programs is thus that it is relatively easy to get conflicts in the rule sets, especially when authored by relatively non-technical end-users as in our intelligent information agents applications scenarios.

Also, it is desirable in our applications scenarios to facilitate modularity and merging of rule sets (including advice-taking, i.e., automatic merging based on inter-agent knowledge-level communication). This is important because it is relatively expensive in human effort to specify and debug rule sets. Re-use and sharing are highly advantageous; it's nice if a user (or his agent) can swap rule sets with his "friends", e.g., co-workers. The catch, though, is that conflicts can arise relatively easily as a result of merging.

Another difficulty is that the presence of two forms of negation, i.e., having negation-as-failure in addition to classical negation, is potentially quite conceptually confusing, again especially for relatively non-technical end-users.

For inspiration in grappling with these challenges, we have drawn on the idea of *prioritized defaults* (e.g., [24] [21] [11] [14] [12] (ch. 2 includes a literature review), and [3] (also includes a literature review)) from the field of general non-monotonic reasoning. As has been explored there (and in the related knowledge representation and common-sense reasoning literatures), it is often easier and more natural, especially for non-technical end-users, to specify rules in the manner of prioritized defaults. "Default" roughly means that a rule antecedent can succeed without the rule consequent succeeding: it may be that the rule consequent is blocked by another conflicting rule. "Prioritized" roughly means that in case of conflict between two rules, the rule with (strictly) higher priority has its consequent succeed, and the rule with lower priority does not.

We are attracted to partially-ordered prioritization in that it is relatively weak, qualitative information, yet it suffices to resolve conflicts. It can be specified by pairwise comparison of rules.

Prioritized defaults suffice as a representational approach for many interesting cases of conflictful reasoning, including: updating in (deductive-)database-flavor fashion, where more recent premises override previous premises; specificity dominance and inheritance with exceptions in which a more specific rule overrides a less specific rule; and legalistic regulations in which a rule whose source has greater authority (e.g., jurisdictional) overrides a rule whose source has less authority.

Taking all this together, we are motivated to provide a mechanism that can not only represent classical negation, but also handle conflicts and priorities in fashion akin to prioritized defaults. Speaking philosophically and slangily, we might say that extended logic programs "give up" in the face of conflicts, whereas we want in developing courteous logic programs to "deal with" conflicts, take them in stride, even "munch on" them.

The courteous logic program formalism meets our desiderata to a considerable extent. First, it preserves overall consistency in the presence of conflict. Conclusions not affected by the conflict are still inferred. (It "does something reasonable" until the the rule set is "totally debugged".)

Second, it provides a simple way to specify override: an optional label for each rule, plus a reserved binary predicate *Overrides* that takes rule labels as arguments. An *Overrides* fact as part of the overall logic program then specifies a pairwise priority comparison.

Third, inferencing in the formalism is tractable, under the Datalog restriction. By contrast, conflict handling in most expressively powerful formalisms for prioritized default reasoning (e.g., based in Default Logic [28] or circumscription [23]) is an additional source of NP-hard complexity beyond the base reasoning [10] [6]. Tractability makes applications practical beyond small scale.

Fourth, there is a unique answer set (i.e., set of conclusions). This helps provide a conceptually simple semantics, which facilitates understandability, especially by non-technical end-users. By contrast, many expressively powerful non-monotonic reasoning formalisms have multiple extensions (e.g., Prioritized Default Logic variants; see [3] for review).

Fifth, reassuringly, the (acyclic) courteous logic programs class includes (acyclic) consistent extended logic programs as a sub-class, both syntactically and semantically. (Acyclic) general logic programs [1] are essentially a sub-class of consistent extended logic programs (the only difference is that in the usual definition, $LP \not\vdash atom$ in general LP's is treated also as $LP \vdash \neg atom$, i.e., the closed world assumption is applied to all atoms).

Sixth, the courteous formalism enables one to avoid many typical uses of negation-as-failure, e.g., closed world assumption, blocking a less specific rule when a more specific rule applies, or blocking a less recent rule when updating with a more recent rule. The expressive mechanisms of classical negation, defaults, and priorities provide a more disciplined and modular way to achieve the same effect, in many cases. Obviating the need for negation-as-failure helps reduce the potential confusion, especially for non-technical end-users, caused by the presence of two forms of negation.

We have found in our previous work on ABE/RAISE that the acyclic Datalog restriction suffices for many interesting applications. Motivated by that work, we are especially interested in exhaustive forward inferencing, i.e., in computing the entire answer set. This can be viewed as a kind of *deductive database*.

Key to the courteous formalism's computational and conceptual simplicity is that conflicts are resolved **locally**: by refutation and skepticism among rules that mention (positively or negatively) the same head atom.

Tractability and uniqueness of the answer set are highly attractive properties, in our view. They make reasoning be practical: not only exhaustive forward inferencing, but also rapidly iterated belief revision. But more than that, they make authoring rules (knowledge acquisition) be more natural. They make it much easier to understand and predict the reasoning behavior, and thus to debug and to trust the program. Locality is a major help too. The author of rules (e.g., a non-technical end-user) need focus only on the set of rules in a locale, in a modular fashion. Tractability and locality enable a human to "simulate in his head" what the rules will "do" and thus what they "mean", even in relatively large rule sets. Modularity, understandability, and predictability are often crucial requirements for practical usage, e.g., as we have found at IBM in our agent-building experience.

---

[1] under the usual, e.g., stratified, semantics; see Theorem 5.2 for details

2 Preliminary Definitions; Extended LP's

Each *rule* r in an *extended* logic program $\mathcal{E}$ has the form:

$$L_0 \leftarrow L_1 \wedge \ldots \wedge L_m \wedge \sim L_{m+1} \wedge \ldots \wedge \sim L_n$$

where $n \geq m \geq 0$, and each L_i is a literal.

We will define courteous LP's' rule syntax to be similar but not identical to that of extended LP's.

Notation and Terminology: A *literal* is a formula of the form A or $\neg A$, where A is an atom. $\neg$ stands for the *classical negation* operator symbol, and $\sim$ for the *negation-as-failure* operator symbol. In English, we read the former as "not" and the latter as "fail". We say that an unnegated literal (i.e., an atom) is *positive*. A ground rule with empty body is called a *fact*. Syntactically, a "*general*" logic program is one in which each literal L_j above is an atom, i.e., where no classical negation is permitted.

The semantics of extended LP's treats a rule with variables as shorthand for the set of its ground instances. We will do likewise with courteous LP's. We write $\mathcal{E}^{instd}$ to stand for the LP that results when each rule in $\mathcal{E}$ having variables has been replaced by the set of all its possible ground **instantiations**. The semantics of extended LP's is further defined using the concept of an **answer set** (i.e., set of conclusions); again, we will do likewise with courteous LP's. An answer set is a subset of the ground literals. We write $\models$ to stand for truth relative to an answer set.

As we discussed in section 1, as Gelfond & Lifschitz define its semantics, an extended LP may be *contradictory*, i.e., **inconsistent**: it may have an inconsistent answer set. An answer set is inconsistent if it contains a pair of complementary literals; indeed in their semantics, an inconsistent extended LP has one answer set which is the set of all ground literals. For example, the extended LP consisting of the two conflicting rules

$$p \leftarrow \quad , \quad \neg p \leftarrow$$

is inconsistent. The answer set contains both the literals p and $\neg p$.

Observe that restricting extended LP's to be acyclic or stratified (and/or Datalog) does *not* ensure their consistency, e.g., as in the above example.

3 Definition: Courteous Logic Programs

Syntactically, a courteous logic program is defined as a restricted class of extended logic programs in which, additionally, rules have labels. These labels are used as handles for specification of prioritization between rules.

Definition 3.1 (Labelled Rule)

A *labelled rule* has the form:

$$\langle lab \rangle \quad L_0 \leftarrow L_1 \wedge \ldots \wedge L_m \wedge \sim L_{m+1} \wedge \ldots \wedge \sim L_n$$

where *lab* is the rule's label (and, as before, $n \geq m \geq 0$, and each L_i is a literal). The label is optional. If omitted, the label is said to be *empty*. The label is not required to be unique within the scope of the overall logic program; i.e., two rules may have the same label. The label is treated as a

0-ary function symbol. The label is preserved during instantiation; all the ground instances of the rule above have label *lab*. □

Definition 3.2 (Prioritization Predicate)

A special binary predicate *Overrides* is used to specify prioritization. *Overrides*(i, j) specifies that the label i has (strictly) higher priority than the label j. □

Definition 3.3 (Prioritization Sub-Program)

A *prioritization sub-program* is defined as a set, possibly empty, of positive ground facts about *Overrides*. Each of these is called a *prioritization fact*.

The prioritization relation *Overrides* specified by the prioritization sub-program is required to be a **strict partial order**, i.e., transitive and anti-symmetric (and irreflexive). □

Since each prioritization fact is a rule of the program, it may in principle have a label. As we will see, however, such labels are effectively ignored semantically.

Definition 3.4 (Courteous LP: Syntax)

A courteous logic program $\mathcal{C}$ is defined as the disjoint union of a main (sub-)program with a prioritization sub-program:

$$\mathcal{C} = \mathcal{C}_{main} \ \dot{\cup} \ \mathcal{C}_{Overrides}$$

Overrides is syntactically reserved: it must not appear in $\mathcal{C}_{main}$ but rather appear only within the prioritization sub-program.

$\mathcal{C}$ (i.e., its ground-*atom* dependency graph) is required to be **acyclic**. [2] □

Note that the prioritization predicate *Overrides* and the labels are treated as part of the language of the logic program, similarly to other predicate and function symbols appearing in $\mathcal{C}$.

Note that adding a prioritization sub-program does not affect the acyclicity of a program.

Terminology: Relative to $\mathcal{C}$: the **definitional locale** for a ground *atom* p, written as $Defn(p)$, is defined as the (possibly empty) subset of rules within $\mathcal{C}^{instd}$ in which p appears in the rule head (positively or negatively).

Let $\rho = p_1, \ldots, p_m$ be a sequencing of all the (ground) atoms of $\mathcal{C}^{instd}$. We say that ρ is a **total stratification** of the atoms when ρ is a reverse-direction topological sort of the atom dependency graph. "Reverse" here means that body comes before head. Associated with the total ordering of the atoms is the associated totally ordered partition of $\mathcal{C}^{instd}$'s rules into definitional atom locales $Defn(p_1), \ldots, Defn(p_m)$. Each *stratum*, i.e., element in this partition, is a single atom's definitional locale. □

Definition 3.5 (Courteous LP: Semantics)

---

[2] Acyclicity (our terminology follows [2]) prevents recursion among ground atoms, hence is often also called **non-recursiveness** in the literature. This is a cause of some confusion, however, in that strictly speaking, acyclicity does *not* prevent recursion among *predicates*.

$\mathcal{C}$ has a unique answer set S, defined as follows. Let ρ be a total atom stratification of $\mathcal{C}$, such that all of the prioritization (i.e., *Overrides*) atoms come before all the other (i.e., main) atoms. (There may be several such total stratifications; the choice among them does not matter.)

Let p_i stand for the ith (ground) atom in this sequence ρ. The answer set is constructed iteratively:
$$S_0 = \emptyset \quad ; \quad S_i = \bigcup_{j=1,\ldots,i} T_j \ , \quad i \geq 1 \quad ; \quad S = \bigcup_i T_i$$
where $\emptyset$ stands for the empty set, $\quad T_i =$
$$\{\sigma p_i \mid Cand_i^\sigma \neq \emptyset \ , \ \forall k \in Cand_i^{\neg\sigma} . \ \exists j \in Cand_i^\sigma . \ S_{i-1} \models Overrides(j,k)\}$$
$$Cand_i^\sigma = \{j \mid labels(j,r) \ , \ Head(r) = \sigma p_i \ , \ S_{i-1} \models Body(r)\}$$
Here, σ stands for a classical sign, either positive (sometimes written as $+$) or negative ($\neg$, also written as $-$). $labels(j,r)$ stands for: j is the label for rule r. $Head(r)$ and $Body(r)$ stand for the head and body of rule r, respectively. Note that $Head(r) = \sigma p_i$ implies that $r \in Defn(p_i)$.

Every rule with empty label is interpreted as having the same catch-all label *empty_label*, which is treated as a new symbol (i.e., new with respect to the rest of $\mathcal{C}$'s language). □

Explanatory Description: The answer set is defined incrementally and constructively, by means of a series of partial answer sets S_i, that are built up by iterating along a total atom stratification, generating conclusions for each ground atom (and thus each predicate) along the way.

The ith stratum in the total atom stratification contributes an increment T_i to the answer set. Recall that a stratum corresponds to the atom p_i's definitional locale. T_i is the **conclusion**, if any, resulting from the rules in that atom locale. The set T_i either consists of a single ground literal, or is empty. The literal is of positive sign, i.e., p_i, or it is of negative sign, i.e., $\neg p_i$.

T_i is the **winner**, if any, that results from **prioritized competition among candidate arguments**. A candidate argument is generated by a rule $r \in Defn(p_i)$ whose body $Body(r)$ successfully "fires" in the sense of being true in the previous answer set iterate S_{i-1}, in which iterate the earlier strata's conclusions have accumulated. Such a rule has either p_i or $\neg p_i$ as its head $Head(r)$. Candidates are represented by their labels and are collected into two sets. There is one such set for each sign σ: $Cand_i^\sigma$, which can be viewed as a **team** arguing for the same conclusion, namely σp_i.

The prioritized competition among candidates can be viewed in terms of these two **opposing** teams. If both teams are empty, then there is no winner. Otherwise, if one team is empty, then the other (non-empty) team wins. The most interesting case is when both teams are non-empty. This case corresponds to **conflict**. In extended logic programs, conflict results in inconsistency. In this case (and only in this case), the prioritization *Overrides* comes into play. **One team wins iff every member of the opposing team is refuted. Refutation is based on prioritization:** one candidate argument with label j refutes another candidate argument with label k iff j has higher priority than k, i.e., if $Overrides(j,k)$ is true in the previous answer set iterate S_{i-1}. Note that $Overrides(j,k)$ is true iff

$$Overrides(j,k) \leftarrow$$

is present as a prioritization fact in the prioritization sub-program $\mathcal{C}_{Overrides}$. If neither team is refuted, then neither team wins: i.e., the **teams can defeat each other**. (Note that due to the strict partial order property of the prioritization $Overrides$, it cannot happen that both teams refute each other.) This outcome of mutual defeat corresponds to **skepticality**: if there are unrefuted candidate arguments both for p_i and for $\neg p_i$, then no conclusion about p_i is drawn; intuitively, there is then no strong justification to believe either, so no "commitment" is made.

Remarks: Our definition of courteous logic programs is as a pure formalism. It therefore supports inferencing in both the **forward** direction (as in the intelligent agents applications discussed in section 1) and the **backward** direction, i.e., query-answering (as in Prolog).

The prioritization ($Overrides$), refutation, and skepticality are **local**, in the sense that they apply directly only within the scope of each atom locale, then ramify indirectly to the entire program.

If a locale contains only rules whose heads share the same sign, then we say that the locale is **one-sided**. If a locale is one-sided, then there can be no conflict within it, and the prioritization within it is irrelevant.

In particular, since the prioritization sub-program is one-sided, its rules' labels and the prioritization among them (if, indeed, it has any) are irrelevant, and can thus be omitted equivalently.

Since $empty\_label$ cannot appear in the prioritization sub-program, any rule with empty label effectively does not participate in strict prioritization. More generally, if the prioritization sub-program is empty, then labels are superfluous.

In general, the prioritization relation $Overrides$ may compare two labels i and j that belong to different locales. Such priority is ignored by the semantics. Similarly, prioritization facts mentioning non-label arguments may be permitted, but are ignored.

4 Examples

Example 4.1 (Molluscs; Inheritance; Specificity Priority)

Etherington & Reiter's [7] example of a default inheritance hierarchy about molluscs can be straightforwardly represented, with prioritization corresponding to specificity, as the following program. There is no need to add the extra "interaction" conditions that make the defaults be semi-normal there (in Default Logic, the formalism they used).

$\langle Mol \rangle \quad ShellBearer(x) \leftarrow Mollusc(x)$

$\langle Cep \rangle \quad \neg ShellBearer(x) \leftarrow Cephalopod(x)$

$\langle Nau \rangle \quad ShellBearer(x) \leftarrow Nautilus(x)$

$Mollusc(x) \leftarrow Cephalopod(x) \quad , \quad Cephalopod(x) \leftarrow Nautilus(x)$

$Overrides(Nau, Cep) \leftarrow \quad , \quad Overrides(Cep, Mol) \leftarrow$

$Overrides(Nau, Mol) \leftarrow$

For example, with

$Mollusc(Molly) \leftarrow$, $Cephalopod(Sophie) \leftarrow$, $Nautilus(Natalie) \leftarrow$

the answer set for the $ShellBearer$ predicate locale is

$\{ShellBearer(Molly), \neg ShellBearer(Sophie), ShellBearer(Natalie)\}$. □

Next, we give an example of a rule base that controls handling of e-mail in a personal intelligent agent. One aspect of such handling is classifying mail into high importance vs. lower importance.

Example 4.2 (Mail Importance: Stores and Deliveries)
Karen has some rule-form knowledge she wants her agent to implement on her behalf. Mail from a retail store should be treated as not highly important (typically, it's junk). Mail from someplace from which Karen is awaiting a delivery should be treated as highly important. These two rules can be represented as:

$\langle Jun \rangle\ \neg Important(msg)\ \leftarrow\ From(msg, x) \wedge Retailer(x)$

$\langle Del \rangle\ \ Important(msg)\ \leftarrow\ From(msg, x)$
$\qquad\qquad\qquad\qquad\qquad \wedge AwaitingDeliveryFrom(Karen, x)$

Also, Karen has various other facts and knowledge, e.g.,

$\qquad AwaitingDeliveryFrom(Karen, ParisCo)$

In addition, Karen has access to a shared background knowledge base containing facts about organizations. She includes this information in her knowledge base. E.g.,

$Retailer(FaveCo) \leftarrow$, $Retailer(BabyCo) \leftarrow$, $Retailer(ParisCo) \leftarrow$

Now Karen receives a mail item:

$\qquad From(msg54, BabyCo)\ \leftarrow$

The courteous program draws the conclusion $\neg Important(msg54)$. So far, so good — Karen is pleased when she inspects a trace of what her agent has done on her behalf. After a while, another mail item arrives:

$\qquad From(msg81, ParisCo)\ \leftarrow$

The courteous program has a conflict between the first two rules, and hence skeptically and consistently draws no conclusion about $Important(msg81)$. When Karen inspects the trace, she exclaims "Oops!". She wants this kind of item to be treated as high importance — the delivery rule should win over the junk rule. This is easy to remedy: all she has to do is to add the prioritization fact

$\qquad Overrides(Del, Jun)\ \leftarrow$

Things go smoothly until after a while arrives the mail item

$\qquad From(msg117, FaveCo)\ \leftarrow$

The courteous program concludes $\neg Important(FaveCo)$. However when Karen inspects the trace, she again exclaims "Oops!". She wants this kind of item to be treated as high importance — because it is from FaveCo, one of her favorite stores. Again, this is easy to remedy: all she has to do is to add a new rule, and prioritize it as an exception override to the junk rule:

$\langle Fav \rangle\ \ Important(msg)\ \leftarrow\ From(msg, FaveCo)$

$\qquad Overrides(Fav, Jun)\ \leftarrow$ □

Example 4.3 (Basics; Localization of Conflict; Chaining)

Next, we illustrate some basics of how courteous LP's behave, even with empty prioritization. The rule set

$$p\leftarrow \ , \quad \neg p\leftarrow \ , \quad q \ \leftarrow \ p \ , \quad r \ \leftarrow \ \neg p$$

$$\neg u \ \leftarrow \ s \wedge \neg t \wedge \sim v \ , \quad \neg t\leftarrow \ , \quad s\leftarrow \ , \quad w \ \leftarrow \ \neg u \wedge \sim \neg p$$

has answer set $\{s, \neg t, \neg u, w\}$. The unresolved conflict about p is localized in its impact: other conclusions are entailed (without *all* propositions being entailed as in extended LP's), including by some chaining. $\neg p$'s failure helps the last rule fire. (If formalized instead in Default Logic (as "normal" defaults), by contrast, there would be two "extensions": the first including p and thus q; the second including $\neg p$ and thus r.)

5 Well-Behavior; Inferencing Algorithm

Theorem 5.1 (Consistency)

Every courteous LP has exactly one answer set which is consistent. $\square$

Since the labels and prioritization sub-program may be empty, one can take any acyclic extended LP and interpret it as a courteous LP. However, the **courteous interpretation of an extended LP is always consistent**.

Theorem 5.2 (Agreement with Extended and General LP's)

If a courteous LP $\mathcal{C}$'s main part $\mathcal{C}_{main}$ is consistent when interpreted semantically as an extended LP $\mathcal{E}_{main}$, then $\mathcal{C}$'s answer set is identical to $\mathcal{E}_{main}$'s answer set.

A special case is when $\mathcal{C}$ is a general logic program: each of its locales is one-sided. $\square$

Remark: Here, we interpret general LP's under the locally stratified semantics [1] [27], the stable semantics [8], or the well-founded semantics [30]. These semantics all coincide for the acyclic case since that is a special case of locally stratified (see, e.g., [2] for review of relevant concepts and literature). General LP's are syntactically a special case of extended LP's. Semantically, they are essentially a special case of extended LP's; the only difference is that in the usual definition, $LP \not\vdash atom$ in general LP's is treated also as $LP \vdash \neg atom$, i.e., the closed world assumption is applied to all atoms.

Next, we discuss inferencing and its computational complexity.

We begin by reviewing a few facts about how instantiation affects size. Let n stand for the size of $\mathcal{C}$. Let m stand for the size of $\mathcal{C}^{instd}$. An interesting question is how much larger m is than n. If $\mathcal{C}$ has no free variables, e.g., is propositional, then $m = n$. A common restriction in practice for logic programs is the **Datalog** condition, i.e., that there are no function symbols with arity greater than 0. Another common restriction in practice for logic programs is that there is a finite upper bound v on the number of variables appearing in any one rule. Taken together, the Datalog and variables-bound conditions on $\mathcal{C}$ imply that the size of the Herbrand base is $O(n)$, and that m is $O(n^{v+1})$.

Theorem 5.3 (Tractability of Inferencing; Algorithm)

Suppose $\mathcal{C}^{instd}$ is finite. Let its size be m. Then $\mathcal{C}$'s entire answer set can be computed in time $O(m^2)$ [3].

As a special case, suppose $\mathcal{C}$ obeys the Datalog restriction and has a bounded number v of variables per rule. Let $\mathcal{C}$'s size be n. Then $\mathcal{C}$'s entire answer set can be computed in time $O(n^{2 \cdot (v+1)})$. □

A conceptually simple **algorithm** (for exhaustive forward inferencing) is to implement directly the answer set construction that we gave in defining courteous programs.

Discussion: The core of the extra computational cost, relative to (acyclic) general LP's or consistent extended LP's, is the refutation process. For conflict-free programs, this overhead is absent. More generally, suppose the size of the smaller of the two teams of candidates in each locale is bounded by $O(f(m))$, where $f(m)$ is smaller than m, e.g., $f(m) = m^{\alpha}$ where $0 \leq \alpha < 1$. Then the overhead is $O(f(m))$, i.e., overall cost is $O(m \cdot f(m))$.

6 Discussion and Related Work

Courteous LP's have a relatively simple way to **force a conclusion** q: simply add a new fact $q\leftarrow$, at highest priority within its locale. Related to this point is the following property. Courteous LP's are **cumulative** in the sense of [22] [20]: if p is a conclusion of $\mathcal{C}$, then adding the fact $p\leftarrow$ to $\mathcal{C}$ results in a $\mathcal{C}'$ that has the same answer set as $\mathcal{C}$.

Database-flavor updating; recency priority: A common principle in databases and deductive databases is that more recent "update" information overrides less recent information. The update may overturn a previous conclusion directly, or may imply indirectly that it should be overturned. This is simple to represent in courteous LP's: by adding the more recent rules (e.g., facts), and prioritizing them higher than the previous rules. This has several virtues compared to general or extended LP's. Negation-as-failure is not required. Moreover, the previous rules do not have to be modified at all — the update is modular in that sense. As a bonus, a group of rules (e.g., a "module") can share a label, thereby reducing the number of prioritization facts needed to specify the overriding preference for recency.

The **closed world assumption** (CWA) for any given literal (e.g., predicate), can be represented in a simple fashion using priority plus classical negation. To achieve the effect of minimizing the predicate p after all the other rules "have had their say", include the rule $\neg p(x)$ with lowest priority within its locale.

By contrast, [9] give an approach in extended LP's — they represent the CWA for p by the rule $\neg p(x)\leftarrow\sim p(x)$. Observe that this employs negation-as-failure, and also creates a cycle in the dependency graph.

As our examples illustrated, courteous LP's have more expressive power on several dimensions than default inheritance systems in the vein of [29]:

---

[3]ignoring log factors, e.g., for insertion or retrieval of an element in a list

e.g., multiple body conditions, multiple variables, prioritization beyond specificity, and appearance of negation (including by failure) in the body. An interesting issue that we are pursuing in current work is how to automatically infer implicitly the higher priority of more specific rules.

Brewka [4] has a form of prioritized extended LP's that is closely related to courteous LP's. Courteous LP's (first introduced in [15] whose content partially overlaps with this paper) and Brewka's approach were developed independently. Brewka's syntax is similar to courteous LP's; however, he is concerned with two additional directions of expressive generality: cyclic dependencies, especially negative (through $\sim$); and reasoning about the prioritization itself, e.g., cf. [13] [3] [14]. He modifies the well-founded semantics to strengthen its conclusions; prioritization specifies how rules defeat each other via negation-as-failure. For comparison, each courteous LP rule r is most appropriately treated as "seminormal", i.e., as including additional body literal $\sim head(r)$. His semantics, including for priorities, behaves differently from courteous LP's, in general, even for some expressively simple cases. Worth considering is the example

$\langle a \rangle \quad p \leftarrow$, $\langle b \rangle \quad \neg p \leftarrow$, $Overrides(a, b) \leftarrow$
$\langle c \rangle \quad p \leftarrow$, $\langle d \rangle \quad \neg p \leftarrow$, $Overrides(c, d) \leftarrow$

which in courteous results in conclusion p but in Brewka's apparently does not [4]. [5] His formalism, like courteous, has the great virtue of computational tractability; conclusions can be computed in $O(n^3)$ time, as compared to $O(n^2)$ for courteous. Unlike courteous, his approach can result in an inconsistent conclusion set; he gives no consistency guarantee even for restricted cases. Space prevents a more detailed comparison here.

Next, we summarize Brewka's review of three other relevant approaches. Praaken & Sartor [26] has an argument-theoretic approach very similar to Brewka's. Buccafurri, Leone, & Rullo's [5] ordered LP's use an inheritance hierarchy as the basis of priority, but allow only one form of negation. Kowalski & Sadri [19] has a conflict handling approach in which rules that are "exceptions" to others are treated as having implicit preference.

Baral & Gelfond [2] discuss techniques for achieving some of the effects of priorities within extended LP's, e.g., via abnormalities, but do not give a general method. Pereira *et al* [25] address the issues of consistency, and priorities between abnormalities, in extended LP's. Their approach forces in $\sim$ literals contrapositively.

Hierarchical Constraint Logic Programming (HCLP) [31] has a notion somewhat similar to defaults with priorities, used abductively.

Concluding Remarks: A key to courteous logic programs' computational simplicity is that the prioritization and conflict resolution is local, pairwise, and atomic. In many other systems for default reasoning (e.g., circumscription and Default Logic and their prioritized versions), by contrast,

---

[4] confirmation awaits further communication with Brewka
[5] See the discussion of merging in [15], especially Example 10.

conflict may involve $k > 2$ default instances together constituting a minimal conflict set (e.g., potentially any subset of the overall set of defaults).

The value of the courteous approach to logic programming, in our view, is in *finding a definition* such that the resulting formalism is simple conceptually and computationally, yet useful expressively. (This definition combines expressive generalization, e.g., about prioritization, with expressive restriction, e.g., about dependencies.) The lack of tremendous mathematical complexity is thus a feature and virtue, and is no accident — it is closely related to the simplicity with which the courteous knowledge representation can be explained to, or explained by, a new rules-writer.

7 Current Work

In current work, we are implementing courteous logic programs (acyclic Datalog case) as an improved fundamental knowledge representation in RAISE, for use in building commercial intelligent agent applications (recall section 1). A RAISE **prototype is currently running**.

Our directions of generalizing representationally include: permitting recursion; implicit specificity priority, inheritance, and integrity constraints; and rich reasoning about the prioritization relation.

Our directions for interactive knowledge acquisition include analyzing conflict statically and dynamically, soliciting prioritization rules from users, and inter-agent advice-taking (prioritized merging of rule sets).

Acknowledgements

Thanks to Hoi Y. Chan, my co-conspirator in the RAISE implementation. Thanks also to Leora Morgenstern, Chitta Baral, Gerhard Brewka, Jeffrey Kephart, and anonymous reviewers for discussions and encouragement.

References

[1] K. Apt, H. Blair, and A. Walker. Towards a theory of declarative knowledge. In J. Minker, editor, *Foundations of Deductive Databases and Logic Programming*, pages 89–148. Morgan Kaufmann, Los Altos, CA, 1987.

[2] Chitta Baral and Michael Gelfond. Logic programming and knowledge representation. *Journal of Logic Programming*, 19,20:73–148, 1994. Includes extensive review of literature.

[3] Gerhard Brewka. Reasoning about priorities in default logic. In *Proceedings of the Twelfth National Conference on Artificial Intelligence (AAAI-94)*, pages 940–945, Menlo Park, CA / Cambridge, MA, 1994. AAAI Press / MIT Press.

[4] Gerhard Brewka. Well-founded semantics for extended logic programs with dynamic preferences. *Journal of Artificial Intelligence Research*, 4:19–36, 1996.

[5] F. Buccafurri, N. Leone, and P. Rullo. Stable models and their computation for logic programming with inheritance and true negation. *Journal of Logic Programming*, 27(1):5–43, 1996.

[6] Marco Cadoli and Marco Schaerf. A survey on complexity results for non-monotonic logics. *Journal of Logic Programming*, 17:127–160, 1993.

[7] D. Etherington and R. Reiter. On inheritance hierarchies with exceptions. In *Proceedings of the Second National Conference on Artificial Intelligence (AAAI-83)*, pages 104–108, Washington, D.C., 1983.

[8] Michael Gelfond and Vladimir Lifschitz. The Stable Model Semantics for Logic Programming. In *Logic Programming: Proceedings of the Fifth International Conference and Symposium*, pages 1070–1080, 1988.

[9] Michael Gelfond and Vladimir Lifschitz. Classical negation in logic programs and disjunctive databases. *New Generation Computing*, 9:365–385, 1991.

[10] Georg Gottlob. Complexity results for nonmonotonic logics. *Journal of Logic and Computation*, 2:397–425, 1992.

[11] Benjamin N. Grosof. Generalizing Prioritization. In *Proceedings of the Second International Conference on Principles of Knowledge Representation and Reasoning (KR-91)*, pages 289–300, April 1991.

[12] Benjamin N. Grosof. *Updating and Structure in Non-Monotonic Theories*. PhD thesis, Computer Science Dept., Stanford University, October 1992. Published by University Microfilms, Inc.. Also available as IBM Research Report RC 20683, dated Jan. 1997.

[13] Benjamin N. Grosof. Prioritizing Multiple, Contradictory Sources in Common-Sense Learning by Being Told; or, Advice-Taker Meets Bureaucracy. In Leora Morgenstern, editor, *Proceedings of the Second Symposium on Logical Formalizations of Common-Sense Reasoning (Common-Sense '93)*, IBM T.J. Watson Research Center, P.O. Box 704, Yorktown Heights, NY 10598, 1993. Available as an IBM Research Report. Copies of the Proceedings are available via the editor (wider publication being arranged). Held Guest Quarters Hotel, Austin, Texas, Jan. 11-13, 1993.

[14] Benjamin N. Grosof. Conflict Resolution in Advice-Taking and Instruction. In Diana Gordon, editor, *Proceedings of the ML-95 Workshop on Agents that Learn From Other Agents*. Proceedings are available at http://www.cs.wisc.edu/~shavlik/ml95w1/ . Extended Version available as IBM Research Report RC 20123., July 1995. Workshop held at the 1995 International Conference on Machine Learning.

[15] Benjamin N. Grosof. Practical prioritized defaults via logic programs. In *Proceedings of the Sixth International Workshop on Nonmonotonic Reasoning*. http://www.kr.org/nm/nm96.html and http://www.cs.utexas.edu/users/vl/, 1996. Extended version available as IBM Research Report RC 20464.

[16] Benjamin N. Grosof. Building Commercial Agents: An IBM Research Perspective (Invited Talk). In *Proceedings of the Second International Conference and Exhibition on Practical Applications of Intelligent Agents and Multi-Agent Technology (PAAM97)*, http://www.demon.co.uk./ar/PAAM97, April 1997. Practical Application Company Ltd. Held London, UK. Also available as IBM Research Report RC 20835.

[17] Benjamin N. Grosof and Davis A. Foulger. Globenet and RAISE: Intelligent Agents for Networked Newsgroups and Customer Service Support. In *Proceedings of the 1995 AAAI Fall Symposium on AI Applications in Knowledge*

Navigation and Retrieval, http://www.aaai.org, November 1995. American Association for Artificial Intelligence. Also available as IBM Research Report RC 20226.

[18] Benjamin N. Grosof, David W. Levine, Hoi Y. Chan, Colin P. Parris, and Joshua S. Auerbach. Reusable Architecture for Embedding Rule-Based Intelligence in Information Agents. In *Proceedings of the ACM Conference on Information and Knowledge Management (CIKM-95) Workshop on Intelligent Information Agents*, http://www.cs.umbc.edu/iia/, December 1995. Also available as IBM Research Report RC 20305.

[19] Robert Kowalski and Fariba Sadri. Logic programs with exceptions. *New Generation Computing*, 9:387–400, 1991.

[20] S. Kraus, D. Lehmann, and M. Magidor. Preferential models and cumulative logics. *Artificial Intelligence*, 44:167–207, 1990.

[21] V. Lifschitz. Computing circumscription. In *Proceedings IJCAI-85*, pages 121–127, Los Angeles, CA, 1985.

[22] D. Makinson. General theory of cumulative inference. In M. Reinfrank *et al.*, editor, *Proceedings of the Second International Workshop on Non-Monotonic Reasoning*, pages 1–18, Berlin, Germany, 1989. Springer Lecture Notes on Computer Science.

[23] J. McCarthy. Circumscription—a form of non-monotonic reasoning. *Artificial Intelligence*, 13:27–39, 1980.

[24] J. McCarthy. Applications of circumscription to formalizing commonsense knowledge. *Artificial Intelligence*, 28:89–116, 1986.

[25] Luis Moniz Pereira, Joaquim N. Aparicio, and Jose J. Alferes. Non-monotonic reasoning with logic programming. *Journal of Logic Programming*, 17:227–263, 1993.

[26] Henry Prakken and Giovanni Sartor. On the relation between legal language and legal argument: Assumptions, applicability, and dynamic priorities. In *Proceedings of the International Conference on AI and Law*, 1995. Washington.

[27] Teodor Przymusinski. On the declarative semantics of deductive databases and logic programs. In J. Minker, editor, *Foundations of Deductive Databases and Logic Programming*. Morgan Kaufmann, San Francisco, CA., 1988.

[28] R. Reiter. A logic for default reasoning. *Artificial Intelligence*, 12:81–132, 1980.

[29] D. Touretzky. *The Mathematics of Inheritance Systems*. Pitman, London, 1986.

[30] A. Van Gelder, K. Ross, and J. Schlipf. The well-founded semantics for general logic programs. *Journal of ACM*, 38(3):620–650, 1991.

[31] Molly Wilson and Alan Borning. Hierarchical constraint logic programming. *Journal of Logic Programming*, 16:277–318, 1993.

A Procedure for Mediation of Queries to Sources in Disparate Contexts[1]

S. Bressan[†], Cheng Hian Goh[‡], T. Lee[†], S. Madnick[†], M. Siegel[†]

[†] Sloan School of Management
Massachusetts Institute of Technology
50 Memorial Drive, E53-320
Cambridge, MA 02139, USA
Email: context@mit.edu

[‡] Dept of Info Sys & Comp Sc
National Univ of Singapore
Kent Ridge, Singapore 119260
Singapore
Email: gohch@iscs.nus.edu.sg

Abstract

This paper discusses the algorithm we are using for the *mediation* of queries to disparate information sources in a *Context Interchange* system, where information sources may have different interpretations arising from their respective *context*. Queries are assumed to be formulated without regard for semantic heterogeneity, and are rewritten to corresponding *mediated queries* by taking into account the semantics of data codified in axioms associated with sources and receivers (the corresponding *context theories*). Our approach draws upon recent advances in abductive logic programming and presents an integration of techniques for query rewriting and semantic query optimization. We also demonstrate how this can be efficiently implemented using the constraint logic programming system ECLiPSe.

1 Introduction

Context Interchange [GBMS96] is a novel approach towards the achievement of *semantic interoperability* of *heterogeneous information systems* [SL90]. Using this strategy, queries to disparate systems can be constructed without regard for (potentially) conflicting representations or interpretations of data across different systems: for example, when comparing the room rates of two hotels on different sides of the US-Canadian border, the user asking the query need not be concerned with whether or not prices are reported using the same currency, or whether the prices reported are inclusive of applicable taxes. Loosely speaking, query mediation can be simplified to the following scheme: for a query expressed in the terms of a *receiver*[2], an equivalent query, in the terms of the component systems providing the data must be composed, and a plan for the resulting query must be constructed, optimized and executed.

Our goal of this paper is to provide a logical interpretation of the query mediation step and to demonstrate how this is realized in a prototype implementation [BFG+97a] using the constraint logic programming system ECLiPSe. The inferences underlying query mediation can be characterized using an *abductive framework* [KKT93] and points to some interesting connection between integrity constraint checking and classical work in *semantic query optimization* [CGM90].

---

[1]This work is supported in part by ARPA and USAF/Rome Laboratory under contract F30602-93-C-0160, the International Financial Services Research Center (IFSRC), the PROductivity From Information Technology (PROFIT) project at MIT, and NUS research grant RP970628.

[2]i.e. under the assumptions and knowledge of the receiver issuing the query. Note that this receiver can either be a user or an application.

The remainder of this paper is organized as follows. In section 2, we summarize the novelty of our approach and describe the translation between a COIN (COntext INterchange) framework and a program (or, logical theory) written in COINL (the COIN language). In section 3, we present and discuss the Abductive Logic Programming framework and some aspects of the duality between abduction and deduction. We set the requirements for our procedure and discuss the possible interpretations of its results. In section 4, we outline the algorithm and discuss its implementation in the Logic Programming environment ECLiPSe [ECL96]. In particular, we discuss the implementation of the consistency checking phase of the abductive procedure as *Constraint Logic Programming* propagation [JM96] using *Constraints Handling Rules* [FH93]. We also discuss the relationship between consistency checking with integrity constraints and *Semantic Query Optimization* [CGM90]. Finally, we conclude in section 5 on some more general aspects of our project and on future work.

We assume that the reader is familiar with notations of first order logic (for instance, at the level of [Llo87]). We refer the reader to [KLW95] and [GBMS96] respectively for formal definitions of the F-Logic and the syntax and semantics of our logical language COINL. Where appropriate, we will explain those constructs used in the examples which are necessary for the understanding of the discussion. Finally, we use the symbol $\models$ to represent logical consequence in the model theory and the symbol $\vdash$ for the application of an inference rule (the acronym of the rule is subscripted when ambiguous).

2 Context Mediation

Before describing what context mediation entails, it is necessary to provide a summary of the motivation behind the architecture of a Context Interchange system, presented in the form of a COIN *framework*. Following which, we introduce an example which illustrates what context mediation entails. Finally, we show how the different components of a Context Interchange system can be used in the construction of a logical theory which may take the form of a *normal (Horn) program* [Llo87].

2.1 The Context Interchange Framework

Traditionally, two different approaches have been adopted for providing integrated access to disparate information sources. The *tight-coupling* approaches rely on the *a priori* creation of federated views on heterogeneous information sources. Although they provide better support for data access, they do not scale-up efficiently given the complexity inherent in the construction and maintenance of a shared schema for a large number of autonomously administered sources. *Loose-coupling* approaches rely on the user's intimate knowledge of the semantic conflicts between the sources and the conflict resolution procedures. This flexibility becomes a drawback for scalability since the amount of knowledge required of users increases exponentially with the number of sources, and may require frequent revisions as and when the semantics and structure of underlying sources undergo changes.

The Context Interchange approach takes a middle ground between these two approaches. Unlike the loose-coupling approaches, queries in such a system need not be concerned with differences in data representation or interpretation across sites; i.e., it allows queries to be formulated on multiple sources *as if* these were fragments of a homogeneous distributed database. Although it requires a common lexicon (called a *domain model*) for disambiguating types and role names, it is no longer mandatory for all conflicts to be resolved a priori in one place (e.g., as in the tight-coupling approaches). Instead, sources and receivers need only provide a declarative specification of the semantics of data pertaining to itself, while deferring conflict detection and resolution to the time when a query is actually submitted (when the sites involved in data exchange is identified). The *Context Mediator* takes on the role of conflict detection and resolution: this process is referred to as *context mediation.*

To support the functionalities described above, information about data sources and the semantics of data therein are captured in a Context Interchange system in a slightly more complex way. Loosely speaking, a Context Interchange system, as characterized by a COIN framework, comprises of a *domain model* (which provides a lexicon of types and *modifiers* corresponding to each type), a collection of *sources* corresponding to heterogeneous extensional databases (which we assume to be relational without any loss of generality), a collection of source-specific *elevation theories* (each comprising a collection of elevation axioms which define the types corresponding to the data domains in a source), a collection of *context theories* (each of which is a collection of declarative statements (in COINL) which either provide for the assignment of a value to a modifier, or identify a *conversion function* which can be used as the basis for converting the values of objects across different contexts), and finally, a *mapping function* mu which maps sources to contexts (suggesting that several different sources can share the same context, thus providing greater economy of expression and allowing context theories to be shared and reused).

Our primary motivation behind this structuring of a Context Interchange system is to provide the transparency of tight-coupling systems without the burden of reconciling all conflicts in one or more federated views. We argue that by allowing data semantics to be declaratively and independently captured in the form of context theories, changes in a local site can be better contained: in most instances, these changes require only modification of the context theory pertaining to the given site and have no repercussions on the global system. An interesting "side-effect" is that receivers too can have context: by associating a query with a context theory, we can request for answers to be returned in a form that is meaningful with respect to the stated context. Finally, notice that evolution in membership of sources has no effect the system: the addition or retraction of a source only involve the introduction or retraction of the corresponding elevation theory (and possibly the introduction of a new context theory). This compares favorably to current tight-coupling systems where the view definition needs to be modified corresponding to every of these changes.

2.2 Example

We consider a simple example where a user poses a query to a source (**security**), which provides historical financial data about a stock exchange. The user and the source have different assumptions regarding the interpretation of the data. These assumptions are captured in their respective contexts $c1$ and $c2$. The Domain Model defines the semantic types **moneyAmount**, **date**, **currencyType**, and **companyName**. The following query requests the price of the IBM security on March, 12th 1995:

```
Q1: select security.Price
    from security
    where security.Company = "International Business Machines"
    and security.Date = "12/03/95";
```

Suppose the user's context $c1$ indicates that money amounts are assumed to be in French Francs, dates are to be reported in the European format, and that currency conversions should be based on the date corresponding to that for which the price is reported for. Among other reasons, this information is needed to avoid the confusion between March, 12th and December, 3rd 1995. The remaining context information are present for circumventing other forms of ambiguity.

Let us assume, on the other hand, that the source context $c2$ report money amounts in the source in "US Dollars", and dates are reported in the American format. Under these circumstances, the Context Mediator will rewrite the query to incorporate the proper currency conversion (as of March, 12th 1995, using ancillary source (cc) for the conversion rates), and also make the appropriate transformations on dates to ensure that the query is correctly interpreted. In addition, if both contexts use different naming conventions for companies involved, then appropriate mapping between two naming conventions will be needed. For example, $c1$ may assume the full company name ("International Business Machines") while $c2$ uses company ticker symbol ("IBM"). Under the above circumstances, the mediated query corresponding to Q1 will be given by Q2 as shown below:

```
select security.Price * cc.Rate
    from security, cc
    where security.Company = "IBM"
    and security.Date = "03/12/95"
    and cc.source = "USD"
    and cc.target = "FRF"
    and cc.date = security.Date;
```

A primary goal of this paper is to demonstrate that the kind of transformations which we have exemplified can be understood as a special type of logical inference, which is sometimes characterized as *abduction* [KKT93]. The next section describes the representations in a Context Interchange framework in somewhat more detail, and illustrates how this can be transformed to a logical theory (comprising only of normal Horn clauses), thereby setting the stage for the subsequent sections of this paper.

2.3 A Logical Interpretation of Context Mediation

The axioms in a Context Interchange framework are represented using a deductive object-oriented formalism called the COIN language (COINL), which is a variant of F-logic [KLW95]. The collection of axioms present in an instance of this framework constitute a COINL program. Mediation of a query submitted to a Context Interchange system proceeds as follows. First, the user query and the COINL program are compiled into a goal (a negative Horn clause) and a normal logic program respectively. Following this, the goal is evaluated against the logic program using the *mediation procedure* (which we will describe shortly) which returns the answer consisting of a set of conjunctive clauses and the corresponding variable substitutions. These are then translated back to SQL, which can then be evaluated using a distributed database engine. In the remainder of this discussion, we will focus on the query mediation procedure. An in-depth description of the query evaluation framework can be found in [GBMS96].

Figure 1 illustrates the approach taken towards the representation of contextual information. Each data element (be it a data element stored in a source database, or a constant introduced in a user query, or a value present in the answer anticipated by

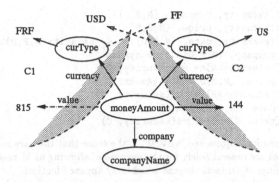

Figure 1: A summary of the COIN Framework.

a user) corresponds to a *semantic-object* or equivalently, an instance of a *semantic-type* defined in the domain model. In the above figure, we show only a portion of the domain model with the semantic-types **moneyAmount** and **curType** (for currency type). The semantic types may be arranged in a type hierarchy. The information on what types exist, their relationship to one another, and the signature of methods (called *modifiers*) defined on each type are defined in the domain model using COINL, examples of which are shown below:

```
moneyAmt :: number.
curType :: string.
moneyAmt[currency(ctx) => curType].
```

The above assertions state that **moneyAmt** is a subtype of **number**, whereas **curType** is a subtype of **string**. In addition, the semantic-type **moneyAmt** is modified by a method **currency** which returns an instance of the type **curType**

Semantic-objects are instantiated through the use of elevation axioms. For each relation R exported by a source, a *semantic relation* **R'** is defined. The semantic relation **R'** is *isomorphic* to the extensional relation R in the sense that it has the same *arity* m (i.e., number of arguments) and for every tuple $r(x_1, \ldots, x_m) \in R$, there exists a tuple $\mathbf{r'}(o_1, \ldots, o_m) \in \mathbf{R'}$ such that the value of o_i in the context corresponding to R is given by x_i. For instance, for the relation **security(company, price)**, the corresponding semantic relation is given by **security'(companyName, moneyAmt)**, where **companyName** and **moneyAmt** are semantic-types. Semantic-objects are syntactic constructs (Skolem functions) of the relation, the attribute, and the tuple. For instance:

$$O_1 = f(\text{security, company, ["IBM", 144, "03/12/95"]}).$$

is a semantic-object. The value of this object in the source context (of the relation **security**) is **"IBM"**. This is expressed in the elevation theory for the particular source by the following axioms. The first axiom defines the semantic relation and the semantic objects for **security**. The three other axioms define the respective values and attributes of the semantic objects. Notice that the value is a function of the context. The context associated with **security** is given by the **mu** function, which is defined for each source when the latter joins the mediation system.

```
security'( f(security, company, [N,P,D]),
          f(security, price, [N,P,D]),
          f(security, date, [N,P,D]) ) <- security(N,P,D).
f(security, company, [N,P,D]):companyName
          [value(C)->N]<- mu(security, C).
f(security, price, [N,P,D]):moneyAmount
          [value(C)->P] <- mu(security, C).
f(security, date, [N,P,D]):date
          [value(C)->D]<- mu(security, C).
```

Notice that semantic-objects are "virtual" in the sense that they are never actually instantiated but are present solely for the purpose of allowing us to reason with the different meanings of syntactic tokens which may appear identical.

In addition to the above, integrity constraints on sources can also be introduced to facilitate their use in semantic optimization of the mediated queries. For example, we may introduce the functional dependency company → price via the following assertion:

```
security(N, P1, D), security(N, P2, D) -> P1 = P2.
```

As we will see later, such constraints allow superfluous references to extensional data sources to be pruned and can result in significant savings.

Intuitively, a semantic-object is a syntactic construction which allows information in a source to be abstracted from the peculiarities of its representation and from the assumptions underlying its interpretation. For example, the same semantic-object may have different "values" in different contexts because different currencies are used for their reporting. In general the assumptions can be characterized by a number of orthogonal concepts (e.g. unit, scalefactor, format, rounding etc). To each semantic-type, and therefore to each semantic object, we associate a *modifier* corresponding to each of the relevant notion defining the interpretation of the data. In Figure 1, the semantic-object o of type moneyAmt has a modifier currency which may take on different values (e.g., "French Francs" or "US Dollars") in distinct contexts, thus allowing the same monetary quantity to take on different symbolic representations in different contexts.

A *context theory* is the set of definitions for the modifiers corresponding to semantic types in the domain model (context inheritance allows the reuse and specialization of context definitions). In our example, the contexts c1 and c2 define the *currency* modifiers as returning strings (also a semantic-type) whose values will be "United States Dollar" and "Japanese Yen" respectively. Notice that the modifiers are themselves semantic-objects whose values are to be interpreted in a context. Indeed, different contexts may represent the data element for United States Dollar as, for instance, "USD", or "$", or "US", etc. In complex situations we may use *modifiers of modifiers*. Let us consider a simple situation and give the axioms for the modifier *currency* in the context c1.

```
X : moneyAmount[currency(c1)->currency(c1,X)].
currency(c1,X):string[value(c1)->"FRF"].
```

Notice that the modifier is a function of the context. The semantic-object currency($c1,X$) (assigned to the modifier currency of X) is created by the first axiom. The second axiom assigns the value of this object which must be a printable string.

Conversion functions define the the mapping of a value to its corresponding counterpart under different assumptions, i.e. for different values of the modifiers. Typically, a conversion function for the currency conversion is multiplying the money amount by the currency exchange rate. Administrators and users contribute to a library of conversion functions.

The process of mediation consists, for each data element encountered in mediating a query, of the following steps. The source and associated context of the corresponding semantic object are identified. They are retrieved from the information in the Skolem function identifying the semantic object. The target context, i.e. the context in which the data element needs to be interpreted is identified. It is primarily given by the context in which the query is asked. Then the modifier values of the semantic objects are compared. For each mismatch in the modifier values, the corresponding conversion function is introduced. This mechanism is expressed by built-in axioms.

A user queries the relations exported by the component sources directly; however, such queries are expressed under the assumptions of the receivers, i.e. in her context. Before any mediation can take place, the query Q1 (as introduced in the example from Section 1) needs to be rewritten to take these assumptions into account. This transformation results in the following query $Q1'$,

```
answer(P) <- security'(O1, O2, O3),
             O1[value(c1)->"International Business Machines"],
             O3[value(c1)->"12/03/95"],
             O2[value(c1)->P].
```

which indicates explicitly the user's intention to query about the values of the semantic objects in the relation *security'* in her context ($c1$).

The above query constitutes a goal for the program composed of all the basic axioms, elevation axioms and context axioms. It is evaluated by the mediation procedure which is described in this paper. The answers are the mediated queries which only contain atoms from the component databases and the conversion functions as we have shown in the introduction.

We have chosen to implement the mediation process by separating it into a general purpose procedure and the explicit set of axioms. The generic mediation axioms and the application contexts, conversions, and elevation axioms are expressed in COINL and compiled into Datalog [ALUW93].

3 An Abductive Framework for Context Mediation

3.1 Background

Abduction [KKT93] is a form of reasoning initially defined by C.S. Pierce as the inference of the case from the rule and the result. For example, from the observation of G and the knowledge of the rule $D \to G$, one can infer D by abduction.

$$G \wedge (D \to G) \vdash_{abd} D$$

We can more generally define abductive inferences in terms of model semantics; thus, we say that

$$(T \wedge G) \vdash_{abd} D$$

if and only if

$$(T \cup D) \models G$$

In consideration of the above, we may say that D is a *"logical antecedent"* of G under T.

In order to make a practical use of abduction as a reasoning mechanism, we also want to avoid non-constructive inferences such as $G \vdash_{abd} D$ where D contains literals which are not "interesting" for the application. A trivial example could be a situation where D is G itself. We therefore add to our definition the condition that only certain literals are acceptable in the sentence D. Such literals are called *abducible literals*. They are identified as such from their predicate name which are explicitly defined as *abducible predicates* and be declared in a set called P_{abd}.

Furthermore we notice that a formula F such that $T \cup F$ is inconsistent ($T \cup F \models \Box$) is a logical antecedent of anything. Indeed, for all formulae G: $\Box \models G$ and therefore $T \cup F \models G$. We add to our definition the requirement that $T \cup F$ is consistent. Thus, we can enrich this framework by considering a set of integrity constraints IC, i.e a set of formulae that are statements about the universe of discourse. We assume that these statements are consistent with our theory T. We also require in our definition that $T \cup IC \cup D$ is consistent.

We can now give the complete definition for the abduction framework. Given a set of sentences T called a theory, a set of sentences IC called integrity constraints, a sentence G called the observation, and a set of predicates P_{abd}, given that $T \cup IC$ is consistent, we say infer D by abduction from T and G under IC:

$$(T \cup G) \vdash_{abd}^{(IC)} D$$

if and only if

(P1) $T \cup D \models G$;

(P2) $T \cup IC \cup D$ is consistent; and

(P3) all predicates used to form literals in D belong to P_{abd}.

Our characterization of an abductive framework is similar to the one presented Kowalski et al. We refer the reader to [KKT93] for a survey of recent work in abduction and their applications.

3.2 Context Mediation as Abductive Reasoning

The COINL program resulting from the definition of a domain model, elevation axioms and contexts for the integration of a set of disparate information sources can be equivalently transformed to a normal Horn program (equivalently, a Datalog^{neg} program). Similar transformations of object-oriented logical formalisms to predicate calculus based languages have been described in several places (for example, [ALUW93]). Let us call this program T.

In this paper, we consider an integrity theory composed of integrity constraint statements expressed in $Datalog^{neg}$[3] on the exported schemas of the sources. We restrict ourselves to constraints of the form $l_1 \wedge \ldots \wedge l_n \to l_0$ where the l_i are atoms and l_0 is a constraint literal. This form is equivalent to $l_1 \wedge \ldots \wedge l_n \wedge \overline{l_0} \to$ where $\overline{l_0}$

---

[3]$Datalog^{neg}$ is a subset of COINL. (For brevity, we will refer to the target language as simply Datalog.)

is $\neg l_0$. Integrity constraints are Horn clauses without positive literals, i.e. denials. Let us call the set of integrity constraints IC.

A query to be mediated is transformed into a COINL and further into a Datalog query. This transformation is not a logical transformation. The query is interpreted with respect to the user contexts. We refer the reader to the example in the previous section. Let us call the Datalog rule Q. Let us assume that Q is of the form $G \rightarrow answer(\vec{X})$ where $\vec{X}$ is the vector of variables projected out.

Let us assume that the set of data in the disparate information sources is a single database DB. G is a query on the deductive database $< P, DB >$ where P is the intensional database and DB the extensional database. $DB \cup IC$ is consistent by definition of IC. An answer to the query G is a substitution θ such that $T \cup DB \models \theta(G)$. Such an answer is usually found by refutation: one looks for θ such that $T \cup DB \cup \neg \theta(G) \models \Box$. For Horn clause programs, resolution is a complete inference rule for refutation [Llo87]. For non-recursive Datalog programs, SLD-resolution is a complete inference rule for refutation [GM78]. A SLD-resolution proof will also construct the substitution θ:

$$T \cup DB \cup \neg \theta(G) \vdash_{SLD} \Box$$

Let us assume that we want to separate the resolution with clauses from T from the resolution with facts in the database DB. In other words, let us assume that we want to rewrite the query according to the intensional database before we access the extensional database. Since T is a non-recursive program, we should be able to achieve this objective by performing some kind of unfolding of the query against the program and only keeping certain literals. This can be accomplished by modifying the literal-selection function in classic SLD-resolution. Specifically, we shall postpone indefinitely the resolution of literals in the query which correspond to literals of the extensional database DB and delay the resolution of the constraints unless they are ground (when they can be evaluated e.g. $2 > 1$). Once all the possible resolutions have been attempted, we remain with a resolvant containing extensional database literals and constraints literals that could not be evaluated because they are non-ground.

To illustrate the preceding remarks, consider the program $T = \{p(X, Y) \wedge r(X, Z) \rightarrow q(X, Y, Z), p(a, Y) \wedge Y > 10 \rightarrow r(a, Y)\}$ and the extensional database relation $p(X, Y, Z)$ and the query $q(U, 9, V)$. The modified SLD-resolution terminates with the resolvant

$$p(a, 9), p(a, Z), Z > 10$$

and the substitution $\theta = \{U/a, V/Z\}$. A resolvant $\neg G'$ obtained with this procedure is such that: $T \cup \neg \theta(G) \vdash_{SLD} \neg G'$ and therefore: $T \cup \neg \theta(G) \models \neg G'$ or $T \cup G' \models \theta(G)$.

In other words, if we describe the literals of the extensional database as abducible, and consider G as an observation for an abductive proof, G' is an *abductive answer* for G against T, we have:

$$T \models G' \rightarrow answer(\theta(\vec{X}))$$

The union of all the formulae $G' \rightarrow answer(\theta(\vec{X}))$, as well as the substitution θ corresponding to each successful branch of the modified SLD-resolution tree, is a program which is equivalent to T for the processing of Q against the extensional database. The completeness of the result is given by the completeness of SLD-resolution for refutation of the type of programs we consider. In other words, instead of evaluating Q over $T \cup DB$, it now suffices to evaluate $\cup G'$ over DB.

If we are able to restrict the answers G' to those consistent with the integrity constraints, we will be able to filter out the mediated queries which would result in an empty answer if evaluated against the extensional database. It must be clear that in the context of mediation of queries to disparate information sources, where the sources are remote, such an elimination of useless network access is a crucial optimization. In addition, any propagation of the constraints that can be performed in the process of consistency checking can also increase the performance of the mediation service by pushing more selections to the remote sources and potentially leading to smaller amounts of data transported over the network. Note that integrity constraints are used here for logical optimization. If the consistency test is not performed, the subsequent query evaluation would still provide sound and complete answers. For this reason we can satisfy ourselves with a sound test as opposed to a sound and complete test; thus, we are able to compromise property (P2) in the definition of an abductive framework.

To illustrate this in the context of the earlier example, consider a functional dependency (a special type of integrity constraints) on p expressed in Datalog by the clause: $p(X, Y) \wedge p(X, Z) \wedge Y \neq Z \rightarrow$, meaning Y and Z cannot be different for the same value X of the first attribute of p. The resolvent $p(a, 9), p(a, Z), Z > 10$ can be simplified in three stages. First the integrity constraint is used to determine that Z must be equal to 9: $p(a, 9), p(a, 9), 9 > 10$. Second, one of the two syntactically identical literals $p(a, 9)$ can be eliminated: $p(a, 9), 9 > 10$. Third, the constraint solver for inequalities on integers figures out that $9 > 10$ is inconsistent. The resolvant is inconsistent with the integrity constraints and can be rejected altogether. In this instance, we are able to infer that the query evaluates to a null answer without actually evaluating it against the extensional database.

4   The Procedure

The procedure we propose is therefore a modified SLD-resolution where literals corresponding to constraints or relations in the remote data sources are not evaluated. From the point of view of abduction, they are abducible (`abducible` boolean function below).

The definition of the abductive framework suggests an algorithm which generates the candidate abductive answers and subsequently tests the consistency against the integrity constraints. Following the Constraint Logic Programming framework [JM96], we argue that, if the consistency testing can be done incrementally during the construction of the SLD-tree, we are likely to have an improvement of the performance of the algorithm. This is a heuristic which depends on the shape of the proof tree.

We replace the *generate and test* procedure by a *constraint and generate* procedure [JM96]. From such a point of view, the resolvant is a constraint store whose consistency is maintained by a propagation algorithm.

Figure 2 presents the pseudo-code for the main algorithm of the abduction procedure. `.tail` and `.head` respectively access the tail and the head of a list or the body and the head of a Horn clause. □ is the empty list. `append` and `add` respectively append two lists and add an element to list. We assume that lists can have a boolean value `False` different from □ or other values of lists with elements.

The input `Goal` is a list of atoms corresponding to the initial query (a conjunctive query). Initially, the store `Store` (the data structure used for propagation) is empty. `Rules` is a data structure containing the program. `Abducted` contains the result of the procedure. It is the list of lists that contains the conjunctive components of the mediated query and is initially □. The unification procedure **unify** returns a substitution in the form of a list of equalities if the arguments do unify; otherwise, it returns **False**. The propagation procedure, **propagation** tests the consistency of the store and returns **false** if it detects an inconsistency. Otherwise, it returns the store which may have been modified by the propagation.

The idea of the algorithm is to traverse the resolution tree. We opted for a depth first traversal. This basic component is implemented by the **if** and **elsif** clauses. When the goal is emptied (**if** clause), a leaf of the resolution tree is reached. One can collect the answer from the store. Indeed, all abducible atoms have been posted to the store in the **else** clause. Notice that the algorithm assumes that abducibles can not be heads of rules.

```
Procedure abduct(Goal, Store){
  if (Goal eq [])
    {Abducted := append(Abducted, Store);}
  elsif (!(abducible(Goal.head))
    {foreach Rule (Rules))
    {Substitutions := unify(Rule.head, Goal.head);
    if (Substitutions)
      {NewGoal := Goal.tail;
       Store := add(Store, Goal.head);
       Store := propagation(Store);
        if (Store) {abduct(NewGoal, Store);}}}}
  else (abducible(Goal.head))
    {NewGoal := Goal.tail;
     Store := add(Store, Goal.head);
     Store := propagation(Store);
     if (Store) {abduct(NewGoal, Store);}}
}
```

Figure 2: Pseudo Code Procedure

Variant algorithms for this procedure correspond to variant strategies for the traversal of the proof tree. For a depth first strategy, they correspond to the various Prolog meta interpreters described in the literature [SS94]. As a matter of fact the procedure is straightforward in Prolog, since the basic control of Prolog is exactly what we are trying to realize here. Any of the classical vanilla interpreter can be used and extended; an example of this will be described in the next subsection.

4.1 Implementation of Constraint Propagation and Consistency Checking

For abductive answers evaluated in an abductive framework to be sound, we require the set of integrity constraints to include Clark's Free Equality axioms (i.e. the axioms defining the consistency of a set of equations between variables and constants). These are needed to manage the consistency of the store with regard to the substitutions produced by the **unify** procedure. From an implementation perspective, we can rely on Prolog's unification in producing a failure when an inconsistency occurs. It is important to realize that the introduction of a new (equality) constraint to the store may require its propagation both within and outside the store. The latter has the effect of allowing the additional equality constraints to be accounted for in the next rule selection and unification phase of the resolution.

In general a consistency procedure for the class of integrity constraints we propose to use can be implemented by means of a production system in which constraints take the form $B(\vec{X}) \rightarrow A(\vec{Y})$ where $\vec{Y} \subset \vec{X}$. The consistency procedure controls the application of the propagation rules in a fixpoint iteration. For the prototype implementation [BFG+97a], we made use of the *Constraint Handling Rules* (CHR) library [FH93] of the ECLiPSe parallel logic programming platform for this purpose[4]. An example of a constraint solver for inequalities can be found in [FH93].

In the context of our problem, each integrity constraint of the form $B(\vec{X}) \rightarrow A(\vec{Y})$ where $\vec{Y} \subset \vec{X}$ is compiled into a CHR propagation rule. For instance, the functional dependency $p(X, Y_1) \wedge p(X, Y_2) \rightarrow Y_1 = Y_2$ is compiled into `p(X, Y1), p(X, Y2) ==> Y1 = Y2`.

It is sufficient to declare the different abducible predicate as constraints and to post them into the store (`post/1`). The consistency checking and constraint propagation will be performed automatically and triggered, as we wished, by constraint posting and unification. When the search tree traversal terminates, the constraints are collected from the store by the predicate `store/1`. This procedure is shown in Figure 3. It should be obvious that classical SLD-resolution is not only the skeleton of the search tree traversal strategy but is actually implemented directly by the first and second clauses of `sub_abduct/1`.

```
abduct(Goal, Result) :-
  setof(Store, abduct_and_collect(Goal, Store), Result).

abduct_and_collect(Goal, Store):-
          sub_abduct(Goal),
          store(Store).

sub_abduct([]).
sub_abduct([Head|Tail]):-
          rule([Head|RTail]),
          append(RTail, Tail, NewGoal),
          sub_abduct(NewGoal).
sub_abduct([Head|Tail]):-
          abducible(Head),
          post(Head),
          sub_abduct(Tail).
```

Figure 3: A Vanilla implementation of the propagation procedure using Prolog and CHR.

4.2 Semantic Query Optimization as Abductive Reasoning

Semantic Query Optimization as described in [CGM90], is the process of optimizing (increasing the potential for an efficient evaluation) database queries using the semantic information contained in the integrity constraints. In the degenerate case,

---

[4]CHR is a language extension of ECLiPSe for the definition of constraint solvers. Rules in a program correspond to individual propagations operated on the store. The host language, Prolog, posts constraints into the store. The propagation is automatically triggered by the posting of a new constraint or an event such as the unification of a variable involved in the store.

it may be possible to infer that a query cannot be satisfied and this will eliminate the need for even accessing the extensional databases. When accessing the database cannot be avoided, the potential for the evaluation of a query can still be improved by the introduction or elimination of elements.

Chakravarthy et al. [CGM90] present a method for compiling integrity constraints into residues attached to the rules (view definitions) of a deductive database program and show how to exploit the residues at the query optimization stage to identify opportunities for the application of one of the six cases. The compilation of the residue for a rule is based on a partial subsumption algorithm. There are four different types of residue in their framework: the null clause, a goal clause, a unit clause, a Horn clause with non-empty body and head.

In comparison, our algorithm is based on a plain subsumption because it is used during the resolution rather than at compile time. There is no significant loss in efficiency: indeed, our constraint propagation also implements the decision of which transformation is to be made. This is possible because of the current restrictions we made to the integrity constraints; specifically, we aim at detecting inconsistencies which, in our case, not only optimize the subsequent evaluation of the query but also optimize, because of the early detection in the traversal of the search tree, the mediation process itself. We need however to guarantee that the constraint solver we use is sound and converges. Minimality of the result and completeness of the solver are wishable properties but are not necessary.

For the above reason, we only compile integrity constraints into propagation rules which propagate constraint literals. However, it is clear that, if we can decide on a strategy to apply other transformations such as join introduction or join elimination, we can compile the integrity constraint into simplification or "simpagation" constraints handling rules [ECL96]. For instance let us assume a situation where we are querying two relations in two separate sources:

- $r_1(cname, revenue, currency)$, a relation reporting for several companies their revenue and the currency the revenue is expressed in;

- $r_2(cname, ticker, last)$ a relation reporting for the same companies as above their ticker name (the company identification code in the stock exchange) and the last price of the share.

Let us consider the query:

```
select r1.cname, r2.last from r1, r2 where r1.cname=r2.cname;
```

An integrity constraint expressing that the correspondence between company names and tickers is also accessible from a third relation $r_3(cname, ticker)$ can be used to generate the transformed query:

```
select r1.cname, r2.last from r1, r2, r3
     where r1.cname=r2.cname
     and r3.cname = r1.cname
     and r3.ticker = r2.ticker;
```

The constraint in Datalog: $r_1(N, R, C) \wedge r_2(N, T, L) \rightarrow r_3(C, N)$ is compiled into a propagation rule of the form `r1(N, R, C), r2(N, T, L) => r3(C, N)`. which will add $r_3(C, N)$ to the store whenever r_1 and r_2 tuples matching the rule are found. Such a join introduction is not only interesting if r_2 is indexed on the ticker value but also, as it is the case with information sources such as on-line services (e.g., web-sites) for which the capabilities of the source are limited [PGH96]. In this case the auxiliary relation r_3 provides a means to generate values for the ticker before querying r_2. This type of use of the semantic query optimization mechanism available in our system is part of our future plans. The question being to determine the strategy guiding the compilation of integrity constraints.

5   Conclusion

We have described in this paper a novel approach to information integration combining results from distinct sub-disciplines, including theorem proving, abductive logic programming, deductive databases and semantic query optimization. These have been appropriated in the unifying framework of abductive logic programming to yield a procedure used in mediating queries to disparate information sources.

The resulting algorithm is powerful yet it has a particularly simple implementation (Figure 3) when one uses state of the art, industrial strength, constraint logic programming technology. The simplicity arises from the fact that the logic of mediation is declaratively encoded in a COINL program, and remains distinct from a general purpose inference engine which determines what conflicts exist and how they should be resolved. This was made possible by the deductive and object oriented features of the COIN language which constitutes an appropriate and expressive support for both the representation of semantic knowledge and the reasoning about semantic heterogeneity. These findings have encouraged us to explore opportunities for extending our approach to new areas such as query planning, integrity management, and update management. We have good guidelines for these endeavors since a number of extensions of the generic abductive framework to these types of non-monotonic problems have already been proposed.

The procedure we have presented is operational in a complete mediation prototype environment which has been discussed [BFG+97b] and demonstrated [BFG+97a]. The prototype is used in several application domains such as financial analysis and logistic in collaboration with our industry partners.

Acknowledgment

We like to thank H Decker for his help in pointing us to the relevant literature on abductive logic programming.

References

[ALUW93] S. Abiteboul, G. Lausen, H. Uphoff, and E. Walker. Methods and rules. In *Proceedings of the ACM SIGMOD Conference*, pages 32–41, Washington, DC, May 1993.

[BFG+97a] S. Bressan, K. Fynn, C.H. Goh, M. Jakobisiak, K. Hussein, H. Kon, T. Lee, S. Madnick, T. Pena, J. Qu, A. Shum, and M. Siegel. The COntext INterchange mediator prototype. In *Proc. ACM SIGMOD/PODS Joint Conference*, Tuczon, AZ, 1997.

[BFG+97b] S. Bressan, K. Fynn, Cheng Hian Goh, Stuart E Madnick, Tito Pena, and Michael D. Siegel. Overview of a prolog implementation of the context interchange mediator. In *Proc. of the Fifth Intl. Conf. on Practical Applications of Prolog*, pages 83–93, April 1997.

[CGM90]   U. S. Chakravarthy, J. Grant, and J. Minker. Logic-based approach to semantic query optimization. *ACM Trans. on Database Sys.*, 15(2), 1990.

[ECL96]   ECRC. *ECRC parallel constraint logic programming system*, 1996.

[FH93]   T. Frühwirt and P. Hanschke. Terminological reasoning with constraint handling rules. In *Terminological Reasoning with Constraint Handling Rules*, 1993.

[GBMS96]   C.H. Goh, S. Bressan, S. Madnick, and M. Siegel. Context interchange: Representing and reasoning about data semantics in heterogeneous systems. Working Paper #3928, Sloan Sch of Mgt, MIT, Oct 1996. Submitted for publication.

[GM78]   H. Gallaire and J. Minker, editors. *Logic and Data Bases*. Plenum Press, 1978.

[JM96]   J. Jaffar and M.J. Maher. Constraint logic programming: A survey. *J. of Logic Programming*, 1996.

[KKT93]   A. C. Kakas, R. A. Kowalski, and F. Toni. Abductive logic programming. *Journal of Logic and Computation*, 2(6):719–770, 1993.

[KLW95]   M. Kifer, G. Lausen, and J. Wu. Logical foundations of object-oriented and frame-based languages. *JACM*, 4:741–843, 1995.

[Llo87]   J.W. Lloyd. *Foundations of logic programming*. Springer Verlag, 1987.

[PGH96]   Y. Papakonstantinou, A. Gupta, and L. Haas. Capabilities-based query rewriting in mediator systems. In *Proc. of the 4th Intl. Conf. on Paralled and Distributed Information Systems*, 1996.

[SL90]   A. Sheth and J. Larson. Federated database systems for managing distributed, heterogeneous, and autonomous databases. *ACM Computing Surveys*, 22(3):183–236, 1990.

[SS94]   L. Sterling and E. Shapiro. *The Art of Prolog*. MIT Press, 1994.

Calculi for Disjunctive Logic Programming

Peter Baumgartner and Ulrich Furbach

Universität Koblenz, Institut für Informatik

Rheinau 1, 56075 Koblenz

Germany

E-mail: {peter,uli}@informatik.uni-koblenz.de

Abstract

In this paper we investigate relationships between top-down and bottom-up approaches to computation with disjunctive logic programs (DLPs). The bottom-up calculus considered, hyper tableaux, is depicted in its ground version and its relation to fixed point approaches from the literature is investigated. For the top-down calculus we use restart model elimination (RME) and show as our main result that hyper tableaux provide a bottom-up semantics for it. This generalizes the well-known result linking the T-operator to SLD-resolution for *definite* programs towards *disjunctive* programs. Furthermore we discuss that hyper tableaux can be seen as an extension of SLO-resolution.

Keywords: Disjunctive Logic Programming, Fixpoint Semantics, SLO

1 Introduction

For disjunctive logic programs (DLPs) there are several proposals for defining interpreters, like the nearHorn-Prolog family [Lov87], SLI-Resolution [LMR92], SLO-Resolution [Raj89], model tree construction [FM91] or restart model elimination (RME) [BF94a, BFS95]. There have also been different approaches to assign least fixpoints to DLPs, like the state semantics [MR90], a semantics based on model trees [FM91] and approaches to give a fixed point semantics to special interpreters, e.g. in [Fur92, Dec91, RS90].

This paper is concerned with relationships among these approaches.

In previous work the authors introduced the family of RME calculi as goal oriented interpreters for positive disjunctive logic programs [BF94a]; more recently, we investigated variants of RME for computing *answers* to queries for DLPs [BFS95]. RME is related to Plaisted's MPRF [Pla88] and Loveland's nearHorn Prolog [Lov87]. The idea throughout these calculi is to enter a clause $A_1 \vee \cdots \vee A_m \leftarrow B_1 \wedge \cdots \wedge B_n$ only through one of the head literals $A_1, \ldots, A_m$, but never through one of the body literals $B_1, \ldots, B_n$. Thus, a natural procedural reading of clauses is better supported than in e.g. model elimination [Lov78].

RME can be implemented by using the PTTP [Sti90] technique. This offers the advantage that in case of Horn programs the procedure *is the underlying PROLOG* system. Only the non-Horn part of a disjunctive logic program is treated by a compiler such that at run time a PROLOG program is executed by an efficient PROLOG system (for details see [BF94b]).

Recently a bottom-up proof procedure for non-ground positive DLPs, the hyper tableaux calculus, was presented in [BFN96]. The present paper shows that this proof procedure can be understood as a direct implementation of the most prominent fixpoint iteration techniques. Since it suffices for our purposes to restrict to the ground case of Hyper tableaux, and Hyper tableaux coincide in this case with the well-known SATCHMO procedure [MB88], our results apply to SATCHMO as well.

In Section 2 we summarize the bottom-up ground hyper tableaux calculus from [BFN96] and in the subsequent Section 3 we compare this calculus to fixpoint iteration techniques from [MR90] and [FM91].

In Section 4 we will show how a hyper tableaux refutation can be transformed into a RME refutation. This result links the bottom-up to a top-down semantics for DLPs, and thus generalizes the standard result in [Llo87] saying that any finite iteration of the T-operator for *definite* programs can be simulated top-town in a SLD-refutation. In Section 5 we relate SLO-Resolution to Hyper tableaux, and conclude that Hyper tableaux are more general.

Preliminaries

Clauses, i.e. multisets of literals, are usually written as the disjunction $A_1 \vee \cdots \vee A_m \vee \neg B_1 \vee \cdots \vee \neg B_n$ or as an implication $A_1, \ldots, A_m \leftarrow B_1, \ldots, B_n$ ($m \geq 0, n \geq 0$). A clause with $m \geq 1$ is also called a *program clause*, and a clause with $m = 0$ is called a *negative* clause. A *ground* clause or literal contains no variables. With $\overline{L}$ we denote the complement of a literal L. Two literals L and K are *complementary* if $\overline{L} = K$. As usual, an *interpretation* for an (implicitly) given signature is always represented by the set of atoms being *true* in it. A clause C' is *the smallest factor of* clause C iff C' is the shortest subclause of C such that $C \equiv C'$.

We consider finite ordered trees T where every node is labeled with a literal, except the root. Such trees are also called *tableaux*. The labeling function is denoted by λ_T, or simply λ, but in the sequel we will often confuse nodes with their labels. A *branch* of a tableau T is a sequence $N_0, \ldots, N_n$ ($n \geq 0$) of nodes in T such that N_0 is the root of T, N_i is the immediate predecessor of N_{i+1} for $0 \leq i < n$, and N_n is a leaf of T. A branch $b = N_0, \ldots, N_n$ is called *regular* iff $\lambda(N_i) \neq \lambda(N_j)$ for $1 \leq i, j \leq n$ and $i \neq j$, otherwise it is called *irregular*. A tableau is *regular* iff each of its branches is regular, otherwise it is *irregular*. The set of *branch literals* of b is $\text{lit}(b) = \{\lambda(N_1), \ldots, \lambda(N_n)\}$. We find it convenient to use a branch in place where a literal set is required, and mean its branch literals. For instance, we will write expressions like $A \in b$ instead of $A \in \text{lit}(b)$. A clause C is called a *tableau clause (in T)* iff there is a node N in T with $\lambda(N_1) \vee \cdots \vee \lambda(N_n) = C$, where $\{N_1, \ldots, N_n\}$ are all children of N. By $T\delta$ we mean the tableaux T' which results from T by updating the labeling function such that $\lambda_{T'}(N) = (\lambda_T(N))\delta$, where δ is some substitution (i.e. we apply δ to the labels).

A *selection function* is a total function f which maps an open tableau to one of its open branches. If $f(T) = b$ we also say that b *is selected in T by f*. Fortunately, there is no restriction on which selection function to use. For instance, one can use a selection function which always selects the "leftmost" branch.

2 Hyper Tableaux

In [BFN96] we introduced a variant of clausal normal form tableaux called "hyper tableaux". Hyper tableaux keep many desirable features of analytic tableaux (structure of proofs, reading off models in special cases) while taking advantage of central ideas from (positive) hyper resolution. In the ground case, hyper tableaux coincide with the well-known SATCHMO [MB88] procedure; for the first-order case, hyper tableaux have significant advantages (see [BFN96]). For the purposes of the present paper, however, where we use hyper tableaux to model a semantics of positive disjunctive programs, it is sufficient to treat the ground case only. A top-down proof procedure, which is able to handle the first order case and, hence, to compute answers is given later in Section 4.

In order to make the present paper self-contained we will recall a simplified ground version of the calculus. For the rest of this paper S always denotes a possibly infinite[1] ground clause set, unless stated otherwise; S is also referred to as the *input clause set*.

Definition 2.1 (Hyper Tableaux)
Let f be a selection function. We consider tableaux where each branch is labeled as either "open" or "closed". *Hyper tableaux* for S are inductively defined as follows[2]:

Initialization Step: The empty tree, consisting of the root node only, is a hyper tableau for S. Its single branch is labeled as "open".

Hyper Extension Step: If

1. T is an open hyper tableau for S, $f(T) = b$ (i.e. b is the open branch selected in T by f), and

2. $C = A_1, \ldots, A_m \leftarrow B_1, \ldots, B_n$ is a clause from S ($m \geq 0$, $n \geq 0$), called *extending clause* in this context, and

3. $\{B_1, \ldots, B_n\} \subseteq b$ (referred to as *hyper condition*)

then the tree T' is a hyper tableau for S, where T' is obtained from T by *extension of b by C*: replace b in T by the *new* branches

$$(b, A_1) \ldots, (b, A_m), (b, \neg B_1) \ldots, (b, \neg B_n)$$

and then label every new branch $(b, A_1) \ldots, (b, A_m)$ with positive leaf as "open", and label every new branch $(b, \neg B_1) \ldots, (b, \neg B_n)$ with negative leaf as "closed".

We will write the fact that T' can be obtained from T by a hyper extension step in the way defined as $T \vdash_{b,C} T'$, and say that C is *applicable* to b (or T). Note that the selection function does not appear explicitly in this relation; instead we prefer to let f be given implicitly by the context.

A hyper tableau is *closed* if each of its branches is closed, otherwise it is *open*.

□

---

[1] The ability to handle *infinite* sets of clauses allows easy treatment of the first-order case.

[2] The inductive definition will be such that a branch is closed iff it contains a pair of complementary literals.

The hyper condition of an extension expresses that *all* (which are possibly zero) body literals have to be satisfied by the branch to be extended. This similarity to hyper *resolution* coined the name "hyper tableaux".

The central property of an open branch b is that it can be mapped to an interpretation in the usual way, i.e. by taking the positive literals of b as *true* and all others as *false*; for infinite derivations we take the chain limit of the increasing branches. Together with an appropriate *fairness* notion for derivations (roughly: at least one open branch has to be expanded as long as possible without violating regularity) we get the completeness of hyper tableaux (see again [BFN96]).

Definition 2.2 (Hyper Tableaux Derivation)
Let f be a selection function. A (possible infinite) sequence $T_1, \ldots, T_n, \ldots$ of hyper tableaux for S is called a *(hyper tableaux) derivation from* S iff T_1 is obtained by an initialization step, and for $i > 1$, $T_{i-1} \vdash_{b_{i-1}, C_{i-1}} T_i$ for some clause $C_{i-1} \in S$. This is also written as

$$T_1 \vdash_{b_1, C_1} T_2 \cdots T_n \vdash_{b_n, C_n} T_{n+1} \cdots$$

A derivation is called *regular* iff every tableau in the derivation is regular (cf. Section. 1), otherwise it is *irregular*. A derivation is called a *(hyper tableaux) refutation* if it contains a closed tableau. $\square$

Note that extension steps are no longer applicable to a closed hyper tableaux.

Figure 1 shows an example refutation. This example also demonstrates that hyper tableaux handle more than one negative clause. By this it is possible to have integrity constraints in the input clause set, and not just program clauses.

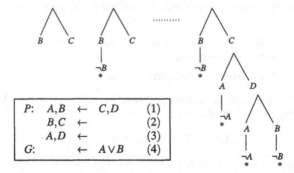

Figure 1: A hyper tableau for P and G given in the figure. Notice that the formula G stands for the two clauses $\leftarrow A$ and $\leftarrow B$. For simplicity of presentation, negative leaf nodes stemming from program clauses are not drawn.

3   States and Model Trees

In this section we relate hyper tableaux to the fixpoint semantics.

3.1 States

We summarize state semantics from [LMR92]. Let S^+ be a possibly infinite set of ground program clauses.

DHB, the disjunctive Herbrand base for S^+ is the set of disjunctions that can be formed by atoms of the Herbrand base of S^+. The transformation $\Gamma : 2^{DHB} \to 2^{DHB}$ is given by[3]

$$\Gamma(D) = \{C \in DHB \mid C' \leftarrow B_1, \dots, B_n \in S^+, \quad \forall 1 \leq i \leq n : B_i \lor C_i \in D,$$
$$C'' = C_1 \lor \dots \lor C_n \lor C', \quad C \text{ is the smallest factor of } C''\}$$

A *state* for S^+ is a subset of *DHB*. An *expanded state ST* for S^+ is a state, such that $ST = exp(ST)$, where

$$exp(ST) = \{C \in DHB \mid C \in ST \text{ or } \exists C' \in ST : C' \text{ is a subclause of } C\}$$

In [LMR92] it is shown that the operator Γ is continuous, hence its least fixpoint exists and the *lfp*-Operator yields $\Gamma \uparrow \omega$.

We do not introduce model states explicitly, moreover we use their characterization as fixpoints and logical consequences:

Theorem 3.1 (Lobo et al. 92)
Let S^+ be a set of program clauses and $C \in DHB$. Then $S^+ \models C$ iff $C \in exp(lfp(\Gamma))$.

Definition 3.2 (Cut of T)
Let T be a hyper tableau for S. A clause C is a *cut of T* iff

    (1) $\forall b$ open branch of T : $\exists N \in b$: $\exists L \in C$ such that $\lambda(N) = L$, and
    (2) $\forall L \in C$: $\exists b$ open branch of T : $\exists N \in b$: $\lambda(N) = L$.

□

That is, in order to get a cut we pick a literal from every open branch.

Now assume that S is in *goal normal form*. By this we mean the transformation of every clause of the form $\leftarrow B_1, \dots, B_n$ into $G \leftarrow B_1, \dots, B_n$, where G is a new predicate symbol, and furthermore adding the clause $\neg G$ as the only goal. By S^+ we denote the set S without the purely negative clauses. Then S^+ consists of program clauses only and consequently is satisfiable.

The following lemma relates hyper tableaux derivations to Γ-iterations.

Lemma 3.3
For every i and $C \in \Gamma \uparrow i$ there is a hyper tableau T such that there is a cut C' of T were C is the smallest factor of C'.

---

[3]Obviously, this operator is dependent of the program S^+; we assume this will be clear from the context.

Proof. Induction on i.

Induction start $i = 0$: The set $\Gamma \uparrow 0$ contains all smallest factors of (disjunctive) facts from S^+. Let $A_1, \ldots, A_n \leftarrow$ be such a fact, then construct a hyper tableau with an initial step and a hyper extension step using this fact. The cut $A_1, \ldots, A_n \leftarrow$ of this tableau has the desired property.

Induction step $i \to i + 1$: If $C \in \Gamma \uparrow i+1$, we know by definition of Γ that C is the smallest factor of $C_1 \vee \ldots \vee C_n \vee C'$, such that $C' \leftarrow B_1, \ldots, B_n \in S^+$ and $\{B_1 \vee C_1, \ldots, B_n \vee C_n\} \subseteq \Gamma \uparrow i$. The induction hypothesis gives us that there exist hyper tableaux $T_1, \ldots, T_n$, such that $B_j \vee C_j$ is the smallest factor of a cut $B_j \vee C'_j$ of T_j.

All we have to do is to link these tableaux together to one hyper tableau: Select a branch b_j from tableau T_j which contains the literal B_j. Take the leaf N_j of this branch and use it as the new root of the tableau T_{j+1}. The result is again a hyper tableau. If this linking is done for j from 1 to n we get with T_{n+1} a hyper tableau which contains a branch with literals $B_1, \ldots, B_n$. Hence, the clause $C' \leftarrow B_1, \ldots, B_n$ is applicable, and in the resulting tableau there is a cut $C' \vee C'_1 \vee \cdots C'_n$ with smallest factor C. Q.E.D.

As an example, assume the following set of clauses $S^+ = \{b \vee c, a \leftarrow b, a \leftarrow c\}$. There is a hyper tableau which consists of the two branches with $\{b, a\}$ and $\{c, a\}$ as sets of labels of its nodes. A set of cuts of this tree is $\{a \vee a, a \vee b, b \vee c, a \vee c\}$. Note that there is no sequence assumed in which the literals from different branches have to occur within a cut. The iteration of the Γ-operator gives $\Gamma \uparrow 0 = \{b \vee c\}$, $\Gamma \uparrow 1 = \{b \vee c, a \vee c, a \vee b\}$ and $\Gamma \uparrow 2 = \{b \vee c, a \vee c, a \vee b, a\} = \Gamma \uparrow \omega$.

Having this close relation between hyper tableaux and the fixpoint iteration over states we can use this result to prove completeness of ground hyper tableaux. Note that a proof for full first order clauses is given from scratch in [BFN96], which includes a fairness consideration. Here we only want to establish the close relationship between the approaches.

Theorem 3.4 (Completeness of Hyper Tableaux)
For every unsatisfiable ground clause set S in goal normal form there is a closed hyper tableau for S.

Proof. Clearly, $S^+ \models G$. From Theorem 3.1 we learn that $G \in exp(lfp(\Gamma))$. Since G is an atom it must be contained in $lfp(\Gamma)$ alone. Since Γ is continuous, we can apply a standard result from fixpoint theory to conclude $lfp(\Gamma) = \Gamma \uparrow \omega$. Hence there is an i such that $G \in \Gamma \uparrow i$.

Lemma 3.3 gives us the existence of a hyper tableau T with a cut C', such that G is the smallest factor of C'. Hence C' has the form $G \vee \ldots \vee G$; in other words every branch of the tableau contains the literal G. This tableau can be closed by using the goal clause $\neg G$. Q.E.D.

3.2 Model Trees

The other approach we want to relate hyper tableaux to, is that of bottom-up evaluation of disjunctive deductive databases. In [FM91] and [Fur92] a bottom-up consequence operator Γ^M for disjunctive deductive databases is given which acts on sets of interpretations, thus yielding models for the given set of clauses. In [SMR95] this approach is related to the consequence operator on states which we discussed above. Fernandez and Minker also introduce model trees as a calculus to compute this operator, this is done in detail in [LMR92]. We will demonstrate that this is related closely to the hyper tableaux calculus.

The consequence operator Γ^M over sets of Herbrand interpretations is given by

$$\Gamma^M : \quad 2^{2^{HB}} \to 2^{2^{HB}} \qquad \Gamma^M(I) = \min(\Gamma^{INT}(I))$$
$$\Gamma^{INT} : \quad 2^{2^{HB}} \to 2^{2^{HB}} \qquad \Gamma^{INT}(I) = \bigcup_{I \in \mathcal{I}} MOD(\Gamma(I))$$

where MOD gives all models of a state and min filters out the minimal models. The latter operator looks harmless; however this is a rather costly step. Its definition is given by: $\min(\mathcal{I}) = \{I \in \mathcal{I} \mid \neg \exists J \in \mathcal{I} : J \subset I\}$. In [BFN96] we gave a proof that the branches of a hyper tableau correspond to partial models of the program and in particular that in fair derivations branches correspond to models. In [Nie96] it is demonstrated how the computation of the min-operator based on this definition can be avoided.

In the following we additionally depict the relation between one step with the Γ^M operator and hyper extension.

Definition 3.5
Let T be a hyper tableau and b an open branch. A *complete extension of T at b wrt. a set of program clauses S^+* is a tree T' which can be obtained from T by applying as long as possible[4] hyper extension steps with clauses from S^+ such that (a) only branches b' are selected which contain b as a prefix, and (b) in the hyper condition only literals from b are used, and (c) no extension step introduces an irregular branch. □

The following lemma establishes the connection of partial branches, i.e. models from a hyper tableau to the iterations using the Γ^M operator.

Lemma 3.6
Let T be a hyper tableau consisting of one single branch b and let T' be a complete extension of T at b wrt. a set of program clauses S^+. Then $\{lit(b') \mid b' \in T'\} \subseteq MOD(\Gamma(lit(b)))$

Note that since b is a single branch of a hyper tableau for S^+ each literal from $lit(b)$ is contained in S^+ as a positive unit clause.

4 Hyper Tableaux and Restart Model Elimination

Unlike hyper tableaux, the RME calculus is a goal oriented interpreter for positive disjunctive logic programs [BF94a, BFS95]. It is a very simple extension of model elimination, which allows a procedural reading of disjunctive clauses. This is possible, because the calculus does not need any contrapositives. For a discussion of

---

[4]Obviously, as S^+ can be infinite, this derivation is possibly infinite. In this case we take the chain limit of a branch to define the interpretation assigned to it; see [BFN96] for details.

these aspects the reader is referred to the above cited literature. Here we are interested only in the relation between RME to hyper tableaux, and therefore we only present its simplest variant.

RME is implemented by using the PTTP technique and hence it offers the advantage that in case of Horn programs the procedure *is the underlying PROLOG* system. Only the non-Horn part of a disjunctive logic program is treated by a compiler such that at run time a PROLOG program is executed by an efficient PROLOG system (for details see [BF94b]).

RME is a *top-town* calculus, i.e. derivations start with a (negative) goal clause and end at the (positive) facts. Our main result below shows how any closed hyper tableau can be transformed into a RME refutation. This transformation will essentially "reverse" a hyper tableau from the leaves to the root, where a splitting in hyper tableaux corresponds to a "restart step" in RME.

This result is in close relationship to the standard result in [Llo87] saying that any finite iteration of the T-operator over *definite* programs can be simulated top-town in a SLD-refutation. In fact, we generalize this result to the non-Horn case.

4.1 Restart Model Elimination

We will briefly review the RME calculus as presented in [BF94a]. However, for ease of presentation we will use a slightly different notation based on tableaux (Section 1) and following the style of Definition 2.1.

Definition 4.1 (Restart Model Elimination)
Let S be a finite, but not necessarily ground, clause set. We assume that S can be partitioned in[5] $S = P \uplus \{ \leftarrow Q \}$, where the *query* $\leftarrow Q$ is a purely negative clause, i.e. it is of the form $\leftarrow B_1, \ldots, B_n$, and P is satisfiable.

Restart model elimination tableaux (RME tableaux) with substitution σ *for* S are inductively defined as follows:

Initialization step: A clausal tableau obtained by extending the root node of the empty tree by the query $\leftarrow Q \in S$ is a hyper tableau for S with substitution $\sigma = \varepsilon$ (the empty substitution). In this context $\leftarrow Q$ is also called the *goal clause* of the tableau. All branches are labeled as "open".

Linked extension step: If

1. T is an open RME tableau for S with substitution σ_T, $f(T) = b$ (i.e. b is selected in T by f) with negative open leaf node $\neg A$, and

2. $C = A_1, \ldots, A_m \leftarrow B_1, \ldots, B_n$ is a new variant of a clause from S ($m \geq 1$, $n \geq 0$), called *extending clause* in this context, and

3. σ is a most general unifier for A and some A_i (where $1 \leq i \leq m$),

then the literal tree $T'\sigma$ is a RME tableau for S with substitution $\sigma_T\sigma$, where T' is obtained from T by extending b by C, and then labeling the new branches

$$(b, A_1), \ldots, (b, A_{i-1}), (b, A_{i+1}), \ldots, (b, A_m), \ldots, (b, \neg B_1), \ldots, (b, \neg B_n)$$

---

[5] "$\uplus$" denotes disjoint union.

as "open", and labeling the new branch (b, A_i) as "closed".

Reduction step: If

1. T is an open RME tableau for S with substitution σ_T, $f(T) = b$ with negative open leaf node $\neg A$, and

2. $A' \in b$ is a positive literal in b, and

3. σ is a most general unifier for A and A',

then the literal tree $T'\sigma$ is a RME tableau for S with substitution $\sigma_T\sigma$, where T' is obtained from T by labeling b as "closed"[6]

Restart step: If

1. T is an open RME tableau for S with substitution σ, $f(T) = b$ (i.e. b is selected in T by f) with positive open leaf node A, and

2. $C = \leftarrow B_1, \ldots, B_n$ is a new variant of some negative clause from S,

then the literal tree T' is a RME tableau for S with substitution σ_T, where T' is obtained from T by extending b by C.

The notions of *derivation* and *refutation* are taken from Definition 2.2. □

As an example consider the clause set in Figure 1 again. Figure 2 contains a RME refutation.

In [BFS95] we investigated the computation of answers by means of variants of RME. For the present paper we only restate one answer completeness result. For this we need the notion of an answer: if $\leftarrow Q$ is a query, and $\theta_1, \ldots, \theta_m$ are substitutions for the variables from Q, then $Q\theta_1 \vee \ldots \vee Q\theta_m$ is an *answer* (for P) An answer $Q\theta_1 \vee \ldots \vee Q\theta_m$ is a *correct answer* if $P \models \forall(Q\theta_1 \vee \ldots \vee Q\theta_m)$. Now let a RME refutation of S with goal clause $\leftarrow Q$ and substitution σ be given. Assume that this refutation contains m occurrences of the query, i.e. it contains one initial-

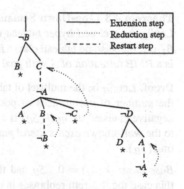

Figure 2: A RME refutation of the clause set of Example 5.

ization step and $m - 1$ restart steps with the clause $\leftarrow Q\rho_i$, where ρ_i is the renaming substitution of this step (ρ_i is the empty substitution for the initialization step). Let $\sigma_i = \rho_i\sigma|_{dom(\rho_i)}$. Then $Q\sigma_1 \vee \ldots \vee Q\sigma_m$ is a *computed answer* (for P).

That is, we simply collect applications of the instantiated query clause to obtain the answer. This idea is, of course, not new. For resolution, question answering was invented in the early paper [Gre69]; the idea is to attach answer literals to trace the usages of the query in the resolution proof (see also [CL73]).

---

[6]Here, reduction steps are applied from negative leaf literals to positive ancestor literals; it would also be sound (but not neccessary for completeness) to allow reduction steps from positive leaf literals to negative ancestor literals. See [BF94a].

Theorem 4.2 (Answer-completeness of RME)
Let S, P and $\leftarrow Q$ as in Definition 4.1, and let f be a selection function; let $Q\theta_1 \vee \ldots \vee Q\theta_l$ be a correct answer for P. Then there exists a RME refutation of S with computed answer $Q\sigma_1 \vee \ldots \vee Q\sigma_m$ such that $Q\sigma_1 \vee \ldots \vee Q\sigma_m$ entails $Q\theta_1 \vee \ldots \vee Q\theta_l$, i.e.

$$\exists \delta \forall i \in \{1, \ldots, m\} \, \exists j \in \{1, \ldots, l\} \, Q\sigma_i\delta = Q\theta_j.$$

Informally, the theorem states that for every given correct answer we can find a computed answer which can be instantiated by means of a *single* substitution δ to a subclause of the given answer, and hence implies it. To obtain this result we have to demand *one single* substitution δ which maps any of the instantiated query clauses $\leftarrow Q\rho_i\sigma$ used in extension steps to the respective clause on the ground level. Refinements and improvements of this result can be found in [BFS95].

4.2 Mapping Hyper Tableaux to Restart Model Elimination

As mentioned in the introduction to this section, our main result is a mapping from hyper tableaux to RME. Together with the results of the previous sections we thus have a top-down interpreter for the fixpoint semantics of positive disjunctive programs.

Theorem 4.3 (Top-Down Semantics for Hyper Tableaux)
Let T_H be a closed hyper tableau containing the tableau clauses S[7]. Let $G = \leftarrow B_1, \ldots, B_n$ be some tableau clause in T_H (which hence closes a branch). Then there is a RME refutation of S with goal clause G.

Proof. Let S_H be the multiset of tableau clauses occurring in T_H. Let $k(S_H)$ denote the number of occurrences of positive literals in S_H minus the number of non-negative clauses[8] in S_H ($k(S_H)$ is a measure for the "Hornness" of S_H; it is related to the well-known *excess literal parameter*). Now we prove the claim by induction on $k(S_H)$.

Base case: $k(S_H) = 0$. S_H and thus also S must be a set of Horn clauses. In this case the theorem rephrases in our setting the well-known corresponding result from [Llo87], which links the T-operator for definite programs to SLD-Resolution. A proof from scratch is in the full version of this paper.

Induction step: $k(S_H) > 0$. As the induction hypothesis assume the result to hold for closed hyper tableau for clause sets S_H' satisfying $k(S_H') < k(S_H)$. Figure 3 depicts the proof.

Some ancestor node A of the tableau clause $G = \leftarrow B_1, \ldots, B_n$ must have one or more positive brother nodes, because otherwise S_H would be a Horn multiset. Let $C = (A_1, \ldots, A_m, A \leftarrow \mathcal{B}) \in S_H$ be the tableau clause where the node A is contained in. Here, $\mathcal{B}$ is understood as a (possibly empty) sequence of positive literals. Below we will also write expressions like $\neg \mathcal{B}$ and mean the clause $\bigvee_{B \in \mathcal{B}} \neg B$.

---

[7]The notion *tableau clause* is defined in the "Preliminaries" section

[8]A *non-negative clause* is a clause containing at least one positive literal.

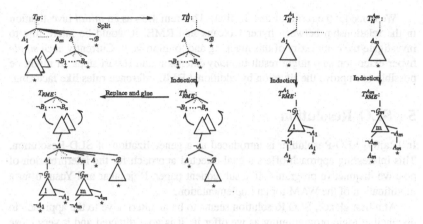

Figure 3: Proof of Theorem 4.3.

We split T_H into $m+1$ closed hyper tableaux: the hyper tableaux T_H^A is obtained from T_H by replacing the tableau clause C by $A \leftarrow \mathcal{B}$ (and thus deleting the subtrees below $A_1, \ldots, A_m$), and the hyper tableaux $T_H^{A_i}$ is obtained from T_H by replacing C by A_i (for $i = 1, \ldots, m$). The other parts of T_H are kept unchanged for for the splitted tableaux.

Let $\mathcal{S}_H^A$ and $\mathcal{S}_H^{A_i}$ be the tableau clause multisets corresponding to T_H^A and $T_H^{A_i}$. It holds that $k(\mathcal{S}_H^A) < k(\mathcal{S}_H)$ and $k(\mathcal{S}_H^{A_i}) < k(\mathcal{S}_H)$. Notice that T_H^A still contains G. Hence, by the induction hypothesis, there is a RME refutation T_{RME}^A [9] of $\mathcal{S}_H^A$ with goal clause G.

Similarly, by applying the induction hypotheses m times we learn that there are RME refutations $T_{RME}^{A_i}$ of $\mathcal{S}_H^{A_i}$ with some respective goal clauses $\leftarrow G_i \in \mathcal{S}_H^{A_i}$. Since splitting does not affect the negative clauses it holds that $\leftarrow G_i \in \mathcal{S}$. Hence, $T_{RME}^{A_i}$ is a RME refutation of $\mathcal{S} \cup \{A_i \leftarrow\}$. Notice that positive unit clauses like $A_i \leftarrow$ can be used in RME refutations only to close branches, without introducing new subgoals (as indicated in Figure 3).

Now we can put things together. Consider T_{RME}^A again. It (possibly) uses the clause $A \leftarrow \mathcal{B}$. However, this clause is (possibly) not contained in $\mathcal{S}$. In order to turn T_{RME}^A into a RME refutation of $\mathcal{S}$, we first replace every occurrence of the tableau clause $A \leftarrow \mathcal{B}$ in T_{RME}^A by C. This leaves us with open branches ending in (possibly several occurrences of) $A_1, \ldots, A_m$. Now, at each of these branches ending in A_i we can restart with the clause $\leftarrow G_i$. Then we append below the upcoming tableau clause $\neg G_i$ the refutation $T_{RME}^{A_i}$ *and* we replace possible extension steps in $T_{RME}^{A_i}$ with $A_i \leftarrow$ by reduction steps to the branch literal A_i where the restart occurred. As a result we get the desired RME refutation T_{RME} of $\mathcal{S}$ with goal clause G.   Q.E.D.

---

[9]To be precise, there is a RME refutation having T_{RME}^A as its last element; but we will confuse this.

We consider the result of this Section –Theorem 4.3– as an *initial* investigation in the relationship between hyper tableaux and RME. It would be interesting to investigate the complexity of this mapping and to improve it. Currently each *single* hyper extension step might result in *many* extension and restart steps. It might be possible to improve the situation by additional RME inference rules like factoring.

5   SLO-Resolution

In [Raj89] SLO-Resolution is introduced as a generalization of SLD-Resolution. This interesting approach offers a goal-directed approach for the interpretation of positive disjunctive programs. In a subsequent paper, Rajesakar and Yusuf offer a modification of the WAM for an implementation.

At a first glance, SLO Resolution seems to be an alternative to the approach to disjunctive logic programming as we offer it. It is goal directed and it very close related to the state semantics. In fact the completeness proof is very much as the one from SLD-resolution, only the fixpoint semantics is different.

However there are two drawbacks which are fixed by our approach:

- When restricted to Horn clauses, the calculus is not equivalent to SLD-resolution, and

- there is only a ground completeness result; it is clear that SLO-resolution can not answer the query $\leftarrow p(x)$ with respect to the program $p(a), p(b) \leftarrow$.

RME is an extension of SLD-resolution and we have answer completeness of various variants. In this section we will demonstrate that SLO-resolution is very close related to bottom-up hyper tableaux. We show how to simulate SLO-resolution, by simply inverting the signs of all literals and then apply hyper tableaux. We do not claim that this transformation is original, it has been used e.g. in [Yah96] to turn a bottom-up prover into a goal-directed top-down one; moreover we want to point out that this simple technique can be used to simulate and to extend SLO-resolution.

The following definitions are taken from [Raj89].

A *goal* for a disjunctive program is of the form $\leftarrow (C_1, \ldots, C_n)$, where $n \geq 0$ and the C_i are positive clauses.

Definition 5.1
Let P be a positive disjunctive logic program and let G be a goal. An SLO-derivation from P with goal G consists of a (finite or infinite) sequence of goals $G_0 = G, G_1, ..$, such that for all $i \geq 0$, G_{i+1} is obtained from $G_i = \leftarrow (C_1, \ldots, C_m, \ldots, C_k)$ as follows:

1. C_m is a clause in G_i. C_m is called the selected clause.

2. $C \leftarrow B_1, \ldots, B_q$ is a program clause in P.

3. C subsumes C_m with most general unifier θ.

4. G_{i+1} is the goal $\leftarrow (C_1, \ldots, C_{m-1}, B_1 \vee C_m, \ldots, B_q \vee C_m, C_{m+1}, \ldots, C_k)\theta$

As usual derivations of the empty clause from G using P are called refutations; one also says that the goal G succeeds for P.

□

In [Raj89], Rajesakar gives a ground completeness result by induction over the fixpoint operator Γ on states. Without loss of generality we assume in the following only goals of the form $\leftarrow C$ where C is a positive disjunction. Note that a negative clause $\leftarrow A_1, \ldots, A_n$ is different from a goal $\leftarrow A_1 \vee \ldots \vee A_n$; the latter is standing for a set of negative units.

Definition 5.2

The dual P^d of a clause $P = A_1, \ldots, A_n \leftarrow B_1, \ldots, B_m$ is obtained by inverting the arrow, i.e. $P^d = B_1, \ldots, B_m \leftarrow A_1, \ldots, A_n$. This could be alternatively formulated, by saying that signs of every literal in $P = A_1 \vee \ldots \vee A_n \vee \neg B_1 \vee \ldots \vee \neg B_m$ are complemented to get $P^d = \neg A_1 \vee \ldots \vee \neg A_n \vee B_1 \vee \ldots \vee B_m$.

Note that the dual of a goal $G = \leftarrow A_1 \vee \ldots \vee A_n$ is the set of clauses $\{A_1 \leftarrow , \ldots, A_n \leftarrow \}$, since G, written in clause form is the set of negative units $\{\leftarrow A_1, \ldots, \leftarrow A_n\}$. This transformation is extended to set of clauses in an obvious way. □

It is very easy to see that this transformation leaves unsatisfiability invariant. The following is a SLO-derivation of P with goal G from Example 1.

$$\leftarrow A \vee B \tag{5}$$
$$\leftarrow C \vee A \vee B, \quad D \vee A \vee B \qquad \text{from 5) and 1)} \tag{6}$$
$$\leftarrow D \vee A \vee B \qquad \text{from 6) and 2)} \tag{7}$$
$$\leftarrow \qquad \text{from 7) and 3)} \tag{8}$$

In order to use the hyper tableaux calculus to simulate this derivation we construct the dual program P^d and goal G^d.

$$P^d: \quad C, D \leftarrow A, B$$
$$\leftarrow B, C$$
$$\leftarrow A, D$$
$$G^d: \quad A \leftarrow \qquad\qquad B \leftarrow$$

Applying hyper tableaux to this clause set gives a closed tableau depicted on the right. The starting goal 5 in the SLO-refutation corresponds to the fist two extension steps with the two facts $A \leftarrow$ and $B \leftarrow$ from the dual goal G^d, resulting in the tableau with the two nodes A and B. The SLO-step yielding in line 6 the goal $\leftarrow C \vee A \vee B, \quad D \vee A \vee B$ corresponds to a hyper extension step with $C, D \leftarrow A, B$. The two branches from the tableau in the

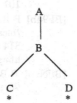

right figure are coded in line 6 by the two clauses in the goal. The step resulting in goal 7 corresponds to the extension step with $\leftarrow B, C$ and the last step to the extension with $\leftarrow A, D$.

Lemma 5.3
Given a ground SLO-derivation from P with ground goal $\leftarrow C$ and derived goal $\leftarrow C_1, \ldots, C_m$. Then there is a hyper tableau T for P^d and a substitution σ such that for all $b \in T$ there is a C_i containing $L\sigma$, for any label L from b.

Based on the previous lemma we are currently investigating how SLO-resolution can be improved by applying the concepts of hyper tableaux. By this it is possible to make SLO-resolution complete with respect to logical consequences and to get rid of some of the rigidly treated variables.

6 Conclusion

We investigated the relation between the top-down restart model elimination (RME) and the bottom-up hyper tableaux calculus. As our main results, we demonstrated that this hyper tableaux calculus can be seen as a fixpoint semantics for DLPs and that restart model elimination provides a corresponding top-down proof procedure.

We want to point out that hyper tableaux can be used as well for efficient model generation. This is of particular interest, when non-monotonic extensions for DLP have to be implemented. As a base for this, we are currently investigating two kinds of minimal reasoning. One uses the hyper tableaux calculus for computing minimal models: in [Nie96] it is shown how minimal models can be computed *without* keeping and comparing models in memory, by means of hyper tableaux. The other approach from [Ara96] uses RME as a base calculus to compute the generalized closed world assumption.

Future work will be the incorporation of negation into DLPs and to investigate more closely the relation between hyper tableaux and RME.

References

[Ara96] C. Aravindan. An abductive framework for negation in disjunctive logic programming. In *Proc. JELIA 96*, number 1126 in LNAI. European Workshop on Logic in AI, Springer, 1996.

[BF94a] P. Baumgartner and U. Furbach. Model Elimination without Contrapositives and its Application to PTTP. *Journal of Automated Reasoning*, 13:339–359, 1994. Short version in: Proceedings of CADE-12, Springer LNAI 814, 1994, pp 87–101.

[BF94b] P. Baumgartner and U. Furbach. PROTEIN: A *PRO*ver with a *T*heory *E*xtension *I*nterface. In A. Bundy, editor, *Automated Deduction – CADE-12*, volume 814 of *LNAI*, pages 769–773. Springer, 1994. Available in the WWW, URL: http://www.uni-koblenz.de/ag-ki/Systems/PROTEIN/.

[BFN96] P. Baumgartner, U. Furbach, and I. Niemelä. Hyper Tableaux. In *Proc. JELIA 96*, number 1126 in LNAI. European Workshop on Logic in AI, Springer, 1996.

[BFS95] P. Baumgartner, U. Furbach, and F. Stolzenburg. Model Elimination, Logic Programming and Computing Answers. In *14th International Joint Conference on Artificial Intelligence (IJCAI 95)*, volume 1, 1995.

[CL73] C. Chang and R. Lee. *Symbolic Logic and Mechanical Theorem Proving*. Academic Press, 1973.

[Dec91] H. Decker. A model-theoretic and a fixpoint-semantic foundation of first order databases. Siemens AG, München, 1991.

[FM91] J.A. Fernandez and J. Minker. Bottom-up evaluation of hierarchical disjunctive deductive databases. In Koichi Furukawa, editor, *Proc. 8th International Conference on Logic Programming*, pages 660–675, 91.

[Fur92] U. Furbach. Computing answers for disjunctive logic programs. In Pearce and Wagner, editors, *Logics in AI, JELIA'92*. Springer, LNAI 633, 1992.

[Gre69] C. Cordell Green. Theorem-Proving by Resolution as a basis for Question-Answering Systems. In Bernard Meltzer and Donald Michie, editors, *Machine Intelligence 4*, pages 183–205. American Elsevier Publishing Company, Inc., 1969.

[Llo87] J.W. Lloyd. *Foundations of Logic Programming*. Symbolic Computation. Springer, second, extended edition, 1987.

[LMR92] J. Lobo, J. Minker, and A. Rajasekar. *Foundations of Disjunctive Logic Programming*. MIT Press, 1992.

[Lov78] D.W. Loveland. *Automated Theorem Proving - A Logical Basis*. North Holland, 1978.

[Lov87] D.W. Loveland. Near-Horn Prolog. In J.-L. Lassez, editor, *Proc. of the 4th Int. Conf. on Logic Programming*, pages 456–469. The MIT Press, 1987.

[MB88] R. Manthey and F. Bry. SATCHMO: a theorem prover implemented in Prolog. In *Proc. 9th CADE*. Argonnee, Illinois, Springer LNCS, 1988.

[MR90] J. Minker and A. Rajasekar. A fixpoint semantics for disjunctive logic programs. *J. Logic Programming*, 9:45–74, 1990.

[Nie96] I. Niemelä. A Tableau Calculus for Minimal Model Reasoning. In P. Moscato, U. Moscato, D. Mundici, and M. Ornaghi, editors, *Theorem Proving with Analytic Tableaux and Related Methods*, number 1071 in Lecture Notes in Artificial Intelligence. Springer, 1996.

[Pla88] D. Plaisted. Non-Horn Clause Logic Programming Without Contrapositives. *Journal of Automated Reasoning*, 4:287–325, 1988.

[Raj89] A. Rajasekar. *Semantics for Disjunctive Logic Programs*. PhD thesis, University of Maryland, 1989.

[RS90] D.W. Reed and B.T. Smith. A case-analysis based fixpoint semantics for disjunctive propgrams. Extended abstract for the Workshop on 'Non-Hornclause programming' during NACLP'90, 1990.

[SMR95] D. Seipel, J. Minker, and C. Ruiz. Model generation and state generation for disjunctive logic programs. Technical report, Univ. of Tübingen, 1995.

[Sti90] M. Stickel. A Prolog Technology Theorem Prover. In M.E. Stickel, editor, *Proc CADE 10, LNCS 449*, pages 673–675. Springer, 1990.

[Yah96] A. Yahya. Query Answering in Disjunctive Deductive Databases. Dagstuhl-Seminar on *Disjunctive logic programming and databases: Non-monotonic aspects*, 1996.

A Characterization
Of The Partial Stable Models
For Disjunctive Deductive Databases

Dietmar Seipel
University of Würzburg, Dept. of Computer Science
Am Hubland, D – 97074 Würzburg, Germany
seipel@informatik.uni-wuerzburg.de

Jack Minker
University of Maryland, Dept. of Computer Science
and Institute for Advanced Computer Studies
College Park, MD 20742, USA
minker@cs.umd.edu

Carolina Ruiz
Worcester Polytechnic Institute, Dept. of Computer Science
Worcester, MA 01609, USA
ruiz@cs.wpi.edu

Abstract

We give a *characterization* of the partial stable models of a disjunctive deductive database $\mathcal{P}$ in terms of the total stable models of a suitably transformed database $\mathcal{P}^{tu}$. The transformation is based on *annotating* the atoms in the given database by the truth values *true* ("t") and *undefined* ("u").

Currently many *fast algorithms* are being developed for computing the total stable models of disjunctive deductive databases. Based on the new characterization given in this paper, these algorithms can also be used for computing partial stable models.

1 Introduction

To define the semantics of a disjunctive database the ground atoms are assigned truth values. Three truth values are used: *true* ("t"), *false* ("f"), and *undefined* ("u"). Herbrand interpretations that use the two classical truth values t and f only are called *total*, while Herbrand interpretations that use all three truth values are called *partial*.

To define the semantics of *normal databases*, i.e. databases that may contain negation but do not contain disjunctions, either total or partial Herbrand interpretations have been used. The most prominent semantics that is based on total interpretations is the semantics of *stable models*, which has been introduced by Gelfond and Lifschitz [5]. Van Gelder, Ross and Schlipf [14] have used partial interpretations, and have defined the so–called *well–founded model*, which is unique for each normal database. Przymusinski defined *partial stable models* by extending the definition of stable models to three truth values [11]. Then it could be shown that the well–founded model is the unique least partial stable model in the knowledge ordering. The knowledge ordering is very essential, since the minimal models in this ordering determine the consequences of a set of models based on skeptical reasoning.

For *disjunctive databases* (databases that may contain disjunctions and negation), the semantics of stable and partial stable models can be defined also, cf. [6, 11]. In the disjunctive case there are usually both many stable and many partial stable models, and there is no unique least partial stable model in the knowledge ordering. Also several extensions of the well–founded semantics to the disjunctive case have been proposed [8].

The different approaches to define the semantics of a disjunctive database can be compared as follows: the semantics of stable models is always stronger than the semantics of partial stable models in that it derives more consequences – where the consequences are defined by skeptical reasoning as those formulas that are *true* in all models that belong to the semantics of the database. But sometimes there do not exist stable models of a disjunctive database, due to *local inconsistencies* in the database. In this case the stable model semantics is called inconsistent. The partial stable model semantics is more robust in these cases. It can assign the truth value *undefined* to atoms in an inconsistent part of the database, while atoms in other parts are assigned classical truth values *true* or *false*. Thus, for many examples the semantics of partial stable models gives a useful interpretation, while the semantics of stable models does not.

Recently, several *algorithms* for computing the (total) stable models of disjunctive databases have been proposed, e.g. cf. [1, 2, 3, 7, 10]. Brass and Dix [2] show how the stable models can be computed based on *partial evaluation*. Since partial evaluation can be computed efficiently based on the well–known hyperresolution operator $\mathcal{T}_P^s$ of Minker and Rajasekar [9], this gives a way of computing stable models of disjunctive databases. For normal databases without disjunctions, efficient algorithms have been developed by Niemelä and Simons, cf. [10].

The paper is organized as follows: In Sections 2 and 3 we review the basic definitions and notation for disjunctive databases, partial Herbrand interpretations and partial stable models. In Section 4 we introduce a concept of *transforming* a disjunctive database $\mathcal{P}$ into a suitable disjunctive database $\mathcal{P}^{tu}$. It is based on suitably *annotating* the atoms in the given database by the truth values "t" and "u". Then, in Section 5 we give a *characterization* of the partial stable models of $\mathcal{P}$ in terms of the total stable models of the transformed database $\mathcal{P}^{tu}$. This reduces the problem of computing partial stable models to the problem of computing total stable models, i.e., the algorithms that were mentioned above to construct total stable models can also be used for computing partial stable models. Finally, in Section 6 we show that *partial evaluation* in general can change the partial stable models of a disjunctive database, but based on the transformed database $\mathcal{P}^{tu}$ it can be used for computing partial stable models as well.

2   Basic Definitions and Notations

Given a first order language $\mathcal{L}$; a *disjunctive database* $\mathcal{P}$ consists of logical inference rules of the form

$$r = A_1 \vee \ldots \vee A_k \leftarrow B_1 \wedge \ldots \wedge B_m \wedge not\, C_1 \wedge \ldots \wedge not\, C_n, \quad (1)$$

where A_i, $i \in \langle 1, k \rangle$, B_i, $i \in \langle 1, m \rangle$, and C_i, $i \in \langle 1, n \rangle$, are (positive) atoms in the language $\mathcal{L}$, $k, m, n \in I\!N_0$, and *not* is the negation–by–default operator.[1] A rule is called a fact if $m = 0$ and $n = 0$. The set of all *ground instances* of the rules and facts in $\mathcal{P}$ is denoted by $gnd\,(\mathcal{P})$. A rule (or database) is called *positive–disjunctive* if it does not contain default negation (i.e. $n = 0$). A disjunctive rule r of the form (1) above is denoted as:

$$r = \alpha \leftarrow \beta \wedge not \cdot \gamma,$$

where $\alpha = A_1 \vee \ldots \vee A_k$, $\beta = B_1 \wedge \ldots \wedge B_m$, and $\gamma = C_1 \vee \ldots \vee C_n$. Note that γ is a disjunction, and thus the negation $not \cdot \gamma$ is taken to be the conjunction $not\, C_1 \wedge \ldots \wedge not\, C_n$.[2]

Herbrand Interpretations and Partial Herbrand Interpretations

The Herbrand base $H_{B_\mathcal{P}}$ of a disjunctive database $\mathcal{P}$ contains all ground atoms over the language of $\mathcal{P}$. A *partial Herbrand interpretation* of $\mathcal{P}$ is given by a mapping $I\colon H_{B_\mathcal{P}} \to \{\,t, f, u\,\}$ that assigns a truth value t, f or u to each atom in $H_{B_\mathcal{P}}$. Thus, partial Herbrand interpretations are also called three–valued Herbrand interpretations. I is called a *total*

---

[1] By $I\!N_+$ we denote the set $\{\,1, 2, 3, \ldots\,\}$ of positive natural numbers, whereas $I\!N_0$ denotes the set $\{\,0, 1, 2, \ldots\,\}$ of all natural numbers. $\langle n, m \rangle$ denotes the interval $\{\,n, n+1, \ldots, m\,\}$ of natural numbers.

[2] I.e., by convention we assume that the operator *not* satisfies De Morgan's laws.

Herbrand interpretation, if all atoms A are mapped to classical truth values t or f.

Equivalently, partial Herbrand interpretations can be represented by using the concept of *annotated atoms*. Given an atom $A = p(t_1, \ldots, t_n)$ and a truth value $v \in \{\, t, f, u \,\}$, by $A^v = p^v(t_1, \ldots, t_n)$ we denote an annotated atom. Here, p^v is taken to be a new predicate symbol. We will use two ways of representing a partial Herbrand interpretation I as a set of annotated atoms, either by specifying the *true* and *false* atoms or by specifying the *true* and *undefined* atoms:

$$
\begin{aligned}
\text{tf–}Representation: \quad & I^{tf} = I^t \cup I^f, \\
\text{tu–}Representation: \quad & I^{tu} = I^t \cup I^u,
\end{aligned}
$$

where the sets I^t, I^u and I^f are given by:

$$
\begin{aligned}
I^t &= \{\, A^t \mid A \in HB_\mathcal{P} \wedge I(A) = t \,\}, \\
I^f &= \{\, A^f \mid A \in HB_\mathcal{P} \wedge I(A) = f \,\}, \\
I^u &= \{\, A^u \mid A \in HB_\mathcal{P} \wedge (\, I(A) = t \vee I(A) = u \,) \,\}.
\end{aligned}
$$

Note that in the tu–representation every *true* atom A is recorded as A^t and as A^u, which will become important later. Note also that the tf–representation is essentially the same as the conventional representation of I as a *set of literals*, where A^t becomes the atom A itself and A^f becomes the negative literal $\neg A$. For collections $\mathcal{I}$ of interpretations we will use the same notations: $\mathcal{I}^v = \{\, I^v \mid I \in \mathcal{I} \,\}$, for $v \in \{\, tf, tu \,\}$.

Consider for instance the Herbrand base $HB_\mathcal{P} = \{\, a, b, c, d \,\}$. Then the partial Herbrand interpretation I with $I(a) = t$, $I(b) = t$, $I(c) = f$, and $I(d) = u$, is represented as follows:

$$
I^{tf} = \{\, a^t, b^t, c^f \,\}, \quad I^{tu} = \{\, a^t, b^t, a^u, b^u, d^u \,\}.
$$

Obviously, a total Herbrand interpretation I can simply be represented by the set $J = \{\, A \in HB_\mathcal{P} \mid I(A) = t \,\}$ of *true* atoms. Conversely, any set $J \subseteq HB_\mathcal{P}$ of ground atoms *induces* a total Herbrand interpretation I, where $I(A) = t$ iff $A \in J$.

Truth Ordering and Knowledge Ordering

There are two common *partial orderings on truth values*, the truth ordering and the knowledge ordering [4]. They are shown by Figure 1:

$$
\begin{aligned}
\textit{Truth Ordering } \leq_t: \quad & f \leq_t u, \ u \leq_t t, \\
\textit{Knowledge Ordering } \leq_k: \quad & u \leq_k f, \ u \leq_k t.
\end{aligned}
$$

Given $v_1, v_2 \in \{\, t, f, u \,\}$, by $v_1 \geq_x v_2$ we denote the fact that $v_2 \leq_x v_1$, for $x \in \{\, t, k \,\}$.

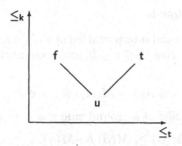

Figure 1: Truth Ordering and Knowledge Ordering

These partial orderings can be generalized (pointwise) to partial Herbrand interpretations as follows: for $x \in \{t, k\}$,

$$I_1 \leq_x I_2, \text{ iff } I_1(A) \leq_x I_2(A), \text{ for all } A \in HB_P.$$

Also, we say $I_1 <_x I_2$, iff $I_1 \leq_x I_2$, and $I_1 \neq I_2$. Thus, the truth ordering on partial Herbrand interpretations corresponds to the subset ordering on their tu–representations:

$$I_1 \leq_t I_2 \text{ iff } I_1^{tu} \subseteq I_2^{tu}.$$

$\wedge$	t	f	u
t	t	f	u
f	f	f	f
u	u	f	u

$\vee$	t	f	u
t	t	t	t
f	t	f	u
u	t	u	u

$\neg$	
t	f
f	t
u	u

Figure 2: Boolean operations in three-valued logic

The *Boolean operations* "$\vee$", "$\wedge$" and "$\neg$" on truth values are defined based on the truth ordering. The corresponding truth tables are given by Figure 2. Given truth values $v_i \in \{t, u, f\}$, $1 \leq i \leq k$, the truth values of the disjunction $\varphi = v_1 \vee \ldots \vee v_k$ and the conjunction $\psi = v_1 \wedge \ldots \wedge v_k$ are defined as the *maximum* and the *minimum*, respectively, of the truth values $v_1, \ldots, v_k$ in the *truth ordering*:

$$v_1 \vee \ldots \vee v_k = max_t(\{ v_i \mid 1 \leq i \leq k \} \cup \{f\}),$$
$$v_1 \wedge \ldots \wedge v_k = min_t(\{ v_i \mid 1 \leq i \leq k \} \cup \{t\}).$$

In particular, empty disjunctions φ (i.e. $k = 0$) evaluate to f and empty conjunctions ψ (i.e. $k = 0$) evaluate to t.

Models and Partial Models

Let M be a partial Herbrand interpretation of a disjunctive database $\mathcal{P}$. For ground atoms $A_i \in HB_{\mathcal{P}}$, $1 \leq i \leq k$, and a connective $\otimes \in \{ \vee, \wedge \}$ we define

$$M(A_1 \otimes \ldots \otimes A_k) = M(A_1) \otimes \ldots \otimes M(A_k).$$

M is called a *partial model* of a ground rule $r = \alpha \leftarrow \beta \wedge not \cdot \gamma$ if

$$M(\alpha) \geq_t M(\beta) \wedge \neg M(\gamma).$$

M is called a *partial model* of $\mathcal{P}$ if M is a partial model of all ground instantiations of all rules $r \in \mathcal{P}$. This is denoted by $M \models_3 \mathcal{P}$.

Minimality of partial models is defined w.r.t. the truth ordering. M is called *partial minimal model* of $\mathcal{P}$ if M is a partial model of $\mathcal{P}$ and there is no other partial model I of $\mathcal{P}$ such that $I <_t M$. The set of all partial minimal models of $\mathcal{P}$ is denoted by $\mathcal{MM}_3(\mathcal{P})$.

A partial model M of a disjunctive database $\mathcal{P}$ that is total is called a *model* of $\mathcal{P}$, denoted by $M \models_2 \mathcal{P}$. If M additionally is a partial minimal model of $\mathcal{P}$, then M is called a *minimal model* of $\mathcal{P}$. The set of all minimal models of $\mathcal{P}$ is denoted by $\mathcal{MM}_2(\mathcal{P})$.

3 Partial Stable Models

The *Gelfond–Lifschitz–transformation* (GL–Transformation) of a disjunctive database $\mathcal{P}$ w.r.t. a partial Herbrand interpretation M is obtained from the ground instance $gnd(\mathcal{P})$ of $\mathcal{P}$ by replacing in every rule that contains default negation in the body the negated literals "*not A*" by their truth value "$\neg M(A)$" w.r.t. M.[3]

Definition 3.1 (Gelfond–Lifschitz–Transformation, [5, 11]) Let M be a partial Herbrand interpretation of a disjunctive database $\mathcal{P}$.

(i) For a disjunctive rule $r = \alpha \leftarrow \beta \wedge not \cdot \gamma \in gnd(\mathcal{P})$ we define

$$r^M = \alpha \leftarrow \beta \wedge \neg M(\gamma).$$

(ii) The *Gelfond–Lifschitz–transformation* of $\mathcal{P}$ is $\mathcal{P}^M = \{ r^M \mid r \in gnd(\mathcal{P}) \}$.

The GL–transformation $\mathcal{P}^M$ of a disjunctive database $\mathcal{P}$ is a ground positive–disjunctive database that has as additional atoms the truth values t, f and u. Note that these new atoms must evaluate to *true*, *false* and *undefined*, respectively, under all partial Herbrand interpretations I of $\mathcal{P}^M$.

---

[3]If the negative body evaluates to true w.r.t. M, then the truth value "t" of the negative body can be deleted.

Example 3.2 (GL–Transformation) For the disjunctive database
$$\mathcal{P}_1 = \{\, a \vee b, \ q \leftarrow not\, a, \ r \leftarrow not\, b \,\},$$
and the partial Herbrand interpretation $M^{\mathrm{tf}} = \{\, a^t, r^t, b^f, q^f \,\}$ we get
$$\mathcal{P}_1^M = \{\, a \vee b, \ q \leftarrow \mathbf{f}, \ r \leftarrow \mathbf{t} \,\}.$$

Definition 3.3 (Partial Stable Models, Stable Models) Let M be a partial Herbrand interpretation of a disjunctive database $\mathcal{P}$.

(i) M is called a *partial stable model* of $\mathcal{P}$ if $M \in \mathcal{MM}_3(\mathcal{P}^M)$. The set of all partial stable models of $\mathcal{P}$ is denoted by $\mathcal{S}_{TABLE_3}(\mathcal{P})$.

(ii) A partial stable model M of $\mathcal{P}$ that is a total Herbrand interpretation of $\mathcal{P}$ is called *stable model* of $\mathcal{P}$. The set of all stable models of $\mathcal{P}$ is denoted by $\mathcal{S}_{TABLE_2}(\mathcal{P})$.

Example 3.4 (Partial Stable Models)

(i) For the disjunctive database
$$\mathcal{P}_1 = \{\, a \vee b, \ q \leftarrow not\, a, \ r \leftarrow not\, b \,\},$$
of Example 3.2 we get the following set of partial stable models:
$$\mathcal{S}_{TABLE_3}(\mathcal{P}_1)^{\mathrm{tf}} = \{\, \{\, a^t, r^t, b^f, q^f \,\}, \ \{\, b^t, q^t, a^f, r^f \,\} \,\}.$$
Here $\mathcal{S}_{TABLE_3}(\mathcal{P}_1) = \mathcal{S}_{TABLE_2}(\mathcal{P}_1)$, i.e. all partial stable models are also stable models. Since the database is stratified, the stable models coincide with the *perfect models*.

(ii) For the disjunctive database
$$\mathcal{P}_2 = \mathcal{P}_1 \cup \{\, p \leftarrow q \wedge r, \ e \leftarrow p \wedge not\, f, \ f \leftarrow not\, e \,\},$$
all partial stable models are also stable models, i.e. $\mathcal{S}_{TABLE_3}(\mathcal{P}_2) = \mathcal{S}_{TABLE_2}(\mathcal{P}_2)$, and
$$\mathcal{S}_{TABLE_3}(\mathcal{P}_2)^{\mathrm{tf}} = \{\, \{\, a^t, f^t, r^t, b^f, e^f, q^f, p^f \,\}, \ \{\, b^t, f^t, q^t, a^f, e^f, r^f, p^f \,\} \,\}.$$

(iii) For the disjunctive database
$$\mathcal{P}_3 = \{\, a \leftarrow not\, b, \ b \leftarrow not\, a \,\},$$
we get the following set $\mathcal{S}_{TABLE_3}(\mathcal{P}_3)$ of partial stable models, where only the first two partial stable models are total:
$$\mathcal{S}_{TABLE_2}(\mathcal{P}_3)^{\mathrm{tf}} = \{\, \{\, a^t, b^f \,\}, \{\, b^t, a^f \,\} \,\},$$
$$\mathcal{S}_{TABLE_3}(\mathcal{P}_3)^{\mathrm{tf}} = \mathcal{S}_{TABLE_2}(\mathcal{P}_3)^{\mathrm{tf}} \cup \{\, \emptyset \,\}.$$

(iv) For the disjunctive database
$$\mathcal{P}_4 = \{\, a \vee b \vee c, \ a \leftarrow not\, b, \ b \leftarrow not\, c, \ c \leftarrow not\, a \,\},$$
there are no partial stable models: $\mathcal{S}_{TABLE_3}(\mathcal{P}_4) = \mathcal{S}_{TABLE_2}(\mathcal{P}_4) = \emptyset$.

4 Annotation of Disjunctive Databases

In this section we describe how to annotate disjunctive rules in such a way that the annotation encodes the condition that a partial Herbrand interpretation must fulfill to be a model of the rule – see below for further explanation.

Given a truth value $v \in \{t, u\}$, for a disjunction $\alpha = A_1 \vee \ldots \vee A_k$ and a conjunction $\beta = B_1 \wedge \ldots \wedge B_m$ of atoms we define $\alpha^v = A_1^v \vee \ldots \vee A_k^v$ and $\beta^v = B_1^v \wedge \ldots \wedge B_m^v$.

Definition 4.1 (Annotation of Databases)

(i) For a disjunctive rule $r = \alpha \leftarrow \beta \wedge not \cdot \gamma$ we define

$$
\begin{aligned}
r^u &= \alpha^u \leftarrow \beta^u \wedge not \cdot \gamma^t, \\
r^t &= \alpha^t \leftarrow \beta^t \wedge not \cdot \gamma^u.
\end{aligned}
$$

(ii) For a disjunctive database $\mathcal{P}$ we define

$$
\mathcal{P}^u = \{ r^u \mid r \in \mathcal{P} \}, \quad \mathcal{P}^t = \{ r^t \mid r \in \mathcal{P} \},
$$

and $\mathcal{P}^{tu} = \mathcal{P}^t \cup \mathcal{P}^u \cup \{ A^u \leftarrow A^t \mid A \in HB_\mathcal{P} \}.$

Thus, for each disjunctive rule r in a disjunctive database $\mathcal{P}$ we get two rules r^t and r^u in the annotated database $\mathcal{P}^{tu}$.

Example 4.2 (Annotation of Databases) The disjunctive database $\mathcal{P}_2$ of Example 3.4 is annotated as follows:

$$
\begin{aligned}
\mathcal{P}_2^u = \{ \quad & a^u \vee b^u, & p^u &\leftarrow q^u \wedge r^u, \\
& q^u \leftarrow not\, a^t, & e^u &\leftarrow p^u \wedge not\, f^t, \\
& r^u \leftarrow not\, b^t, & f^u &\leftarrow not\, e^t \quad \}, \\[6pt]
\mathcal{P}_2^t = \{ \quad & a^t \vee b^t, & p^t &\leftarrow q^t \wedge r^t, \\
& q^t \leftarrow not\, a^u, & e^t &\leftarrow p^t \wedge not\, f^u, \\
& r^t \leftarrow not\, b^u, & f^t &\leftarrow not\, e^u \quad \}.
\end{aligned}
$$

Now we want to give a brief motivation for the construction of the annotated database $\mathcal{P}^{tu}$. A partial Herbrand interpretation M is a partial Herbrand model of a ground rule $r = \alpha \leftarrow \beta \wedge not \cdot \gamma$, iff it holds that

$$
M(\alpha) \geq_t M(\beta) \wedge \neg M(\gamma).
$$

This is equivalent to the following:

$$
\begin{aligned}
&(\, (\, M(\beta) \geq_t u \ \wedge \ \neg M(\gamma) \geq_t u \,) \implies M(\alpha) \geq_t u \,) \ \wedge \\
&(\, (\, M(\beta) = t \ \wedge \ \neg M(\gamma) = t \,) \implies M(\alpha) = t \,),
\end{aligned}
$$

where $(\neg M(\gamma) \geq_t u) \iff \neg(M(\gamma) \geq_t t)$, and $(\neg M(\gamma) = t) \iff \neg(M(\gamma) \geq_t u)$.

Properties of the Annotated Database

It can be shown that annotation preserves stratification: Given a disjunctive database $\mathcal{P}$, the annotated disjunctive database $\mathcal{P}^{tu}$ is *stratified* if and only if $\mathcal{P}$ is stratified. Based on this, one can give an alternative proof of the well–known fact (see [11]) that the partial stable models of a stratified–disjunctive database $\mathcal{P}$ coincide with the perfect models of $\mathcal{P}$. This fact implies in particular that the partial stable models of a stratified–disjunctive database $\mathcal{P}$ are total.

The annotated database $\mathcal{P}^{tu}$ can be seen as a database over two predicate symbols "t" and "u". Then annotated atoms A^t and A^u in the annotated rules r^t and r^u can be represented by atoms $\mathsf{t}(A)$ and $\mathsf{u}(A)$, respectively, where "A" is seen as a term now. In this representation the (possibly infinite) set $\{\, A^u \leftarrow A^t \mid A \in HB_{\mathcal{P}}\,\}$ of rules can simply be represented by one rule $\mathsf{u}(X) \leftarrow \mathsf{t}(X)$, where "$X$" is a variable symbol for atoms. Then $\mathcal{P}^{tu}$ has the size of $2 \cdot n + 1$ rules if $\mathcal{P}$ consists of n rules. This compact representation has been used for an implementation dealing with the annotated database $\mathcal{P}^{tu}$.

5   Characterization of Partial Stable Models

In this section we prove that the partial stable models of a disjunctive database $\mathcal{P}$ correspond to the stable models of $\mathcal{P}^{tu}$.

For any partial Herbrand interpretation I of the original disjunctive database $\mathcal{P}$ we introduce the notation I^{TU} for the total Herbrand interpretation of the annotated database $\mathcal{P}^{tu}$ that is induced by I^{tu}:

$$I^{TU}(A^v) = \begin{cases} \mathsf{t} \text{ iff } A^v \in I^{tu}, \\ \mathsf{f} \text{ iff } A^v \in HB_{\mathcal{P}^{tu}} \setminus I^{tu}, \end{cases}$$

where $v \in \{\, \mathsf{t}, \mathsf{u}\,\}$. Note that this construction is necessary, since I^{tu} is just a set of ground atoms for the annotated database $\mathcal{P}^{tu}$, while I^{TU} is the corresponding total Herbrand interpretation. Note also that given two partial Herbrand interpretations I and J,

$$I_1 \leq_t I_2 \text{ iff } I_1^{tu} \subseteq I_2^{tu} \text{ iff } I_1^{TU} \leq_t I_2^{TU}.$$

For proving our main result we need the following lemma that relates the partial models of the GL–transformation of a disjunctive database $\mathcal{P}$ w.r.t. a partial Herbrand interpretation M to the total models of the GL–transformation of the annotated database $\mathcal{P}^{tu}$ w.r.t. the total Herbrand interpretation M^{TU}.

Lemma 5.1 (GL–Transformation) *Given a disjunctive database $\mathcal{P}$, and any two partial Herbrand interpretations I and M. Then*

$$I \models_3 \mathcal{P}^M \text{ iff } I^{TU} \models_2 (\mathcal{P}^{tu})^{M^{TU}}.$$

Proof: Given a rule $r = \alpha \leftarrow \beta \wedge not\cdot\gamma \in \mathcal{P}$ and its derivates

$$r^u = \alpha^u \leftarrow \beta^u \wedge not\cdot\gamma^t, \quad r^t = \alpha^t \leftarrow \beta^t \wedge not\cdot\gamma^u.$$

Let $r_m = r^M$, $r_u = (r^u)^{M^{TU}}$, $r_t = (r^t)^{M^{TU}}$. We show the equivalence

$$\text{(EQ)}: \quad I \models_3 r_m \quad \text{iff} \quad (I^{TU} \models_2 r_u \text{ and } I^{TU} \models_2 r_t).$$

We will use the following equivalence, which holds for all $v \in \{t, u\}$ and all formulas φ:

$$I(\varphi) \geq_t v \iff I^{TU} \models_2 \varphi^v.$$

(i) Assume that $M(\gamma) = t$. Then

$$r_m = \alpha \leftarrow \beta \wedge f, \quad r_u = \alpha^u \leftarrow \beta^u \wedge f, \quad r_t = \alpha^t \leftarrow \beta^t \wedge f.$$

Since the rules r_m, r_u, r_t all contain "f" in their bodies, they are all modelled by any partial Herbrand interpretation, and we get the desired result (EQ).

(ii) Assume that $M(\gamma) = u$. Then

$$r_m = \alpha \leftarrow \beta \wedge u, \quad r_u = \alpha^u \leftarrow \beta^u \wedge t, \quad r_t = \alpha^t \leftarrow \beta^t \wedge f.$$

Since r_t contains "f" in its body, it is modelled by any partial Herbrand interpretation. Thus, for r_m and r_u we get

$$
\begin{aligned}
I \models_3 r_m \iff & (I(\beta) \geq_t u \implies I(\alpha) \geq_t u) \\
\iff & (I^{TU} \models_2 \beta^u \implies I^{TU} \models_2 \alpha^u) \iff I^{TU} \models_2 r_u.
\end{aligned}
$$

This shows the equality (EQ).

(iii) Assume that $M(\gamma) = f$. Then

$$r_m = \alpha \leftarrow \beta \wedge t, \quad r_u = \alpha^u \leftarrow \beta^u \wedge t, \quad r_t = \alpha^t \leftarrow \beta^t \wedge t.$$

Thus, we get

$$
\begin{aligned}
I \models_3 r_m \iff & ((I(\beta) \geq_t u \implies I(\alpha) \geq_t u) \wedge \\
& (I(\beta) \geq_t t \implies I(\alpha) \geq_t t)), \\
I^{TU} \models_2 r_u \iff & (I^{TU} \models_2 \beta^u \implies I^{TU} \models_2 \alpha^u), \\
I^{TU} \models_2 r_t \iff & (I^{TU} \models_2 \beta^t \implies I^{TU} \models_2 \alpha^t),
\end{aligned}
$$

which shows the equality (EQ).

Finally, note that the rules $A^u \leftarrow A^t$ for atoms $A \in H_{B_{\mathcal{P}}}$ are also fulfilled in I^{TU} because of the structure of I^{tu}. $\qquad\square$

Based on the previous lemma, we can relate the partial models of a disjunctive database $\mathcal{P}$ to the models of the annotated database $\mathcal{P}^{tu}$.

Lemma 5.2 (Partial Models) *Given a disjunctive database $\mathcal{P}$, and a partial Herbrand interpretation I. Then*

$$I \models_3 \mathcal{P} \text{ iff } I^{\mathsf{TU}} \models_2 \mathcal{P}^{\mathsf{tu}}.$$

Proof: From the definition of the GL–transformation it follows that (1) $I \models_3 \mathcal{P}$ iff $I \models_3 \mathcal{P}^I$ and (2) $I^{\mathsf{TU}} \models_2 \mathcal{P}^{\mathsf{tu}}$ iff $I^{\mathsf{TU}} \models_2 \mathcal{P}^{\mathsf{tu}^{I^{\mathsf{TU}}}}$. Using the previous Lemma 5.1 for $I = M$ we get that (3) $I \models_3 \mathcal{P}^I$ iff $I^{\mathsf{TU}} \models_2 (\mathcal{P}^{\mathsf{tu}})^{I^{\mathsf{TU}}}$. By chaining the three equivalences (1), (2) and (3) we get the desired result. $\square$

The following theorem shows that the tu–representation of the partial stable models of a disjunctive database corresponds to the total stable models of the tu–transformation of the database.

Theorem 5.3 (Partial Stable Models) *Given a disjunctive database $\mathcal{P}$, then*

$$STABLE_3(\mathcal{P})^{\mathsf{TU}} = STABLE_2(\mathcal{P}^{\mathsf{tu}}).$$

Proof: Consider partial Herbrand interpretations I and M of $\mathcal{P}$. From Lemma 5.1 we know $I \models_3 \mathcal{P}^M$ iff $I^{\mathsf{TU}} \models_2 (\mathcal{P}^{\mathsf{tu}})^{M^{\mathsf{TU}}}$. For partial Herbrand interpretations, minimizing in the truth ordering corresponds to minimizing in the subset ordering for their tu–representations. Thus, $M \in \mathcal{MM}_3(\mathcal{P}^M)$ iff $M^{\mathsf{TU}} \in \mathcal{MM}_2((\mathcal{P}^{\mathsf{tu}})^{M^{\mathsf{TU}}})$. That is, M is a partial stable model of $\mathcal{P}$ iff M^{TU} is a stable model of $\mathcal{P}^{\mathsf{tu}}$. $\square$

Example 5.4 (Partial Stable Models)

(i) For the disjunctive database $\mathcal{P}_1$ of Example 3.4 we get the following annotated disjunctive database:

$$\mathcal{P}_1^{\mathsf{tu}} = \{\ a^{\mathsf{u}} \vee b^{\mathsf{u}},\ q^{\mathsf{u}} \leftarrow not\ a^{\mathsf{t}},\ r^{\mathsf{u}} \leftarrow not\ b^{\mathsf{t}},$$
$$a^{\mathsf{t}} \vee b^{\mathsf{t}},\ q^{\mathsf{t}} \leftarrow not\ a^{\mathsf{u}},\ r^{\mathsf{t}} \leftarrow not\ b^{\mathsf{u}},$$
$$a^{\mathsf{u}} \leftarrow a^{\mathsf{t}},\ b^{\mathsf{u}} \leftarrow b^{\mathsf{t}},\ q^{\mathsf{u}} \leftarrow q^{\mathsf{t}},\ r^{\mathsf{u}} \leftarrow r^{\mathsf{t}}\ \}.$$

Thus, we get $STABLE_3(\mathcal{P}_1)^{\mathsf{tu}} = \{\ \{\ a^{\mathsf{t}}, r^{\mathsf{t}}, a^{\mathsf{u}}, r^{\mathsf{u}}\ \},\ \{\ b^{\mathsf{t}}, q^{\mathsf{t}}, b^{\mathsf{u}}, q^{\mathsf{u}}\ \}\ \}$.

(ii) For the disjunctive database $\mathcal{P}_3$ of Example 3.4 we get the following annotated disjunctive database:

$$\mathcal{P}_3^{\mathsf{tu}} = \{\ a^{\mathsf{u}} \leftarrow not\ b^{\mathsf{t}},\ b^{\mathsf{u}} \leftarrow not\ a^{\mathsf{t}},$$
$$a^{\mathsf{t}} \leftarrow not\ b^{\mathsf{u}},\ b^{\mathsf{t}} \leftarrow not\ a^{\mathsf{u}},$$
$$a^{\mathsf{u}} \leftarrow a^{\mathsf{t}},\ b^{\mathsf{u}} \leftarrow b^{\mathsf{t}}\ \}.$$

Thus, we get $STABLE_3(\mathcal{P}_3)^{\mathsf{tu}} = \{\ \{\ a^{\mathsf{t}}, a^{\mathsf{u}}\ \},\ \{\ b^{\mathsf{t}}, b^{\mathsf{u}}\ \},\ \{\ a^{\mathsf{u}}, b^{\mathsf{u}}\ \}\ \}$.

6 Partial Stable Models and Partial Evaluation

Let $\mathcal{P}$ be a disjunctive database. A ground rule $\alpha \leftarrow not \cdot \gamma$ such that α and γ are disjunctions of atoms from the Herbrand base $HB_\mathcal{P}$ is called *conditional fact* over $\mathcal{P}$. Note, that by our convention $not \cdot \gamma$ will be a conjunction of negative literals. The *conditional disjunctive Herbrand base* $DHB_\mathcal{P}^*$ is the set of all conditional facts over $\mathcal{P}$. A subset $S \subseteq DHB_\mathcal{P}^*$ is called *conditional disjunctive Herbrand state*.

Definition 6.1 (Consequence Operator $\mathcal{T}_\mathcal{P}^s$) Let $\mathcal{P}$ be a disjunctive database, and let $S \subseteq DHB_\mathcal{P}^*$. The disjunctive *consequence operator*

$$\mathcal{T}_\mathcal{P}^s : 2^{DHB_\mathcal{P}^*} \to 2^{DHB_\mathcal{P}^*}$$

of $\mathcal{P}$ is defined as

$$
\begin{aligned}
\mathcal{T}_\mathcal{P}^s(S) = \{ &\alpha \vee \alpha_1 \vee \ldots \vee \alpha_m \leftarrow not \cdot \gamma \wedge not \cdot \gamma_1 \wedge \ldots \wedge not \cdot \gamma_m \mid \\
&\text{there is a rule } \alpha \leftarrow B_1 \wedge \ldots \wedge B_m \wedge not \cdot \gamma \in gnd(\mathcal{P}) : \\
&\forall i \in \langle 1, m \rangle : B_i \vee \alpha_i \leftarrow not \cdot \gamma_i \in S \}.
\end{aligned}
$$

This consequence operator generalizes the consequence operator of Minker and Rajasekar, which had been defined for positive–disjunctive databases (i.e. databases without default negation) only [9]. Just like the operator of Minker and Rajasekar, the new operator is *monotonic* and *continuous*. Thus, it reaches its *least fixpoint* in at most ω steps. The least fixpoint of $\mathcal{T}_\mathcal{P}^s$ is called the *partial evaluation* of $\mathcal{P}$, and is denoted by $\mathcal{P}^*$. $\mathcal{P}^*$ is a conditional disjunctive Herbrand state, i.e. a disjunctive database that consists of ground conditional facts only.

It has been shown by Brass and Dix, cf. [2], that partial evaluation does not change the set of (total) stable models of a disjunctive database. In [2] this property is called the *generalized principle of partial evaluation (GPPE)*, and it is argued that GPPE is a very important property that every semantics should have.

Theorem 6.2 (Partial Evaluation and Stable Models, [2]) *Given a disjunctive database $\mathcal{P}$, then*

$$STABLE_2(\mathcal{P}) = STABLE_2(\mathcal{P}^*).$$

Unfortunately, the following example shows that the set of partial stable models is changed by partial evaluation. That is, the semantics of partial stable models does not fulfill GPPE.

Example 6.3 (Partial Evaluation and Partial Stable Models) For the disjunctive database

$$\mathcal{P}_5 = \{ a \vee b, \; u \leftarrow not \, u, \; c \leftarrow a \wedge not \, u \},$$

we get the following set of partial stable models:

$$STABLE_3(\mathcal{P}_5)^{\text{tf}} = \{\, \{\, a^t, b^f \,\}, \{\, b^t, a^f, c^f \,\}\, \},$$

which is equivalent to $STABLE_3(\mathcal{P}_5)^{\text{tu}} = \{\{\, a^t, a^u, c^u, u^u \,\}, \{\, b^t, b^u, u^u \,\}\}$. It can be seen that in the partial stable models one of a and b is *true* and the other is *false*. Also, u is *undefined* in both partial stable models, because it is defined by the rule $u \leftarrow not\, u$ that contains u in the head and in the positive body. If a is *true*, the third rule $c \leftarrow a \wedge not\, u$ supports c being *undefined*, while c is *false* in the second partial stable model, where a is *false*. By partial evaluation of $\mathcal{P}_5$ we derive

$$\mathcal{P}_5^* = \{\, a \vee b, \; u \leftarrow not\, u, \; b \vee c \leftarrow not\, u \,\}.$$

The third rule has been derived by resolving the fact $a \vee b$ with the rule $c \leftarrow a \wedge not\, u$ on the atom a. The partial stable models of $\mathcal{P}_5^*$ are derived as follows: Again, u is *undefined* in all partial stable models – the defining rules for u haven't changed. But now there are two rules defining b. The new rule $b \vee c \leftarrow not\, u$ can support c being *undefined* or it can support b being *undefined*. Thus, we get two partial stable models models with a being *true*, where the *truth* of a is based on the fact $a \vee b$. In the case that b is taken to be *true* based on the fact, we get that c is *false*, since the new rule cannot support c now:

$$STABLE_3(\mathcal{P}_5^*)^{\text{tf}} = STABLE_3(\mathcal{P}_5)^{\text{tf}} \cup \{\, \{\, a^t, c^f \,\}\, \},$$

which is equivalent to $STABLE_3(\mathcal{P}_5^*)^{\text{tu}} = STABLE_3(\mathcal{P}_5)^{\text{tu}} \cup \{\{\, a^t, a^u, b^u, u^u \,\}\}$. The additional model is due to the strange new rule that supports the *undefinedness* of b based on the *undefinedness* of u. That support was not present in $\mathcal{P}_5$.

The unfavorable behavior of partial evaluation in the three–valued setting can be overcome by our method of annotating the database. For the annotated database $\mathcal{P}^{\text{tu}}$ we can first perform partial evaluation and then (two–valued) stable models computation to obtain the set of partial stable models of $\mathcal{P}$. This is expressed by the following theorem, which is a consequence of the Theorems 5.3 and 6.2.

Theorem 6.4 (Partial Evaluation and Partial Stable Models)
Given a disjunctive database $\mathcal{P}$, then

$$STABLE_3(\mathcal{P})^{\text{TU}} = STABLE_2((\mathcal{P}^{\text{tu}})^*).$$

Example 6.5 (Annotation and Partial Evaluation) For the disjunctive database $\mathcal{P}_5$ of Example 6.3 we get

$$\begin{aligned}
\mathcal{P}_5^{\text{tu}} = \{ \; & a^t \vee b^t, \; u^t \leftarrow not\, u^u, \; c^t \leftarrow a^t \wedge not\, u^u, \\
& a^u \vee b^u, \; u^u \leftarrow not\, u^t, \; c^u \leftarrow a^u \wedge not\, u^t, \\
& a^u \leftarrow a^t, \; b^u \leftarrow b^t, \; c^u \leftarrow c^t, \; u^u \leftarrow u^t \, \}.
\end{aligned}$$

By partial evaluation we get the following disjunctive database:

$$(\mathcal{P}_5^{tu})^* = \{ \ a^t \vee b^t, \ a^t \vee b^u, \ a^u \vee b^t, \ a^u \vee b^u,$$
$$u^t \leftarrow not\, u^u, \ u^u \leftarrow not\, u^u, \ u^u \leftarrow not\, u^t,$$
$$b^t \vee c^t \leftarrow not\, u^u, \ b^t \vee c^u \leftarrow not\, u^u,$$
$$b^u \vee c^t \leftarrow not\, u^u, \ b^u \vee c^u \leftarrow not\, u^u,$$
$$b^t \vee c^u \leftarrow not\, u^t, \ b^u \vee c^u \leftarrow not\, u^t \ \}.$$

For $(\mathcal{P}_5^{tu})^*$ we can see that u^u is *true* in all stable models and u^t is *false* in all stable models. This renders many rules useless, where $not\, u^u$ is contained in the body. The problematic partial Herbrand interpretation induced by $I^{tu} = \{ \ a^t, a^u, b^u, u^u \ \}$, mentioned in Example 6.3, is not a stable model of $(\mathcal{P}_5^{tu})^*$, since the rule $b^t \vee c^u \leftarrow not\, u^t$ and the fact that u^t is *false* require b^t or c^u to be *true*.

Finally, based on a known result on *supported models*, we can conclude that a partially evaluated database $\mathcal{P}^*$ can be transformed to a normal database by moving positive head atoms to the negative body without changing the total stable models. Thus, the efficient algorithms of Niemelä and Simons [10] can be applied for computing total and partial stable models as well.

7 Conclusions

The computation of partial stable models based on the **tu**–*transformation* described in this paper has been implemented within the system DISLOG for efficient reasoning in disjunctive databases, cf. [13]. Especially the fact that we could use the technique of *partial evaluation* turned out to speed up the computation drastically.

Another approach to computing the partial stable models of a disjunctive database based on a program transformation has been developed by Ruiz and Minker, cf. [12]. In that paper, a disjunctive database $\mathcal{P}$ is translated into a constraint positive–disjunctive database $\mathcal{P}^{3S}$, the *3S–transformation* of $\mathcal{P}$, in such a way that the total minimal models of $\mathcal{P}^{3S}$ that additionally fulfill the constraints coincide with the partial stable models of $\mathcal{P}$.

An advantage of the new approach, i.e. the **tu**–transformation, is that *efficient algorithms* developed for the total stable semantics can be used for computing partial stable models, that the **tu**–transformation does not need constraints, and that the size of the translated program is only twice the size of the original program plus one.

Acknowledgements: This research was supported in part by the National Science Foundation under grant number IRI9300691.

References

[1] *C. Bell, A. Nerode, R. Ng, V.S. Subrahmanian:* Implementing Stable Semantics by Linear Programming, Proc. Second Intl. Workshop on Logic Programming and Non–Monotonic Reasoning, MIT Press, 1993, pp. 23–42.

[2] *S. Brass, J. Dix:* Characterizations of the Disjunctive Stable Semantics by Partial Evaluation, Proc. Third Intl. Conference on Logic Programming and Non–Monotonic Reasoning, Springer LNCS 928, 1995, pp. 85–98.

[3] *J.A. Fernández, J. Lobo, J. Minker, V.S. Subrahmanian:* Disjunctive LP + Integrity Constrains = Stable Model Semantics, Annals of Math. and AI, vol. 8 (3–4), 1993, pp. 449–474.

[4] *M. Fitting:* Bilattices and the Semantics of Logic Programs, Journal of Logic Programming, vol. 11, 1991, pp. 91–116.

[5] *M. Gelfond, V. Lifschitz:* The Stable Model Semantics for Logic Programming, Proc. Fifth Intl. Conference and Symposium on Logic Programming, MIT Press, 1988, pp. 1070–1080.

[6] *M. Gelfond, V. Lifschitz:* Classical Negation in Logic Programs and Disjunctive Databases, New Generation Computing, vol. 9, 1991, pp. 365–385.

[7] *K. Inoue, M. Koshimura, R. Hasegawa:* Embedding Negation as Failure into a Model Generation Theorem Prover, Proc. Eleventh Intl. Conference on Automated Deduction, Springer LNAI 607, 1992, pp. 400–415.

[8] *J. Lobo, J. Minker, A. Rajasekar:* Foundations of Disjunctive Logic Programming, MIT Press, 1992.

[9] *J. Minker, A. Rajasekar:* A Fixpoint Semantics for Disjunctive Logic Programs, Journal of Logic Programming, vol. 9(1), 1990, pp. 45–74.

[10] *I. Niemelä, P. Simons:* Efficient Implementation of the Well–founded and Stable Model Semantics, Proc. Joint Intl. Conference and Symposium on Logic Programming 1996, MIT Press, 1996, pp. 289–303.

[11] *T.C. Przymusinski:* Stable Semantics for Disjunctive Programs, New Generation Computing, vol. 9, 1991, pp. 401–424.

[12] *C. Ruiz, J. Minker:* Computing Stable and Partial Stable Models of Extended Disjunctive Logic Programs, Proc. Workshop on Nonmonotonic Extensions of Logic Programming 1995, Springer LNCS 927, 1995, pp. 205–229.

[13] *D. Seipel, H. Thöne:* DisLog – A System for Reasoning in Disjunctive Deductive Databases, Proc. Intl. Workshop on the Deductive Approach to Information Systems and Databases, 1994, pp. 325–343, available on the WWW at "http://www-info1.informatik.uni-wuerzburg.de/databases/DisLog".

[14] *A. Van Gelder, K.A. Ross, J.S. Schlipf:*, Unfounded Sets and Well–Founded Semantics for General Logic Programs, Proc. Seventh ACM Symposium on Principles of Database Systems, 1988, pp. 221–230.

Lower-bound Time-complexity Analysis of Logic Programs

Andy King[1], **Kish Shen**[2] and **Florence Benoy**[1]
[1]University of Kent at Canterbury,   [2]University of Manchester,
CT2 7NF, UK.   M13 9PL, UK.
{a.m.king, p.m.benoy}@ukc.ac.uk   kish@cs.man.ac.uk

Abstract

The paper proposes a technique for inferring conditions on goals that, when satisfied, ensure that a goal is sufficiently coarse-grained to warrant parallel evaluation. The method is powerful enough to reason about divide-and-conquer programs, and in the case of quicksort, for instance, can infer that a quicksort goal has a time complexity that exceeds 64 resolution steps (a threshold for spawning) if the input list is of length 10 or more. This gives a simple run-time tactic for controlling spawning. The method has been proved correct, can be implemented straightforwardly, has been demonstrated to be useful on a parallel machine, and, in contrast with much of the previous work on time-complexity analysis of logic programs, does *not* require any complicated difference equation solving machinery.

1 Introduction

Automatic time-complexity analysis is useful to the programmer for algorithmic considerations but has a special rôle in the development of efficient parallel programs [9, 6, 7, 12, 15]. The execution of a parallel program can break down into processes which are too fine-grained for a multiprocessor. This can present a mismatch of granularity between the program and the multi-processor which, in turn, can degrade performance. Time-complexity analysis enables fine-grained processes to be identified and coalesced into more coarse-grained units at run-time in a fully automatically way. This can unburden the programmer from awkward, machine-dependent and error-prone tactical programming decisions like deciding which processes to spawn.

Automatic time-complexity analysis was first suggested as a way of controlling granularity for logic programs in [21] where a simple, heuristic-based analysis was proposed. The analysis, however, was crude and did not satisfactorily model recursive predicates. Recursive predicates present difficulties because the quantity of computation (and therefore the granularity) is data-dependent and is therefore difficult to determine at compile-time. Useful complexity information can still be derived, however, by automatically inferring complexity expressions formulated as functions on the size of the data [7]. Once the size of the data is known at run-time, the time-complexity (and therefore the granularity) can be simply calculated. Specifically, the size of the data can be checked against a threshold to determine whether or not the goal should be evaluated in parallel.

```
Qs(l, s) <- Qs(l, s, []).        Pt([], _, [], []).
Qs([], l, l).                    Pt([x | xs], m, [x | l], g) <-
Qs([x | xs], h, t) <-                x ≤ m, Pt(xs, m, l, g).
    Pt(xs, x, l, g),             Pt([x | xs], m, l, [x | g]) <-
    Qs(l, h, [x | m]),               m < x, Pt(xs, m, l, g).
    Qs(g, m, t).
```

To illustrate, consider the quicksort predicate implemented with difference-lists, and suppose that the first argument of Qs/3 is known to be input. This, for example, might have been inferred through mode analysis. (Note that Gödel notation is used throughout: variables are denoted by identifiers beginning with a lower case letter whereas constants begin with an upper case letter.) The time-complexity of a Qs/3 goal, t, depends on the length, l, of its first argument. To be more precise, if time is measured by counting the number of resolution steps, then $t_{min}(l) \leq t \leq t_{max}(l)$ where $t_{min}(l)$ and $t_{max}(l)$ are the lower- and upper-bounds on the time-complexity,

$$t_{min}(0) = 1 \qquad\qquad\qquad\qquad t_{max}(0) = 1$$
$$t_{min}(l) = 1 + l + t_{min}(\lfloor \tfrac{l-1}{2} \rfloor) + t_{min}(\lceil \tfrac{l-1}{2} \rceil) \qquad t_{max}(l) = 1 + l + t_{max}(0) + t_{max}(l - 1)$$

and $\lfloor . \rfloor$ and $\lceil . \rceil$ denote the floor and ceiling integer rounding functions. Since the input list is ground, we assume perfect indexing between the Pt/4 clauses so that failing computation paths do not need to be considered. Granularity can be controlled by clamping $t_{min}(l)$ and $t_{max}(l)$ with closed-form expressions, $l(\lfloor \log_2(\tfrac{l}{3}) \rfloor - \tfrac{2}{3}) \leq t_{min}(l)$ and $t_{max}(l) = 1 + \tfrac{l(l+5)}{2}$ (either derived by hand or derived automatically) and then only sequentialising goals for which $t_{max}(l) \leq d_{max}$ [7] where d_{max} is granularity spawning threshold that depends on the underlying machine architecture which, for example, relates to the cost of forking a process. Another strategy for throttling the granularity is to only spawn goals with $d_{min} \leq t_{min}(l)$ where d_{min} is another machine dependent threshold.

The $t_{max}(l) \leq d_{max}$ method is the dual of the $d_{min} \leq t_{min}(l)$ strategy [9]. Interestingly, if $t_{max}(l)$ is not a tight upper bound on d_{max}, then the first technique can still spawn fine-grained tasks. Thus there is no guarantee that the first strategy will actually improve the performance of a parallel system. In an extreme situation a parallel system might actually run slower than an equivalent sequential system. On the other hand, if $t_{min}(l)$ is not a tight lower bound on d_{min}, then there is no guarantee that any processes will be spawned with the second method. Note, however, that the parallel system is unlikely to lead to slow-down. The practicality of either technique depends on the inequalities $t_{max}(l) \leq d_{max}$ and $d_{min} \leq t_{min}(l)$ being solved for useful, non-trivial values of l.

Our contribution is to show how the $d_{min} \leq t_{min}(l)$ inequality can be solved straightforwardly for useful, non-trivial values of l by bottom-up abstract interpretation. For example, with $d_{min} = 64$, our analysis can infer for Qs/2 that if $t_{min}(l) \leq d_{min}$ then $l \leq 9$. Interpreted negatively, this means that if $10 < l$ then $64 = d_{min} < t_{min}(l)$. This is not an exercise in aesthetics but has a number of important and practical implications:

precision – our analysis can straightforwardly solve $d_{min} \leq t_{min}(l)$ for useful values of l even for a number of divide-and-conquer problems, including quicksort, which are difficult to reason about requiring, for example, extra analysis machinery in the difference equation approach [9].

implementation – in terms of practicality, our analysis builds on the argument-size analysis of [2] and, like the analysis described in [2], the analysis can be implemented straightforwardly in a language with constraint support. In fact the initial prototype analyser is less than 200 lines of code and took just two weeks to code and debug. Furthermore, the analysis does not require difference equation support to solve the equations that normally arise in time-complexity analysis [6, 7]. The analysis reduces to solving and projecting systems of constraints and machinery for these operations is provided and already implemented in systems like CLP($\mathcal{R}$) and SICStus version 3.

correctness – time-complexity analysis is potentially very complicated and therefore the correctness of an analysis is a real issue. For the analysis described in this paper, safety has been formally proved through abstract interpretation. In more pragmatic terms it means that the thresholding conditions inferred by the analysis guarantee that fine-grained processes are never spawned.

Note, however, that not spawning fine-grained processes is not always enough to guarantee a speedup (or even a no slowdown) since even the largest parallel machine will eventually saturate!

The exposition is structured as follows. Section 2 outlines the analysis with a worked example. Section 3 presents some preliminary theory. Sections 4 and 5 describe the transformation and the fixpoint calculation that make up the body of the analysis. Section 6 describes how an implementation of the analysis has been used on a parallel machine and sections 7 and 8 present the related and future work. Finally section 9 summarises the work. The paper assumes some familiarity with the s-semantics for CLP [3].

2 Worked example

Consider a time-complexity analysis for the predicate $\mathrm{Qs}/2$ where $d_{min} = 16$. Analysis divides into two stages: a fixpoint calculation that characterises how the time complexity relates to argument sizes; and a post-processing phase that infers conditions for the time complexity of a goal to exceed d_{min} resolution steps. By applying program transformation (abstract compilation [13, 14]) time complexity analysis can be recast as the problem of inferring invariants of a $CLP(\mathcal{R})$ program. Analysis then, in effect, reduces to evaluating the concrete (bottom-up) semantics of the $CLP(\mathcal{R})$ program. The $\mathrm{Qs}/2$ program listed below, for example, is a $CLP(\mathcal{R})$ program that is obtained from $\mathrm{Qs}/2$ by a syntactic transformation in which each term in the first program is replaced by its size with respect to list length. Note, however, that the first argument of each predicate in the $CLP(\mathcal{R})$ (abstract) program corresponds to a counter, d, that records the time-complexity. d is the sum of the resolution steps required to solve the body goals with an increment for the single resolution step implicit in goal-head unification. d is clamped by the constraint $d \leq d_{min}$ to ensure that goals whose time-complexity exceeds d_{min} are not considered in bottom-up evaluation.

All arguments but the first of an abstract predicate define an n-ary tuple of argument sizes. The n-tuple represents the sizes of the n arguments of the corresponding (concrete) predicate. Time-complexity analysis is performed by inferring relationships between the time argument and the size arguments of the n-tuple. Other measures of term size, for instance, term depth, can also be used [10, 19] to generate the abstract program.

```
Qs(d, l, s) <-                      Pt(d, 0, _, 0, 0) <-
    d ≤ 16, d = 1 + d₁,                 d ≤ 16, d = 1.
    Qs(d₁, l, s, 0).                Pt(d, 1 + xs, m, 1 + l, g) <-
                                        d ≤ 16, d = 1 + d₁,
Qs(d, 0, l, l) <- d ≤ 16, d = 1.        Pt(d₁, xs, m, l, g).
Qs(d, 1 + xs, h, t) <-              Pt(d, 1 + xs, m, l, 1 + g) <-
    d ≤ 16, d = 1 + d₁ + d₂ + d₃,        d ≤ 16, d = 1 + d₁,
    Pt(d₁, xs, _, l, g),                Pt(d₁, xs, m, l, g).
    Qs(d₂, l, h, 1 + m),
    Qs(d₃, g, m, t).
```

Suppose that the abstract program is denoted $P^{\mathcal{A}}$. The fixpoint phase of the analysis amounts to computing $T_{Lin,P^{\mathcal{A}}} \uparrow \omega = \cup_{i=0} T_{Lin,P^{\mathcal{A}}} \uparrow i$ where $T_{Lin,P^{\mathcal{A}}}$ is the immediate consequence operator of the s-semantics for CLP instantiated for Herbrand equations and linear inequations [3] and $T_{Lin,P^{\mathcal{A}}} \uparrow i + 1 = T_{Lin,P^{\mathcal{A}}}(T_{Lin,P^{\mathcal{A}}} \uparrow i)$. Each iteration in the fixpoint calculation takes an $T_{Lin,P^{\mathcal{A}}} \uparrow i$, dubbed an interpretation, as input and generates an $T_{Lin,P^{\mathcal{A}}} \uparrow i + 1$, as output. $T_{Lin,P^{\mathcal{A}}} \uparrow 0 = \emptyset$ is the empty interpretation. To compute $T_{Lin,P^{\mathcal{A}}} \uparrow i + 1$, the body atoms of each clause of the program are unified with the atom abstractions in interpretation $T_{Lin,P^{\mathcal{A}}} \uparrow i$. Since $T_{Lin,P^{\mathcal{A}}} \uparrow 0$ is empty, however, $T_{Lin,P^{\mathcal{A}}} \uparrow 1$ will represent only those argument and time-complexity relationships embodied in the clauses of $P^{\mathcal{A}}$ that do not have user-defined body atoms.

$$T_{Lin,P^{\mathcal{A}}} \uparrow 1 = T_{Lin,P^{\mathcal{A}}} \uparrow 0 \cup \{ \texttt{Qs}(1, 0, x_2, x_3) \leftarrow x_2 = x_3. \quad \texttt{Pt}(1, 0, x_2, 0, 0) \leftarrow true. \}$$

The relationships asserts that if a $\texttt{Qs/3}$ goal can be solved in one resolution step, then the first argument must (ultimately) be bound to $[\,]$ and the second and third arguments must (ultimately) be of equal length. Similarly, for the $\texttt{Pt/4}$ goal to solved in one step, the first, third and fourth must be bound to $[\,]$. Since the $\texttt{Pt/4}$ and $\texttt{Qs/2}$ predicates each have only one unit clause, only one abstract atom for $\texttt{Pt/4}$ and $\texttt{Qs/2}$ is included in $T_{Lin,P^{\mathcal{A}}} \uparrow 1$. In calculating $T_{Lin,P^{\mathcal{A}}} \uparrow 2$, however, two abstract atoms are generated from the two recursive clauses of $\texttt{Pt/4}$.

$$\left\{ \begin{array}{ll} \texttt{Qs}(2, 0, 0) \leftarrow true. & \texttt{Pt}(2, 1, x_2, 1, 0) \leftarrow true. \\ \texttt{Qs}(4, 1, x_2, x_3) \leftarrow x_2 = 1 + x_3. & \texttt{Pt}(2, 1, x_2, 0, 1) \leftarrow true. \end{array} \right\}$$

To keep the size of each $T_{Lin,P^{\mathcal{A}}} \uparrow i$ small and manageable, the sets of inequalities for each predicate are collected and approximated by an over-estimate, the convex hull. The convex hull can itself be expressed as a single set of inequalities so that $T_{Lin,P^{\mathcal{A}}} \uparrow i$ needs only to maintain one set of inequalities for each predicate at each depth. For example, to calculate $T_{Lin,P^{\mathcal{A}}} \uparrow 2$ the convex hull is computed for two equation sets that define the argument sizes for $\texttt{Pt/4}$ at depth 2, that is,

$$\text{hull} \left(\left\{ \begin{array}{l} x_1 = 1, x_3 = 1, \\ x_4 = 0 \end{array} \right\}, \left\{ \begin{array}{l} x_1 = 1, x_3 = 0, \\ x_4 = 1 \end{array} \right\} \right) = \left\{ \begin{array}{ll} x_1 = 1, & 0 \le x_3, \\ x_3 \le 1, & x_4 = 1 - x_3 \end{array} \right\}$$

The first equation set $x_1 = 1, x_3 = 1, x_4 = 0$ defines the second, fourth and fifth arguments in the first abstract $\texttt{Pt/5}$ atom whereas $x_1 = 1, x_3 = 0, x_4 = 1$ defines the arguments in the second atom. The two equation sets are over-approximated with a single equation set thereby leading to

$$T_{Lin,P^{\mathcal{A}}} \uparrow 2 = T_{Lin,P^{\mathcal{A}}} \uparrow 1 \cup \left\{ \begin{array}{c} \texttt{Qs}(2, 0, 0) \leftarrow true. \\ \texttt{Qs}(4, 1, x_2, x_3) \leftarrow x_2 = 1 + x_3. \\ \texttt{Pt}(2, 1, x_2, x_3, x_4) \leftarrow 0 \le x_3, x_3 \le 1, x_4 = 1 - x_3. \end{array} \right\}$$

Although the convex hull operation computes an approximation, useful argument size relationships are still preserved since the convex hull corresponds to the smallest convex space enclosing the spaces defined by the sets of inequalities. In the case of $\texttt{Pt/4}$, for example, $T_{Lin,P^{\mathcal{A}}} \uparrow 2$ asserts that if a $\texttt{Pt/4}$ goal can be solved in exactly two resolution steps then the first argument is a list of length one, and the third and fourth arguments are lists of length either zero or one. (Interestingly, the convex hull operation often produces deep and unexpected argument size relationships [2].) The convex hull calculation is used in the ensuing iterates.

$$T_{Lin,P^{\mathcal{A}}} \uparrow 3 = T_{Lin,P^{\mathcal{A}}} \uparrow 2 \cup \left\{ \begin{array}{c} \texttt{Qs}(5, 1, 1) \leftarrow true. \\ \texttt{Qs}(8, 2, x_2, x_3) \leftarrow x_2 = 2 + x_3. \\ \texttt{Pt}(3, 2, x_2, x_3, x_4) \leftarrow 0 \le x_4, x_4 \le 2, x_3 = 2 - x_4. \end{array} \right\}$$

$$\ldots$$

$$T_{Lin,P^{\mathcal{A}}} \uparrow 16 = T_{Lin,P^{\mathcal{A}}} \uparrow 15 \cup \{ \texttt{Pt}(16, 15, x_2, x_3, x_4) \leftarrow 0 \le x_4, x_4 \le 15, x_3 = 15 - x_4 \}$$
$$T_{Lin,P^{\mathcal{A}}} \uparrow 17 = T_{Lin,P^{\mathcal{A}}} \uparrow 16$$

The iteration sequence will always converge within $d_{min} + 1$ iterations because of the $d \leq d_{min}$ constraints and since there are a finite number of clauses in the abstract program. Thus fixpoint termination techniques like widening are not required [4]. To use $T_{Lin,P^A} \uparrow \omega$ to control spawning, however, we want to deduce conditions that guarantee that the time complexity of a goal exceeds d_{min} resolution steps. A bounding box approximation of $T_{Lin,P^A} \uparrow \omega$ makes these conditions explicit.

$$\left\{ \begin{array}{l} \texttt{Qs}(d, x_1, x_2) \leftarrow \\ \quad 0 \leq d, \quad d \leq 14, \quad 0 \leq x_1, \quad x_1 \leq 3, \quad 0 \leq x_2, \quad x_2 \leq 3. \\ \texttt{Qs}(d, x_1, x_2, x_3) \leftarrow \\ \quad 0 \leq d, \quad d \leq 13, \quad 0 \leq x_1, \quad x_1 \leq 3, \quad 0 \leq x_2, \quad x_2 \leq 3. \\ \texttt{Pt}(d, x_1, x_2, x_3, x_4) \leftarrow \\ \quad 0 \leq d, \quad d \leq 16, \quad 0 \leq x_1, \quad x_1 \leq 15, \quad 0 \leq x_3, \quad x_3 \leq 15, \quad 0 \leq x_4, \quad x_4 \leq 15. \end{array} \right\}$$

Note how each argument, including d, is approximated as an interval so that the argument sizes are represented as a box in the space $\mathbf{R}^n$. The abstraction asserts (among other things) that if the time-complexity of a $\texttt{Qs}/2$ goal is less or equal to d_{min} steps, then the first and second arguments must ultimately be bound to lists with a length of less than four. Put another way, if the length of argument is known to be greater or equal to four, then the computation must either exceed d_{min} resolution steps or fail. Possible failure (or equivalently definite non-failure) can be detected with a query-dependent non-failure analysis [8]. Thus if the program is queried with a $\texttt{Qs}/2$ goal where the first argument is known to be a list of integers, say, then non-failure can be deduced [8]. Hence, if the argument is also known to have a length of greater or equal to four, then the goal is guaranteed to lead to a computation that exceeds d_{min} resolution steps.

3 Preliminaries

Syntax of logic programs Let $Func$, $Pred$ and Var respectively denote the set of function symbols, predicate symbols and a denumerable set of variables. The non-ground term algebra over $Funct$ and Var is denoted $Term$, where the set of atoms constructed from the predicate symbols $Pred$ is denoted $Atom$. A goal is a sequence of atoms. A logic program is a finite set of clauses. A clause has the form $h \leftarrow \vec{b}$ where h, the head, is a atom and $\vec{b}$, the body, is a finite sequence of atoms. Also $var(o)$ denotes the set of variables in a syntactic object o, :: denotes concatenation, whereas $\pi_i(.)$ denotes vector projection, that is, $\pi_i(\langle x_1, \ldots, x_n \rangle) = x_i$.

The set of idempotent substitutions from Var to $Term$ is denoted Sub and the set of renamings (which are bijective substitutions) is denoted Ren. A substitution ϕ will sometimes be represented as a finite set of pairs $\phi = \{u_1 \mapsto t_1, \ldots, u_n \mapsto t_n\}$. Sub and Ren extend in the usual way from functions from variables to terms, to functions from terms to terms, to functions from atoms to atoms, and to functions from clauses to clauses. Syntactic objects, o and o', are variants of one another, denoted $o \approx o'$, if there exists $\rho \in Ren$ such that $\rho(o) = o'$. The equivalence class of o under $\approx$ is denoted $[o]_\approx$. The restriction of a substitution ϕ to a set of variables U and the composition of two substitutions ϕ and φ, are denoted by $\phi \upharpoonright U$ and $\phi \circ \varphi$ respectively, and defined such that: $\phi \upharpoonright U = \{u \mapsto t \in \phi \,|\, u \in U\}$ and $(\phi \circ \varphi)(u) = \phi(\varphi(u))$.

An equation is an equality constraint of the form $a = b$ where a and b are terms or atoms. Let Eqn denote the set of finite sets of equations. There is a natural mapping from substitutions to equations, that is, $eqn(\phi) = \{u = t \,|\, u \mapsto t \in \phi\}$, and $mgu(E)$ denotes the set of most general unifiers for an equation set E.

Operational semantics of logic programs An operational semantics is introduced to argue correctness. The semantics is described in terms of a transition system that defines reductions between states. The set of states is defined by $State = Atom^* \times Sub$.

Definition 3.1 Let P be a logic program. The transition system $\langle State, \rightarrow \rangle$ where $\rightarrow \subseteq State \times State$ is the least relation such that

$$s \rightarrow s' \Leftrightarrow \begin{cases} s = \langle \vec{a}, \phi \rangle \quad \wedge \quad h \leftarrow \vec{b} \in P \quad \wedge \quad h \leftarrow \vec{b} \approx h' \leftarrow \vec{b}' \quad \wedge \\ var(h' \leftarrow \vec{b}') \cap var(s) = \emptyset \quad \wedge \quad \varphi = mgu(\{\phi(a_i) = h'\}) \quad \wedge \\ s' = \langle \langle a_1, \ldots, a_{i-1} \rangle :: \vec{b}' :: \langle a_{i+1}, \ldots, a_n \rangle, \varphi \circ \phi \rangle \end{cases}$$

The notion of answer for a goal g are defined in terms of a transition system. Depth corresponds to the number of resolution steps and is used as a measure of computational complexity, that is, if $\langle \vec{a}_1, \phi_1 \rangle \rightarrow \langle \vec{a}_2, \phi_2 \rangle \rightarrow \langle \vec{a}_3, \phi_3 \rangle \ldots$ then $\langle \vec{a}_1, \phi_1 \rangle \rightarrow^d \langle \vec{a}_{1+d}, \phi_{1+d} \rangle$.

Definition 3.2 (answers and partial answers at a depth)

- A goal g has a partial answer g' at depth d iff $\langle g, \epsilon \rangle \rightarrow^d \langle g', \phi \rangle$ and $g' \approx \phi(g)$;

- A goal g has an answer g' at depth d iff $\langle g, \epsilon \rangle \rightarrow^d \langle true, \phi \rangle$ and $g' \approx \phi(g)$.

Fixpoint s-semantics of constraint logic programs The semantics of the abstract program is formalised in terms of the concrete s-style semantics for constraint logic programs [3] and therefore, to make the paper reasonably self-contained, the semantics is summarised below. The semantics is parameterised over a computational domain, C, of constraints. We write $c \models c'$ iff c entails c' and also $c = c'$ iff $c \models c'$ and $c' \models c$. The interpretation base B_C for the language defined by a program P is the set of unit clauses of the form $p(\vec{x}) \leftarrow c$ quotiented by equivalence. Equivalence, again denoted $\approx$, is defined by: $p(\vec{x}) \leftarrow c \approx p(\vec{x'}) \leftarrow c'$ iff $c \upharpoonright var(\vec{x}) = (c' \wedge (\vec{x} = \vec{x'})) \upharpoonright var(\vec{x})$ where $\upharpoonright$ denotes projection. If C is the domain of equations over Herbrand terms, $Herb$ say, then $\approx$ is variance and $\upharpoonright$ is restriction. The fixpoint semantics of a program P is defined in terms of an immediate consequence operator like so: $\mathcal{F}_C[\![P]\!] = lfp(T_{C,P})$.

Definition 3.3 (fixpoint s-semantics for CLP [3]) The immediate consequence operator $T_{C,P} : B_C \rightarrow B_C$ is defined by:

$$T_{C,P}(I) = \left\{ [p(\vec{x}) \leftarrow c']_\approx \left| \begin{matrix} w \in P \quad \wedge \quad w = p(\vec{t}) \leftarrow c, p_1(\vec{t}_1), \ldots, p_n(\vec{t}_n) \quad \wedge \\ [w_i]_\approx \in I \quad \wedge \quad w_i = p_i(\vec{x}_i) \leftarrow c_i \quad \wedge \\ \forall i.var(w) \cap var(w_i) = \emptyset \quad \wedge \quad \forall i \neq j.var(w_i) \cap var(w_j) = \emptyset \quad \wedge \\ c' = \wedge_{i=1}^n (\vec{x}_i = \vec{t}_i \wedge c_i) \wedge (\vec{x} = \vec{t}) \wedge c \quad \wedge \quad c' \text{ is solvable} \end{matrix} \right. \right\}$$

For the abstract programs of the analysis the domain C is Lin, that is, sets of (non-strict) inequalities between linear expressions and equations between Herbrand terms. Thus, for example, $\{f(a) = f(b), x \leq y + z\} \in Lin$.

Fixpoint depth semantics for logic programs Correctness of the analysis is argued in terms of the depth semantics of [1] since, although it was originally devised to reason about termination, the semantics also expresses a natural notion of complexity. Again, to keep the paper self-contained, we briefly summarise the relevant aspects of the depth semantics [1]. The interpretation base, denoted B_{Time} for clarity, is the set of depth and clause pairs where clauses are quotiented by variance, that is, $\langle d, [h \leftarrow \vec{b}]_\approx \rangle$. Informally, the pair $\langle d, [h \leftarrow \vec{b}]_\approx \rangle$

represents a partial (incomplete) computation from the atomic goal h to the goal $\vec{b}$ in d steps. Empty partial computations correspond to the set $\Phi_P = \{\langle 0, [p(\vec{x}) \leftarrow p(\vec{x})]_\approx\rangle \mid p \in Pred\}$ [1]. The set of partial answers for a depth d can be characterised with another immediate consequence operator $T_{Time,P}$.

Definition 3.4 (fixpoint clausal semantics with depth [1]) The immediate consequence operator $T_{Time,P} : B_{Time} \rightarrow B_{Time}$ is defined by:

$$T_{Time,P}(I) =$$

$$\left\{ \langle d, [\varphi(h \leftarrow \vec{b_1} :: \ldots :: \vec{b_n})]_\approx\rangle \;\middle|\; \begin{array}{ll} w \in P & \wedge \; w = h \leftarrow \vec{b} \quad \wedge \\ \langle d_i, [w_i]_\approx\rangle \in I \cup \Phi_P \wedge w_i = h_i \leftarrow \vec{b_i} \wedge \\ \forall i.var(w) \cap var(w_i) = \emptyset & \wedge \\ \forall i \neq j.var(w_i) \cap var(w_j) = \emptyset & \wedge \\ d = 1 + \sum_{i=1}^n d_i & \wedge \\ \varphi = mgu(\{\vec{b} = \langle h_1, \ldots, h_n\rangle\}) & \end{array} \right\}$$

$T_{Time,P}$ is continuous and defines the fixpoint semantics of a program P like so $\mathcal{F}_{Time}[\![P]\!]$ $= lfp(T_{Time,P})$. $\mathcal{F}_{Time}[\![P]\!]$ is consistent with $\mathcal{F}_{Herb}[\![P]\!]$ in that $\mathcal{F}_{Herb}[\![P]\!] = \{[h]_\approx \mid \langle d, [h \leftarrow true]_\approx\rangle \in \mathcal{F}_{Time}[\![P]\!]\}$ [1]. The following theorem, adapted from [1], formally asserts the relationship between partial answers and the fixpoint semantics.

Theorem 3.1 Let P be a logic program. A goal g is a partial answer at depth d for g' iff there exists $\langle d_i, [h_i \leftarrow true]_\approx\rangle \in \mathcal{F}_{Time}[\![P]\!]$ such that $\forall i.var(h_i) \cap var(g') = \emptyset$ and $\forall i \neq j.var(h_i) \cap var(h_j) = \emptyset$, $\varphi = mgu(\{g' = \vec{h}\})$, $g \approx \varphi(g')$ and $d = \sum_{i=1} d_i$.

4 Abstract compilation

By applying program transformation (abstract compilation [13, 14]) the problem of inferring how time complexity depends on argument size is recast as the problem of inferring the invariants of a CLP($\mathcal{R}$) program. Our transformation is dubbed α. Size, as usual [10, 19], is expressed in terms of norms that map terms to (possibly non-ground) constraint in Lin. In the case of the list length norm [22, 19], for example, $\|[]\|_{leng} = 0$, $\|[x]\|_{leng} = 1$ and $\|[x|y]\|_{leng} = 1 + y$. In addition, to ensure that the norm is always defined, if t cannot be instantiated to a list we define $\|t\|_{leng} = z$ where z is a free (fresh) variable.

Definition 4.1 (program abstraction α)

$$\alpha[\![w_1, \ldots, w_m]\!] =$$
$$\alpha_{clause}[\![w_1]\!], \ldots, \alpha_{clause}[\![w_m]\!]$$

$$\alpha_{clause}[\![p(\vec{t}) \leftarrow p_1(\vec{t_1}), \ldots, p_m(\vec{t_m})]\!] =$$
$$\left\{ \begin{array}{l} p(d :: \vec{x}) \leftarrow \\ \quad d \leq d_{min}, d = 1 + \sum_{i=1}^m d_i, \\ \quad \alpha_{eqns}[\![eqn(mgu(\vec{x} = \vec{t} \wedge \vec{x_1} = \vec{t_1} \wedge \ldots \wedge \vec{x_m} = \vec{t_m}))]\!], \\ \quad p_1(d_1 :: \vec{x_1}), \ldots, p_m(d_m :: \vec{x_m}) \end{array} \right.$$

$$\alpha_{eqns}[\![e_1, \ldots, e_m]\!] =$$
$$\alpha_{eqn}[\![e_1]\!], \ldots, \alpha_{eqn}[\![e_m]\!]$$

$$\alpha_{eqn}[\![x = t]\!] =$$
$$\left\{ \begin{array}{l} x = \vec{y}, \\ \quad x_1 = \vec{y_1}, \ldots, x_m = \vec{y_m}, \\ \quad \|\phi_1(x)\|_1 = \|\phi_1(t)\|_1, \ldots, \|\phi_n(x)\|_n = \|\phi_n(t)\|_n \end{array} \right.$$

where w_i and e_i respectively denote a clause and an equation, $var(t) = \{x_1, \ldots, x_m\}$, $\phi_i = \{x \mapsto \pi_i(\vec{y}), x_1 \mapsto \pi_i(\vec{y_1}), \ldots, x_m \mapsto \pi_i(\vec{y_m})\}$ and the variables d, d_i and vectors of variables $\vec{x}$, $\vec{x_i}$, $\vec{y}$ and $\vec{y_i}$ are fresh and distinct. The arities of $\vec{y}$ and $\vec{y_i}$ are both n.

Note that the transform is parameterised by the machine dependent granularity constant d_{min} and the n norms $\|\cdot\|_1, \ldots, \|\cdot\|_n$. Multiple norms are useful when a unique norm cannot be matched to an argument position, for example, because of a lack of type declarations or because a type analysis is imprecise. The worked example corresponds to a (simplified) special case for when $n = 1$ and $\|\cdot\|_1 = \|\cdot\|_{\text{leng}}$. Abstracting equations, α_{eqn}, is the most subtle part of the program abstraction α and so example 4.1 illustrates how α_{eqn} is applied.

Example 4.1 Consider $\alpha_{\text{eqn}}[\![x = [x_1|x_2]]\!]$ when $n = 2$ and in particular $\|\cdot\|_1 = \|\cdot\|_{\text{leng}}$. and $\|\cdot\|_2 = \|\cdot\|_{\text{size}}$ where $\|\cdot\|_{\text{size}}$ counts the number of function symbols in a term. If $\vec{y} = \langle y_1, y_2 \rangle$, $\vec{y_1} = \langle y_{1,1}, y_{1,2} \rangle$ and $\vec{y_2} = \langle y_{2,1}, y_{2,2} \rangle$ then $\phi_1 = \{x \mapsto y_1, x_1 \mapsto y_{1,1}, x_2 \mapsto y_{2,1}\}$ and similarly $\phi_2 = \{x \mapsto y_2, x_1 \mapsto y_{1,2}, x_2 \mapsto y_{2,2}\}$ so that $(\|\phi_1(x)\|_1 = \|\phi_1([x_1|x_2])\|_1)$ $= (\|y_1\|_{\text{leng}} = \|[y_{1,1}|y_{2,1}]\|_{\text{leng}}) = (y_1 = 1 + y_{2,1})$ and $(\|\phi_2(x)\|_2 = \|\phi_2([x_1|x_2])\|_2) =$ $(\|y_2\|_{\text{size}} = \|[y_{1,2}|y_{2,2}]\|_{\text{size}}) = (y_2 = 1 + y_{1,2} + y_{2,2})$. Hence

$$\alpha_{\text{eqn}}[\![x = [x_1|x_2]]\!] = \left\{ \begin{array}{lll} x = \langle y_1, y_2 \rangle, & x_1 = \langle y_{1,1}, y_{1,2} \rangle, & x_2 = \langle y_{2,1}, y_{2,2} \rangle, \\ y_1 = 1 + y_{2,1}, & y_2 = 1 + y_{1,2} + y_{2,2} \end{array} \right\}$$

In practise, the abstract programs generated by α tend to include equations that can be eliminated, combined or simplified. Since the clauses of $\alpha[\![P]\!]$ are used repeatedly to compute a fixpoint, we have found it beneficial to simplify $\alpha[\![P]\!]$ in a partial evaluation (local simplification) phase that precedes the fixpoint calculation.

Example 4.2 Consider the `Leng/2` predicate, listed in the left-hand column, which computes the length of a list. Its (partially evaluated) abstract program is listed in the right-hand column. The two norms are $\|\cdot\|_{leng}$ and $\|\cdot\|_{num}$ where the latter gives the numeric value of an integer. By using both norms together useful time complexity can often be inferred even in an absence of type information [10, 19]. Our prototype analyser, for example, does not perform type analysis and simply measures size with a set of pre-defined norms.

```
Leng([], 0).                 Leng(1, ⟨0,_⟩, ⟨_,0⟩).
Leng([_ | ys], l) <-         Leng(d, ⟨z_1,_⟩, ⟨_,z_2⟩) <-
  Leng(ys, ls),                d ≤ d_min, d = 2+d_1, z_1 = 1+z_3, z_2 = 1+z_4,
  l = ls + 1.                  Leng(d_1, ⟨z_3,_⟩, ⟨_,z_4⟩).
```

Note that the depth equation $d = 2 + d_1$ reflects the presence of the builtin $=/2$ in the clause. Each builtin requires one addition resolution step. The partial evaluation phase has applied the equations to the head and body of the clause to reduce the numbers of equations that have to be solved at analysis time. This explains, for example, why the arguments of the heads are not variables.

To formalise the relationship between a concrete program and its abstract program, the concretisation mapping is introduced.

Definition 4.2 (γ) Concretisation $\gamma : \wp(B_{Lin}) \to \wp(B_{Time})$ is defined by:

$$\gamma(I) = \left\{ \langle d, [p(\vec{t})]_{\approx} \rangle \;\middle|\; \begin{array}{l} [p(x' :: \vec{x}) \leftarrow c \wedge (\wedge_{i=1} \pi_i(\vec{x}) = \vec{y_i})]_{\approx} \in I \quad \wedge \\ x' = d \wedge (\wedge_{i=1} \wedge_{j=1}^n \pi_j(\vec{y_i}) = \|t_i\|_j) \models c \end{array} \right\}$$

Example 4.3 Suppose $n = 2$ where $\|.\|_1 = \|.\|_{\text{leng}}$ and $\|.\|_2 = \|.\|_{\text{num}}$. If $c = (x' = y_{1,1} + 1) \wedge (x_1 = \langle y_{1,1}, y_{1,2} \rangle) \wedge (y_{2,2} = y_{1,1}) \wedge (x_2 = \langle y_{2,1}, y_{2,2} \rangle)$ then

$$\gamma(\{[\text{Leng}(x', x_1, x_2) \leftarrow c]_{\approx}\}) =$$
$$\{\langle d, [\text{Leng}(t_1, t_2)]_{\approx} \rangle \mid d = |t_1|_{\text{leng}} + 1 \wedge |t_2|_{\text{num}} = |t_1|_{\text{leng}}\}$$

The concretisation mapping is used to link $\mathcal{F}_{Time}[\![P]\!]$ with $\mathcal{F}_{Lin}[\![\alpha[P]\!]]$ in the following safety theorem. The theorem explains how the abstract program can be used to characterise the time behaviour of the concrete program.

Theorem 4.1 (safety I)

$$\{\langle d, [h \leftarrow true]_{\approx}\rangle \in \mathcal{F}_{Time}[\![P]\!] \mid d \leq d_{min}\} \subseteq \gamma(\mathcal{F}_{Lin}[\![\alpha[P]\!]])$$

Because each clause in the abstract program includes the constraint $d \leq d_{min}$, $\mathcal{F}_{Lin}[\![\alpha[P]\!]]$ can be finitely computed within $d_{min} + 1$ iterations. Thus termination techniques, like widening [4], are not required to induce iteration. Finally, the corollary relates $\mathcal{F}_{Lin}[\![\alpha[P]\!]]$ to the operational semantics.

Corollary 4.1 (safety II) Let P be a logic program. If an atomic goal g had an answer g' at depth d then there exists $\langle d, [h \leftarrow true]_{\approx}\rangle \in \gamma(\mathcal{F}_{Lin}[\![\alpha[P]\!]])$ such that $var(h) \cap var(g) = \emptyset$, $\varphi = mgu(\{g = h\})$ and $g' \approx \varphi(g)$.

5 Fixpoint computation

Although $\mathcal{F}_{Lin}[\![\alpha[P]\!]]$ can always be computed within $d_{min} + 1$ iterations, the number of atoms in an interpretation (iterate) can become large. Thus, to constrain the growth of interpretations, the sets of inequalities for each predicate are collected together and approximated by their convex hull. To be more precise, the convex hull is used to over-approximate the argument sizes for atoms at the same depth.

Example 5.1 Returning to the worked example, recall that the convex hull operation collapses together the constraints for the two argument relationships for depth 2

$$\text{hull}\left(\left\{\begin{matrix} [\text{Pt}(x' :: \vec{x}) \leftarrow x' = 1, x_1 = 0, x_3 = 0, x_4 = 0]_{\approx} \\ [\text{Pt}(x' :: \vec{x}) \leftarrow x' = 2, x_1 = 1, x_3 = 1, x_4 = 0]_{\approx} \\ [\text{Pt}(x' :: \vec{x}) \leftarrow x' = 2, x_1 = 1, x_3 = 0, x_4 = 1]_{\approx} \end{matrix}\right\}\right) =$$
$$\left\{\begin{matrix} [\text{Pt}(x' :: \vec{x}) \leftarrow x' = 1, x_1 = 0, x_3 = 0, x_4 = 0]_{\approx} \\ [\text{Pt}(x' :: \vec{x}) \leftarrow x' = 2, x_1 = 1, 0 \leq x_3, x_3 \leq 1, x_4 = 1 - x_3]_{\approx} \end{matrix}\right\}$$

The hull operator is defined in terms of convex hull operation on sets of constraint sets.

Definition 5.1 (hull) The approximation operator hull : $B_{Lin} \rightarrow B_{Lin}$ is defined by:

$$\text{hull}(I) = \{[p(x' :: \vec{x}) \leftarrow c_{p,n}]_{\approx} \mid p \in Pred \wedge n \in \mathbf{N}\}$$

where $c_{p,n} = \text{hull}_{var(x' :: \vec{x})}(\{c \restriction var(x' :: \vec{x}) \mid [p(x' :: \vec{x}) \leftarrow c]_{\approx} \in I \wedge c \models (x' = n)\})$, $\text{hull}_X(\emptyset) = false$ and $\text{hull}_X(\{c_1, \ldots, c_n\}) = \text{hull}_X(c_1, \text{hull}_X(\{c_2, \ldots, c_n\}))$.

The binary hull_X can be computed straightforwardly with a relaxation adapted from disjunctive constraint logic programming [5]. For simplicity, consider calculating

$\text{hull}_{var(\vec{x})}(c_1, c_2)$ where $\vec{x}$ is an n-ary vector and the constraints c_i are represented in standard form $A_i \vec{x} \leq \vec{b_i}$, where A_i is an $m \times n$ matrix and $\vec{b_i}$ in an m-ary vector. The convex hull of the spaces defined by c_1 and c_2 can be computed by:

$$\left\{ \begin{array}{c} \vec{x} = \vec{x_1} + \vec{x_2} \ \wedge \ \sigma_1 + \sigma_2 = 1 \ \wedge \\ A_1 \vec{x_1} \leq \sigma_1 \vec{b_1} \ \wedge \ A_2 \vec{x_2} \leq \sigma_2 \vec{b_2} \ \wedge \\ -\sigma_1 \leq 0 \quad \wedge \quad -\sigma_2 \leq 0 \end{array} \right\} \upharpoonright var(\vec{x})$$

Since the system of inequations is linear, the convex hull can be calculated by simply imposing the equations on the store of a constraint language and then applying projection [2].

Example 5.2 Continuing with example 5.1, combining the $x_1 = 1, x_3 = 1, x_4 = 0$ and $x_1 = 1, x_3 = 0, x_4 = 1$ equations for the $\mathtt{Pt/5}$ atoms amounts to solving:

$$\left\{ \begin{array}{c} \vec{x} = \vec{x_1} + \vec{x_2} \qquad\qquad \wedge \qquad\qquad \sigma_1 + \sigma_2 = 1 \qquad\qquad \wedge \\ \begin{bmatrix} 1,0, & 0, & 0 \\ -1,0, & 0, & 0 \\ 0,0, & 1, & 0 \\ 0,0, & -1, & 0 \\ 0,0, & 0, & 1 \\ 0,0, & 0, & -1 \end{bmatrix} \vec{x_1} \leq \sigma_1 \begin{bmatrix} 1 \\ -1 \\ 1 \\ -1 \\ 0 \\ 0 \end{bmatrix} \wedge \begin{bmatrix} 1,0, & 0, & 0 \\ -1,0, & 0, & 0 \\ 0,0, & 1, & 0 \\ 0,0, & -1, & 0 \\ 0,0, & 0, & 1 \\ 0,0, & 0, & -1 \end{bmatrix} \vec{x_2} \leq \sigma_2 \begin{bmatrix} 1 \\ -1 \\ 0 \\ 0 \\ 1 \\ -1 \end{bmatrix} \wedge \\ -\sigma_1 \leq 0 \qquad \wedge \qquad -\sigma_2 \leq 0 \end{array} \right\} \upharpoonright var(\vec{x})$$
$$= \{ \ x_1 = 1, 0 \leq x_3, x_3 \leq 1, x_4 = 1 - x_3 \ \}$$

The post-processing phase of the analysis boils down to computing a bounding box abstraction for the fixpoint that defines the maximum and minimum sizes of the arguments that can occur for goals with a complexity between 1 and d_{min} resolution steps. The bounding box approximation is the obvious lifting of a bounding box operator on sets of constraint sets to interpretations.

Definition 5.2 (box) The approximation operator $box : B_{Lin} \to B_{Lin}$ is defined by:

$$box(I) = \{[p(\vec{x}) \leftarrow c_p]_{\approx} \, | \, p \in Pred\}$$
$$\text{where } c_p = box_{var(\vec{x})}(\{c \upharpoonright var(\vec{x}) \, | \, [p(\vec{x}) \leftarrow c]_{\approx} \in I\})$$

As with the convex hull, $box_X(\emptyset) = false$. There are several ways of calculating box_X. One tactic that can be coded very simply in a constraint language offering projection and an entailment check is to use $box_{var(\vec{x})}(c, c') = \wedge_{i=1} (\{e \, | \, e \in c \upharpoonright var(\pi_i(\vec{x})) \wedge c' \models e\} \cup \{e' \, | \, e' \in c' \upharpoonright var(\pi_i(\vec{x})) \wedge c \models e'\})$. Note that c and c' are themselves regarded as sets of inequations e and e'. The final safety theorem states that the convex hull and bounding box approximations do not compromise safety. When combined with the earlier safety results, the theorem gives an efficient way of characterising fine-grained goals.

Theorem 5.1 (safety III)

$$\gamma(\mathcal{F}_{Lin}[\![P^{\mathcal{A}}]\!]) \subseteq \gamma(box(hull(T_{Lin, P^{\mathcal{A}}}) \uparrow \omega))$$

Thresholding tests can then be inferred to test whether the input arguments of a goal permit the goal to be a member of $\gamma(box(hull(T_{Lin, P^{\mathcal{A}}}) \uparrow \omega))$ and therefore possibly a member of $\{\langle d, [h \leftarrow true]_{\approx}\rangle \in \mathcal{F}_{Time}[\![P]\!] \, | \, d \leq d_{min}\}$. If not, then the goal must either lead to a computation that exceeds d_{min} steps or the goal must eventually fail. Input arguments can be deduced with mode analysis whereas the non-failing goals can be detected by non-failure analysis [8]. Thus the program can be annotated with granularity thresholding tests that ensure that goals are only spawned when their granularity is guaranteed to exceed d_{min}.

6   Experimental results

The purpose of the experiment presented here is to study the effect of different granularity sizes has on many programs, under different configurations of queries, and number of processors used to run the program. The analysis was implemented in SICStus Prolog, and used to infer thresholding tests for grains sizes of 16, 64, 256 and 1024 resolution steps for the Fibonacci, Hanoi and quicksort programs. $Fib(n, f)$ calculates the n'th Fibonacci number f; $Hanoi(n, l)$ computes a list of moves, l, for n disks in the towers of Hanoi problem; and $Qsort(l, s)$ quicksorts a random list l of length n to give s. Hanoi and Fibonacci are good candidates for granularity control since the parallelism is fine-grained whereas quicksort is less predictable generating both fine-grained and course-grained processes. The programs were hand annotated with the thresholding tests, and then timings where taken on a Sequent Symmetry for 1, 2, 4 and 9 processors. We have used similar benchmark programs to [12], and the same 20MHz 80386 processor Sequent. The and-parallel Prolog system DASWAM [20] was used. The programs used were limited to independent and-parallelism, because suspension complicates the granularity question for general dependent and-parallelism. The programs were executed with different queries, which affected the execution times of the program, but not the relationship between threshold and grain-sizes.

#	none	16	64	256	1024
			fib(17), 1108.1±0.3		
1	1702.9±1.4	1688.2±4.4	1338.0±4.5	1177.1±1.4	1139.3±0.9
2	862.4±5.6 (1.97×)	848.8±4.0 (1.99×)	670.1±1.8 (2.00×)	589.9±1.4 (2.00×)	583.8±12.3 (1.95×)
4	440.2±1.6 (3.87×)	429.6±1.1 (3.92×)	341.1±1.1 (3.92×)	300.5±2.1 (3.92×)	331.1±0.2 (3.44×)
9	203.4±1.2 (8.37×)	201.0±3.4 (8.40×)	156.9±0.2 (8.53×)	140.5±0.2 (8.38×)	167.9±1.0 (6.79×)
			fib(19), 2898.5±0.4		
1	4470.8±1.9	5048.4±0.2	3476.1±3.3	3040.4±3.0	2949.2±1.1
2	2257.5±7.1 (1.98×)	2544.4±4.3 (1.98×)	1761.1±1.9 (1.97×)	1536.9±1.3 (1.98×)	1483.2±0.2 (1.99×)
4	1140.0±4.6 (3.92×)	1277.9±1.8 (3.95×)	882.1±1.7 (3.94×)	775.9±2.0 (3.92×)	766.2±6.5 (3.85×)
9	516.5±1.0 (8.66×)	577.8±2.0 (8.74×)	398.8±17.0 (8.72×)	351.4±2.5 (8.65×)	365.4±6.2 (8.07×)
			hanoi(10), 441.7±0.3		
1	727.0±4.0	522.0±2.6	466.3±1.4	454.5±0.4	453.1±0.1
2	363.1±2.0 (2.00×)	260.2±0.1 (2.01×)	230.9±0.2 (2.02×)	224.4±0.6 (2.02×)	223.1±0.1 (2.03×)
4	185.7±2.3 (3.92×)	132.1±0.2 (3.95×)	117.4±0.3 (3.97×)	114.5±0.4 (3.97×)	223.4±0.8 (2.03×)
9	87.8±1.1 (8.28×)	63.9±0.4 (8.17×)	60.6±0.3 (7.69×)	59.5±0.1 (7.63×)	224.2±1.9 (2.02×)
			hanoi(16), 28061.6±11.6		
1	46509.5±60.8	33054.6±11.5	29391.0±12.8	28656.4±14.8	28323.3±4.8
2	23210.6±138.1 (2.00×)	16522.3±2.7 (2.00×)	14730.9±4.2 (2.00×)	14273.7±3.4 (2.01×)	14322.9±16.5 (1.98×)
4	11594.8±15.3 (4.01×)	8265.5±9.8 (4.00×)	7376.2±4.5 (3.98×)	7147.9±2.7 (4.01×)	7092.9±4.3 (3.99×)
9	5209.6±14.5 (8.93×)	3694.6±3.4 (8.95×)	3287.6±2.1 (8.94×)	3191.9±2.4 (8.98×)	3298.3±2.8 (8.59×)
			qsort(300), 816.8±1.5		
1	909.5±0.1	912.6±2.9	888.9±2.3		
2	509.7±0.6 (1.78×)	512.7±3.2 (1.78×)	498.5±0.7 (1.78×)		
4	330.6±11.8 (2.75×)	334.2±9.0 (2.73×)	332.3±17.8 (2.68×)		
9	272.1±0.6 (3.34×)	274.8±0.9 (3.32×)	278.0±0.8 (3.20×)		
			qsort(3200), 12239.1±3.1		
1	13474.8±29.9	14083.9±3.2	13197.2±2.4		
2	7452.1±3.5 (1.81×)	7701.4±3.2 (1.83×)	7337.8±1.4 (1.80×)		
4	4822.6±9.8 (2.79×)	4925.5±26.5 (2.86×)	4771.9±19.9 (2.77×)		
9	3724.0±10.1 (3.62×)	3766.6±29.8 (3.74×)	3741.6±4.7 (3.53×)		

The table summarises our results. Timings, in milliseconds, were averaged over five runs and are given with the standard deviation. Entries are not given for quicksort for grain sizes of 256 and 1024 because the prototype analyser cannot infer the thresholds within a minute and, we believe that for an optimisation to be practical, it should be reasonably fast. The problem stems from the repeated computations in the fixpoint calculation. We believe that this overhead can be removed by considering the strongly connected components of the call graph of the program. More usually, thresholds can be inferred within a minute even for the larger grain sizes for the benchmark3.tar.Z programs obtained from UPM Madrid.

The execution time for DASWAM running in sequential mode is given in the headings. The results confirm those of [12], showing that granularity control is useful even for a Sequent Symmetry which has relatively low task creation overheads. The results show, as expected, that controlling the granularity has two main effects:

- It reduces the total execution time for the program by reducing the frequency of parallel execution and thus parallel overheads. The larger the granularity threshold, the smaller the parallel overhead. The limit is the sequential case, with no parallel overhead at all.

- It reduces the amount of available parallelism. The larger the granularity threshold, the lesser the available parallelism.

Reducing the parallel overhead tends to improve the total amount of computation (work and overhead), but at the same time, it reduces parallelism. These two factors need to be balanced to give the best results. For any program, the best granularity size can be affected by the particular query being solved and the number of workers the system is using. In addition, the best size changes from program to program, and we also expect it to change from system to system. For some programs, such as quicksort, the overhead of testing for the threshold can be sufficiently expensive so that it actually degrades performance instead of improving it. Thus what is best for one configuration is not necessarily best for another.

It may be possible to take some of these factors into account (such as the type of threshold test being performed), but some factors cannot be controlled, such as what query the user want to solve, and to a lesser extent, how many workers the user choose to use. Thus, a compromise threshold has to be chosen that works well (but not best) for a range of configurations. Looking at the results in general, if the grain size is set too high, say 1024 resolution steps, then the granularity control mechanism limits the parallelism to the extent that the processors are not properly utilised. hanoi(10) on 9 processors is one extreme example. Conversely, if the grain size is set too low, say 16 resolution steps, then the cost of the threshold check is not repaid by reduced task creation, so the overall performance is worse with granularity control than without. The grain size should thus balance machine utilisation against reduced task creation overheads. For the Sequent and the programs that we have analysed and tested, grain sizes of around 64 resolution steps seem to give consistently good results for our granularity control scheme. Moreover, since the Sequent has low task creation overheads, a granularity control scheme is also likely to be useful (and perhaps even more useful) on a more coarse-grained multiprocessor such as a loosely-coupled system.

7 Related work

Imperative programming Cousot and Halbwachs [4] mention how extra counters can be added to loops and how polyhedral abstractions might be used to infer bounds for the number of iterations of a loop. The link with time-complexity analysis is not reported.

Functional programming Most similar to our work is that of Huelsbergen, Larus and Aiken [15] in the context of parallel functional programming. The analysis reported in [15], like ours, is based on an abstract semantics that calculates lower bounds on the time complexity by instrumenting the semantics with counters. Termination, again, is not an issue since the depth of computations is bounded. Coincidently, a granularity control experiment is reported for quicksort, coded in SML, on an eight processor Sequent Symmetry. Our work adds weight to theirs since Huelsbergen *et al.* conclude that with lower bound time complexity analysis "large reductions (> 20%) in execution time" are possible. Interestingly, the thresholds used in the experiment do not seem to be derived automatically [15]. Our experiments suggest that this is because non-trivial thresholds cannot be derived without convex hull approximations. Convex hull approximations are, in fact, essential if the analysis is to be collapsed into something manageable. Furthermore, we have shown how an analysis for logic programs can be formulated elegantly as abstract compilation, established correctness, and shown how it can be implemented straightforwardly in a language with constraint support.

Logic programming Time-complexity analyses [6, 7] for logic programs have tended to cast the problem of inferring argument relationships in terms of solving difference equations. The analyses focus on deriving upper bound time complexity expressions like, for example $1 + \frac{l(l+5)}{2}$, for quicksort. Mode analysis is first applied to trace the input and output arguments of a clause and derive a data dependency graph for the clause literals. Prototype difference equations are then extracted from the recursive clauses, boundary conditions derived from the non-recursive clauses, and finally a difference equation is solved to yield a closed-form time-complexity expression. Although, the difference equation method is potentially useful, it requires sophisticated machinery just to manipulate and solve the equations. By way of contrast, our approach is formulated in terms of linear constraints. Also, divide and conquer algorithms can be particularly difficult to reason about with difference equations requiring special techniques [9, 18]. Moreover, additive argument size relationships, like $x_1 = x_3 + x_4$ for Pt/4, cannot be expressed [18]. On the other hand, the efficiency of the difference equation approach does not depend on the grain size whereas our approach may well become inefficient for coarse-grained systems, like multi-processor farms, that may require a very high granularity threshold.

A lower-bound time-complexity calculation for Fib/2 is sketched in [12]. Difference equations are used to derive a non-trivial time complexity expression but what is not clear is the extent to which the method can be automated. The paper also discusses the cost analysis for or-parallelism, and reports some granularity control experiments. The authors justify granularity analysis by demonstrating that it is possible to obtain improved performance on a fixed configuration of four processors for different grain sizes [16]. The question of variations with different program sizes and range of number of processors and programs, does not seem to have been considered. For a configuration of four processors Sequent, a threshold test of n > 15 (which corresponds to ≫ 4096 resolution steps if builtins are assumed to have a non-zero cost) was found to be useful for solving the query Fib(19, f). Our experiments have found that although the threshold is close to ideal for Fib(19, f) on four processors, it gives practically no parallelism for Fib(17, f) and severely limits parallelism for Fib(19, f) on more than four processors. Our work suggests that (for DASWAM at least) a much lower threshold is necessary if granularity control is to be useful across a range of processors numbers and goal sizes, and that these thresholds can be inferred automatically. The lower-bound time-complexity work of [12] is further developed in [9] which develops some special tactics for reasoning about divide-and-conquer algorithms. The methodology can infer a useful lower bound of $4n + 1$ for quicksort (where n is the length of the first argument). It is not yet clear whether or not our method can improve on this degree of precision.

A technique for reducing the cost of calculating term size is proposed in [17]. The technique is based on finding predicates which are called before a term size test and which traverses the terms whose size need to be determined. As we basically use the same annotation methods as [12], we expect this technique to be applicable to our work.

Very recently, Gallagher and Lafave [11] have shown abstract programs can instrumented with trace terms that abstract the shape of the computation to derive control flow information for program specialisation. The depth counter, d, is another way to abstract the shape of the computation.

8 Future work

The prototype analyser cannot (yet) infer thresholds for coarse grained loosely coupled systems very quickly and future work is required on the implementation to make the approach fast and efficient. Furthermore, integration with a norm derivation analysis [10] and a non-failure analysis is required [8]. Orders of magnitude speedup are possible, however, by carefully limiting the size of the interpretation. The tradeoff is between speed and safety. This unusual tradeoff is possible since, when used for granularity control, the analysis does not affect program correctness only program efficiency. All that matters is that the threshold is reasonably precise. Future work will examine how limiting the enumeration impacts on precision and analysis time. This is likely to be a study within itself. We also suspect that computation size alone may not be the best metric to use for controlling granularity, and we intend to research into other metrics. Finally, we shall also investigate how the method can be adapted to infer closed-form time-complexity expressions.

9 Summary

An analysis has been presented for inferring size conditions on goals that, when satisfied, ensure that a goal is sufficiently coarse-grained to warrant parallel evaluation. The analysis is precise enough to infer useful thresholding conditions even for a number of problematic divide-and-conquer programs, can be implemented straightforwardly in a language with constraint support, and, finally, has been proved correct.

Acknowledgements

Thanks are due to Nai-Wei Lin, Jon Martin and Andy Verden for stimulating discussions that motivated the investigation; Pedro López García for his comments and suggestions; Manuel Hermenegildo and Vítor Santos Costa for hosting some of the work; and Mats Carlsson and Christian Holzbaur for their invaluable help with SICStus.

References

[1] R. Barbuti, M. Codish, R. Giacobazzi, and M. Maher. Oracle Semantics for Prolog. *Information and Computation*, 22(2):178–200.

[2] F. Benoy and A. King. Inferring Argument Size Relationships with CLP($\mathcal{R}$). In *LOPSTR'96*. Springer-Verlag, 1996.

[3] A. Bossi, M. Gabbrielli, G. Levi, and M. Martelli. The s-semantics approach: theory and applications. *Journal of Logic Programming*, 1991.

[4] P. Cousot and N. Halbwachs. Automatic discovery of linear restraints among variables of a program. In *POPL'78*, pages 84–97, 1978.

[5] B. De Backer and H. Beringer. A CLP language handling disjunctions of linear constraints. In *ICLP'93*, pages 550–563. MIT Press, 1993.

[6] S. Debray and N.-W. Lin. Cost Analysis for Logic Programs. *ACM TOPLAS*, July 1992.

[7] S. Debray, N.-W. Lin, and M. Hermenegildo. Task Granularity Analysis in Logic Programs. In *PLDI'90*, White Plains, New York, 1990. ACM.

[8] S. Debray, P. López García, and M. Hermenegildo. Non-Failure Analysis of Logic Programs. In *ICLP'97*. MIT Press, 1997.

[9] S. Debray, P. López García, M. Hermenegildo, and N. Lin. Lower Bound Cost Estimation for Logic Programs. Technical Report TR Number CLIP20/95.0, T.U. of Madrid (UPM), Facultad Informática UPM, 28660-Boadilla del Monte, Madrid-Spain, 1995.

[10] S. Decorte, D. De Schreye, and M. Fabris. Automatic Inference of Norms: A Missing Link in Termination Analysis. In *ICLP'93*, pages 420–436. MIT Press, 1993.

[11] J. Gallagher and L. Lafave. Regular Approximation of Computational Paths in Logic and Functional Languages. In *Partial Evaluation*, pages 115–136. Springer-Verlag, 1996.

[12] P. López García, M. Hermenegildo, and S.K. Debray. A Methodology for Granularity Based Control of Parallelism in Logic Programs. *Journal of Symbolic Computing*, 11(3–4):217–242, 1996.

[13] R. Giacobazzi, S. K. Debray, and G. Levi. Generalized Semantics and Abstract Interpretation for Constraint Logic Programs. *Journal of Logic Programming*, 3(25):191–248, 1995.

[14] M. Hermenegildo, R. Warren, and S. K. Debray. Global Flow Analysis as a Practical Compilation Tool. *JLP*, 13(4):349–366, 1992.

[15] L. Huelsbergen, J. R. Larus, and A. Aiken. Using the Run-Time Sizes of Data Structures to Guide Parallel-Thread Creation. In *LFP'94*. ACM Press, 1994.

[16] P. López García. Personal communication on granularity control for &-Prolog with a Sequent. December 1996.

[17] P. López García and M. Hermenegildo. Efficient Term Size Computation for Granularity Control. In *ICLP'95*, pages 647–661. MIT Press, 1995.

[18] P. López García and N.-W. Lin. E-mail exchanges on argument size analysis and time complexity analysis of divide and conquer algorithms. September 1996.

[19] J. Martin, A. King, and P. Soper. Typed Norms for Typed Logic Programs. In *LOPSTR'96*. Springer-Verlag, 1996.

[20] K. Shen. Overview of DASWAM: Exploitation of Dependent And-parallelism. *JLP*, 29(1–3), 1996.

[21] E. Tick. Compile-time Granularity Analysis for Parallel Logic Programming Languages. *New Generation Computing*, 7:325–337, 1990.

[22] A. Van Gelder. Deriving constraints among argument sizes in logic programs. *Annals of Mathematics and Artificial Intelligence*, 3, 1991.

Recursive Modes for Precise Analysis of Logic Programs

Jichang Tan
Department of Information Engineering
KaoHsiung Polytechnic Institute, KaoHsiung 84008, Taiwan
jctan@csie.ntu.edu.tw

I-Peng Lin
Department of Computer Science and Information Engineering
National Taiwan University, Taipei 10764, Taiwan

Abstract

We present a method to improve the precision of mode analysis of logic programs. The idea is to refine the approximation of non-variable terms into a lattice of *recursive modes* so the recursive data types having proper but not ground instantiation states can be analyzed more precisely. This refinement is significant since the incomplete data structures are a useful technique in logic programming, but the analysis for its applications is usually inaccurate without using the much more expensive domains like type graphs. Because the modes are important to many other analyses, the improvements in the precision can have significant overall benefits. In particular, this idea can improve the precision of analysis for reference-chain patterns and the generalized type synthesis. Perhaps more interesting is that it suggests a method to describe and reason about the modes more precisely without depending on the notion of types. In this paper, we shall demonstrate how to develop a simple abstract domain of recursive modes as an application of the Galois connection approach to abstract interpretation. To evaluate the benefits, a generic analyzer has been designed and implemented.

1 Introduction

In logic programming, the mode information is concerned with the instantiation states of variables at runtime. Since the first compiler-based Prolog system, it has been used for optimizations [34]. To free the users from declaring the information, there have been many work about automatic inference of modes, including the frameworks developed in [2, 8, 19], but the basic set of modes remains rather stable. Based on the approach of abstract interpretation [4], we can classify the set of all runtime terms into the *de facto* standard set of modes: {any, var, nv, gnd, ∅} where any denotes the set of all runtime terms, var denotes the set of variables, nv denotes the set of non-variable terms, and gnd denotes the set of ground terms. To avoid the problem of variable aliasing [8, 14, 22], the var mode can be restricted to a subset called *uninitialized variables* or uninit mode so to approximate the runtime variables which do not refer to another variable [1, 29, 33]. The result of this classification is the domain of modes implemented in the Aquarius Prolog compiler [12, 33].

But unlike the programming in other paradigms, the logic variables can be partially instantiated for various useful purposes in addition to being in the modes of pure input (gnd) or output (var/uninit). Unfortunately, the non-variable mode (nv) is oversimplified about this and the analyses based on the standard set of modes cannot infer the incomplete data structures accurately. This can be found in several analyzers where it ends up with no information (any) when the non-variable terms are recursively processed in the analyzed program [3, 27, 29, 33]. Due to this problem, many applications using the technique of partially instantiated terms would either run in a comparatively lower efficiency or be rewritten to be more functional-like as suggested in [33]. For better precision, the analyzer can incorporate an abstract domain like *type graphs* [2, 14] for an integrated analysis of modes and types, but the cost is much higher on both theoretical and practical sides [14, 21, 31].

In this paper, we shall present the idea of *recursive modes* to improve the precision of mode analysis directly while keeping the analysis efficient enough to be incorporated in a fast compiler. Since the mode information is known to be the basis for many other analyses [11, 23], the improvements in its precision can have significantly overall benefits. In particular, this idea can improve the precision of analysis for reference-chain patterns – the analysis that has been integrated into several Prolog implementations [17, 30, 33]. The precise modes can also improve the precision of information inferred by the generalized *type synthesis* [28]. Perhaps more interesting is that it suggests a method to describe and reason about the modes more precisely without depending on the notion of types.

The basic idea of recursive modes is given as follows. Many of the popular incomplete data types are recursive data structures with "proper" but not ground instantiation states [24]. To analyze the modes more precisely, there should be elements in the abstract domain to approximate the sets of terms with similar recursive patterns of instantiation states. For example, we can introduce the modes lg, rg, or lrg to approximate the set of terms recursively instantiated in the left-most, the right-most, or both subterms. Thus rg can better approximate non-ground lists like *list*(any) disregarding the exact details in the cars, and lrg can better approximate types like binary trees *tree*/3 whose contents are unknown. There can be more elements in the domain or the representation can be more elaborated so to capture the recursive patterns better than the singletons. In this paper, however, we shall only develop a simple set of recursive modes illustrated as the right hand side lattice in Figure 1. The development of these modes is an application of the techniques of abstract interpretation [4, 5] and conventional parsing [13].

To evaluate the benefits, a generic analyzer has been designed and implemented. It is generic in that it can incorporate any finite domain under 256 elements which does not need to maintain the information about variable aliasings. We have implemented several such domains for analysis of recursive modes and dereferencing information where the simplest one is the domain used by the Aquarius Prolog compiler (as the baseline of our comparison). Even though the set of recursive modes used is rather simple, the analysis results with this refinement show that a significant portion of incomplete data structures can be inferred (13.6% out of 38.3% arguments in the benchmarks which are not purely input or output). In general, the analysis time increases when the results are more precise (7% more time to analyze with the domain of recursive modes). However the performance is still quite acceptable in compared to the Aquarius and so making it practical for inclusion in a fast optimizing compiler.

In the following sections we shall demonstrate how to develop a simple set of recursive modes based on the approach of Galois connection to abstract interpretation [4, 5]. Specifically we shall derive the semantic specification (for γ) in Section 2, the simplification procedure (for α) in Section 3, and the abstract unifications over the

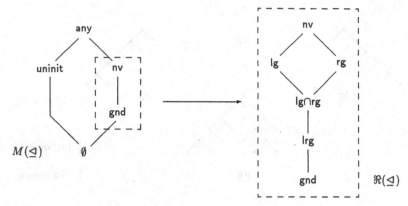

Figure 1: The lattice of recursive modes.

domain (*unify*) in Section 4. The implementation and evaluation of a generic analyzer for recursive modes is given in Section 5. We conclude this paper by discussing the possibility of obtaining even more precise analysis in Section 6.

2 The Semantics for a Set of Recursive Modes

In this section, we shall give an intuitive development of a simple set of recursive modes. For illustration, we begin with the data types *lists* and *binary trees* with proper instantiation status, i.e. whose instances are required to be instantiated only on the skeletons. Based on the formalisms of regular terms [25], type graphs [14], or the Mercury-style instantiatedness trees [26], they can be described as:

$$list \rightarrow \text{`·'}(any, list) \mid []. \qquad list = \{[], [any], [any, any], ...\}$$
$$tree \rightarrow tree(tree, any, tree) \mid void. \qquad tree = \{void, tree(void, any, void), ...\}$$

where the right-hand side shows the enumeration of the instances. If we consider the abstraction of *list* and *tree* over the standard set of modes, i.e. disregarding of the specific functors and constants used, the rules can be rewritten as:

$$mode_{list} \rightarrow f(any, mode_{list}) \mid gnd.$$
$$mode_{tree} \rightarrow f(mode_{tree}, any, mode_{tree}) \mid gnd.$$

where $mode_t$ denotes the mode patterns for type t and f represents the universal functor. To cover more general sets of runtime terms, the arity (2 for *list* and 3 for *tree*) can also be abstracted away:

$$rg \rightarrow f(any^*, rg) \mid gnd. \qquad rg = \{gnd, f(any^*, gnd), f(any^*, f(any^*, gnd)), ...\}$$
$$lrg \rightarrow f(lrg, any^*, lrg) \mid f(lrg) \mid gnd. \qquad lrg = \{gnd, f(gnd), f(gnd, any^*, gnd), ...\}$$

where any^* denotes zero or more subterms of any. The mode patterns for *list* and *tree* are now replaced by the more general modes rg and lrg, respectively. In a similar way, the rules for modes lg (which approximates the runtime terms recursively instantiated in the left-most subterms), nv and gnd can also be defined. In summary, the extended set of modes forms a complete lattice $M(\trianglelefteq)$ where $M = \{any, uninit, nv, lg, rg, lrg, gnd, \emptyset\}$ and ordered by set inclusion over the sets of

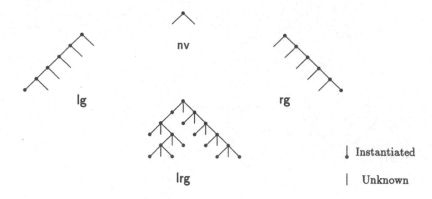

Figure 2: Term-tree instances of recursive modes: nv, lg, rg and lrg.

terms *Term* denoted by the modes (see the right-hand side diagram in Figure 1). The orderings can be formally written as:

$$m_1 \trianglelefteq m_2 \quad \text{iff} \quad \gamma(m_1) \subseteq \gamma(m_2) \qquad m_1, m_2 \in M$$

where $\gamma : M \mapsto 2^{Term}$ is the concretization function. In particular, we are interested in the sub-lattice of recursive modes $\Re(\trianglelefteq)$ where $\Re = \{$nv, lg, rg, lrg, gnd$\}$, nv is the top and gnd is the bottom:

nv $\to$ $f(\text{any}, \text{any}^*)$ | gnd.   lg $\to$ $f(\text{lg}, \text{any}^*)$ | gnd.
rg $\to$ $f(\text{any}^*, \text{rg})$ | gnd.   lrg $\to$ $f(\text{lrg}, \text{any}^*, \text{lrg})$ | $f(\text{lrg})$ | gnd.
gnd $\to$ $f(\text{gnd}, \text{gnd}^*)$ | *const*.

The instances of the major elements in $\Re$ are illustrated in Figure 2. Let $T(F)$ or simply T be the set of trees constructed by the function symbols $F = \{const, \text{any}, f\}$, where *const* and any are nullary and f is positive. The recursive modes considered then simply denote the subsets of T that can be defined by the least fixed point of the function $\mathcal{F} : \mathcal{T}^n \mapsto \mathcal{T}^n$ for the set of rules given above:

$$\mathcal{F}(r_1, r_2, .., r_n) = (\{f(\text{any}, \text{any}^*)\} \cup r_n, \{f(r_2, \text{any}^*)\} \cup r_n, .., \{f(r_n, r_n^*)\} \cup \{const\})$$

where $\mathcal{T} = 2^T$ is the powerset of trees and n is the size of the lattice $\Re$ (5 in this case). That is, the tuple (nv, lg, rg, lrg, gnd) $\stackrel{\text{def}}{=} \bigcup_{k \geq 0}^n \mathcal{F}^k(\emptyset^n)$ is the least solution of the equation $X = \mathcal{F}(X)$ where $\mathcal{F}^0(X) \stackrel{\text{def}}{=} X$ and $\mathcal{F}^{k+1} \stackrel{\text{def}}{=} \mathcal{F}(\mathcal{F}^k(X))$. The solution of the equation is guaranteed to exist by Kleen's fixed point theorem since $\mathcal{F}$ is continuous over the complete lattice $(\mathcal{T}^n, \subseteq^n, \cap^n, \cup^n, \mathcal{T}^n, \emptyset^n)$ [4, 5, 7, 18]. In this simple set of recursive modes, we are only concerned with the instantiation patterns in the left-most and the right-most subterms. The analysis for more precise modes will be discussed in Section 6.

3 Developing the Simplification Procedure

To practically implement the abstraction function $\alpha : 2^{Term} \mapsto M$, which is needed at analysis time, we fall back on the formalism of context-free grammars (see e.g.

[13]). The available technique of regular tree or term automata as those used in the work like [6, 15, 16, 20] cannot recognize the recursive modes since they accept *regular* subsets of terms, but indefinite number of subterms (i.e. any*) is patterned in the recursive modes. The ubiquitous software tools for string parsing also justify a reformulation.

3.1 The Context-Free Grammar for the Recursive Modes

We rewrite the previous set of rules for recursive modes into the CFG $G = (V, T, P, S)$, where:

- *Variables* $V = \{S,\ nv,\ lg,\ rg,\ lrg,\ gnd,\ sany,\ slg,\ srg,\ slrg\}$.
- *Terminals* $T = \{any,\ const,\ f,\ \text{'('},\ \text{','},\ \text{')'}\}$.
- *Productions* P consists of the following rules:

$S \rightarrow nv \mid lg \mid rg \mid lrg \mid gnd.$ (S is the start symbol.)

$nv \rightarrow f(sany, sany^*) \mid gnd.$ $lg \rightarrow f(slg, sany^*) \mid gnd.$

$rg \rightarrow f(sany^*, srg) \mid gnd.$ $lrg \rightarrow f(slrg, sany^*, slrg) \mid f(slrg) \mid gnd.$

$gnd \rightarrow f(gnd, gnd^*) \mid const.$

The terminal *const* represents any constant, *any* represents any (uninitialized or aliased) variable, and non-terminals *sany, slg, srg, slrg* generate the strings denoted by the modes any, lg, rg, lrg respectively:

$sany \rightarrow any \mid nv \mid ... \mid gnd.$ (symbols for any mode except $\emptyset$)

$slg \rightarrow lg \mid ... \mid gnd.$ (symbols for any mode m: gnd $\trianglelefteq m \trianglelefteq$ lg)

$srg \rightarrow rg \mid ... \mid gnd.$ (symbols for any mode m: gnd $\trianglelefteq m \trianglelefteq$ rg)

$slrg \rightarrow lrg \mid ... \mid gnd.$ (for any mode m: gnd $\trianglelefteq m \trianglelefteq$ lrg)

The semantics for $L(G)$ and the variables V can also be defined by the function $\psi : (2^\tau)^n \mapsto (2^\tau)^n$, where $\tau \stackrel{\text{def}}{=} T^*$ (the strings of terminal symbols) and $n = |V|$ (see [18]), like the function $\mathcal{F}$ for the trees.

3.2 Resolving the Problem of Ambiguity

The reformulated grammar is unfortunately ambiguous. In general, this means that the results of the analysis can be less precise than they should be. For example, the string $f(const, any)$ can be accepted by either rule lg or nv. Formally speaking, mode m_1 is more precise than m_2, i.e. $m_1 \trianglelefteq m_2$, if the set of runtime terms denoted by m_1 is smaller than that by m_2. Based on the grammar, a ground term can be classified less precisely to one of nv, lg, rg and lrg. But being ambiguous like this is not a real problem since we can always reduce to the symbol denoted by the smallest element in the conflict set, so the string $f(const, any)$ will be accepted by lg and a ground term is always classified to gnd.

The grammar is however ambiguous in another way, e.g. there is a conflict in reducing $f(lg, any, rg)$ to lg or rg. Since neither lg $\trianglelefteq$ rg nor rg $\trianglelefteq$ lg is true, it is not clear which reduction eventually leads to more precise results. This is illustrated in Figure 3 where the term is an lg in its left subterms and an rg in its right subterms. A straightforward method to resolve this problem is to include a new element "lg∩rg" into the abstract domain denoting the intersection of $\gamma(lg)$ and $\gamma(rg)$ such that lg∩rg $\trianglelefteq$ lg, lg∩rg $\trianglelefteq$ rg, and lrg $\trianglelefteq$ lg∩rg. In other words, the mode lg∩rg should be defined as follows:

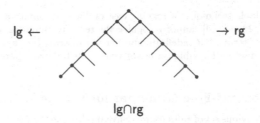

lg ←   → rg

lg∩rg

Figure 3: The problem of ambiguity in abstracting an instance of lg∩rg.

$lg∩rg → f(lg, any^*, rg) \mid f(lg∩rg) \mid gnd.$ $lg∩rg = \{gnd, f(lg∩rg), f(lg, any, rg), ...\}$

and the relevant rules for lg∩rg in the grammar G can be similarly obtained as:

$S → nv \mid lg \mid rg \mid lg∩rg \mid lrg \mid gnd.$ (S is the start symbol.)

$lg∩rg → f(slg, sany^*, srg) \mid f(slg∩rg) \mid gnd.$

$slg∩rg → lg∩rg \mid ... \mid gnd.$ (for any mode m: $gnd \trianglelefteq m \trianglelefteq lg∩rg$)

where the rule for the start symbol S has been modified, and two new non-terminals $lg∩rg$ and $slg∩rg$ have been added. Note that lg∩rg, $lg∩rg$ and $slg∩rg$ are just names, though they are deliberately chosen to remind the semantic significance. By the introduction of lg∩rg, the sub-lattice $\{nv, gnd\}$ is completely refined into $\Re(\trianglelefteq) = \{nv, lg, rg, lg∩rg, lrg, gnd\}$ as illustrated earlier in Figure 1.

3.3   The Procedure for Term Simplification

By removing the inherent ambiguities, we can always decide which mode in $\Re$ approximates a non-variable term best. Since the structures of the terms are available at analysis time, we can have a specialized pushdown automaton than the one for recognizing the strings generated by $L(G)$. That is, we only have to be concerned with the simplification of the "flat" non-variable terms, and recursively reduce the given term tree in a bottom-up way. This is outlined in Figure 4 as the function *simplify* that returns a recursive mode (*mode*) for a term tree (*term*). The recursive type *term* is either a symbol in $\Sigma \stackrel{\text{def}}{=} \{any, const\} \cup \{nv, .., gnd\}$ or an n-ary structure $f(t_1, .., t_n)$ where $t_1, .., t_n$ are also instances of *term*. The primitive function *mode* (line 9) returns the mode of a term in atomic form:

$$mode(t) = \begin{cases} gnd & \text{if } t = const \quad \text{(atoms and numbers)} \\ any & \text{if } t = any \quad \text{(uninitialized or aliased variables)} \\ t & \text{otherwise} \quad (t \in \{nv, .., gnd\} \approx \Re) \end{cases}$$

The function *reduce* (line 7) returns the mode of a flat term $f(m_1, .., m_n)$ where $m_1, .., m_n$ are symbols in Σ and can be implemented by the finite state automata with output (i.e, a Moore Machine) that accepts the regular sets derived from the grammar G.

Specifically, the *reduce* function can be implemented by the finite state machine $\mathcal{M}(\Sigma, L, \Lambda)$ where Σ is the alphabet, L is the set of regular expressions $\{L_{nv}, L_{lg}, L_{rg}, L_{lg∩rg}, L_{lrg}, L_{gnd}\}$, Λ is the mapping from L to Σ with $\Lambda(L_s) = s$ for $s \in \{nv, lg, rg, lg∩rg, lrg, gnd\} \subset \Sigma$, and the regular expressions follow:

```
1   function simplify(t : term) : mode;        { simplify returns the mode of a term }
2   begin
3      if t = f(t_1, .., t_n) then              { if t is an f/n term }
4         for i ←1 to n do                      { for every subterm }
5            m_i ←simplify(t_i)                  { get simplification by recursion }
6         od ;
7         return reduce(f(m_1, .., m_n))         { simplification of the "flat" term }
8      else
9         return mode(t)                         { if t is in atomic form }
10     fi
11  end
```

Figure 4: The procedure for term simplification.

$$L_{nv} = sany\ sany^* \qquad\qquad L_{lg} = slg\ sany^*$$
$$L_{rg} = sany^* srg \qquad\qquad L_{lg \cap rg} = slg\ sany^* srg\ |\ slg \cap rg$$
$$L_{lrg} = slrg\ sany^* slrg\ |\ slrg \qquad L_{gnd} = gnd\ gnd^*$$

where the symbols $sany$, .., $slrg$ represent the unions of symbols in Σ based on the grammar G. Note that for each non-ground recursive mode, the base case (i.e., gnd) in the production is redundant and has been removed from the regular expression. If the state machine $\mathcal{M}$ returns more than one output, the function $reduce$ simply chooses the one with the smallest concretization in the ordering of $\trianglelefteq$.

Example 3.1 Consider abstracting a complex term $[pair(1, X), pair(2, Y)]$ with the procedure:

$$
\begin{aligned}
&[pair(1, X), pair(2, Y)]\\
=\ &`\cdot'/2(pair(1, X), `\cdot'/2(pair(2, Y), [\,]))\\
\Leftarrow\ &f(f(gnd, any), f(f(gnd, any), gnd))\\
\Leftarrow\ &f(lg, f(lg, gnd))\\
\Leftarrow\ &f(lg, lg \cap rg)\\
\Leftarrow\ &lg \cap rg
\end{aligned}
$$

where the first "$\Leftarrow$" is the result of several recursive applications of $simplify$ with $mode$ (line 9), and the next ones are each one or two applications of $reduce$ (line 7) of the flat subterms. □

Lattice-theoretically speaking, the introduction of $lg \cap rg$ into the recursive modes $\Re$ or M makes the complete lattice an *intersection structure* (or $\cap$-structure) on the set of runtime terms where the *meet* '$\triangle$' is just set intersection, but in general the *join* '$\triangledown$' is not set union [7]. For example, in the case of $\Re(\trianglelefteq)$, $\gamma(lg) \cup \gamma(rg) = \gamma(nv) - \gamma(f(any, any^*)) \subset \gamma(nv)$. For $M(\trianglelefteq)$, $\gamma(nv) \cup \gamma(uninit) \subset \gamma(any)$ since we have intentionally excluded the aliased variables from the analysis. If an abstract domain $\mathcal{D}$ is an $\cap$-structure, it is obvious that there is no inherent ambiguities for simplification of terms over $\mathcal{D}$; if any term $t \in \gamma(m_i)$ for a set of elements $m_i \in \mathcal{D}, i = 1..n > 1$, then there is a unique minimum $m \in \mathcal{D}$ such that $m = \triangle_{i=1}^n m_i = \alpha(\bigcap_{i=1}^n \gamma(m_i))$, which best approximates t.

unify	any	uninit	$\Re$
any	any	any	$\Re$
uninit	any	any	$\Re$
$\Re$	$\Re$	$\Re$	$\triangle_{\Re}$

$\triangle_{\Re}$	nv	lg	rg	lg∩rg	lrg	gnd
nv	nv	lg	rg	lg∩rg	lrg	gnd
lg	lg	lg	lg∩rg	lg∩rg	lrg	gnd
rg	rg	lg∩rg	rg	lg∩rg	lrg	gnd
lg∩rg	lg∩rg	lg∩rg	lg∩rg	lg∩rg	lrg	gnd
lrg	lrg	lrg	lrg	lrg	lrg	gnd
gnd	gnd	gnd	gnd	gnd	gnd	gnd

Table 1: The abstract unifications for recursive modes.

4 Abstract Unification for Recursive Modes

To implement the analysis, we also need to know how to perform abstract unifications over the recursive modes. Since each abstract element represents a set of runtime terms, the abstract unifications can be characterized by *set unification* as follows:

$$set\_unify(T_1, T_2) = \{unify(t_1, t_2) \mid t_1 \in T_1 \text{ and } t_2 \in T_2 \text{ are unifiable}\}$$

where T_1 and T_2 are sets of terms. Based on the Galois connection approach to abstract interpretation [4, 5], abstract unification unify for abstract elements e_1 and e_2 can be defined in terms of set_unify:

$$\begin{aligned} unify(e_1, e_2) &= (\alpha \circ set\_unify \circ \gamma)(e_1, e_2) \\ &= \alpha \circ set\_unify(T_1, T_2) \qquad \text{if } \gamma(e_1) = T_1 \text{ and } \gamma(e_2) = T_2 \end{aligned}$$

For the abstract domain considered, the abstract unifications can be summarized as follows:

$$unify(m_1, m_2) = \begin{cases} \text{any} & \text{if } m_1 = m_2 = \text{uninit} \\ m_1 & \text{if } m_1 \neq \text{uninit} \wedge m_2 = \text{uninit} \\ m_2 & \text{if } m_1 = \text{uninit} \wedge m_2 \neq \text{uninit} \\ m_1 \triangle m_2 & \text{otherwise} \end{cases}$$

where the intersection closure of $\Re$ and M is necessary for $unify(m_1, m_2)$ to be *soundly* approximated by $m_1 \triangle m_2$ (see, e.g., [9]) when m_1 and m_2 are not uninit; without the mode lg∩rg, the best approximation for $unify(\text{lg}, \text{rg})$ can be either lg or rg, a case of ambiguity again, so that it can result in a less precise analysis. We tabulate the values of unify for every pair of modes in Table 1. Based on set_unify, the definition can also be extended to those for specialized abstract unifications. In particular, we have:

$$unify(m, f(X_1, .., X_n)) = \begin{cases} f & \text{with } \theta = \{\} & (n = 0) \\ f(m_1, .., m_n) & \text{with } \theta = \{X_1/m_1, .., X_n/m_n\} & (n > 0) \end{cases}$$

where θ is the abstract substitution and $f(X_1, ..., X_n)$ is an f/n term with n variable subterms. If the mode $m \in \Re$, then the modes $m_1, ..., m_n$ can be found directly from the semantic rule R for mode m that covers arity n. For example, if $n > 1$, m_1 is the left-most subterm of R; m_n is the right-most subterm of R; m_i is any, for $1 < i < n$. If the mode $m \in \{\text{any}, \text{uninit}\}$, then $m_i = m$ for $1 \leq i \leq n$, as usual. In general, arbitrary unify can be computed by recursively flattening complex terms and applying the primitive and specialized unify's. The following example shows how this is done in the top-down abstract interpretation of a calling mode lrg for a clause-head structure like $tree(L, pair(1, X), R))$.

Example 4.1 Consider the unify of lrg and a complex term $tree(L, pair(gnd, X), R)$:

(0) $unify(lrg, tree(L, pair(gnd, X), R))$
    $= unify(lrg, tree(L, T, R))$ let $T = pair(gnd, X)$ and recurse on (1)
    $= tree(lrg, any, lrg)$ $\theta_0 = \{L/lrg,\ T/any,\ R/lrg\}$.

(1) $unify(any, pair(gnd, X))$ the recursion of $unify(any, T)$
    $= unify(any, pair(S, X))$ let $S = gnd$ and recurse on (2)
    $= pair(any, any)$ $\theta_1 = \{S/any,\ X/any\}$

(2) $unify(any, gnd)$ the recursion of $unify(any, S)$
    $= gnd$ $\theta_2 = \{\}$

By composing the substitutions $\theta_0, \theta_1, \theta_2$, we get:

    $unify(lrg, tree(L, pair(gnd, X), R))$
    $= tree(lrg, pair(gnd, any), lrg)$ $\theta = \{L/lrg,\ X/any,\ R/lrg\}$ □

5 Implementation and Evaluation

5.1 The Implementation

To evaluate the improvements in precision of the analysis based on the recursive modes, we have developed a generic dataflow analyzer for inference of the mode and dereferencing information. Theoretically it works with any finite domain if each element can be encoded in a single word and there is no need to maintain the information about variable aliasings. Practically the number of elements has to be under 256 since the term-tree reducer is produced by a character-string scanner generator (see below). This experimental analyzer is in fact a simplified version of our previous work [27]. Due to the simplification, it is significantly more efficient than the original one with respect to the abstract domains that we have implemented. The analyzer is about 7000 lines of C code: 2500 lines for the generic core, 1500 lines for the abstract domain, and the rest for a few supporting modules.

We have constructed a set of integrated abstract domains each as a Cartesian product of $M \times D$ where M is the domain of modes and D is the domain for dereferencing information. The domains of modes include: M_0, the standard set of modes, and M_1, the domain of recursive modes developed previously. The domains for dereferencing information include: $D_0 = \{any, rderef, \emptyset\}$ and $D_1 = \{any, sderef, rderef, \emptyset\}$ where rderef denotes the recursively dereferenced terms and sderef denotes the terms dereferenced only on the instantiated skeletons. For lack of space, we cannot discuss the details about D_1 but simply note that each recursive mode but gnd has an irreducible product with sderef in the domain (gnd·sderef = gnd·rderef), and can be used to improve the precision of dereferencing information (see the results below). The domain $M_0 \times D_0$ is the one employed by the Aquarius Prolog and the domain $M_0 \times D_1$ is $M_0 \times D_0$ plus the element nv·sderef for toplevel-dereferenced non-variable terms. The domain $M_1 \times D_0$ infers the recursive modes but does not improve the precision of analysis for dereferencing information. The domain $M_1 \times D_1$ is the most precise and therefore the most interesting one in the set.

Since the domains can be developed in a systematic way, we also implemented a simple "domain compiler" to help ensure the correctness of the analyzer. Given the syntactic and semantic descriptions of a domain, the compiler generates a C program file containing the encoding table of the abstract elements, the subterm table, the least-upper-bound (join) table and the unification table. This file is directly included into the analyzer. The domain compiler also generates a `lex` file to implement the state machine for scanning and reducing the flat terms. The `lex` file is processed by `flex` (the `lex` distributed by FSF) and the state machine generated is statically linked with the analyzer. The domain compiler was found to be an indispensable tool since the complexity of the rules grows as the size of the domain grows, in our case, from $|M_0 \times D_0| = 9$ to $|M_1 \times D_1| = 21$. The compiler itself is however very small: less than 200 lines of Prolog code, including the descriptions of the abstract domains.

5.2 The Evaluation of Precision

The input to the analyzer is the WAM code generated by the PLM Prolog compiler[1] for a subset of the Aquarius benchmarks [11, 33] and a subset of the benchmarks used in [31]. The analyzer is compiled with "`cc -O`" command on a Sparc 10/51 Workstation under SunOS 4.1.3. We summarize the results for $M_0 \times D_0$ (the simplest domain) and $M_1 \times D_1$ (the most precise domain) in Table 2 and 3; the results for $M_0 \times D_1$ and $M_1 \times D_0$ are mostly between these two extremes. The size of the benchmarks is measured by the number of arguments in the calling patterns (*num*). The precision of the results from our analyzer is given by the percentages of arguments with any, nv, *full*, and "true" recursive modes. A calling pattern is considered full mode if it is gnd or uninit and it is a true recursive mode ($\Re'$) if it is in $\Re - \{\text{nv}, \text{gnd}\}$. Note that none of the benchmarks has a trivial 100% of full modes. For this set of benchmarks, the any and nv modes inferred are effectively reduced in the domain $M_1 \times D_1$. In spite of the loss of precision in analyzing extra-logical builtins (e.g., the approximation given by the abstract *arg/3* and *func/3* wrt recursive modes is conservative since the arities and subterm numbers are not available), a significant portion of incomplete data structures has been uncovered (13.6% out of 38.3% non full-mode arguments). Among them, over 85% is skeletal-dereferenced (sderef) but less than 3% can be inferred as recursive-dereferenced (not shown in the table). The appearing reduction of full modes in some benchmarks is due to the fact that the analyzer collects *multiple-specialized* patterns. While some of the any and nv modes are better approximated to be recursive modes, the number of full modes does not always increase proportionally as the number of the patterns increases, and as a result causes the percentages to decrease slightly.

5.3 The Evaluation of Efficiency

The timings of the dataflow analyzer for both domains (A_{00} and A_{11}) have been measured with a resolution of 0.1 mSec; the results are the average execution times of 500 to 1000 iterations. The timings of the Aquarius Prolog compiler (APC) have been measured with the execution times reported from the command "`apc -tb -st -v`" with two sets of compiler options: "`:- option(analyze).`" and "`:- notoption(analyze).`"; the results are the average of 5 iterations. To avoid

---

[1] The original code was from Peter Van Roy [32] and modified by Hervé Touati.

benchmark	Domain $M_0 \times D_0$				Domain $M_1 \times D_1$				
	num	any	nv	full	num	any	nv	$\mathfrak{R}'$ (sderef)	full
serialise	16	37.5	6.3	56.2	18	16.6	0.0	33.3 (17)	50.0
zebra	10	40.0	50.0	10.0	13	0.0	23.0	69.2 (56)	7.7
fast_mu	38	2.6	15.7	81.5	38	2.6	0.0	15.7 (67)	81.5
boyer	81	51.8	17.2	30.8	81	50.6	4.9	13.5 (100)	30.8
browse	49	30.6	4.1	65.3	49	24.4	0.0	10.2 (80)	65.3
prover	22	31.8	27.2	40.9	25	28.0	36.0	0.0 (n/a)	36.0
reducer	113	53.0	7.9	38.9	116	50.8	6.9	2.6 (100)	39.6
meta_qsort	17	52.9	11.7	35.2	17	47.0	11.7	0.0 (n/a)	41.1
chat_parser	1039	28.2	3.8	67.8	1024	18.3	0.0	13.7 (98)	67.3
cs_o	97	13.4	15.4	17.1	99	9.1	1.0	20.2 (95)	69.6
disj_r	60	18.3	8.3	73.3	60	15.0	0.0	11.6 (100)	73.3
gabriel	59	33.8	5.1	61.0	59	32.2	1.7	5.1 (33)	61.0
kalah_r	130	21.5	15.3	63.0	139	20.1	13.6	2.2 (100)	64.0
peep	65	12.3	1.5	86.1	68	11.7	0.0	1.5 (100)	86.7
pg	36	25.0	16.6	58.3	31	25.8	3.2	16.1 (80)	54.8
plan	38	26.3	39.5	34.2	46	17.4	6.5	41.3 (68)	34.8
press1	149	31.5	29.5	38.9	177	16.9	2.8	32.2 (72)	48.0
read_o	145	28.2	6.9	64.8	153	28.1	4.6	2.6 (25)	64.7
% of args	100	28.8	9.5	61.7	100	21.7	3.1	13.6 (85)	61.6

Table 2: The evaluation of precision.

benchmark	APC (sec)	A_{00} (msec)	A_{11} (msec)
serialise	0.12	2.1	3.0
zebra	0.22	2.7	2.45
fast_mu	0.68	1.8	1.85
boyer	1.88	13.6	13.4
browse	0.88	3.0	2.7
prover	0.68	3.5	3.5
reducer	3.76	11.8	12.1
meta_qsort	0.50	3.75	3.75
chat_parser	25.5	77.8	94.7
cs_o	1.68	4.25	4.3
disj_r	0.82	3.25	3.25
gabriel	0.58	4.25	4.0
kalah_r	2.08	11.5	13.2
peep	5.12	15.6	15.6
pg	0.34	1.3	1.25
plan	0.08	2.0	2.9
press1	3.28	18.7	27.4
read_o	2.44	23.6	23.7
geo. mean	177	1	1.07

Table 3: The evaluation of efficiency.

skewing the results, both runs also include the switch ":- notoption(compile)."
[12]. In compared to the Aquarius compiler, our analyzer is typically two orders
faster in the analysis time (geo. mean 166 to 177 times faster). In general, the
analyzer does pay slightly more time for more precise information (177/166 is about
7% more analysis time). If the precision is significantly improved (e.g. *serialise*,
chat_parser, *plan*, and *press1*), it takes significantly more time to analyze. On the
other extreme (e.g. *prover*, *meta_qsort*, *peep*), it takes almost the same time for
either analysis. In fact, the analyzer does not appear to consume any more CPU
time when the results are not improved. For several benchmarks (e.g. *zebra*), it
however shows the interesting anomaly that slightly less time is required for similar
or more precise results.

6 Discussion

The domain of recursive modes developed until now is special in that it only works
on the instantiation patterns in the left-most and right-most subterms. It may therefore be considered rather ad-hoc and be quite "fragile" in the analysis of certain
kinds of programs. For example, the domain is too coarse to precisely analyze the
applications using incomplete data structures that have a different recursion pattern or have more than two recursive sub-structures (e.g., see [24]). It is also unable
to accurately capture the instantiation patterns in *list*(uninit) and *tree*(*list*(any)).
A general but efficient way to incorporate these and other refinements is to have
a full-fledged domain compiler so the users can customize the analyzer to improve
the precision while keeping the compiler fast enough in the developing cycles. Another way to improve the precision is to go beyond the representation of modes by
singletons, e.g. using a pair of numbers (p, q) to represent $p + q$ partial trees or the
n-tuple of $\Re$ (i.e. $\Re^n$) for n-dimensional incomplete structures.

Despite of the concerns about the general effectiveness, the evaluation however
shows that the domain is actually not fragile for various kinds of applications in
the benchmarks. The question is therefore whether the cost of a more elaborated
implementation can be justified. For ordinary applications, it may not worth much
extra effort due to the diminishing return of the benefits. For large applications,
e.g. a library code or a production software, a precise but fast compiler is probably justified – even though the programs may eventually be analyzed with a very
expensive domain and get highly optimized before it is released to the users.

The package, including the analyzer, the abstract domains, and the benchmarks,
is available by the URL http://www.csie.ntu.edu.tw/~jctan/amanda.

Acknowledgement

We would like to thank the anonymous referees for their useful comments and
suggestions on this and earlier versions of the paper.

References

[1] J. Beer. The Occur-Check Problem Revisited. *Jour. of Logic Programming*,
1988:5:243-261.

[2] M. Bruynooghe and G. Janssens. An Instance of Abstract Interpretation Integrating Type and Mode Inferencing. *Proc. of 5th Int'l Logic Programming Conf.*, 1988.

[3] F. Bueno, M. García de la Banda, and M. Hermenegildo. The PLAI Abstract Interpretation System. *Tech. Report CLIP2/94.0*, Computer Sci. Dept., Tech. U. of Madrid (UPM), Feb. 1994.

[4] P. Cousot and R. Cousot. Abstract Interpretation: a Unified Lattice Model for Static Analysis of Programs by Constructions of Fixed Points. *Conf. Rec. of 4th POPL,* pp. 78-88, 1977.

[5] P. Cousot and R. Cousot. Abstract Interpretation and Application to Logic Programs. *Technical Report LIENS-92-12*, Laboratoire d'Informatique, URA 1327 du CNRS, Ecole Normale Supérieure, June 1992. Also *Jour. of Logic Programming*, Special Issue on Abstract Interpretation, 1992.

[6] P. Cousot and R. Cousot. Formal Languages, Grammar and Set-Constraint-Based Program Analysis by Abstract Interpretation. *Conf. Rec. of ACM/FPCA 1995*, La Jolla, California, June 1995.

[7] B. A. Davey and H. A. Priestley. *Introduction to Lattices and Order*, Cambridge University Press, New York, 1990.

[8] S. K. Debray and D. S. Warren. Automatic Mode Inference for Prolog Programs. *Proc. of 3rd Symp. on Logic Programming*, Salt Lake, 1986.

[9] S. K. Debray. Efficient Dataflow Analysis of Logic Programs. *Jour. of the ACM*, 39:4:949-984, 1992.

[10] S. K. Debray. On the Complexity of Dataflow Analysis of Logic Programs. *Proc. of 19th Int'l Colloq. on Automata, Languages, and Programming*, Vienna, July 1992. LNCS Series.

[11] T. W. Getzinger. The Costs and Benefits of Abstract Interpretation-Driven Prolog Optimization. *Proc. of 1994 Int'l Static Analysis Symposium*, 1994.

[12] R. Haygood. *The Aquarius Prolog User's Manual*, Department of Computer Science, University of South California, April 1993.

[13] J. E. Hopcroft and J. D. Ullman. *Introduction to Automata Theory, Languages, and Computation*, Addison-Wesley Publishing Company, 1979.

[14] G. Janssens. Deriving Run Time Properties of Logic Programs by Means of Abstract Interpretation, *Ph. D. Dissertation*, Department of Computer Science, Katholieke Universiteit, Leuven, Belgium 1990.

[15] N. D. Jones and S. S. Muchnick. Flow Analysis and Optimization of LISP-like Structures. *Proc. of 6th Symp. Principles of Programming Languages*, 1979.

[16] D. Kozen and J. Palsberg. Efficient Recursive Subtyping. *Proc. of 20th Symp. Principles of Programming Languages*, 1993.

[17] A. Krall and T. Berger. Incremental Global Compilation of Prolog with the Vienna Abstract Machine. *Proc. of '95 Int'l Conf. on Logic Programming*, Kanakawa, Japan, June 1995.

[18] E. G. Manes and M. A. Arbib. *Algebraic Approaches to Program Semantics*, Springer-Verlag New York Inc., 1986.

[19] C. S. Mellish. The Automatic Generation of Mode Declarations for Prolog Programs, *DAI Research Paper No. 163*, 1981.

[20] P. Mishra and U. S. Reddy. Declaration-free Type Checking. *Proc. of 12th Symp. of Principles of Programming Languages,* 1985.

[21] A. Mulkers, W. Winsborough, and M. Bruynooghe. Live-Structure Dataflow Analysis for Prolog. *ACM Trans. on Programming Languages and Systems,* 16(2), 1994.

[22] K. Muthukumar and M. Hermenegildo. Determination of Variable Dependence Information Through Abstract Interpretation. *Proc. of North America Conf. on Logic Programming,* 1989.

[23] L. Naish. A Declarative View of Modes. *Proc. of JICSLP '96,* Bonn Germany, September 1996.

[24] R. A. O'Keefe. *The Craft of Prolog,* In Series of Logic Programming, MIT Press, 1990.

[25] *Types in Logic Programming,* F. Pfenning, editor, MIT Press, 1992.

[26] Z. S. Somogyi, F. Henderson and T. Conway. The execution algorithm of Mercury, an efficient purely declarative logic programming language. To appear at *Journal of Logic Programming.*

[27] J. Tan and I.-P. Lin. Compiling Dataflow Analysis of Logic Programs. *Proc. of '92 ACM/SIGPLAN Conf. on Programming Language Design and Implementation,* San Francisco, June 1992.

[28] J. Tan and I.-P. Lin. Type Synthesis for Logic Programs. *Proc. of JICSLP '96,* Bonn Germany, September 1996.

[29] A. Taylor. Removal of Dereferencing and Trailing in Prolog Compilation. *Proc. of 6th Int'l Conf. on Logic Programming,* Lisbon, June 1989.

[30] A. Taylor. LIPS on a MIPS: Results from a Prolog Compiler for a RISC. *Proc. of 7th Int'l Conf. on Logic Programming,* Jerusalem, 1990.

[31] P. Van Hentenryck, A. Cortesi and B. Le Charlier. Type Analysis of Prolog Using Type Graphs. *Jour. of Logic Programming,* 1995:22:179-209.

[32] P. Van Roy. *A Prolog Compiler for the PLM,* Report No. UCB/CSD 84/203, UC Berkeley, November 1984.

[33] P. Van Roy. Can Logic Programming Execute as Fast as Imperative Programming? *Ph. D. Dissertation,* Department of Computer Science, UCB, Nov. 1990.

[34] D. H. D. Warren. Applied Logic - its Use and Implementation as a Programming Tool. *Ph. D. Thesis,* Univ. Edinburgh, Scotland, 1977.

[35] R. Warren, M. Hermenegildo and S. K. Debray. On the Practicality of Global Flow Analysis of Logic Programs. *Proc. of 5th Int'l Conf. on Logic Programming,* 1988.

Lower Bound Cost Estimation for Logic Programs

Saumya Debray
Department of Computer Science
University of Arizona
Tucson, AZ 85721, U.S.A.
debray@cs.arizona.edu

Pedro López-García, Manuel Hermenegildo
Facultad de Informática
Universidad Politécnica de Madrid
E-28660 Madrid, Spain
pedro@dia.fi.upm.es, herme@.fi.upm.es

Nai-Wei Lin
Department of Computer Science and Information Engineering
National Chung Cheng University
Chiayi, 62107, Taiwan, R.O.C.
naiwei@cs.ccu.edu.tw

Abstract

It is generally recognized that information about the runtime cost of computations can be useful for a variety of applications, including program transformation, granularity control during parallel execution, and query optimization in deductive databases. Most of the work to date on compile-time cost estimation of logic programs has focused on the estimation of upper bounds on costs. However, in many applications, such as parallel implementations on distributed-memory machines, one would prefer to work with lower bounds instead. The problem with estimating lower bounds is that in general, it is necessary to account for the possibility of failure of head unification, leading to a trivial lower bound of 0. In this paper, we show how, given type and mode information about procedures in a logic program, it is possible to (semi-automatically) derive non-trivial lower bounds on their computational costs. We also discuss the cost analysis for the special and frequent case of divide-and-conquer programs and show how —as a pragmatic short-term solution —it may be possible to obtain useful results simply by identifying and treating divide-and-conquer programs specially. Finally, we present experimental results from a preliminary implementation of the proposed approach, applied to automatic parallel task size control.

Keywords: Cost Analysis, Lower Bound Estimation, Granularity Control, Parallelism.

1 Introduction

It is generally recognized that information about the runtime cost of computations can be useful for a variety of applications. For example, it is useful for granularity control, i.e., dynamic control of thread creation in parallel implementations of logic and functional languages [14, 4, 16, 9, 15, 12], and for query optimization in deductive databases [5]. In the context of logic programming, the work on cost estimation has generally focused on upper bound cost analyses [6]. However, in many cases one would prefer to work with lower bounds instead. As an example, consider a distributed memory implementation of Prolog: suppose that the work involved in spawning a task on a remote processor takes 1000 instructions, and that we infer that a particular procedure call in a program will execute no more than 5000 instructions. This suggests that it *may be* worth executing this call on a remote processor, but provides no assurance that doing so will not actually produce a performance degradation relative to a sequential execution (the call might terminate after executing only a small number of instructions). On the other hand, if we know that a call will execute at least 5000 instructions, we can be assured that spawning a task on a remote processor to execute this call is worthwhile. Thus, while upper bound cost information is better than no information at all, lower bounds may be more useful than upper bounds.

The biggest problem with the inference of lower bounds on the computational cost of logic programs is the possibility of failure. Any attempt to infer lower bounds has to contend with the possibility that a goal may fail during head unification, yielding a trivial lower bound of 0. An obvious solution would be to try and rule out "bad" argument values by considering the types of predicates. However, most existing type analyses provide upper approximations, in the sense that the type of a predicate is a superset of the set of argument values that are actually encountered at runtime. Unfortunately, straightforward attempts to address this issue, for example by trying to infer lower approximations to the calling types of predicates, fail to yield nontrivial lower bounds for most cases.

In [3], we showed how, given mode and (upper approximation) type information, we can detect procedures and goals that can be guaranteed to not fail. Our technique is based on an intuitively very simple notion, that of a (set of) tests "covering" the type of a variable. We showed that the problem of determining a covering is undecidable in general, and is co-NP-hard even if we have only finite types and simple equality tests. We then gave an algorithm for checking whether a set of tests covers a type, that is complete for *tuple-distributive regular types*, sound, and efficient in practice.

Based on this information, we showed how to identify goals and procedures that can be guaranteed to not fail at runtime. Note that this information is interesting in its own right, in the context of program transformations (for example, we may want to execute possibly-failing goals ahead of non-failing goals where possible) and in systems that exploit speculative parallelism.

The main contributions of this paper are as follows: (*i*) we show how non-failure information can be used to infer lower bounds on the computational costs of goals; (*ii*) discuss how to bound the chromatic polynomial of a graph from below, and thereby show how to infer lower bounds on the number of solutions a predicate can generate (this information is useful, for example, for estimating communication costs in distributed-memory implementations); (*iii*) show how information about the number of solutions computed can be used to improve lower bound estimates when all solutions to a goal are required; and (*iv*) show how to obtain improved lower bound estimates for a simple but common class of divide-and-conquer programs. We discuss the application of our ideas to granularity control for parallel programs: in this case, the use of lower bound cost estimates guarantees that no slowdowns will occur, even in systems with significant overheads associated with parallel execution. Our ideas have been implemented and the resulting lower bound cost estimates, given in Section 7, can be seen to be quite precise, especially for an automatic analysis tool. Experimental results with granularity control using lower bound cost estimates indicate that significant performance improvements can be attained using our approach.

Despite a suggestive similarity in names, our work is quite different from Basin and Ganzinger's work on complexity analysis based on ordered resolution [1]. They consider resolution based on a well-founded total ordering on ground atoms, and use this to examine the complexity of determining, given a set of Horn clauses N and a ground Horn clause C, whether $N \models C$. Our work, by contrast, is based on an operational formulation of logic program execution that is not restricted to ground queries (or, for that matter, to Horn programs, since it is easy to handle features such as cuts and negation by failure). Because operational aspects of program execution are modeled more accurately in our approach, the results obtained are considerably more precise.

2 Lower-Bound Cost Analysis: The One-Solution Case

If only one solution is required of any computation, it suffices to know whether a computation will generate at least one solution, i.e., will not fail. Assuming that this information is available, for example by using the technique mentioned in the previous section, cost analysis for a particular predicate can then proceed as follows:

1. We first determine the relative sizes of variable bindings at different program points in a clause by computing lower bounds on output argument sizes as functions of input argument sizes. This is done by solving (or estimating lower bound solutions to) the resulting difference equations: the approach is very similar to that discussed in [6], the only difference being that whereas [6] estimated upper bounds on argument sizes using the *max* function across the output sizes of different clauses in a cluster, we use the *min* function across clauses to estimate lower bounds on argument sizes.

2. The (lower bound) computational cost of a clause is then expressed as a function of the input argument size, in terms of the costs of the body literals in that clause.

    Consider a clause $C \equiv$ '$H :- B_1, \ldots, B_m$'. Let n be the r-tuple which represents the sizes of the r input arguments for the head of the clause, and let (lower bounds on) the input argument sizes for the body literals $B_1, \ldots, B_m$ be $\phi_1(n), \ldots, \phi_m(n)$ respectively. Assume that the cost of head unification and tests for this clause is at least $h(n)$, and let $Cost_{B_i}(x)$ denote a lower bound on the cost of the body literal B_i. Then, if B_k is the rightmost body literal that is guaranteed to not fail, the following gives a lower bound on the cost $Cost_C(n)$ of the clause C on an input of size n:

$$h(n) + \sum_{i=1}^{k} Cost_{B_i}(\phi_i(n)) \leq Cost_C(n).$$

    If the clause C corresponds to a non-failing predicate, then we take $k = m$.

3. A lower bound on the cost $Cost_p(n)$ of a predicate p on an input of size n is then given by

$$\min\{Cost_C(n) \mid C \text{ is a clause defining } p\} \leq Cost_p(n).$$

As discussed in [6], recursion is handled by expressing the cost of recursive goals symbolically as a function of the input size. From this, we can obtain a set of difference equations that can be solved (or approximated) to obtain a lower bound on the cost of a predicate in terms of the input size.

Given a predicate defined by m clauses $C_1, \ldots, C_m$, we can improve the precision of this analysis by noting that clause C_i will be tried only if clauses $C_1, \ldots, C_{i-1}$ fail to yield a solution. For an input of size n, let $\delta_i(n)$ denote the least amount of work necessary to determine that clauses $C_1, \ldots, C_{i-1}$ will not yield a solution and that C_i must be tried: the function δ_i obviously has to take into account the type and cost of the indexing scheme being used in the underlying implementation. In this case, the lower bound for p can be improved to:

$$\min\{Cost_{C_i}(n) + \delta_i(n) \mid 1 \leq i \leq m\} \leq Cost_p(n).$$

The pruning operator can also be taken into account, so that clauses which are after the first clause, say C_i, which has a non-failing sequence of literals just before the cut, are ignored, and the lower bound on the cost of the predicate is then the minimum of the costs of the clauses preceding the clause C_i and this clause itself.

3   Lower-Bound Cost Analysis: All Solutions

In many applications, it is reasonable to assume that all solutions are required. For example, in a distributed memory implementation of a logic programming system, the cost of sending or receiving a message is likely to be high enough that it makes sense for a remote computation to compute all the solutions to a query and return them in a single message instead of sending a large number of messages, each containing a single solution. For such cases, estimates of the computational cost of a goal can be improved greatly if we have lower bounds on the number of solutions—indeed, as the example of a distributed memory system suggests, in some cases the number of solutions may itself be a reasonable measure of cost.

If we obtain lower bounds on the number of solutions that can be generated by the literals in a clause (this problem is addressed in next section), we can use this information to improve lower bound cost estimates for the case where all solutions to a predicate are required. Consider a clause '$p(\bar{x}) :- B_1, \ldots, B_n$' where B_k is the rightmost literal that is guaranteed to not fail. Let the input argument size for the head of the clause be n, and let (lower bounds on) the input argument sizes for the body literals $B_1, \ldots, B_m$ be $\phi_1(n), \ldots, \phi_m(n)$ respectively. Assume that the cost of head unification and tests for this clause is at least $h(n)$, and let $Cost_{B_i}(x)$ denote a lower bound on the cost of the body literal B_i. Now consider a body literal B_j, where $1 \leq j \leq k + 1$, i.e., all the predecessors of B_j are guaranteed to not fail. The number of times B_j will be executed is given by the total number of solutions generated by its predecessors, i.e., the literals $B_1, \ldots, B_{j-1}$. Let this number be denoted by N_j : we can estimate N_j using Theorem 5.1 (or extensions thereof), e.g., by considering a clause whose body consists of the literals $B_1, \ldots, B_{j-1}$, and where the output variables in the head are given by $vars(B_1, \ldots, B_{j-1}) \cap vars(B_j, \ldots, B_n)$. Assume that the cost of head unification and tests for this clause is at least $h(n)$, and let $Cost_{B_i}(x)$ denote a lower bound on the cost of the body literal B_j. Then, a lower bound on the execution cost of the clause to obtain all solutions is given by

$$h(n) + \sum_{i=1}^{k}(N_i \times Cost_{B_i}(\phi_i(n))) \leq Cost_C(n).$$

4 Number of Solutions: The Single-Clause Case

In this section we address the problem of estimating lower bounds on the number of solutions which a predicate can generate.

4.1 Simple Conditions for Lower Bound Estimation

It is tempting to try and estimate a lower bound on the number of solutions generated by a clause '$H :- B_1, \ldots, B_n$' from lower bounds on the number of solutions generated by each of the body literals B_i, possibly using techniques analogous to those used in [6] for the estimation of upper bounds on the number of solutions. Unfortunately, this does not work. For example, given a clause '$p(X) :- q(X), r(X)$', where X is an output variable, and assuming that q and r generate n_q and n_r bindings, respectively, for X, then $min(n_q, n_r)$ is not a lower bound on the number of solutions the clause can generate. To see this, consider the situation where q can bind X to either a or b, while r can bind X to either b or c: thus, $min(n_q, n_r) = min(2, 2) = 2$, but the number of solutions for the clause is 1.

The following gives a simple sufficient condition for estimating a lower bound on the number of solutions generated by a clause.

Theorem 4.1 *Let $x_1, \ldots, x_m$ be distinct unaliased output variables in the head of a clause such that each of the x_i occurs at most once in the body of the clause, and x_i and x_j do not occur in the same body literal for $i \neq j$. If n_i is a lower bound on the number of bindings that can be generated for x_i by the clause body, then $\prod_{i=1}^{m} n_i$ is a lower bound on the number of solutions that can be generated by the clause.*

This result can be generalized in various ways: we do not pursue them here due to space constraints. The utility of this theorem is shown in Example 5.1.

4.2 Handling Equality and Disequality Constraints

This section presents a simple algorithm for computing a lower bound on the number of solutions for predicates which can be "unfolded" into a conjunction of binary equality and disequality constraints on a set of variables. The constraints are in the form of $X = Y$ or $X \neq Y$ for any two variables X and Y. The types of the variables in a predicate are assumed to be the same and to be given as a finite set of atoms. The problem of computing the number of bindings that satisfy a set of binary equality and disequality constraints on a set of variables with the same type can be transformed into the problem of computing the *chromatic polynomial* of a graph G, denoted by $C(G, k)$, which is a polynomial in k and represents the number of different ways G can be colored by using no more than k colors (see [6]).

Unfortunately, the problem of computing the chromatic polynomial of a graph is NP-hard, because the problem of k-colorability of a graph G is equivalent to the problem of deciding whether $C(G, k) > 0$ and the problem of graph k-colorability is NP-complete [11]. Therefore, we will develop an approximation algorithm to compute a lower bound on the chromatic polynomial of a graph. The basic idea is to start with a subgraph that consists of only a single vertex of the graph, then repeatedly build larger and larger subgraphs by adding a vertex at a time into the previous subgraph. When a vertex is added, the edges connecting that vertex to vertices in the previous subgraph are also added. At each iteration, a lower bound on the number of ways of coloring the newly added vertex can be determined by the number of edges accompanied with the vertex. Accordingly, a lower bound on the chromatic

Let $G = (V, E)$ be a graph of order n. The algorithm proceeds as follows:

begin
    compute the degree for each vertex in V;
    generate an ordering $\omega = v_1, \ldots, v_n$ of V by sorting the vertices in
        decreasing order on their degrees using the radix sort;
    $C(G, k) := k$;
    $G_1 := (\{v_1\}, \emptyset)$;
    for $i := 2$ **to** n **do**
        compute the order $|G_i'|$ of the interfacing subgraph G_i';
        $C(G, k) := C(G, k) \times (k - |G_i'|)$;
        construct the accumulating subgraph G_i;
    od
end

Figure 1: An approximation algorithm for computing the chromatic polynomial of a graph

polynomial for the corresponding subgraph can be determined using the bound on the polynomial for the previous subgraph and the bound on the number of ways of coloring the newly added vertex.

We now describe the algorithm more formally. The *order* of a graph $G = (V, E)$, denoted by $|G|$, is the number of vertices in V. Let G be a graph of order n. Suppose $\omega = v_1, \ldots, v_n$ is an ordering of V. We define two sequences of subgraphs of G according to ω. The first is a sequence of subgraphs $G_1, \ldots, G_n$, called *accumulating subgraphs*, where $G_i = (V_i, E_i)$, $V_i = \{v_1, \ldots, v_i\}$, and E_i is the set of edges of G that join the vertices of V_i, for $1 \leq i \leq n$, The second is a sequence of subgraphs $G_2', \ldots, G_n'$, called *interfacing subgraphs*, where $G_i' = (V_i', E_i')$, V_i' is the set of vertices of G_{i-1} that are adjacent to vertex v_i, and E_i' is the set of edges of G_{i-1} that join the vertices of V_i', for $2 \leq i \leq n$.

The algorithm for computing the chromatic polynomial of a graph, based on the construction of accumulating subgraphs and interfacing subgraphs, is shown in Figure 1. This algorithm constructs the accumulating subgraphs according to an ordering of the set of vertices. At each iteration, the number of ways of coloring the newly added vertex is computed based on the order of the corresponding interfacing subgraph.

Theorem 4.2 *Let $G = (V, E)$ be a graph of order n and ω be an ordering of V. Suppose the interfacing subgraphs of G corresponding to ω are $G_2', \ldots, G_n'$. Then:*

$$k \prod_{i=2}^{n} (k - |G_i'|) \leq C(G, k).$$

The proof of this theorem is given in [13]; we omit it here due to space constraints. Since the bound obtained from this may depend on the ordering chosen for the vertices in the graph, we use a heuristic to find a "good" ordering. The intuition behind the heuristic is that if the maximum order of the interfacing subgraphs is smaller, then we can get a nontrivial lower bound ($\neq 0$) on $C(G, k)$ for more values of k. Therefore, we use the ordering that sorts the vertices in the decreasing order on the degrees of vertices.

Let the graph under consideration have n vertices and m edges. First, the computation for the degrees of vertices in the graph can be performed in $O(n + m)$.

Second, since the degrees of vertices in the graph are at most $n - 1$, we can sort the vertices using radix sort in $O(n)$. Third, the total cost for the construction of accumulating subgraphs G_i, $i \leq i \leq n$, is $O(n + m)$ because each edge in the graph is examined only twice. Finally, since only the orders of the interfacing subgraphs are needed to compute the chromatic polynomial, it is not necessary to construct the interfacing graphs. The orders of the interfacing subgraphs can be obtained as a by-product of constructing the accumulating graphs. Therefore, the complexity of the whole algorithm is $O(n + m)$.

5 Number of Solutions: Multiple Clauses

The previous section discussed the estimation of lower bounds on the number of solutions computed by a single clause. In this section we discuss how we can estimate the number of solutions for a group of clauses.

Theorem 5.1 *Consider a set of clauses $S = \{C_1, \ldots, C_n\}$ that all have the same head unification and tests. If n_i is a lower bound on the number of solutions generated by C_i, $1 \leq i \leq n$, then $\sum_{i=1}^{n} n_i$ is a lower bound on the total number of (not necessarily distinct) solutions generated by the set of clauses S.*

The restrictions in this theorem can be relaxed in various ways: we do not pursue this here due to space constraints. We can use the result above to estimate a lower bound on the number of solutions generated by a predicate for an input of size n as follows: partition the clauses for the predicate into clusters such that the clauses in each cluster have the same head unification and tests, so that Theorem 5.1 is applicable, and compute lower bound estimates of the number of solutions for each cluster. Then, if a number of different clusters—say, clusters $C_1, \ldots, C_k$, with number of solutions at least $n_1, \ldots, n_k$ respectively, may be applicable to an input of size n, then the number of solutions overall for an input of size n is given by $min(n_1, \ldots, n_k)$. The utility of this approach is illustrated by the following example.

Example 5.1 Consider the following predicate to generate all subsets of a set represented as a list:

```
subset([], X) :- X = [].
subset([H|L], X) :- X = [H|X1], subset(L, X1).
subset([H|L], X) :- subset(L, X).
```

As discussed in Section 2, recursion is handled by initially using a symbolic representation to set up difference equations, and then solving, or estimating solutions to, these equations. In this case, let (a lower bound on) the number of solutions computed by subset/2 on an input of size n be symbolically represented by $S(n)$. The first clause for the predicate yields the equation

$$S(0) = 1.$$

From Theorem 4.1, on an input of size n, $n > 0$, the second and third clauses each yield at least $S(n-1)$ solutions. Since they have the same head unification and tests, Theorem 5.1 is applicable, and the number of solutions given by these two clauses taken together is therefore at least $S(n-1) + S(n-1) = 2S(n-1)$. Thus, we have the equation

$$S(n) = 2S(n-1).$$

These difference equations can be solved to get the lower bound $S(n) = 2^n$ on the number of solutions computed by this predicate on an input of size n. □

6 Cost Estimation for Divide-and-Conquer Programs

A significant shortcoming of the approach to cost estimation presented is its loss in precision in the presence of divide-and-conquer programs in which the sizes of the output arguments of the "divide" predicates are dependent. In the familiar quicksort program (see Example 6.1), for example, since either of the outputs of the partition predicate can be the empty list, the straightforward approach computes lower bounds under the assumption that both output can *simultaneously* be the empty list, and thereby significantly underestimates the cost of the program. In some sense, the reason for this loss of precision is that the approach outlined so far is essentially an independent attributes analysis [10]. However, even if we came up with a relational attributes analysis that kept track of relationships between the sizes of different output arguments of a predicate, it is not at all obvious how we might, systematically and from first principles, use this information to improve our lower bound cost estimates. For the quicksort program, for example, if the input list has length n, then the two output lists of the partition predicate have lengths m and $n - m - 1$ for some m, $0 \leq m < n$. The resulting cost equation for the recursive clause is of the form

$$C(n) = C(m) + C(n - m - 1) + \ldots \qquad (0 \leq m \leq n - 1)$$

In order to determine a worst-case lower bound solution to this equation we need to determine the value of m that minimizes the function $C(n)$, and doing this automatically, when we don't even know what $C(n)$ looks like, seems nontrivial. As a pragmatic solution, we argue that it may be possible to get quite useful results simply by identifying and treating common classes of divide-and-conquer programs specially.

In many of these programs, the sum of the sizes of the input for the "divide" predicates in the clause body is equal to the size of the input in the clause head minus some constant. This size relationship can be derived in some cases by the approach presented in [6]. However, this is not possible in other cases, since in this approach the size of each output argument is treated as a function only of the input sizes, independently of the sizes of other output arguments, and, as a result, relationships between the sizes of different output arguments are lost (consider for example the partition/4 predicate defined in example 6.1). Although the analysis does not break down for these cases, it can lose precision. A possible solution to improve precision is to use one of the recently proposed approaches for inferring size relationships for this class of programs [2, 7].

Assuming that we have the mentioned size relationship for these programs, in the cost analysis phase we obtain an expression of the form:

$y(0) = C$,
$y(n) = y(n - 1 - k) + y(k) + g(n)$ for $n > 0$, where k is an arbitrary value such that $0 \leq k \leq n - 1$, C is a constant and $g(n)$ is any function.

where $y(n)$ denotes the cost of the divide-and-conquer predicate for an input of size n and $g(n)$ is the cost of the part of a clause body which does not contain any call to the divide-and-conquer predicate.

For each particular computation, we obtain a succession of values for k. Each succession of values for k yields a value for $y(n)$.

In the following we discuss how we can compute lower/upper bounds for expressions such as that for $\text{Cost}_{\text{qsort}}(n)$ in Example 6.1. Consider the expression:

$$y(0) = C,$$
$$y(n) = y(n-1-k) + y(k) \text{ for } n > 0, \text{ where k is an arbitrary value such}$$
that $0 \leq k \leq n-1$ and C is a constant.

A *computation tree* for such an expression is a tree in which each non-terminal node is labeled with $y(n)$, $n > 0$, and has two children $y(n-1-k)$ and $y(k)$ (left- and right-hand-side respectively), where k is an arbitrary value such that $0 \leq k \leq n-1$. Terminal nodes are labeled with $y(0)$ and have no children. Assume that we construct a tree for $y(n)$ following a depth-first traversal. In each non-terminal node, we (arbitrarily) chose a value for k such that $0 \leq k \leq n-1$. We say that the *computation succession* of the tree is the succession of values that have been chosen for k in chronological order, as the tree construction proceeds.

Lemma 6.1 *Any computation tree corresponding to the expression:*

$$y(0) = C,$$
$$y(n) = y(n-1-k) + y(k) \text{ for } n > 0, \text{ where } k \text{ is an arbitrary value such}$$
that $0 \leq k \leq n-1$ and C is a constant,

has $n+1$ terminal nodes and n non-terminal nodes.

Proof By induction on n. For $n = 0$ the theorem holds trivially. Let us assume that the theorem holds for all m such that $0 \leq m \leq n$, then, we can prove that for all m such that $0 \leq m \leq n+1$ the theorem also holds by reasoning as follows: we have that $y(n+1) = y(n-k) + y(k)$, where k is an arbitrary value such that $0 \leq k \leq n$. Since $0 \leq k \leq n$, we also have that $0 \leq n-k \leq n$, and, by induction hypothesis, the number of terminal nodes in any computation tree of $y(n-k)$ (respectively $y(k)$) is $n-k+1$ (respectively $k+1$). The number of terminal nodes in any computation tree of $y(n+1)$ is the sum of the number of terminal nodes in the children of the node labeled with $y(n+1)$, i.e. $(n-k+1) + (k+1) = n+2$. Also, the number of non-terminal nodes in any computation tree of $y(n-k)$ (respectively $y(k)$) is $n-k$ (respectively k). The number of non-terminal nodes of any computation tree of $y(n+1)$ is the sum of the number of non-terminal nodes of the children of the node labeled with $y(n+1)$ plus one (the node $y(n+1)$ itself, since it is non-terminal) i.e. $1 + (n-k) + k = n+1$. ∎

Theorem 6.2 *For any computation tree corresponding to the expression:*

$$y(0) = C,$$
$$y(n) = y(n-1-k) + y(k) \text{ for } n > 0, \text{ where } k \text{ is an arbitrary value such}$$
that $0 \leq k \leq n-1$ and C is a constant,

it holds that $y(n) = (n+1) \times C$.

Proof By Lemma 6.1, any computation tree has $n+1$ terminal nodes labeled with $y(0)$ and the evaluation of each of these terminal nodes is C. ∎

Theorem 6.3 *Given the expression:*

$$y(0) = C,$$
$$y(n) = y(n-1-k) + y(k) + g(k) \text{ for } n > 0, \text{ where } k \text{ is an arbitrary value}$$
such that $0 \leq k \leq n-1$, C is a constant and $g(k)$ a function,

for any computation tree corresponding to it, it holds that $y(n) = (n+1) \times C + \sum_{i=1}^{n} g(k_i)$, where $\{k_i\}_{i=1}^{n}$ is the computation succession of the tree.

Proof By Lemma 6.1, any computation tree has $n + 1$ terminal nodes and n non-terminal nodes. The evaluation of each terminal node yields the value C and each time a non-terminal node i is evaluated, $g(k_i)$ is added. ∎

In order to minimize (respectively maximize) $y(n)$ we can find a succession $\{k_i\}_{i=1}^n$ that minimizes (respectively maximizes) $\sum_{i=1}^n g(k_i)$. This is easy when $g(k)$ is a monotonic function, as the following corollary shows.

Corollary 6.1 *Given the expression:*

$y(0) = C,$
$y(n) = y(n - 1 - k) + y(k) + g(k)$ *for $n > 0$, where k is an arbitrary value such that $0 \leq k \leq n-1$, C is a constant and $g(k)$ an increasing monotonic function,*

Then, the succession $\{k_i\}_{i=1}^n$, where $k_i = 0$ (respectively $k_i = n-1$) for all $1 \leq i \leq n$ gives the minimum (respectively maximum) value for $y(n)$ of all computation trees.

Proof It follows from Theorem 6.3 and from the fact that $g(k)$ is an increasing monotonic function. ∎

It follows from Corollary 6.1 that the solution of the difference equation (obtained by replacing k by 0):

$y(0) = C,$
$y(n) = y(n - 1) + y(0) + g(0)$ for $n > 0,$

i.e. $(n + 1) \times C + n \times g(0)$ is the minimum of $y(n)$, and the solution of the difference equation:

$y(0) = C,$
$y(n) = y(0) + y(n - 1) + g(n - 1)$ for $n > 0,$

i.e. $(n + 1) \times C + n \times g(n - 1)$ is the maximum of $y(n)$.

Note that we can replace $g(k)$ by any lower/upper bound on it to compute a lower/upper bound on $y(n)$. We can also take any lower/upper bound on each $g(k_i)$. For example, if $g(k)$ is an increasing monotonic function then $g(k_i) \leq g(n - 1)$ and $g(k_i) \geq g(0)$ for $1 \leq i \leq n$, thus, $y(n) \leq (n + 1) \times C + n \times g(n - 1)$ and $y(n) \geq (n + 1) \times C + n \times g(0)$.

Let's now assume that the function g depends on n and k:

Corollary 6.2 *Given the expression:*

$y(0) = C,$
$y(n) = y(n - 1 - k) + y(k) + g(n, k)$ *for $n > 0$, where k is an arbitrary value such that $0 \leq k \leq n - 1$, C is a constant and $g(n, k)$ a function.*

Then, the solution of the difference equation:

$f(0) = C,$
$f(n) = f(n - 1) + C + L$ *for $n > 0$,*

where L is a lower/upper bound on $g(n, k)$, is a lower/upper bound on $y(n)$ for all $n \geq 0$ and for any computation tree corresponding to $y(n)$. In particular, if $g(n, k)$ is an increasing monotonic function, then $L \equiv g(1, 0)$ (respectively $L \equiv g(n, n - 1)$) is a lower (respectively upper) bound on $g(n, k)$.

Example 6.1 Let us see how, using the described approach for divide-and-conquer programs, the lower-bound cost analysis can be improved. We first consider the analysis without the incorporation of the optimization, and then we compare with the result obtained when the optimization is used.

Consider the predicate `qsort/2` defined as follows:

```
qsort([], []).
qsort([First|L1], L2) :-
      partition(L1, First, Ls, Lg),
      qsort(Ls, Ls2), qsort(Lg, Lg2),
      append(Ls2, [First|Lg2], L2).


partition([], F, [], []).
partition([X|Y], F, [X|Y1], Y2) :-
      X =< F,
      partition(Y, F, Y1, Y2).
partition([X|Y], F, Y1, [X|Y2]) :-
      X > F,
      partition(Y, F, Y1, Y2).


append([], L, L).
append([H|L], L1, [H|R]) :- append(L, L1, R).
```

Let $\text{Cost}_p(n)$ denote the cost (number of resolution steps) of a call to predicate p with an input of size n (in this example, the size measure used for all predicates is list length [6]). The estimation of cost functions proceeds in a "bottom-up" way as follows:

The difference equation obtained for `append/3` is:

$$\text{Cost}_{\text{append}}(0, m) = 1 \text{ (the cost of head unification)},$$
$$\text{Cost}_{\text{append}}(n, m) = 1 + \text{Cost}_{\text{append}}(n - 1, m).$$

where $\text{Cost}_{\text{append}}(n, m)$ is the cost of a call to `append/3` with input lists of lengths n and m (first and second argument, respectively). The solution to this equation is: $\text{Cost}_{\text{append}}(n, m) = n + 1$. Since this function depends only on n, we use the function $\text{Cost}_{\text{append}}(n)$ instead.

The difference equation for `partition/4` is:

$$\text{Cost}_{\text{partition}}(0) = 1 \text{ (the cost of head unification)},$$
$$\text{Cost}_{\text{partition}}(n) = 1 + \text{Cost}_{\text{partition}}(n - 1).$$

where $\text{Cost}_{\text{partition}}(n)$ gives the cost of a call to `partition/4` with an input list (first argument) of length n. The solution to this equation is: $\text{Cost}_{\text{partition}}(n) = n + 1$. For `qsort/2`, we have:

$$\text{Cost}_{\text{qsort}}(0) = 1 \text{ (the cost of head unification)},$$
$$\text{Cost}_{\text{qsort}}(n) = 1 + \text{Cost}_{\text{partition}}(n - 1) + 2 \times \text{Cost}_{\text{qsort}}(0) + \text{Cost}_{\text{append}}(0)$$

because the computed lower bound for the size of the input to the calls to `qsort` and `append` is 0. Thus, the cost function for `qsort/2` is given by:

$$\text{Cost}_{\text{qsort}}(0) = 1,$$
$$\text{Cost}_{\text{qsort}}(n) = n + 4, \text{ for } n > 0.$$

Now, we use the described approach for divide-and-conquer programs. Assume that we use the expression:

$\text{Cost}_{\text{qsort}}(0) = 1,$

$\text{Cost}_{\text{qsort}}(n) = 1 + \text{Cost}_{\text{partition}}(n-1) + \text{Cost}_{\text{qsort}}(k)$
$\qquad + \text{Cost}_{\text{qsort}}(n-1-k) + \text{Cost}_{\text{append}}(k), \text{ for } 0 \leq k \leq n-1 \text{ and } n > 0.$

Replacing values, we obtain:

$\text{Cost}_{\text{qsort}}(n) = n + k + 2 + \text{Cost}_{\text{qsort}}(k) + \text{Cost}_{\text{qsort}}(n-1-k),$
$\qquad \text{for } 0 \leq k \leq n-1.$

According to Corollary 6.2, by giving to n and k the minimum possible value, i.e. 1 and 0 respectively, we have that $n + k + 2 \geq 3$, and thus we replace $n + k + 2$ by 3 in order to obtain a lower bound on the former expression, which yields:

$\text{Cost}_{\text{qsort}}(n) = 3 + \text{Cost}_{\text{qsort}}(k) + \text{Cost}_{\text{qsort}}(n-1-k), \text{ for } 0 \leq k \leq n-1.$

which is equivalent to the difference equation:

$\text{Cost}_{\text{qsort}}(n) = 3 + 1 + \text{Cost}_{\text{qsort}}(n-1), \text{ for } n > 0.$

The solution of this equation is $\text{Cost}_{\text{qsort}}(n) = 4n + 1$, which is an improvement on the former lower bound. $\square$

The previous results can be easily generalized to cover multiple recursive divide-and-conquer programs and programs where the sum of the sizes of the input for the "divide" predicates in the clause body is equal to the size of the input in the clause head minus some constant which is not necessarily 1.

7 Implementation

We have implemented a prototype of a lower bound size/cost analyzer, by recoding the version of CASLOG [6] currently integrated in the CIAO system [8]. The analysis is fully automatic, and only requires type information for the program entry point. Types, modes and size measures are automatically inferred by the system. Table 1 shows some accuracy and efficiency results of the lower bound cost analyzer. The second column of the table shows the cost function (which depends on the size of the input arguments) inferred by the analysis. T_{tms} is the time required by the type, mode, and size measure analysis (SPARCstation 10, 55MHz, 64Mbytes of memory), T_{nf} the time required by the non-failure analysis, and T_s and T_{ca} are the time required by the size and cost analysis respectively. **Total** is the total analysis time ($Total = T_{tms} + T_{nf} + T_s + T_{ca}$). All times are given in milliseconds.

8 Application to Automatic Parallelization

As briefly mentioned in the introduction, one of the most attractive applications of lower bound cost analysis is implementing granularity control in parallelizing compilers, an issue on which we expand in this section. Parallel execution of a task incurs various overheads, e.g. overheads associated with process creation and scheduling, the possible migration of tasks to remote processors and the associated communication overheads, etc. In general, a goal should not be a candidate for parallel execution if its granularity, i.e., the "work available" underneath it, is less than the work necessary to create a separate task for that goal. While the overheads for spawning goals in parallel in some architectures are small (e.g. in small shared memory multiprocessors), in many other architectures (e.g. distributed memory multiprocessors,

Program	Cost function	T_{tms}	T_{nf}	T_s	T_{ca}	Total
fibonacci	$\lambda x. 1.447 \times 1.618^x + 0.552 \times (-0.618)^x - 1$	90	10	20	20	140
hanoi	$\lambda x. x2^x + 2^{x-1} - 2$	430	30	60	60	580
qsort	$\lambda x. 4x + 1$	420	50	70	50	590
nreverse	$\lambda x. 0.5x^2 + 1.5x + 1$	220	20	30	30	300
mmatrix	$\lambda \langle x, y \rangle. 2xy + 2x + 1$	350	90	90	90	620
deriv	$\lambda x. x$	1010	80	170	120	1,380
addpoly	$\lambda \langle x, y \rangle. x + 1$	220	70	40	30	360
append	$\lambda x. x + 1$	100	20	10	10	140
partition	$\lambda x. x + 1$	175	30	30	20	255
substitute	$\lambda \langle x, y, z \rangle. x$	70	50	110	100	330
intersection	$\lambda \langle x, y \rangle. x + 1$	150	130	20	30	260
difference	$\lambda \langle x, y \rangle. x + 1$	140	90	20	40	290

Table 1: Accuracy and efficiency of the lower bound cost analysis

workstation "farms", etc.) such overheads can be very significant. The consequence is that automatic parallelization cannot be achieved realistically in the latter without some form of granularity control.

As we have already pointed out, all of the previous work that we know of in this context involves estimating upper bounds on the cost of goals. Given a program that is already parallelized, upper bound cost information can be used to produce a program in which some of the parallel goals are forced to run sequentially, in such a way that the resulting execution can be guaranteed to be faster (or, at least, no slower) than that of the original parallel program. However, the problem faced by parallelizing compilers is in fact exactly the converse: what needs to be guaranteed is that the parallel execution will be more efficient than that of the original sequential program, rather than the other way around. This type of granularity control can be performed applying essentially the same techniques as when using upper bound information [14], but, of course, *lower bound* information on the cost of each goal is required instead, and this is where the techniques proposed in this paper fit in. The usefulness of lower bounds was already clear when the work presented in [4] was developed, but the determination of useful lower bounds was deemed too difficult at the time. Using lower bounds allows obtaining *guaranteed speedups* (or, at least, ensuring that no *slow-downs* will occur) from automatic parallelization, even in architectures for which parallel execution involves a significant overhead. We know of no other approach which can achieve this.

We have interfaced the cost analysis stage (see Section 7) with the granularity control system described in [14] (which is also integrated in the CIAO system as another stage, and which includes an annotator which transforms programs to perform granularity control). The result is a complete program parallelizer with (lower bound cost based) granularity control. Since our objective herein is simply to study the usefulness of the lower bound estimates produced, only a very simple granularity control strategy has been selected: goals are always executed in parallel provided their grain sizes are estimated to be greater than a given fixed threshold, which is a constant for all programs. Also, the versions of the programs that perform granularity control are simple source-to-source transformations which add granularity control tests to the original versions. A discussion of more advanced strategies that include variable thresholds (which depend on parameters such as data transfer cost, number of processor, system load, etc.), lower level transformations, and performing goal groupings to increase granularity can be found in [14].

programs	seq	ngc	gclb(175)	gclb(959)
mmatrix(100)	52.389	74.760 (0.70)	29.040 (1.80)	27.981 (1.87)
mmatrix(50)	6.469	5.978 (1.08)	3.378 (1.92)	3.758 (1.72)
fib(19)	0.757	1.458 (0.52)	0.128 (5.93)	0.103 (7.32)
hanoi(13)	1.442	1.464 (0.98)	0.677 (2.13)	0.619 (2.33)
qsort(1000)	0.475	0.414 (1.15)	0.230 (2.06)	0.314 (1.51)
qsort(3000)	4.142	2.423 (1.71)	1.094 (3.79)	1.575 (2.63)

Table 2: Granularity control results for benchmarks on ECL^{i}PS^e.

We have performed some preliminary experiments in which a series of benchmarks have been parallelized automatically, with the compiler option corresponding to inclusion of granularity control both enabled and disabled. The resulting programs have been executed on the ECL^{i}PS^e system using 10 workers, and running on a SUN SPARC 2000 SERVER with 10 processors. We have chosen this system, which implements and-parallelism on top of or-parallelism, because it has considerably greater parallel task execution overhead than systems which implement and-parallelism natively (such as, for example, the &-Prolog engine used in the CIAO system). As a result, this system offers an interesting challenge – it proved very difficult to achieve and-parallel speedups on it automatically with previous parallelizers.

Table 2 presents the results. It shows wall-clock execution times in seconds. Results are given for the sequential execution (seq), the parallel execution without granularity control (ngc), and the versions which perform granularity control (gclb(175) and gclb(959)). The two numbers correspond to two different choices of threshold, and illustrate the comparatively low sensitivity of the results to the choice of this parameter that we have observed.

The results of the experiments appear promising, in the sense that the granularity control does improve speedups in practice, in a quite challenging situation. On systems with higher overheads, such as distributed systems, the benefits can be much larger, although it may be difficult to achieve actual speedups in some cases (i.e., given high enough overheads, the result of the granularity analysis can often be simply a sequential program). In any case, we believe that it is possible to improve these results significantly by using more sophisticated control strategies, as mentioned above.

Acknowledgements

The work of S. Debray was supported in part by the National Science Foundation under grant CCR-9123520. The work of M. Hermenegildo and P. López-García was supported in part by ESPRIT project LTR 22532 "DiSCiPl" and CICYT proyect number TIC96-1012-C02-01. The work of N.-W. Lin was supported in part by the NSC of ROC under grant NSC83-0408-E-194-010.

References

[1] D. Basin and H. Ganzinger. Complexity Analysis based on Ordered Resolution *Proc. 11th. IEEE Symposium on Logic in Computer Science*, 1996.

[2] F. Benoy and A. King. Inferring Argument Size Relationships with CLP(R). *Proc. 6th International Workshop on Logic Program Synthesis and Transformation*, Stockholm University/Royal Intitute of Technology, 1996, pp. 134–153.

[3] S. Debray, P. López García, and M. Hermenegildo. Non-Failure Analysis for Logic Programs. In *1997 International Conference on Logic Programming*, pages 48–62, Leuven, Belgium, June 1997. MIT Press, Cambridge, MA.

[4] S. K. Debray, N.-W. Lin, and M. Hermenegildo. Task Granularity Analysis in Logic Programs. In *Proc. of the 1990 ACM Conf. on Programming Language Design and Implementation*, pages 174–188. ACM Press, June 1990.

[5] S.K. Debray and N.-W. Lin. Static estimation of query sizes in horn programs. In *Third International Conference on Database Theory*, Lecture Notes in Computer Science 470, pages 515–528, Paris, France, December 1990. Springer-Verlag.

[6] S.K. Debray and N.W. Lin. Cost analysis of logic programs. *ACM Transactions on Programming Languages and Systems*, 15(5):826–875, November 1993.

[7] R. Giacobazzi, S.K. Debray, and G. Levi. Generalized Semantics and Abstract Interpretation for Constraint Logic Programs. *Journal of Logic Programming*, 25(3):191–248, 1995.

[8] M. Hermenegildo, F. Bueno, M. García de la Banda, and G. Puebla. The CIAO Multi-Dialect Compiler and System: An Experimentation Workbench for Future (C)LP Systems. In *Proceedings of the ILPS'95 Workshop on Visions for the Future of Logic Programming*, Portland, Oregon, USA, December 1995. Available from http://www.clip.dia.fi.upm.es/.

[9] L. Huelsbergen, J. R. Larus, and A. Aiken. Using Run-Time List Sizes to Guide Parallel Thread Creation. In *Proc. ACM Conf. on Lisp and Functional Programming*, June 1994.

[10] Neil D. Jones and Steven S. Muchnick. Complexity of flow analysis, inductive assertion synthesis, and a language due to Dijkstra. In Steven S Muchnick and Neil D Jones, editors, *Program Flow Analysis: Theory and Applications*, chapter 12, pages 380–393. Prentice-Hall, 1981.

[11] R. M. Karp. Reducibility among Combinatorial Problems. *Complexity of Computer Computations*, R. E. Miller and J. W. Thatcher (eds), Plenum Press, New York, 1972, pp. 85–103.

[12] S. Kaplan. Algorithmic Complexity of Logic Programs. In *Logic Programming, Proc. Fifth International Conference and Symposium, (Seattle, Washington)*, pages 780–793, 1988.

[13] N.-W. Lin. Approximating the Chromatic Polynomial of a Graph. *Proc. Nineteenth International Workshop on Graph-Theoretic Concepts in Computer Science*, Amsterdam, June 1993.

[14] P. López García, M. Hermenegildo, and S.K. Debray. A Methodology for Granularity Based Control of Parallelism in Logic Programs. *Journal of Symbolic Computation, Special Issue on Parallel Symbolic Computation*, (22):715–734, 1996.

[15] F. A. Rabhi and G. A. Manson. Using Complexity Functions to Control Parallelism in Functional Programs. Res. Rep. CS-90-1, Dept. of Computer Science, Univ. of Sheffield, England, Jan 1990.

[16] X. Zhong, E. Tick, S. Duvvuru, L. Hansen, A.V.S. Sastry, and R. Sundararajan. Towards an Efficient Compile-Time Granularity Analysis Algorithm. In *Proc. of the 1992 International Conference on Fifth Generation Computer Systems*, pages 809–816. Institute for New Generation Computer Technology (ICOT), June 1992.

Constraint Logic Programming with Hereditary Harrop Formulas

Javier Leach, Susana Nieva and Mario Rodríguez-Artalejo

Dpto. de Sistemas Informáticos y Programación

Univ. Complutense de Madrid

28040 Madrid, Spain

{leach,nieva,mario}@dia.ucm.es

Abstract

Constraint Logic Programming (*CLP*) and Hereditary Harrop Formulas (*HH*) are two well-known ways to enhance the expressivity of Horn clauses. In this paper, we present a novel combination of these two approaches. We show how to enrich the syntax and proof theory of *HH* with the help of a given constraint system, in such a way that the key property of *HH* as a logic programming language (namely, the existence of uniform proofs) is preserved. We also present a procedure for goal solving, showing its soundness and completeness for computing answer constraints. As a consequence of this result, we obtain a new strong completeness theorem for *CLP* that avoids to build disjunctions of computed answers, as well as a more declarative formulation of a known completeness theorem for *HH*.

KEYWORDS: constraint systems, hereditary Harrop formulas, uniform proofs, goal solving.

1 Introduction

Traditionally, the logic of Horn clauses has been considered as the basis for logic programming [20]. In spite of its Turing completeness [1], the lack of expressivity of Horn clauses for programming purposes is widely acknowledged. During the last decade, different extensions of Horn clauses have been proposed, with the aim of increasing expressivity without sacrificing the declarative character of pure logic programming. Among such extensions, two important approaches are Constraint Logic Programming (*CLP*) and Hereditary Harrop Formulas (*HH*).

The *CLP* scheme [7] goes beyond the limitations of the Herbrand universe by providing the ability to program with Horn clauses over different computation domains, whose logical behaviour is given by *constraint systems*. *CLP* languages keep all the good semantic properties of pure logic programming, including soundness and completeness results [9]. Their implementation relies on the combination of *SLD* resolution with dedicated algorithms for constraint entailment, solving and simplification. Therefore, efficient and yet declarative programs can be written to solve complex combinatorial problems. See [8] for a survey of the foundations, implementation issues and applications of *CLP* languages.

On the other hand, the *HH* approach [14] overcomes the inability of Horn clauses to provide a logical basis for several constructions commonly found in modern programming languages, such as scoping, abstraction and modularity. This is achieved by extending Horn clauses to a richer fragment of intuitionistic logic that allows us to use disjunctions, implications and quantifiers in goals. In fact, *HH* is a typical example of an *abstract logic programming language*, in the sense of [15]. Abstract logic programming languages are characterized by the fact that the declarative meaning of a program, given by provability in a deduction system, can be interpreted operationally as goal-oriented search for solutions. Technically, the existence of *uniform proofs* for all provable goal formulas enables the search interpretation of provability. The implementation of programming languages based on *HH*, such as λ-Prolog [13, 17], requires the resolution of the problem of unifying terms occurring under the scope of arbitrary quantifier prefixes. Correct unification algorithms for such problems have been studied in [12, 16]. Moreover, [16] shows in detail the soundness and completeness of a goal solving procedure for the first-order *HH* language.

The aim of this paper is to present a framework for the combination of the *CLP* and *HH* approaches. We will enrich the syntax of first-order *HH* with constraints coming from a given constraint system, and we will present an amalgamated proof system that combines inference rules from intuitionistic logic with constraint entailment, in such a way that the key property of an abstract logic programming language is preserved. Moreover, we will also present a sound and complete procedure for goal solving. In the particular case of the *Herbrand* constraint system, our completeness result boils down to a more declarative formulation of the completeness theorem in [16]. In the case of *CLP* programs using only Horn clauses with constraints, our goal solving procedure reduces to constrained resolution, and our completeness theorem yields a form of strong completeness for success that avoids the need to build disjunctions of computed answers, in contrast to [11], Th. 2 (see also [9], Th. 4.12). The reason for this discrepancy is that our amalgamated proof system uses more constructive inference mechanisms to deduce goals from program clauses.

The rest of this paper is organized as follows: In Section 2 we recall the notion of a constraint system and we define the syntax of *HH* with constraints. In Section 3 we present two proof systems for *HH* with constraints, showing the existence of uniform proofs. A sound and complete procedure for goal solving is presented as a transformation system in Section 4. In Section 5 we summarize conclusions and possible lines for future research.

Some proofs have been omitted due to lack of space; they appear in [10].

2   Hereditary Harrop Formulas with Constraints

As explained in the Introduction, the framework presented in this paper requires the enrichment of the syntax of *Hereditary Harrop Formulas* (shortly, *HH*) [14, 15] with constraints coming from a given *constraint system*. Following [18], we view a constraint system as a pair $C = (\mathcal{L}_C, \vdash_C)$, where $\mathcal{L}_C$ is the set of formulas allowed as constraints and $\vdash_{\mathcal{C}} \subseteq \mathcal{P}(\mathcal{L}_{\mathcal{C}}) \times \mathcal{L}_{\mathcal{C}}$ is an *entailment relation*. Therefore, $\Gamma \vdash_{\mathcal{C}} C$ means that the constraint C is entailed by the set of constraints Γ. We write just $\vdash_{\mathcal{C}} C$ if Γ is empty. $\mathcal{L}_{\mathcal{C}}$ and $\vdash_{\mathcal{C}}$ are required to satisfy certain minimal assumptions, mainly related to the behaviour of the logical symbols. We assume:

- $\mathcal{L}_{\mathcal{C}}$ is a set of formulas including $\top$ (true), $\bot$ (false) and all the equations $t \approx t'$ between terms over a fixed signature, and closed under $\wedge, \Rightarrow, \exists, \forall$ and the application of substitutions of terms for variables.

- $\vdash_{\mathcal{C}}$ is *compact*, i.e. $\Gamma \vdash_{\mathcal{C}} C$ holds iff $\Gamma_0 \vdash_{\mathcal{C}} C$ for some finite $\Gamma_0 \subseteq \Gamma$. $\vdash_{\mathcal{C}}$ is also *generic*, i.e. $\Gamma \vdash_{\mathcal{C}} C$ implies $\Gamma \sigma \vdash_{\mathcal{C}} C \sigma$ for every substitution σ.

- All the inference rules related to $\wedge, \Rightarrow, \exists, \forall$ and equality valid in the intuitionistic fragment of first-order logic are also valid to infer entailments in the sense of $\vdash_{\mathcal{C}}$.

The notation $C\sigma$ used above, with $\sigma=[t_1/x_1, \ldots, t_n/x_n]$, means application of a substitution σ to a constraint C, using proper renaming of the variables bound in C to avoid capturing free variables from the terms t_i, $1 \le i \le n$. This notation will be also used for any class of formula.

$\vdash_{\mathcal{C}}$ is not restricted to represent deducibility in some intuitionistic theory; on the contrary, our assumptions allow us to consider constraint systems $\mathcal{C}$ such that $\mathcal{L}_{\mathcal{C}}$ is a full first-order language with classical negation, and $\Gamma \vdash_{\mathcal{C}} C$ holds iff $Ax_{\mathcal{C}} \cup \Gamma \vdash C$, where $Ax_{\mathcal{C}}$ is a suitable set of first-order axioms and $\vdash$ is the entailment relation of classical first-order logic with equality. In particular, three important constraint systems of this form are: $\mathcal{H}$, where $Ax_{\mathcal{H}}$ is Clark's axiomatization of the Herbrand universe [2]; $\mathcal{CFT}$, where $Ax_{\mathcal{CFT}}$ is Smolka and Treinen's axiomatization of the domain of *feature trees* [19]; and $\mathcal{R}$, where $Ax_{\mathcal{R}}$ is Tarski's axiomatization of the real numbers [21]. In these three cases, the constraint system is known to be *effective*, in the sense that the validity of entailments $\Gamma \vdash_{\mathcal{C}} C$, with finite Γ, can be decided by an effective procedure. Note that these three systems include the use of disjunctions; nevertheless, our results do not rely on the assumption that $\mathcal{L}_{\mathcal{C}}$ is closed under $\vee$.

In the sequel, we assume an arbitrarily fixed effective constraint system $\mathcal{C}$. By convention, the notation $\Gamma \vdash_{\mathcal{C}} \Gamma'$ will mean that $\Gamma \vdash_{\mathcal{C}} C$ holds for all $C \in \Gamma'$. Also, we will say that a constraint C with free variables $x_1, \ldots, x_n$ is $\mathcal{C}$-satisfiable when $\vdash_{\mathcal{C}} \exists x_1 \ldots \exists x_n C$.

All constructions and results in the rest of the paper are valid for any constraint system $\mathcal{C}$. Therefore, we can speak of a *scheme HH(X)* with *instances HH(C)*, as in *CLP*. In order to define the syntax of first-order formulas of *HH(C)*, we assume a set of ranked predicate symbols (disjoint from the symbols occurring in $\mathcal{L}_{\mathcal{C}}$) which are used to build atomic formulas A of the form $P(t_1, \ldots, t_n)$.

Definition 2.1 *The set of* definite clauses, *with elements noted D, and the set of* goals, *with elements noted G, are defined by the following syntactic rules:*

$D := A \mid D_1 \wedge D_2 \mid G \Rightarrow A \mid \forall x D$

$G := A \mid C \mid G_1 \wedge G_2 \mid G_1 \vee G_2 \mid D \Rightarrow G \mid C \Rightarrow G \mid \exists x G \mid \forall x G$ □

In comparison to first-order *HH* as defined e.g. in [16], notice that constraints can occur in goals of the forms C and $C \Rightarrow G$, and therefore also in definite clauses of the form $G \Rightarrow A$. In the rest of the paper, by a *program* we understand any finite set Δ of definite clauses. This includes both *CLP* programs and first-order *HH* programs as particular cases. As in *CLP*, the result of solving a goal G using a program Δ will be an *answer constraint R* such that G can be deduced from Δ and R by means of the proof system which will be presented in Section 3.

The following simple program Δ and goal G belong to the instance $HH(\mathcal{R})$. The formula R turns out to be a correct and computable answer constraint, as we will see later. We will refer to this as the *disc example* in the rest of the paper.

$$\boxed{\begin{aligned} \Delta &\equiv \{\forall x \forall y (x^2 + y^2 \leq 1 \Rightarrow disc\,(x,y))\} \\ G &\equiv \forall y(y^2 \leq 1/2 \Rightarrow disc\,(x,y)) \\ R &\equiv x^2 \leq 1/2 \end{aligned}}$$

As usual in the *HH* framework, we need a technical device (so-called *elaboration*) for decomposing the clauses of a given program into a simple form. This is useful for a natural formulation of goal solving procedures.

Definition 2.2 *We define the* elaboration *of a program Δ as a set:*
$elab(\Delta) = \bigcup_{D \in \Delta} elab(D)$, *where $elab(D)$ is defined by case analysis in the following way:*
  $elab(A) = \{\top \Rightarrow A\}$; $elab(D_1 \wedge D_2) = elab(D_1) \cup elab(D_2)$;
  $elab(G \Rightarrow A) = \{G \Rightarrow A\}$; $elab(\forall x D) = \{\forall x D' \mid D' \in elab(D)\}$. □

Note that all clauses in $elab(\Delta)$ have the form $\forall x_1 \ldots \forall x_n (G \Rightarrow A), n \geq 0$. A *variant* of such a formula consists in the same formula where the quantified variables $x_1, \ldots, x_n$ have been renamed with variables that do not occur free in it.

3 Proof Systems

In this section we present an amalgamated proof system $\mathcal{IC}$ that combines the usual inference rules from intuitionistic logic with the entailment relation $\vdash_c$ of a constraint system $\mathcal{C}$. We will derive sequents of the form $\Delta; \Gamma \vdash G$ where Δ is a program, Γ represents a finite set of constraints and G is an arbitrary goal. We also show that $\mathcal{IC}$ enjoys the existence of uniform proofs, and we present a second proof system $\mathcal{UC}$ which is equivalent to $\mathcal{IC}$ in deductive power, but is tailored to build uniform proofs only.

3.1 The calculus $\mathcal{IC}$

$\mathcal{IC}$ stands for an <u>I</u>ntuitionistic sequent calculus for $HH(\mathcal{C})$ to deduce a goal from defined clauses in the presence of <u>C</u>onstraints. The proof system $\vdash_{\mathcal{IC}}$ is defined as follows. $\Delta; \Gamma \vdash_{\mathcal{IC}} G$ if and only if the sequent $\Delta; \Gamma \vdash G$ has a proof using the rules of $\mathcal{IC}$ shown below. A proof of a sequent is a tree whose root is the sequent and whose leaves match axioms of the calculus. The rules regulate the pass from the sons to the parent.

- Axioms to deal with constraints or atomic goals:

$$\frac{}{\Delta; \Gamma \vdash C} \; (C_R) \;\; \text{if } \Gamma \vdash_c C \qquad \frac{}{\Delta, A; \Gamma \vdash A'} \; (Atom) \;\; \text{if } \Gamma \vdash_c A \approx A'$$

A, A' are atomic formulas beginning with the same predicate symbol $-A \equiv P(t_1, \ldots, t_n)$, $A' \equiv P(t'_1, \ldots, t'_n)-$, $A \approx A'$ represents the conjunction of the equations $t_i \approx t'_i$, $1 \le i \le n$.

- Rules introducing the connectives and quantifiers of the Hereditary Harrop formulas:

$$\frac{\Delta; \Gamma \vdash G_i}{\Delta; \Gamma \vdash G_1 \vee G_2} \; (\vee_R) \; (i = 1, 2) \qquad \frac{\Delta; \Gamma \vdash G_1 \quad \Delta; \Gamma \vdash G_2}{\Delta; \Gamma \vdash G_1 \wedge G_2} \; (\wedge_R)$$

$$\frac{\Delta, D_1, D_2; \Gamma \vdash G}{\Delta, D_1 \wedge D_2; \Gamma \vdash G} \; (\wedge_L) \qquad \frac{\Delta; \Gamma \vdash G_1 \quad \Delta, A; \Gamma \vdash G}{\Delta, G_1 \Rightarrow A; \Gamma \vdash G} \; (\Rightarrow_L)$$

$$\frac{\Delta, D; \Gamma \vdash G}{\Delta; \Gamma \vdash D \Rightarrow G} \; (\Rightarrow_R) \qquad \frac{\Delta; \Gamma, C \vdash G}{\Delta; \Gamma \vdash C \Rightarrow G} \; (\Rightarrow_{R_C})$$

$$\frac{\Delta; \Gamma, C \vdash G[y/x]}{\Delta; \Gamma \vdash \exists x G} \; (\exists_R) \;\; \text{if } \Gamma \vdash_c \exists y C,$$

and y does not appear free in the sequent of the conclusion.

$$\frac{\Delta, D[y/x]; \Gamma, C \vdash G}{\Delta, \forall x D; \Gamma \vdash G} \; (\forall_L) \;\; \text{if } \Gamma \vdash_c \exists y C,$$

and y does not appear free in the sequent of the conclusion.

$$\frac{\Delta; \Gamma \vdash G[y/x]}{\Delta; \Gamma \vdash \forall x G} \; (\forall_R)$$

where y does not appear free in the sequent of the conclusion.

Note that this calculus is similar to those defined for HH in the literature (see e.g. [15, 16]), but the presence of constraints induces some modifications. Of particular importance are the modifications introduced to $(\exists_R)$ and $(\forall_L)$. A simply reformulation of the traditional version of $(\exists_R)$, using a constraint $y \approx t$ instead of a substitution $[t/x]$ could be

$$\frac{\Delta; \Gamma, y \approx t \vdash G[y/x]}{\Delta; \Gamma \vdash \exists x G} \;\; \text{if } y \text{ does not occur in } t,$$

and y does not appear free in the sequent of the conclusion.

In our constraint-oriented formulation of $(\exists_R)$ we allow any satisfiable constraint C (not necessary of the form $y \approx t$) instead of the substitution. Example 3.2 below will show that this extra generality is necessary. On the other hand, our definition of $(\forall_L)$ is the dual correspondence of $(\exists_R)$ as commonly.

The notion of size of a proof given next will be used in the sequel.

Definition 3.1 *The size of a proof is defined by recursion on its height viewed as a tree. If the tree is a single leaf, then the size is 1. Otherwise if the last inference rule has one upper sequent whose size proof is l, then the size is $l + 1$. If the last rule has two upper sequents whose size proofs are l_1 and l_2 respectively, then the size of the entire proof is $l_1 + l_2 + 1$.* □

The following lemmas show two interesting properties of $\vdash_{IC}$.

Lemma 3.1 *For any Δ, Γ, G, if Γ' is a set of constraints such that $\Gamma' \vdash_C \Gamma$ and $\Delta; \Gamma \vdash_{IC} G$, then $\Delta; \Gamma' \vdash G$ has a IC-proof of the same size.*

Lemma 3.2 *For any Δ, Γ, C, G, if $\Delta; \Gamma, C \vdash_{IC} G$ and x is a variable that does not appear free in Δ, Γ, G, then $\Delta; \Gamma, \exists x C \vdash_{IC} G$.*

We are aiming at an *abstract logic programming language* in the sense of [15]. This means that *uniform proofs* must exist for all provable sequents. Here the idea of uniform proof consists in breaking down a goal in its components until obtaining an atomic formula or a constraint, before using the rules for introduction of connectives on the left or resorting to constraint entailment. In the next subsection we define a new sequent calculus that always uses uniform deductions, and which is the basis of the goal solving procedure to be presented in the next section. Moreover both sequent calculi are equivalent, as we will prove. This equivalence is based on the following two lemmas.

Lemma 3.3 (Uniform Proofs) *If G is a goal, Δ a program and Γ a set of constraint formulas, such that $\Delta; \Gamma \vdash G$ has a proof of size l then:*

1. *For $G \equiv A$, there are constraints $C_1, \ldots, C_n$ ($n \geq 0$) and a variant of a formula in $elab(\Delta)$, $\forall x_1 \ldots \forall x_n (G' \Rightarrow A')$, such that $x_1, \ldots, x_n$ are new distinct variables not appearing free in Δ, Γ, A; A' begins with the same predicate symbol as A. In addition it holds:*
   (a) $\Gamma \vdash_C \exists x_1 C_1$, $\Gamma, C_1 \vdash_C \exists x_2 C_2, \ldots, \Gamma, C_1, \ldots, C_{n-1} \vdash_C \exists x_n C_n$.
   (b) $\Gamma, C_1 \ldots, C_n \vdash_C A \approx A'$.
   (c) $\Delta; \Gamma, C_1, \ldots, C_n \vdash G'$ has a proof of size less than l, or $G' \equiv \top$.

2. *If $G \equiv C$, then $\Gamma \vdash_C C$.*

3. *If $G \equiv G_1 \wedge G_2$, then $\Delta; \Gamma \vdash G_1$ and $\Delta; \Gamma \vdash G_2$ have proofs of size less than l.*

4. *If $G \equiv G_1 \vee G_2$, then $\Delta; \Gamma \vdash G_i$ has a proof of size less than l, $i = 1$ or 2.*

5. *If $G \equiv D \Rightarrow G_1$, then $\Delta, D; \Gamma \vdash G_1$ has a proof of size less than l.*

6. *If $G \equiv C \Rightarrow G_1$, then $\Delta; \Gamma, C \vdash G_1$ has a proof of size less than l.*

7. *For $G \equiv \exists x G_1$, if y is a variable not appearing free in Δ, Γ, G, then there is a constraint formula C such that:*
   (a) $\Gamma \vdash_C \exists y C$. (b) $\Delta; \Gamma, C \vdash G_1[y/x]$ has a proof of size less than l.

8. *For $G \equiv \forall x G_1$, if y is a variable that does not appear free in Δ, Γ, G, then $\Delta; \Gamma \vdash G_1[y/x]$ has a proof of size less than l.*

This lemma is proved by induction on the size of the proof, using the permutability of the rules for connectives on the left and on the right. A similar proof for first-order *HH* can be found in [16]. This permutability is also possible in $\mathcal{IC}$ in spite of constraints, because the conditions assumed for $\vdash_C$.

Lemma 3.4 (Elaboration) *For any Δ, Γ, A and $F \in elab(\Delta)$:*

$$\text{If } \Delta, F; \Gamma \vdash_{\mathcal{IC}} A, \text{ then } \Delta; \Gamma \vdash_{\mathcal{IC}} A.$$

Since $F \in elab(\Delta)$, there will be $D \in \Delta$ such that $F \in elab(D)$. The proof of the lemma is by induction on the size of the proof of $\Delta, F; \Gamma \vdash A$, using case analysis according to the structure of D.

3.2 The calculus $\mathcal{UC}$

$\mathcal{UC}$ stands for an intuitionistic sequent calculus for $HH(\mathcal{C})$ to building <u>U</u>niform proofs in the presence of <u>C</u>onstraints. $\Delta; \Gamma \vdash_{uc} G$ if and only if the sequent $\Delta; \Gamma \vdash G$ has a proof using the following rules.

- Axiom to deal with constraints:

$$\frac{}{\Delta; \Gamma \vdash C} \ (C_R) \ \text{ if } \Gamma \vdash_C C$$

- Rule for atomic goals:

$$\frac{\Delta; \Gamma \vdash \exists x_1 \ldots \exists x_n ((A \approx A') \wedge G)}{\Delta; \Gamma \vdash A'} \ (Clause)$$

A, A' begin with the same predicate symbol and $\forall x_1 \ldots \forall x_n (G \Rightarrow A)$ is a variant of a formula of $elab(\Delta)$, where $x_1, \ldots, x_n$ do not appear free in the sequent of the conclusion.

- Rules introducing the connectives and quantifiers of the goals: $(\vee_R), (\wedge_R), (\Rightarrow_R), (\Rightarrow_{R_C}), (\exists_R), (\forall_R)$. Defined as in the system $\mathcal{IC}$.

Our aim is to allow only proofs directed by the goal as the ones built using the system $\mathcal{UC}$ but without losing any possible derivation of $\mathcal{IC}$. The following theorem guarantees this result.

Theorem 3.5 *The deduction systems $\mathcal{IC}$ and $\mathcal{UC}$ are equivalent. That means, for any program Δ, for any set of constraints Γ, and for any goal G it holds:*

$$\Delta; \Gamma \vdash_{\mathcal{IC}} G \text{ if and only if } \Delta; \Gamma \vdash_{uc} G.$$

This theorem can be proved by induction on the size of the proofs by case analysis. The proof of $\Rightarrow$) is a direct consequence of Uniform Proofs Lemma. Proving $\Leftarrow$), Elaboration Lemma is used for the atomic case, the other are immediate from the definition of the calculi $\mathcal{UC}$, $\mathcal{IC}$.

From now on we will work only with the calculus $\mathcal{UC}$. The following examples illustrate its deductive power.

Example 3.1 The following is a $\mathcal{UC}$-proof of the sequent $\Delta; R \vdash G$, where Δ, G and R correspond to our *disc* running example.

$$\cfrac{\cfrac{\cfrac{\cfrac{x^2 \leq 1/2, y^2 \leq 1/2 \vdash_{\mathcal{R}} \exists u \exists v (x \approx u \wedge y \approx v \wedge u^2 + v^2 \leq 1)}{\Delta; x^2 \leq 1/2, y^2 \leq 1/2 \vdash \exists u \exists v (x \approx u \wedge y \approx v \wedge u^2 + v^2 \leq 1)} \ (C_R)}{\Delta; x^2 \leq 1/2, y^2 \leq 1/2 \vdash disc\ (x, y)} \ (Clause)}{\Delta; x^2 \leq 1/2 \vdash y^2 \leq 1/2 \Rightarrow disc\ (x, y)} \ (\Rightarrow_{R_C})}{\Delta; x^2 \leq 1/2 \vdash \forall y (y^2 \leq 1/2 \Rightarrow disc\ (x, y))} \ (\forall_R)$$

$\square$

Example 3.2 This example motivates the use of constraints in our inference rule $(\exists_R)$. It is based on $HH(\mathcal{R})$. Consider

$\Delta \equiv \{\forall x (x^2 \approx 2 \Rightarrow r(x))\}$,
$G \equiv \exists x\ r(x)$.

The sequent $\Delta; \vdash G$ is expected to be derivable. However, the traditional formulation of $(\exists_R)$ does not work, because no term t in the language $\mathcal{L}_{\mathcal{R}}$ denotes a square root of 2. With our $(\exists_R)$, choosing the $\mathcal{R}$-satisfiable constraint $C \equiv x^2 \approx 2$, the problem is reduced to the easy derivation of the sequent $\Delta; x^2 \approx 2 \vdash r(x)$. $\square$

Example 3.3 This example is borrowed from [11]. It belongs to the instance $HH(\mathcal{H})$ given by the Herbrand constraint system, and it will be used at the end of Section 4 to explain why our completeness theorem for goal resolution does not need to consider disjunctions of computed answer constraints. Consider

$\Delta \equiv \{D_1, D_2\}$, with $D_1 \equiv p(a, b)$, $D_2 \equiv \forall x (x \not\approx a \Rightarrow p(x, b))$,
$G \equiv p(x, y)$, $R \equiv y \approx b$.

Up to trivial syntactic variants, this is a $CLP(\mathcal{H})$-program. According to the model theoretic semantics of $CLP(\mathcal{H})$, we get $\Delta; R \models_{\mathcal{H}} G$, because either $x \approx a$ or $x \not\approx a$ will hold in each $\mathcal{H}$-model of $\Delta \cup \{R\}$. In contrast to this, in $\mathcal{UC}$ we only can derive $\Delta; R \wedge x \approx a \vdash G$ (using D_1) and $\Delta; R \wedge x \not\approx a \vdash G$ (using D_2). But we do not obtain $\Delta; R \vdash_{\mathcal{UC}} G$. Since $R \not\vdash_{\mathcal{H}} x \approx a$, $R \not\vdash_{\mathcal{H}} x \not\approx a$, neither D_1 nor D_2 can be used to build a $\mathcal{UC}$-proof. $\square$

4   A Goal Solving Procedure

In $HH(\mathcal{C})$, solving a goal G using a program Δ means to find a $\mathcal{C}$-satisfiable constraint R such that $\Delta; R \vdash_{\mathcal{UC}} G$. Any constraint R with this property is called a *correct answer constraint*. For instance, $R \equiv x^2 \leq 1/2$ is a correct answer constraint for the *disc* example, as shown by Example 3.1.

We will present our goal solving procedure as a transition system. Goal solving will proceed by transforming an initial state through a sequence of intermediate states, ending in a final state where no goal remains to be solved.

Definition 4.1 *A* state *w.r.t. a finite set of variables V, written S, has the form $\Pi[S\square\mathcal{G}]$ where: $\mathcal{G}$ is a multiset of triples $\langle \Delta, C, G \rangle$ (local program, constraint and goal, respectively). Π is a quantifier prefix $Q_1 x_1 \ldots Q_k x_k$, where $x_1, \ldots, x_k$ are distinct variables not belonging to V, and every Q_i, $1 \leq i \leq k$, is the quantifier $\forall$ or $\exists$. S is the* global constraint. $\square$

This complex notion of state is needed because the goal solving transformations, presented below, introduce local clauses and local constraints. Of course, local clauses also arise in *HH*, see [16].

We say that a *state* $\Pi[S\square\mathcal{G}]$ is *satisfiable* iff the associated constraint formula $\Pi.S$, also called *partially calculated answer constraint*, is $\mathcal{C}$-satisfiable.

If Π', Π are quantifier prefixes such that Π' coincides with the first k elements of Π, $0 \leq k \leq n$, where n is the number of elements of Π, then $\Pi - \Pi'$ represents the result of eliminating Π' of Π.

Definition 4.2 Rules for transformation of states. *The transformations permitting to pass from a state w.r.t. a set of variables V, S, to another state w.r.t. V, S', written as $S \Vdash S'$, are the following:*

i) Conjunction.

$$\Pi[S\square\mathcal{G} \cup \{\langle \Delta, C, G_1 \wedge G_2 \rangle\}] \Vdash \Pi[S\square\mathcal{G} \cup \{\langle \Delta, C, G_1 \rangle, \langle \Delta, C, G_2 \rangle\}].$$

ii) Disjunction.

$$\Pi[S\square\mathcal{G} \cup \{\langle \Delta, C, G_1 \vee G_2 \rangle\}] \Vdash \Pi[S\square\mathcal{G} \cup \{\langle \Delta, C, G_i \rangle\}], \textit{for } i = 1 \textit{ or } 2$$
(don't know choice).

iii) Implication with local clause.

$$\Pi[S\square\mathcal{G} \cup \{\langle \Delta, C, D \Rightarrow G \rangle\}] \Vdash \Pi[S\square\mathcal{G} \cup \{\langle \Delta \cup \{D\}, C, G \rangle\}].$$

iv) Implication with local constraint.

$$\Pi[S\square\mathcal{G} \cup \{\langle \Delta, C, C' \Rightarrow G \rangle\}] \Vdash \Pi[S\square\mathcal{G} \cup \{\langle \Delta, C \wedge C', G \rangle\}].$$

v) Existential quantification.

$$\Pi[S\square\mathcal{G}\cup\{\langle \Delta, C, \exists x G \rangle\}] \Vdash \Pi\exists w[S\square\mathcal{G}\cup\{\langle \Delta, C, G[w/x] \rangle\}], \textit{where } w \textit{ does not appear in } \Pi \textit{ nor in } V.$$

vi) Universal quantification.

$$\Pi[S\square\mathcal{G}\cup\{\langle \Delta, C, \forall x G \rangle\}] \Vdash \Pi\forall w[S\square\mathcal{G}\cup\{\langle \Delta, C, G[w/x] \rangle\}], \textit{where } w \textit{ does not appear in } \Pi \textit{ nor in } V.$$

vii) Constraint.

$\Pi[S\square\mathcal{G}\cup\{\langle\Delta, C, C'\rangle\}]\Vdash\Pi[S\wedge(C\Rightarrow C')\square\mathcal{G}]$.
If $\Pi(S\wedge(C\Rightarrow C'))$ *is* $\mathcal{C}$-*satisfiable.*

viii) Clause of the program.

$\Pi[S\square\mathcal{G}\cup\{\langle\Delta, C, A'\rangle\}]\Vdash\Pi[S\square\mathcal{G}\cup\{\langle\Delta, C, \exists x_1\ldots\exists x_n((A\approx A')\wedge G)\rangle\}]$.
Provided that $\forall x_1\ldots\forall x_n(G\Rightarrow A)$ *is a variant of some clause in* elab(Δ)
(don't know choice), $x_1,\ldots,x_n$ *do not appear in* Π *nor in* V, *and* A, A'
begin with the same predicate symbol. □

Definition 4.3 *The* initial state *for a program* Δ *and a goal* G *is a state w.r.t. the
set of free variables of* Δ *and* G *consisting in* $S_0\equiv[\top\square\{\langle\Delta, \top, G\rangle\}]$.

A *resolution of a goal* G *from a program* Δ *is a finite sequence of states w.r.t.
the free variables of* Δ *and* G, $S_0,\ldots, S_n$, *such that:*

– S_0 *is the initial state for* Δ *and* G.
– $S_{i-1}\Vdash S_i$, $1\leq i\leq n$, *by means of any of the transformation rules.*
– *The final state* S_n *has the form* $\Pi_n[S_n\square\emptyset]$.

The constraint $\Pi_n S_n$ *is called the* answer constraint *of this resolution.* □

For *CLP* programs, the goal transformations ii), iii), iv) and vi) can never be
applied. Therefore, the state remains of the the form $\Pi[S\square\mathcal{G}]$, where Π includes
only existential quantifiers and $\mathcal{G}$ is a multiset of triples $\langle\Delta, C, G\rangle$ such that Δ is the
global program. For states of this kind, the goal transformations i), v), vii) and viii)
specify constrained *SLD* resolution, as used in *CLP*; see e.g. [8, 9]. On the other
hand, traditional *HH* programs can be emulated in our framework by using the Herbrand constraint system $\mathcal{H}$ and avoiding constraints in programs and initial goals.
Then transformation iv) becomes useless, and the remaining goal transformations
can be viewed as a more declarative formulation of the goal solving procedure
from [16]. Transformation viii) introduces equational constraints in intermediate
goals, and in transformation vii) the local constraint C is simply $\top$. Therefore,
$\Pi(S\wedge(C\Rightarrow C'))$ is equivalent to $\Pi(S\wedge C')$, where $S\wedge C'$ can be assumed to be
a conjunction of equations. Checking $\mathcal{H}$-satisfiability of $\Pi(S\wedge C')$ corresponds to
solving a unification problem under a mixed prefix in [16].

Admittedly, the labeled unification algorithm presented in [16] is closer to an
actual implementation, while our description of goal solving is more abstract. Note,
however, that the goal solving transformations are open to efficient implementation
techniques. In particular, when vii) adds a constraint to the global constraint S, the
satisfiability of the new partially calculated answer constraint should be checked
incrementally, without repeating all the work previously done for ΠS.

4.1 Soundness

Soundness of the goal solving procedure indicates that if R is the answer constraint
of a resolution of a goal G from a program Δ, then the sequent $\Delta; R\vdash G$ has a
proof in the system $\mathcal{UC}$. The soundness theorem is based on the following result.

Lemma 4.1 *Let $S_0, \ldots, S_n$ be a resolution of a goal G from a program Δ, and V the set of free variables of Δ and G. Then, for any i, $0 \leq i \leq n$, if $S_i \equiv \Pi_i[S_i \square \mathcal{G}_i]$, then the following properties are satisfied:*
1. The free variables of the formulas of $\mathcal{G}_i$, and S_i are in Π_i or in V.
2. S_i is satisfiable.
3. Let $R_i \equiv (\Pi_n - \Pi_i)S_n$, then for any $\langle \Delta', C', G' \rangle \in \mathcal{G}_i$, $\Delta'; R_i, C' \vdash_{\mathcal{UC}} G'$.

Proof Properties 1 and 2 are easily proved due to the procedure used to build the prefix and the partially calculated answer constraint for any state.

To prove 3, we use induction on the construction of $S_0, \ldots, S_n$, but beginning from the last state. The basic case is obvious because $\mathcal{G}_n = \emptyset$. For the induction step, we suppose the result for $S_{i+1}, \ldots, S_n$, and we prove it for S_i. We analyze the different cases, according to the transformation applied to S_i to obtain S_{i+1}. Let us see some cases (others are proved analogously).

Let $\langle \Delta', C', G' \rangle \in \mathcal{G}_i$, if implication with local constraint transformation was applied then $R_i \equiv R_{i+1}$. Let us prove the case $\langle \Delta', C', G' \rangle \notin \mathcal{G}_{i+1}$ (the opposite is trivial), then $G' \equiv C \Rightarrow G_1$ and $\langle \Delta', C' \wedge C, G_1 \rangle \in \mathcal{G}_{i+1}$. By induction hypothesis, since $R_i \equiv R_{i+1}$, we have $\Delta'; R_i, C' \wedge C \vdash_{\mathcal{UC}} G_1$, hence $\Delta'; R_i, C', C \vdash_{\mathcal{UC}} G_1$, using Lemma 3.1. Now we conclude $\Delta'; R_i, C' \vdash_{\mathcal{UC}} G'$, applying $(\Rightarrow_{R_C})$.

If existential quantification transformation was applied, then $\Pi_{i+1} \equiv \Pi_i \exists w$, with w a new variable w.r.t. Π_i and V. Therefore $R_i \equiv \exists w R_{i+1}$. Besides, by item 1, w is not free in Δ', C', G'. If $\langle \Delta', C', G' \rangle \in \mathcal{G}_{i+1}$, by induction hypothesis, $\Delta'; R_{i+1}, C' \vdash_{\mathcal{UC}} G'$. Then $\Delta'; R_i, C' \vdash_{\mathcal{UC}} G'$ by Lemma 3.2, because w is not free in Δ', C', G'. If $\langle \Delta', C', G' \rangle \notin \mathcal{G}_{i+1}$, $G' \equiv \exists x G_1$ and $\langle \Delta', C', G_1[w/x] \rangle \in \mathcal{G}_{i+1}$. By induction hypothesis, $\Delta'; R_{i+1}, C' \vdash_{\mathcal{UC}} G_1[w/x]$, and by Lemma 3.1 $\Delta'; R_i, R_{i+1}, C' \vdash_{\mathcal{UC}} G_1[w/x]$. Consequently, applying $(\exists_R)$, $\Delta'; R_i, C' \vdash_{\mathcal{UC}} G'$, since $R_i, C' \vdash_{\mathcal{C}} \exists w R_{i+1}$. ∎

Theorem 4.2 (Soundness) *Let Δ be any program. If G is a goal such that there is a resolution $S_0, \ldots, S_n$ of G from Δ with answer constraint $R \equiv \Pi_n S_n$, then R is $\mathcal{C}$-satisfiable and $\Delta; R \vdash_{\mathcal{UC}} G$.*

Proof Straightforward from the previous lemma. $\mathcal{C}$-satisfiability of R is a consequence of item 2. From item 3, for $n = 0$, we obtain $\Delta; R \vdash_{\mathcal{UC}} G$, since $\mathcal{G}_0 = \{ \langle \Delta, \top, G \rangle \}$ and $R_0 \equiv (\Pi_n - \Pi_0)S_n \equiv \Pi_n S_n \equiv R$. ∎

4.2 Completeness

Completeness of the goal solving procedure states that given a program Δ, and a goal G such that $\Delta; R_0 \vdash_{\mathcal{UC}} G$ for a $\mathcal{C}$-satisfiable constraint R_0, there is a resolution of G from Δ with answer constraint R that is entailed by R_0 in the constraint system $\mathcal{C}$, i.e. $R_0 \vdash_{\mathcal{C}} R$.

The completeness theorem is based on the following auxiliary result.

Lemma 4.3 *Let $S \equiv \Pi[S \square \mathcal{G}]$ be a non final state w.r.t. a set of variables V and let R be a constraint such that ΠR is C-satisfiable and $R \vdash_C S$. If $\Delta; R, C \vdash_{UC} G$ for all $\langle \Delta, C, G \rangle \in \mathcal{G}$, and if $\tau_R(\Delta, C, G)$ is the size of the shortest UC-proof of the sequent $\Delta; R, C \vdash G$ and $\mathcal{M}_{\mathcal{G}R}$ is the multiset constituted by $\tau_R(\Delta, C, G)$ for $\langle \Delta, C, G \rangle \in \mathcal{G}$, then we can find a rule transforming S in a state $S' \equiv \Pi'[S' \square \mathcal{G}']$ ($S \Vdash S'$) and a constraint R' such that:*

1. *$\Pi R \vdash_C \Pi' R'$ and $R' \vdash_C S'$.*

2. *$\Delta'; R', C' \vdash_{UC} G'$ for all $\langle \Delta', C', G' \rangle \in \mathcal{G}'$. Moreover $\mathcal{M}_{\mathcal{G}'R'} << \mathcal{M}_{\mathcal{G}R}$ where $<<$ is the well-founded multiset ordering [6] induced by the ordering $<$ over the natural numbers.*

Proof. Let us choose any $\langle \Delta, C, G \rangle \in \mathcal{G}$; we reason by induction on the structure of G. We show here only some cases.

- If G has the form $\exists x G_1$, applying the transformation v) we obtain S'. Let w be the variable used in the substitution involved in this transformation, w does not appear in Π, V, and we can choose it also not free in R. By hypothesis $\Delta; R, C \vdash \exists x G_1$ has a proof of size l, then by the definition of UC, there is a constraint formula C_1 such that $\Delta; R, C, C_1 \vdash G_1[w/x]$ has a proof of size less than l and $R, C \vdash_C \exists w C_1$. Let $R' \equiv R \wedge (C \Rightarrow C_1)$.
  1. Since w is not free in R, C, and $R, C \vdash_C \exists w C_1$, we obtain $R \vdash_C \exists w (R \wedge (C \Rightarrow C_1))$, therefore $\Pi R \vdash_C \Pi' R'$, because $\Pi' \equiv \Pi \exists w$ and $R' \equiv R \wedge (C \Rightarrow C_1)$. Moreover, $S' \equiv S$, $R' \vdash_C R$ and $R \vdash_C S$ implies $R' \vdash_C S'$.
  2. Let $\langle \Delta', C', G' \rangle \in \mathcal{G}'$, if $\langle \Delta', C', G' \rangle \in \mathcal{G}$, then $\Delta'; R, C' \vdash_{UC} G'$ by hypothesis, and therefore $\Delta'; R', C' \vdash_{UC} G'$, with $\tau_{R'}(\Delta', C', G') = \tau_R(\Delta', C', G')$, because $R' \vdash_C R$ and Lemma 3.1. If $\langle \Delta', C', G' \rangle \notin \mathcal{G}$, then $G' \equiv G_1[w/x]$, $\Delta' \equiv \Delta$, $C' \equiv C$. Since $\Delta; R, C, C_1 \vdash G_1[w/x]$ has a proof of size less than l, $\Delta; R', C \vdash G_1[w/x]$ will also have such a proof, because $R', C \vdash_C R, C, C_1$ and Lemma 3.1. So $\Delta'; R', C' \vdash_{UC} G'$ for all $\langle \Delta', C', G' \rangle \in \mathcal{G}'$, $\tau_{R'}(\Delta', C', G_1[w/x]) < \tau_R(\Delta, C, G)$, and then $\mathcal{M}_{\mathcal{G}'R'} << \mathcal{M}_{\mathcal{G}R}$.

- If G is atomic $G \equiv A'$, by hypothesis $\Delta; R, C \vdash A'$ has a proof of size l, then by reason of the form of UC, if $x_1, \ldots, x_n$ are new variables not free in Δ, R, C neither in A', then there is a variant of a formula from $elab(\Delta)$, $\forall x_1 \ldots \forall x_n (G_1 \Rightarrow A)$, with A and A' beginning with the same predicate symbol, such that $\Delta; R, C \vdash \exists x_1 \ldots \exists x_n ((A \approx A') \wedge G_1)$ has a proof of size less than l. We transform S in S' by means of the rule viii), using $\forall x_1 \ldots \forall x_n (G_1 \Rightarrow A)$. Assume now $R' \equiv R$. Since $S \equiv S'$ and $\Pi \equiv \Pi'$, the proof of 1. is immediate.
  2. Let $\langle \Delta', C', G' \rangle \in \mathcal{G}'$, if $\langle \Delta', C', G' \rangle \in \mathcal{G}$, then $\Delta'; R, C' \vdash_{UC} G'$ by hypothesis and therefore $\Delta'; R', C' \vdash_{UC} G'$, besides $\tau_{R'}(\Delta', C', G') = \tau_R(\Delta', C', G')$. If $\langle \Delta', C', G' \rangle \notin \mathcal{G}$, then $G' \equiv \exists x_1 \ldots \exists x_n ((A \approx A') \wedge G_1)$, $C' \equiv C$ and $\Delta' \equiv \Delta$. As we have noted before $\Delta; R', C' \vdash G'$ has a proof

of size less than l. So $\tau_{R'}(\Delta', C', G') < \tau_R(\Delta, C, G)$, and 2. is also proved in this case. ∎

Theorem 4.4 (Completeness) *Let Δ be a program, G a goal and R_0 a C-satisfiable constraint such that $\Delta; R_0 \vdash_{UC} G$. Then there is a resolution of G from Δ with answer constraint R such that $R_0 \vdash_C R$.*

Proof Using the previous lemma, we prove that there is a resolution of G from Δ, $\mathcal{S}_0 \Vdash \mathcal{S}_1 \ldots \Vdash \mathcal{S}_n$, and a sequence of constraints, $R_0, \ldots, R_n$ satisfying that for all $i, 1 \le i \le n$, $R_0 \vdash_C \Pi_i R_i$, $R_i \vdash_C \mathcal{S}_i$, $\Delta'; R_i, C' \vdash_{UC} G'$, for all $\langle \Delta', C', G' \rangle \in \mathcal{G}_i$. We prove it by an inductive construction that is guaranteed to terminate thanks to the well founded ordering $<<$. Let $\mathcal{S}_0 \equiv [\top \square \{\langle \Delta, \top, G \rangle\}]$ be the initial state for Δ and G, which we know is not final, if we take R_0 as the constraint given by the theorem's hypothesis, we obtain $R_0 \vdash_C \Pi_0 R_0$ and $R_0 \vdash_C \mathcal{S}_0$, since Π_0 is empty and $\mathcal{S}_0 \equiv \top$. Moreover, by hypothesis, $\Delta; R_0 \vdash_{UC} G$ is satisfied, and then also $\Delta; R_0, \top \vdash_{UC} G$ by reason of $R_0, \top \vdash_C R_0$.

Assume the result true for $\mathcal{S}_0, \ldots, \mathcal{S}_i$, if the state $\mathcal{S}_i$ is not final, then $\mathcal{S}_i$ and R_i fulfill the hypothesis of the previous lemma, by which there will be a state $\mathcal{S}_{i+1}$, with $\mathcal{S}_i \Vdash \mathcal{S}_{i+1}$, and a constraint R_{i+1} such that $\Pi_i R_i \vdash_C \Pi_{i+1} R_{i+1}$ (†) and $R_{i+1} \vdash_C \mathcal{S}_{i+1}$. Furthermore, for all $\langle \Delta', C', G' \rangle \in \mathcal{G}_{i+1}$, $\Delta'; R_{i+1}, C' \vdash_{UC} G'$ and $\mathcal{M}_{\mathcal{G}_{i+1} R_{i+1}} << \mathcal{M}_{\mathcal{G}_i R_i}$. Therefore, by the induction hypothesis, $R_0 \vdash_C \Pi_i R_i$, and with (†) we obtain $R_0 \vdash_C \Pi_{i+1} R_{i+1}$. By successive iteration, as $<<$ is a well founded order, we must eventually get a final state $\mathcal{S}_n$ that will in fact satisfy $R_0 \vdash_C \Pi_n R_n$ and $R_n \vdash_C \mathcal{S}_n$ and so $R_0 \vdash_C \Pi_n \mathcal{S}_n$, where $R \equiv \Pi_n \mathcal{S}_n$ is the answer constraint of $\mathcal{S}_0, \ldots, \mathcal{S}_n$. In this way we conclude $R_0 \vdash_C R$. ∎

Example 4.1 Using Δ, G and R as given in the *disc* example it is possible to find a resolution of G from Δ with answer constraint R as it is shown below.

$[\top \square \{\langle \Delta, \top, \forall y(y^2 \le 1/2 \Rightarrow disc\,(x, y))\rangle\}] \Vdash_{vi)}$

$\forall y[\top \square \{\langle \Delta, \top, y^2 \le 1/2 \Rightarrow disc\,(x, y)\rangle\}] \Vdash_{iv)}$

$\forall y[\top \square \{\langle \Delta, y^2 \le 1/2, disc\,(x, y)\rangle\}] \Vdash_{viii)}$

$\forall y[\top \square \{\langle \Delta, y^2 \le 1/2, \exists u \exists v(x \approx u \wedge y \approx v \wedge u^2 + v^2 \le 1/2)\rangle\}] \Vdash_{vii)}$

$\forall y[y^2 \le 1/2 \Rightarrow \exists u \exists v(x \approx u \wedge y \approx v \wedge u^2 + v^2 \le 1)\square\emptyset]$

since $\forall y(y^2 \le 1/2 \Rightarrow \exists u \exists v(x \approx u \wedge y \approx v \wedge u^2 + v^2 \le 1))$ is $\mathcal{R}$-satisfiable. So the answer constraint is: $\forall y(y^2 \le 1/2 \Rightarrow \exists u \exists v(x \approx u \wedge y \approx v \wedge u^2 + v^2 \le 1))$ that in the system $\mathcal{R}$ can be successively simplified to $\forall y(y^2 \le 1/2 \Rightarrow x^2 + y^2 \le 1)$ and then to $x^2 \le 1/2$. □

For $HH(\mathcal{H})$ programs without constraints in the left of implications and in the initial goals, Theorem 4.4 implies an alternative formulation of the completeness theorem given in [16] for a goal solving procedure for first-order HH: using constraints and constraint satisfiability instead of substitutions and unification under a mixed prefix, we gain a more declarative presentation. For *CLP* programs, Theorem 4.4 becomes a stronger form of completeness, in comparison to the strong completeness theorem for success given in [11], Th. 2 (see also [9], Th. 4.12). There, assuming $\Delta; R \models_{\mathcal{C}} G$, the conclusion is that $R \vdash_{\mathcal{C}} \bigvee_{i=1}^{m} R_i$ where $R_1, \ldots, R_m$ are answer constraints computed in m different resolutions of G from Δ. Example 3.3 was used in [11] to illustrate the need of considering disjunctions of computed answers. In fact, there is no single computed answer R_0 such that $R \vdash_{\mathcal{H}} R_0$. However, this fact doesn't contradict Theorem 4.4, because $\Delta; R \vdash G$ is not $\mathcal{UC}$-derivable, as we have seen in Example 3.3. In the same example we have seen that $\Delta; R \wedge x \approx a \vdash G$ and $\Delta; R \wedge x \not\approx a \vdash G$ were derivable. It is easy to check that both answers $R \wedge x \approx a$ and $R \wedge x \not\approx a$ can be computed by the goal solving transformations. We can conclude that $\mathcal{UC}$-provability is more constructive than the classical model-theoretic semantics of *CLP*, and its behaviour resembles constrained *SLD* resolution more closely.

5   Conclusions and Future Work

We have proposed a novel combination of Constraint Logic Programming (*CLP*) with first-order Hereditary Harrop Formulas (*HH*). Our framework includes a proof system with the uniform proofs property and a sound and complete goal solving procedure. Our results are parametric w.r.t. a given constraint system $\mathcal{C}$, and they can be related to previously known results for *CLP* and *HH*. Therefore, we can speak of a scheme whose expressivity sums the advantages of *CLP* and *HH*.

As far as we know, our work is the first attempt to combine the full expressivity of *HH* and *CLP*. A related, but more limited approach, can be found in [5]. This paper presents an integrated logic that combines the Horn fragment of intuitionistic logic with the entailment relation of a given constraint system, showing the existence of uniform proofs as well as soundness and completeness of constrained *SLD* resolution w.r.t. the proof system. The more general case of *HH* is not studied. Moreover, the presentation of constrained *SLD* resolution is not fully satisfactory, because the *backchaining* transition rule (see [5]) guesses an arbitrary instance of a program clause, instead of adding unification constraints to the new goal.

Several interesting issues remain for future research. Firstly, some concrete evidence on potential application areas should be found. We are currently looking for *CLP* applications where greater *HH* expressivity may be useful, as well as for typical *HH* applications that can benefit from the use of numeric and/or symbolic constraints. Secondly, tractable fragments of our formalism (other than *CLP* and *HH* separately) should be discovered. Otherwise, constraint satisfiability and constraint entailment may become intractable or even undecidable. Our broad notion of constraint system includes any first-order theory based on arbitrary equational axiomatization. Such theories are sometimes decidable (see [3, 4]), but most often restricted fragments must be chosen to ensure decidability. Last but not least, our framework should be extended to higher-order *HH* as used in many λ-Prolog applications.

Acknowledgements. This work has been partially supported by the Spanish National Project TIC 95-0433-C03-01 *CPD* and the Esprit BRA Working Group EP-22457 *CCLII*. We are grateful to the anonymous referees for their constructive criticisms.

References

[1] H. Andréka and I. Németi. *The generalized completeness of Horn predicate logic as a programming language.* Acta Cybernetica 4:3-10, 1978.

[2] K.L. Clark. *Negation as Failure.* In H. Gallaire and J. Minker (Eds.), *Logic and Databases*, Plenum Press, 293-322, 1978.

[3] H. Comon. *Complete axiomatizations of some quotient term algebras.* Theoretical Computer Science 118, 1993, 167-191.

[4] H. Comon, M. Haberstrau and J.P. Jouannaud. *Cycle-Syntacticness, and Shallow Theories.* Information and Computation 111, 1994, 154-191.

[5] J. Darlington and Y. Guo. *Constraint Logic Programming in the Sequent Calculus.* Proc. LPAR'94, Springer LNAI 822, 1994, 200-213.

[6] N. Dershowitz and Z. Manna. *Proving Termination with Multiset Ordering.* Comm. of the ACM 22(8):465-476, 1979.

[7] J. Jaffar and J.L. Lassez. *Constraint logic programming.* Proc. POPL'87, 1987, 111-119.

[8] J. Jaffar and M.J. Maher. *Constraint logic programming: A survey.* Journal of Logic Programming 19(20):503-581, 1994.

[9] J. Jaffar, M.J. Maher, K. Marriott and P. Stuckey. *The Semantics of Constraint Logic Programs.* Techn. Rep. TR 96/39, Dept. of Comput. Sci., Univ. of Melbourne, 1996.

[10] J. Leach, S. Nieva and M. Rodríguez-Artalejo. *Constraint Logic Programming with Hereditary Harrop Formulas.* Technical Report SIP 60/97, Univ. Complutense de Madrid, 1997.

[11] M. Maher. *Logic Semantics for a Class of Committed-Choice Programs.* Proc. ICLP'87, MIT Press, 1987, 858-876.

[12] D. Miller. *Unification under a mixed prefix.* Journal of Symbolic Computation 14:321-358, 1992.

[13] D. Miller and G. Nadathur. *Higher-order logic programming.* Proc. ICLP'86. Springer LNCS 225, 1986, 448-462.

[14] D. Miller, G. Nadathur and A. Scedrov. *Hereditary Harrop Formulas and Uniform Proof Systems.* Proc. LICS'87, IEEE Comp. Soc. Press, 1987, 98-105.

[15] D. Miller, G. Nadathur, F. Pfenning and A. Scedrov. *Uniform proofs as a foundation for logic programming.* Annals of Pure and Applied Logic 51:125-157, 1991.

[16] G. Nadathur. *A proof procedure for the logic of hereditary Harrop formulas.* Journal of Automated Reasoning 11:115-145, 1993.

[17] G. Nadathur and D. Miller. *An overview of λ-Prolog.* Proc. ICLP'88, MIT Press, 1988, 810-827.

[18] V. Saraswat. *The Category of Constraint Systems is Cartesian Closed.* Proc. LICS'92. IEEE Comp. Soc. Press, 1992, 341-345.

[19] G. Smolka and R. Treinen. *Records for Logic Programming.* Journal of Logic Programming 1994:18:229-258.

[20] M.H. van Emden and R.H. Kowalski. *The semantics of predicate logic as a programming language.* J. ACM 23(4):733-742, 1976.

[21] A. Tarski. *A Decision Method for Elementary Algebra and Geometry.* University of California Press, 1951.

On T Logic Programming

Agostino Dovier
Università di Verona, Ist. Policattedra
Strada Le Grazie 3, 37134 VERONA (I).
dovier@sci.univr.it

Andrea Formisano
Università di Roma *"La Sapienza"*, Dip. di Scienze dell'Informazione
Via Salaria 113, 00198 ROMA (I).
formisan@dsi.uniroma1.it

Alberto Policriti
Università di Udine, Dipartimento di Matematica e Informatica
Via delle Scienze 206, 33100 UDINE (I).
policrit@dimi.uniud.it

Abstract

T-resolution parametrically generalizes standard resolution with respect to a first-order theory T (the parameter). The inherent power of its derivation rule, however, makes it difficult to develop efficient unrestricted T-resolution based systems. $CLP(\mathcal{X})$ parametrically extends Horn clause logic programming with respect to a domain of computation $\mathcal{X}$. The theory T underlying the domain $\mathcal{X}$ is fixed *a-priori* and can not be modified (extended) by the user.

In this paper we present the parametric logic programming language T *logic programming (TLP)* which extends the CLP-scheme by giving the possibility of acting on the theory T. The scheme is embedded into (linear) T-resolution; however, its syntax ensures that three rules (simple instances of the general T-resolution rule) are sufficient to implement the derivation process.

Keywords: Theorem Proving, Constraint Logic Programming, Foundations.

1 Introduction

The main motivation of this work is to establish a link between automated deduction and logic programming on the basis of the T-resolution approach to the theory reasoning.

T-resolution ([12]) parametrically generalizes standard resolution with respect to a first-order theory T (the parameter). It was introduced to provide a general theorem-proving framework in which the power of the basic inference rule can grow with the underlying theory T. Another motivation was to establish criteria to classify first-order theories with respect to their suitability for theorem proving. In the framework obtained, the parts of a proof which are carried out entirely within the theory are hidden inside the manager of the theory. Being binary, the T-resolution inference rule is simpler than the previously proposed *Theory-resolution* rule ([14]) and more suitable for integration with refinements already proposed of (classical) resolution. Moreover, the T-resolution rule ensures a complete independence between the background level (the T-decider) of the theorem prover and the foreground reasoner. This could not be the case for Theory-resolution, where the background reasoner plays an active role in the inference steps (*residues generation* [14]).

$CLP(\mathcal{X})$-scheme (cf., e.g., [9]) integrates the paradigms of *constraint solving* and *logic programming*. $CLP(\mathcal{X})$ parametrically extends Horn clause logic programming with respect to a specific domain of computation $\mathcal{X}$.

The theory T, on which an instance $CLP(\mathcal{X})$ of the CLP-scheme is based, is given *a-priori*. A privileged model $\mathcal{D}$ of T is chosen and model-theoretic, fixpoint, as well as operational semantics of the program are strongly based on $\mathcal{D}$. However, in CLP there is no way to affect the theory T by adding semantics to predicate and functional symbols. For instance, having a $CLP(\mathcal{R})$ system, one can compute in logic on a real domain. However, for an uninterpreted functional symbol f, there is no way to impose, for example, that $0 < f(X)$ for any X real.

In this paper, we present the parametric logic programming language, T-logic programming (TLP). TLP is an instance of the general T-resolution scheme and extends Constraint Logic Programming by providing a way for handling programs (consistently) extending T. In particular, we will provide inference rules instantiating the general T-resolution rule, realizing a simpler inference mechanism which behaves as the standard $CLP(T)$ one when the program is a CLP-program.

An exemplary advantage of our approach is the following: a CLP inference step must necessarily manipulate the equality literals and the only manner to share/exchange information between the theory and the program is through the use of such a relator. In TLP, the theory T need not to include the equality predicate symbol. Moreover, deduction steps are not bound to involve only pairs of literals, but the entire clause can be usefully employed.

Section 2 recalls basic definitions and results of T-resolution. Section 3 presents syntax and model-theoretic semantics of the TLP language, and in Section 4 soundness and completeness results for the deduction system are proved. In Section 5 some further lines of research are drawn.

2 Preliminaries

We assume standard first-order logic notions, such as: formula, model, substitution, unifier, variant, etc. (see e.g., [10]). Let T be a (consistent) first-order theory whose axioms are in fully Skolemized form, Σ be a first-order signature, and P a set of formulas. A formula φ is said to be T-unsatisfiable if for any model M of T it holds that $M \not\models \vec{\exists}\varphi$. We write: $T, P \vdash \varphi$ if and only if $P \cup \{\neg\varphi\}$ is T-unsatisfiable.

If T is the predicate calculus and α and β are clauses, then Robinson's resolution inference rule is a binary rule:

$$\frac{\alpha \quad \beta}{\gamma}$$

preserving T-satisfiability (i.e., $\alpha \wedge \beta$ is T-satisfiable implies γ is T-satisfiable). T-resolution extends such methodology to any general theory T, provided a simple satisfiability test for T is available. A similar approach, *Theory resolution*, is presented in [14]; but in that case, an infinite number of rules is required by the author.

Given a first-order theory T, the following two rules define the *T-resolution* inference system:

Definition 2.1 *Given two clauses $\alpha = \alpha_1 \vee \alpha_2$ and $\beta = \beta_1 \vee \beta_2$, γ is said to be a T-resolvent of α and β if there exists a substitution μ such that one of the following conditions holds:*

1. *$\gamma = (\alpha_1 \vee \beta_1)\mu$ and $T \vdash \vec{\forall}((\alpha_2 \wedge \beta_2 \rightarrow \alpha_1 \vee \beta_1)\mu)$,*

2. *$\gamma = (\alpha \vee L)\mu$ where either L or $\neg L$ occurs in β.*

Item (2) above presents two possibilities: the case in which L is a disjunct of β is a particular case of (1) and is included for the sake of uniformity; the case of $\neg L$ in β is essential to guarantee the completeness of the rule (see [5]). We refer to such a rule as *loading*; the literal $L\mu$ is said *loaded*.

The rationale behind such rule can be understood assuming that $(\alpha_1 \vee \alpha_2) \wedge (\beta_1 \vee \beta_2)$ holds. The following cases are possible: if α_1 is true, then $\alpha_1 \vee \beta_1$ is true. Else, α_1 is false, hence α_2 must be true and we have two further cases: if β_1 is true, then again $\alpha_1 \vee \beta_1$ is true; otherwise, if β_2 is true, since it holds: $T \vdash (\alpha_2 \wedge \beta_2) \rightarrow (\alpha_1 \vee \beta_1)$, then $\alpha_1 \vee \beta_1$ is true.

Definition 2.2 *Given a set P of clauses, a sequence $\gamma_1, \ldots, \gamma_n$ is a derivation of γ_n from P by T-resolution if every γ_i for $i \in \{1, \ldots, n\}$ is either in P or is a T-resolvent of γ_j and γ_k for $j, k < i$. γ_j and γ_k are said parent-clauses of γ_i. If $j = i - 1$, then the derivation is said linear; γ_j and γ_k are said center-clause and side-clause, respectively. Moreover, if each side-clause γ_k belongs to P, then the linear derivation is said linear-input derivation.*

Remark 2.3 *Standard resolution is subsumed by T-resolution: if μ is a unifier of $s_1 = t_1, \ldots, s_n = t_n$, then it holds:*

$$T \vdash \vec{\forall}((\neg p(s_1, \ldots, s_n) \wedge p(t_1, \ldots, t_n))\mu \to (\alpha_1 \vee \beta_1)\mu),$$

since the l.h.s. formula of the implication is always false. This means that resolution inference rule:

$$\frac{\alpha_1 \vee \neg p(s_1, \ldots, s_n) \qquad \beta_1 \vee p(t_1, \ldots, t_n)}{(\alpha_1 \vee \beta_1)\mu}$$

is an instance of the T-resolution one.

Differently from other parametrical inference mechanisms (such as, e.g., CLP ([9])), T-resolution can be used for non-equational theories, as well:

Example 2.4 *Assume that T is a fragment of set theory dealing with $\in$ and $\cap$, and that $P = \{a \in b \cap c\}$. T-resolution allows to infer that $T, P \vdash a \in c$.*

$$\frac{a \in b \cap c \qquad a \notin c}{\square} \qquad T \vdash a \in b \cap c \wedge a \notin c \to \mathtt{false}$$

since $T \vdash a \in b \cap c \to a \in c$ holds.

T-resolution generalizes such concepts as *semantic unification* already introduced for equational theories ([13]): if T contains the standard equality axioms, and $T \vdash \vec{\forall}(s_1 = t_1 \wedge \ldots \wedge s_n = t_n)\mu$, then, as an instance of the general rule, we have:

$$\frac{\alpha_1 \vee \neg p(s_1, \ldots, s_n) \qquad \beta_1 \vee p(t_1, \ldots, t_n)}{(\alpha_1 \vee \beta_1)\mu} \qquad T \vdash \vec{\forall}(s_1 = t_1 \wedge \ldots \wedge s_n = t_n)\mu$$

It should be noticed that the power of the basic T-resolution rule allows to introduce trivial forms of linearity: in fact, given two clauses α and β, each of them can be obtained as T-resolvent of the pair. This possibility allows to consider each derivation by T-resolution as "linear". For instance, Figure 1 illustrates how we could systematically map every T-derivation into a "linear" one: suppose $\mathcal{D}$ is a derivation of γ and let α and β be the parent-clauses of γ. Having two "linear" derivations $\mathcal{D}_1$ and $\mathcal{D}_2$ of α and β respectively, we could combine them obtaining a "linear" derivation of γ simply deriving the top-clause δ_2 of $\mathcal{D}_2$ from α and δ_2.

This phenomenon destroys the main purpose of linear refinements and prevents any restriction/cut of the search space. We need a more restrictive concept of T-resolvent suitable to support non-trivial linearity. We say that a clause $\ell_1 \vee \ldots \vee \ell_m$ *includes* a clause $r_1 \vee \ldots \vee r_n$ if for all $i \in \{1, \ldots, n\}$ there is $j \in \{1, \ldots, m\}$ such that $\ell_j = r_i$.

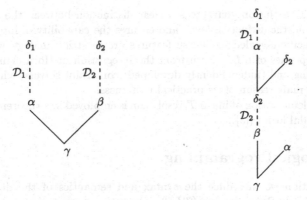

Figure 1: Trivial linearization.

Definition 2.5 *Given a linear derivation, a clause γ is said to be a strict T-resolvent of the center-clause α and the side-clause β if there exists a substitution μ such that one of the following conditions holds:*

1. $\gamma = (\alpha_1 \vee \beta_1)\mu$ *and* $T \vdash \vec{\forall}((\alpha_2 \wedge \beta_2 \to \alpha_1 \vee \beta_1)\mu)$, *such that* $(\alpha_1 \vee \beta_1)\mu$ *does not include a variant of* β;

2. $\gamma = (\alpha \vee L)\mu$ *where either* L *or* $\neg L$ *occurs in* β.

A *strict linear derivation is a linear derivation in which each derived clause is a strict T-resolvent.*

Strict linear T-resolution is shown to be sound and complete, as well as other T-generalizations of standard resolution refinements ([5]).

Theorem 2.6 *Let T be a first-order theory. A set of clauses is T-unsatisfiable if and only if a T-unsatisfiable ground instance is derivable from it by strict linear T-resolution.*

Proof: (Sketch) The key point consists in showing that from any linear derivation by standard ground resolution of a clause γ from a set of ground clauses $S \cup T'$ (where T' is a set of ground instances of theorems in T), we can obtain a linear ground T-derivation of γ from S. This is shown by induction on the length of the derivation. The ground completeness result is then lifted to the general case of T-resolution. (For the complete proof, see [5]) □

The correctness and completeness result above does not depend from effectiveness of rule application. As for the *CLP*-scheme, a satisfiability test for simple formulas of T is needed (solvability, cf. [12]) to ensure mechanizability.

Linear T-resolution guarantees a clear distinction between the calculation level and the deduction level, and ensures the capability of integrating domain specific knowledge. These features are in strict analogy with the similar properties of CLP, born from the integration of Horn clause logic programming and (independently developed) constraint solvers, which represents the main reason of its practical usefulness.

An implementation of linear T-resolution is employed in a theorem prover for polymodal logics ([3]).

3 T Logic Programming

In this section we introduce the syntax and semantics of the deduction scheme T Logic Programming (TLP). Operational semantics and a completeness theorem are given in the Section 4.

3.1 Syntax

Let $\Sigma = \Sigma_C \cup \Sigma_P$ be a first-order signature. Σ_C is the *constraint* signature and Σ_P is the *program* signature. We assume that $\Sigma_C \cap \Sigma_P = \emptyset$, $\Sigma_C = \Pi_C \cup \mathcal{F}_C$, and $\Sigma_P = \Pi_P \cup \mathcal{F}_P$, where Π denotes a set of predicate symbols and $\mathcal{F}$ a set of functional (and constant) symbols. A Π-*atom* is an atom $p(t_1, \ldots, t_n)$, where $p \in \Pi$ and $t_1, \ldots, t_n$ are terms built from $\mathcal{F}_C \cup \mathcal{F}_P$ and a denumerable set of variables. A Π-*literal* is either a Π-atom or the negation of a Π-atom. There are cases in which T deals with all possible functional symbols; in such cases, clearly, $\mathcal{F}_P = \emptyset$.

Definition 3.1 *The general form of a T-Logic Programming program clause is $B_0 \leftarrow B_1, \ldots, B_n$ where B_i can be either a Π_P-atom, or a Π_C-literal. If B_0 is a Π_C-literal, then the clause is said to be a T-head clause. If $B_0, B_1, \ldots, B_n$ are all Π_C-literals, then the clause is said to be a constraint clause. A goal is a clause with empty head.*

As opposed to predicate symbols in Π_P, predicates in Π_C are (partially) defined in T which is a generic first-order theory. Moreover, they may occur in a negative literal either in the head or in the body of a TLP-program clause.

3.2 Model-theoretic semantics issues

The model-theoretic semantics of a definite program is based on the uniqueness of the least Herbrand model. Models of $CLP(\mathcal{X})$-programs, dealing with interpreted functional and predicate symbols over the domain $\mathcal{X}$, are not always Herbrand models. In general, $\mathcal{X}$ is provided with a first-order theory T which can have several independent minimal models; a privileged model $\mathcal{D}_T$ of T is often chosen.

By using a CLP program there is no way to act on the theory T in order to modify the semantics of predicate and functional symbols. For instance, having a $CLP(\mathcal{R})$ system and two uninterpreted functional symbols $f, g \in \mathcal{F}_P$, we can not impose that $g(X, X) < f(X)$ for any $0 < X < 1$.

The possibility of writing TLP-clauses with interpreted heads allows to overcome such a restriction. We can classify such program clauses in three types:

1. clauses that add (consistent) information to T. For instance, if T is a theory of natural numbers and the symbol '$<$' belongs to Π_C:

$$(0 < X) \leftarrow (1 < X).$$

2. Clauses which cause the inconsistency of $T \cup P$. With respect to the above theory T, for instance:

$$(x * x < 0) \leftarrow (0 < x)$$

or, more implicitly, if T is a set theory with foundation axiom:

$$(a \in b) \leftarrow$$
$$(b \in a) \leftarrow .$$

3. Clauses which contain the functional symbols in $\mathcal{F}_P$ or $\mathcal{F}_C$ and consistently extend T, such as, for instance:

$$(f(X) < f(Y)) \leftarrow (X < Y).$$

Clauses of type 1) could be introduced in order to give a higher priority to the use of some theorems in T during the inference process.

We leave to the programmer the task of avoiding situations of type 2).

Clauses of type 3) allow to express T-properties of program-defined functional symbols.

Considering constraint clauses only, we can characterize these three kinds of clauses in model-theoretic terms: clauses of type 1) have, as models, all the models of T; none of the models of clauses of type 2) is model of T; only a proper subset of the models of T are models of clauses of kind 3).

A possibility offered by TLP is that of using program-defined predicates to give semantics to new constants, as shown in the following example.

Example 3.2 *Consider a program containing the TLP-clause:*

$$X \in c \leftarrow X \in a, r(X)$$

where $r(X)$ is a program defined atom (i.e., a Π_P-atom). The above TLP-clause characterizes the constant c imposing that in each T-model of the program P it holds that: $\{X \in a \mid r(X)\} \subseteq c$.

The next example shows how this feature can be used, for instance, to collect answers to CLP-like goals.

Example 3.3 *Let T be a fragment of set theory, and consider the program:*

$$
\begin{aligned}
num(\emptyset) &\leftarrow \\
num(X \cup \{X\}) &\leftarrow num(X) \\
(X \in \omega) &\leftarrow num(X)
\end{aligned}
$$

The (minimal) semantics for the constant symbol ω is exactly the (infinite) set of all numerals à la Von Neumann.

Our aim is to give a semantics to a program P which extends a CLP-program, by giving meaning to symbols in $\mathcal{F}_P$ or adding meaning to those in $\mathcal{F}_C$, when $T \cup P$ is consistent.

Let $\mathcal{D}_T$ be a model of T. A simple-minded solution would consist in looking for a privileged structure $\mathcal{D}$ which models $P \cup T$ and such that the structure $\mathcal{D}_T$ is $\mathcal{D}$ restricted to Σ_C. Unfortunately, $P \cup T$ may extend T without guaranteeing the uniqueness of $\mathcal{D}$. Below we illustrate with a few simple examples some of the reasons behind this phenomenon.

Since constraint clauses could contain negative Π_C-literals, typical semantical problems related to negation can arise: consider this example based on a set theory T:

$$
\begin{aligned}
(X \in a) &\leftarrow (X \notin b) \\
(X \in b) &\leftarrow (X \notin a).
\end{aligned}
$$

The program is non-stratifiable ([1]) and infinitely many minimal independent models are possible. For instance: $[a \mapsto \{\emptyset\}, b \mapsto \emptyset]$ and $[a \mapsto \emptyset, b \mapsto \{\emptyset\}]$ are two possibilities.

Even for stratified program, there could be no unique model. Consider, for example, the following two clauses

$$
\begin{aligned}
(0 \leq f(X)) &\leftarrow \\
(f(X) \leq f(Y)) &\leftarrow (X \leq Y)
\end{aligned}
$$

stating that f is a monotone function whose co-domain is composed by elements greater than or equal to 0. There are infinitely many minimal interpretations for f.

In this paper we have not addressed the problem of providing suitable restrictions (for instance, of syntactical nature) on TLP-programs to ensure a precise semantical characterization in terms of uniqueness of the minimal model. In general, to force a unique minimal model of a TLP-program it is necessary that for each functional symbol $f \in \mathcal{F}_P$ enough knowledge is embedded in the program in order to guarantee/identify a unique interpretation. The two clauses of the following example give the expected semantics to the functional symbol $abs \in \mathcal{F}_C$:

Example 3.4 *Consider a theory T dealing with numbers, and the program P:*

$$abs(X) = X \quad \leftarrow \quad X \geq 0$$
$$abs(X) = -X \quad \leftarrow \quad X < 0$$

Observe that in any model of $P \cup T$, if X is interpreted with a number, then $abs(X)$ is mapped on $|X|$.

In Example 4.6 we will show how from this program it is possible to obtain a "functional-like" answer.

4 Operational Semantics

In this section we introduce a restriction of the general *linear* T-resolution rule (Definition 2.5) and we prove in Theorems 4.7 and 4.8 that it is suitable for our purposes.

For the sake of simplicity, in the following rules the sequence $L_1, \ldots, L_k$ of literals in a goal $\leftarrow L_1, \ldots, L_k$ is considered as a multiset instead of a list. In this manner, splitting a multiset into L_1 and $L_2, \ldots, L_n$ is the same as splitting arbitrarily a list into L_i and $L_1, \ldots, L_{i-1}, L_{i+1}, \ldots, L_n$.

Definition 4.1 (TLP derivation rules) *Let μ denote a substitution and $\leftarrow H_1, \ldots, H_k$ denote a goal which plays the role of the center-clause (see Definition 2.2).*

R1: *If $B_0 \leftarrow B_1, \ldots, B_n$ is a TLP-clause, and B_0 and H_1 are Π_P-atoms,*

$$\frac{\leftarrow H_1, \ldots, H_k \quad B_0 \leftarrow B_1, \ldots, B_n}{\leftarrow (H_2, \ldots, H_k, B_1, \ldots, B_n)\mu}$$

provided $T \vdash ((\neg H_1 \wedge B_0) \rightarrow$
$\qquad\qquad (\neg H_2 \vee \cdots \vee \neg H_k) \vee (\neg B_1 \vee \cdots \vee \neg B_n))\mu$

R2: *If $\leftarrow B_0, \ldots, B_n$ is a T-head clause (i.e., the program clause: $\neg B_i \leftarrow B_0, \ldots, B_{i-1}, B_{i+1}, \ldots, B_n$) or a previously derived goal,*

$$\frac{\leftarrow H_1, \ldots, H_k \quad \leftarrow B_0, \ldots, B_n}{\leftarrow (H_1, \ldots, H_r, B_0, \ldots, B_s)\mu}$$

provided $T \vdash ((\neg H_{r+1} \vee \cdots \vee \neg H_k) \wedge (\neg B_{s+1} \vee \cdots \vee \neg B_n) \rightarrow$
$\qquad\qquad (\neg H_1 \vee \cdots \vee \neg H_r) \vee (\neg B_0 \vee \cdots \vee \neg B_s))\mu$
where $H_{r+1}, \ldots, H_k, B_{s+1}, \ldots, B_n$ are all Π_C-literals and
$\leftarrow (H_1, \ldots, H_r, B_0, \ldots, B_s)\mu$ *does not include a variant of $\leftarrow B_0, \ldots, B_n$.*

Loading: *Let α be program clause, and L be a Π_C-literal,*

$$\frac{\leftarrow H_1, \ldots, H_k \quad \alpha}{\leftarrow (H_1, \ldots, H_k, L)\mu} \quad \text{with } L \text{ in } \alpha \text{ or } \neg L \text{ in } \alpha$$

Rules **R1** and **R2** constitute a proper refinement of the general T-resolution rule. **R1** operates on pairs of Π_P-literals in a classical fashion; however the rule generalizes the standard Prolog inference step since uses knowledge embedded in the theory and in the whole parent-clauses. Rule **R2**, on the other hand, uses the full power of T-resolution and deals only with the "T-part" of the TLP-program. We discuss in more detail the features of this rule in the Section 5.

Remark 4.2 *Observe that strictness condition (Definition 2.5) holds for rule **R1**, **R2** and **Loading**. Moreover, notice that the parts of a TLP-derivation (see below) built using rule **R1** actually have a linear-input character (as Horn clauses—pure Prolog—derivations have). This is the main reason justifying the introduction of two different instances (i.e., **R1** and **R2**) of the general T-resolution rule.*

Definition 4.3 *Given a program P and a goal G, a TLP-derivation is a sequence of goals $G = G_0, \ldots, G_n$ such that, for each $i \in \{1, \ldots, n\}$, G_i is obtained from G_{i-1} and:*

- *a program clause using rule **R1** or **Loading**,*

- *a T-head program clause, or a goal G_k, $k < i$, using rule **R2**.*

A TLP-refutation is a derivation of a goal $G_n = \leftarrow H_1, \ldots, H_k$, with H_j Π_C-literal (for all $j \in \{1, \ldots, k\}$), such that $H_1 \wedge \cdots \wedge H_k$ is T-satisfiable. For each $i \in \{1, \ldots, n\}$, let μ_i be the substitution employed obtaining G_i from G_{i-1}. The pair consisting of $\mu_1 \circ \cdots \circ \mu_n$ and $H_1 \wedge \cdots \wedge H_k$ is the computed answer.

In T-resolution it is not required to perform the satisfiability test for the constraint part (i.e., Π_C-literals) of each derived goal. Such a test was mandatory in the original definition of the CLP-scheme ([8]) and optional (apart for the last derived goal) in the more recent overview paper ([9]). However, in all implementations of T-resolution such a test is performed (see [5, 11]) to improve efficiency and cut the search tree.

A possibility offered by CLP is to perform the simplification of the derived goals removing the valid Π_C-literals. This step can be viewed as an application of the following rule:

$$\textbf{Simpl}: \quad \frac{\leftarrow H_1, \ldots, H_k}{\leftarrow (H_1, \ldots, H_r)\mu} \quad T \vdash \vec{\forall}((H_{r+1} \wedge \cdots \wedge H_k)\mu)$$

Simpl actually, turns out to be an instance of rule **R2** with $B_0, \ldots, B_n = H_1, \ldots, H_k$ and $s = r - 1$.

Rules **R1** and **Simpl** are sufficient to simulate any CLP derivation.

Example 4.4 *Let T a theory over the reals dealing with $\leq$ and $\in$. Consider the simple program P defined by the following clauses:*

$$X \in a \quad \leftarrow \quad 2 \leq X$$
$$p(X) \quad \leftarrow \quad X \in a, X \leq 2$$

The first clause semantically characterizes the constant symbol a in terms of $\in$, stating that a has to be interpreted as a set containing at least all numbers greater or equal to 2. The second clause defines a Π_P-literal (namely, $p(X)$) in terms of the new constraint $X \in a$. Submitting the goal: $\leftarrow p(X)$, few inference steps yield the goal $\leftarrow 2 \leq X, X \leq 2$.

Recently, primitives aimed to allow intensional definitions of sets (namely, by providing the property characterizing their elements), have been introduced in (constraint) logic programming (e.g., $\mathcal{LDL}$ [2], Gödel [6], {log} [4]). However, in all such approaches, dealing with infinite sets may generate infinite computations. *TLP* allows a better handling of such sets:

Example 4.5 *Let T deal with natural numbers and with sets. Consider the following TLP-program (notice that the first five clauses are in fact CLP-clauses):*

1) $even(0)$
2) $even(X) \quad \leftarrow \quad X = Y + 2, even(Y)$
3) $prime(X) \quad \leftarrow \quad X \geq 2, non\_div(2, X)$
4) $non\_div(X, X)$
5) $non\_div(N, X) \quad \leftarrow \quad X \bmod N \neq 0, M = N + 1, non\_div(M, X)$
6) $X \in a \quad \leftarrow \quad even(X)$
7) $X \in b \quad \leftarrow \quad prime(X)$

and the goal:

$$\leftarrow \emptyset \neq a \cap b.$$

From this goal, loading the literals $X \in a$ and $X \in b$, we obtain:

$$\leftarrow \emptyset \neq a \cap b, X \in a, X \in b$$

from which, since $T \vdash \vec{\forall}(X \in a \wedge X \in b \rightarrow \emptyset \neq a \cap b)$, we can derive the goal:

$$\leftarrow X \in a, X \in b$$

With two further steps involving the clauses defining the two constants a and b, we obtain the following goal:

$$\leftarrow even(X), prime(X).$$

*A sequence of applications of rule **R1** yields to a TLP-refutation of the original goal:*

$$\leftarrow X = Y + 2, even(Y), prime(X). \qquad using\ 2)$$
$$\leftarrow X = 0 + 2, prime(X). \qquad using\ 1)$$
$$\leftarrow X = 0 + 2, X \geq 2, non\_div(2, X). \qquad using\ 3)$$
$$\leftarrow 2 = 0 + 2, 2 \geq 2. \qquad using\ 4)$$

An application of rule **Simpl** *yields to an empty goal. Notice that the two sets denoted by the constant symbols a and b are actually infinite sets.*

Example 4.6 *Consider the program P of Example 3.4 and the goal*

$$\leftarrow abs(-1997) = Y.$$

Rule **R2** *can be applyed using the clause:*

$$abs(X) = -X \leftarrow X < 0.$$

since it holds that:

$$T \vdash \vec{\forall}((\neg abs(-1997) = Y \wedge abs(X) = -X \rightarrow \neg(X < 0))\mu),$$

with $\mu = [X/1997, Y/1997]$, *we obtain the goal* $\leftarrow -1997 < 0$, *from which the empty goal is obtained using rule* **Simpl**.

Below we prove soundness and completeness results for the three rules introduced above:

Theorem 4.7 (Soundness) *Rules* **R1**, **R2**, *and* **Loading** *preserve T-satisfiability.*

Proof: It is immediate to see that the three rules are instances of the general T-resolution inference rule. Therefore, the soundness follows from Theorem 3.1 of [12]. □

Theorem 4.8 (Completeness) *Let P be a TLP-program, and G be a goal. If* $P \cup \{G\}$ *is a T-unsatisfiable set of clauses, then there exists a (strict) TLP-refutation of G.*

Proof: The proof will follow the classical pattern of proving ground completeness and then lifting the result to the general case.

To prove ground completeness we make use of the completeness of ground $SL\text{-}T$-resolution ([5]) (Subsumption Linear T-resolution, a refinement of linear T-resolution—cf. Section 2). Suppose that $P \cup \{G\}$ is a T-unsatisfiable set of ground clauses and that G is essential to T-unsatisfiability (i.e., P is T-satisfiable), then there exists a $SL\text{-}T$-refutation of $P \cup \{G\}$ with top-clause G: $G_0 = G, \dots, G_n$. This $SL\text{-}T$-refutation has some useful properties: only loading, standard resolution, and the following instance of rule **R2**:

$$\frac{\alpha \quad \leftarrow H_1, \dots, H_k}{\leftarrow H_2, \dots, H_k} \quad T \vdash \vec{\forall}(\neg H_1 \wedge \alpha \rightarrow (\neg H_2 \vee \cdots \vee \neg H_k))$$

(where α is an auxiliary arbitrarily chosen T-head clause) called *unloading*, are used. Moreover, loading and unloading steps are performed on Π_C-literals only, and only standard resolution steps are performed on Π_P-literals. Notice that (viewing the program clauses and goals as disjunctions of literals) G consists of negative literals and that if a clause in P contains Π_P-literals, then exactly one of them is positive (the head of the clause). Those literals are the only positive Π_P-literals occurring in $P \cup \{G\}$. This ensures that each Π_P-literal occurring in any derived center-clause (i.e., G_i) is negative. To obtain a TLP-refutation from the given SL-T-refutation, the following steps are performed:

- standard resolution step on Π_P-literals: from the above argument, it follows that each of these steps must involve, as side-clause, a clause in P. Hence, these steps come out to be applications of rule **R1**;

- unloading and loading steps: these are particular cases of our TLP-rules (i.e., **R2** and **Loading**, respectively);

- standard resolution step on Π_C-literals: in this case we employ rule **R2** to perform exactly the same inference step. □

Notice that the derivation considered in the previous theorem are *strict*, in the sense introduced by Definition 2.5.

Even though the proof of the above result is a direct consequence of the completeness of SL-T-resolution, the restrictions imposed on the T-resolution rule and on the kind of program clauses allowed in the context of TLP, make Theorem 4.8 rather significant. As a matter of fact, the two main differences between TLP and SL-T-resolution are the following:

1. TLP deals with sets of clauses built from two different (disjoint) sets of symbols (namely, Σ_C and Σ_P);

2. the part of the derivation relative to Π_P-literals is in fact a linear-input derivation. In other words, the inference process relative to Π_P-literals proceeds in a "Prolog-like fashion" (see also Remark 4.2).

Both these characteristics are not achievable in the general context of SL-T-resolution.

5   Concluding Remarks and Further Directions

Rule **R2** and **Loading** are the main sources of inefficiency in a TLP-derivation.

As far as rule **R2** is concerned, the problem is that, in general, previously derived goals have to be considered as possible side-clauses ($\leftarrow B_0, \ldots, B_n$). Therefore, the resulting TLP-derivation may not be an input-derivation. There are different possibilities to overcome this problem, each of them offers interesting starting points for research. One approach could be to introduce the introduction of a stronger rule in place of **R.2**, allowing as side-clauses only the clauses in P. This rule should be proposed together with a characterization (by means of syntactical or semantical restrictions) of the class of those first-order theories for which the completeness results still hold. Another possibility could be to consider an approach in the style of Model Elimination ([10]). In this case a suitable use, by means of particular literals inserted in the derived goals, of knowledge about the previous derivation steps, allows to preserve completeness even considering input derivations only.

Loading is needed for the completeness of the T-resolution procedure. A simple restriction that preserves completeness consists in loading only instances of literals occurring (positively or negatively) in the program ([5]). Two heuristics to handle loading are currently object of study:

- load any literal at most one time, and

- perform all loading steps that you consider useful on a single input-clause.

The freedom of using literals based on interpreted predicate symbols in the heads of clauses, allows, in particular, to write programs in the *Equational Logic Programming* style (see [7]; an example is the definition of the semantics of the functional symbol *abs* in Example 3.4). Therefore, ELP represents a class of TLP programs with a well-defined semantics; moreover, TLP can be seen as an extension of ELP in which negative information can be defined. Even though, a (necessarily) general-purpose implementation of TLP can not compete with ELP one in efficiency.

At present, different implementations of inference systems based on T-resolution are object of research. Namely, a Model Elimination variant of T-resolution is described in [5]. A theorem prover for modal logic has been introduced and tested in [15]. Moreover, an approach combining refutational and model-building methods in the context of T-theorem proving is being developed. A further step in this research will be the development of implementations of TLP that, for CLP-programs, adopts the same search strategy (i.e., equivalent proof trees and constraint checks) as standard CLP interpreters.

Acknowledgements

We thank the anonymous referees for their comments. This work enjoyed support of the C.N.R. of Italy, Research Project No. 95.00411.CT12 (S.E.T.A.). Agostino Dovier is partially supported by C.N.R. grant No. 201.15.08.

References

[1] K. R. Apt and R. Bol. Logic Programming and Negation: a Survey. *J. of Logic Programming*, 19,20:9–71, 1994.

[2] C. Beeri, S. Naqvi, O. Shmueli, and S. Tsur. Set Constructors in a Logic Database Language. *J. of Logic Programming*, 10(3):181–232, 1991.

[3] J. Benthem van, G. D'Agostino, A. Montanari, and A. Policriti. Modal deduction in second-order logic and set theory - I. *J. of Logic and Computation*, 7(2):251–265, 1997.

[4] A. Dovier, E. G. Omodeo, E. Pontelli, and G. Rossi. {log}: A Language for Programming in Logic with Finite Sets. *J. of Logic Programming*, 28(1):1–44, 1996.

[5] A. Formisano and A. Policriti. T-resolution: Refinements and Model Elimination. Research Report 32/95, Dipartimento di Matematica e Informatica, Università di Udine, 1995. Available in: ftp://ftp.dimi.uniud.it/pub/formisan/papers/TR32_12_95.ps.gz.

[6] P. M. Hill and J. W. Lloyd. *The Gödel Programming Language.* The MIT Press, Cambridge, Mass., 1994.

[7] S. Hölldobler. *Foundations of Equational Logic Programming.* Lecture Notes in Artificial Intelligence, 353, Springer-Verlag, 1987.

[8] J. Jaffar and J.-L. Lassez. Constraint Logic Programming. Technical report, Dept. of Computer Science, Monash University, June 1986.

[9] J. Jaffar and M. J. Maher. Constraint Logic Programming: A Survey. *J. of Logic Programming*, 19–20:503–581, 1994.

[10] D. W. Loveland. *Automated Theorem Proving.* North-Holland, 1978.

[11] F. Masier. Ottimizzazione di algoritmi di soddisfacibilità mediante T-risoluzione. Master's thesis, Univ. di Udine, Dip. di Matematica e Informatica, 1996. (In Italian)

[12] A. Policriti and J. T. Schwartz. T-theorem proving I. *J. of Symbolic Computation*, 20(3):315–342, 1995.

[13] J. H. Siekmann. Unification Theory. *J. of Symbolic Computation*, 7, 1989.

[14] M. E. Stickel. Automated deduction by theory resolution. *J. of Automated Reasoning*, I, 1985.

[15] D. Turchetti. Sistemi di deduzione per logiche modali. Master's thesis, Univ. di Udine, Dip. di Matematica e Informatica, 1996. (In Italian)

Best-first search for property maintenance in reactive constraints systems

Narendra Jussien and **Patrice Boizumault**
École des Mines de Nantes – Département Informatique
4 Rue Alfred Kastler – BP 20722
F-44307 Nantes Cedex 03 – France
Narendra.Jussien@emn.fr, Patrice.Boizumault@emn.fr

Abstract

Real-life dynamic problems may lead to inconsistent constraints systems for which
a solution must be found even if constraints have to be relaxed. In this paper, we
propose a best-first search to handle such problems. Classical backtracking search
algorithms are extended in two ways: identification of good backtrack points as in
Intelligent Backtracking techniques and maximum use of independant work (that
would have been discarded with a mere *backtrack*). We first describe an operational
semantics for our search method. Then we specialize it to handle constraint relaxation over finite domains. The practical use of this approach is demonstrated by
theoretical complexity analysis and experiments.

1 Introduction

Constraints are nowadays widely used for solving problems arising in various fields
such as Artificial Intelligence, Operations Research, ... Constraint Programming
Languages and Systems are mainly designed to handle *static* problems. But, many
real life problems are *dynamic*: the problem evolves throughout modifications induced by the outside environment (*e.g.* consider the necessity of on-line rescheduling
when a machine is damaged or not usable). Performing a complete reexecution from
scratch is not realistic. First, the amount of work can be prohibitive if many modifications are to be taken into account. Second, the resulting solution may be far
away from the initial one. It seems more efficient to use the previous computation
to ease the search of a solution.

In order to handle dynamic problems, Fages *et al.* [5] have proposed an extension
of Constraint Logic Programming to *reactive systems* [8]. The objective of such a
system is not to produce a single *input-output* relation, but to maintain a given
property of the considered system through any modification. Hence, incrementality
is a key aspect of reactive systems.

When considering large amounts of modifications, dynamic problems can lead to
inconsistent constraint systems (they are over-constrained). In many cases, a solution is required even if constraints (that are considered as not being important) are
not taken into account *i.e.* relaxed. Despite many works handling over-constrained
static problems have been developped [6; 20], very few can handle *dynamic* problems
[12] without a mere complete reexecution.

In this paper, we present an algorithmic scheme to handle over-constrained
problems in a dynamic environment. Our approach consists in considering the
constraint solver over a domain $\mathcal{D}$ as a reactive system which interacts with the
outside environment by continuously maintaining a property $\mathcal{P}$ over the current

constraint system[1]. When this property is not verified, some constraints will be relaxed according to their relative importance. Our approach relies on the notion of configuration : a *configuration* is the splitting of the constraints of the problem in two sets: active and relaxed ones. A user-defined comparator enables discrimination between configurations.

We define a best first search method over the configurations space that is well suited for dynamic problems because it actively uses past computations to ease future computation. This search step is performed when a contradiction occurs during the property maintenance. A configuration that is not contradictory and suits the user's preferences is determined. The key idea is to benefit from the past computation *i.e.* to provide a search method that combines *intelligent* backtracking with avoiding *thrashing*: recomputation of already explored parts of the search space. This search method is parameterized by the *domain* on which constraints are defined and by the *property* maintained during the computation.

The paper is organized as follows: in section 2, we introduce definitions related to over-constrained problems. In section 3 we briefly recall related works. In section 4, we present our search method for which an operational semantics is given section 5. Section 6 shows how our method can be successfully instantiated for constraints over Finite Domains and the property of Arc-Consistency, and efficiently implemented using a Deduction Maintenance System. Complexity issues and experimental results are addressed in section 7.

2 Definitions

In order to *solve* over-constrained problems, **preferences** over the constraints of the problem should be specified by the user. Such a preference[2] represents the will of the user regarding the activation of the constraints. When grouping constraints by preference levels, an **hierarchy** is built upon the constraints.

A **configuration** is a split of a given constraints system in two sets: the set A of active constraints and the set R of relaxed ones. It is noted: $\langle A, R \rangle$.

We consider a property $\mathcal{P}$ that is defined for sets of constraints[3]. $\mathcal{P}$ is necessary (but not necessarily sufficient) for the satisfiability of the constraints system. It thus represents a certain level of consistency. A configuration $\langle A, R \rangle$ is called $\mathcal{P}$-**satisfiable** is $\mathcal{P}$ holds for A and $\mathcal{P}$-**contradictory** otherwise.

The user provides a **comparator** based upon the hierarchy. Such a comparator enables selection betweens $\mathcal{P}$-satisfiable configurations. More precisely, a comparator is a partial order relation upon configurations. It must respect the hierarchy [20] defined from the user preferences. We can consider the following comparator used in [17]:

Definition 2.1 (The C_{MM} comparator)
Let $C_1 = \langle A_1, R_1 \rangle$ and $C_2 = \langle A_2, R_2 \rangle$ two configurations.

$$C_{MM}(C_1, C_2) \quad \equiv \quad \begin{array}{l} \exists k > 0, \text{tel que} \\ \forall i < k, R_{1[i]} = R_{2[i]} \\ R_{1[k]} = \varnothing \text{ and } R_{2[k]} \neq \varnothing \end{array} \tag{1}$$

where $R_{[\ell]}$ is the restriction of R to the constraints with a preference[4] level ℓ in the hierarchy.

---

[1] This property could be Arc-consistency for finite domains, B-Consistency for Intervals, *"full"* consistency for linear constraints over rationals, ...

[2] A preference can be considered as a *weight* on the constraint.

[3] For example, one can consider global consistency for rationals or local consistencies for finite domains or intervals.

[4] The higher the preference level, the less important is the constraint.

A *C*-solution for an over-constrained problem is then defined as a $\mathcal{P}$-satisfiable configuration maximum for a given comparator C.

3   Related Works

Hierarchical Constraint Logic Programming (HCLP) [20] is an extension of CLP handling constraints hierarchies. The operational behavior of HCLP is like building a *tower of constraints*. Constraints are introduced level by level in the constraint store (from the most important to the less important ones) until an inconsistency occurs. This approach needs to completely know the constraints system before resolution (this is not suitable for dynamic environments).

In order to handle dynamic problems within the HCLP framework, Menezes and Barahona [12] proposed the IHCS (Incremental Hierarchical Constraint Solver) system. This approach uses works on Intelligent Backtracking. As all backtracking techniques do, this approach suffers from the *thrashing* behavior: recomputation of already explored parts of the search space. Furthermore, despite its incremental handling of constraint addition, constraint relaxations are handled in the *hard* way: using a *backtrack* and not incrementally. IHCS is then not a completely satisfactory answer to handle over-constrained problems arising in dynamic environments.

As mentioned in the introduction, Fages *et al.* proposed an extension of CLP to reactive systems [5]. A reactive system allows interactions between the user and the solver. The aim is not only to give a solution to an instance of a problem but also to maintain such a solution throughout interactions with the user. The framework proposed in [5] handles constraint addition or suppression but unfortunately does not consider over-constrained systems[5]. Indeed, constraints to be suppressed must be explicitly specified by the user. Our proposal provides the necessary machinery to handle those problems and from this point of view extends Fages' proposal.

Local propagation is well suited for solution maintenance on dynamic functional constraints systems. A constraint is *functional* if, for each of its constrained variables v, there is a unique value of v that will satisfy the constraint, given values for the other variables. Such a constraint is defined by the set of functions than compute this value for each set of fixed variables. Local propagation algorithms for functional constraints handling constraint hierarchies with no cycle in the constraint graph provide efficient constraint solvers. Recent works include the DeltaBlue and SkyBlue algorithms [16], and QuickPlan [19]. But such techniques are not so well adapted for dynamic non functional constraints systems. Recently, Borning *et al.* proposed the Indigo system [3] to handling inequality constraints (a particular case of non functional constraints) using local propagation techniques. Unfortunately, such a method seems not suited for a dynamic environment; as said by the authors: *producing an incremental version of Indigo does not seem to be straightforward.*

From another view point, the CSP (Constraint Satisfaction problems) community is used to handle dynamic problems [1; 14]. They mainly implement Maintenance Systems inherited from the TMS community [4]. But, unfortunately no satisfactory handling of over-constrained dynamic CSPs has ever been proposed. Indeed, works such as [2; 6; 17] are meant for static problems and do not provide fully incremental systems for dynamic ones. Nevertheless, the idea of maintaining information seems the wisest thing to do when handling dynamic CSP.

---

[5] When such a system arises, it just says no solution.

4   A best-first search

We present here a search method over the configurations space that ensures that as soon as a $\mathcal{P}$-satisfiable configuration is identified, this configuration is the best one regarding the user-defined comparator (thus providing a C-solution). The idea of the search inherits from the *Dynamic Backtracking* algorithm[6] [7]. Standard backtracking is enhanced in two ways: first, upon failure, a relevant choice point is reconsidered instead of merely considering the last choice point (this is *Intelligent bactracking*), and, second, *thrashing* is avoided by keeping information gathered between the backtrack point and the current point that is independant from the failure. Of course, conditions of *backtrack* must be recorded in order to ensure the completeness of the search.

4.1   The configurations space

The configurations space can be considered as a binary tree. Each node is a constraint whose children represent the two possible states: active or relaxed. This tree is built considering the entrance order of the constraints (the problem is dynamic).

For a node associated with a constraint c_a, an outcoming edge is labeled a (*resp.* a') for the active state (*resp.* relaxed state). Figure 1 shows such a tree for three constraints c_a, c_b and c_c.

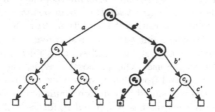

Figure 1: Configurations space for $\{c_a, c_b, c_c\}$.

Each leaf (or path from the root to a leaf) of this tree represents a *configuration*. For example, the bold branch ($a'bc$) in figure 1 represents the configuration: $\langle\{c_b, c_c\}, \{c_a\}\rangle$.

Solving an over-constrained problem requires to find the best (considering the comparator C) $\mathcal{P}$-satisfiable leaf (configuration).

4.2   Classical Explorations

Explorations based upon backtracking (standard backtracking or *intelligent backtracking* [5; 12]) have two main drawbacks: on one hand, an optimality proof step is required as a $\mathcal{P}$-satisfiable configuration is found; and on the other hand, these approaches suffer from *thrashing*.

We claim here that by recording the same information as in *intelligent backtracking* techniques, the search can be improved by not only computing good backtrack points but also avoiding *thrashing* by using previously gathered information.

---

[6] *Dynamic Backtracking* is an enumeration algorithm designed for CSPs. Enumeration is done here on the state of the constraints (active or relaxed). Moreover, unlike in *Dynamic Backtracking*, constraint propagation is considered. Finally, our proposal is meant for over-constrained problems which *Dynamic Backtracking* cannot deal with.

4.3 A best first approach

Our search method does not perform backtracks but *jumps*. These *jumps* lead to a non classical exploration of the search space that is complete and optimum. The proposed approach is a general method that can be applied to different constraints domain and for different consistency techniques. We suppose from now on that the following three functions are given: `explain-contradiction`, `best-configuration` and `change-configuration`. Section 6 provides complete definitions of these functions for finite domains.

4.3.1 Contradiction explanations

Our method relies upon the key concept of **contradiction explanation**[7]. A *contradiction explanation* is a set of constraints whose conjunction leads to a contradiction. It is a *justification* for the contradiction. This notion is strongly related to the property $\mathcal{P}$ maintained throughout the computation for the current set of active constraints.

Definition 4.1 (contradiction explanation)
Let $\langle A, R \rangle$ be the current configuration. Let us suppose that this configuration has been identified as over-constrained i.e. $\mathcal{P}(A)$ does not hold. Let $E \subset A$ a set of constraints.
*E is a **contradiction explanation** iff $\mathcal{P}(E)$ does not hold.*

Contradiction explanations are learnt from the identification of a contradiction. The function `explain-contradiction` computes such a contradiction explanation from a $\mathcal{P}$-contradictory configuration[8].

4.3.2 Promising configurations

Let $\mathcal{E}_c$ be the set of all the contradiction explanations determined so far during the computation. We can search the C-solution of the considered problem amongst the *promising configurations*.

Definition 4.2 (Promising configuration)
*Let $C_f = \langle A, R \rangle$ a configuration. C_f is a **promising configuration** iff*

$$\forall E \in \mathcal{E}_c, R \cap E \neq \varnothing \qquad (2)$$

*In other words, a **promising configuration** covers the set of contradiction explanations.*

A configuration that is not promising is necessarily $\mathcal{P}$-contradictory because its set of active constraints contains an identified contradiction explanation.

The `best-configuration` function computes the best (regarding the given comparator C) promising configuration from the current configuration taking into account the contradiction explanations in $\mathcal{E}_c$. This leads to solve a set covering problem. Note that set covering is an NP-hard problem in general. We will adress this issue on section 6.

4.3.3 A best first exploration

Let C_f be the current configuration. As the problem has been identified as over-constrained, C_f is $\mathcal{P}$-contradictory. Let $\mathcal{E}_c$ be the set of computed contradiction explanations so far (from the beginning of the dynamic process). The main idea is to use the information gathered throughout the computation (the set $\mathcal{E}_c$) to directly

---

[7] We do not use the term *nogood* (partial affectation not found in any solution) because a contradiction explanation is more general.

[8] The simplest contradiction explanation is the set A of active constraints but such an explanation is inefficient. Section 6 will precise the function for finite domains.

explore the best promising configurations. Implicit information embedded within the contradiction explanations (parts of the search tree that lead to contradiction) are thus actively used.

Let us consider the following algorithm:

Algorithm 4.1 (Best-first search)
```
        % We start from a promising configuration C_f that
        % became P-contradictory after a modification
(1)  begin
(2)      while C_f is P-contradictory do
(3)          add explain-contradiction(C_f) to E_c
(4)          change-configuration(C_f,best-configuration(C_f,E_c))
(5)      endwhile //C_f is a C-solution //
(6)  end
```

The `change-configuration` function performs the configuration *jump* at minimal cost: the system is in the target configuration as it would have been if it had been explored first. This *jump* avoids as much as possible *thrashing*.

This algorithm presents a search method that does not require any optimality proof step. As soon as the explored configuration verifies property $\mathcal{P}$, it is a C-solution. Such an exploration can be characterized as a best first search.

The presented search method does not use any backtrack. Only configuration *jumps* are performed. All the exploration relies in the same level in the tree. This approach implicitly cuts branches leading to a $\mathcal{P}$-contradiction at each identification of a contradiction explanation. This supplementary information is used to compute promising configurations. Thus, redundant work is as much as possible avoided.

This algorithm terminates because:

- Only new contradiction explanations are produced (only new configurations will then be explored) (see theorem 6.1);

- The number of existing configurations is finite (2^e where e is the number of constraints in the problem);

- There exists at least one $\mathcal{P}$-satisfiable configuration: all the constraints are relaxed.

The proposed algorithm is correct because as soon as a $\mathcal{P}$-satisfiable configuration is obtained, it is the best possible one giving thus a C-solution.

4.4 Example

Let us consider the following example involving 4 constraints: (c_a, c_b, c_c, c_d). We suppose that the constraints are introduced in the reverse order of their importance *i.e.* c_d is the most important one and c_a is the least important one. Moreover, we will use a comparator based upon a set of preferences that leads to systematically prefer the relaxation of any set of less important constraints against the relaxation of a single more important one. For example, the relaxation of constraints $\{c_a, c_b, c_c\}$ will be preferred against the relaxation of $\{c_d\}$.

Let us suppose that property $\mathcal{P}$ is verified by $\{c_a, c_b, c_c\}$ but when adding c_d $\mathcal{P}$ does not hold. The problem is over-constrained. The exploration is depicted in figure 2.

- The current configuration C_f (path $abcd$ in the tree) is $\mathcal{P}$-contradictory. We suppose that `explain-contradiction`$(C_f) = (c_a, c_b, c_d)$. Then `best-configuration`$(\mathcal{E}_c) = a'bcd$. The constraint c_a, being the least important constraint in the contradiction explanation, is chosen to be relaxed. The following explored configuration (path) is then $a'bcd$.

- We suppose that $C_f = a'bcd$ is $\mathcal{P}$-contradictory and that `explain-contra-diction`$(C_f) = (c_b, c_d)$. Then `best-configuration`$(\mathcal{E}_c) = ab'cd$. Relaxing c_a is no more needed because the contradiction explanation (c_a, c_b, c_d) is *covered* by the relaxation of c_b. Note that when exploring this configuration a *back*[9] jump is performed. Such an unusual behavior would not have been authorized by a classical backtrack-based method but thanks to the set $\mathcal{E}_c$ it is possible here.

- Let us suppose that $C_f = ab'cd$ is also $\mathcal{P}$-contradictory and that `explain--contradiction`$(C_f) = (c_c, c_d)$. Then `best-configuration`$(\mathcal{E}_c) = ab'c'd$.

- At last, let us suppose that $C_f = ab'c'd$ is $\mathcal{P}$-satisfiable. There exists no better configuration regarding the user-defined comparator. This last configuration is thus a C-solution for the considered problem.

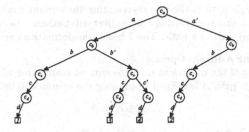

Figure 2: Best first search. Leafs are numbered in their exploration order.

5 An operational semantics for the exploration

In this section, we give an operational semantics for the `change-configuration` function. This semantics explicitly shows the main key-points of our approach: efficient identification of constraints to relax and the avoiding of a thrashing behavior.

5.1 Changing the current configuration

A configuration change is performed in three steps:

- Identification of parts of the current path (current configuration) that will not be modified in the next configuration and that are independant from the relaxed constraints.

- Effective relaxation of the selected constraint(s) and propagation of this relaxation (*cf.* section 6.5 for an implementation for finite domains),

- Reintroduction of the constraints that are relaxed in the current configuration but that are active in the next one (as shown in section 4.4, *cf.* configuration $a'bcd$).

---

[9]To the left of the current position.

5.2 Modifying the search tree

The example depicted in figure 2 does not emphasize the reuse part of the proposed computations. We give now an operational semantics of the configuration change that enlightens the properties of our approach. This semantics is based upon transformations of the search tree.

The idea of the transformations relies on this statement: if the relaxed constraints were the last ones, a standard backtrack would have been efficient. As the order of introduction of the constraints does not modify the set of solutions (or C-solutions) for a problem, the search tree can be transformed in such a way that every constraint whose status has changed (active to relaxed, or relaxed to active) is put at the "*end*" of the tree (the part of computation that will be recomputed).

Thus, the operational behavior of the configuration becomes explicit and the reused parts from the previous computation can be more clearly seen.

5.2.1 Transformation Operators

As only a path in the tree is considered at a given time, our operators are defined considering a single path in the tree representing the current configuration.

Let • be the **concatenation** operation over sub-paths: $ab \bullet cd = abcd$. In the following, x is any part of a path. The 3 basic transformations are:

- **Constraint Adding:** Operator $\oplus$
  The adding of the constraint c_c in the current search tree whose current configuration is path A is defined from using the operator $\oplus$ by:
  $$A \oplus c_c = A \bullet c$$

- **Constraint Relaxation (or deletion):** Operator $\ominus$
  The relaxation of constraint c_c in the current configuration is recursively defined as:
  $$(x \bullet A) \ominus c_c = \left| \begin{array}{ll} A \bullet c' & \text{if } x = c \\ x \bullet (A \ominus c_c) & \text{otherwise} \end{array} \right.$$

- **Constraint Reintroduction:** Operator $\odot$
  The reintroduction of constraint c_c in the current configuration is recursively defined as:
  $$(x \bullet A) \odot c_c = \left| \begin{array}{ll} A \bullet c & \text{if } x = c' \\ x \bullet (A \odot c_c) & \text{otherwise} \end{array} \right.$$

When considering a configuration change, the comparison of the current $\mathcal{P}$-contradictory configuration (path A) and the target configuration (given by **best--configuration**) defines two sets: a set of constraints to relax $c_{k_1}, \ldots, c_{k_n}$ and a set of constraints to reintroduce $c_{\ell_1}, \ldots, c_{\ell_m}$. Using the operators, the new current configuration is thus defined as:

$$A \ominus c_{k_1} \cdots \ominus c_{k_n} \odot c_{\ell_1} \cdots \odot c_{\ell_m}$$

5.2.2 Graphical Illustration

Let us take back the example presented section 4.4.

- From the first explored configuration $abcd$ which is $\mathcal{P}$-contradictory, the function **best-configuration** gives the configuration $a'bcd$. There is only one constraint to relax (c_a) in this configuration and none to reintroduce. The performed transformation is thus:

$$abcd \ominus c_a = bcda' \qquad (3)$$

This new path defines a new tree for the search (*cf.* figure 3 (left)). Note that part of this new tree has been already explored (bold). Indeed, everything on the left of the current configuration leads to a $\mathcal{P}$-contradictory configuration. The figure describes what part of the tree has been reused without modification.

- The next configuration is $ab'cd$. The transformation is:

$$bcda' \ominus c_b \odot c_a = cdb'a \qquad (4)$$

The resulting tree is depicted figure 3 (right).

- The next and final configuration is $ab'c'd$. The transformation is:

$$cdb'a \ominus c_c = db'ac' \qquad (5)$$

The resulting tree is depicted figure 4. Note that the method implicitly excludes here any part of the graph that is on the left of the current configuration. This is due to the the used comparator.

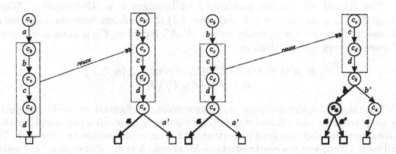

Figure 3: Transformations of the search tree – Transformation (3) (left) – Transformation (4) (right)

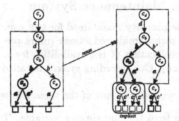

Figure 4: Transformations of the search tree – Transformation (5)

6 Specialization for finite domains and Arc-consistency

In this section, we present the specialization of the three functions explain-contradiction, change-configuration and best-configuration in order to handle CSP (Constraint Satisfaction Problems) *i.e.* Finite Domains problems.

Let us recall that a CSP can be defined as a set $\mathcal{V}$ of variables; the set $\mathcal{D}$ of their respective domains (discrete finite set of the possible values for each variable) and the set $\mathcal{C}$ of constraints specifying acceptable combinations of values for the variables of the problem.

6.1 The best-configuration function

As precised in definition 4.2, the new best promising configuration must *cover* the set $\mathcal{E}_c$ of *contradiction explanations* whilst optimizing the comparator-based partial order.

This problem can be modeled as the determination of a set covering in the hypergraph $\mathcal{H}$:

Definition 6.1 (The Hypergraph $\mathcal{H}$)
The hypergraph $\mathcal{H}$ is defined from the set $\mathcal{E}_c$ of contradiction explanations. *Each constraint appearing in any element of $\mathcal{E}_c$ is a vertex in $\mathcal{H}$. Each* contradiction explanation E *is an hyper-edge in $\mathcal{H}$.*

The general set covering problem in an hypergraph is NP-complete. When using the C_{MM} comparator (*cf.* definition 2.1) this problem becomes polynomial. Indeed, the best promising configuration $\langle A', R' \rangle$ regarding C_{MM} computed from a $\mathcal{P}$-contradictory configuration is:

$$R' = \{c \in A \cup R \mid \exists E \in \mathcal{E}_c, c = \min_{\text{pref}}\{c_i \in E\}\}$$
$$\text{and } A' = (A \cup R) \setminus R'$$

Note that using this comparator, best promising configurations can be computed in an incremental and efficient way ($O(e)$ – number of constraints) by simply adding a constraint to relax (the least important of the new *contradiction explanation*). We call such a comparator a **contradiction-local** one. A contradiction-local comparator is interesting for the complexity results (*cf.* section 7) that can therefore be obtained. It is also of great use when all the preferences associated with constraints are not known; they can be specified only when required.

6.2 A Deduction Maintenance System

Arc-consistency is the property maintained for CSP using domain reduction. We suggest here to *record* such domain reductions (more precisely their *explanation*) in order to provide identification of responsibilities for a contradiction (function **explain-contradiction**). Our recording system is called a **deduction maintenance system** (DMS).

A **deduction** is associated with any of the three following actions:

- Removing a value from the domain of a variable. The deduction associated with the removal of the value a from the domain d_x of the variable x is denoted: $\delta_{(x \neq a)}$.

- Removing a constraint from the constraint store (relaxing). The deduction associated with the relaxation of the constraint c is denoted: $\delta_{(\bar{c})}$.

- Raising a contradiction (the domain of a variable becomes empty). The associated deduction is denoted $\delta_{(\perp)}$.

Let Δ be the set of deductions performed during the resolution.

A **deduction explanation** E, for a deduction δ, is a set of constraints whose conjunction leads to perform the action associated with the deduction.

Definition 6.2 (Deduction explanation)

Let E be a set of constraints.

- *E is a **deduction explanation** for a deduction $\delta_{(x \neq a)}$ iff a is removed from d_x when achieving $\mathcal{P}$ for the set of constraints E.*

- *E is a **deduction explanation** for a deduction $\delta_{(\perp)}$ iff the configuration $\langle E, \varnothing \rangle$ is P-contradictory.*

- *E is a **deduction explanation** for a deduction $\delta_{(\delta)}$ iff the configuration $\langle \{c\} \cup E, \varnothing \rangle$ is $\mathcal{P}$-contradictory.*

A *deduction explanation* E is **valid** in a given configuration $\langle A, R \rangle$ if $E \subset A$.

A configuration becomes $\mathcal{P}$-contradictory as soon as the domain of a variable becomes empty, *i.e.* all the deduction explanations of the removal of each value in the domain are valid.

6.3 Providing deduction explanations

The simplest *deduction explanation* for any deduction is the complete set of the active constraints of the current configuration. This kind of *deduction explanation* is obviously of no use and would lead to a complete enumeration process of all the possible configurations (that we try to avoid).

The *best deduction explanation* is the minimal set of constraints that verifies the definition 6.2. When using a particular algorithm during property $\mathcal{P}$ enforcement, a *good deduction explanation* must reflect the knowledge used by this algorithm to perform any deduction. We detail possible *deduction explanation* when achieving arc-consistency.

Using the AC4 algorithm: The AC4 algorithm [13] uses two main steps to remove unsupported values from the domain of the variables. The first step performs value removals directly due to a unique constraint (thus, the *deduction explanation* is built from this constraint). In the second step, indirect removals are performed, they are the consequence of the removals in the first step (the *deduction explanation* is then the applied constraint associated with the *deduction explanation* of the propagated removal).

Using the AC5 algorithm: The AC5 algorithm [18] actively uses the semantics of the handled constraints. This leads to a better *deduction explanation* system. For example, when filtering a constraint $x > y$ considering that the current domain of x is $\{..., a\}$, values greater than a will be removed from d_y and the *deduction explanation* for these removals is $E = \bigcup_{b \in d_u, b > a} E_{\delta_{x \neq b}}$ where E_δ represents an explanation for deduction δ.

6.4 Function explain-contradiction

When a contradiction (deduction $\delta_{(\perp)}$) occurs, the domain of at least one variable is empty. Let x be such a variable. Let note E_δ the *deduction explanation* associated with the deduction δ. Thus $E_{\delta_{(\perp)}} = \bigcup_{a \in d_x} E_{\delta_{(x \neq a)}}$.

Theorem 6.1 (New contradiction explanation)

When computing a new contradiction explanation for a (previously promising) $\mathcal{P}$-contradictory configuration, only a new contradiction explanation is produced i.e. $E_{\delta_{(\perp)}} \not\subset \mathcal{E}_c$.

Proof: As $E_{\delta_{(\perp)}}$ is valid, it cannot be an already computed *contradiction explanation* because the current configuration would not have been a promising one (not covering the current set of *contradiction explanations*). □

6.5 Function `change-configuration`

When performing a configuration change, we compute the set C_α of new active constraints and the set C_β of the new relaxed constraints.

Relaxing a constraint The relaxation of any element of C_β needs to be propagated. The aim of this propagation is to delete the past effects of the relaxed constraints. We present here an extension of DNAC4 (which performs incremental constraint deletions for dynamic CSP) [1].

First of all, a *deduction explanation* can be added for the removal of the constraint c_c. It consists in the invalidated *contradiction explanation* in $\mathcal{E}_c$ (except c).

Let c be an element of C_β. Let $\alpha(c)$ be the subset of Δ (the deductions of the problem) whose validity relies upon c. $\alpha(c) = \{\delta \in \Delta \mid c \in E_\delta\}$. Our extension of DNAC4 proceeds in two steps:

- in the first step, values considered in $\alpha(c)$ are put back in their respective domain,

- in the second step, each of these values are considered through arc-consistency achievement to see if they can be removed with a new explanation. If it is possible, the associated value removal is propagated as usual.

Completing the jump In order to terminate the jump, every constraint in C_α needs to be introduced in the constraint system. Note that when using our comparator (C_{MM}) no constraint in C_α needs to be reintroduced.

6.6 Enumeration and Relaxation

Enumeration can be modeled as the dynamic addition/removal of equality constraints (*eg.* $x = a$ for $a \in d_x$). This is completely transparent in our approach. After each addition of such a constraint, the property $\mathcal{P}$ is enforced and if the current configuration is $\mathcal{P}$-contradictory then the constraint relaxation process is initiated by handling enumeration constraints in the same way as the other ones. The preference associated to such constraints is the lowest possible; so in case of failure, enumeration constraints will be relaxed in priority.

In fact, our algorithm is extended in order to enforce the introduction of another constraint (testing another value) when relaxing an equality constraint due to the enumeration. This leads to model an exclusive disjunction between equality constraints.

During this process, informations (namely the explanations associated with constraint removals) are kept as in *Dynamic Backtracking* [7] in order to ensure the completeness of the approach.

7 Complexity issues

Let n be the number of variables, e the number of constraints and d the maximum size of the domains. There are $c = e + n \times d$ possible constraints in the problem (we add the equality constraints produced by the enumeration process). Note that there are only $c' = e + n$ active constraints at a given time of computation since a variable can only be assigned to a single value.

The good complexity results presented here are due to the properties of contradiction-local comparators (such as C_{MM} – *cf.* section 6.1).

7.1 Space Complexity

The space occupation is related to the *deduction explanations* recording. Thus, the overall space complexity is defined as the number of possible deductions multiplied by the worst-case size of an explanation.

A *deduction explanation* can contain at most $e+n$ constraints since it is a subset of the active constraints. There are $O(a) = O(n \times d + e + 1)$ possible deductions in the system:

- one for each value removal *i.e.* $n \times d$ in the worst case;

- one for each constraint removal *i.e.* e *real* constraints plus $n \times d$ enumeration-related constraints;

- one for the last contradiction (when using comparator C_{MM}, only the last contradiction need to be kept).

Hence, in the worst case, we encounter $O(n \times d + e)$ *deduction explanations*.

This leads to the following worst case space complexity:

$$O(c' \times a) = O((n + e) \times (n \times d + e))$$

7.2 Time complexity

In the worst-case, the overall complexity of the search is obviously exponential since solving a CSP is NP-complete. As usual, we will give the time complexity of the basic steps of our approach:

- the arc-consistency management is dependent from the used arc-consistency algorithm used augmented with the providing of explanations. For example, when using an AC4-based algorithm, explanations are computed in $O(d)$ (from the supporting values). Hence, the resulting complexity of the algorithm is in $O(e \times d^2 \times d)$ because AC4 is in $O(e \times d^2)$;

- computing a contradiction explanation can be computed in $O(d)$ as explained before;

- determining a constraint to relax is done in $O(e+n)$: the size of an explanation;

- performing the constraint removal is achieved in $O(e \times d^2 \times d)$ since DNAC4 gives the same complexity for constraint addition or removal.

7.3 Experimental results

DECORUM (Deduction-based Constraint Relaxation Management) is an implementation (done in C++) which provides a constraint solver for over-constrained CSPs. The efficient complexities enabled by our Deduction Maintenance System allow the handling of large CSPs: hundred of variables for thousand of constraints.

We give here experimental results on large random problems since the main worry when dealing with a Deduction Maintenance System is practability. We will focus on single examples. Random problems are classically categorized using 4 parameters : the number of variables, the uniform size of their domain, the density of the constraint graph and the tightness[10] of the constraints.

Here are some results that give a hint of how our system behaves for large problems[11]:

---

[10] Ratio between the number of allowed combinations of value and the total number of such combinations ($d \times d$ for binary constraints).

[11] The problems considered here are very over-constrained because of the high value of the tightness of constraints. This explains the large number of relaxed constraints.

- a $\langle 700, 2, 0.05, 0.5 \rangle$ which involves 12500 constraints is solved in 27s. This boolean satisfaction problem (binary domains) is solved using 211320 constraint checks and a space occupation of 17368.[12] 5967 constraints need to be relaxed. The enumeration step is done without *backtrack*[13].

- a $\langle 120, 5, 0.32, 0.6 \rangle$ which thus involves 2300 constraints is solved in 51s with 172070 constraint checks and using a 49581 space. The search requires 1240 *backtracks* and 1297 constraint relaxations.

- a $\langle 50, 10, 0.49, 0.75 \rangle$ which involves 600 constraints is solved in 260s using 927587 constraint checks and using a 31229 space. The search requires 1980 *backtracks* and 362 constraint relaxations.

- a $\langle 50, 25, 0.20, 0.32 \rangle$ which involves 200 constraints is solved in 113s using 615117 constraint checks and using a 23547 space. The search requires 16 *backtracks* and no constraint is relaxed.

These results simply show that large problems can be dealt with using DECORUM. Our various experiments [10] show that the behavior of DECORUM on a large set of random problems conforms to the well known phase transition [15] despite the relaxation process. Other experiments [9] show that the search provided by DECORUM is of much interest on *structured* problems (with set of relatively independant variables, ...).

8 Conclusion

We have proposed a best first search on the configurations space that is well suited for dynamic problems. This search method is parameterized by the *domain* on which constraints are defined and by the *property* maintained during the computation. This method has been instantiated for finite domains and the property of arc-consistency. Algorithms, a complexity analysis and an implementation have shown the efficiency of the approach. Our current works lie on two topics:

- the use of DECORUM to solve real-life dynamic resource allocation problems for military purposes and for communication networks;

- the instantiation of our search method maintaining the property of B-consistency [11] for intervals also processed by domain reduction; therefore, the proposed approach (including the DMS) seems easily adaptable to intervals.

References

[1] Christian Bessière. Arc consistency in dynamic constraint satisfaction problems. In *Proceedings AAAI'91*, 1991.

[2] Stefano Bistarelli, Hélène Fargier, Ugo Montanari, Francesca Rossi, Thomas Schiex, and Gérard Verfaillie. Semiring-based csps and valued csps: basic properties and comparison. In *Over-Constrained Systems*, number 1106 in LNCS, pages 111–150, 1996.

[3] Alan Borning, Richard Anderson, and Bjorn Freeman-Benson. Indigo: A local propagation algorithm for inequality constraints. In *ACM Symposium on User Interface Software and Technology*, pages 129–136, 1996.

---

[12] The space occupation is represented by the number of constraints references in all the explanations of the system.

[13] Since no *real* backtrack occur in DECORUM, we call backtrack each constraint relaxation related to enumeration.

[4] J. Doyle. A truth maintenance system. *Artificial Intelligence*, 12:231–272, 1979.

[5] François Fages, Julian Fowler, and Thierry Sola. A reactive constraint logic programming scheme. In *International Conference of Logic Programming, ICLP'95*, Tokyo, 1995.

[6] Eugene C. Freuder and Richard Wallace. Partial constraint satisfaction. In *Over-Constrained Systems*, number 1106 in LNCS, pages 63–110, 1996.

[7] Matthew L. Ginsberg. Dynamic backtracking. *Journal of Artificial Intelligence Research*, 1:25–46, 1993.

[8] D. Harel and A. Pnueli. On the development of reactive systems. In K. R. Apt, editor, *Logics and Models of Concurrent Systems*, volume F13 of *NATO ASI Series*. Springer Verlag, January 1985.

[9] Narendra Jussien. *Relaxation de Contraintes pour les problèmes dynamiques*. PhD thesis, Université de Rennes 1, 1997. In french, to appear.

[10] Narendra Jussien and Patrice Boizumault. A best first approach for solving over-constrained dynamic problems. In *IJCAI'97 posters session*, Nagoya, Japan, August 1997. (also available as Technical Report 97-6-INFO at the École des Mines de Nantes).

[11] Olivier Lhomme, Arnaud Gotlieb, Michel Rueher, and Patrick Taillibert. Boosting the interval narrowing algorithm. In *JICSLP'96*, Bonn, Germany, 2–6September 1996.

[12] Francisco Menezes and Pedro Barahona. Defeasible constraint solving. In *Over-Constrained Systems*, number 1106 in LNCS, pages 151–170, 1996.

[13] R. Mohr and T. C. Henderson. Arc and path consistency revisited. *Artificial Intelligence*, 28:225–233, 1986.

[14] Bertrand Neveu and Pierre Berlandier. Arc-consistency for dynamic constraint satisfaction problems: an RMS free approach. In *Proc. ECAI-94, Workshop on Constraint satisfaction issues raised by practical applications*, Amsterdam, The Netherlands, 1994.

[15] Patrick Prosser. An empirical study of phase transitions in binary constraint satisfaction problems. Technical Report AISL-49-94, Department of Computer Science, University of Strathclyde, Glasgow, Scotland, 1994.

[16] Michael Sannella. The SkyBlue constraint solver and its applications. In Paris Kanellakis, Jean-Louis Lassez, and Vijay Saraswat, editors, *PPCP'93: First Workshop on Principles and Practice of Constraint Programming*, Providence RI, 1993.

[17] Thomas Schiex. Possibilistic constraint satisfaction problems or "How to handle soft constraints ?". In *8th International Conference on Uncertainty in Artificial Intelligence*, Stanford, July 1992.

[18] Pascal Van Hentenryck, Yves Deville, and Choh-Man Teng. A generic arc-consistency algorithm and its specializations. *Artificial Intelligence*, 57(2–3):291–321, October 1992.

[19] Brad Vander Zanden. An incremental algorithm for satisfying hierachies of multi-way dataflow constraints. *ACM transactions on Programming Languages and Systems*, 18(1):30–72, January 1996.

[20] Molly Wilson and Alan Borning. Hierarchical constraint logic programming. *Journal of Logic Programming*, 16(3):277–318, July 1993.

From Functional Specifications to Logic Programs

Michael Gelfond, Alfredo Gabaldon
Department of Computer Science
University of Texas at El Paso
El Paso, TX 79968, USA
{mgelfond,alfredo}@cs.utep.edu

Abstract

The paper investigates a methodology for representing knowledge in logic programming using functional specifications. The methodology is illustrated by an example formalizing several forms of inheritance reasoning. We also introduce and study a new specification constructor which corresponds to removal of the closed world assumption from input predicates of functional specifications.

1 Introduction

> *"The only effective way to raise the confidence level of a program significantly is to give a proof of its correctness. But one should not first make the program and then prove its correctness, because then the requirement of providing the proof would only increase the poor programmer's burden. On the contrary: the programmer should let correctness proof and program grow hand in hand. ...If one first asks oneself what the structure of a convincing proof would be and, having found this, then construct a program satisfying this proof's requirements, then these correctness concerns turn out to be a very effective heuristic guidance."*
>
> E. Dijkstra, The Humble Programmer

This paper continues the mathematical investigation of the *process* of representing knowledge in declarative logic programming (DLP). We are looking for some insights into the ways to specify knowledge, to gradually transfer an initial specification into an executable (and eventually efficient) logic program and to insure the correctness of this transformation. We hope that such insights will help to facilitate the construction of correct and efficient knowledge based systems. In this paper we leave out some of the important aspects of the process of representing knowledge and focus our attention on specific types of representational problems. In particular, we concentrate on the early stages of program development and almost completely ignore the question of elaborating executable (but possibly inefficient) specifications into their efficient counterparts[1]. We are primarily interested in what is entailed by our program and not in specific algorithms used to compute this

---

[1]Our use of the term "specification" follows [Mor90] which eliminates the distinction between programs and specifications.

entailment. In this sense our approach is complementary to the work on program development in Prolog (see for instance [Dev90]) which concentrates on properties of a particular inference engine. We further simplify our task by limiting attention to a special type of knowledge representation problem which consists in formalizing (possibly partial) definitions of new relations between objects of the problem domain given in terms of old, known relations between these objects. We call such problems *functional KR problems*. They frequently occur in the development of databases when new relations (views) are defined in terms of basic relations stored in the database tables. They are also typical in artificial intelligence (see [Lif93]), e.g., in formalizing knowledge about action and change when we need to define the state of the world at a given moment in terms of its initial (known) state.

The restriction to functional problems allows us to start the programming process with formalizing a natural language description of a problem in terms of functional specifications (f-specifications) [GP96] - functions which map collections of facts about known relations from the domain into collections of facts about new, defined relations. Such specifications can be defined by a specifier directly in a simple set-theoretic language, or they can be built from previously defined specifications with the help of specification constructors - simple mappings from specifications to specifications. After the construction of an f-specification f the designer of the system is confronted with the task of representing f in a logical language with a precisely described entailment relation. [GP96] advocates the use of a language $\mathcal{L}$ of logic programs with two types of negations and the answer set semantics. The choice is determined by the ability of $\mathcal{L}$ to represent default assumptions, i.e., statements of the form "Elements of the class A normally have property P", epistemic statements "P is unknown", "P is possible", and other types of statements needed for describing commonsense domains. Other important factors are the simplicity of the semantics, the existence of a mathematical theory providing a basis for proving properties of programs in $\mathcal{L}$, and the availability of query answering systems which can be used for rapid prototyping. The alternative approach which uses logic programs with well-founded semantics and its extensions can be found in [AP96].

At the end of the second stage of the program development the implementor will have a logic program π_f which, taken in conjunction with a collection X of facts about known relations of f, will entail exactly those facts about the new relations which belong to $f(X)$. Programs of this sort are called lp-functions. In [GP96] the authors suggest that the construction of π_f from f can be substantially facilitated by so called realization theorems which relate specification constructors to some operations on logic programs. They can provide an implementor with a useful heuristic guidance and the means to establish the correctness of his programs. Several examples of such theorems and their applications will be given in the paper.

At the last stage of the process, the lp-function π_f representing f-specification f will be transfered into an efficient logic program Π_f computing (or approximating) the entailment relation of π_f. Unlike π_f, the construction of Π_f will depend significantly on the choice of the query answering system used by the implementors.

Space limitations preclude us from giving any serious comparison with other methodologies of representing knowledge. Moreover, we believe that such comparison can only be done when all of these methodologies are more fully-developed. Still a short remark is in order. At the moment, the specification language most frequently used for the first formal refinement of a problem is probably the language of first-order logic (FOL). As others before us we conjecture that FOL is not fully adequate for our purpose. Its expressive power is insufficient to define even fairly simple f-specifications such as transitive closure of database relations. It also doesn't seem to be the best language for representing defaults, epistemic statements, and other types of "commonsense" knowledge. These observations are well known and led to various extensions and modifications of FOL. One of such modifications, DLP, is used by us at the second stage of the programming process. Why not to use it directly? There are two reasons for it. The first advantage of the language of f-specifications over DLP is its simplicity. The construction of f requires knowledge of a simple set-theoretic notation together with definitions of a (hopefully small) collection of specification constructors. The specifier involved at the first stage of the process does not need to know anything about semantics of DLP. Another possible advantage of translating a natural language description of a functional KR problem into an f-specification f is the ability to use the structure of f and the corresponding realization theorems for reducing the construction of π_f to the construction of simpler programs. Examples of such reductions can be found in [GP96].

The previous discussion shows that the success of our approach depends to a large extent on our ability to discover a collection of specification constructors which can serve as building blocks for the construction of f-specifications. This paper is a continuation of a search for such constructors. We introduce and study a new specification constructor, called input opening, which is defined on f-specifications of KR problems which assume the closed world assumption (CWA) [Rei78] on its input predicates. Informally, the input opening f° of f is the result of the removal of this assumption. The notion of input opening is closely related to the notion of interpolation of a logic program from [BGK93]. Interpolation can be viewed as a particular case of input opening defined for specifications which assume the CWA for their outputs as well as inputs and whose input relations are independent from each other. There are many interesting domains which do not satisfy these assumptions, which led us to the introduction of input opening. We give a definition of the constructor, show how it can be decomposed into simpler ones, and prove some useful realization theorems. The use of input opening (in combination with several previously defined constructors) is illustrated by the design of a concise, but fairly powerful program representing a "classical" KR problem associated with inheritance hierarchies. Our solution generalizes previously suggested solutions to this problem by allowing information about class membership in hierarchies to be incomplete. The program development is accompanied by a simultaneous proof of its correctness. We find that our confidence level in the correctness of the result was significantly improved by this approach. The paper is organized as follows. Section 2 contains the definitions of f-specification and lp-function. Their use is illustrated by formalizing a simple hierarchical reasoning problem under CWA. In Section 3 we define input opening and use this constructor to represent several other problems related to inheritance reasoning in the absence of CWA.

2 F-specifications and lp-functions

2.1 Definitions

A signature is a triple of disjoint sets called object constants, function constants, and predicate constants. Signature $\sigma_1 = \{O_1, F_1, P_1\}$ is a sub-signature of signature $\sigma_2 = \{O_2, F_2, P_2\}$ if $O_1 \subseteq O_2$, $F_1 \subseteq F_2$ and $P_1 \subseteq P_2$; $\sigma_1 + \sigma_2$ denotes signature $\{O_1 \cup O_2, F_1 \cup F_2, P_1 \cup P_2\}$. Terms over σ are built as in the first-order language; positive literals (atoms) have the form $p(t_1, \ldots, t_n)$, where the t's are terms and p is a predicate symbol of arity n; negative literals are of the form $\neg p(t_1, \ldots, t_n)$. Literals of the form $p(t_1, \ldots, t_n)$ and $\neg p(t_1, \ldots, t_n)$ are called contrary. By $\bar{l}$ we denote the literal contrary to l. Literals and terms not containing variables are called ground. The sets of all ground terms, atoms and literals over signature σ are denoted by $terms(\sigma)$, $atoms(\sigma)$ and $lit(\sigma)$ respectively. For a list of predicate symbols $p_1, \ldots, p_n$ from σ, $atoms(p_1, \ldots, p_n)$ $(lit(p_1, \ldots, p_n))$ denote the sets of ground atoms (literals) of σ formed with predicates $p_1, \ldots, p_n$. Consistent sets of ground literals over signature σ are called *states* of σ and denoted by $states(\sigma)$.

A four-tuple $f = \{f, \sigma_i(f), \sigma_o(f), dom(f)\}$ where

1. $\sigma_i(f)$ and $\sigma_o(f)$ are signatures;

2. $dom(f) \subseteq states(\sigma_i(f))$;

3. f is a function which maps $dom(f)$ into $states(\sigma_o(f))$

is called *f-specification* with input signature $\sigma_i(f)$, output signature $\sigma_o(f)$ and domain $dom(f)$. States over $\sigma_i(f)$ and $\sigma_o(f)$ are called input and output states respectively.

By a logic program π over signature $\sigma(\pi)$ we mean a collection of rules of the form

(r) $l_0 \leftarrow l_1, \ldots, l_m, not\, l_{m+1}, \ldots, not\, l_n$

where l's are literals over $\sigma(\pi)$ and *not* is negation as failure [Cla78, Rei78]. $head(r) = \{l_0\}$, $pos(r) = \{l_1, \ldots, l_m\}$, $neg(r) = \{l_{m+1}, \ldots, l_n\}$. $head(\pi)$ is the union of $head(r)$ for all rules from π. Similarly for *pos* and *neg*. We say that a literal $l \in lit(\sigma(\pi))$ is entailed by π ($\pi \models l$) if l belongs to all answer sets of π. A program with a consistent answer set is called consistent.

A four-tuple $\pi = \{\pi, \sigma_i(\pi), \sigma_o(\pi), dom(\pi)\}$ where

1. π is a logic program (with some signature $\sigma(\pi)$);

2. $\sigma_i(\pi), \sigma_o(\pi)$ are sub-signatures of $\sigma(\pi)$ called input and output signatures of π respectively;

3. $dom(\pi) \subseteq states(\sigma_i(\pi))$

is called *lp-function* if for any $X \in dom(\pi)$ program $\pi \cup X$ is consistent, i.e., has a consistent answer set. For any $X \in dom(\pi)$,

$$\pi(X) = \{l : l \in lit(\sigma_o(\pi)), \pi \cup X \models l\}.$$

We say that an lp-function π *represents* an f-specification f if π and f have the same input and output signatures and domains and for any $X \in dom(f)$, $f(X) = \pi(X)$.

2.2 An Example

In this section, we illustrate the notions of functional specification and lp-function by solving a knowledge representation problem associated with a simple type of taxonomic hierarchies called the *is-nets*. The problem of specifying and representing is-nets is commonly used to test strengths and weaknesses of various nonmonotonic formalisms. Logic programming approaches to this problem (which assume completeness of its domain) can be found in [AP96] and [Lin91]. Modifications of this example will be used throughout this paper.

An is-net N can be viewed as a combination of graphs N_s and N_d where N_s describes the subclass relation between classes and N_d consists of positive and negative links connecting classes with properties. These links represent defaults "elements of class c normally satisfy (do not satisfy) property p". To simplify the presentation we will assume that N_s is acyclic and that a class c and a property p can be connected by at most one link. We use (possibly indexed) letters o, c, p, and d to denote objects, classes, properties and defaults respectively. Fig 1a gives a pictorial representation of a net. Here $c_0, \ldots, c_5$ are classes and p is a property. Links from c_5 to p and from c_4 to p represent positive and negative defaults while the other links represent subclass relationships.

There are many knowledge representation problems which can be associated with a net N. We start with the simplest one when N is viewed as an

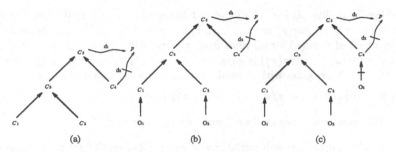

Figure 1: A simple taxonomic hierarchy

informal specification of a function f_N which takes as an input *complete* collections of ground literals formed by predicate symbol *is* and computes all possible conclusions about relation *has* which a rational agent can obtain from this net.[2] Pictorially, the input to f_N is represented by positive links from objects to classes (see Fig 1b). It is assumed that an object o is an element of a class c iff N_s contains a path from o to c.

We are interested in applying our methodology for providing a rigorous specification of this function and for finding its logic programming representation. Later we consider more complex functions which can also be associated with N.

• We start by playing the role of a specifier and give a precise definition of function f_N using the language of f-specifications. To this goal, we first identify graphs N_s and N_d with some encoding of collections of literals of the form $subclass(c_1, c_2)$, $default(d, c, p, +)$, $default(d, c, p, -)$ specified by these graphs. (The last parameter in $default$ is used to distinguish positive and negative defaults.) For instance, a net N_s may be encoded by a logic program consisting of rules

$subclass_0(c_i, c_j).$ (where c_i, c_j are classes connected by a link of N_s.)

$subclass(C_i, C_j) \leftarrow subclass_0(C_i, C_j)$

$subclass(C_i, C_j) \leftarrow subclass_0(C_i, C_k), subclass(C_k, C_j)$

or by some other means. N_d for the net from Fig 1 consists of two statements:

$default(d_1, c_5, p, +).$ $default(d_2, c_4, p, -).$

Since we assume that our information about the membership relation *is* is complete, i.e., for any object o and class c, $is(o, c)$ or $\neg is(o, c)$ belongs to the net's input, we call f_N a *closed domain* specification of N. (To simplify the notation we will from now on omit the index N whenever possible). A closed domain f-specification f of a net N can be defined as follows.

_____

[2]$is(o, c)$ stands for "object o is an element of class c"; $has(o, p)$ means that "object o has property p". Both predicates are typed.

1. Input signature $\sigma_i(f)$ of f consists of object constants for objects and classes of the hierarchy and the predicate symbol *is*; output signature $\sigma_o(f)$ consists of object constants for the hierarchy objects and properties and predicate symbol *has*.

2. $dom(f)$ consists of complete states of $\sigma_i(f)$ which satisfy the constraints:[3]

$$\leftarrow is(O, C_1), subclass(C_1, C_2), \neg is(O, C_2) \tag{1}$$

3. For any $X \in dom(f)$, $has(o, p) \in f(X)$ iff there are d_1 and c_1 s.t.

    (a) $default(d_1, c_1, p, +) \in N$

    (b) $is(o, c_1) \in X$

    (c) for any $default(d_2, c_2, p, -) \in N$,

$$\neg is(o, c_2) \in X \text{ or } subclass(c_1, c_2) \in N$$

Similarly for $\neg has(o, p)$.

Note that this definition does not require any sophisticated mathematics. In particular, it presupposes no knowledge of logic programming.

• Now let us assume the role of an implementor, who just received a description of N and f and is confronted with the task of building an executable lp-function representing f. To simplify the discussion let us assume that we will only be interested in getting answers to ground queries formed by predicate *has*. According to our methodology, we will first ignore the executability requirement and proceed with the construction of an lp-function π representing the f-specification f. We start with considering a program π:

$$
\left.
\begin{aligned}
has(X, P) &\leftarrow default(D, C, P, +),\\
&\quad is(X, C),\\
&\quad not\ exceptional(X, D, +).\\
\neg has(X, P) &\leftarrow default(D, C, P, -),\\
&\quad is(X, C),\\
&\quad not\ exceptional(X, D, -)\\
exception(E, D_1, +) &\leftarrow default(D_1, C, P, +),\\
&\quad default(D_2, E, P, -),\\
&\quad not\ subclass(C, E).\\
exception(E, D_1, -) &\leftarrow default(D_1, C, P, -),\\
&\quad default(D_2, E, P, +),\\
&\quad not\ subclass(C, E).\\
exceptional(X, D, S) &\leftarrow exception(E, D, S),\\
&\quad is(X, E).\\
N_s \cup N_d
\end{aligned}
\right\} \pi
$$

---

[3]A constraint is a rule of the form $\leftarrow \Delta$ where Δ is a list of literals from some signature σ. A set $X \in states(\sigma)$ *satisfies* the constraint $\leftarrow \Delta$ if $\Delta \not\subseteq X$. X satisfies a collection C of constraints if it satisfies every constraint in C.

(Here N_s and N_d are logic programming encodings of the corresponding nets.) We would like π to be viewed as an lp-function whose input and output signatures are the same as in f and whose domain is $dom(f)$, i.e., we need the following

Proposition 2.1 For any $X \in dom(f)$, program $\pi \cup X$ is consistent.

Now we can show the correctness of our construction.

Proposition 2.2 Lp-function π represents f, i.e., for any $X \in dom(f)$, $\pi(X) = f(X)$.

The next refinement of our program will address the question of specifying its input X. We decided that the input to f will be represented by positive links from objects to classes and that an object o is an element of a class c iff N_s contains a path from o to c. It is easy to check that, under this assumption, we can replace a complete input X to our lp-function π by a program π_X consisting of atoms of the form $is_0(o, c)$ for any link from o to c which is present in the graph ($is_0(o_1, c_1)$ and $is_0(o_2, c_2)$ in Fig 1b), together with three rules:

$$is(O, C) \leftarrow is_0(O, C)$$

$$is(O, C_2) \leftarrow is_0(O, C_1), subclass(C_1, C_2)$$

$$\neg is(O, C) \leftarrow not\ is(O, C)$$

It is also easy to show that for ground queries the program $\pi \cup \pi_X$ is executable by a simple modification of a Prolog interpreter which replaces $\neg has(O, P)$ by a new predicate symbol $\hat{has}(O, P)$. Since our focus in this paper is on the first two steps of the development process we will not discuss this question further. Instead we introduce another KR-problem associated with is-nets and demonstrate how a specification constructor, called *input opening*, can be used to specify and represent this problem.

3   Opening closed domain specifications

3.1   Specifying the problem

So far we assumed that the net N is used in conjunction with complete lists of ground literals characterizing the relation *is*. In the process of development and modification of the system this assumption may become too strong and the specifier may decide to remove it from his specification. Now the net N will be used in conjunction with a possibly incomplete set X of ground literals formed by predicate *is*. As before, X must satisfy the constraint (1). Pictorially, the input to the net will be represented by positive and negative links from objects to classes (see Fig 1c). Now the net N can be viewed as a function F° which takes X as an input and returns all conclusions about relations *is* and *has* which a rational agent can obtain from N and X. (f° will be called the *open domain* specification of N.) The problem is to precisely define the set of all such conclusions. In order to do that the specifier may use a closed domain f-specification f of N together with a specification constructor called the input opening of f. To define this constructor we need the following terminology.

Let D be a collection of states over some signature σ. A set $X \in states(\sigma)$ is called *D-consistent* if there is $\hat{X} \in D$ s.t. $X \subseteq \hat{X}$; $\hat{X}$ is called a *D-cover* of X.

If, for instance, σ is a signature associated with net N_s from Fig 1 and D is the collection of complete sets from $lit(is)$ which satisfy the constraint (1) then $\{is(o_1, c_1), is(o_2, c_2)\}$ is D-consistent while $\{is(o_1, c_1),\ is(o_2, c_2),\ \neg is(o_2, c_3)\}$ is not.

The set of all D-covers of X is denoted by $c(D, X)$. The set of all D-consistent states of σ is called the *interior* of D and is denoted by D°. An f-specification f defined on a collection of complete states of $\sigma_i(f)$ is called *closed domain specification*.

Definition 3.1 *(Input Opening)* Let f be a closed domain specification with domain D. An f-specification f° is called the *input opening* of f if

$$\sigma_i(f^\circ) = \sigma_i(f) \qquad \sigma_o(f^\circ) = \sigma_i(f) + \sigma_o(f) \tag{2}$$

$$dom(f^\circ) = D^\circ \tag{3}$$

$$f^\circ(X) = \bigcap_{\hat{X} \in c(D,X)} f(\hat{X}) \ \cup \bigcap_{\hat{X} \in c(D,X)} \hat{X} \tag{4}$$

Now the open domain f-specification f_N° of a net N can be defined as the input opening of its closed domain specification f_N. (Again, we will omit the index whenever possible).

Our next problem is to find an lp-function representing f°. To do that we will show how the input opening of f can be expressed as a composition of two simpler specification constructors called *interpolation* and *domain completion*. We need the following definitions.

Definition 3.2 A set $X \in states(\sigma)$ is called *maximally informative* w.r.t. a set $D \subseteq states(\sigma)$ if X is D-consistent and

$$X = \bigcap_{\hat{X} \in c(D,X)} \hat{X} \tag{5}$$

By $\tilde{D}$ we denote the set of states of σ maximally informative w.r.t. D.

Consider the net N from Fig 1b. The set $\{is(o_1, c_1),\ is(o_1, c_3),\ is(o_1, c_5),$ $is(o_2, c_2),\ is(o_2, c_3),\ is(o_2, c_5)\}$ is maximally informative w.r.t. the set of all complete input states of N, while the set $\{is(o_1, c_1),\ is(o_2, c_2)\}$ is not.

Definition 3.3 *(Interpolation)* Let f be a closed domain f-specification with domain D. F-specification $\tilde{f}$ with the same signatures as f and the domain $\tilde{D}$ is called the *interpolation* of f if

$$\tilde{f}(X) = \bigcap_{\hat{X} \in c(D, X)} f(\hat{X}) \tag{6}$$

This is a slight generalization of the notion of interpolation introduced in [BGK93], where the authors only considered interpolations of functions defined by general logic programs.

Definition 3.4 *(Domain Completion)*
Let D be a collection of complete states over signature σ. The *domain completion* of D is a function $\tilde{f}_D$ which maps D-consistent states of σ into their maximally informative supersets.

Specifications f and g s.t. $\sigma_o(f) = \sigma_i(g)$ and $lit(\sigma_i(g)) \cap lit(\sigma_o(g)) = \emptyset$ can be combined into a new f-specification $g \circ f$ by a specification constructor $\circ$ called *incremental extension* [GP96]. Function $g \circ f$ with domain $dom(f)$, $\sigma_i(g \circ f) = \sigma_i(f)$, $\sigma_o(g \circ f) = \sigma_o(f) + \sigma_o(g)$ is called the *incremental extension* of f by g if for any $X \in dom(g \circ f)$, $g \circ f(X) = f(X) \cup g(f(X))$. The following proposition follows immediately from the definitions.

Proposition 3.1 For any closed domain f-specification f with domain D

$$f^\circ = \tilde{f} \circ \tilde{f}_D \tag{7}$$

3.2 Realization theorems for domain completion and interpolation

The above proposition shows that a representation for f° can be constructed from lp-functions representing $\tilde{f}$ and $\tilde{f}_D$. In the construction of these functions we will be aided by realization theorems for domain completions and interpolations.

Let C be a collection of constraints of the form $\leftarrow \Delta$ where $\Delta \subset lit(\sigma)$. A constraint is called *binary* if Δ consists of two literals. We say that a domain D is defined by C if D consists of complete sets from $states(\sigma)$ satisfying C. Let C be a set of binary constraints and D be the closed domain defined by C. Let $\tilde{\pi}_D$ be a program obtained from C by replacing each rule $\leftarrow l_1, l_2$ by the rules $\neg l_1 \leftarrow l_2$ and $\neg l_2 \leftarrow l_1$.

Theorem 3.1 *(Realization Theorem for Domain Completion)*
If for every $l \in lit(\sigma)$ there is a set $Z \in D$ not containing l then a four-tuple $\{\tilde{\pi}_D, \sigma, \sigma, D^\circ\}$ is an lp-function which represents domain completion $\tilde{f}_D$ of D.

To give a realization theorem for the interpolation we need some auxiliary definitions.

Let D be a collection of complete states over a signature σ. Function f defined on the interior of D is called *separable* if

$$\bigcap_{\hat{X} \in c(D,X)} f(\hat{X}) \subseteq f(X)$$

or, equivalently, if for any $X \in dom(f)$ and any output literal l s.t. $l \notin f(X)$ there is $\hat{X} \in c(D, X)$ s.t. $l \notin f(\hat{X})$.

The following examples may help to better understand this notion.

Example 3.1 Let D be the set of complete states over some signature σ_i and let π be an lp-function defined on $D^\circ = states(\sigma_i)$, s.t.

1. The sets of input and output predicates of π are disjoint and input literals do not belong to the heads of π;

2. for any $l \in \sigma_i$, $l \notin lit(\pi)$ or $\bar{l} \notin lit(\pi)$. (By $lit(\pi)$ we mean the collection of all literals which occur in the rules of the ground instantiation of π.)

Then π is separable.

The next example shows that the last condition is essential.

Example 3.2 Let $D = \{\{p(a)\}, \{\neg p(a)\}\}$ and consider a function f_1 defined on D° by the program

$q(a) \leftarrow p(a)$

$q(a) \leftarrow \neg p(a)$

Let $X = \emptyset$. Obviously, $f_1(X) = \emptyset$ while $\bigcap_{\hat{X} \in c(D,X)} f_1(\hat{X}) = \{q(a)\}$ and hence f_1 is not separable.

Example 3.3 In some cases to establish separability of an lp-function π it is useful to represent π as the union of its independent components and to reduce the question of separability of π to separability of these components. Let π be an lp-function with input signature σ_i and output signature σ_o. We assume that the input literals of π do not belong to the heads of rules of π. We say that π is decomposable into independent components $\pi_0, \ldots, \pi_n$ if $\pi = \pi_0 \cup \ldots \cup \pi_n$ and $lit(\pi_k) \cap lit(\pi_l) \subseteq lit(\sigma_i)$ for any $k \neq l$. It is easy to check that, for any $0 \leq k \leq n$, four-tuple $\{\pi_k, \sigma_i, \sigma_o, dom(\pi)\}$ is an lp-function, and that if all these functions are separable then so is π. This observation can be used for instance to establish separability of function f_2 defined on the interior of the set D from the previous example by the program

$q_1(a) \leftarrow p(a)$

$q_2(a) \leftarrow \neg p(a)$

(The output signature of f_2 consists of a, q_1 and q_2).

□

Now we are ready to formulate our next theorem.

Theorem 3.2 *(Realization Theorem for Interpolation)* Let f be a closed domain specification with domain D represented by an lp-function π and let $\tilde{\pi}$ be the program obtained from π by replacing some occurrences of input literals l in $pos(\pi)$ by $not\ \bar{l}$. Then $\{\tilde{\pi}, \sigma_i(f), \sigma_o(f), dom(\tilde{f})\}$ is an lp-function and if $\tilde{\pi}$ is separable and monotonic then $\tilde{\pi}$ represents $\tilde{f}$.

3.3   Representing the open domain specification of N

As before, we now need to address the task of constructing an lp-function π° representing f°. We already know that $f^\circ = \tilde{f} \circ \tilde{f}_D$ where D is the domain of f. This means that we need to find representation $\tilde{\pi}$ of $\tilde{f}$ and $\tilde{\pi}_D$ of $\tilde{f}_D$. An important heuristic guidance in this task will be provided to us by the corresponding realization theorems. To find the representation of $\tilde{f}$ we use Theorem 3.2. The program $\tilde{\pi}$ can be obtained from π by replacing the rule defining predicate *exceptional* by the rule

$$
\begin{aligned}
exceptional(X, D, S) \leftarrow \ &exception(E, D, S), \\
&not\ \neg is(X, E).
\end{aligned}
\tag{8}
$$

(which is the only way to turn π into a signed program using the transformation from Theorem 3.2.) We may show that $\tilde{\pi}$ is separable and hence:

Proposition 3.2 $\tilde{\pi}$ represents $\tilde{f}$

To complete the construction of π° we need to find the representation $\tilde{\pi}_D$ of the domain completion of $D = dom(f)$. We use Theorem 3.1. The corresponding program $\tilde{\pi}_D$ consists of the rules

$$
is(O, C_2) \leftarrow is(O, C_1), subclass(C_1, C_2)
\tag{9}
$$

$$
\neg is(O, C_1) \leftarrow \neg is(O, C_2), subclass(C_1, C_2)
\tag{10}
$$

Proposition 3.3 $\tilde{\pi}_D$ represents $\tilde{f}_D$

Finally, using Propositions 3.2, 3.3 and the realization theorem for incremental extension from [GP96] we can prove:

Proposition 3.4 π° represents f°

Proposition 3.4 shows the correctness of π° w.r.t. our specification. However, due to the left recursion in the rules 9, 10 π° cannot be run with the Prolog interpreter. It was however run under a simple meta-interpreter based on the SLG inference engine [CSW95] which is sound w.r.t. our semantics. Of course, the left recursion can be eliminated by introducing a new predicate is_0 but we will not do it here due to the space limitations.

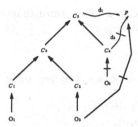

Figure 2: Hierarchy with links from objects to properties

3.4 A simple generalization

In this section we generalize the KR problem associated with a net N by allowing strict (non-defeasible) links from objects to properties to belong to the net's input (see Fig 2). We show that this generalization can be easily incorporated into the design. To do that we use another specification constructor from [GP96]. We will recall the following definitions from [GP96].

Definition 3.5 Let f be a functional specification with disjoint sets of input and output predicates. A f-specification f^* with input signature $\sigma_i(f) + \sigma_o(f)$ and output signature $\sigma_o(f)$ is called *input extension* of f if

1. f^* is defined on elements of $dom(f)$ possibly expanded by consistent sets of literals from $\sigma_o(f)$,

2. for every $X \in dom(f)$, $f^*(X) = f(X)$,

3. for any $Y \in dom(f^*)$ and any $l \in lit(\sigma_o(f))$,

    (i) if $l \in Y$ then $l \in f^*(Y)$

    (ii) if $l \notin Y$ and $\bar{l} \notin Y$ then $l \in f^*(Y)$ iff $l \in f(Y \cap lit(\sigma_i(f))$

Definition 3.6 Let π be an lp-function. The result of replacing every rule

$$l_0 \leftarrow l_1, \ldots, l_m, not\ l_{m+1}, \ldots, not\ l_n$$

of π with $l_0 \in lit(\sigma_o(f))$ by the rule

$$l_0 \leftarrow l_1, \ldots, l_m, not\ l_{m+1}, \ldots, not\ l_n, not\ \bar{l}_0$$

is called the *guarded version* of π and is denoted by $\hat{\pi}$.

Theorem 3.3 ([GP96]) *(Realization Theorem for Input Extension)*
Let f be a specification represented by lp-function π with signature σ. If the set $U = lit(\sigma) \setminus lit(\sigma_o)$ is a splitting set of π dividing π into two components $\pi_2 = top(\pi, U)$ and $\pi_1 = base(\pi, U)$ then lp-function $\pi^* = \pi_1 \cup \hat{\pi}_2$ represents the input extension f^* of f.

Now we can give a specification of the third function associated with a net N. It is defined by a specification

$$f^* = \tilde{f}^* \circ f_D$$

and the representation π^* is obtained by replacing the *has* rules in π° by

$$\left.\begin{array}{rl} has(x,p) \leftarrow & default(d,c,p,+), \\ & is(x,c), \\ & not\ exceptional(x,d,+), \\ & not\ \neg has(x,p). \\ \neg has(x,p) \leftarrow & default(d,c,p,-), \\ & is(x,c), \\ & not\ exceptional(x,d,-) \\ & not\ has(x,p). \end{array}\right\}$$

The following proposition follows immediately from the construction of π^* and Theorem 3.3

Proposition 3.5 π^* represents f^*

Again, specification constructors and their realization theorems provided a useful heuristic guidance and allowed to build a program provenly satisfying the corresponding specification.

4   Conclusion

The main contributions of this paper consist in

• Introducing the input opening of a closed domain specification and proving some properties of this constructor;

• Providing a case study for our methodology.

Somewhat surprisingly, the resulting class of programs formalizes inheritance reasoning with incomplete information which was not previously formalized. Unfortunately, the size limitations do not allow us to include proofs. They can be found in [GG97].

Acknowledgments

We would like to thank the referees for valuable comments. The first author acknowledges the support of NASA under grant NCCW-0089.

References

[AP96]   J.J. Alferes and L.M. Pereira. *Reasoning with Logic Programming*, Lecture Notes in Artificial Intelligence. Springer. 1996.

[BGK93]   C. Baral, M. Gelfond, and O. Kosheleva. Approximating general logic programs, *Proc. ILPS*, pp. 181-198, 1993.

[CSW95]   W. Chen, T. Swift and D. Warren. Efficient top-down computation of queries under the well-founded semantics, *Journal of Logic Programming*, 24,3:161–201, 1995.

[Cla78]   K. Clark. Negation as failure. In H. Gallaire and J. Minker, eds., *Logic and Data Bases*, pp. 293–322. Plenum Press, NY, 1978.

[Dev90]   Y. Deville. *Logic Programming: systematic program development*, Clark, K., series editor, Addison-Wesley Publishing Co., 1990.

[GG97]   M. Gelfond and A. Gabaldon. From functional specifications to logic programs. Technical report. Available from: http://cs.utep.edu/gelfond/gelfond.html

[GL91]   M. Gelfond and V. Lifschitz. Classical Negation in Logic Programs and Disjunctive Databases. *New Generation Computing*, 9:365–385, 1991.

[GP96]   M. Gelfond and H. Przymusinska. Towards a theory of elaboration tolerance: logic programming approach. *Int'l Journal of Software Engineering and Knowledge Engineering*, 6(1):89-112, 1996.

[Kun89]   K. Kunen. Signed data dependencies in logic programs. *Journal of Logic Programming*, 7(3):231-245, 1989.

[Lif93]   V. Lifschitz. Restricted Monotonicity. In *Proc. of AAAI-93*, pp. 432–437, 1993.

[LT94]   V. Lifschitz and H. Turner. Splitting a Logic Program. In P. Van Hentenryck, editor, *Proc. 11th ICLP*, pp. 23–38, 1994.

[Lin91]   F. Lin. *A study of nonmonotonic reasoning*, Ph.D. Thesis, Stanford U., 1991.

[Mor90]   C. Morgan. In C.A.R. Hoare, series ed., *Programming from specifications*, Prentice Hall, 1990.

[Rei78]   R. Reiter. On closed world data bases. In H. Gallaire and J. Minker, eds., *Logic and Data Bases*, Plenum Press, NY, pp. 119–140, 1978.

[Tur93]   H. Turner. A monotonicity theorem for extended logic programs. In D. S. Warren, ed., *Proc. 10th ICLP*, pp. 567–585, 1993.

[Tur94]   H. Turner. Signed Logic Programs. In Bruynooghe, M., ed., *Proc. ILPS*, pp. 61–75, 1994.

Compositionality of normal open logic programs

Sofie Verbaeten, Marc Denecker, Danny De Schreye
Department of Computer Science, K.U.Leuven,
Celestijnenlaan 200A, B-3001 Heverlee, Belgium.
{sofie, marcd, dannyd}@cs.kuleuven.ac.be

Abstract

Compositionality of programs is an important concern in knowledge representation and software development. In the context of Logic Programming, up till now, the issue has mostly been studied for *definite* programs only. Here, we study compositionality in the context of *normal open logic programming*. This is a very expressive logic for knowledge representation of uncertainty and incomplete knowledge on concepts and on problem domain, in which the compositionality issue turns up very naturally. The semantics of the logic is a generalisation (allowing non-Herbrand interpretations) of the well-founded semantics.

We provide a number of results which offer different sufficient conditions under which the models of the composition of two theories can be related to the intersection of the models of the composing theories. In particular, under these conditions, logical consequence will be preserved under composition.

1 Introduction

The compositionality issue arises in a situation where two or more experts cooperate to axiomatise a certain domain of application; they have more or less disjunct subdomains of expertise and they represent their expert knowledges independently in distinct logical theories. Ideally, once this stage is finished the problem arises how to combine the *knowledge modules* in one united theory. In general, there may be different modes in which the modules can be composed, but certainly the most important one seems to take the *logical conjunction* of their knowledges; i.e. to construct a new theory which contains exactly the sum of the knowledges of the component modules.

By the nature of the situation, the modules designed by the experts are incomplete representations of the problem domain; they contain uncertainty about the problem domain. Typically, experts will have two sorts of ignorance in their theories: ignorance on concepts, some of which are defined by the other experts; ignorance about the objects some of which are defined by other experts. A suitable logic to represent knowledge modules should allow to represent these forms of uncertainty.

In this paper, we investigate the compositionality issue in the logic of *normal Open Logic Programs* (OLP) and *First Order Logic* (FOL) [10]. [10] presents this logic from a Knowledge Representation perspective and illustrates its suitability for representing uncertainty of similar nature as cooperating experts have to face: incomplete knowledge on the definitions of certain concepts and on the problem domain.

A theory $\mathcal{T}$ in this logic is a pair $(\mathcal{T}_d, \mathcal{T}_c)$ of a First Order Logic theory $\mathcal{T}_c$ and a normal open logic program $\mathcal{T}_d$, i.e. a set of normal program clauses $p \leftarrow q_1, .., q_n, \neg r_1, .., \neg r_m$. Normal open logic programs will further on also be called logic programs briefly. $\mathcal{T}_d$ represents a set of *definitions*. Predicates occuring in the head of a clause of $\mathcal{T}_d$ are called *defined*. The other predicates, occuring at the most in the body of program clauses, are called *open*. Intuitively, they represent concepts for which no definitions are given. Partial knowledge about these predicates can be expressed in the set of FOL axioms $\mathcal{T}_c$. The model semantics of OLP-FOL is an extension of the well-founded semantics [21] and of the extended well-founded semantics [19] and was defined in [11]. This logic has a *possible state semantics*, that is, a model correspond to a state in which the problem domain might occur according to the (incomplete) expert knowledge (and not a *belief set*, a set of believed atoms, as in answer set semantics of Extended Logic Programming). At the level of the semantics, uncertainty on the definition of a concept is modeled by allowing models which give to the open predicates an arbitrary interpretation which satisfies the set of FOL axioms $\mathcal{T}_c$ (and not e.g. by having truth value *unknown* for these open predicates as in a belief set semantics). Uncertainty on the level of the domain of discourse (no Domain Closure) is modeled by allowing general, non-Herbrand models.

Compositionality of logic programs has been investigated by a number of researchers. We refer to the discussion section for explicit references. In the context of OLP-FOL, the problem of correct composition of different independently designed modules has a natural formulation which differs from the formalisation as presented in much of the existing research. In the context of a logic with *possible state semantics*, the *compositionality criterion* that a logic theory $\mathcal{T}$ contains precisely the sum of the knowledges in the modules $\mathcal{T}_1, \mathcal{T}_2$ has a natural formalisation: that the class of models of $\mathcal{T}$ is precisely the intersection of the classes of models of $\mathcal{T}_1$ and of $\mathcal{T}_2$. Note that this criterion is the one expressed by the semantics of classical logic conjunction: models of the conjunction $F \wedge G$ of arbitrary FOL formulas F, G are precisely the models of F and of G.

In this paper, we investigate conditions in which the simple union of two OLP-FOL theories $\mathcal{T}_1, \mathcal{T}_2$ yields a theory which satisfies the natural compositionality criterion. A more formal description of the problem investigated is as follows. We use the following notations. The composition of two OLP-FOL theories $\mathcal{T}_1 = (\mathcal{T}_{1d}, \mathcal{T}_{1c})$ and $\mathcal{T}_2 = (\mathcal{T}_{2d}, \mathcal{T}_{2c})$ is defined as the theory $\mathcal{T}_1 \cup \mathcal{T}_2 = (\mathcal{T}_{1d} \cup \mathcal{T}_{2d}, \mathcal{T}_{1c} \cup \mathcal{T}_{2c})$. Also, given a class of interpretations $\mathcal{J}$, the class of members of $\mathcal{J}$ which are models of the OLP-FOL theory $\mathcal{T}$ is denoted $Mod^{\mathcal{J}}(\mathcal{T})$. Using this notation, the compositionality problem considered in this paper is formalised as follows.

- Given is a class $\mathcal{J}$ of interpretations, representing a priori knowledge shared by the experts. In general, this class may be the class of models of a logical theory representing the a priori knowledge. E.g. this theory can describe knowledge on the domain of discourse (a Domain Closure Axiom) or simple programming concepts such as definitions of membership of lists, appending of lists, etc.,

- given also is a pair of OLP-FOL theories T_1, T_2 representing the modules of the experts with separate sets of defined predicates,

we investigate conditions on T_1, T_2 such that:

$$Mod^{\mathcal{J}}(T_1 \cup T_2) = Mod^{\mathcal{J}}(T_1) \cap Mod^{\mathcal{J}}(T_2).$$

After a section 2 with preliminaries, section 3 gives us a first result, stating that for correct theories, the class of models of the composition is contained in the intersection of the classes of models of the two separate theories. In section 4, we give a very general condition (the justification condition) on T_1 and T_2 to obtain the equality $Mod^{\mathcal{J}}(T_1 \cup T_2) = Mod^{\mathcal{J}}(T_1) \cap Mod^{\mathcal{J}}(T_2)$. In the next section, some less general, but more syntactical conditions are given. In 5.2 we study for instance conservative extensions. We conclude with a discussion in section 6, where we give some related works. For the proofs of the theorems we refer to [22].

2 Preliminaries

We assume familiarity with basic concepts of logic and logic programming such as logical languages $\mathcal{L}$, atoms, literals, (normal) program clauses or rules based on $\mathcal{L}$, ground instances of rules w.r.t. a language $\mathcal{L}$, 2-valued and 3-valued interpretations, Herbrand interpretations of $\mathcal{L}$. We refer to [17]. We assume some familiarity with the well-founded semantics [21] as well.

We introduce some auxiliary concepts. Each language $\mathcal{L}$ is assumed to contain propositional predicates $\top$ and $\bot$; in each interpretation I of $\mathcal{L}$, $\top$ is true and $\bot$ is false. $\mathcal{H}_{\mathcal{L}}$ (or $\mathcal{H}$ if $\mathcal{L}$ is clear from the context) denotes the class of all Herbrand interpretations of the language $\mathcal{L}$. Atomic rules are denoted $A \leftarrow \top$. Given a language $\mathcal{L}$ and an interpretation I with domain D, define the language $\mathcal{L}_D$ as the extension of $\mathcal{L}$ by adding all elements of D as constants to $\mathcal{L}$. A literal of the form $p(d_1, \ldots, d_n)$ or $\neg p(d_1, \ldots, d_n)$, where $d_1, \ldots, d_n \in D$ is called a *fact*. For a ground literal $F = p(t_1, \ldots, t_n)$ in $\mathcal{L}_D$, $\tilde{I}(F)$ denotes the fact $p(\tilde{I}(t_1), \ldots, \tilde{I}(t_n))$, where $\tilde{I}$ is the mapping which assigns to each ground term in $\mathcal{L}_D$ the corresponding domain element of the interpretation I. The truth function of I (i.e. the function which maps positive facts to $\{\mathbf{f}, \mathbf{u}, \mathbf{t}\}$) is denoted by $\mathcal{H}_I$. In this paper we describe a truth function as a set of tuples of facts with truth value (e.g. $\{p^{\mathbf{f}}, q^{\mathbf{u}}, r^{\mathbf{t}}\}$, meaning that $\mathcal{H}_I(p) = \mathbf{f}, \mathcal{H}_I(q) = \mathbf{u}$ and $\mathcal{H}_I(r) = \mathbf{t}$). 2-valued Herbrand interpretations are denoted in the conventional notation, as a subset of the Herbrand base.

A theory T in the OLP-FOL logic is a pair (T_d, T_c) with T_d a set of normal program clauses and T_c a set of FOL formulas. A predicate p is *defined* in T_d or in T iff p occurs in the head of a rule of T_d (it is possible that this rule is of the form $p(t_1, \ldots, t_n) \leftarrow \bot$). *Open* predicates are predicates of $\mathcal{L}$ which are not defined. An open logic program T_d (or a theory T) is *complete* if each predicate symbol of $\mathcal{L}$ except equality $=$, $\top$ and $\bot$ is defined, otherwise it is *incomplete*.

The semantics of the OLP-FOL logic is an extension of well-founded semantics based on general interpretations. Well-founded semantics can be easily *lifted* to general interpretations by extending the well-known notion of the *grounding of a logic program*. The grounding of an open logic program $\mathcal{T}_d$ w.r.t. a given 3-valued interpretation I is denoted as $\mathcal{G}round_I(\mathcal{T}_d)$ and is defined as the following set of program clauses:

$\{\tilde{I}(F) \leftarrow \tilde{I}(F_1), .., \tilde{I}(F_n) | F \leftarrow F_1, .., F_n$ ground instance of a rule in $\mathcal{T}_d$ in $\mathcal{L}_D\}$
$\cup \{F \leftarrow \top | F$ is a positive fact of an open predicate and F is true in $I\}$

Definition 2.1 *An interpretation M is a model of $\mathcal{T}_d$ iff M is a well-founded model of the grounding of $\mathcal{T}_d$ w.r.t. M. M is a model of $\mathcal{T} = (\mathcal{T}_d, \mathcal{T}_c)$ iff M is a model of $\mathcal{T}_d$ and M is a model of $\mathcal{T}_c$ in the normal FOL sense.*
A formula is a consequence of a theory $\mathcal{T}$ if it is true in every model of $\mathcal{T}$.

Note that a model is necessarily 2-valued on the open predicates. Note also that the grounding of an open logic program $\mathcal{T}_d$ w.r.t. to a Herbrand interpretation corresponds to the conventional notion of the grounding of a logic program. It trivially follows that the Herbrand model of a complete logic program is the well-founded model. Also, a Herbrand model of an incomplete logic program is an extended well-founded model [19].

An open logic program $\mathcal{T}_d$ is interpreted as a definition of the defined predicates in terms of open predicates. Recall that uncertainty is delt with by having multiple models, not by having undefined facts in models. The occurrence of an undefined fact in a model of $\mathcal{T}_d$ reveals an ambiguity or a local inconsistency in the definition. This motivates the following definition.

Definition 2.2 *Given is an open logic program $\mathcal{T}_d$ and a class of interpretations $\mathcal{J}$. Then $\mathcal{T}_d$ is called a correct definition (or correct) w.r.t. $\mathcal{J}$ iff each model of $\mathcal{T}_d$ which belongs to $\mathcal{J}$ is 2-valued. A theory $\mathcal{T} = (\mathcal{T}_d, \mathcal{T}_c)$ is correct w.r.t. $\mathcal{J}$ iff $\mathcal{T}_d$ is a correct definition w.r.t. $\mathcal{J}$.*

In case $\mathcal{J}$ is the class of all interpretations, we simply call $\mathcal{T}$ *correct*. With $\mathcal{M}od(\mathcal{T})$ we will denote the class of models of a theory $\mathcal{T}$. If $\mathcal{J}$ is a class of interpretations, then $\mathcal{M}od^{\mathcal{J}}(\mathcal{T})$ denotes the class of models of $\mathcal{T}$ which belong to $\mathcal{J}$ (i.e. $\mathcal{M}od^{\mathcal{J}}(\mathcal{T}) = \mathcal{M}od(\mathcal{T}) \cap \mathcal{J}$).

The basic theorem of this paper, which gives weakest conditions under which two OLP-FOL theories can be composed, uses the concept of *justification*. For a detailed discussion, we refer to [11]. Below, we denote the complement of a fact F by $\sim F$; i.e. if F is a positive fact, then $\sim F$ denotes $\neg F$; vice versa $\sim \neg F$ denotes F. We define $\sim \top = \bot$ and vice versa.

We now define the concepts of elementary justification and justification given an open logic program $\mathcal{T}_d$ based on $\mathcal{L}$ and an interpretation I of $\mathcal{L}$.

Definition 2.3 *Given is a defined positive fact F in I.*
For any rule $F \leftarrow F_1, .., F_n \in \mathcal{G}round_I(\mathcal{T}_d)$ we call $\{F_1, .., F_n\}$ an elementary justification for F. If no such ground instance exists for F, then we call $\{\bot\}$ an elementary justification for F.

Each positive defined fact has an elementary justification. Also, an elementary justification is never empty (recall atomic rules are denoted as $A \leftarrow \top$). An elementary justification is always finite. The concept of an elementary justification can be defined also for negative facts.

Definition 2.4 *A set J is called an elementary justification for a negative fact $\neg F$ of a defined predicate iff each elementary justification J^+ of F contains a fact F' such that $\sim F' \in J$.*

Analogously as for positive facts, each negative fact $\neg F$ has an elementary justification and an elementary justification is never empty. It can be infinite.

Definition 2.5 *A justification J for F (given $\mathcal{T}_d$ and I) is a (possibly infinite) tree of facts with F in the root. Each non-leaf node contains a defined fact F' such that the set of direct descendants of the node is an elementary justification for F' and no leaf contains a defined fact.*

The leaves of a justification are $\top, \bot$ or positive or negative open facts. A justification of a fact is always defined w.r.t. a logic program $\mathcal{T}_d$. Therefore, when necessary, we explicitly talk about a justification in $\mathcal{T}_d$ rather than a justification. A *branch* in a justification J is a maximal sequence of facts $(F_0, F_1, \ldots)$ with F_0 in the root of J, and each F_i a direct descendant of F_{i-1} in J. A *positive* (resp. *negative*) *loop* is a branch with an infinite number of positive (resp. negative) facts and a finite number of negative (resp. positive) facts. A *loop over negation* is a branch with an infinite number of positive and negative facts. Next we define the value of a justification as a measure for its success.

Definition 2.6 *Let I be an interpretation.*
Let B be a branch in a justification. If B is finite and has F as leaf then the value of B under I is the truth value of F under I. With respect to infinite branches, we define the value of a positive loop as $\mathbf{f}$, the value of a loop over negation as $\mathbf{u}$ and the value of a negative loop as $\mathbf{t}$. We denote the value of B under I by $val_I(B)$.
Let J be a justification. The value of J under I is $\min\{val_I(B)|B$ is a branch of $J\}$. We denote J's value by $val_I(J)$. J is false, weak, strong under I if $val_I(J)$ is $\mathbf{f}$, $\mathbf{u}$, $\mathbf{t}$ respectively.

In [11] you can find how justifications provide an alternative characterisation of models[1] in the sense of definition 2.1.

3 No loss of information

Given is a first order language $\mathcal{L}$ and two theories $\mathcal{T}_1 = (\mathcal{T}_{1d}, \mathcal{T}_{1c})$ and $\mathcal{T}_2 = (\mathcal{T}_{2d}, \mathcal{T}_{2c})$ based on $\mathcal{L}$. As mentioned in the introduction, we will suppose, for the rest of the paper, that $\mathcal{T}_1$ and $\mathcal{T}_2$ define disjunct sets of predicates. Then all the predicate symbols of $\mathcal{L}$ defined in $\mathcal{T}_1$ (resp. $\mathcal{T}_2$) are open in $\mathcal{T}_2$ (resp. $\mathcal{T}_1$). Denote the union of $\mathcal{T}_1$ and $\mathcal{T}_2$ by $\mathcal{T}_1 \cup \mathcal{T}_2 = (\mathcal{T}_{1d} \cup \mathcal{T}_{2d}, \mathcal{T}_{1c} \cup \mathcal{T}_{2c})$

---

[1]Namely, models are interpretations in which the truth value of each fact is identical to the value of its best justification.

(where $\cup$ is just the normal union of sets; $\mathcal{T}_{id}$ a set of clauses, $\mathcal{T}_{ic}$ a set of FOL axioms, $i \in \{1,2\}$).

The crucial question in this paper is the following: 'When are the consequences of $\mathcal{T}_1 \cup \mathcal{T}_2$ exactly those formulas which are true in all the interpretations which are model of $\mathcal{T}_1$ and of $\mathcal{T}_2$?'. Since a formula is a consequence of a theory iff it is true in every model of the theory, we can reformulate this question in terms of models :'When is $Mod(\mathcal{T}_1 \cup \mathcal{T}_2) = Mod(\mathcal{T}_1) \cap Mod(\mathcal{T}_2)$?'. The equality doesn't always hold, as is shown by the following example.

Example 3.1

$$\mathcal{T}_1 \; : \; alive \leftarrow not\_dead$$
$$\mathcal{T}_2 \; : \; not\_dead \leftarrow alive$$

Because not_dead is open in $\mathcal{T}_1$, $\mathcal{T}_1$ has two models, $I_1 = \{not\_dead^{\mathbf{t}}, alive^{\mathbf{t}}\}$ and $I_2 = \{not\_dead^{\mathbf{f}}, alive^{\mathbf{f}}\}$. $\mathcal{T}_2$ has the same two models ($alive$ is open in $\mathcal{T}_2$). But only the interpretation I_2 is a model of $\mathcal{T}_1 \cup \mathcal{T}_2$. We see that $\neg alive$ and $\neg not\_dead$ are consequences of the union $\mathcal{T}_1 \cup \mathcal{T}_2$, whereas they are not true in I_1, which is a model of $\mathcal{T}_1$ and of $\mathcal{T}_2$.

Athough the equality doesn't always hold, for *correct* theories, $\mathcal{T}_1, \mathcal{T}_2$ and $\mathcal{T}_1 \cup \mathcal{T}_2$, the inclusion $Mod(\mathcal{T}_1 \cup \mathcal{T}_2) \subseteq Mod(\mathcal{T}_1) \cap Mod(\mathcal{T}_2)$ already holds. This means that formulas which are true in every interpretation which is a model of $\mathcal{T}_1$ and $\mathcal{T}_2$ are consequences of $\mathcal{T}_1 \cup \mathcal{T}_2$ (but it is possible that $\mathcal{T}_1 \cup \mathcal{T}_2$ has more consequences, see example 3.1).

Theorem 3.1 (no loss of information)
Given are two theories $\mathcal{T}_1$ and $\mathcal{T}_2$ such that $\mathcal{T}_1, \mathcal{T}_2$ and $\mathcal{T}_1 \cup \mathcal{T}_2$ are correct. Then $Mod(\mathcal{T}_1 \cup \mathcal{T}_2) \subseteq Mod(\mathcal{T}_1) \cap Mod(\mathcal{T}_2)$.

We want to remark that it is not always the case that the union of two correct theories is correct or that two theories whose union is correct are correct. Recall that we made the assumption that each predicate symbol is defined in at most one theory $\mathcal{T}_1$ or $\mathcal{T}_2$. This assumption is necessary. Look for instance at the theory $\mathcal{T}_1 = \{p \leftarrow q, q \leftarrow p\}$, with $Mod(\mathcal{T}_1) = \{p^{\mathbf{f}}, q^{\mathbf{f}}\}$. When we compose $\mathcal{T}_1$ with the theory $\mathcal{T}_2 = \{p \leftarrow \top\}$, we get another unique model, namely $Mod(\mathcal{T}_1 \cup \mathcal{T}_2) = \{p^{\mathbf{t}}, q^{\mathbf{t}}\}$.

For some theories we are only interested in a certain class of interpretations (like for instance Herbrand interpretations). In this case, we have the following result, which is a generalisation of theorem 3.1:

Theorem 3.2 Given a class of interpretations $\mathcal{J}$ and two theories $\mathcal{T}_1$ and $\mathcal{T}_2$ such that $\mathcal{T}_1, \mathcal{T}_2$ and $\mathcal{T}_1 \cup \mathcal{T}_2$ are correct w.r.t. $\mathcal{J}$. Then $Mod^{\mathcal{J}}(\mathcal{T}_1 \cup \mathcal{T}_2) \subseteq Mod^{\mathcal{J}}(\mathcal{T}_1) \cap Mod^{\mathcal{J}}(\mathcal{T}_2)$.

Example 3.2

$$\mathcal{T}_1 \; : \; \begin{cases} even(0) \leftarrow \top \\ even(s(s(X))) \; \leftarrow \; \neg odd(X) \end{cases}$$
$$\mathcal{T}_2 \; : \; \begin{cases} odd(s(0)) \leftarrow \top \\ odd(s(s(X))) \; \leftarrow \; \neg even(X) \end{cases}$$

It is easily seen that $\mathcal{T}_1$ and $\mathcal{T}_2$ are correct. But $\mathcal{T}_1 \cup \mathcal{T}_2$ has a 3-valued (non-Herbrand) model. Indeed, let J_0 be the pre-interpretation with domain the disjunct union $\mathbb{N} \cup \mathbb{Z}$, the interpretation of 0 (constant) $0 \in \mathbb{N}$ and the interpretation of $s/1$ the union of the successor functions on the natural numbers and on the integers. Define the interpretation I with pre-interpretation J_0 as follows: the interpretation of $even/1$ is

$$\left\{ even(2 \times n)^{\mathbf{t}}, even(2 \times n + 1)^{\mathbf{f}} \mid n \in \mathbb{N} \right\} \quad \cup \quad \left\{ even(z)^{\mathbf{u}} \mid z \in \mathbb{Z} \right\},$$

and the interpretation of $odd/1$ is

$$\left\{ odd(2 \times n)^{\mathbf{f}}, odd(2 \times n + 1)^{\mathbf{t}} \mid n \in \mathbb{N} \right\} \quad \cup \quad \left\{ odd(z)^{\mathbf{u}} \mid z \in \mathbb{Z} \right\}.$$

Then I is a 3-valued model of $T_1 \cup T_2$. It is obvious though, that only Herbrand interpretations are relevant w.r.t. this theory, and it is clear that $T_1 \cup T_2$ has only 2-valued Herbrand models. In fact, there is only one, namely

$$\left\{ even(s^{2n}(0)), odd(s^{2n+1}(0)) \mid n \in \mathbb{N} \right\}.$$

Hence, the conditions of theorem 3.2 with $\mathcal{J} = \mathcal{H}$ are satisfied and the inclusion $Mod^{\mathcal{H}}(T_1 \cup T_2) \subseteq Mod^{\mathcal{H}}(T_1) \cap Mod^{\mathcal{H}}(T_2)$ holds. (In fact, as we will see later, we have an equality here (theorem 4.1, with $\mathcal{J} = \mathcal{H}$).)

4 The justification condition

The aim of this section is to provide a general condition on T_1 and T_2, so that the equality

$$Mod(T_1 \cup T_2) = Mod(T_1) \cap Mod(T_2) \qquad (*)$$

holds, or equivalently, so that the consequences of $T_1 \cup T_2$ are exactly those formulas which are true in every interpretation which is a model of T_1 and of T_2. We first give some motivating examples.

4.1 Motivating examples

In the first example the predicates defined in T_2 are all 'new', that is, they don't occur in T_{1d}.

Example 4.1

$$T_1 : \begin{cases} parent(X, Y) & \leftarrow & father(X, Y) \\ parent(X, Y) & \leftarrow & mother(X, Y) \\ father(a, b) \leftarrow \top \\ mother(b, c) \leftarrow \top \end{cases}$$

$$T_2 : \begin{cases} anc(X, Y) & \leftarrow & parent(X, Y) \\ anc(X, Y) & \leftarrow & anc(X, Z), parent(Z, Y) \end{cases}$$

The first theory T_1 defines the predicate $parent/2$ in terms of the predicate $father/2$ and $mother/2$, for which there are given some facts. The second theory T_2 defines the predicate $anc/2$ in terms of itself and $parent/2$.

In this case the equality $(*)$ holds. Looking for instance at Herbrand interpretations, we see that the only Herbrand interpretation which is a model of T_1 and of T_2 is the interpretation $I = \{ father(a, b), mother(b, c), parent(a, b), parent(b, c), anc(a, b), anc(b, c), anc(a, c) \}$. It is easily seen that I is the unique Herbrand model of $T_1 \cup T_2$.

Next we give an example in which clauses of T_2 have predicates in their body which are defined in T_1, and vice versa (hence, there is a kind of mutual dependency between T_1 and T_2). In this example the equality (∗) doesn't hold, and we have a strict inclusion.

Example 4.2

$$T_1 \;:\; \begin{cases} parent(X) & \leftarrow & father(X) \\ parent(X) & \leftarrow & mother(X) \end{cases}$$

$$T_2 \;:\; \begin{cases} father(X) & \leftarrow & parent(X), male(X) \\ mother(X) & \leftarrow & parent(X), female(X) \\ male(a) \leftarrow \top \end{cases}$$

In T_1 parent/1 is defined in terms of father/1 and mother/1, while in T_2 father/1 and mother/1 are defined in terms of parent/1.

The Herbrand interpretation $I = \{male(a), parent(a), father(a)\}$ is a model of both T_1 and T_2, but it is not a model of $T_1 \cup T_2$. The only Herbrand model of $T_1 \cup T_2$ is $I' = \{male(a)\}$.

Example 4.2 suggests that the condition to be put on T_1 and T_2 to obtain the equality (∗) is that only 'new' predicates (i.e. predicates not occuring in T_{1d}) can be defined in T_2. This condition is surely sufficient (see theorem 5.3 in section 5), but is not necessary, as is shown by the following example.

Example 4.3

$$T_1 \;:\; \{grpar(X,Y) \leftarrow parent(X,Z), parent(Z,Y)$$

$$T_2 \;:\; \begin{cases} gr\_grpar(X,Y) & \leftarrow & grpar(X,Z), parent(Z,Y) \\ parent(a,b) \leftarrow \top \\ parent(b,c) \leftarrow \top \\ parent(c,d) \leftarrow \top \end{cases}$$

T_2 defines gr_grpar/2 in terms of grpar/2 and parent/2, and grpar/2 is defined in T_1 in terms of parent/2, which is defined in T_2.

The equality (∗) holds. For instance, the only Herbrand interpretation which is a model of T_1 and of T_2 is $\{parent(a,b), parent(b,c), parent(c,d), grpar(a,c), grpar(b,d), gr\_grpar(a,d)\}$, and this is the unique Herbrand model of $T_1 \cup T_2$.

Comparing the last two examples, we see that in example 4.2 the dependency between the defined predicates in T_1 and the defined predicates in T_2 is an 'infinite' one:

parent/1 (T_1) is defined in terms of father/1 (T_2),
father/1 (T_2) is defined in terms of parent/1 (T_1),
parent/1 (T_1) is defined in terms of father/1 (T_2), ...

Whereas in example 4.3, the dependency is a 'finite' one:

gr_grpar/2 (T_2) is defined in terms of grpar/2 (T_1),
grpar/2 (T_1) is defined in terms of parent/2 (T_2),
parent/2 (T_2) is defined totally in T_2.

A condition in terms of dependency relations is discussed in the next sections. We now give an example which requires a more general condition. The equality (∗) holds, although the dependency between the defined predicates in T_1 and the defined predicates in T_2 is an infinite one.

Example 4.4
$$T_1 : \begin{cases} dead & \leftarrow \neg alive, \neg dancing \\ dancing & \text{(FOL axiom)} \end{cases}$$
$$T_2 : \{ alive \leftarrow \neg dead$$

The predicates $dead$ (T_1) and $alive$ (T_2) depend on each other, but the equality $Mod(T_1 \cup T_2) = Mod(T_1) \cap Mod(T_2)$ holds. Indeed, the intersection of $Mod(T_1)$ and $Mod(T_2)$ consists of one interpretation $\{dancing^t, alive^t, dead^f\}$, which is the only model of $T_1 \cup T_2$.

In Event Calculus, there is a broad class of examples for which, like example 4.4, the equality $(*)$ holds, although there is an infinite kind of dependency between the defined predicates in T_1 and the defined predicates in T_2 (for an example, see [22]). These examples require a more general condition, the justification condition, defined in the following subsection.

4.2 The justification condition

Definition 4.1 *Given a class of interpretations $\mathcal{J}$. Two theories T_1 and T_2 satisfy the justification condition w.r.t. $\mathcal{J}$ if for each interpretation of $\mathcal{J}$ which is a model of the FOL axioms $T_{1c} \cup T_{2c}$ it holds that for any fact F, if there is a justification of F in $T_{1d} \cup T_{2d}$ with only true leaves (or no leaves) and an infinite branch with an infinite number of facts defined in T_1 and an infinite number of facts defined in T_2, then there is a strong justification of F in $T_{1d} \cup T_{2d}$.*

Theorem 4.1 *Given a class of interpretations $\mathcal{J}$ and two theories T_1 and T_2 correct w.r.t. $\mathcal{J}$. If T_1 and T_2 satisfy the justification condition w.r.t. $\mathcal{J}$, then $Mod^{\mathcal{J}}(T_1 \cup T_2) = Mod^{\mathcal{J}}(T_1) \cap Mod^{\mathcal{J}}(T_2)$.*

Hence, in particular, if T_1 and T_2 are correct w.r.t. $\mathcal{J}$ and satisfy the justification condition w.r.t. $\mathcal{J}$, then $T_1 \cup T_2$ is also correct w.r.t. $\mathcal{J}$.

Example 4.5 *Reconsider example 3.2. T_1 and T_2 don't satisfy the justification condition (w.r.t. the class of all interpretations). Indeed, for each interpretation with pre-interpretation J_0, the justification of a fact $even(z)$ (analogously $odd(z)$), $z \in \mathbb{Z}$, is an infinite branch with infinitely many facts defined in T_1 (the even-facts) and infinitely many facts defined in T_2 (the odd-facts), and there is no justification for $even(z)$ (analogously for $odd(z)$) with value t. As was already shown in example 3.2, the only model of $T_1 \cup T_2$ with pre-interpretation J_0 is 3-valued and the equality $(*)$ doesn't hold.*

But, as we mentioned before, the only interpretations that really matter here are the Herbrand interpretations. Looking at Herbrand interpretations only, we can see that every justification of a fact is finite. Hence, T_1 and T_2 satisfy the justification condition w.r.t. $\mathcal{H}$ and it holds that $Mod^{\mathcal{H}}(T_1 \cup T_2) = Mod^{\mathcal{H}}(T_1) \cap Mod^{\mathcal{H}}(T_2)$.

The justification condition is a very general condition from which many other conditions can be deduced. In the next section we introduce some simpler, more syntactical, but less general conditions on the theories T_1 and T_2 such that $(*)$ holds. All these syntactical conditions are special cases of the justification condition, such that the correctness theorems of these conditions are simple corollaries of theorem 4.1.

5 More syntactical conditions

5.1 Condition in terms of dependency relation

Let $Ground(T_1 \cup T_2)$ denote the grounding of $T_1 \cup T_2$ (i.e. of the logic program part and of the FOL axioms) w.r.t. the Herbrand universe. We will consider the dependency relation, denoted $\succ$, on the ground atoms of $Ground(T_1 \cup T_2)$. Recall that the dependency relation is the transitive closure of the relation $\succ_1$, with $p \succ_1 q$ if there's a clause in $Ground(T_{1d} \cup T_{2d})$ with head p, and q or $\neg q$ in the body. If $p \succ q$, we say that p depends on q. The following theorem is a direct consequence of the definition of a justification (definition 2.5), the definition of justification condition (definition 4.1) and theorem 4.1, with $\mathcal{J} = \mathcal{H}$.

Theorem 5.1 *Given two theories T_1 and T_2 which are correct w.r.t. $\mathcal{H}$. Consider the dependency relation on the ground atoms of $Ground(T_1 \cup T_2)$. If for each descending sequence K of ground atoms, there is an $i \in \{1,2\}$ such that there's only a finite number of elements of K defined in $Ground(T_{id})$, then $Mod^{\mathcal{H}}(T_1 \cup T_2) = Mod^{\mathcal{H}}(T_1) \cap Mod^{\mathcal{H}}(T_2)$.*

And hence $T_1 \cup T_2$ is also correct w.r.t. $\mathcal{H}$. Sometimes it is not enough to consider only Herbrand interpretations. For this reason, let's define in the usual way the dependency relation $\succ$ on the predicate symbols of $T_1 \cup T_2$.

Theorem 5.2 *Given a class of interpretations $\mathcal{J}$ and two theories T_1 and T_2 correct w.r.t. $\mathcal{J}$. Consider the dependency relation on the predicate symbols of $T_1 \cup T_2$. If for each descending sequence K of predicate symbols there is an $i \in \{1,2\}$ such that there's only a finite number of elements of K defined in T_{id}, then $Mod^{\mathcal{J}}(T_1 \cup T_2) = Mod^{\mathcal{J}}(T_1) \cap Mod^{\mathcal{J}}(T_2)$.*

Hence $T_1 \cup T_2$ is also correct w.r.t. $\mathcal{J}$. Examples 4.1 and 4.3 of section 4 satisfy the conditions of theorem 5.2, with $\mathcal{J}$ the class of all interpretations, whereas example 4.2 does not. We give another nice example.

Example 5.1

$$T_1 \;:\; \begin{cases} even(0) \leftarrow \top \\ even(s(X)) \quad\leftarrow\; odd(X) \end{cases}$$
$$T_2 \;:\; \{odd(s(X)) \leftarrow even(X)\}$$

First note that the equality $Mod(T_1 \cup T_2) = Mod(T_1) \cap Mod(T_2)$ does not hold. Indeed, consider the 2-valued non-Herbrand interpretation I with pre-interpretation J_0 (see example 3.2), the interpretation of even/1

$$\left\{ even(2 \times n)^{\mathbf{t}}, even(2 \times n + 1)^{\mathbf{f}} \mid n \in \mathbb{N} \right\} \;\cup\; \left\{ even(z)^{\mathbf{t}} \mid z \in \mathbb{Z} \right\},$$

and the interpretation of odd/1

$$\left\{ odd(2 \times n)^{\mathbf{f}}, odd(2 \times n + 1)^{\mathbf{t}} \mid n \in \mathbb{N} \right\} \;\cup\; \left\{ odd(z)^{\mathbf{t}} \mid z \in \mathbb{Z} \right\}.$$

Then I is a non-Herbrand model of T_1 and of T_2. But I is not a model of $T_1 \cup T_2$, because the only model of $T_1 \cup T_2$ with pre-interpretation J_0 assigns truth value $\mathbf{f}$ to all facts $even(z), odd(z)$ with $z \in \mathbb{Z}$.
But again, the only interpretations which are important w.r.t. these theories are the Herbrand interpretations. And for these interpretations the equality

holds, i.e. $Mod^{\mathcal{H}}(\mathcal{T}_1 \cup \mathcal{T}_2) = Mod^{\mathcal{H}}(\mathcal{T}_1) \cap Mod^{\mathcal{H}}(\mathcal{T}_2)$. *To prove this, we take the grounding of* $\mathcal{T}_1 \cup \mathcal{T}_2$ *and check that the conditions of theorem 5.1 are satisfied. It is easily seen that* $\mathcal{T}_1 \cup \mathcal{T}_2$ *has a unique 2-valued Herbrand model given by* $\{even(s^{2n}(0)), odd(s^{2n+1}(0)) \mid n \in \mathbb{N}\}$.

Note that we can not apply theorem 5.2 (with $\mathcal{J} = \mathcal{H}$*) to obtain the same result, because* $\mathcal{T}_1$ *and* $\mathcal{T}_2$ *don't satisfy the conditions of that theorem (there is an infinite descending sequence* $even/1 \succ odd/1 \succ even/1 \succ \ldots$*, with* $even/1$ *defined in* $\mathcal{T}_1$ *and* $odd/1$ *in* $\mathcal{T}_2$*).*

5.2 Conservative extensions

In this subsection and the next one, we give some even stronger, syntactical conditions to obtain (∗). For the first result we need some notation. Given a theory $\mathcal{T} = (\mathcal{T}_d, \mathcal{T}_c)$. Let $Head(\mathcal{T}_d)$ denote the set of all predicate symbols occuring in the head of a clause of $\mathcal{T}_d$, i.e. the set of the defined predicate symbols of $\mathcal{T}$. Let $Pred(\mathcal{T}_d)$ denote the set of all predicate symbols occuring in $\mathcal{T}_d$. The following theorem is a direct consequence of theorem 5.2.

Theorem 5.3 *Given a class of interpretations* $\mathcal{J}$ *and two theories* $\mathcal{T}_1$ *and* $\mathcal{T}_2$ *correct w.r.t.* $\mathcal{J}$*. If* $Head(\mathcal{T}_{2d}) \cap Pred(\mathcal{T}_{1d}) = \emptyset$ *, then* $Mod^{\mathcal{J}}(\mathcal{T}_1 \cup \mathcal{T}_2) = Mod^{\mathcal{J}}(\mathcal{T}_1) \cap Mod^{\mathcal{J}}(\mathcal{T}_2)$*.*

The condition $Head(\mathcal{T}_{2d}) \cap Pred(\mathcal{T}_{1d}) = \emptyset$ means that only predicate symbols not occuring in $\mathcal{T}_{1d}$ can be defined in $\mathcal{T}_{2d}$. Hence, predicate symbols defined in $\mathcal{T}_{1d}$ can not depend on predicate symbols defined in $\mathcal{T}_{2d}$ (the converse is possible though). An example was given in section 4, example 4.1.

Under the conditions of theorem 5.3, we are given a way to construct every model of $\mathcal{T}_1 \cup \mathcal{T}_2$ by successively finding a model of $\mathcal{T}_1$ and $\mathcal{T}_2$. Let us be more precise. Suppose two correct logic programs $\mathcal{T}_{1d}$ and $\mathcal{T}_{2d}$ are given and $\mathcal{T}_{1d}$ does not refer to the predicate symbols defined in $\mathcal{T}_{2d}$. Suppose $\mathcal{T}_{1d} \cup \mathcal{T}_{2d}$ is complete. Because $\mathcal{T}_{1d}$ does not refer to predicates defined in $\mathcal{T}_{2d}$, every predicate occuring in $\mathcal{T}_{1d}$ is also defined in $\mathcal{T}_{1d}$. Given a pre-interpretation J, denote the set of models of $\mathcal{T}_{1d}$ with pre-interpretation J by $\mathcal{M}_J$. It is clear that each model in $\mathcal{M}_J$ has the same truth function on predicate symbols defined in $\mathcal{T}_{1d}$. In the set $\mathcal{M}_J$ there is exactly one interpretation M which is also a model of $\mathcal{T}_{2d}$. Because of the equality, $Mod(\mathcal{T}_{1d} \cup \mathcal{T}_{2d}) = Mod(\mathcal{T}_{1d}) \cap Mod(\mathcal{T}_{2d})$, M is a model of $\mathcal{T}_{1d} \cup \mathcal{T}_{2d}$ and every model of $\mathcal{T}_{1d} \cup \mathcal{T}_{2d}$ can be obtained in this way. If $\mathcal{T}_{1d} \cup \mathcal{T}_{2d}$ is incomplete, then, instead of starting with a given pre-interpretation only, we also fix a 2-valued truth function on the predicate symbols open in $\mathcal{T}_{1d} \cup \mathcal{T}_{2d}$ and then repeat the same reasoning. The reasoning remains valid when adding FOL axioms $\mathcal{T}_{1c}$ and $\mathcal{T}_{2c}$ to the logic programs. This is because of the monotonicity of FOL; not satisfying $\mathcal{T}_{1c}$ or $\mathcal{T}_{2c}$ is equivalent with not satisfying $\mathcal{T}_{1c} \cup \mathcal{T}_{2c}$.

In a way, the logic program $\mathcal{T}_d = \mathcal{T}_{1d} \cup \mathcal{T}_{2d}$ is split into two parts. In [16] Lifschitz and Turner discuss this idea of splitting a logic program in the context of answer set semantics for disjunctive logic programs with classical negation. They call $\mathcal{T}_{1d}$ the bottom of $\mathcal{T}_d$ and $\mathcal{T}_{2d}$ the top of $\mathcal{T}_d$.

A corollary to theorem 5.3 is a property which is in literature often called the *conservative extension property*. If we extend an initial correct logic program T_{1d} by a correct logic program T_{2d}, which gives only definitions for 'new' predicate symbols (i.e. not occuring in T_{1d}), then for every formula φ, consisting only of predicate symbols defined in T_{1d}, φ is a consequence of T_{1d} if and only if φ is a consequence of $T_{1d} \cup T_{2d}$. This can be proven by induction on the length of the formula φ, using theorem 5.3.

Conservative extensions were studied by Lifschitz and Turner in the context of disjunctive logic programming with classical negation [16], by Gelfond and Przymusinska in the context of extended logic programming [13] and in the context of epistemic specifications [14] .

5.3 Hierarchical and acyclic programs

The last results concern hierarchical and acyclic programs. For more details about this kind of programs, see [17] and [1] . We just give their definitions.

Definition 5.1 *A logic program T_d is hierarchical, if there exists a mapping $|\ |$ from $Pred(T_d)$ to the natural numbers such that for every clause $p(t_1,\ldots,t_n) \leftarrow L_1,\ldots,L_m$ in T_d, $|p|$ is greater than the value under $|\ |$ of each predicate symbol occuring (positively or negatively) in the body.*

It is obvious that hierarchical programs cannot have 3-valued models (they are correct) and that each subset of clauses of a hierarchical program is itself hierarchical. Combining these proporties together with theorem 5.2, with $\mathcal{J}$ the class of all interpretations, we obtain:

Theorem 5.4 *Given a theory $T = (T_d, T_c)$ with T_d a hierarchical logic program. Then for every $T_1 = (T_{1d}, T_{1c})$ and $T_2 = (T_{2d}, T_{2c})$ such that $T = T_1 \cup T_2$ (and such that every predicate is defined in at most one theory, either T_1 or T_2), the equality $Mod(T) = Mod(T_1) \cap Mod(T_2)$ holds.*

Using induction, we can extend this theorem to split a theory into a finite number of theories. We refer to the very similar case of acyclic programs below for an example of how this is done.

When only Herbrand interpretations are relevant w.r.t. the theory, we can put a more general, syntactical restriction on the theory.

Definition 5.2 *A logic program T_d is acyclic, if there exists a mapping $|\ |$ from the Herbrand base to the natural numbers such that for every clause $A \leftarrow B_1,\ldots,B_m, \neg B_{m+1},\ldots,\neg B_n$ in $Ground(T_d)$, $|A| > |B_i|$ for every $1 \le i \le n$.*

Analogously to the case of hierarchical programs, an acyclic logic program is correct and each subset of clauses of an acyclic logic program is acyclic. Together with theorem 5.1 this gives us:

Theorem 5.5 *Given a theory $T = (T_d, T_c)$ with T_d an acyclic logic program. Then for every $T_1 = (T_{1d}, T_{1c})$ and $T_2 = (T_{2d}, T_{2c})$ such that $T = T_1 \cup T_2$ (and such that every predicate is defined in at most one theory, either T_1 or T_2), the equality $Mod^{\mathcal{H}}(T) = Mod^{\mathcal{H}}(T_1) \cap Mod^{\mathcal{H}}(T_2)$ holds.*

Again, we can extend this theorem to split T into a finite number of theories.

Example 5.2

$$\mathcal{T}_1 \; : \; \begin{cases} even(0) \leftarrow \top \\ even(s(X)) \;\;\; \leftarrow \;\; odd(X) \end{cases}$$

$$\mathcal{T}_2 \; : \; \{odd(s(X)) \leftarrow even(X)\}$$

$$\mathcal{T}_3 \; : \; \begin{cases} nat(X) \;\; \leftarrow \;\; even(X) \\ nat(X) \;\; \leftarrow \;\; odd(X) \end{cases}$$

It is clear that $\mathcal{T}_1 \cup \mathcal{T}_2 \cup \mathcal{T}_3$ is acyclic. Indeed, consider the mapping $| \; |$, $|even(s^n(0))| = n$, $|odd(s^n(0))| = n$, $|nat(s^n(0))| = n+1$, with $n \in \mathbb{N}$ and $s^0(0) = 0$. Then for every clause in $Ground(\mathcal{T}_1 \cup \mathcal{T}_2 \cup \mathcal{T}_3)$ the value under $| \; |$ of the head is greater than the value of the atom in the body.
The intersection of $\mathcal{M}od^{\mathcal{H}}(\mathcal{T}_1), \mathcal{M}od^{\mathcal{H}}(\mathcal{T}_2)$ and $\mathcal{M}od^{\mathcal{H}}(\mathcal{T}_3)$ gives us (see also example 5.1) the unique Herbrand model of $\mathcal{T}_1 \cup \mathcal{T}_2 \cup \mathcal{T}_3$:
$\{even(s^{2n}(0)), odd(s^{2n+1}(0)), nat(s^n(0)) \mid n \in \mathbb{N}\}.$

6 Discussion

Our study differs from existing works on composing logic programs in one or more of the following 3 aspects: its position w.r.t. compositionality versus nonmonotonicity, the results concerning composing programs with negation and the representation of uncertainty in modules.

In [20] it is observed that compositionality of a semantics and nonmonotonicity are to some extent irreconcilable aspects. Compositionality requires that the old knowledge is maintained when new knowledge is added; nonmonotonicity is defined as exactly the opposite. In some studies, compositionality of the semantics is seen as a first rank requirement. However, from a knowledge representation point of view, such a semantics is too weak for common sense knowledge representation. The union operator on OLP-FOL theories is not compositional, and, in general, it shouldn't be.

As opposed to most of the works about compositionality, this paper considers logic programs which may contain negation in the body of their clauses. In section 5.2 we mentioned three works [16], [13] and [14] which also allow negation, though in the context of a quite different LP-extension (two negations, epistemic operator). Other exceptions which also consider negation are [12], [20], [8]. However, either they consider a weaker compositional semantics based on completion semantics [20], or the results are restricted either to hierarchical dependencies between modules, as in [12], or to the case of one module representing a conservative extension of another module [8].

By allowing predicates to be open in a logic program, we deal with incomplete knowledge on predicates. In [12], whose approach leanst closest to ours, they consider programs with import predicates (called units); import predicates correspond to open predicates in our approach. In [7], [6] they work with a different notion of open predicates to capture the possible composition with other programs. Their semantics of admissable Herbrand models for definite programs is suited for compositionality problems, but seems less suitable for knowledge representation. In [5] this semantics is extended to normal logic programs by transforming them to open positive programs. Though in this semantics the compositionality problem can be handled elegantly, the semantics is much weaker than ours and seems not suited for knowledge representation and nonmonotonic reasoning. In [2] an OR-compositional semantics (i.e. compositional w.r.t. program union) of open programs is defined. As opposed to most of the works, computed answer substitutions are taken here as observables.

A special place in the compositionality research is taken by [3], where each definite program is denoted by its immediate consequence operator T_P and not by its set of models. The union of two definite programs can be proven to correspond to a certain operation on the corresponding T_P operators. The result is a highly abstract sort of semantics of a program, which is not really suitable for studying knowledge representation problems, but which allows [3] to define many different composition operators, all in terms of different ways of composing the T_P operators of the distinct modules. In comparison, we investigate only one operator, namely the operator which joins the knowledge of the modules (though we expect that this operator is the most relevant one in practical situations). Recently, this algebraic approach was extended for normal logic programs ([4]) using Fittings 3-valued completion operator.

Besides uncertainty on predicates, one can also have incomplete knowledge on the domain of discourse. By considering general interpretations, like in [20], we take into account this kind of uncertainty. Other approaches either do not allow to model this kind of incomplete knowledge or model it by allowing Herbrand interpretations of arbitrary extensions of the module language.

In the previous discussed approaches and also in our approach, module composition is seen as a metalinguistic mechanism. Another main direction in the research of compositionality of logic programming formalisms is of a linguistic nature and is seen for instance in [18], [15]. They extend the formalism of Horn clause logic with modal operators in order to provide a richer support for modular programming. For a survey we refer to [9].

Note that we did not consider problems such as: parametrised modules, several experts designing definitions for the same concepts, several experts overloading the same predicate symbol to represent different concepts, ... These are topics for future work.

References

[1] K.R. Apt and M. Bezem. Acyclic programs. In *Proc. of the International Conference on Logic Programming*, pages 579–597. MIT press, 1990.

[2] A. Bossi, M. Gabbrielli, G. Levi, and M.C. Meo. Contributions to the Semantics of Open Logic Programs. In ICOT, editor, *Proc. of the International Conference on Fifth Generating Computer Systems*, 1992.

[3] A. Brogi. *Program Construction in Computational Logic*. PhD thesis, Dipartimento di Informatica Universita di Pisa, 1993.

[4] A. Brogi, S. Contiero, and F. Turini. Composing General Logic Programs. *to appear in Proc. of LPNMR*, 1997.

[5] A. Brogi, E. Lamma, P. Mancarella, and P. Mello. Normal Logic Programs as Open Positive Programs. In K. Apt, editor, *Proc. of JICSLP*, pages 783–797, 1992.

[6] A. Brogi, E. Lamma, and P. Mello. Open Logic Theories. In L.-H. Eriksson, L. Hallnas, and P. Schroeder-Heister, editors, *Proc. of the Second International Workshop on Extensions of Logic Programming*, pages 73–88. Springer-Verlag, 1991.

[7] A. Brogi, E. Lamma, and P. Mello. Compositional Model-Theoretic Semantics for Logic Programs. *New Generation Computing*, 11(1):1–21, 1992.

[8] F. Bry. A Compositional Semantics for Logic Programs and Deductive Databases. In M. Maher, editor, *Proc. of JICSLP*, pages 453–467, 1996.

[9] M. Bugliesi, E. Lamma, and P. Mello. Modularity in logic programming. *Journal of Logic Programming*, 20:443–502, 1994.

[10] M. Denecker. A Terminological Interpretation of (Abductive) Logic Programming. In V.W. Marek, A. Nerode, and M. Truszczynski, editors, *International Conference on Logic Programming and Nonmonotonic Reasoning*, pages 15–29. Springer, Lecture notes in Artificial Intelligence 928, 1995.

[11] M. Denecker and D. De Schreye. Justification semantics: a unifying framework for the semantics of logic programs. In *Proc. of the Logic Programming and Nonmonotonic Reasoning Workshop*, pages 365–379, 1993.

[12] A. Lallouet G. Ferrand. A Compositional Proof Method of Partial Correctness for Normal Logic Programs. In J. Lloyd, editor, *Proc. of ISLP*, pages 210–223, 1995.

[13] M. Gelfond and H. Przymusinska. Towards a Theory of Elaboration Tolerance: Logic Programming Approach. *to appear in Journal on Software and Knowledge Engineering*.

[14] M. Gelfond and H. Przymusinska. Definitions in Epistemic Specifications. In A. Nerode, W. Marek, and V. S. Subrahmanian, editors, *Proc. of the First International Workshop on Logic Programming and Non-monotonic Reasoning*, pages 245–259, 1991.

[15] L. Giordano and A. Martelli. A modal reconstruction of blocks and modules in logic programming. In *Proc. of the International Logic Programming Symposium*, pages 239–253. The MIT Press, 1991.

[16] V. Lifschitz and H. Turner. Splitting a Logic Program. In P. Van Hentenrijck, editor, *Proc. of the Eleventh International Conference on Logic Programming*, pages 23–38, 1994.

[17] J.W. Lloyd. *Foundations of Logic Programming*. Springer-Verlag, 1987.

[18] L. Monteiro and A. Porto. Contextual Logic Programming. In G. Levi and M. Martelli, editors, *Proc. of the Sixth International Conference on Logic Programming*, 1989.

[19] L. M. Pereira, J.N. Aparicio, and J.J. Alferes. Hypothetical reasoning with well founded semantics. Technical report, AI Centre, Uninova, Portugal, 1990.

[20] F. Teusink S. Etalle. A Compositional Semantics for Normal Open Programs. In M. Maher, editor, *Proc. of JICSLP*, pages 468–482, 1996.

[21] A. Van Gelder, K.A. Ross, and J.S. Schlipf. The Well-Founded Semantics for General Logic Programs. *Journal of the ACM*, 38(3):620–650, 1991.

[22] S. Verbaeten, M. Denecker, and D. De Schreye. Compositionality of normal open logic programs. Technical Report 254, Department of Computer Science, K.U.Leuven, 1997.

Approximate reasoning about actions in presence of sensing and incomplete information

Chitta Baral and **Tran Cao Son**
Department of Computer Science
University of Texas at El Paso
El Paso, TX 79968
{chitta,tson}@cs.utep.edu

Abstract

Sensing actions are important for planning with incomplete information. A solution for the frame problem for sensing actions was proposed by Scherl and Levesque. They adapt the possible world model of knowledge to situation calculus. In this paper we propose a high level language in the spirit of the language $\mathcal{A}$, that allows sensing actions. We then present two approximation semantics of this language and their translation to logic programs. Unlike, $\mathcal{A}$, where states are two valued interpretations, and unlike the approach in Scherl and Levesque where states are Kripke models, in our approach states are three valued interpretations.

1 Introduction and Motivation

Sensing actions are important for planning with incomplete information [2, 5, 8, 7]. Consider a robot which is asked to get milk. The robot does not know if there is milk in the fridge or not, and of course would prefer to get the milk from the fridge rather than from the neighborhood 24 hr store. A conditional plan of the robot to get milk would be to go to the fridge, open it and sense (or look) if there is milk in it and then bring the milk if it is there; otherwise it has to go to the store and get the milk from there. This conditional plan involves sensing and to generate such a plan the robot has to be able to reason about its sensing actions.

Scherl and Levesque [12] propose an elegant solution to the frame problem in presence of sensing actions. (Sensing actions are also referred to as knowledge producing actions.) To formalize knowledge they adapt the standard possible world model of knowledge to situation calculus. Although elegant, their formulation would require a planner based on it to keep track of the accessibility relations and thus increase the complexity of the planner. (Note that if there are n fluents originally then the number of possible worlds may be 2^n – the number of fluent interpretations – and then the accessibility relation would be a subset of 2^{n+1} elements. So keeping track of the change in the accessibility relation would be expensive.) Moreover, in presence of temporally extended goals [1], their formulation would result in having two kind of modal operators, a knowledge operator, and an operator for temporal goals.

We take a simpler approach using Lukasiewicz's three valued logic [10]. In Lukasiewicz's logic a proposition may have three truth values: *true* (T), *false* (F) or *unknown* (U). For any proposition p, if p is *true*, then $K(p)$ will be *true*, if p is *false*, then $K(p)$ will be *false* (but $K(\neg p)$ will be true), and if p is unknown, then both $K(p)$ and $K(\neg p)$ will be false. The truth table for the other connectives and operators are defined as follows:

$\wedge$	T	F	U
T	T	F	U
F	F	F	F
U	U	F	U

$\vee$	T	F	U
T	T	T	T
F	T	F	U
U	T	U	U

$\neg$	
T	F
F	T
U	U

Although, at first glance, this simple formulation seems an intuitive representation of knowledge, there is one problem lurking underneath. In this formulation $K(p \vee \neg p)$ has the truth value *false*, when p is *unknown*, which seems unintuitive. Although, this was pointed out to Lukasiewicz, he stuck to his convictions in his lifetime, and argued that for some modal operators his formulation makes sense.

In our approach a state of the world is represented as a 3-valued interpretation of the fluents in the world. We denote it by a pair $\langle T, F \rangle$, where T is the set of fluents that have truth value *true*, F is the set of fluents that have truth value *false*, and T and F are disjoint. The rest of the fluents in the world have truth value *unknown*. This is more general than states in $\mathcal{A}$, which are 2-valued interpretation of the fluents in the world. But, states in the formulation of Scherl and Levesque [12] are Kripke models and in the formulation of Lobo, Taylor and Mendez [9] are sets of 3-valued interpretations of fluents in the world. Our states being simpler than the last two approaches, result in loss of expressibility. *Nevertheless, we present two approximate reasoning methods to reason about actions in presence of sensing and incomplete information.*

Our most approximate approach, which we refer to as the, *0-semantics,* directly corresponds to the logic of Lukasiewicz. We justify the apparent fallacy of reasoning $K(p \vee \neg p)$ to be *false* when p is *unknown*, by saying that reasoner (or the robot) does not have the resources (time) to adequately reason (by cases) and makes a hasty decision.

Our next approximate approach, which we refer to as the, *1-semantics,* avoids the above mentioned fallacy by treating the truth value U in a different way. A proposition with truth value U, can either be *true* or *false*. I.e., with additional knowledge it may turn out to be *true* or it may turn out to be *false*. Consider a formula $F(P, P_u)$ composed of two sets of propositions P, and P_u. Suppose the truth values of the propositions in P are either *true* and *false* and the truth value of the propositions in P_u are *unknown*. Let

$I(P_u)$ be the set of all possible two valued interpretation of P_u. We define the truth value of the formula F as the truth value of

$$\wedge_{I \in I(P_u)} F(P, I)$$

Based on this definition, $K(p \vee \neg p)$ has the truth value *true*, when p is *unknown*.

In the next section we present the syntax of a high level language, in the spirit of $\mathcal{A}$ [4], that allows specification of effects of sensing actions. In later sections we discuss the 1-semantics and the 0-semantics of this language and present translation to disjunctive logic programming. We also discuss when our approximate semantics fail to reason intuitively.

2 A high level language with sensing actions: Syntax

Our language $\mathcal{A}_K$ has two distinct parts. One that is used to define descriptions in the language and another that is used to define queries.

A *description* of an action domain in the language $\mathcal{A}_K$ consists of "propositions" of three kinds. A "v-proposition" specifies the value of a fluent in the initial situation. An "ef-proposition" describes the effect of an action on the truth value of a fluent. A "k-proposition" describes the effect of an action on the knowledge about a fluent's truth value.

We begin with two disjoint nonempty sets of symbols, called *fluent names* and *action names*. A *fluent literal* is either a fluent name or a fluent name preceded by $\neg$. For a fluent literal l, by $\bar{l}$ we denote the fluent literal $\neg l$, and we shorten $\neg\neg l$ to l.

A *v-proposition* is an expression of the form

$$\textbf{initially} \quad f \tag{1}$$

An *ef-proposition* is an expression of the form

$$a \textbf{ causes } f \textbf{ if } p_1, \ldots, p_n \tag{2}$$

where a is an action name, and each of $f, p_1, \ldots, p_n$ ($n \geq 0$) is a fluent literal. The set of fluent literals $\{p_1, \ldots, p_n\}$ is referred to as the *precondition* of the ef-proposition and f is referred to as the *effect* of this ef-proposition. About this proposition we say that it *describes the effect of a on f*, and that $p_1, \ldots, p_n$ are its *preconditions*. If $n = 0$, we will drop **if** and write simply a **causes** f.

Two ef-propositions with preconditions $p_1, \ldots, p_n$ and $q_1, \ldots, q_m$ respectively are said to be *contradictory* if they describe the effect of the same action a on complementary fs, and $\{p_1, \ldots, p_n\} \cap \{\overline{q_1}, \ldots, \overline{q_m}\} = \emptyset$

A *k-proposition* is an expression of the form

$$a \textbf{ determines } f \textbf{ if } q_1, \ldots q_n \tag{3}$$

where a is an action name, and each of f and $q_1, \ldots, q_n$ ($n \geq 0$) is a fluent literal. The set of fluent literals $\{p_1, \ldots, p_n\}$ is referred to as the *precondition* of the k-proposition and f is referred to as the *k-effect* of this k-proposition. About this proposition we say that it stipulates that if a is executed in a situation where $q_1, \ldots, q_n$ are true, then in the resultant state the truth value of f becomes known.

A *proposition* is a v-proposition, ex-proposition, or an k-proposition. A *domain description*, or simply *domain*, is a set of propositions which does not contain contradictory ef-propositions.

Example 1 We have a robot which can perform the actions: *go_to_fridge*, *look_at_fridge*, *open_fridge*, *look_into_fridge*, *get_milk_from_fridge*, and *get_milk_from_store*. Intuitively, if the robot performs the action *go_to_fridge* then it will be near the fridge. If it is near the fridge, it can look at the fridge to find out if the fridge is open or not. By performing the action *open_fridge*, the fluent *fridge_open* becomes true. We can formally represent the above (and some additional knowledge) by the following domain description D_1:

> *go_to_fridge* **causes** *near_fridge*
> *look_at_fridge* **determines** *fridge_open* **if** *near_fridge*
> *open_fridge* **causes** *fridge_open* **if** *near_fridge*
> *look_into_fridge* **determines** *milk_in_fridge*
>   **if** *fridge_open*, *near_fridge*
> *get_milk_from_fridge* **causes** *has_milk*
>   **if** *milke_in_fridge*, *fridge_open*, *near_fridge*
> *get_milk_from_store* **causes** *has_milk*
> *get_milk_from_store* **causes** ¬*near_fridge*   □

In the presence of incomplete information and knowledge producing actions, we need to extend the normal definition of a plan as a sequence of actions. If we would like to make a plan to have milk w.r.t. the above domain, our plan will not be a sequence of actions, rather it would contain conditional statements. In the following definition we formalize this notion.

Definition 1 Conditional Plan
(i) An empty sequence of action, denoted by [ ], is a conditional plan.
(ii) If a is an action then a is a conditional plan.
(iii) If c_1 and c_2 are conditional plans, then $c_1; c_2$ is a conditional plan.
(iv) If $c_1, \ldots, c_n$ are conditional plans and $p_{i,j}$'s are fluents then the following is a conditional plan. (Such a plan is referred to as a *case plan*).

Case

$$p_{1,1}, \ldots, p_{1,m_1} \rightarrow c_1$$

$$\vdots$$

$$p_{n,1}, \ldots, p_{n,m_n} \rightarrow c_n$$

Endcase

where $\{p_{1,1}, \ldots, p_{1,m_1}\}, \ldots, \{p_{n,1}, \ldots, p_{n,m_n}\}$ are mutually exclusive (but not necessary exhaustive).

(v) Nothing else is a conditional plan.

Example 2 Following is a conditional plan[1] c_1 which will achieve the goal of the robot having milk, w.r.t. the description in D_1.

go_to_fridge;
look_at_fridge;
Case
$\neg fridge\_open \rightarrow open\_fridge;$
   look_into_fridge;
   Case
    milk_in_fridge $\rightarrow$ *get_milk_from_fridge*
    $\neg milk\_in\_fridge \rightarrow get\_milk\_from\_store$
   Endcase
$fridge\_open \rightarrow look\_into\_fridge;$
   Case
    milk_in_fridge $\rightarrow$ *get_milk_from_fridge*
    $\neg milk\_in\_fridge \rightarrow get\_milk\_from\_store$
   Endcase
Endcase   □

A query is an expression of the form f **after** c (4)
where f is a fluent and c is a conditional plan.

Example 3 To find out if c_1 indeed achieves the goal of having milk w.r.t. D_1, we need to pose the query   *has_milk* **after** c_1 to D_1 □

In the following sections we define two approximate semantics of domain descriptions in $\mathcal{A}_k$. In the process we define two entailment relations between domain descriptions and queries of $\mathcal{A}_k$.

3   1-Semantics and its properties

In $\mathcal{A}$ [4] a state is defined as a set of fluents, and corresponds to a state of the world at a particular moment. Here, a state corresponds to the state of the robots knowledge at a particular moment. Hence, it may be incomplete. Formally, a *state* is a pair of disjoint sets of fluent names. Given a fluent name f and a state $\sigma = \langle T, F \rangle$, we say that f *holds* in σ (we sometime denote it by $\sigma \models f$) if $f \in T$; $\neg f$ *holds* in σ if $f \in F$; otherwise both f and $\neg f$ are said to be *unknown* in σ. A *transition function* is a mapping Φ from the set of pairs (a, σ), where a is an action name and σ is a state, into the power set of states. Intuitively, $\Phi(a, \sigma)$ encodes the set of states the robot may reach after executing an actions a in a state σ. A *state* is said to be *complete* if $T \cup F$ is the set of all the fluents in the language. A *structure* is a pair (σ_0, Φ), where σ_0 is a state (the *initial state* of the structure), and Φ is a transition function.

---

[1]This plan can be made simpler and compact. The reason we present this particular plan without simplifying it is because it was automatically generated by our planner.

Before we define when a structure is a model of a domain description, we have the following notations:

- $E_a^+(\langle T, F\rangle)$ denotes the set $\{f \mid f$ is a fluent name and there exists an ef-proposition in our domain description whose action is a, effect is f, and whose preconditions are satisfied in $\langle T, F\rangle\}$.

- $E_a^-(\langle T, F\rangle)$ denotes the set $\{f \mid f$ is a fluent name and there exists an ef-proposition in our domain description whose action is a, effect is $\neg f$, and whose preconditions are satisfied in $\langle T, F\rangle\}$.

- For complete states $\langle T, F\rangle$, if for any action a, $E_a^+(\langle T, F\rangle) \cap E_a^-(\langle T, F\rangle) = \emptyset$, we say $Res(a, \langle T, F\rangle) = \langle T \cup E_a^+(\langle T, F\rangle) \setminus E_a^-(\langle T, F\rangle), F \cup E_a^-(\langle T, F\rangle) \setminus E_a^+(\langle T, F\rangle)\rangle$, otherwise we say $Res(a, \langle T, F\rangle)$ is undefined. (Note that, since we restrict our domain description to only contain non-contradicting ef-propositions, the function Res is always defined.)

- Let $\sigma_1 = \langle T_1, F_1\rangle$, and $\sigma_2 = \langle T_2, F_2\rangle$ be two states. We say the state $\langle T_1, F_1\rangle$ extends the state $\langle T_2, F_2\rangle$ if $T_2 \subseteq T_1$ and $F_2 \subseteq F_1$. $\sigma_1 \cap \sigma_2$ is defined as $\langle T_1 \cap T_2, F_1 \cap F_2\rangle$ and $\sigma_1 \setminus \sigma_2$ denotes the set $(T_1 \setminus T_2) \cup (F_1 \setminus F_2)$. For a set of fluent names X we write $X \setminus \langle T, F\rangle = X \setminus (T \cup F)$.

- For an incomplete state $\langle T, F\rangle$, $\mathcal{R}es(a, \langle T, F\rangle)$ denotes the state $\bigcap_{\sigma \in S(\langle T, F\rangle)} Res(a, \sigma)$ where $S(\langle T, F\rangle)$ is the collection of all complete states that extend $\langle T, F\rangle$.

- For a complete state $\langle T, F\rangle$, $K(a, \langle T, F\rangle)$ denotes the set $\{f : f$ is a fluent name and there exists a k-proposition whose action is a, whose k-effect is either f or $\neg f$, and whose preconditions are satisfied in $\langle T, F\rangle\}$.

- For an incomplete state $\langle T, F\rangle$, $\mathcal{K}(a, \langle T, F\rangle)$ denotes the set $\bigcap_{\sigma \in S(\langle T, F\rangle)} K(a, \sigma)$

Example 4 Consider the domain description D_1 from Example 1. The effects of actions, the result functions, and the extended result functions for some actions in D_1 are given below.

$E_{go\_to\_fridge}^+(\langle T, F\rangle) = \{near\_fridge\}$ and $E_{go\_to\_fridge}^-(\langle T, F\rangle) = \emptyset$;
$E_{look\_at\_fridge}^+(\langle T, F\rangle) = E_{look\_at\_fridge}^-(\langle T, F\rangle) = \emptyset$.
$Res(go\_to\_fridge, \langle T, F\rangle) = \langle T \cup \{near\_fridge\}, F \setminus \{near\_fridge\}\rangle$
$Res(look\_at\_fridge, \langle T, F\rangle) = \langle T, F\rangle$
$\mathcal{R}es(go\_to\_fridge, \langle T, F\rangle) = \langle T \cup \{near\_fridge\}, F \setminus \{near\_fridge\}\rangle$
$\mathcal{R}es(look\_at\_fridge, \langle T, F\rangle) = \langle T, F\rangle$ □

Definition 2 A transition function Φ of a domain description D is a mapping of a pair of action a and state σ into a set of states, denoted by $\Phi(a, \sigma)$, where

(i) for a complete state σ, $\Phi(a, \sigma) = \{Res(a, \sigma)\}$, and

(ii) for an incomplete state σ, $\Phi(a, \sigma) = \{\sigma' \mid \sigma'$ extends $Res(a, \sigma)$ and $\sigma' \setminus Res(a, \sigma) = \mathcal{K}(a, \sigma) \setminus Res(a, \sigma)\}$. $\qquad\square$

Note the difference between the definition of transition function above and the definition of transition function in $\mathcal{A}$, where we do not have any sensing actions. In $\mathcal{A}$, the transition function is defined in terms of the Res function. Here, $Res(a, \sigma)$, only specifies what is known to be true and what is known to be false in all states that may be reached by executing a in the state σ. The transition function Φ takes into account Res and $\mathcal{K}$ to define the set of states that may be reached by executing a in σ.

Example 5 The domain description D_1 has a unique model (σ_0, Φ_1), where $\sigma_0 = \langle \emptyset, \emptyset \rangle$, and Φ_1 is specified for every possible pair of states $\langle T, F \rangle$ and actions a. For example,

$\Phi_1(go\_to\_fridge, \langle T, F \rangle) = Res(go\_to\_fridge, \langle T, F \rangle)$ (see Example 4) and

$$\Phi_1(look\_at\_fridge, \langle T, F \rangle) = \begin{cases} \{\langle T \cup \{fridge\_open\}, F \rangle, \\ \quad \langle T, F \cup \{fridge\_open\} \rangle\} \\ \quad \text{if } fridge\_open \notin T \cup F \\ \quad \text{and } near\_fridge \in T \\ \{\langle T, F \rangle\} \quad \text{otherwise} \end{cases}$$

In general, a domain description D might have many transition functions but if the actions in D are deterministic then D has a unique transition function as the function Res is also unique.

Definition 3 Given a domain description D, we say a structure (σ_0, Φ) is a model of D if

(i) for any fluent literal f, f is true w.r.t. σ_0 iff **initially** $f \in D$,

(ii) Φ is a transition function of D. $\qquad\square$

Note that if a is a non-sensing action (i.e., there is no k-proposition whose action is a) then $\mathcal{K}(a, \langle T, F \rangle) = \emptyset$ for every state $\langle T, F \rangle$. Hence, $\Phi(a, \langle T, F \rangle) = \{Res(a, \langle T, F \rangle)\}$ for every state $\langle T, F \rangle$.

Definition 4 For any transition function Φ, we define an extended transition function $\hat{\Phi}$ from conditional plans, and sets of states to power set of states, in the following way:

$$\hat{\Phi}(a, S) = \bigcup_{\sigma \in S} \Phi(a, \sigma)$$

(ii) $\hat{\Phi}(c_1; c_2, S) = \hat{\Phi}(c_2, \hat{\Phi}(c_1, S))$

(iii) Let c be a conditional case plan; then $\hat{\Phi}(c, S)$ is defined as the set

$$\bigcup_{i \leq n} \left(\bigcup_{\sigma \in S, \sigma \models p_{i1}, \dots p_{im_i}} \hat{\Phi}(c_i, \sigma) \right)$$

Example 6 Consider the conditional plan c_1 in Example 2 and the transition function Φ_1 in Example 5. We can easily compute that
$$\hat{\Phi}_1(c_1, \langle \emptyset, \emptyset \rangle) = \{\langle \{fridge\_open, near\_fridge, milk\_in\_fridge, has\_mik\}, \emptyset \rangle,$$
$$\langle \{fridge\_open, has\_milk\}, \{near\_fridge, milk\_in\_fridge\} \rangle \}.$$

Definition 5 Let $M = (\sigma_0, \Phi)$ be a model of a domain description D. We say the query f **after** c is true w.r.t. M, if f is true in all the states in $\hat{\Phi}(c, \sigma_0)$. We say $D \models f$ **after** c, if the query f **after** c is true w.r.t. all models of D. $\square$

Proposition 1 $D_1 \models has\_milk$ **after** c_1

Proof : It is easy to see that D_1 has a unique model of the form $M = (\langle \emptyset, \emptyset \rangle, \Phi_1)$ where Φ_1 is computed in Example 5. Since
$$\hat{\Phi}_1(c_1, \langle \emptyset, \emptyset \rangle) = \{\langle \{near\_fridge, fridge\_open, milk\_in\_fridge, has\_milk\}, \emptyset \rangle,$$
$$\langle \{fridge\_open, has\_mik\}, \{near\_fridge, milk\_in\_fridge\} \rangle \},$$
has_milk is true in every state of $\hat{\Phi}_1(c_1, \langle \emptyset, \emptyset \rangle)$.
Hence, $D_1 \models has\_milk$ **after** c_1. $\square$

3.1 Translation to Disjunctive Logic Programming

In this section we present a translation from a domain description D in $\mathcal{A}_K$ into a disjunctive logic program πD and show that the translation (using answer semantics [3]) is sound w.r.t the entailment relationship in D.

The translation πD of a domain description D, uses variables of three sorts: *situation* variables $S, S', \ldots$, *fluent* variables $F, F', \ldots$, and *action* variables $A, A', \ldots$. Lower case letters are used to denoted constants of the same sort as its upper case counterpart.

In the following we write $R\_holds(L, S)$ ($Holds(L, S)$) to represent $r\_holds(L, S)$ ($holds(L, S)$) if L is a fluent name and $\neg r\_holds(\bar{L}, S)$ ($\neg holds(\bar{L}, S)$) if L is a negative fluent literal where $\bar{L}$ denotes the complementary literal of L. Basically, $holds(F, S)$ ($\neg holds(F, S)$) means that the fluent F is true (false) in the state S and $r\_holds(F, S)$ ($\neg r\_holds(F, S)$) means that the robot knows that the fluent F is true (false) in the state S.

Given a domain description D in $\mathcal{A}_K$ the disjunctive logic program πD corresponding to D will contain following rules.

(i) In the world fluents are either true or false. Hence, for every fluent f in D

$$holds(f, s_0) \vee \neg holds(f, s_0) \leftarrow \tag{5}$$

is a rule in πD.

(ii) The robot knows only what is correct:

$$Holds(F, S) \leftarrow R\_holds(F, S) \tag{6}$$

(iii) For every v-proposition **initially** f

$$R\_holds(f, s_0). \tag{7}$$

is a rule in πD.

(iv) For every ef-proposition a **causes** f **if** $p_1, \ldots, p_n$, the following rules are added to πD.

$$R\_holds(f, Res(a, S)) \quad \leftarrow \quad Holds(p_1, S), \ldots, Holds(p_n, S)$$
$$ab(\bar{f}, a, S) \quad \leftarrow \quad Holds(p_1, S), \ldots, Holds(p_n, S) \tag{8}$$

Intuitively, the above rules encode what the robot thinks is true in the state $Res(a, S)$. But, it tries to reason by cases about the preconditions. For that reason, we have $Holds$, instead of R_holds in the body of the rules.

(v) The inertia axioms

$$R\_holds(F, Res(A, S)) \quad \leftarrow \quad R\_holds(F, S), \; not\; ab(F, A, S)$$
$$Holds(F, Res(A, S)) \quad \leftarrow \quad Holds(F, S), \; not\; ab(F, A, S) \tag{9}$$

(vi) For every k-proposition a **determines** f **if** $p_1, \ldots, p_n$, the program πD will contain the following rule.

$$r\_holds(f, Res(a, S)) \vee \neg r\_holds(f, Res(a, S)) \quad \leftarrow \quad Holds(p_1, S), \ldots,$$
$$Holds(p_n, S) \tag{10}$$

We prove the consistency and soundness of πD in the next propositions.

Proposition 2 (Consistency of πD) Let D be a consistent domain description. Then, the program πD is consistent.

Proposition 3 (Soundness of πD) Let D be a consistent domain description and s_0 be its initial state. Then, for every fluent name f and action a in D, if $\pi D \models r\_holds(f, res(a, s_0))$ (resp. $\pi D \models \neg r\_holds(f, res(a, s_0))$) then $D \models f$ **after** a (resp. $D \models \neg f$ **after** a).

The following example shows that the logic programming translation does not capture the 1-semantics of $\mathcal{A}_K$ completely.

Example 7 Consider the domain description D_2 consisting of the following ef-proposition: a **causes** f **if** $\neg f$.

Suppose that the initial state of D_2 is $s_0 = \langle \emptyset, \emptyset \rangle$. There are two complete extensions of s_0: $s_1 = \langle \{f\}, \emptyset \rangle$ and $s_2 = \langle \emptyset, \{f\} \rangle$. Since $Res(a, s_1) = Res(a, s_2) = s_1$, $Res(a, s_0) = \langle \{f\}, \emptyset \rangle$. It is easy to see that D has only one model Φ in which $\Phi(a, s_0) = \langle \{f\}, \emptyset \rangle$. Therefore, $D_2 \models f$ **after** a.

On the other hand, the unique answer set of πD_2 is $\emptyset$. Hence, $\pi D_2 \not\models r\_holds(f, res(a, s_0))$. $\qquad \square$

We now present an even weaker semantics of $\mathcal{A}_K$, which we call the 0-semantics, that more closely follows Lukasiewicz's logic. We show that the translation π is stronger than this weaker semantics. *One advantage of the 0-semantics is that we have a sound and complete translation of it to disjunctive logic programming.*

4   0-semantics of $\mathcal{A}_K$

Let D be a domain description, $\langle T, F \rangle$ be a state, and f be a fluent name in D. f (resp. $\neg f$) is said to be *possibly correct* in $\langle T, F \rangle$ iff $f \notin F$ (resp. $f \notin T$). A set of fluents $\{f_1, \ldots, f_n\}$ is *possibly correct* in $\langle T, F \rangle$ iff for all i, f_i is possibly correct in $\langle T, F \rangle$. We define,

- $e_a^+(\langle T, F \rangle)$ denotes the set $\{f \mid f$ is a fluent name and there exists an ef-proposition in our domain description whose action is a, effect is f, and whose preconditions are satisfied in $\langle T, F \rangle \}$.

- $e_a^-(\langle T, F \rangle)$ denotes the set $\{f \mid f$ is a fluent name and there exists an ef-proposition in our domain description whose action is a, effect is $\neg f$, and whose preconditions are satisfied in $\langle T, F \rangle \}$.

- $F_a^+(\langle T, F \rangle)$ denotes the set $\{f \mid f$ is a fluent name and there exists an ef-proposition in our domain description whose action is a, effect is f, and whose preconditions are possibly correct in $\langle T, F \rangle \}$.

- $F_a^-(\langle T, F \rangle)$ is defined similarly.

- $k_a(\langle T, F \rangle)$ denotes the set $\{f \mid f$ is a fluent name there exists an k-proposition a **determines** f $(or \neg f)$ **if** $p_1, \ldots, p_n$ in our domain description whose preconditions are satisfied in $\langle T, F \rangle \}$.

It is easy to see that if D does not contain contradictory ef-propositions then $e_a^+(\langle T, F \rangle) \cap F_a^-(\langle T, F \rangle) = \emptyset$ and $e_a^-(\langle T, F \rangle) \cap F_a^+(\langle T, F \rangle) = \emptyset$. The result function is then defined as $Res_W(a, \langle T, F \rangle) = \langle T \cup e_a^+ \setminus F_a^-, F \cup e_a^- \setminus F_a^+ \rangle$. The transition function is then defined as follows.

Definition 6 Given a domain description D, the transition function Φ_W of D is defined by $\Phi_W(a, \langle T, F \rangle) = \{\sigma \mid \sigma$ extends $Res_W(a, \langle T, F \rangle)$ and $\sigma \setminus Res_W(a, \langle T, F \rangle) = k_a(\langle T, F \rangle) \setminus Res_W(a, \langle T, F \rangle)\}$.   □

Definition 7 Given a domain description D, we say a structure (σ_0, Φ_W) is a weak-model of D if
(i) for any fluent literal f, f is true w.r.t. σ_0 iff **initially** $f \in D$,
(ii) Φ_W is a transition function of D.
  Entailment w.r.t. weak models is referred to as weak entailment and is denoted by $\models_w$.   □

The next example shows that the 0-semantics and 1-semantics agrees on the domain D_1.

Proposition 4 $D_1 \models_w has\_milk$ **after** c_1.   □

We now present a logic programming translation π' which exactly captures the weak entailment w.r.t. domain descriptions.

4.1 The translation $\pi'D$

The program $\pi'D$ differs from the program πD in that it only represents and reasons about what the robot knows. The notation $R\_holds(F,S)$ has the same meaning as in πD. $\overline{R\_holds(L,S)}$ stands for $\neg r\_holds(L,S)$ if L is a fluent name and $r\_holds(\bar{L},S)$ if L is a negative fluent literal. Given a domain description D in $\mathcal{A}_K$ the disjunctive logic program $\pi'D$ corresponding to D contains the following rules:

(i) Initially, the robot knows what is given. Hence, for every v-proposition **initially** f

$$R\_holds(f,s_0). \tag{11}$$

is a rule in $\pi'D$.

(ii) For every ef-proposition a **causes** f **if** $p_1,\ldots,p_n$, the following rules are added to $\pi'D$.

$$
\begin{aligned}
R\_holds(f,res(a,S)) &\leftarrow R\_holds(p_1,S),\ldots,R\_holds(p_n,S) \\
ab(\bar{f},a,S) &\leftarrow not\ \overline{R\_Holds(p_1,S)},\ldots,not\ \overline{R\_Holds(p_n,S)}
\end{aligned} \tag{12}
$$

(iii) The inertia axioms

$$R\_holds(F,res(A,S)) \leftarrow R\_holds(F,S),\ not\ ab(F,A,S) \tag{13}$$

(iv) For every k-proposition a **determines** f **if** $p_1,\ldots,p_n$, the program $\pi'D$ will contain the following rule.

$$
\begin{aligned}
r\_holds(f,res(a,S)) \vee \neg r\_holds(f,res(a,S)) &\leftarrow \\
R\_holds(p_1,S),\ldots,R\_holds(p_n,S)
\end{aligned} \tag{14}
$$

In the next propositions we state the consistency, and the soundness and completeness of $\pi'D$ with respect to the weak semantics $\models_w$. (We will present the proof in the full version of the paper.)

Proposition 5 (Consistency of $\pi'D$) Let D be a consistent domain description. Then, the program $\pi'D$ is consistent.

Proposition 6 (Soundness and Completeness of $\pi'D$ w.r.t. $\models_w$) Let D be a consistent domain description and s_0 be its initial state s_0. Then, for every fluent name f and action a in D, $\pi'D \models r\_holds(f,res(a,s_0))$ (resp. $\pi'D \models \neg r\ holds(f,res(a,s_0))$) if and only if $D \models_w f$ **after** a (resp. $D \models_w \neg f$ **after** a).

We now state the relation between the 0-semantics and the 1-semantics of domain descriptions of $\mathcal{A}_K$.

Proposition 7 (Soundness of 0-semantics w.r.t. 1-semantics) For every state $\sigma' \in \Phi_w(a,\sigma)$, there exists a state $\sigma^* \in \Phi(a,\sigma)$ such that $\sigma' \subseteq \sigma^*$.

The next example shows that 1-semantics is more powerful than the 0-semantics.

Example 8 Consider the domain description D_3 with two ef-propositions:

a **causes** f **if** p and a **causes** f **if** $\neg p$.

Suppose that the initial state is $s_0 = \langle \emptyset, \emptyset \rangle$. It is easy to see that in every complete extension of s_0, p is either true or false. Hence, in the 1-semantics, we have $\mathcal{R}es(a, s_0) = \langle \{f\}, \emptyset \rangle$. Furthermore, we can prove that D_3 has only one model Φ (w.r.t. the 1-semantics) where $\Phi(a, s_0) = \langle \{f\}, \emptyset \rangle$. Therefore, $D_3 \models f$ **after** a.

However, in the 0-semantics, we have $e_a^+(s_0) = e_a^-(s_0) = \emptyset$. Hence, $Res_W(a, s_0) = s_0$. It is easy to see that D_3 has a unique model Φ_W (w.r.t. the 0-semantics) where $\Phi_W(a, s_0) = \{s_0\}$. So, $D_3 \not\models_w f$ **after** a.

5 Weakness of the 1-semantics

In the previous example, we showed that the 1-semantics is stronger than the 0-semantics. This is because the 1-semantics reasons by cases, while the 0-semantics does not. On the other hand we have a sound and complete translation of the 0-semantics to disjunctive logic programming, while we only[2] have a sound translation for the 1-semantics. In the next section we discuss why even the 1-semantics is not strong enough to completely capture our intuition.

5.1 Reasoning about preconditions

Suppose we have the k-proposition a **determines** f **if** p and in the initial state p is unknown. In our formulation after executing a our state remains the same. A stronger semantics may reason that either p is true or p is false. If p is true then there would be two sates $\langle \{p, f\}, \emptyset \rangle$, and $\langle \{p\}, \{f\} \rangle$; and if p is false then there would be the state $\langle \emptyset, \{p\} \rangle$. This is what the semantics of [9] does.

We believe this leads to additional complexity and prefer the relative simplicity of our approach. Nevertheless, we can simulate the above reasoning by thinking that the action a actually is sequentially composed of two actions a_1 and a_2, where a_1 **determines** p and a_2 **determines** f **if** p. Then our approach captures the suggested meaning.

5.2 Reasoning about sequences of actions

A more serious weakness of 1-semantics[3] (and consequently also of the 0-semantics) manifests when reasoning about a sequence of actions in presence of completeness.

---

[2] We have not been able to find a complete translation to disjunctive logic programming. We suspect that no such translation exists, and we need logic programming with epistemic operators for a complete translation.

[3] We thank the anonymous AAAI97 reviewer who pointed this out. It should be also noted that this paper and [9] were independently done around the same time.

Example 9 Consider the following domain description D_4:

a **causes** p **if** r ; a **causes** q **if** $\neg r$

b **causes** f **if** p ; b **causes** f **if** q

Suppose that the initial state is $\langle \emptyset, \emptyset \rangle$, where p, q, r, and f are unknown. Although, intuitively, after executing a followed by b in the initial state, f should be true, our 1-semantics is not able to capture this. This is because, the 1-semantics reasons by cases only upto 1-level. Since after reasoning by cases for 1-level, it summarizes its reasoning to a pair $\langle T, F \rangle$ of sets, it is not able to capture the fact that after executing a in the initial state $p \vee q$ is true.   □

Note that, the above example does not have any sensing actions, and even the semantics of $\mathcal{A}$ [4] is able to capture the intuitive meaning. But in $\mathcal{A}$, there is no separation between what is true in the world and what is known to the reasoner. *Since we incorporate sensing, our semantics captures what is known to the reasoner.*

For the reasoner to more accurately reason about his beliefs, he needs either carry more information from one state to another, or he needs to reason by cases for multiple levels. The first approach is taken in [9], and [12], where states are sets of 3-valued interpretations, and Kripke models, resp.

We prefer the second approach, and can define n-semantics (for any number n), where the reasoner does reasoning by cases, for n-levels, guaranteeing intuitive reasoning skills (equivalent to [9]) upto sequences of n actions. The reason we prefer this approach is that the reasoner depending on the time it has can choose the appropriate n. This corresponds to the notion of anytime-reasoning in AI. We will further discuss this issue and present the general formulation of n-semantics in the full paper.

6 Properties of 1-semantics and 0-semantics

In this section we prove some general results about 0-semantics and 1-semantics that show their intuitiveness in capturing the meaning of sensing actions. Sherl and Levesque prove similar results for their formalization in [12].

We first show that a knowledge producing action a does not normally (formalized precisely in Proposition 8) change the truth value of a fluent f whose truth value is either *true* or *false* in the state before the execution of a. We then show that our formalization ensures that there will be no unwanted knowledge change when actions are executed.

Let a be an action and s be a state in the domain description D. We say that a does not affect a fluent f in a state s if the following condition holds:

    (i) For every ef-proposition a **causes** f **if** $p_1, \ldots, p_n$

        $\{p_1, \ldots, p_n\}$ *is not possibly correct in s and*

    (ii) For every k-proposition a **determines** f **if** $p_1, \ldots, p_m$

$\{p_1, \ldots, p_m\}$ *is not possibly correct in* s.

Furthermore, for a fluent f and a state $\langle T, F \rangle$ in D, we define

$$\mathbf{Knows}(f, \langle T, F \rangle) \;\stackrel{def}{\equiv}\; f \in T \cup F$$

Intuitively, $\mathbf{Knows}(f, \langle T, F \rangle)$ holds when we know the truth value of the fluent f in the situation s.

Proposition 8 (Knowledge Producing Effects of 1-semantics and 0-semantics) Consider a consistent domain description D with a model (σ_0, Φ) (resp. (σ_0, Φ_W)). Let a be a knowledge producing action and s be a state in D such that there exists no ef-proposition in D whose action is a and whose preconditions are possibly correct in s. Then, if f is true (or false) w.r.t. s then f is true (or false) w.r.t. every state s' in $\Phi(a, s)$ (resp. $\Phi_W(a, s)$).

The above proposition points out the difference between non-deterministic actions (see e.g. [6]) and knowledge producing actions. A knowledge producing action a, that is only supposed to determine the truth value of a fluent f, does not change the truth value of fluent f if its truth value is either *true* or *false* before a is executed. On the other hand the truth value of f may change when executing a non-deterministic action that non-deterministically changes the truth value of f.

Proposition 9 (Knowledge Inertial Effects of 1-semantics and 0-semantics) Consider a consistent domain description D with a model (σ_0, Φ) (resp. (σ_0, Φ_W)). Let a be an action and a state s in D. Then, for every fluent f, if $\mathbf{Knows}(f, s)$ $(\neg\mathbf{Knows}(f, s))$ and a does not affect f in s then $\mathbf{Knows}(f, s')$ $(\neg\mathbf{Knows}(f, s))$ for $s' \in \Phi(a, s)$ (resp. $s' \in \Phi_W(a, s)$).

7 Conclusion

In this paper we presented two approximate formulations of sensing actions in terms of 3-valued logic. Our formulation was first at the level of a high level language and later we presented translations to disjunctive logic programs.

Although, translation of action theories to disjunctive logic programs were done for non-sensing action theories, the current translation has the novelty that we have disjunctions about non-initial states. Earlier translations only required disjunctions about the initial state.

Our language $\mathcal{A}_K$ differs from the language GOLOG (see e.g. [11] and the references therein) in several respects. GOLOG is a language for describing and executing complex plans, whereas $\mathcal{A}_K$ is a high-level language for reasoning about sensing and non-sensing actions, and conditional plans. Second, our conditional plan does not allow loop, whereas complex plans in GOLOG are more general and allow loops.

Our use of three valued logic to capture knowledge was driven by the goal of simplifying the process of planning with incomplete information. As it is,

planning with complete information is expensive, and having Kripke-models or set of 3-valued interpretations as states is going to make it much more expensive to plan in presence of incomplete information. Hence we choose approximations that have states as 3-valued interpretations. The only widely available planner that plans with sensing actions seem to agree with us. In [5] the authors say:
"In UWL (and in SADL) individual literals have truth values expressed in a three-valued logic: T, F, U." Moreover, our approximation semantics can be extended to be equivalent to [9] upto any levels of reasoning. In the full paper we will formally state this result.

References

[1] F. Bacchus, F. Kabanza. Planning for Temporally Extended Goals. In *Proc. of AAAI '96*, 1215–1222, 1996.

[2] O. Etzioni et al. An approach to planning with incomplete information. In *Proc. of KR'92*, 115–125, 1992.

[3] M. Gelfond and V. Lifschitz. Logic Programs with Classical Negation. In *Proceeding of the 7th ICLP, MIT Press*, 579 –597, 1990.

[4] M. Gelfond and V. Lifschitz. Representing actions and change by logic programs. *Journal of Logic Programming*, 17(2,3,4):301–323, 1993.

[5] K. Golden and D. Weld. Representing sensing actions: the middle ground revisited. In *Proc. of KR'96*, pages 174-185, 1996.

[6] G.N. Kartha. A mathematical investigation of reasoning about actions. *Ph.D dissertation. University of Texas at Austin*, 1995.

[7] K. Krebsbach, D. Olawsky, and M. Gini. An empirical study of sensing and defaulting in planning. In *First Conference of AI Planning Systems*, 136–144, 1992.

[8] H.J. Levesque. What is planning in the presence of sensing. In *Proc. of AAAI'96*, 1139–1146, 1996.

[9] J. Lobo, S. Taylor, and G. Mendez. Adding knowledge to the action description language $\mathcal{A}$. To appear in Proc. of AAAI'97.

[10] J. Lukasiewicz. A system of modal logic. *Journal of Computing Systems* 1, 111-149.

[11] Levesque, H., Reiter, R., Lesperance, Y., Lin, F. and Scherl, R. Golog: A Logic programming language for dynamic domains. *Journal of Logic Progamming* 31, 59–84, 1997.

[12] R. Scherl and H.J. Levesque. Knowledge Producing Actions. In *Proc. of KR*, 1139-1146, 1994.

[13] D. Weld. An introduction to least commitment planning. *AI magazine*, 27–61, Winter 94.

Poster Abstracts

On Well-Behaved Semantics Suitable for Aggregation

Jürgen Dix
University of Koblenz, Dept. of CS,
Rheinau 1, 56075 Koblenz, Germany
dix@informatik.uni-koblenz.de

Mauricio Osorio
Universidad de las America
Dept. de Ingenieria en Sistemas Computacionales
Sta. Catarina Martir, Cholula, Puebla,
72820 Mexico, Mexico
osorio@cs.buffalo.edu

Abstract

In this paper we study semantics WFS^0, WFS^1 for DATALOG programs by extending the calculus of Brass and Dix ([1, 2]) with more transformation rules. These extended calculi still share the same nice properties as the base calculus: they are confluent and terminating. In addition, WFS^0 is *rational*, *well-behaved* and *polynomial-time computable*. Even more important, our experiments suggest that such semantics can be used for potential applications in modelling *aggregation* in deductive databases. Previous work has been done by the second author recently ([3]).

References

[1] Stefan Brass and Jürgen Dix. Characterizations of the Disjunctive Stable Semantics by Partial Evaluation. *Journal of Logic Programming*, 32(3):207–228, 1997.

[2] Stefan Brass and Jürgen Dix. Characterizations of the Disjunctive Well-founded Semantics: Confluent Calculi and Iterated GCWA. *Journal of Automated Reasoning*, to appear, 1998.

[3] Mauricio Osorio and Bharat Jayaraman. Aggregation and WFS^+. In J. Dix, L. Pereira, and T. Przymusinski, editors, *Nonmonotonic Extensions of Logic Programming*, LNAI 1216, pages 71–90. Springer, Berlin, 1997.

OPENLOG: A logical language to program reactive and rational agents

Jacinto A. Dávila

jacinto@ing.ula.ve
CESIMO - Universidad de Los Andes
Mérida, 5101A, Venezuela
http://www.ing.ula.ve
Phone: +58 74 40 28 79 Fax: +58 74 40 11 16

Abstract

This poster introduces a language to program a reactive and rational agent such as that described in [2], [3] and [1]. The new programming language, called OPENLOG, has its semantics described as a logic program which can also work as the interpreter for the language. One of the innovations in OPENLOG is that between any two actions in a program sequence it is always possible to "insert" a third event without disrupting the semantics of the programming language. The language is OPEN in the sense that programs written in it can be interrupted at anytime to allow for assimilation of inputs.

The language is based on a *background theory* of actions that supports logical descriptions of dynamic universes with fluents, event concurrency and synergistic effects. The background theory can be formalised using either the Situation Calculus [5] or the Event Calculus [4].

References

[1] Jacinto Dávila. *Agents in Logic Programming*. PhD thesis, Imperial College, London, May 1997.

[2] Robert Kowalski. Using metalogic to reconcile reactive with rational agents. In K. Apt and F. Turini, editors, *Meta-Logics and Logic Programming*. MIT Press, 1995. (Also at http://www-lp.doc.ic.ac.uk/UserPages/staff/rak/recon-abst.html).

[3] Robert Kowalski and Fariba Sadri. Towards a unified agent architecture that combines rationality with reactivity. 1997. To appear. (Also at http://www-lp.doc.ic.ac.uk/UserPages/staff/fs/unify.html).

[4] Robert Kowalski and Marek Sergot. A logic-based calculus of events. *New Generation Computing*, 4:67–95, 1986.

[5] J. McCarthy and P. Hayes. Some philosophical problems from the standpoint of artificial intelligence. *Machine Intelligence*, 4:463–502, 1969.

Type Inference for CLP($\mathcal{FD}$)[1]

Paweł Pietrzak
Department of Computer and Information Science
Linköping University
S-581 83 Linköping, Sweden
pawpi@ida.liu.se

Abstract

We describe an approach to types in CLP($\mathcal{FD}$) (we consider a programming language CHIP restricted to finite domains) [Hen89] and show a method of type inference. We treat the type of a particular variable as a set of its all possible values, that is as a set of ground terms. These sets are specified by a regular grammar or equivalently by a *regular unary logic* program. We also allow types for finite domain variables. A type for such a variable is its domain (i.e the set of all values it can take). These finite domain types can occur as leaves of terms denoting regular types.

To perform type inference for CLP($\mathcal{FD}$) we propose to adopt and extend the system described in [SG95]. In this approach the programmer may impose (polymorphic) types on selected symbols. It is also possible to introduce a set of pre-defined, built-in types. The analysis applies a fixpoint bottom-up algorithm based on the *regular approximation* method.

We have extended the above system wrt finite domains. Pre-defined types for finite domains and some types for most common terms (like lists) are introduced. We also impose types for built-in predicates operating on finite domain variables. Then we add an extra step on the very beginning of the analysis. In this stage the system performs propagation of finite domains in a scope of a single clause. It is an application of the *looking ahead inference rule* restricted to one clause. Then the system replaces domain variables by terms describing respective types. Finite domain types are described simply by lists containing domains or by intervals.

A prototype version of our type inference system has been implemented.

References

[Hen89] P. Van Hentenryck. *Constraint Satisfaction in Logic Programming.* MIT Press, 1989.

[SG95] H. Saglam and J. Gallagher. Approximating Constraint Logic Programs Using Polymorphic Types and Regular Descriptions. Technical Report CSTR-95-017, Department of Computer Science, University of Bristol, 1995.

---

[1]This work was supported by ESPRIT project DiSCiPl (22532).

Disjunctive Completion Is Not "Optimal"

Helmut Seidl
FB IV - Informatik, University of Trier, Germany,
seidl@uni-trier.de

Christian Fecht
Department of Computer Science, Universität des Saarlandes,
Saarbrücken, Germany, fecht@cs.uni-sb.de

Enhancing ordinary analysis of Prolog with abstract domain D by using disjunctive completion $\mathcal{P}(D)$ instead of D [1] may gain precision, but still is at most as precise as abstract OLDT-resolution with D [2, 3]. While OLDT with $\mathcal{P}(D)$ gains nothing over OLDT with D, we give an example which proves that ordinary analysis with $\mathcal{P}(D)$ may *lose* information against OLDT with D and hence cannot be "optimal". Consider program:

$$s(X,Y,Z) \leftarrow a(X,Y,Z), p(X,Y,Z). \qquad a(X,Y,Z) \leftarrow X = Y.$$
$$p(X,Y,Z) \leftarrow . \qquad a(X,Y,Z) \leftarrow Y = Z.$$

for query $s(X,Y,Z)$ and assume we would like to compute *pair-sharing* information with pair-sharing domain PS of Søndergaard [4]. The possible sharing arriving before the call to p is given between X and Y or Y and Z, respectively. OLDT-resolution for the call to p propagates these two values separately and therefore returns just these values also for the program point behind the call to p. On the contrary, ordinary analysis using $\mathcal{P}(\text{PS})$, cannot propagate the two values separately. Instead, it *combines* all possible return values for p with all possible values *before* the call. Therefore, it introduces a further possible sharing, namely between X and Z – and thus loses precision.

References

[1] Gilberto Filé and Francesco Ranzato. Improving Abstract Interpretations by Systematic Lifting to the Powerset. In *SLP'94*, 655–669. MIT Press, 1994.

[2] Pascal Van Hentenryck, Olivier Degimbe, Baudouin Le Charlier, and Laurent Michel. Abstract Interpretation of Prolog Based on OLDT Resolution. Tech. Rep. CS-93-05, Brown University, Providence, RI 02912, 1993.

[3] Helmut Seidl and Christian Fecht. Interprocedural Analysis Based on PDAs. Tech. Rep. 97-06, Trier, 1997.

[4] Harald Søndergaard. An Application of Abstract Interpretation of Logic Programs: Occur Check Reduction. In *ESOP'86*, 327–338. LNCS 213, 1986.

Controlling the Search in Tabled Evaluations

Juliana Freire   David S. Warren

Department of Computer Science
State University of New York at Stony Brook
Stony Brook, NY 11794-4400
{juliana,warren} @cs.sunysb.edu

Abstract

Tabled evaluation ensures termination for programs with finite models by distinguishing calls to tabled subgoals. Given several variant subgoals in an evaluation, only the first (the generator) will use program clause resolution, the rest (consumers) must perform answer resolution using answers computed by the original invocation. This use of answer resolution prevents the possibility of infinite looping for Datalog programs, which sometimes occurs in SLD. As variant subgoals can be called at different stages of the evaluation, there is an intrinsic asynchrony between the generation and consumption of answers. Given this asynchrony, implementations of tabled logic programs face an important scheduling choice not present in traditional top-down evaluation: When to return answers to consumer subgoals.

We have experimented with different orders of scheduling the return of answers to consumer nodes as well as the resolution of tabled subgoals, and have derived a number of different scheduling strategies (see e.g., [2] and [3]). Each of these strategies has very specific characteristics. Local Scheduling, for instance, by following the dynamic dependencies between subgoals avoids non-productive computation in the presence of answer subsumption and thus, achieves good performance for applications such as aggregate computations and program analyses. Even though Local Scheduling performs well in general, there are cases where it leads to unacceptable performance, and the same can be said of other scheduling strategies. Since different applications have different requirements, the ability to use multiple strategies in an evaluation is likely to be beneficial. We discuss the issues involved in combining scheduling strategies in an SLG evaluation [1] and describe an implementation which provides engine-level support for integrating different strategies at the predicate level.

References

[1] W. Chen and D.S. Warren. Tabled Evaluation with Delaying for General Logic Programs. *JACM*, 43(1):20–74, January 1996.

[2] J. Freire, T. Swift, and D.S. Warren. Beyond depth-first: Improving tabled logic programs through alternative scheduling strategies. *Journal of Functional and Logic Programming*, 1997. To appear.

[3] J. Freire, T. Swift, and D.S. Warren. Taking I/O seriously: Resolution reconsidered for disk. In *Proceedings of the International Conference on Logic Programming (ICLP)*, pages 198–212, 1997.

Post-Conference Workshops

Specialization of Declarative Programs and its Applications

Michael Leuschel (workshop coordinator)
Department of Computer Science, Katholieke Universiteit Leuven
Celestijnenlaan 200A, B-3001 Heverlee, Belgium
michael@cs.kuleuven.ac.be

Program Committee

Saumya Debray, University of Arizona, USA
John Gallagher, University of Bristol, UK
Manuel Hermenegildo, University of Madrid, Spain
Neil Jones, University of Copenhagen, Denmark
Michael Leuschel, University of Leuven, Belgium

Workshop Overview

Program specialization [2, 3], also called *partial evaluation* [1, 5, 6], *partial deduction* [7] or *supercompilation* [4], is an automatic tool for program optimization, similar in concept to, but in several ways stronger than highly optimizing compilers. The central idea is to specialize a given source program for a particular application domain. This is (mostly) done by a well-automated application of parts of the Burstall and Darlington unfold/fold transformation framework [8].

Program specialization encompasses traditional compiler optimization techniques, such as *constant folding* and *in-lining* used in compilers, but uses more aggressive transformations, yielding both (much) greater speedups and more difficulty in controlling the transformation process. Program specialization can be used to speed up existing programs for certain application domains, sometimes achieving speedups of several orders of magnitude. It however also allows the user to write programs at a higher level using a more secure, readable and maintainable style. The program specializer then takes care of transforming this readable, but inefficient program into an efficient one.

Declarative programming languages, are high-level programming languages in which one only has to state *what* is to be computed and not necessarily *how* it is to be computed. Because of their clear (and often simple) semantical foundations, declarative languages offer significant advantages for the design of semantic based program analyzers, transformers and optimizers.

The aim of this workshop is to discuss new trends, ideas and developments concerning the specialization of declarative languages, especially geared towards trying to exploit the advantages of these languages in practice. The workshop is thereby not limited to the field of logic programming — contributions from other fields involved with the declarative programming paradigm, like e.g. functional programming, will be presented and cross-fertilization is sought.

The proceedings will be published as a technical report of the University of Leuven and will also be available on the world-wide-web via: `http://www.cs.kuleuven.ac.be/~michael/workshop.html` or `http://www.cs.kuleuven.ac.be/~lpai`.

References

[1] C. Consel and O. Danvy. Tutorial notes on partial evaluation. In *Proceedings of ACM Symposium on Principles of Programming Languages (POPL'93)*, Charleston, South Carolina, January 1993. ACM Press.

[2] D. De Schreye, M. Leuschel, and B. Martens. Tutorial on program specialisation (abstract). In J. W. Lloyd, editor, *Proceedings of ILPS'95, the International Logic Programming Symposium*, Portland, USA, December 1995. MIT Press.

[3] J. Gallagher. Tutorial on specialisation of logic programs. In *Proceedings of PEPM'93, the ACM Sigplan Symposium on Partial Evaluation and Semantics-Based Program Manipulation*, pages 88–98. ACM Press, 1993.

[4] R. Glück and M. H. Sørensen. A roadmap to supercompilation. In O. Danvy, R. Glück, and P. Thiemann, editors, *Proceedings of the 1996 Dagstuhl Seminar on Partial Evaluation*, LNCS 1110, pages 137–160, Schloß Dagstuhl, 1996. Springer-Verlag.

[5] N. D. Jones. An introduction to partial evaluation. *ACM Computing Surveys*, 28(3):480–503, September 1996.

[6] N. D. Jones, C. K. Gomard, and P. Sestoft. *Partial Evaluation and Automatic Program Generation*. Prentice Hall, 1993.

[7] J. Komorowski. An introduction to partial deduction. In A. Pettorossi, editor, *Proceedings Meta'92*, LNCS 649, pages 49–69. Springer-Verlag, 1992.

[8] A. Pettorossi and M. Proietti. Transformation of logic programs: Foundations and techniques. *The Journal of Logic Programming*, 19& 20:261–320, May 1994.

Workshop DYNAMICS 97: (Trans)Actions and Change in Logic Programming and Deductive Databases

Anthony Bonner
University of Toronto, Dep. of Computer Science
Toronto, Ontario M5S 3H5, Canada
bonner@db.toronto.edu

Burkhard Freitag
University of Passau, Dep. of Computer Science
D-94030 Passau, Germany
freitag@fmi.uni-passau.de

Laura Giordano
University of Torino, Dep. of Computer Science
Corso Svizzera 185, I-10149 Torino, Italy
laura@di.unito.it

Robert Kowalski
Imperial College, Dep. of Computing
180 Queen's Gate, London SW7 2BZ, UK
rak@doc.ic.ac.uk

Abstract

The static semantics of logic programming languages and the evaluation of queries is well understood. However, there is no consensus about the appropriate treatment of dynamic behaviour, i.e., the evolution of databases or even entire programs with time. Thus, in spite of substantial progress in the theory and implementation of logic programming and deductive databases, they are likely to be ruled out as platforms for information systems unless viable and widely accepted solutions are found to the question of dynamics. In addition, the need is not only for complex rule bases, but also for standard database functionality, such as concurrent access, transaction isolation and atomicity, large amounts of data, data distribution, recovery from system failures, etc. The problems to be solved span all of logic programming and databases, from theory to implementation.

Among others, the following topics have to be addressed: abduction, active logic databases, concurrency, consistency and integrity, cooperation, communication, and interaction between actions, distributed (trans)actions, dynamic agents, dynamic constraints, dynamics of logic and database systems, the frame problem, hypothetical query answering, implementation issues, logical transactions and updates, planning, reactive systems, reasoning about update programs, reasoning about workflows, semantics and proof theory, transaction specification, updating incomplete information, updates vs revision, and workflow specification.

Fortunately, a number of solid approaches to dynamic behavior are beginning to emerge. This workshop is intended to bring together researchers in the field and to stimulate discussion on the foundations of (trans)actions and change in logic programming and deductive databases.

Tools and Environments for (Constraint) Logic Programming

Germán Puebla (coordinator)
Technical University of Madrid (UPM), Spain
german@fi.upm.es

Marco Comini
University of Pisa, Italy
comini@di.unipi.it

Wlodek Drabent
Polish Academy of Sci., and Linköping University, Sweden
wdr@mimuw.edu.pl

Mireille Ducassé
IRISA / INSA de Rennes, France
Mireille.Ducasse@irisa.fr

Massimo Fabris
ICON, Italy
fabris@icon.it

Christian Schulte
DFKI GmbH, Saarbruecken, Germany
schulte@dfki.uni-sb.de

Micha Meier
Germany
mmeier@gmtag.de

1   Description

Logic Programming presents in many cases important advantages over imperative programming and other declarative paradigms. The last few years have witnessed the development of many useful extensions to logic programming such as support for parallel, concurrent, and distributed programming or the constraint logic programming paradigm, with clear industrial applications. However, although the industrial impact of (constraint) logic programming is substantial compared to other new programming paradigms, it is still far from widespread. One of the factors that can presumably make the use of logic programming and its extensions more pervasive by industry is the availability of advanced programming environments which facilitate the development, debugging, and exploitation of systems based on these paradigms. Moreover, some of the extensions to logic programming make understanding the performance of program execution more difficult. This workshop aims at fostering interaction among different researchers and groups currently working on the design and implementation of practical tools and environments for the development of (constraint) logic programs and related paradigms.

2 Papers to be Presented at the Workshop

- *Type Inference for CLP(FD).* Paweł Pietrzak.

- *MOGUL: a Graphical environment for developing the LOGFLOW parallel Prolog system.* P. Kacsuk, J. Kovacs, and N. Podhorszki.

- *On the Design of an Automatic Tool for Prolog Program Verification.* A. Cortesi, B. Le Charlier, C. Leclère, and S. Rossi.

- *An operational model for the SCLP language.* Stefano Bistarelli and Elvinia Riccobene.

- *Modular Abstract Diagnosis.* Marco Comini, Giorgio Levi, and Giuliana Vitiello.

- *An Assertion Language for Debugging of Constraint Logic Programs.* Germán Puebla, Francisco Bueno, and Manuel Hermenegildo.

- *The TUFF train scheduler.* P. Kreuger, M. Carlsson, J. Olsson, T. Sjöland, and E. Åström.

- *The ECCE Partial Deduction System.* Michael Leuschel.

- *Towards a Structuration of the Constraint Store.* Frédéric Benhamou and Frédéric Goualard.

- *The DiSCiPl Project: Debugging Systems for Constraint Programming.* Pierre Deransart (Invited talk).

3 Proceedings

Informal proceedings will be available at the workshop and electronic versions of abstracts accepted for presentation will be collected in the WWW at http://www.clip.dia.fi.upm.es/Tools_Environ/proceedings.html and will remain available after the workshop.

Logic Programming and Knowledge Representation (LPKR'97)

Jürgen Dix
University of Koblenz, Dept. of CS,
Rheinau 1, 56075 Koblenz, Germany
dix@informatik.uni-koblenz.de

Teodor C. Przymusinski
University of California at Riverside,
Dept. of CS, Riverside, CA 92521, USA
teodor@cs.ucr.edu

Luís Moniz Pereira
Universidade Nova de Lisboa, Dept. of CS
2825 Monte da Caparica, Portugal
lmp@di.fct.unl.pt

General Description

The development of machines that are able to reason and act intelligently is one of the most challenging and desirable tasks ever attempted by humanity. It is therefore not surprising that the investigation of techniques for representing and reasoning about knowledge has become an area of paramount importance to the whole field of Computer Science. Due to logic programming's declarative nature, and its amenability to implementation, it quickly became a prime candidate for a knowledge representation language. Impressive research progress of the past decade made the role of logic programming as a major knowledge representation tool even more apparent by establishing close relationships between logic programs, deductive databases and other non-monotonic reasoning formalisms. This impressive progress, coupled with the advent of low cost multiprocessor machines and significant advances in logic programming implementation techniques, now provides us with a great opportunity to bring to fruition computationally efficient implementations of extended logic programming and use it as a powerful knowledge representation tool.

This is the third (after ICLP'94 and JICSLP'96) in a series of workshops which we are organizing in conjunction with Logic Programming conferences. However, as shown by the following list of suggested topics, its scope is significantly broader than the previous ones.

Programme Committee and Programme

The following 11 papers were selected out of 17 from the PC consisting of the organizers and *Phan Minh Dung Thailand, Robert Kowalski (UK), Vladimir Lifschitz (USA), Jack Minker (USA), Chiaki Sakama (Japan), Mirek Truszczynski (USA) and David Warren (USA)*.

Accepted Papers: G. Brewka: *Preferred Answer Sets*, H. Decker: *A Model Based Semantics for Integrity in Deductive Databases*, M. Gelfond and T.C. Son: *Reasoning with Prioritized Defaults*, S. Greco, N. Leone and F. Scarcello: *Disjunctive Datalog with Nested Rules*, E. Lamma, M. Milano, P. Mello and F. Riguzzi: *A System for Learning Abductive Logic Programs*, J. Leite and L. Pereira: *Generalizing Updates: From Models to Programs*, R. Li, L. Pereira and V. Dahl: *Refining Action Theories Through Abductive Logic Programming*, D. Seipel: *Partial Evidential Stable Models for Disjunctive Databases*, K. Wang: *Abduction, argumentation and bi-disjunctive LP*, A. Yahya: *Updates in Disjunctive Deductive Databases: A Minimal Model Based Approach*, L.-Y. Yuan and J.-H. You: *An Introspective Logic of Belief*.

Proceedings and Suggested Topics

The topics of the workshop are *LP Functionalities:* abduction, communication, contradiction removal, declarative debugging, knowledge and belief revision, learning, reasoning about actions, updates. *LP Integrations:* coupling knowledge sources, combining functionalities, logical agent architecture, multi-agents architecture. *LP Language Extensions:* constructive default negation, disjunctive programs, default and epistemic extensions, metalevel programming, object-oriented programming, paraconsistency, reactive rules, strong and explicit negation. *LP Applications to Knowledge Representations:* heterogeneous databases, model-based diagnosis, modeling production systems, planning, reactive databases, relations to non–monotonic formalisms, software engineering. *LP Implementations:* computational procedures, implementations.

The preliminary proceedings will be available by October 1 from the following address `http://www.uni-koblenz.de/~dix/LPKR97/`. Like for the preceding workshops ([1] and [2]) we plan proceedings to be published by Springer. There will be a separate refereeing process where all participants of the workshop are allowed to submit papers.

[1] J. Dix, L. Pereira, and T. Przymusinski, editors. *Non-Monotonic Extensions of Logic Programming*, LNAI 927, Berlin, 1995. Springer.

[2] J. Dix, L. Pereira, and T. Przymusinski, editors. *Non-Monotonic Extensions of Logic Programming*, LNAI 1216, Berlin, 1997. Springer.

ILPS'97 Post-Conference Workshop on

Verification, Model Checking and Abstract Interpretation

Organizing Committee:

Annalisa Bossi (Coordinator)
University Ca' Foscari of Venice, Italy
bossi@dsi.unive.it

Dennis Dams
Eindhoven Univ. of Technology, The Netherlands
wsindd@win.tue.nl

Gilberto Filé
University of Padova, Italy.
gilberto@math.unipd.it

Elena Marchiori
University Ca' Foscari of Venice, Italy
elena@dsi.unive.it

Motivations and Goals

Program verification aims at proving that programs meet their specifications, i.e., that the actual program behaviour coincides with the desired one. *Abstract interpretation* is a method for designing and comparing semantics of programs, expressing various types of programs properties. In particular, it has been successfully used to infer run-time program properties that can be valuable to optimize programs. *Model checking* is a specific approach to the verification of temporal properties of reactive and concurrent systems, which has proven successful in the area of finite-state programs.

Clearly, among these three methods, there are similarities concerning their goals and their domains of applications. Furthermore, while much research has been performed in the area of abstract interpretation of logic programs, connections between model checking and logic programming have hardly been investigated as yet; at the same time it seems that there may be interesting directions in this area. Besides model checking of (concurrent) logic programs, one may also think of the use of specialized constraint (logic) solvers to tackle the model checking problem.

The main goal of the workshop is to enhance cross-fertilization among these areas and in this way to clarify their relationships.

Contributions

The main topics covered by the submitted papers are as follows.

- **Comparison of abstract interpretation and verification of logic programs**: it is shown that abstract interpretation can be viewed as an automatic method for logic program verification in some abstract axiomatic semantics; moreover, a framework based on abstract interpretation is proposed for the design and evaluation of verification methods.

- **Declarative analysis and verification of logic programs**: an experimental tool for deriving fine-grained descriptions of the declarative behaviour of logic programs is introduced; a declarative method for the verification of logic programs is compared with proof methods based on pre/post assertions.

- **Interprocedural analysis**: a framework for the interprocedural analysis of imperative and logic programs based on pushdown automata is investigated.

- **Abstract model-checking**: abstract interpretation is used for model-checking of process algebra.

- **Techniques for verification, abstract interpretation and model-checking applied to concurrent languages**: implementation of a model checker in a logic program; refinement methods for abstractions; over- and under-approximations to explicitly treat negation in specifications; a calculus based on assertional reasoning for the development of systems in a specific coordination model.

- **Formalisms for the verification of systems where the notion of time is relevant**: a framework for specifying and automatically verifying real time systems is proposed. Temporal epistemic logic is shown to be a suitable logic for verification of knowledge-based systems.

Proceedings

The proceedings are published as a technical report of the University of Venice and are available on the world-wide-web.
See http://www.dsi.unive.it/~bossi/VMCAI.html for further information.

Author Index

Logic Programming

Ehud Shapiro, editor

Koichi Furukawa, Jean-Louis Lassez, Fernando Pereira, and David H. D. Warren, associate editors

The Art of Prolog: Advanced Programming Techniques, Leon Sterling and Ehud Shapiro, 1986

Logic Programming: Proceedings of the Fourth International Conference (volumes 1 and 2), edited by Jean-Louis Lassez, 1987

Concurrent Prolog: Collected Papers (volumes 1 and 2), edited by Ehud Shapiro, 1987

Logic Programming: Proceedings of the Fifth International Conference and Symposium (volumes 1 and 2), edited by Robert A. Kowalski and Kenneth A. Bowen, 1988

Constraint Satisfaction in Logic Programming, Pascal Van Hentenryck, 1989

Logic-Based Knowledge Representation, edited by Peter Jackson, Han Reichgelt, and Frank van Harmelen, 1989

Logic Programming: Proceedings of the Sixth International Conference, edited by Giorgio Levi and Maurizio Martelli, 1989

Meta-Programming in Logic Programming, edited by Harvey Abramson and M. H. Rogers, 1989

Logic Programming: Proceedings of the North American Conference 1989 (volumes 1 and 2), edited by Ewing L. Lusk and Ross A. Overbeek, 1989

Logic Programming: Proceedings of the 1990 North American Conference, edited by Saumya Debray and Manuel Hermenegildo, 1990

Logic Programming: Proceedings of the Seventh International Conference, edited by David H. D. Warren and Peter Szeredi, 1990

The Craft of Prolog, Richard A. O'Keefe, 1990

The Practice of Prolog, edited by Leon S. Sterling, 1990

Eco-Logic: Logic-Based Approaches to Ecological Modelling, David Robertson, Alan Bundy, Robert Muetzelfeldt, Mandy Haggith, and Michael Uschold, 1991

Warren's Abstract Machine: A Tutorial Reconstruction, Hassan Aït-Kaci, 1991

Parallel Logic Programming, Evan Tick, 1991

Logic Programming: Proceedings of the Eighth International Conference, edited by Koichi Furukawa, 1991

Logic Programming: Proceedings of the 1991 International Symposium, edited by Vijay Saraswat and Kazunori Ueda, 1991

Foundations of Disjunctive Logic Programming, Jorge Lobo, Jack Minker, and Arcot Rajasekar, 1992

Types in Logic Programming, edited by Frank Pfenning, 1992

Logic Programming: Proceedings of the Joint International Conference and Symposium on Logic Programming, edited by Krzysztof Apt, 1992

Concurrent Constraint Programming, Vijay A. Saraswat, 1993

Logic Programming Languages: Constraints, Functions, and Objects, edited by K. R. Apt, J. W. de Bakker, and J. M. M. Rutten, 1993

Logic Programming: Proceedings of the Tenth International Conference on Logic Programming, edited by David S. Warren, 1993

Constraint Logic Programming: Selected Research, edited by Frédéric Benhamou and Alain Colmerauer, 1993

A Grammatical View of Logic Programming, Pierre Deransart and Jan Maluszyński, 1993

Logic Programming: Proceedings of the 1993 International Symposium, edited by Dale Miller, 1993

The Gödel Programming Language, Patricia Hill and John Lloyd, 1994

The Art of Prolog: Advanced Programming Techniques, second edition, Leon Sterling and Ehud Shapiro, 1994

Logic Programming: Proceedings of the Eleventh International Conference on Logic Programming, edited by Pascal Van Hentenryck, 1994

Logic Programming: Proceedings of the 1994 International Symposium, edited by Maurice Bruynooghe, 1994

Logic Programming: Proceedings of the Twelfth International Conference, edited by Leon Sterling, 1995

Logic Programming: Proceedings of the 1995 International Symposium, edited by John Lloyd, 1995

Inductive Logic Programming: From Machine Learning to Software Engineering, Francesco Bergadano and Daniele Gunetti, 1995

Meta-Logics and Logic Programming, Krzysztof Apt and Franco Turini, 1995

Logic Programming: Proceedings of the 1996 Joint International Conference and Symposium on Logic Programming, edited by Michael Maher, 1996

Logic Programming: Proceedings of the 14th International Conference on Logic Programming, edited by Lee Naish, 1997

Logic Programming: Proceedings of the 1997 International Symposium, edited by Jan Maluszyński, 1997

Printed in the United States
by Baker & Taylor Publisher Services

Printed in the United States
by Baker & Taylor Publisher Services